JEWS, GENTILES,
AND THE OPPONENTS OF PAUL

Jews, Gentiles, and the Opponents of Paul

The Pauline Letters

B. J. OROPEZA

Apostasy in the New Testament Communities

VOLUME 2

CASCADE *Books* · Eugene, Oregon

JEWS, GENTILES, AND THE OPPONENTS OF PAUL
The Pauline Letters

Apostasy in the New Testament Communities, vol. 2

Cascade Books
An imprint of Wipf and Stock Publishers
199 W. 8th Ave., Suite 3
Eugene, OR 97401

www.wipfandstock.com

ISBN 13: 978-1-61097-290-1

Cataloging-in-Publication data for series:

Oropeza, B. J., 1961–

    Apostasy in the New Testament Communities / B. J. Oropeza.

    xviii + 406 p. ; 25.4 cm. Includes bibliographical references and indexes.
    Contents:
    v. 1, In the Footsteps of Judas and Other Defectors: The Gospels, Acts, and Johannine Letters.
    v. 2, Jews, Gentiles, and the Opponents of Paul: The Pauline Letters.
    v. 3, Churches under Siege of Persecution and Assimilation: The General Epistles and Revelation.

    ISBN 13: 978-1-61097-289-5 (v. 1); 978-1-61097-290-1 (v. 2); 978-1-61097-291-8 (v. 3); 978-1-61097-206-2 (vols. 1–3)

    1. Apostasy—Biblical teaching. 2. Apostasy—Christianity. 3. Bible N.T.—Theology. I. Title. II. Series.

BS2395 O55 V.2 2012

Manufactured in the U.S.A.

To Jared and Justin

μειζοτέραν οὐκ ἔχω χαρά

Contents

Preface

This second of my three-volume work continues to endeavor a thorough study on the subject of apostasy in the New Testament; this volume focuses on the canonical letters attributed to Paul, both disputed and undisputed. Only Paul's letter to Philemon is exempt from this study because it does not address the subject of falling away. As in the previous volume, which examined the canonical gospels, Acts, and Johannine letters, the second volume studies the nature and consequences of apostasy. As well, this volume identifies emerging Christian communities of the first century and investigates whether those communities held to diverse viewpoints on the subject of defectors and apostasy.

In the process of producing this set, many have assisted along the way. I wish to thank, first of all, Shirley Decker-Lucke, the former senior editor of Hendrickson Publishers, for first accepting this work for publication. The complete manuscript was finished under her auspices before Baker Book House bought the title in 2010, and then through negotiations Cascade Books has taken up the mantle for its publication. A special thanks goes to Chris Spinks, the editor of these volumes.

Also, a special thanks goes out to my colleagues, friends, and academic readers who over the years have taken time to provide me with feedback and criticisms on various prepublished versions of these chapters. These individuals include Paul Anderson, Richard Ascough, Bart Buhler, Scott Caulley, David deSilva, Don Garlington, Robert Hall, David Horrell, Roy Jeal, Judith Lieu, Fred Long, Lynn Losie, James McGrath, Mark Nanos, C. K. Robertson, Kenneth Schenck, Kay Smith, Jerry Sumney, Kenneth Waters, Robert Webb, Adam Winn, and Karen Winslow.

As well, at Azusa Pacific University I was able to participate at the Center for Research on Ethics and Values (CREV) headed by Carol Lambert, which allowed me time off my teaching load and the ability to present drafts of some of my chapters to fellow colleagues for their feedback. The CREV participants in fall 2006 included Ruth Anna Abigail, Mark Eaton, Carole Lambert, Daniel Park, Carrie

Peirce, Karla Richmond, and Kay Smith; and in fall 2008 the participants were Mark
Eaton, Randy Fall, Emily Griesinger, Craig Keen, Carole Lambert, Annie Tsai, and
Steven Wentland. A special thanks goes out to them all. I hope I have not left out
anyone! I was also fortunate enough to be awarded the Beverly Stanford Hardcastle
Fellowship Award for 2009–2010, which will provide me with an upcoming semes-
ter for research, time off teaching, and a research assistant. I would like to thank
Mark Eaton for chairing the award committee and making this possible, and a very
special thanks to my assistant, Maranatha Wall.

I would also like to thank at APU the School of Theology, headed by David
Wright, Russell Duke, and now Scott Daniels (deans), Bill Yarchin and Kenneth
Waters (assistant deans), and Kay Smith (chair of the Biblical Studies department),
for their support and providing me with various types of assistance, time for research, and great colleagues. Colleagues that I have not mentioned already that deserve special mention for helping me with ideas and resources to this book are Ralph
Martin, Roger Oakland, and Don Thorsen. I also give a warm thanks to administrative assistants Sheryl Lindsay, Pat Losie, Marilyn Moore, and Laura Smith Webb.

Finally, at APU I also wish to thank Kimberly Battle-Waters and again Carol
Lambert for providing me with opportunities to get away to the beautiful Franciscan
monastery in Malibu, California, for the annual Faculty Writer's Retreat. Friends,
students, and assistants that have helped directly or indirectly with this book and
deserve honorable mention include Joel Fowler, Amanda Rudd, Sybil Schlegel,
Eric Ciampa, Breonna Wharton, Garret Granitz, Claire Moellenberndt, and Jessica
Chessum.

For my sabbatical at the University of Tübingen, I wish to thank Professor Dr.
Michael Theobald of the Katholisch-Theologischen Fakultät for graciously invit-
ing me to do research and use the facilities of the Bibliothek des Theologicums,
Dr. Thomas Schmeller of the Universität Frankfurt for helping arrange this connection; and Dr. Thomas Scott Caulley, director of the Institut zur Erforschung des
Urchristentums, and Dr. Hermann Lichtenberger of the Evangelisch-Theologischen
Fakultät, who were kind enough to invite me to present a paper on my research at
their seminar. In Tübingen, Timothy Sailors and Petra Keller also deserve special
mention for their friendship and assisting me with daily living protocols and use of
the university housing and facilities.

B. J. Oropeza

Abbreviations

MODERN SOURCES

AB	Anchor Bible
ABD	*Anchor Bible Dictionary*, edited by D. N. Freedman, 6 vols. (New York: Doubleday, 1992)
ABR	*Australian Biblical Review*
ABRL	Anchor Bible Reference Library
ACCS	Ancient Christian Commentary on Scripture
AGJU	Arbeiten zur Geschichte des antiken Judentums und des Urchristentums
AnBib	Analecta biblica
ANTC	Abingdon New Testament Commentaries
ATANT	Abhandlungen zur Theologie des Alten und Neuen Testaments
AThRSup	Anglican Theological Review Supplement Series
AYB	Anchor Yale Bible
BBET	Beiträge zur biblischen Exegese und Theologie
BDAG	Danker, F. W., W. Bauer, W. F. Arndt, and F. W. Gingrich, *A Greek-English Lexicon of the New Testament and Other Early Christian Literature*, 3rd. ed. (Chicago: University of Chicago Press, 2000)
BDB	Brow, F. S. R. Driver, and C. A. Briggs, *A Hebrew and English Lexicon of the Old Testament* (Oxford: Clarendon, 1907)
BDF	Blass, F. A. Debrunner, and R. W. Funk, *A Greek Grammar of the New Testament and Other Early Christian Literature* (Chicago: University of Chicago Press, 1961)
BECNT	Baker Exegetical Commentary on the New Testament
BETL	Bibliotheca ephemeridum theologicarum lovaniensium
BFCT	Beiträge zur Förderung christlicher Theologie\
BFT	Biblical Foundations in Theology
BibOr	Biblica et Orientalia
BNTC	Black's New Testament Commentaries
BRev	*Bible Review*
BSac	*Bibliotheca sacra*
BTB	*Biblical Theology Bulletin*

BZ	*Biblische Zeitschrift*
BZNW	Beihefte zur Zeitschrift für die neutestamentliche Wissenschaft
CBQ	*Catholic Biblical Quarterly*
CBR	*Currents in Biblical Research*
CC	Continental Commentaries
CNT	Commentaire du Nouveau Testament
CNTOT	*Commentary on the New Testament use of the Old Testament*, edited by G. K. Beale and D. A. Carson (Grand Rapids: Baker Academic, 2007)
ConBNT	Coniectanea biblica, New Testament Series
ConBNT	*Coniectanea neotestamentica*
CRINT	Compendia Rerum Iudaicarum ad Novum Testamentum
CTJ	*Calvin Theological Journal*
CTQ	*Concordia Theological Quarterly*
DJG	*Dictionary of Jesus and the Gospels*, edited by Joel B. Green, Scot McKight, and I. Howard Marshall (Downers Grove, IL: InterVarsity, 1992)
DNTB	*Dictionary of New Testament Background*, edited by Craig A. Evans and Stanley S. Porter (Downers Grove, IL: InterVarsity, 2000)
DPL	*Dictionary of Paul and His Letters*, edited by G. F. Hawthorne, R. P. Martin, and Daniel G. Reid (Downers Grove, IL: InterVarsity, 1993)
EBib	Etudes bibliques
EDNT	*Exegetical Dictionary of the New Testament*, edited by H. Balz, G. Schneider, 3 vols. (Grand Rapids: Eerdmans, 1990–93)
EH	Europäische Hochschulschriften
EpC	Epworth Commentaries
ER	*Encyclopedia of Religion*, edited by Mircea Eliade, 16 vols. (New York: Macmillan, 1995)
ERE	*Encyclopedia of Religion and Ethics*, edited by James Hastings, 12 vols. (Edinburgh: T. & T. Clark, 1908–21)
ESEC	Emory Studies in Early Christianity
ETL	*Ephemerides theologicae Lovanienses*
ETR	*Evangelical Theological Review*
EvQ	*Evangelical Quarterly*
EGGNT	Exegetical Guide to the Greek New Testament
EKKNT	Evangelisch-katholischer Kommentar zum Neuen Testament
ETL	Ephemerides theologicae lovanienses
ExpTim	*Expository Times*
GMP	*The Greek Magical Papyri in Translation, Including the Demotic Spells*, edited by Hans Dieter Betz, 1st ed. (Chicago, University of Chicago Press, 1986)
FF	Foundations and Facets

Fragments	*Fragments of an Unknown Gospel and Other Early Christian Papyri*, edited by H. Idris Bell and T. C. Skeat (London: Trustees of the British Museum, 1935)
FZAW	Beihefte zur Zeitschrift für die alttestamentliche Wissenschaft
HCOT	Historical Commentary on the Old Testament
HCS	Hellenistic Culture and Society
HFT	Helps for Translators
HNT	Handbuch zum Neuen Testament
HNTC	Harper's New Testament Commentaries
HTKNT	Herders theologischer Kommentar zum Neuen Testament
HTR	*Harvard Theological Review*
HTS	Harvard Theological Studies
HUT	Hermeneutische Untersuchungen zur Theologie
IBS	*Irish Biblical Studies*
ICC	International Critical Commentary
IRM	*International Review of Mission*
ISBE	*International Standard Bible Encyclopedia*, edited by Geoffrey W. Bromiley, 4 vols., rev. ed. (Grand Rapids: Eerdmans, 1979–88)
IVPNTC	InterVarsity Press New Testament Commentary Series
JBL	*Journal of Biblical Literature*
JETS	*Journal of the Evangelical Theological Society*
JPT	*Journal of Pentecostal Theology*
JSB	*The Jewish Study Bible*, edited by Adele Berlin and Marc Zvi Brettler (Jewish Publication Society; Oxford: Oxford University Press, 2004)
JSJSup	Supplements to the Journal for the Study of Judaism
JSNT	*Journal for the Study of the New Testament*
JSNTSup	Journal for the Study of the New Testament Supplement Series
JSOTSup	Journal for the Study of the Old Testament Supplement Series
KEK	Kritisch-exegetischer Kommentar über das Neue Testament
LCL	Loeb Classic Library
LD	Lectio divina
LEH	Lust, Johan, Erik Eynikel, and Katrin Hauspie, *A Greek-English Lexicon of the Septuagint*, rev. ed. (Stuttgart: Deutsche Bibelgesellschaft, 2003)
LES	Library of Ecumenical Studies
LNTS	Library of New Testament Studies
LPS	Library of Pauline Studies
LSJ	Liddel, H. G., R. Scott, and H. S. Jones, *A Greek-English Lexicon*, 9th ed. (Oxford: Clarendon, 1996)
LTQ	*Lexington Theological Quarterly*
McMNTS	McMaster New Testament Studies
MTS	Marburger theologische Studien
NA	Neutestamentliche Abhandlungen

NA27	*Novum Testamentum Graece*, edited by Barbara and Kurt Aland, Johannes Karavidopoulos, Carlo M. Martini, and Bruce M. Metzger, 27th ed. (Stuttgart: Deutsche Bibelgesellschaft, n.d.)
NAC	New American Commentary
NCB	New Century Bible
NCBC	New Cambridge Bible Commentary
NEcht	Neue Echter Bibel
Neot	*Neotestamentica*
NIBCNT	New International Biblical Commentary on the New Testament
NICNT	New International Commentary on the New Testament
NICOT	New International Commentary on the Old Testament
NIDNTT	*New International Dictionary of New Testament Theology*, edited by C. Brown, 4 vols. (Grand Rapids: Regency Reference Library, 1975–85)
NIGTC	New International Greek Testament Commentary
NIVAC	NIV Application Commentary
NovT	*Novum Testamentum*
NovTOA	Novum Testamentum et orbis antiquus
NovTSup	Supplements to Novum Testamentum
NSBT	New Studies in Biblical Theology
NTD	Das Neue Testament Deutsch
NTHC	The New Testament in Its Hellenistic Context
NTSI	The New Testament and the Scriptures of Israel
NTL	New Testament Library
NTR	New Testament Readings
NTS	*New Testament Studies*
NTT	New Testament Theology
ÖTKNT	Ökumenischer Taschenbuch-Kommentar zum Neuen Testament
OTP	*The Old Testament Pseudepigrapha*, edited by James A. Charlesworth, 2 vols. (New York: Doubleday, 1983–85. 2 Volumes.)
P&P	*Past and Present*
PNTC	The Pillar New Testament Commentary
PRS	Perspectives in Religious Studies
PS	Pauline Studies
ResQ	*Restoration Quarterly*
RIDA	*Revue internationale des droits de l'antiquité*
RNT	Regensburger Neues Testament
RNTS	Reading the New Testament Series
RTR	*Reformed Theological Review*
SBLDS	Society of Biblical Literature Dissertation Series
SBibL	Studies in Biblical Literature
SC	*Second Century*
SCJ	Studies in Christianity and Judaism

SESJ	Suomen Eksegeettisen Seuran Julkaisuja (Publications of the Finnish Exegetical Society)
SJT	*Scottish Journal of Theology*
SNTSMS	Society of New Testament Studies Monograph Series
SNTW	Studies of the New Testament and Its World
SP	Sacra pagina
SPNT	Studies on Personalities in the New Testament
SR	Studies in Religion
STJ	*Stulos Theological Journal*
Str.B.	Strack, Hermann Leberecht, and Paul Billerbeck, *Kommentar zum Neuen Testament aus Talmud und Midrasch*, 6 vols. (Munich: C. H. Beck, 1922–61)
SUNT	Studien zur Umwelt des Neuen Testaments
SwJT	*Southwestern Journal of Theology*
TDNT	*Theological Dictionary of the New Testament*, edited by G. Kittel and G. Friedrich, translated by G. W. Bromiley, 10 vols. (Grand Rapids: Eerdmans, 1964–76)
TDOT	*Theological Dictionary of the Old Testament*, edited by Johannes Botterweck, Helmer Ringgren, and Heinz-Josef Fabry, rev. ed. translated by John T. Willis, 15 vols. (Grand Rapids: Eerdmans, 1974–2006)
THKNT	Theologischer Handkommentar zum Neuen Testament
THNTC	Two Horizons New Testament Commentary
TJ	*Trinity Journal*
TNTC	Tyndale New Testament Commentaries
UBS	United Bible Society *Greek New Testament*, edited by Kurt Aland, Matthew Black, Carlo M. Martini, Bruce M. Metzger, and Allen Wikgren, 4th ed. (Stuttgart: Deutsche Bibelgesellschaft, 1998)
UBSHS	United Bible Society Handbook Series
VT	*Vetus Testamentum*
WBC	Word Biblical Commentary
WUNT	Wissenschaftliche Untersuchungen zum Neuen Testament
WW	*Word and World*
ZBK	Zürcher Bibelkommentare
ZNW	*Zeitschrift für die neutestamentliche Wissenschaft und die Kunde der älteren Kirche*

SCRIPTURES AND ANCIENT SOURCES

ʿAbod. Zar.	*ʿAbodah Zarah*
1 Clem.	*1 Clement*
1 En.	*1 Enoch*
2 Bar.	*2 Baruch*
Add Esth	Additions to Esther

Abbreviations

Apoc El.	Apocalypse of Elijah
Apoc. Ab.	Apocalypse of Abraham
Apoc. Mos.	Apocalypse of Moses
Apoc. Zeph.	Apocalypse of Zephaniah
Apuleius, Metam.	Metamorphoses
Ascen. Isa.	Martyrdom and Ascension of Isaiah (6–11)
Bel	Bel and the Dragon
CD	Damascus Document
Cicero, Clu.	Pro Cluentio
Cyril, Myst. Cat.	Mystagogical Catechesis
Demosthenes, C. Phorm.	Against Phormio
Dio Chrysostom, Or.	Orations (Discourses)
Did.	Didache
Euripides, Iph. taur.	Iphigeneia at Tauris
Eusebius, Hist. eccl.	Ecclesiastical History
Eusebius, Prep.	Preparation for the Gospel
Gos. Bart.	Gospel (Questions) of Bartholomew
Gos. Phil.	Gospel of Philip
Gos. Thom.	Gospel of Thomas
Herm. Mand.	Shepherd of Hermas, Mandates
Herm. Sim.	Shepherd of Hermas, Similitudes
Herm. Vis.	Shepherd of Hermas, Visions
Hippolytus, Trad. ap.	The Apostolic Tradition
Ign. Eph.	Ignatius, To the Ephesians
Ign. Magn.	Ignatius, To the Magnesians
Ign. Phil.	Ignatius, To the Philadelphians
Ign. Poly.	Ingatius, To Polycarp
Ign. Smyrn.	Ingatius, To the Smyrnaeans
Ign. Trall.	Ignatius, To the Trallians
Irenaeus, Haer.	Against Heresies
Jdt	Judith
John Chrysostom, Hom. 2 Cor.	Homily on the Second Letter to the Corinthians
Jos. Asen.	Joseph and Aseneth
Josephus, Ag. Ap.	Against Apion
Josephus, Ant.	Jewish Antiquities
Josephus, J.W.	Jewish War
Jub.	Jubilees
Justin, Dial.	Dialogue with Trypho
L.A.B.	Liber antiquitatum biblicarum
L.A.E.	Life of Adam and Eve
Lam. Rab.	Lamentations Rabbah
Lev. Rab.	Leviticus Rabbah
LXX	Septuagint
Mart. Pol.	Martyrdom of Polycarp
MT	Masoretic Text

Odes Sol.	*Odes of Solomon*
Origen, *Cels.*	*Against Celsus*
Origen, *Comm. Jo.*	*Commentary on the Gospel of John*
Origen, *Comm. Matt.*	*Commentary on the Gospel of Matthew*
P.Oxy.	*Oxyrhynchus Papyri*
Palladius, *Laus. Hist.*	*Lausiac History*
Pesiq. Rab.	*Pesiqta Rabbati*
Philo, *Abr.*	*On the Life of Abraham*
Philo, *Alleg. Interp.*	*Allegorical Interpretation*
Philo, *Cherubim*	*On the Cherubim*
Philo, *Conf.*	*On the Confusion of Tongues*
Philo, *Creation*	*On the Creation of the World*
Philo, *Decal.*	*On the Decalogue*
Philo, *Embassy*	*On the Embassy to Gaius*
Philo, *Heir*	*Who Is the Heir?*
Philo, *Joseph*	*On the Life of Joseph*
Philo, *Moses*	*On the Life of Moses*
Philo, *Names*	*On the Change of Names*
Philo, *Prelim.*	*On the Preliminary Studies*
Philo, *QE*	*Questions and Answers on Exodus*
Philo, *QG*	*Questions and Answers on Genesis*
Philo, *Rewards*	*On Rewards and Punishments*
Philo, *Spec.*	*On the Special Laws*
Philo, *Virtues*	*On the Virtues*
Philo, *Worse*	*That the Worse Attacks the Better*
Philostratus, *Apoll.*	*Life of Apollonius*
Plutarch, *Quaest. conv.*	*Quaestionum convivialum libri IX*
Plutarch, *Sera*	*De sera numinis vindicta*
Pol. *Phil.*	Polycarp, *To the Philippians*
Pss. Sol.	*Psalms of Solomon*
Quintilian, *Inst.*	*Institutio oratoria*
S. Eli. Rab.	*Seder Eliyahu Rabbah*
Sib. Or.	*Sibylline Oracles*
Suetonius, *Claud.*	*Divus Claudius*
T. Abr.	*Testament of Abraham*
T. Ash.	*Testament of Asher*
T. Ben.	*Testament of Benjamin*
T. Dan	*Testament of Dan*
T. Gad	*Testament of Gad*
T. Iss.	*Testament of Issachar*
T. Jud.	*Testament of Judah*
T. Lev.	*Testament of Levi*
T. Mos.	*Testament of Moses*
T. Naph.	*Testament of Naphtali*
T. Reub.	*Testament of Reuben*
T. Sol.	*Testament of Solomon*

Tertullian, *Nat.*	*To the Heathens*
Tg. Onq.	*Targum Onqelos*
Tg. Ps.-J.	*Targum Pseudo-Jonathan*
Thucydides, *Hist.*	*History of the Peloponnesian War*

Introduction

This study on the Pauline letters intends to provide a thorough examination that aims at more clarity on how the subject of apostasy was perceived in the various New Testament communities. The term "apostasy" I define as a phenomenon that occurs when a religious follower or group of followers turn away from, or otherwise repudiate, the central beliefs and practices they once embraced in a respective religious community.[1] This work focuses on the communities that belonged to or interacted with the Pauline mission, including friends and opponents, Jews and Gentiles.

We begin by looking into the person of Paul and accusations against his own defection from the Jewish sect of the Pharisees. Since Galatians recollects Paul's religious transformation and earliest years, and it provides a natural bridge for conflicts over the Law that we noticed from the Book of Acts (see vol. 1), this letter appears first in the study. Next, I will address the Thessalonian correspondence because these letters are Paul's earliest.[2] The other letters will then be covered in the order in which they were most likely written: 1 Corinthians, 2 Corinthians, Romans, and Philippians.[3] I will then focus on the disputed letters of Ephesians and Colossians before looking into the Pastoral Letters (1 and 2 Timothy, Titus).

My approach is consistent with the other volumes of this study. First, I *identify the communities* from which the exhortations or warnings against apostasy originate. The author, audience, and apostates, or potential apostates, will all be recognized. In Paul's letters, the communities are comprised for the most part of Gentile converts,

---

1. For a more thorough treatment on the subject of the apostasy and my approach in these volumes, see the Introduction of the first volume of this work.

2. That is, unless an early date for Galatians is accepted (c.49 CE). More plausible is a date somewhere between 51 and 54 CE. First Thessalonians was written about 51 CE. I will argue that 2 Thessalonians is an authentic letter from Paul.

3. In Philemon, religious apostasy is not an issue, and so we will not study this letter. Interestingly though, the term ἀποστάτης or "deserter," which sometimes refers to apostates in early Christian sources (e.g., Jas 2:11 [Alexandrinus text]; *Herm. Vis* 1.4.2), can also refer to runaway slaves (e.g., Plutarch, *Romulus* 9), and Paul's letter to Philemon is about a runaway slave (vv. 10–17).

but conflicts over Jewish law will become quite evident, especially in Galatians. A significant amount of Paul's correspondence attempts to dissuade the churches from following his opponents who confess Christ but attempt to lead the congregants away from Pauline teachings. Opponents both inside and outside these churches threaten the spiritual state of the members, and so it will be important for us to identity these opponents and the situation behind the letters.

Second, I ponder on the *perceived nature of apostasy within the respective communities.* The churches under Paul's auspices do not always believe or conduct themselves in a manner that pleases him. Here we will explore the type of apostasy that threatens respective congregations. Possible dangers include vice-doing, persecution, and false teachings. At times, Paul or the Pauline writer must determine who is "in" and who is "out" of the Christ community.

Third, I address the perceived *consequences of apostasy.* What will happen to congregation members who fall away? Expulsion from the community and divine judgment become important options. We will also ponder on whether the apostle encourages the restoration of defectors.

Fourth and finally, I will *compare perspectives on apostasy from the standpoint of certain emergent Christian communities* relevant to Paul's letters. The conclusion of various chapters, as well as the final conclusion, highlight some similarities and dissimilarities between the Pauline viewpoint and other Christ-communities from the first century. Did the communities of Christ interpret apostasy differently? Our conclusions may have ramifications on how we as contemporary readers perceive these communities and their interpretations.[4]

---

4. In volume 3 I will address a final conclusion about what unifies and differentiates all the NT Christ-communities in this regard.

1

Galatians: Paul, the Law,
and the Threat of Opponents

On the road to Damascus Paul's life was forever changed when he encountered the risen Jesus (Acts 9:1–19; 22:6–16; 26:12–18; cf. 1 Cor 9:1; Gal 1:15–17).[1] As a Pharisee he had persecuted followers of "the Way," attempting to get them to renounce their faith in Jesus as the Christ (Acts 26:11; cf. 8:3; 9:1–2; Gal 1:13, 23; 1 Cor 15:9; Phil 3:6; 1 Tim 1:13). Opposition against the early Christ-followers was perhaps motivated by charges similar to those trumped up against emergent Hellenistic-Jewish Christians like Stephen—they allegedly taught against the Law, the temple, and Jewish customs (Acts 6:13–14), and their claim that divine authority was given to Jesus had been interpreted as blasphemy (Acts 7:55–60; Mark 14:61–64).[2] Their affirmation that Jesus rose from the dead likewise became vindication for his innocence of any crime worthy of death, and this claim attested to the wrongful decision of the authorities in determining him guilty of blasphemy and deserving execution (e.g., Acts 5:28–33).

Paul's zeal for the Torah motivated him to persecute the Way; he felt justified that violence against what he considered to be blasphemers of the Law was sanctioned by God (Gal 1:14; Phil 3:6). He was acting very much like the heroes of Israel's

---

1. On Paul's experience of Christ at Damascus and the possible influence it had on Paul's thoughts, see e.g., Hengel and Schwemer, *Paul between Damascus and Antioch*, 91–105; Segal, *Paul the Convert*, 7–16; Kim, *Origin of Paul's Gospel*.

2. On the latter point see Hurtado, "Pre-70 Jewish Opposition," 50–54.

past such as Phineas,[3] Elijah,[4] Simeon and Levi,[5] Jehu,[6] and the Maccabee brothers,[7] who killed rebels or God's enemies.[8] After his encounter with Christ, however, Paul became zealous in a different sort of way as an apostle to the Gentiles (Acts 9:15; 22:21; 26:17, 20, 23; cf. 13:1–3; Gal 2:2, 8–9; Col 1:25–27).

PAUL: APOSTLE AND APOSTATE (GAL 1:13-16; CF. 2 COR 11:24)

Is Paul himself an apostate, a renegade Jew who distorted or abandoned the Law to follow the Way? Much depends on whether he was actually converted through his Damascus experience or merely received his divine commission at this point while remaining a faithful Jew.[9] Alan Segal argues that Paul underwent a conversion involving a drastic change in his experience, and such a transformation involves movement "from one sect or denomination to another within the same religion, if the change is radical."[10] Membership among the Essenes, for example, came by way of conversion only, even though the neophytes were already Jewish.[11] We see something very similar taking place when a group of John the Baptist's disciples in Ephesus convert to the emergent Christian message, receiving the Holy Spirit and getting baptized in the name of the Lord Jesus (Acts 19:1–10).

Paul joined the group he once persecuted and could speak of his former experiences "in Judaism" prior to his change (Gal 1:13–14).[12] His past accomplishments he considered as excrement, including his gains as a Pharisee (Phil 3:4–8). He probably felt much remorse about his former days as a persecutor of the church (1 Cor 15:9; Gal 1:13; cf. 1 Tim 1:13–16).[13] More specifically, Paul considered his transformation

3. Num 25:6–13; cf. Ps 105[106]:30–31; Philo, *Spec.* 1.56–57.

4. 1 Kgs 18:40; Sir 48:1–2; 1 Macc 2:58.

5. Gen 34:1–31; Jdh 9:2–4; *Jub.* 30:1–20.

6. 2 Kgs 10:16–30.

7. 1 Macc 2:23–68.

8. See Hengel, *Zealots*, esp. 146–49.

9. On the divine commission view, see Stendahl, *Paul among Jews and Gentiles*, 7–23. Roetzel, *Paul*, 46, affirms: "Paul was born a Jew, lived as a Jew, and in all likelihood died as a Jew."

10. Segal, *Paul the Convert*, 6. See also Chester, *Conversion at Corinth*, 153–64; Donaldson, *Paul and the Gentiles*, 17; Barrett, *Freedom and Obligation*, 110. Differently, Gaventa, *Darkness to Light*, 37–40, cf. 11, views Paul's experience as neither a call nor a conversion, but a transformation that takes on a new perception of the past without rejecting it.

11. Segal, *Paul the Convert*, 83.

12. The term Ἰουδαϊσμός emerges from the Maccabean era. It marks off Jewish life from outsiders and seems to be highlighted as the antithesis to Hellenism, according to Dunn, *Galatians*, 56–57. It emphasizes separation from the world and understands the Torah as reinforcing this separateness (cf. 2 Macc 2:21; 4:13; 8:1; 14:38; 4 Macc 4:26).

13. See Grindheim, "Apostate Turned Prophet," 552–53.

to be one from Pharisiac Judaism rather than "Judaism" *per se*.[14] That he experienced a conversion when he decided to follow Christ is confirmed by his warnings to the Galatians—if they submit to the works of the Law, something he once did (Gal 1:14; 2:18–19), they will be severed from Christ, and this would be just as bad as if they reverted back to their pre-converted status as unbelieving Gentiles (Gal 4:8–11; 5:2, 4).

Paul is considered an apostate by much of the Jewish community and Jewish Christ-followers who disregarded his commission.[15] In Acts the accusation among certain Jews, including some Christian Jews, is that Paul teaches "apostasy" (ἀποστασία) from the Mosaic Law in relation to circumcision and following the Jewish cultic customs (Acts 21:21; cf. v. 28; 6:14; 15:1; 26:3; 28:17).[16] Paul's own claims of suffering at the hands of fellow Jews, whether by stoning or flogging, attest to his committing some blasphemy or crimes worthy of severe punishment according to ancient Jewish courts (2 Cor 11:24–26; cf. Lev 24:16; *m. Makkot* 3.2, 15; *m. Keritot* 1.1). Punishment by flogging, according to the *Mishnah*, is an appropriate penalty for Sabbath breaking, working on the Day of Atonement, and food or ritual uncleanliness. These are the types of things Paul would be likely to commit with Gentile converts; and yet his submission to Jewish flogging—"forty stripes, save one" (2 Cor 11:24)—would seem to indicate he was not entirely ostracized from the Jewish community. He never abandoned his mission to the Jews.[17]

Stephen Wilson goes further than this by suggesting that Paul is "consciously an apostate" because he intentionally identifies himself with Gentiles in Christ: "The message he conveyed hit at the very heart of Judaism as understood by his Jewish contemporaries, and, I suspect, he abandoned some Jewish practices when living among Gentiles."[18] He suggests that Paul's sudden switch of loyalties may classify him in sociological terms as a precipitate defector, but Paul's vigorous opposition towards his former tradition may lead some to think that he is an antagonistic apostate.[19] To be sure, Paul is not portrayed as a gradual defector in Acts 9: on his way to Damascus to persecute the church, Christ appears to him, and in three days he is baptized,

14. Cf. Dunn, *Theology of Paul*, 346–53.

15. Cf. Segal, *Paul the Convert*, 223. On Jewish Christians considering Paul an apostate in early Christian sources, see e.g., Irenaeus *Haer.* 1.26.2; Origen, *Cels.* 5.65; Eusebius, *Hist. eccl.* 6.38.

16. On "custom" (ἔθος) as referring to Jewish cultic activities or laws, see 2 Macc 11:25; 4 Macc 18:5; Philo, *Spec.* 2.149; Josephus, *Ant.* 9.262–63.

17. See Gallas, "Fünfmal vierzig," 178–91; Harvey, "Forty Strokes," 79–96. Harvey adds that Paul, "having committed an offence and having been found guilty by Jewish courts, he had to discharge the sentence imposed on him before he could be readmitted to the Jewish community and continue preaching where his missionary work had most effect—among the Gentile sympathizers" (92–93).

18. Wilson, *Leaving the Fold*, 51–52.

19. Wilson, 124–25.

filled with the Spirit, and then proclaims Jesus as the Son of God in Damascus, apparently several days afterward! And if we evaluate his zealous turnaround (cf. Gal 1:23) and reaction towards the Law as taught by his opponents (e.g., Gal 5:12), his action and language may certainly suggest antagonism towards his former beliefs. Even so, we should not lose sight of evaluating Paul's defection according to his own perspective. James Dunn opines that Paul thought of himself not as abandoning his Jewish heritage, but fulfilling it as an apostle of Israel to the Gentiles. He is converted and receives a prophetic commission, which he would have understood in terms of being an agent of the *qahal* or "assembly of Israel." He considers it of primary importance to include himself, along with Gentiles, as Abraham's offspring (Gal 3:6–9, 14, 26, 29), and views the gospel as a completion of the Law rather than its abrogation.[20] From Paul's perspective, the Israelites who reject his message have become apostate, not him (cf. Rom 9–11).

John Barclay seems correct when he suggests that Paul shows a limited amount of acculturation and accommodation to Hellenism, but the apostle seems highly assimilated in this way. For Barclay, "Paul is most at home among the particularistic and least Hellenized segments of the Diaspora, yet in his social behaviour he shatters the ethnic mould in which such concepts were formed."[21] Barclay's study concludes that apostasy is a judgment term used by insiders to exclude others. The label seems to be relative to the one who is labeling: "inasmuch as Paul was consistently repudiated as an 'apostate' by his contemporaries, the label fits historical reality. So long as one recognizes that the label is a label, applied as a form of repudiation, not a neutral description of Paul's stance, it may be helpfully retained."[22] From the perspective of his Jewish contemporaries who oppose him, Paul is an apostate, but from Paul's own perspective he is not.

There remains some ambiguity about Paul's identity. He could speak of himself as not under the Law while at the same time embracing both Jewish customs and the Law whenever it might be expedient for him to do so (1 Cor 9:20); and yet he never stops considering himself an Israelite (cf. Rom 9–11). It could be adduced from Galatians that *he regards himself as an Israelite aligned with what God intended for the Israelites all along—that they would become one with the Gentiles, honoring Jesus as Messiah in a new salvific era planned by God and predicted in Israel's scriptures* (Gal 1–3; cf. Rom 1–11). Paul mentions his conversion and calling often within the matrix of his discussions about the Law (Gal 1–2; Philippians 3; cf. 1 Tim. 1). This may suggest that issues about the Law stood at the heart of his calling; a significant

20. Dunn, "Paul: Apostate," 256–71.

21. Barclay, "Paul among Diaspora Jews," 89–120; quote from 108.

22. Barclay, 118.

portion of his Jewish identity seems wrapped around his interpretation of the Law. In his letters to the Galatians and Romans especially, *at stake for Paul as a follower of Christ are his self-identity and the fate of those who interpret the Law similar to how he once did prior to his conversion.*

Paul's emphasis on the Law, primarily in his letters to the Galatians, Romans, and Philippians, suggests that he faces a common nemesis that threatens not only the unity of his churches but the salvific status of members of the congregation who are "in Christ." For Paul, being "in Christ" takes on the meaning that a mystical union and fellowship is occurring between Christ and believers through the Spirit of God; believers participate in Christ, and this takes place on individual and corporate levels so as to foster a oneness between the church and the presence of Christ (Gal 3:27–28; Rom 8:1, 18–25; 1 Cor 12:13, 27; 2 Cor 5:17; Phil 3:9; cf. Gal 2:19–20; Col 1:27). And yet the phrase "in Christ" is used by Paul in other ways also (e.g., Rom 3:24; 6:23; 8:39). The idea of, *being "in Christ" conveys both instrumental and locative meanings: Christ is the agent by whom and sphere in which salvation becomes effectual.*[23] The congregation members experience a salvific relationship with Christ, and as long as they *continue* in this relationship they can be assured of the future hope of final salvation at Christ's second coming.

PAUL'S PROPHETIC COMMISSION
AND ISRAEL'S SCRIPTURES (1:15–16)

Paul frequently cites or alludes to Israel's scriptures when attempting to persuade his readers to accept his way of thinking, whether this comes by way of instruction or warning. Isaiah, Psalms, and the Pentateuch, especially Deuteronomy, dominate his citations.[24] Isaianic and Deuteronomic traditions dominate Paul's writings, it seems, because in these traditions he finds prophetic words and prefigurations for both himself and the community of believers.[25] Related to divine judgment is the motif of blessings and curses—if the people of Israel obey God, they will be blessed and prosper in their endeavors in the place God promised them; if they disobey God, they will be cursed in their endeavors and expelled from the land God promised them (Deut 28–30). Göran Forkman finds several types of activities in Israel's scriptures resulting in expulsion from the community or land. Individuals who committed hei-

---

23. See Longenecker, *Paul*, 160–70; Talbert, *Ephesians and Colossians*, 35–37; Oropeza, *Paul and Apostasy*, 97–99, 205. For a comparison of "in Christ" with similar phrases in Paul, see Bouttier, *Christ*.

24. Cf. e.g., Silva, "Old Testament in Paul," 631; Watson, *Paul*; Hübner, *Vetus*.

25. See examples in Hays, *Echoes of Scripture*; Wilk, *Bedeutung*. The LXX seems to dominate Paul's use of sources.

nous sins were "cut off" (כָּרַת) from the community. The lawbreaker was no longer considered a member of Israel's elect community, and this often meant the offender was put to death.[26] In this manner expulsion became the proper punishment against apostates who were now denied the blessings and protection of the community; they were given over instead to the curses and misfortunes outlined in the Mosaic covenant.[27] Destruction was the proper Mosaic punishment for idolaters who served foreign gods within Israel's community.[28] These notions become relevant for Paul as he declares a "curse" on his opponents (e.g., Gal 1:8–9) and considers expulsion from the community to be the proper sanction against apostates (e.g., 1 Cor 5:1–5).

The writings of Isaiah provide a scheme of Israel's rebellion, God's punishment of apostates, and Israel's future restoration. Divine judgment comes by way of exile (Isa 5) and spiritual blindness and dullness of hearing (Isa 6). But in the imagery of a new creation and exodus-wilderness journey, the Isaianic author anticipates the blind seeing once again and God's people restored.[29] Passages relevant to this theme permeate not only Deutero-Isaiah but the entire Isaianic corpus.[30] In essence these passages affirm God doing a new thing by restoring a remnant of Israel, giving them a leader to guide them on their wilderness journey to Zion, and this trek will include the nations or Gentiles. The new epoch is characterized by God's Spirit and the imagery of water as the source of life and renewal in the desert (Isa 44:3–4; cf. 32:15–19; 34:16–35:10). This pattern from the prophetic tradition finds fertile ground in Paul's perception of the new era, which was ushered in by the coming of Christ. The salvific plan for God's people now includes the Gentiles, and the apostle is commissioned to reach them.

In Galatians Paul considers himself to be like the prophets in the tradition of Israel's scriptures.[31] Two examples will suffice.[32] Similar to the Isaianic Servant, he is called from his mother's womb, commissioned to give good news to the Gentiles,

---

26. Lev 7:20–27; 17:4–14; 20:2–6, 17f; Exod 22:18–19; 31:14; Deut 13:5; 17:1–12; 19:19; 22:21–24; 24:7; cf. 1 Kgs 14:10–14; 21:21; Jer 2:22–23; Ezek 14:7–8; 20:30; Ps 105[106]:37–38.

27. See Forkman, *Limits of the Religious Community*, esp. 17–36.

28. חָרַם: Deut 13:1–18; cf. 2:34; 7:5, 25–26; 20:15–18; Exod 22:20.

29. Isa 40:3–5; 41:17–20; 42:14–17; 43:1–7, 14–21; 48:20–21; 49:8–12; 51:9–10; 52:11–12; 55:12–13; cf. 44:1–5; 44:27; 50:2. For elaboration and important aspects on this theme, see Oropeza, "Echoes of Isaiah," 87–112.

30. E.g., Isa 4:2–6; 10:20–27; 11:10–16; 14:1–6; 26:20; 27:12–13; 31:5; 32:14–20; 34:16–17; 58:8; 60:2; 61:4–7; 63:8–14.

31. On the stereotyped prophetic call, see Stenger, "Biographisches und Idealbiographisches," 123–40.

32. A third example highly relevant to Paul is his commission as the courier of Habakkuk's message of righteousness by faithfulness: see Oropeza, "Running in Vain," 139–50.

and God is glorified in him (Gal 1:12–16, 24/Isa 49:1–5, 16; cf. Acts 13:47). Paul's calling is bound up with the Isaianic Servant, he interprets this figure as the Christ (cf. 1 Cor 15:3/Isa 53:5; Rom 4:25/Isa 53:12; Rom 15:8–12/Isa 11:1–2; Rom 15:20–21/Isa 52:15; cf. Luke 3:22/Isa 49:1–5). If he considers himself crucified with Christ so that he no longer lives but Christ lives in him (Gal 2:20), then his own role as a prophetic servant is in this sense a continuation of the message and mission of Christ. He seems to think of himself as one of the servants of the Isaianic Servant (e.g., Gal 4:11/Isa 49:4; 2 Cor 6:1–2/Isa 49:4, 8).[33] The mission initiated with Christ becomes Paul's mission; his special task includes reaching the Gentiles along with the remnant of Israel.

Even so, the aspects of Paul being set apart (ἀφορίζω) from the womb and God's taking pleasure (εὐδοκέω) in revealing his Son to him echoes Jeremiah's calling to be a prophet to the nations (Gal 1:15–16/Jer 1:5–6, 10).[34] The emphasis on God's activity of selecting the prophet is to show that such commissions are not derived from human origin or by self-appointment; the prophet's authority comes from God (cf. Gal 1:1, 11f). Such calling and commission includes the predestination of an individual in Gal 1:15–16. Paul's point, however, is not about predestination to eternal salvation. An individual who is predestined by God for a special task or appointment, even from the womb, is not exempt from the possibility of being disobedient and committing apostasy, as the examples of Samson (Judg 13–16), Saul (1 Sam 9–16), and Solomon (2 Sam 7:1–17; 12:24–25; 1 Kgs 1–11) would clearly remind Paul from Israel's tradition-history. There is no guarantee of final salvation attached to Paul's appointment; he believed in the possibility of his own apostasy (cf. 1 Cor 9:16b, 24–27).[35]

THE OPPONENTS IN GALATIA
(1:6–9; 2:1–14; 2:17–18; 3:10–13; 4:17; 6:12–13)

The Galatian congregations consist of a large number of uncircumcised Gentiles who are "in Christ." Paul calls them "brothers," a typical designation for the recipients of his letters (1:11; 3:15; 4:12, 28; 5:13; 6:1, 18). They are redeemed, belong to Christ, know God, and operate in the Spirit (3:3, 5, 13, 14, 24–29; 4:7–9; 5:1; cf. 5:18, 25). They already stand in a covenant relationship with Christ, but the apostle's re-

33. Gignilliat, *Paul and Isaiah's Servants*, 53–54, 112–42, stresses the offspring of the Servant (Isa 53:10) and a plurality of righteous ones (56:9—63:6) and servants (54:17; 63:17–18; 65:8f, 13, 15, 20–23).

34. On God taking pleasure (εὐδοκέω) with someone, see 2 Sam 22:20; Ps 43[44]:3–4; Isa 62:4; Ps 146[147]:11. On the concept of setting apart (ἀφορίζω), see Rom 1:1; Acts 13:2.

35. On Paul's calling requiring obedience in Luke, see Acts 26:19.

peated warnings indicate they are in peril of "getting out" of this relationship.[36] Paul warns these congregations against those who teach another gospel that is distorted and leads to being accursed (1:6–9).[37]

Some teachers are influencing these members to follow Jewish customs contrary to Paul's teachings, and they want to "exclude" (ἐκκλείω) the Galatians, from both fellowship and salvation altogether, if they have not been circumcised (4:17; cf. 6:12–13). The fear this might have generated in the congregations may be seen if we compare ταράσσω in Gal 1:7 with passages such as Ps 6:4 LXX; Isa 8:12; Matt 14:26; 1 Pet 3:14; and *Mart. Pol.* 12.1.[38] These opponents had evidently visited the Galatian churches recently and were still persuading some of their members to accept circumcision. After Paul heard about this visit he wrote to the Galatians attempting to dissuade them from this teaching. He primarily uses deliberative rhetoric to do this, with the central thesis or *propositio* contrasting righteousness by faith(fulness) with works of the Law (Gal 2:16–21) and with the supporting proofs (*probatio*) unpackaged in the immediate chapters that follow.

Our view in the Pauline letters is that δικαιοσύνη and δικαιόω normally have the meaning of "righteousness" and "to make righteous," respectively (e.g., Gal 2:16, 17, 21).[39] Sometimes, however, the synonymous terms "justification"/"to justify" will be used, especially when we are highlighting a sense of acquittal before God whether in the present or on judgment day. A forensic aspect to δικαιοσύνη and δικαιόω should not be denied, but a distinction should be made between justification in the present (initial justification/righteousness) and justification on judgment day (final justification/righteousness). For the believer, perseverance is needed to bridge the gap between initial and final justification. Paul and the Galatian congregations experience a sense of salvation in the present era and participation in the righteousness that God has imparted to them by their faith/faithfulness.[40] Their being made

---

36. Notice Witherington, *Grace in Galatia*, 80–81: "getting in" is not the issue but "getting out."

37. The verb μεταστρέφω means to "alter" or "change" and is often used in a negative sense (cf. Exod 14:5; Ps 77[78]:56–57; Sir 11:31; *T. Ash.* 1.8). In Gal 1:7 it means "to distort" (cf. BDAG, 641).

38. Martyn, *Galatians*, 111–12. Differently, Wisdom, *Blessing for the Nations*, 204, relates the term to apostasy, noticing that ταράσσω is used of those who led others into apostasy in 1 Macc 3:5 and 7:22.

39. Sanders, *Paul, the Law*, 6–14, uses to verb "to righteous" to help capture the meaning. All the Pauline studies on justification and righteousness are too laborious to mention here. For a concise discussion on Pauline justification/righteousness, see Horrell, *Study of Paul*, 73–77.

40. Regarding my use of the term πίστις: Gal 2:16 is recalled in 3:11. In 3:11 it is the righteous person's faith/faithfulness that is emphasized (cf. 3:6–9). In a number of cases in Paul's letters, such as Gal 2:16 and 3:11, I believe the objective genitive ("faith in Christ") makes proper sense. This faith stresses more than the idea of merely trusting/believing; it includes the thought of loyal obedience or faithfulness. The two concepts of trust and faithfulness are not mutually exclusive—the allusion from Hab 2:4 would seem to imply for Paul an idea of living by fidelity. Interestingly, *b. Makkot* 23b–24a;

righteous happens as a result of God's grace and their belief in the gospel message centering on Jesus Christ as the sacrificial offering for the remission of their sins.

Who are the opponents? Paul recollects earlier conflicts with "false brothers" (Gal 2:4) and the followers of James from Jerusalem who influenced Peter (Cephas) in Antioch (2:1–15), but it is not at all clear that James, Peter, or even the false brothers are directly associated with the current disturbance in Galatia.[41] Peter is rebuked by Paul for not eating with the Gentile Christians in Antioch after initially doing so (2:11–14); he exemplifies hypocrisy by his action in the context of table fellowship, but this is not the same thing as actively demanding that Christian Gentiles be circumcised. His compelling the Gentiles to live like Jews (2:14) is probably more passive than active. Paul rhetorically attributes this accusation to Peter due to the influence of his bad example, which caused the other believing Jews, Barnabas included, to join the separation. By virtue of Peter's position and fame as one of the main "pillars" of the church, his reverting back to a resemblance of keeping Jewish customs in eating separately from Gentiles placed enormous pressure on Gentile believers to conform to Jewish customs if they wished to maintain table fellowship with Jewish believers. To what extent the Gentile believers would need to conform is not clarified; perhaps they would have to keep stricter dietary rules, be circumcised, or more. The unspoken message would seem to be that these Gentiles had to become essentially like Jews to eat with the Jewish Christ-followers.[42]

Paul claims that Peter stood "condemned" (καταγινώσκω) for his act (2:11), which could mean that he regarded him as condemned before God; but then again Paul may be saying that Peter was simply guilty of wrongdoing.[43] He is not standing in the "truth of the gospel" that ensures Gentiles are receiving the blessing of Abraham without having to keep Jewish Law and become, as it were, Jews.[44] The latter seems more correct in this context given that the "we" who are made righteous in 2:15–17 seems to include Peter and those with him, despite their hypocrisy in Antioch, and Paul could hardly attribute such righteousness to his opponents (1:8–9; 2:21; 3:10,

---

Sanhedrin 81, supports a rabbinic reading of the saying derived from Hab 2:4 as encapsulating all 613 precepts of Moses: cf. Pinker, "Was Habakkuk Presumptuous?," 33.

41. Differently, Goulder, *St. Paul Versus St. Peter*, maintains a view resembling the classic Baur position, having Pauline and Petrine missions in conflict with one another.

42. One possibility along these lines is that the separation between Jew and Gentile could reach a level in which the Gentile believers would be considered excluded from God's people (Israel), a scenario that would pressure Gentiles to become complete converts to the Judaism of the time. See Holmberg, "Jewish *versus* Christian Identity," 404–11.

43. See e.g., Wilckens, "ὑποκρίνομαι," 8.568, for the former case; Burton, *Galatians*, 103, for the latter.

44. For similar thoughts, see Dunn, *Galatians*, 127.

21).[45] Perhaps even the followers of James (2:12) would be included in Paul's "we." In any case Peter and the party of James do not appear to be the false teachers troubling the Galatians. In fact, *Paul does not know the names of the opponents* (3:1; 5:10).

Those who are teaching the false gospel in Galatia are considered accursed by Paul (1:8–9; 3:10; cf. 2:18, 21; 5:2–4, 12; 6:13). The ringleader will give an account for his teachings on judgment day (5:10b),[46] or alternatively, he will be ousted from the congregations (i.e., judged and punished by human means) and then also have to give an account at the final judgment for his disturbing of the Galatians. But more than one person is involved: "some" are disturbing and downright frightening the Galatians with their perverted teachings (1:7).[47] Their message is apparently laced with condemnation—the Gentile Christians must be circumcised to belong to God's people, and without circumcision they would be excluded from God's kingdom (cf. 4:17; 6:12).

The events in Gal 2:1–10 seem to interact with the meeting in Jerusalem in Acts 15:6–29. At this meeting it is determined that Gentile Christians did not need to follow all the precepts from Mosaic Law except for prohibitions against idol foods, fornication, things strangled, and blood (Acts 15:20, 29; see vol. 1 on Luke-Acts). That Paul is referring to the same Jerusalem meeting of Acts 15 in Gal 2:1–10 is not without its problems.[48] Among other things, the meeting seems to be private in Gal 2:1–10 between Paul and Barnabas (from Antioch) and James, Peter, and John (from Jerusalem). In Acts 15 the meeting seems to be open to the apostles, elders, and others (vv. 2–7, 12, 19). We assume that Paul's conversion took place somewhere around 33–34 CE (Gal 1:15–17; Acts 9), and the three plus fourteen years referring to visits to Jerusalem in Gal 1:18 and 2:1, respectively, add up to seventeen years since his conversion. But it is always possible that Paul may be counting parts of years or possibly forgot the exact number. This would seem to suggest that the date for the private meeting in Gal 2:1–10 is compatible with the date for the Jerusalem meeting in Acts 15 (c. 49 CE).[49]

---

45. On this identity of "we" in 2:15 see further Walker, "'We' in Gal 2.15–17," 560–65.

46. Martyn, *Galatians*, 475, correctly relates this verse to the motif of future judgment (cf. Gal 5:2, 5, 21; 6:5, 7–9).

47. Differently, Lührmann, *Galatians*, 97, does not see an anonymous person in Gal 5:10 but an announcement of judgment against anyone proclaiming a different gospel.

48. Problems with comparing Gal 2 with Acts are notorious. For a discussion of various options, see Myllykoski, "James the Just," 90–114.

49. For various chronologies of Paul's life and attempts to synthesize this with emergent Christian history, see Riesner, *Frühzeit des Apostels Paulus*; Jewett, *Chronology*; Donfried, "Chronology: New Testament," 1.1011–22; Alexander, "Chronology of Paul," 115–233.

While it is possible that the decision at the Jerusalem meeting in Acts 15 may have been an invention of Luke, or anachronistic to other events in Acts,[50] such perspectives often presuppose Paul's version is more accurate than Luke's, when both men have biases and intend to persuade their recipients. Both also insist on the veracity of their record (e.g., Luke 1:1–4; Acts 1:1–3; Gal 1:20). Others suggest the three and fourteen years both refer to the date of Paul's conversion, and on this reading the date for the meeting in Gal 2:1–10 may be a couple of years prior to the Jerusalem meeting based on Acts 11:27, 30; 12:25.[51] In this case the event of Peter in Antioch (Gal 2:11–14) may have taken place even before Paul went to Jerusalem in c. 49 CE.[52] Problematic with the earlier date for Gal 2:1–14 is that the fourteen years mentioned in 2:1 would most naturally suggest the number of years between Paul's visits to Jerusalem (cf. Gal 1:18–19), not the amount of years since his conversion.[53] Also, passages such as Acts 11:27–30 and 12:25 suggest a time before Barnabas and Paul's first missionary journey to Asia Minor (Acts 13–14). What is discussed in Gal 2:1–10, however, assumes that Paul has reached many Gentiles with his message, a view that is rather difficult to maintain if his first mission had not yet taken place.

The differences between the two versions of a meeting in Jerusalem are perhaps better explained by comparing Gal 2:1–10 with Acts 15:6–29 and suggesting that either Luke or Paul or both are not completely accurate with the details of the meeting, or that Paul is referring to a private meeting that took place on the same visit but at a different time than the more general meeting described in Acts 15.

If the Jerusalem meeting reflects Gal 2:1–10, then the conflict in Antioch with Peter (2:11–15) seems to have occurred some unknown time after the meeting in Acts 15:6–29. It perhaps took place not too long afterward. Several years after the meeting Paul does not explain whether the conflict between Peter and himself

50. See discussion in Conzelmann, *Acts*, 121, 180–81.

51. Along these lines, see Longenecker, *Galatians*, lxxvii–lxxxiii; Bruce, *Galatians*, 43–56.

52. This view may be seen as complementary with the fact that nowhere in Galatians does Paul mention the four prohibitions decided at the Jerusalem meeting. It could be surmised also from this view that Paul's letter to the Galatians was written shortly before the Jerusalem meeting (c. 49 CE). However, in Acts 15:22, 30–33 the decision in Jerusalem was given to the church in Antioch, not to the churches in Paul's mission field such as in Galatia. Paul may have accepted the decision but was uneasy with its stress on the maintenance of Jewish purity codes related to foods (cf. Lev 17), especially in relation to idol meats. The decision from Jerusalem is not mentioned to the Galatians because: 1) it was not given to these churches, and 2) it might have been counterproductive to Paul's own arguments about the Law if he would bring up that the four prohibitions are maintained by other apostles via the Law.

53. The distinctive visits in both Gal 1:18–19 and 2:1–10 include meetings or conversations with James and Peter, which may help explain why the visit to Jerusalem from Acts 11:27–30; 12:25 is not mentioned—no such meeting with these leaders took place on that occasion. Other possibilities are that Luke is in error or chronologically inaccurate, or Paul forgot about this intermediate visit to Jerusalem when writing Galatians or simply fuses it together with the later meeting.

was resolved, but in 1 Corinthians (c. 55 CE)—which in my view is written after Galatians—there is no sense of animosity between the two apostles (1 Cor 3:22; 9:5; 15:5; cf. 1:12 below). Also, no later conflict between Paul and James is recorded in Acts 21:17–26 (cf. 1 Cor 15:7) even though Luke mentions the prominent influence of the Law among the Jewish Christians, a vast number of whom consider Paul to be an apostate (cf. Acts 21:17–25).

The "false brothers" in Gal 2:4 are intended to be compared with the opponents of Paul in Galatia. If the conflict in Acts 15:1–3 that prompts the Jerusalem meeting beginning in 15:4 reflects the same meeting Paul mentions in Gal 2:1–10, this Jewish party from Judea are probably the same ones who troubled the Gentile Christians in Antioch, insisting they be circumcised to be saved (Acts 15:1, 24; cf. ταράσσω in Gal 1:7).[54] The Pharisaic Christ-followers at the meeting (Acts 15:5) may be the same group as the one mentioned in Acts 15:1; they also agree that Gentile believers must be circumcised.[55] Galatians 2 brings up earlier situations Paul faced in Jerusalem and Antioch as examples of how the Galatians should stand against false teachers from their region and not be pressured to conform to Jewish customs. The "false brothers" in Gal 2:4, then, may not be the same group as the troublemakers in Galatia even though they may have similar beliefs about the Law.[56]

Nevertheless, it is still possible that the false brothers from Judea (2:4) influenced the opponents in Galatia.[57] The ones "from James" that come to Antioch (2:12a) do not appear to be the false brothers in 2:4. This group from James is possibly the same as the circumcision party (2:12c),[58] but more likely these two groups are distinct. The former is sent by James to deliver a message to Peter or give a message to the church in Antioch. The latter group is less clear. They may be a group of Law-abiding, Jewish Christ-followers back in Judea who would get wind of Peter's "Gentile-like" behavior

---

54. Nanos, "Intruding Spies," 59–98, argues that the "pseudo-brethren" are representatives from Jewish groups that do not believe in Jesus Christ. This would be similar to the intra-Jewish sociopolitical climate of inspectors or informants who watched Jesus carefully (cf. Luke 20:20). One weakness with this view is that Paul calls this group "brothers," which in Galatians refers to Christ-followers. To be sure, in passages such as Rom 9:3 (cf. 11:1, 14) Paul uses the term to refer to Jews in general, but in that passage Paul is affirming his own Jewishness and not naming them "false" brothers. The implication in Gal 2:4 seems to be that from Paul's point of view these particular Jewish "brothers" are something they really are not (i.e., they claim to be Christ-followers but they really are not). Other options are that they are false because of what they teach, or they are both fake and teach falsely.

55. The Western text tradition equates the two groups in 15:1, 5; cf. Metzger, *Textual Commentary*, 376–78.

56. Both groups presumably made some profession of belief in Jesus as Christ, but in Paul's view they were not genuine believers.

57. See Martyn, *Galatians*, 218.

58. So Burton, *Galatians*, 107.

once the group sent by James returns and reports what is going on in Antioch (cf. Acts 11:2–3). Perhaps Peter's fear of the circumcision party centers on his not wanting to offend them, or possibly he wants to avoid any trouble they might cause to his reputation in Judea. Equally, bad rumors of Peter's behavior could damper Peter's missionary inroads to reach Jews in other areas.[59] Then again, the circumcision party of Gal 2:12 may be non-Christian Judeans or Zealots pressuring James's church, or even a local group representing the larger Jewish community in Antioch.[60]

The Jerusalem meeting in Acts 15 obviously did not resolve for long much of the tensions between Jewish and Gentile Christ-followers. The prohibitions at the meeting, it seems, were not specific enough in relation to proper food regulations for Gentile believers in Antioch when eating with Jewish believers *from Judea*. Likewise, some issues at the meeting were perhaps interpreted differently by the individuals at the meeting: Paul interpreted the decisions one way, Peter another, and James yet another.[61] Then again, Paul may have been motivated to reject or reinterpret the dietary prohibitions prescribed in Acts 15 because of Peter and the other Jewish believers' hypocrisy in Antioch. For Paul the dietary prohibitions given by James in Jerusalem were causing more division than unity.

The Galatian opponents, in any event, are described as teaching a different gospel that is leading astray Gentile believers in Galatia. They observe Jewish customs related to the Law, especially circumcision, and probably stress Abraham as their forefather (Gal 1:7; 5:2–4; 6:12–13; cf. 2:14; 3:6–9, 29; 4:30). *These opponents advocate the circumcision of Gentile Christ-followers, and they are probably Jewish Christ-followers similar to the "false brothers" in Judea and the Pharisaic believers in Acts 15:1–5.* They seem pressured by the potential of facing persecution by others if they do not get the Gentiles circumcised (6:12; cf. 5:11), and so they impel Gentile followers of Christ to conform to their view and practices related to the Law.[62] It may also be worth mentioning that Paul never says that the opponents squarely reject Jesus as Messiah, adding to the credibility that they believe in Jesus even though they insist the Gentile believers adhere to their interpretation of the Torah.[63]

59. For options on Peter's fear, see Dunn, *Galatians*, 125–26.

60. For the former option see e.g., Longenecker, *Galatians*, xci–xciv, 73–75; for the latter see Nanos, "What Was at Stake," 282–318, and his response to the former position (291).

61. On the possible misunderstandings at the Jerusalem meeting, see Dunn, *Galatians*, 122–24.

62. Some competing reasons for this circumcision include: Winter, *Seek the Welfare of the City*, 133–43 (to identify Christians as holding to formative Judaism and thus a *religio licita* [Gal 6:12]); Jewett, "Agitators," 340–41 (to thwart reprisals from the Zealots); Betz, *Galatians*, 314–16 (to avoid accusations and/or excommunication from "Judaism" for admitting converts without submission to the Torah).

63. Differently Nanos, *Irony of Galatians*, suggests Jews from the local synagogue considered Gentile

Don Garlington interprets Paul's arguments in terms of role reversal with the opponents. In 2:17–18 Paul's interlocutor thinks that justification without the Torah turns a Jew into a "Gentile sinner" outside the covenant. Paul replies that he would see himself as a sinner and apostate if he were to rebuild the things he tore down, that is, the Torah. In 3:10–13 the scriptures cited by Paul address issues related to apostasy and perseverance. Deuteronomy 27:26 LXX, for instance, retains the aspect of "remaining" in the covenant, hence, perseverance;[64] Lev 18:5 stresses "doing" the Law, which suggests a living in and keeping the Torah that is made possible through perseverance (cf. Lev. 18:3–4); and the curse in Deut 21:23 relates to an apostate's death. These same texts that the opponents probably used to encourage Gentiles to adhere to the Law, Paul has turned around and used on them to claim they are unfaithful to God's salvific plan in Christ—they are cursed and apostate for aligning themselves with the epoch of Torah, the wrong era of salvific history.[65] These opponents "have become 'ministers of sin' and 'transgressors' because of their preaching of 'another gospel'. Therefore, the apostasy/perseverance texts of Deut 27.26, Hab 2.4, Lev 18.5 and Deut 21.23 are directly applicable to them by virtue of role reversal."[66]

If so, then their apostasy seems related more to Paul's argumentative strategy of role reversing than their actual, conscious choice to defect from God or Christ. Or, said differently, there is no clear indication from the text that Paul's opponents faithfully served Christ at one time but then turned away from him through their adherence to false teachings. They may have always held to their strict beliefs about the Torah even when first becoming Christ-followers. From their own perspective they might have seen themselves as having always been faithfully serving Christ. Hence, their implied role as apostates seems to be more a vilifying label in Paul's persuasive rhetoric than referring to an actual phenomenon of their renouncing Christ. Either way, Paul makes them comparable with the "false brothers" in 2:4. The Galatians, on

Christians as candidates for the full proselytism, and it is their Gentile converts who are attempting to convince the Galatian Christ-followers. Boyarin, *Radical Jew*, 116 also considers the opponents to be Gentile Christians. Harvey, "Opposition to Paul," 326, interprets the troublemakers in Gal 6:13 as recent Gentile proselytes to Judaism, based on a present participle translation of οἱ περιτεμνόμενοι as "those who get themselves circumcised." The proper meaning, however, may simply be "those who are circumcised." On text variants and translations of the term see Betz, *Galatians*, 316, who concludes, "A decision on this problem is impossible."

64. Cf. ἐμμένω: Sir 2:10; 1 Macc 10:26–27; Philo, *Prelim.* 125; Josephus, *Ag. Ap.* 2.257.

65. Garlington, "Role Reversal," 85–121. On the covenant curse motif in relation to apostasy and idolatry in Israel's scriptures and Second Temple sources, see especially Wisdom, *Blessing for the Nation*, 43–125. Wisdom considers Paul to be cursing the opponents in terms of apostasy and idolatry (e.g., 195, 210–11, 223). On adherence to the Law as idolatry in Galatians, see further Calvert-Koyzis, *Paul, Monotheism*, 85–114.

66. Garlington, "Role Reversal," 110.

the other hand, are viewed by Paul as genuine brothers and sisters who will become apostates if they fully embrace the opponents' teachings.

EXODUS DELIVERANCE AND APOSTASY
IN GALATIANS (1:6–7; 4:1–11; CF. 1:4)

Paul's declaration of the believers' deliverance (ἐξαιρέω) through Christ recalls Israel's exodus from Egypt; instead of deliverance from Pharaoh, however, the Christ-followers are rescued from the present "evil age" (Gal 1:4; cf. Exod 3:8; Acts 7:10; 7:34). Similar to Israel before them, the Galatians are freed from slavery, adopted as God's children, and God's spiritual presence guides them through the new exodus-wilderness journey (Gal 4:1–7; cf. Rom 8:15, 23; 9:24; Eph 1:5). The Galatians, along with all those who are in Christ, are adopted as God's people, the "Israel of God" (6:16). The exodus story has now become the Galatian Christians' story of deliverance, but just as the Israelites fell in the wilderness so now the Galatians are in danger of apostasy before the full realization of God's kingdom has taken place. Todd Wilson correctly maintains that the Galatians face their own "wilderness" in between a type of redemption similar to the exodus but not yet standing at "the future reception of all this is intended to procure."[67] God rescued them, but they are quickly deserting God (Gal 1:4, 6–7/Exod 3:7–8; 32:8; Deut 9:12, 16; Judg 2:17). Although they have been adopted as God's children, they are turning back to become slaves again (Gal 4:3–10/Exod 4:22; 14:10–12; 16:3; 17:3; Num 14:2–4; Neh 9:17; Acts 7:39). Christ set them free, and yet they are in jeopardy of submitting again to a yoke of slavery (Gal 4:21–5:1/Exod 13:3, 14; Lev 26:13, 45; *Passover Haggadah*). They have been "called" to freedom, but they are not to use it for an opportunity to indulge in the "flesh" (Gal 5:13–26/Exod 4:22–23; 19:4–6; cf. chs. 16–17; Num 11:13).

In short, *the Galatians are in danger of committing apostasy, and Paul is exercising whatever "moral leverage" necessary over the problem by embellishing his warnings with words that evoke the tragedy of Israel's apostasy in the wilderness.*[68] He stands amazed at how quickly the Galatians are deserting God to follow a false gospel—their "turning quickly" (ταχέως μετατίθεσθε: Gal 1:6) echoes Israel's turning away from God to worship the golden calf (Exod 32:8).[69] The quick change does

67. Wilson, "Wilderness Apostasy," 552.

68. Wilson, 552–53, 559, 570. Martin, "Apostasy to Paganism," considers Gal 4:8–20 to be evidence of the Galatians' having committed apostasy to paganism; the calendar observances are not Jewish but pagan (437–61). But given the purpose of the letter to persuade the Galatians against following the works of the Law, and allusions to exodus in the background of 4:8–20, the calendar practices are more likely Jewish (Gal 4:10: cf. Gen 1:14; 1 Chr 23:31; *Jub.* 2.9; Justin, *Dial.* 8; 46).

69. See Ciampa, *Presence and Function of Scripture*, 72–74.

not merely describe the rapid manner in which they are apostatizing, but also as relatively new converts who had apparently turned away from false gods to serve the one true God of Israel (cf. Gal 4:8–11), they are now on the verge of abandoning God via a false gospel (1:6–9).[70] They might turn into precipitate defectors similar to the second seed in Jesus' parable of the Sower, but in this case their falling away would not be caused by persecution or affliction but by turning away from the gospel.[71] More precisely, it is *Paul's* version of the gospel that is at stake. The gospels of Peter and James (2:1–10, 14) would seem to be somewhat different than Paul's. The ironic twist in Galatians is that Paul associates the community's desire to observe the Mosaic Law and Jewish customs with their former enslavement to paganism and observance of celestial spiritual powers (στοιχεῖα). For them to follow the works of the Law as propounded by his opponents would be akin to reverting back to their former lifestyles as idolatrous non-believers (4:1–11).[72]

For Paul, if the Galatians follow the works of the Law, this would nullify their redemption in Christ so that his death would be "in vain" as well as Paul's ministerial labor among them (2:21; 4:11; cf. 3:4). Carl Bjerkelund demonstrates through midrash sources and the Septuagint that the concept of *vergeblich* ("vain," "useless") is related to the age to come (Isa 49:1–8; 45:18; 65:23; Hab 2:2–4; Deut 32:47).[73] In light of an eschatological emphasis, this would suggest the possibility of the Galatians' failure to enter into the prophetic "Zion" or the place of rest after their exodus-like deliverance. In essence, they are in danger of being cut off from God's new exodus-wilderness community in Christ. Paul sees his role in this community as a prophetic servant of the new exodus (cf. Gal 1:15–16), and as such, "running . . . in vain" describes his apprehension about his work among the Gentiles turning out to be worthless (2:2)—he would have failed in his prophetic mission if the Galatians backslide (4:11). Differently, the Galatians are described as once "running well" before being hindered by the agitators (5:7);[74] they were living in obedience

---

70. As relatively new converts this would suggest an early date for this letter. If the Galatians were converted on Paul's first missionary journey to Asia Minor (Acts 13–14, assuming the Southern Galatian hypothesis), which probably took place in the late 40s before the Jerusalem meeting (c. 49 CE), and assuming that 2:1–10 reflects that meeting, this letter may have been written around 50 or 51 CE. Betz, *Galatians*, 9–12 suggests a date anywhere from 50 to 55 CE for the writing of Galatians.

71. On this view see also Mussner, *Galaterbrief*, 54–55; Wisdom, *Blessings for the Nations*, 203.

72. In general agreement with Barclay, *Obeying the Truth*, 63–64. For various meanings behind the "elements" (στοιχεῖα) in Gal 4:3, 8–9, see Longenecker, *Triumph*, 46–58; Lührmann, *Galatians*, 83–84; Delling, "στοιχέω," 7.666–87.

73. Bjerkelund, "Vergeblich," 179–82, 189.

74. On 5:7 in relation to the new exodus theme, see Oropeza, "Running in Vain," 146–47.

to God and righteousness by faith(fulness) until Paul's opponents thwarted this by their influence over the congregations.

What is significant about the Galatians' danger of falling away to the "works of the Law" is that Paul seems to be turning the Mosaic covenant on its head (2:16; 5:2–4; cf. 1:8–9). Whereas the original exodus generation was to be safeguarded from apostasy by keeping the Law (Deut 28–32), the Galatians are in danger of committing apostasy, it seems, by doing the very thing the original wilderness generation was supposed to do—keep the Law!

THE WORKS OF THE LAW (1:8–9; 2:16–17; 3:6–25; 4:29–30; 5:10)

Paul's adrenalin runs high in this letter. In the opening section he gives no thanksgiving for the condition of the congregational recipients, unlike what he does in his other letters.[75] He repeats and stresses his warnings (1:8–9; 6:11–13) and wishes the agitators would mutilate themselves (5:12). To follow the false gospel of the opponents is to be accursed with the opponents (1:8–9; cf. 3:10). Kjell Morland rightly considers that the double *anathema* in 1:8–9 amplifies the problem in Galatia as one of seduction and apostasy, and shares some features of Deuteronomic covenant curses (Deut 27–31) and laws against false prophets (Deut 13) to demonstrate that the opponents are accursed by God. Hence, the Galatian congregations are left with a choice after Paul gives the double curse: "They have to choose between the authority of Paul and the authority of the opponents. In the former case they will have to regard the opponents as seducers; in the latter case they will have to regard Paul as a false curser."[76] The confidence he has that the Galatians will choose his viewpoint over his opponents (Gal 5:10a; cf. Phlm 21; 2 Thess 3:4) must be tempered with his fears and uncertainty about them and their potential to commit apostasy (Gal 1:6; 4:11, 16, 19–20). His optimism in 5:10 comes with a deliberative agenda: he wishes to persuade the Galatians to make the right decision, that is, accept his viewpoint and realize that he is on their side.[77] His frank speech is not relentlessly harsh, but he finds room to praise the Galatians in order to foster good will;[78] this is done ultimately to get them to agree with him and turn away from the opponents. Conversely,

---

75. Notice Cosby, "Red-Hot Rhetoric," 296–309, who describes Paul's response to the situation in terms of his honor challenged, his feelings hurt, and his response "like an erupting volcano" (296).

76. Morland, *Rhetoric of Curse*, 236–39.

77. See McKnight, *Galatians*, 252. Contrast Gundry Volf, *Paul and Perseverance*, 215 (cf. 286).

78. See further, Sampley, "Paul and Frank Speech," 293–318.

the opponents are neither on their side nor the Lord's, and they will be judged by God (5:7–10; cf. 1:8–9).[79]

The Galatians are in danger of falling away if they seek to become righteous by following the requirements of the Law, and this is a central concern motivating Paul's strong language (2:16–17; cf. 5:2–4). In Paul's argument the works of the Law do not serve the same function as they once did prior to the new era ushered in by Christ. The Law served its purpose by revealing and dealing with transgressions, but this made culpability greater for people who did wrongful things, and it highlighted the fact that all were prisoners enslaved by the power of sin, until Christ came (3:19–23).[80] The point of this passage does not seem to be centering on the notion that no one can keep the Law perfectly or without sinning. Nowhere in Galatians does Paul explicitly make this claim, and many ancient Jews did not think this way about the Law.[81] Given its sacrificial system of atonement for sins (e.g., Lev 1–5; 16), the Law in fact could be kept to the extent of permitting adherents to be considered blameless (cf. Luke 1:6; 18:20–21).[82] To be sure, one's strict adherence to all the requirements in the Law may have been considered by Paul or his Gentile converts to be a burden (e.g., Acts 15:10),[83] but this reason alone would not seem to be enough to condemn, as does Paul, those who are teaching the Galatians to follow the works of the Law.

For Paul sin seems to be a personified power enslaving everyone prior to the time of Christ, and the Law only amplified this condition; it could not produce righteousness or give "life" (Gal 3:19, 21–22; cf. 2:16, 21). Now that Christ has come, however, the believers are made righteous by faith(fulness) and are no longer kept under the child-guardian (παιδαγωγός) of the Law (2:16; 3:11–12, 24–25). *The old way of keeping the Law has become passé by virtue of the new era in Christ.* It could not bring about righteousness or faith(fulness), and it stresses the aspect of *doing* rather than persistent trust and obedience to God (cf. Gal 3:11–12/Hab 2:4; Lev 18:5). *The works*

79. Or, if one insists on the singular language of this passage, at least the primary agitator in the congregations will be judged.

80. Cf. McKnight, *Galatians*, 182: The law's "function was to declare that the whole world is a prisoner of sin" (Gal 3:22). See also Esler, *Galatians*, 197, for thoughts about how the law made sin greater.

81. For evidence against works righteousness/merit theology in Second Temple literature see e.g., Sanders, *Paul and Palestinian Judaism*; albeit, Second Temple literature may be more diverse on the issue than Sanders had supposed: cf. Carson et al., *Justification and Variegated Nomism*, vol. 1.

82. In the Lukan passages, being righteous and blameless within the Law does not appear to be equated with being perfect or sinless. Zechariah, though righteous and blameless, will be chastised with temporary muteness because he doubted the angel's words (Luke 1), and the rich young ruler, who has kept the Mosaic commandments, will favor his wealth and possessions over following Jesus (Luke 18).

83. An alternative or multifaceted interpretation of Gal 3:10–12 and 5:3 might assume this aspect also. Paul may have believed that keeping the entire Law was possible to do yet burdensome, at least for his Gentile audience.

of the Law specially relevant to the Galatian situation include Jewish precepts related to circumcision, food, and calendar observances (Gal 2:11–14/Acts 10:28; 4:3–11) although other customs or items related to the Law also may be included.[84] Ultimately if the Mosaic covenant itself is insufficient to bring about faith(fulness) and righteousness (Gal 2:21; 3:11–12, 21–22), then in some sense all works apart from the command in Leviticus to love one's neighbor would seem insufficient for the new era of faithfulness (Lev 19:18/Gal 5:6, 14).[85] In the new era the believers are to follow the "law of Christ," which refers to Jesus' adaptation of the Law's command to love one's neighbor as oneself (Gal 6:2; cf. Luke 10:26–28; Mark 12:31; Matt 22:39–40). Rather than practicing the law of love, the Galatians are beginning to observe special days on the Jewish calendar, and Paul considers this a type of enslavement akin to the paganism they once practiced before their redemption (4:3–11).

Paul believes the opponents' teachings to be a threat to his divinely given commission to reach Gentiles. *An implicit solution to this threat is to expel the troublemakers from the community of churches as Hagar and Ishmael were expelled from Abraham* (Gal 4:29–30). The message through the allegory may be subtle, but it does seem to be directed at the opponents who are themselves threatening to exclude the Gentiles believers (cf. 4:17).[86]

WORKS OF THE FLESH AND WORKS OF THE LAW (3:6–13; 5:19–23)

Even though the new era of being in Christ has arrived for Paul and other Christ-followers, we may wish to ask why such a view would be sufficient to condemn those who kept the works of the Law. In Galatians we have in essence two peoples: those who are of faith(fulness) and blessed, and "those" (ὅσος) who are of the works of the Law and cursed (Gal 3:9–11; cf. vv. 13–14).[87] The latter are cursed because they do not keep all things that are written in "the book of the Law" (Gal 3:10/Deut 27:26).

---

84. Dunn, *Theology of Paul*, 358 does not restrict the meaning of Jewish identity markers to the three focal points of circumcision, special days, and food laws.

85. Yet, paradoxically, Paul seems to hold to sexual prohibitions from Leviticus in 1 Cor 5, perhaps based on Gentile prohibitions in Acts 15.

86. The interpretation of this text, however, may not be limited to the opponents: see further Dunn, *Galatians*, 258–59. While it is possible that the opponents used Gen 21:10 against Paul (e.g., Longenecker, *Galatians*, 127), we would seem to be mirror reading the text by affirming this point.

87. Morland, *Rhetoric of Curse*, 202, suggests the plural of ὅσος in Gal 3:10 (translated "those" rather than "as many as") is a pronoun referring to different groups in Galatia (3:27 [Galatians]; 6:12 [opponents]; 6:16 [readers]). Other impersonal pronouns likewise refer to the opponents (see Morland, 111–13, for references, and further Wisdom, *Blessing to the Nations*, 160–64). Morland is basically correct, although 3:27 seems more universal than merely the Galatians. It is probably more accurate to say that ὅσος in Galatians often has a specific group in view without necessarily precluding other groups.

In view of the Deuteronomic sources Paul cites in Gal 3:10–13, cursing happens to those who break God's covenant—they face expulsion from God's community and other calamities mentioned in Deut 28–29.[88] Yet the Abrahamic covenant may still be in view where God curses those who curse Abraham and his children, children which include the "nations" or Gentiles who believe (Gal 3:6–9/Gen 12:3). For Paul, it seems, God's "curse" is also against those who would come against Abraham's posterity.

Paul's somewhat unexpected inclusion of Abraham in Gal 3:6–9 and the curse in 3:10, cited from Deut 27:26, may suggest his opponents used such thoughts to support their view.[89] Perhaps they held up Abraham as a model for circumcision (cf. Gen 17) and frightened the Gentile believers with a curse: if they refuse to be circumcised, they are not part of the elect community and so are subject to the divine wrath warned against in Deut 27–32. Is Paul playing on two nuances of the word "law" with "works of [the] Law" in Gal 3:10a and "Book of the Law" (i.e., Scripture/Pentateuch) in 3:10b (cf. 2:19; 4:21) to accuse the agitators of not living by faith as did Abraham (found in Genesis, before the Mosaic covenant)?[90] If so, then this would strengthen the link between Abraham's faith and blessing in 3:6–9 and the Deuteronomic covenant in 3:10. By the opponents creating a bifurcation between themselves and uncircumcised believers, they either deny or impede the promise of blessing to the nations, which the gospel preached beforehand through Abraham prior to any command relative to circumcision (Gal 3:6–9/Gen 12; cf. 2:11–14; 4:17; 5:12–13, 26; 6:13). Hence the opponents become the enemies of God, cursed for violating Abraham's example of faith found in the Scriptures and cursed for cursing Abraham's posterity that includes Gentiles. They are also covenant breakers subject to God's judgment for doing this, for they do not follow the example of Abraham (in Genesis), which belongs to the "Book of the Law." In ironic fashion these teachers of the Torah contradict the Torah by showing themselves to be enemies of Abraham.

A weakness with this interpretation is that it assumes Paul's Gentile audience—many of whom are recent converts and former idolaters—would have caught the subtle distinction between the Mosaic Law and Genesis as included within the "Book of the Law" in 3:10. On this interpretation, Paul seems to read the phrase "Book of the Law" as the entire Pentateuch, while the context in Deut 27:26 refers to the Mosaic Law alone, specifically, the Deuteronomic covenant. We would have to assume that he reconfigured the "Book of the Law" to include Genesis and Abraham,

88. See Forkman, *Limits of Religious Community*, as explained above.

89. Matera, *Galatians*, 121–22, discusses this issue in relation to his question on how it was expected that Gentiles be familiar with the text traditions in 3:7–13.

90. On the dual meaning of the Law see Morland, *Rhetoric of Curse*, 190, 220–21.

which were prior to the Mosaic Law. Another problem with this view is that it creates tensions with the aspect of "doing" in 3:10, which is related to mimicking Abraham's faith, and "doing" in 3:12, which is the opposite of faith.[91] At best this is twisted logic, though it is not impossible for Paul to argue this way.[92]

Perhaps a better alternative is to argue that the opponents do not themselves keep the Law, as Paul asserts in 6:12–13. The opponents violate the Mosaic command to love their neighbor due to their boastful, divisive and unloving behavior (cf. Gal 5:14/Lev 19:18). Hence they do not adhere to all things written in the Mosaic Law and so are cursed (Gal 3:10/Deut 27:26). This alternative works well *if* Paul expected the Galatians to hear the content of his letter several times so as to connect the dots between 3:10, 5:14, and 6:13. This view does not deny that the "curse" in 3:10 is still, in a secondary sense, associated with the curse against those who oppose Abraham's posterity, implied in the echo of Gen 12:3 in Gal 3:9. The argument in 3:10–14 still evokes the idea that the opponents do not operate by faith(fulness) as do Abraham's children. Moreover, they are void of Abraham's "blessing" because they operate under the old disposition of curse that regulates the Mosaic Law.

If we opt for the traditional viewpoint that in Gal 3:10 Paul is referring to the impossibility of keeping the entire Mosaic Law, we must draw an inference not clearly found in Galatians: that the Galatians, or at least Paul, believed it humanly impossible to keep the commandments of the Law. Against this assumption Paul could speak of his former days as a Pharisee in terms of being "blameless" when it came to his righteousness within the Law (Phil 3:4–6).

Another possibility is for us to consider the curse in 3:10 in nationalistic terms, based on the Deuteronomic curses for disobedience and apostasy (cf. Deut 28–32). With this interpretation in our mind, Israel has failed to obey the Law, and as a result Israel is still in exile by foreign powers despite returning to Jerusalem during the Second Temple Era.[93] Maybe from Paul's perspective Israel remains apostate if it continues to reject living by faith(fulness).[94] This meaning, however, centers on

91. Notice a similar problem raised by Longenecker, *Triumph*, 136–37. Longenecker interprets the works of the Law in terms of both Jewish markers and efforts to keep the entire Mosaic Law. This viewpoint has the advantage of a multifaceted interpretation of the Law of in Galatians, but it also has its setbacks related to Phil 3:4–6.

92. E.g., we notice the conundrum in 3:10: those who perform the works of the Law are cursed, but the citation from Deuteronomy claims that those who do *not* perform the works of the Law are cursed.

93. On the intertextual backdrop of this passage in relation to Deut 27–30, see Waters, *End of Deuteronomy*, 79–130. Waters (100) considers the curse in nationalistic terms. On the exile view, see also Scott, *Exile*; Wright, *Climax of the Covenant*: Jesus as Israel's representative marks the end of the national exile by dying on the cross, taking upon himself the curse of the people, and rising again from the dead.

94. Grindheim, "Apostate Turned Prophet," stresses Israel's apostasy by arguing that Paul sees him-

Israel instead of Paul's opponents, and the entire thrust of the letter, including 3:10–12, seems to argue against Paul's opponents who are Christ-followers, not Israel as a nation or people per se. The exile view, like the other perspectives, is not without critics. Dunn, among other points, argues that Paul did not appear to be aware of such a curse in his robust view of keeping the Law as a Pharisee (Phil 3:4–6; cf. Gal 1:13–14; Rom 2:17–20; 10:2–3).[95] Some sources from the Second Temple Era would seem to agree with their rather positive views of the restored people and worship that seems to be blessed by God (cf. Sir 49:12–50:24; Wis 10:15; *Jub.* 2.19–20).[96]

One final option we will entertain is that perhaps the clearest intention of Gal 3:10–12 is forever shrouded behind Paul's rhetorical goal of denouncing the opponents' view of the Law. He is not a scholastic theologian but an upset pastor and missionary who uses emotional persuasion, loaded language ("curse"), and an appeal to the authority of scriptures (Deut 27:26; Hab 2:4; Lev 18:5; Deut 21:23) to make his points, with the assumption that his congregations would know what he is talking about even though his arguments remain unclear to us.

Some of these viewpoints may be combined so that an eclectic answer from what we can decipher in *3:10 suggests that it is directed primarily at the opponents who are considered covenant violators and cursed primarily for breaking the Mosaic Law to love their neighbors, and in this circumstance their neighbors are the Gentile Christ-followers in Galatia. The believing Gentiles in Galatia are among the blessed children of Abraham who live by faith(fulness).*

More than this, as Paul's argument continues, by insisting on keeping the works of the Law the opponents are condemning uncircumcised Christians, and the Law is being used as an incentive to exclude faithful Gentiles from inheriting God's promises (cf. 1:6; 4:17; 5:10). The works of the Law, then, when imposed on the Gentile Christ-followers, becomes the occasion for divisions among those who profess to believe in Christ. It is not by coincidence that Paul includes vices of division in his list of "works of the flesh" (5:19–21). For Paul the "works of the flesh" are deeds associated with the pre-converted status of individuals void of God's Spirit and subject to the evil era.[97] To indulge in these works is to commit vices and live in a manner

---

self in the role of a Hebrew prophet denouncing Israel's disloyalty to God. He notices that, similar to Paul, Jer 11:3 alludes to Deut 27:10, 26, and Ezek 20 invokes Lev 18:5 to address Israel's problem. Grindheim thinks the apostasy is related to "failure to believe in Jesus" (564). This view works well if Paul has non-Christian Israel in view (as in Rom 9–11), but if Paul's opponents are primarily in view in Gal 3:10–12, and they are Jewish Christians, then they *do* believe in Jesus.

95. Dunn, *Galatians*, 172–74.

96. See further, Wisdom, *Blessing for the Nations*, 157–58. For other criticism of the exile view, see O'Brien, "Was Paul a Covenantal Nomist?" 12–20.

97. For Gentiles, pre-conversion would amount to their status as "pagans"; for a Jew like Paul this

incompatible with the leading of God's Spirit (5:16–18, 22–25). The danger of committing these vices is so grave that a person whose lifestyle is characterized by such activities will be excluded from God's kingdom.[98] The works of the flesh mentioned in these lists may be somewhat conventional, but they are not peripheral to the situation in Paul's respective letters; in fact, they are sometimes extremely relevant to the situation (see on Corinthians below).[99] The warning in 5:21b does not pertain to the opponents, who are already cursed, but to the believers (cf. προεῖπον/προλέγω: 1 Thess 4:6; 2 Cor 13:2; Mark 13:23; Matt 24:25; *1 Clem.* 58.1).[100] *It is the Christ-followers who are in danger of practicing these vices and not inheriting God's kingdom.*

Be that as it may, the Galatians as well as the opponents appear to be committing vices related to division: "strife," "disputes," "dissensions," and "factions" (5:19–21; cf. Gal 4:17; 5:15, 26). To this we might add that Paul did not intend to be exhaustive with his vice list; the sins he mentions are only samplings of the vices one could commit. We notice "such things as these" in 5:19 (cf. Rom 1:32). These "works of the flesh" are committed in social spaces, disrupting unity in the congregations and thus violate the ethical command to "love your neighbor as yourself" (5:14). They are also characteristic of the types of sins those who belong to the "evil age" commit (1:4). For the Galatians *the works of the Law, as imposed by the opponents, become an incentive for division and similar works of the flesh.* The connection between "works of the Law" and "works of the flesh" would not seem to be missed by the original audience (cf. 5:16, 18, 19, 23). Hence, the works of the Law become the great divider among Jewish and Gentile Christians, and division is a work of the flesh leading to apostasy and eschatological separation from God and his kingdom. The opponents' disruptive teachings would seem to place them under a curse that leads to their exclusion from God, and we miss the full explication of the curses in 1:8–9 and 3:10–13 without adding this dimension to it. The "gospel" of the agitators is creating factions among the Galatians.

Those who are delivered from the old era, by contrast, are to operate in the Spirit and practice the "fruit" of love and other virtues (Gal 5:22–23; cf. 2 Cor 6:6; Phil 4:8; Col 3:12). The "fruit" of the Spirit may be contrasted with the "works" of the flesh to suggest that these virtues are gracious benefits that originate with the Galatians' reception of the Spirit, and yet with this foundation intact they are to cul-

---

would include his former lifestyle as a Pharisee hostile towards the Christ-followers.

98. Gal 5:19–21; cf. 5:15–16; 6:7–8; 1 Cor 6:9–11; 5:11; 10:5–10; 2 Cor 12:20–21; Rom 1:29–32; 13:13; Col. 3:5, 8; Eph 4:25–32; 5:3–5.

99. This is one point I stress in Oropeza, "Situational Immorality," 9–10. See also Engberg-Pedersen, "Paul, Virtues, and Vices," 608–9.

100. See e.g., Gal 5:21b NASB: ". . . of which I forewarn [προλέγω] you, just as I have forewarned [προεῖπον] you, that those who practice such things will not inherit the kingdom of God."

tivate the fruit actively.[101] This involves a lifestyle of regular surrender to the Spirit's guidance and control.[102] The contrast between "works" and "fruit," then, does not support a view that the latter is entirely passive, involving no effort on the part of the believer. Elsewhere in Galatians, one must actively work at one's faith (Gal 5:6; 6:4, 10; cf. 1 Thess 1:3; Phil 2:12; Rom 1:5).[103] Paul's instructions here would not fall on deaf ears; the Galatians are no strangers to the Spirit's presence (Gal 3:5; 6:1 cf. 4:29).[104] They must "walk in the Spirit" (5:16, 25; cf. 5:18)—an activity that involves both subjective-relational and ethical dimensions (cf. 3:5; 4:6; 5:22–23)—because those who walk in the Spirit will not cave in to the desires of the flesh. In this sense the Spirit seems to function as the *Halakah* for the new era.

The curse in 3:10 is mostly directed at the opponents in contrast to the faithful in 3:6–9, whereas freedom from the curse in 3:13 centers on believers and especially anticipates 3:14–25 where the apostle brings out how the era of Law was temporarily established to expose transgressions while at the same time it could not bring about righteousness. This all changed with the coming of Christ. The remedy against the works of the Law becomes Christ's atoning sacrifice—he is made a curse "for us" (Gal 3:13/ Deut 21:23). Here "us" refers primarily to Paul and like-minded Jewish Christians who were the first people redeemed by Christ, showing that the gospel and blessings pertaining to it had to come to the Jews first before it came to the Gentiles (Gal 3:14; cf. Rom 15:8–9).[105] After Christ's death redeemed the faithful from exclusion and the punishments prescribed by the Deuteronomic curses, which apparently prefigure eschatological judgment, God's blessing to the Gentiles in Christ could now be fulfilled (Gal 3:14–18).

Christ's crucifixion provides a new means of atonement through his substitutionary death (3:13; cf. 1:4a; 2:20–21; 5:11b). The phrase "for us" (3:13) is most likely echoed from the Isaianic Servant tradition (Isa 52:12—53:12) that occurs in various faith formulas used by early Christ followers, including Paul. Ben Meyers lists a total of five aspects of expiation from Isa 53 that are used as early faith formulas: 1) the eucharistic combinations of "poured out" and "many";[106] 2) the confession formula

---

101. See Betz, *Galatians*, 286–87.

102. Cf. McKnight, *Galatians*, 269. How God/the Spirit and humans can work or cooperate together has been traditionally understood in terms of synergism. However, Barclay, "By the Grace of God," 156–57, suggests another term to describe divine grace at work in active humans: "the placement of one agency 'within' the other," a thought that he names as "energism." In Paul's thinking, "the work of the Spirit does not substitute for but precisely energizes, the work of the believer."

103. Rightly, Longenecker, *Galatians*, 259.

104. See Martyn, *Galatians*, 534–36.

105. See Longenecker, *Triumph*, 90–95.

106. Mark 14:24; cf. Matt 26:28; Luke 22:20; John 6:51/Isa 53:11–12.

"for our sins";[107] 3) the combination of "gave himself for" with a genitive or similar constructions, which are found in Galatians and other passages;[108] 4) "suffering for" with a genitive or something similar;[109] and 5) echoes of Isa 53:10 LXX in Rom 8:3 and 2 Cor 5:21. Although Paul expounds on the meaning of such formulas, they seem to antedate his writings.[110] Here we have hints pointing to the arrival of the Isaianic new era: the deliverance of God's people comes by way of a leader or leaders, one of whom plays the role of the sacrificial servant described in Isa 53.

The act of redeeming (ἐξαγοράζω) in Gal 3:13 is probably economic, combining the imagery of purchasing a slave with God's obtaining of a people from Egypt. To this Paul adds scapegoat imagery: the idea of "curse" transmitted to a victim (cf. Lev 16; 2 Cor 5:21). Paul's blending of these colorful notions is well noted by Stephen Finlan: "He makes the cultic act the *currency* that pays the ransom: Christ redeems *by* becoming a curse. The scapegoat exchange somehow *pays the ransom* . . . [Christ] takes on a negative *ritual* condition so that humanity can take on positive *judicial* and *social* conditions (acquitted and freed)."[111] An implication that may be drawn from this transaction is that *the Law's sacrificial procedure of bringing offerings to atone for guilt and sin has now been fulfilled through the sacrificial death of Christ as God's faithful servant and representative Israelite*; the old method is now rendered insufficient for those who are in Christ.

Paul and other Jews who are in Christ ("us" in 3:13), and who prior to their conversion held to a stricter view of the Law for Gentiles, have been delivered from the curse of the Law. The era of the Mosaic covenant, with its curses and prescriptions against transgressors and its inability to make people righteous or give life (3:19–24), has given way to a new era in which God's people consist of both Jews and Gentiles made righteous by Christ and who live on the basis of faith(fulness), loving others, and being led by God's Spirit (2:16, 20; 3:25–29; 5:16–25; 6:2–4). It should be noted here that the curse related to the "works of the Law" (ἔργων νόμου) in 3:10 is more particularized than the curse "of the Law" (τοῦ νόμου) in 3:13. The former curse targets primarily the opponents and pertains to their teachings and hypocritical deeds; the latter curse is not associated with "works" of the Law but the Law itself. It focuses more on the dispensation of the Mosaic Law that is regulated

107. 1 Cor 15:3–5/Isa 53:5.

108. Gal 1:4; 2:20; Eph 5:2, 25; 1 Tim 2:6; Titus 2:14; Mark 10:45; Matt 20:28/Isa 53:6, 10 LXX; 53:5, 12 Targum.

109. Rom 5:6–8; 2 Cor 5:14–15; 1 Pet 2:21; 3:18/Isa 53.

110. Meyer, "Expiation Motif," 18–19. On Gal 3:10–13 and the subsitutionary death of the Isaianic Servant, see also Merklein, "Bedeutung des Kreuzestodes Christi," 24–25.

111. Finlan, *Problems with Atonement*, 44–48, quote from 45 (emphases original).

by curses on disobedient adherents in contrast to the "blessing" of the Spirit given to those who have faith (cf. 3:14).

In the new era, it seems, Paul considers humanity under two spheres—the old era with its works of the Law that finds its basis in the Mosaic covenant, and the new creation that operates on the basis of faith(fulness) and living "in Christ" through the Spirit (3:23–29 cf. 1:4; 6:15). For those who belong to the new age, the Law has been relegated to a single command to love one's neighbor as oneself (5:13–14). In a very broad sense,[112] then, 3:10, 13 speaks to 3:19: the Law functions as a revealer of transgressions. Galatians 3:11–12 looks forward to 3:21–24: the Law highlighted human transgressions in an epoch ruled by the power of sin.[113] The Law could not give "life" or Spirit-granted power to bring about righteousness; it lacked Christ's redemption and its results. Those under the old evil age operated under the spheres of sin and curse. For Paul, the "stumbling block" (σκάνδαλον: 5:11) of the cross is the message that Jesus as Messiah was wrongly convicted as an apostate, he suffered curse and death and, through his crucifixion, eschatological salvation and righteousness are made possible to both Jews and Gentiles on the basis of faith(fulness) rather than the Torah.[114] Thus *one more implication related to Paul's cursing the opponents appears to be that by their imposing the works of the Law on Gentile Christ-followers, they are essentially nullifying the redemptive work of Christ's death, making it insufficient for saving all people, genders, and social classes* (3:13 cf. 3:19–29).

If there remain loose ends to Paul's view of the Law in Galatians, it may be due primarily to his rhetorical aim. His goal is to discourage the Galatians from accepting the works of the Law, which for him turns out to be more important than the theological consistency of all the reasons he gives for rejecting the works of the Law. The Galatians should not follow the works of the Law because these works lead to condemning and excluding Abraham's Gentile posterity, create division among believers, do not operate on the basis of faith(fulness), make the atoning work of Christ insufficient for redemption, and expose transgressions without bringing about righteousness and spiritual life. If Paul is primarily concerned about winning

112. That is, without our denying the particularized sense of 3:10 as pertaining primarily to the opponents.

113. Among the interpretations of 3:22, "the scripture" may refer to Deuteronomy 27:26 (Longenecker, *Galatians*, 144), the Law (Bruce, *Galatians*, 180), or the collective body of Israel's scriptures that probably includes a catena of verses similar to Rom 3:9–18 (Dunn, *Galatians*, 194). In any case the thought of the Law still seems present from 3:21.

114. The noun form of σκάνδαλον for Paul often interacts with unbelief and apostasy (cf. 1 Cor 1:23; Rom 9:33; 11:9; 14:13; 16:17). Betz, *Galatians*, 270, observes the proper nuance in 5:11: "the Christian message presents the unbeliever with a central and indispensible element of 'provocation' and 'alienation.' Without this element, the Christian message has lost its integrity and identity, i.e., its truth."

the Galatians to his way of thinking, it seems plausible that he would throw at them every reason he could think of to discourage them from following his opponents and thus committing apostasy. In the end, what we are left with in Galatians is a compilation of reasons to reject the works of the Law that appear to make the Mosaic covenant virtually useless in the present era. Had Paul's audience been Jewish Christ-followers from Judea, such as Peter and James, we could speculate that Paul might have tempered his arguments, perhaps affirming that Jewish Christ-followers are not under any curse if they keep the works of the Law, so long as they do not impose such works on Gentile Christians. As it stands in Galatians, Peter or James probably would not have shared Paul's conviction that those who follow the works of the Law are cursed.

MORE WARNINGS OF APOSTASY TO THE GALATIANS (5:2–4; 6:1, 7–9)

The threat of apostasy among the Galatians is conveyed in terms of deserting or changing one's allegiance (μετατίθημι: Gal 1:6; cf. 2 Macc 7:24; *Mart. Pol.* 11.1), being bewitched or influenced by the evil eye (βασκαίνω: Gal 3:1; cf. Deut 28:56; *T. Sol.* 18.39), being hindered (ἐγκόπτω) from one's journey by a different persuasion (Gal 5:7–8; cf. 1 Thess 2:18), and turning back (ἐπιστρέφω) to enslavement and weak spiritual elements (Gal 4:8–9 cf. 2 Pet 2:21; *Barn.* 4:8; *Herm. Sim.* 8.7.5).[115] Paul fears that he may have labored "in vain" (εἰκῇ) for them (Gal 4:11/Isa 49:4) and warns that their seeking to be justified by the Law leads to falling from grace and being cut off from Christ. The end result of this apostasy is that they would once again be subject to the evil age, enslaved by transgressions and external powers, and finally be subject to eschatological destruction (Gal 5:2–4 cf. 1:4; 2:16, 18; 3:19–24; 4:1–11; 5:21; 6:7–8).

Paul warns the Galatians who seek to be circumcised that Christ will be of no benefit to them and they will become debtors to keep "the whole law" (5:2–3),[116] which may be Paul's abbreviated way of saying that circumcision will obligate them to adopt the total manner of Jewish life and customs.[117] This would apparently in-

---

115. The verb ἐπιστρέφω has special significance related to religious conversion either in a negative sense (as in the examples above) or in a positive sense: 2 Cor 3:16; 1 Thess 1:9; Acts 9:35; John 12:40; Jas 5:19–20; 1 Pet 2:25; Deut 30:11; Josephus, *Ant.* 10.53; *1 Clem.* 59.4; BDAG, 382. For further elaboration on concepts related to apostasy in Galatians, see Morland, *Rhetoric of Curse*, 142–48.

116. In the passage compare "benefit" (ὠφελέω) in 1 Cor 13:3; Heb 4:2; Mark 8:36; Luke 9:25.

117. On this view see Sanders, *Paul, the Law*, esp. 27–29. Differently, Hays, *Galatians*, 312, views law and grace as locations, and this passage refers to entering the "sphere where the Law is sovereign." There may also be a hint of Paul considering the observance of the Law in its entirety as a burden (cf.

clude their coming under the jurisdiction of the Jewish courts and risking potential physical punishment, such as flogging, if they committed transgression (e.g., 2 Cor 11:24; Lev 24:16; *m. Makkot* 3).[118] Even so, their potential to undergo human punishment if violating the Law would not seem to account for the full force of Paul's severe words. The assumption here may be that their obligation to the whole Law would require them to follow the Mosaic sacrificial system as the means of atonement from sin—which nullifies, reverts, or renders insufficient the redemptive work of Christ's death on the cross and all it entails (cf. Gal 1:4; 3:13; 3:23–25; 4:4–6). It dismantles a connection between his death and salvation; in essence, Christ would have died in vain (2:18, 21; 3:22). That Christ would be of no use to them suggests that they would no longer benefit from his atoning death and the redemption it provides (5:2; cf. 2:21). As such, they would be without Christ when it comes to receiving a favorable verdict at the final judgment (5:5).[119]

In keeping with the circumcision language, Paul warns that if the Galatians get circumcised and follow the works of the Law they will be severed from Christ (5:3–4).[120] In other words *if the Galatians cut off their foreskins, they will be cut off from Christ.* It may strike us as odd how he could warn the Galatians that their getting circumcised would be tantamount to committing apostasy while at the same time maintaining circumcision as merely ineffectual in comparison to faith working through love (cf. Gal 5:6; 1 Cor 7:18–19). Presumably it is not so much the act of circumcision that cuts off Gentile believers from Christ but what circumcision represents in this case: it becomes a conversion ritual that obligates the neophyte to follow the entire Law (Gal 5:2). If righteousness involves participation "in Christ" and a relationship with him (cf. 1:22; 2:4; 3:26–28; 5:6), then being severed from Christ would be the converse of this: no union or participatory relationship with Christ. An individual with this status does not belong to Christ but with those who are under sin's power in the evil age and will not inherit God's kingdom (1:4; 6:8; cf. 5:21). Moreover, if the Galatians are to "stand" in Christian liberty (5:1), then to be justified by the works of the Law is to "fall" from grace and be enslaved again under the Law (Gal 5:4; cf. Rom 5:2). In this verse grace may be understood as "the entire process of salvation in Christ."[121] The works of the Law nullify grace because such

Longenecker, *Galatians*, 226), but Sanders, 28–29, qualifies that this may be true for Gentiles but not Jews.

118. On this idea for Paul, see Harvey, "Forty Strokes," esp. 87–88.

119. See Dunn, *Galatians*, 264, 269–70.

120. Here καταργέω may be understood as "to take from the sphere of operation" and finds its opposite in Rom 7:6 with those who are discharged or severed from the Law and no longer are enslaved under it but walk in the new life of the Spirit: cf. Delling, "καταργέω," 1.454.

121. Betz, *Galatians*, 126.

works remain bound up with traditions that have already found their full realization in God's salvific plan through Christ.[122] Grace also focuses on Christ's substitutionary death (Gal 2: 20–21) as referenced in the *propositio* of Paul's deliberative argument in Galatians, where righteousness/justification comes by faith(fulness) instead of by the works of the Law (2:16–21). *Falling from grace, then, would be the reversal of justification by faith(fulness); it involves a complete nullifying of the atoning work of Christ in a believer's life and the righteousness this brings.*

Clearly for the Galatians, salvation is a process, and participating in Christ's righteousness does not guarantee a remaining in righteousness and escaping from condemnation at the final judgment if they follow the works of the Law. Final righteousness/justification will come as a result of their continuing in faith and remaining in Christ's righteousness, both of which are exemplified by their living in the Spirit and in love as opposed to practicing the works of the "flesh" related to the old era in which "sowing" or fostering vice-related activities will ultimately "reap" eternal corruption (φθορά), the opposite of eternal life (6:7–8; cf. 5:5, 16, 21; 2 Pet 2:12). The believers are encouraged not to grow weary in doing good, because they will eventually reap eternal life if they persevere and do not give up faith (6:9). If there is a forensic aspect to righteousness by faith(fulness), it seems to rest more on a person being acquitted on judgment day than on the day of his/her conversion-initiation. Barrett asserts that justification "leads to a consummation at the future judgment, when God's initial gracious verdict on the sinner is—or is not—confirmed," and the initially justified sinner "can de-justify himself and secure his condemnation by his flouting of grace."[123]

For those believers who have been overtaken by any sin related to the vices in 5:19–21, there is potential recovery in 6:1. The trespass (παράπτωμα) in 6:1 is considered by Paul as a sin or an immoral act (cf. Rom 4:25; 11:11–12; 2 Cor 5:19; Col 2:13; cf. Matt 6:15). Those who operate in the fruit of the Spirit (i.e., the "spiritual") are to restore such individuals, being mindful that they themselves are susceptible to temptations. The trespass may convey entrapment (προλαμβάνομαι; cf. Josephus, *Ant.* 5.79).[124] If the person were to continue in the vice, the outcome would be their exclusion from God's kingdom (Gal 5:21; 6:7–8); hence, such a person may be considered either an apostate via immorality or headed towards apostasy if not restored. The latter is probably more accurate, given that the trespass is in the singular (τινι παραπτώματι) and it appears in the context of congregation members loving one

122. Cf. Barclay, *Obeying the Truth*, 240.

123. Barrett, *Freedom and Obligation*, 65.

124. So Longenecker, *Galatians*, 272. On this possible nuance for "overtaken" as catching the person by surprise, see Betz, *Galatians*, 295.

another and bearing each other's burdens (6:2–5). Paul does not specify if such an individual is still meeting with the congregation or stopped coming to the gathering. His words would seem to be valid in either case. Paul does not mention whether his opponents could be restored from their false teachings; he focuses instead on the recovery of congregation members from moral failure. Elsewhere he believes that apostate Israel (Rom 11:26–29), apostate vice-doers (1 Cor 5:5), and even divisive individuals who attack him on a personal level (2 Cor 2:5–11) could be forgiven and restored to good standing within a congregation. If some of the vices are directly related to causing divisions, then presumably it is possible to restore the culprits of such divisions.

Given that the works of the flesh lead to ultimate exclusion from God's kingdom (Gal 5:21), vice would seem to lead to apostasy in terms of a reversion back to pre-converted practices. Paul does not explain how this transition or exit ritual from believer to non-believer takes place.[125] *He nowhere teaches some sort of fixed number of sins that must be committed in order to become apostate; such a determination seems better discerned through a person's lifestyle, character, and intentions of heart.*[126] Is this decision based purely on a verdict made by God or Christ on judgment day? Passages such as Rom 14:4 and 2 Cor 5:10 lean in this direction. On the other hand, Paul may assume that sometimes divine judgment can take place against congregational vice-doers before the culmination of the eschaton (cf. 1 Cor 10:1–12). There is also evidence that Paul and other leaders of the church sometimes determine when congregants have crossed over the boundary line into apostasy with their wicked behavior and thus need to be "out" of the community (1 Cor 5:1–5; Titus 3:10–11; Matt 18:15–20). Paul excludes a vice-doer from God's community in Corinth and claims to operate by the authority of Christ to perform the exit ritual. The person was committing this sin willfully, persistently, apparently with a boastful attitude, and it was reaping a negative influence on other congregation members (1 Cor 5:1–5). Clearly, the nature of the trespasser's sin in Gal 6:1 is not of the same caliber, but it nonetheless can lead to apostasy. Similar to the vice-doer in Corinth, on the other hand, the opponents in Galatia who teach the works of the Law are to be cast "out" of the community (4:30).

125. Jas 1:13–15 attempts an explanation, but James's view is not necessarily Paul's.

126. Yinger, *Paul, Judaism, and Judgment*, 19–63, examines motifs related to judgment in the Jewish scriptures and concludes that "the boundary between apostasy and fidelity is nowhere legislated in unambiguous fashion, since it is a matter not of legal boundaries but of the human heart and of sovereign divine freedom. Hence questions as to the quantity of transgressions necessary to activate God's wrath are pointless. The sinner cannot check in any legal code to determine his/her standing with God" (63).

CONCLUSION

The Galatian community to whom Paul writes consists of Gentiles who are Christ-followers and have recently converted from idolatry to serve the God of Israel. A missionary-styled group of Jewish Christ-followers were pressuring them to be circumcised with the threat of exclusion from God's people if they refused. Paul echoes the exodus story when describing how the Galatians have been redeemed through Christ but are now turning away from God to become enslaved to the works of the Law, a phenomenon akin to their former days of enslavement as idolatrous non-believers (Gal 1:6; 4:1–11). Whereas the opponents are attempting to bring these Gentile converts into conformity with the Torah and thus draw them further away from their idolatrous roots, Paul discourages assimilation with Jewish customs by associating the view of the opponents with the Gentiles' idolatrous past. The Galatians face a danger of defecting from Paul's version of the gospel to another gospel that, according to Paul, brings curse and condemnation (1:8–9; 3:10–13). For Paul the works of the Law highlight human transgression and cannot produce righteousness or faith(fulness). Christ's sacrificial death in the new era has made possible righteousness by fidelity that opens the way for both Jews and Gentiles to become one community participating "in Christ" (cf. 3:19–29). Those who operate on the principle of faith(fulness), as did Abraham, are blessed with spiritual life, but the opponents are under a curse for following the Mosaic Law that cannot make them righteous in the new era. It instead reveals them as violators of the Law's fundamental command to love one another. The opponents likewise are cursed for condemning and excluding Abraham's posterity, creating factions among believers, and making the atoning work of Christ insufficient for redemption through their teachings. The Galatians are warned that if they seek to be circumcised and made righteous by the Law, Christ's atoning work on the cross will not profit them and they will fall away from divine grace (5:2–4). This will result in their being cut off from their union with Christ and his community.

Paul's warnings against falling away to vices come to the foreground when confronting Gentile believers under the temptation of reverting back to former practices. Paul's converts in Galatia are discouraged from practicing "works of the flesh." The vice list in Galatians adds various sins of factionalism to the standard list, it seems, because this is the area in which the Galatians are most susceptible, given the false teachers' influence on them (cf. 5:19–21). There is an assumption that members of the congregations are causing divisions. The end result of apostasy, whether it occurs by adhering to the works of the Law or by indulging in the "works of the flesh," amounts to eternal destruction and exclusion from God's kingdom (5:21; 6:7–8).

Restoration is possible for believers ensnared by vices (6:1), but Paul implies through the allegory of Hagar and Ishmael that the teachers of the distorted gospel should be expelled from the churches (4:29–30).

The situations in Galatia and Antioch (2:10–15) suggest that Jewish Christ-followers from Jerusalem maintained circumcision and other Jewish customs. The decision made at the Jerusalem meeting in Acts 15 (cf. Gal 2:1–10) apparently did not change internal Judean Christian practices; it only altered Gentile Christian practices by demarcating the Mosaic rules necessary for them to maintain fellowship with Jewish Christians. Paul, however, is addressing Gentile Christians in Galatia and a network of congregations he personally evangelized and helped convert to Christ. The passion by which he challenges those who are being influenced by the works of the Law seems motivated by his personal ministerial work within this community, as well his own conversion experience from a zealous Pharisee and persecutor of the church to a missionary called by Christ to reach the Gentiles. If Acts helps inform the situation, he probably recognized that many Jews thought he had defected from Mosaic Law by eating with Gentiles and discouraging his converts to get circumcised. Hence, issues directly relevant to the Torah are at the center of his own calling and experiences with God.

The conflict between Jewish and Gentile Christ-followers emphasized in first-century Galatia betrays an emergent Christian movement in which conflicting beliefs and practices related to the Torah were held by those who agreed that Jesus is the Christ. Paul's opponents, as well as his previous encounter with "false brothers" and his open confrontation with Peter in view of the party of James, present us with at least three or four different positions that early Christ-followers held regarding the Torah. Paul championed the gospel of a new era in Christ in which Jews and Gentiles stand on equal religious footing by faith(fulness). On table fellowship James seems to hold to Torah regulations that distinguish Jewish and Gentile believers. Peter's actions at Antioch showed that he was somewhere in between Paul and James on the matter, and the "false brothers" as well as Paul's opponents considered the Law to be mandatory for Gentile Christ-followers. What Paul considers a false gospel would probably not be thought of that way by James and Peter, let alone his opponents. We can determine that Paul would consider the Galatians to be apostates if they decided to get circumcised. It is doubtful that Paul's warnings against the works of the Law would have been wholeheartedly embraced by many Jewish Christians of that time, including James, Peter, and the church in Jerusalem. Here we have another glimpse of inter-Christian and inter-Jewish conflicts in the first century.

Beyond Gal 2, Paul's Law-free gospel is often contrasted with Matthew's gospel, which stresses the importance of keeping the Law and condemning lawlessness. It seems that the Matthean community, which incidentally may have resided in Antioch (or part of the community anyway), would be more at home with James' view of the Torah than Paul's. Perhaps this should be expected because Paul's message is given primarily to Gentile Christians whereas Matthew's gospel is given primarily to Jewish Christians. Although shrouded with different agendas and audiences, these authors nevertheless come relatively close together when stressing that the heart of the Law is maintained by the phrase "love your neighbor as yourself." Paul adds a second major charge for his converts to keep: "walk in the Spirit." Matthew, on the other hand, highlights "love God" as the great command of the Torah.

Differently, the Johannine community's concept of abiding in Christ bears some similarities to Paul's community being "in Christ." Both affirm a mystical union with Christ involving the Spirit, and both emphasize the necessity of persevering in this relationship. In both communities the opponents are mostly other Christ-followers. Whereas the Johannine author assures his community with eternal life and reinforces their identity as God's children in order to prevent members from falling away to false christological teachings, Paul advances a different strategy. He attempts to dissuade the Galatian community from falling away by sternly warning them of consequences related to the works of the Law. They will be cut off from being "in Christ" if they cut off their foreskins. In Acts, the Lukan Paul's passion against false teachers in Ephesus resembles the fervent rhetoric of Paul that we find in Galatians. As Paul's colleague, Luke perhaps had special insights into Paul's character. Even so, their versions of the Jerusalem meeting are dissimilar. Luke's idealistic resolve of the early conflict related to the Law strikes a dissident chord when compared with Paul's perspective.

2

1 and 2 Thessalonians: Persecution, *Parousia*, and *Porneia* in a New Congregation

Paul's original mission to Thessalonica is presented in Acts 17:1–10, and he may have written to the Thessalonian church either from Athens or Corinth (cf. Acts 18:5; 1 Thess 1:1; 3:1). The first epistle to the Thessalonians may be Paul's oldest extant letter if written about 51 CE.[1] It was probably written only several months to about a year after the Thessalonians first converted to the gospel of Christ as proclaimed by Paul. In favor of this view, among other things, is that: 1) Timothy is sent to Thessalonica from Athens[2] and his safe return to Paul has taken place, coinciding with Paul's stay in Corinth in Acts (1 Thess 3:6; cf. 1:1; 2 Thess 1:1; Acts 18:5); 2) Silas is also with Paul,[3] but only during his so-called second missionary journey (2 Cor 1:19; Acts 15–18); and 3) there is no mention in the letter of a special collection, which is typical of the letters he writes during his third mission (1 Cor 16:1–4; 2 Cor 8–9; Rom 15:25–32).[4] The congregation members in Thessalonica, then, are newly converted to the gospel message of Paul, and their turning away from idols suggests they are Gentiles (1 Thess 1:9).

A number of interpreters reject Paul's authorship of 2 Thessalonians. Generally speaking some of the primary reasons include: 1) the eschatology argues against an imminent return of Christ as promoted in 1 Thess 5:1–11, which may be the letter mentioned in 2 Thess 2:2; 2) a pseudonym or forgery may be detected from 2 Thess

---

1. For discussion and date of the letter, see Söding, "Erst Thessalonicherbrief," 180–203; Malherbe, *Thessalonians*, 55–74.

2. 1 Thess 3:1–2; cf. Acts 17:15–34.

3. 1 Thess 1:1; 2 Thess 1:1; cf. Acts 18:5.

4. See further arguments and responses to rejoinders in Best, *Thessalonians*, 7–12.

3:17; 3) on a literary level, it seems to be dependent on 1 Thessalonians; 4) the letter lacks the personal tone of Paul in 1 Thessalonians.[5]

Scholarship, however, is by no means unanimous on this rejection.[6] Support for Paul's authorship include these reasons: 1) Polycarp already refers to this letter in the early second century, and there is insufficient time and no compelling situation for a pseudonym or forgery to gain widespread acceptance in Thessalonica before this time. 2) No persuasive explanation accounts for the "man of lawlessness" sitting in the temple of God (2 Thess 2:2) if, assuming this letter's pseudonymity, the temple was already destroyed in 70 CE. Figurative/symbolic interpretations of this temple sound like cases of special pleading. 3) The apparent tension in eschatological perspective between Thessalonian correspondences may be seen in other early Christian sources that emphasize both visible signs and unknowability regarding the end times/*parousia* (e.g., Mark 13; Matt 24). Such sources, incidentally, are alluded to in both 1 Thess 5 and 2 Thess 2 (see below). Paul could speak of both the imminence of the second coming and yet speculate about the possibility of his own death prior to that time (e.g., Phil 1:21–23; 4:5). 4) Stylistic and linguistic elements may in fact be Pauline, and the difference in tone may only confirm situational differences between the two letters. If the Corinthian correspondences or early and latter portions of Romans were examined by the same scrutiny applied to the Thessalonian letters, we wonder if major portions of these letters would likewise fail the test of Paul's authorship. 5) The forgery hypothesis based on 2 Thess 3:17 is a rather odd notion given that Paul's signature could be compared and verified by ancient readers (cf. Gal 6:11; 1 Cor 16:21; Phlm 19). Moreover, it would seem contradictory of the author of 2 Thessalonians to affirm in a positive way Paul's earlier correspondence to the Thessalonians (2 Thess 2:15) if this author intended to refute the previous correspondence's eschatology in 2 Thess 2:1–12. These are some of the main reasons why the view that 2 Thessalonians is written by someone other than Paul remains unconvincing.

This chapter will read the Thessalonian correspondence together, and we suggest that the second letter was written by Paul perhaps within months of the first.[7] The reason for the second letter, as some scholars have posited, may be due to

5. Relevance to our main agenda does not permit more thorough explanations here. For non-Pauline authorship see, e.g., Trilling, *Untersuchung zum zweiten Thessalonicherbrief*; Hughes, *Early Christian Rhetoric*, 75–95; Menken, *2 Thessalonians*, 27–43.

6. For Pauline authorship see, e.g., Jewett, *Thessalonian Correspondence*, 5–17; Malherbe, *Thessalonians*, 349–75; Wanamaker, *Thessalonians*, 17–28; Marshall, *Thessalonians*, 28–45; Frame, *Thessalonians*, 39–54.

7. Alternatively, Wanamaker, *Thessalonians*, 37–45, defends that 2 Thessalonians was written earlier than 1 Thessalonians, a view that raises criticisms from Green, *Thessalonians*, 64–69; and Witherington, *Thessalonians*, 14–16. In favor of 1 Thessalonians being written first, I add this to the discussion: Paul's

the Thessalonians misinterpreting the first letter on the imminence of the second coming (2 Thess 2:1–2). Then again, some false utterances may have taken place in the congregation, and Paul's signature at the end of the letter intends to safeguard against the possibility of a forged letter in his name.[8] He must, in any case, correct the congregation's imminent perspective on the end times.

PERSECUTION AT THE HANDS OF COMPATRIOTS
(1 THESS 1:6–9; 2:14–16; 3:3–5; 2 THESS 1:4–5)

In hyperbolic fashion Paul commends the Thessalonians for their exemplary model of faith despite opposition; they became examples to other believers "in every place" (1 Thess 1:6–8). The θλῖψις they experience is not merely referring to mental anguish but external opposition.[9] They suffer at the hands of their own compatriots, and yet they continue to persevere in faith (1 Thess 2:14; 3:1–8; 2 Thess 1:4, 6). The tone of 1 Thessalonians in the first half of the letter is primarily one of encouragement and thanksgiving due to the Thessalonians' perseverance despite afflictions. As recent converts who turned from idolatry to serve the God whom Paul proclaims (1:9), they could easily doubt their new faith due to societal pressures. Paul's positive words reinforce the congregation's perseverance through external harassment. Their faithfulness through hardships seems to increase their hope in being delivered from future divine punishment on judgment day (1:3, 10; cf. 5:23).[10] Problems in the congregation and warnings against potential apostasy become more evident in the later chapters. The apostle often considers persecution and afflictions to be beneficial for, and positive confirmation of, both his own and other believers' divine calling, though more often than not his optimism regarding suffering has his own hardships in view rather than those of his congregations (e.g., Rom 8:18–39; 2 Cor

---

confidence that the Thessalonians will not be overcome by Satan in 2 Thess 3:3 has been informed by Timothy's positive report of the congregation in 1 Thess 3:6. Prior to Timothy's return, Paul had apprehensions that Satan would overcome the congregation and they would commit apostasy (1 Thess 3:5).

8. For discussion on these options, see Jewett, *Thessalonian Correspondence*, 181–86, who sides with the misinterpretation view. Mitchell, "1 and 2 Thessalonians," 58–62, posits the danger of apostasy to paganism/idolatry in 1 Thessalonians and "misrepresentation of the authentic Pauline teaching about the end times and appropriate behaviour" in 2 Thessalonians. On the false utterance view see especially Giblin, *Threat to Faith*, 243–44, cf. 151.

9. See Still, *Conflict at Thessalonica*, 208–212, who argues, among other points, that the Thessalonians' imitation of the apostles in this regard (1 Thess 1:6), example to other churches (1 Thess 1:7; 2 Thess 1:4), and comparative suffering with the Judean Christians (1 Thess 2:14) make better sense if θλῖψις refers to external opposition rather than mental anguish. Contrast Malherbe, *Thessalonians*, 115.

10. On the relationship between perseverance and hope see further Denton, "Hope and Perseverance," 313–20.

1:3–7; 11:23–12:10; Phil 1:27–29; Col 1:24). Such affliction builds the endurance of the Thessalonians and marks them out as worthy for God's kingdom (2 Thess 1:4–5; cf. 1 Thess 2:12).[11] Paul also considers the affliction to be inevitable (1 Thess 3:3–4)[12] perhaps in anticipation of prophetic traditions that predicted an increase of tribulation or "messianic woes" before the end takes place (cf. Dan 12:1; *4 Ezra* 5.1–12; *2 Bar.* 70.2–10; *Jub.* 23.13–14; Mark 13:7–13; Matt 24:6–14).[13]

The apostle's words in 1 Thess 3:5 are atypical—he confesses here an anxiety over the possibility that the Thessalonians may be abandoning their faith as a result of their afflictions.[14] When he departed from the city, and prior to the return of Timothy who was sent in order to comfort them and determine their condition (1 Thess 3:1–6), Paul feared that the Tempter, that is, Satan (cf. 1 Cor 7:5; Mark 1:13; Matt 4:1), might have tempted them to abandon their faith, and his missionary labor among them would have been "in vain" (1 Thess 3:5; cf. Gal 4:11; 2 Cor 6:1; Phil 2:16; 1 Cor 15:58). Clearly Paul believes the Christ-confessors in Thessalonica are susceptible to committing apostasy.[15] As recent converts, if such calamity were to occur, this would make them precipitate defectors.

Malina and Pilch see Paul's laboring in vain as conveying shame and "a mark against his honor as change agent."[16] Perhaps so, but Paul seems more concerned about the Thessalonians' welfare than his own reputation. The nature of Satan's temptation for this church could hardly be anticipating Paul's exhortation material against sexually immoral behavior (1 Thess 4:1–8). Rather, Paul was plagued by deep concerns about their succumbing to the temptation of falling away from their faith because of persecution, and such apostasy would have rendered his missionary efforts among them to be useless.[17] Satan apparently influences outsiders to hinder God's work (2:18; 3:5),[18] and he likewise was instigating the Thessalonians' unbe-

11. Cf. Bruce, *Thessalonians*, 149.

12. Cf. Acts 14:22; Matt 10:16–25; John 16:33.

13. See Bammel, "Preparation for the Perils," 91–100; Wanamaker, *Thessalonians*, 129–30.

14. Jervis, *Heart of the Gospel*, 25–26, 29, maintains that Paul's own suffering increases his holiness (1 Thess 2:2–4, 9–10), but it is not clear if he makes this connection for the Thessalonians also.

15. Bruce, *Thessalonians*, 63, ascertains that the aorist ἐπείρασεν ("tempt") in this verse "implies successful temptation, temptation which had succeeded in overthrowing their faith."

16. Malina and Pilch, *Letters of Paul*, 44.

17. Mitchell, "1 and 2 Thessalonians," 54, lists four options that may be causing the temptation: 1) "general pressure" from outsiders who may cause the Thessalonians to regress to a "status quo," 2) aggressive persecution, 3) other missionaries who cause the congregation to doubt Paul's legitimacy, or 4) a combination of the above. Of the four options, number 3 is the only one that does not involve some form of harassment, and it is also the weakest alternative given that nothing explicit in the context of 3:5 seems to support it.

18. Donfried, "Cults of Thessalonica," 347, suggests the Satanic attack is related to the politarch's

lieving compatriots to harass them. The Thessalonians were primarily comprised of Gentiles who turned from τῶν εἰδώλων to serve the living God (1:9). This turning (ἐπιστρέφω) refers to their conversion[19] and may relate to other Jewish traditions that sometimes use ἐπιστρέφω to refer to the Gentiles turning to God (cf. Isa 19:22; Jer 18:8–11; *Jos. Asen.* 11.10–11).[20] Tobit 14:6 has Gentiles turning to God and burying their idols. Paul's use of the word εἴδωλον refers to an image or idol, but in light of his Jewish sentiments he probably assumes that the Thessalonians were committing idolatry and serving false deities before turning to the true and living God.[21] At the same time he assumes that non-Christian Gentiles do not know the one true God, and this has led to their immoral behavior (cf. 1 Thess 4:5; Rom 1:18–32). Doubtless Paul instructed these converts to embrace his position regarding their former relationship with other deities, and there is no indication in the letter that they are struggling with the concept of one God. In a broad sense Ezekiel may serve as a backdrop to his thinking when the prophet discusses the restoration of God's people in the eschaton via God's Spirit and their turning away from idols to serve God (cf. Ezek 11:18–20; 37:14, 23). Like Israel of old, the Thessalonians are identified as God's elect people and cleansed of idolatry through the Spirit in the new era (Ezek 36:25–29 LXX; 37:14).[22] Given this background and his apprehension in 1 Thess 3:5, *Paul's worst nightmare would be for his Gentile converts to turn away from God as a result of persecution and turn to idols once again in order to be reconciled with their Gentile neighbors who reject the God of the Jews and followers of Christ.*[23]

The encouraging report from Timothy that the Thessalonians are standing firm in Christ assuages Paul's fears about their committing apostasy (3:6–8). Because of their perseverance, there is no need to warn the believers of divine judgment; the wrath of God is something that will overtake their persecutors instead of them (1 Thess 5:3, 9; 2 Thess 1:6–9). By the time he writes 2 Thessalonians, his confidence in them remains, and he assures the congregation that the Lord will be faithful to protect them from Satan, the evil one (2 Thess 3:3–5). Later on, however, we read

negative decision against believers.

19. Gal 4:9; 2 Cor 3:16; cf. Acts 3:19; 9:35; 14:15; 15:19.

20. See further, Malherbe, *Thessalonians*, 119.

21. 1 Cor 8:4; 10:19; 12:2; 2 Cor 6:16; cf. Exod 20:1–5; Deut 5:6–9; Lev 19:4; Num 25:2; 1 Macc 1:43; Wis 12:27; *T. Reub.* 4.6; Josephus, *Ant.* 9.273; Philo, *Spec.* 1.332. See more references in Cheung, *Idol Food*, 39–81.

22. See Thielman, *Paul & the Law*, 77. On their election in relation to Israel, see further, Marshall, "Election and Calling," 262.

23. That is, "pagans," but the term conveys a derogatory connotation for some, and so I use it sparingly.

that his anxiety over the potential apostasy of converts in his churches generally remained a burden for him (cf. 2 Cor 11:28–29).

Luke's version of Paul's mission to the Thessalonians locates Paul in the synagogue where both Jews and Gentiles join him (Acts 17:1–4). If Gentiles who were formerly idolaters predominate the congregation by the time Paul writes 1 Thessalonians,[24] Acts does not mention their idolatry prior to conversion. This leads Bart Ehrman to suggest that Luke only knew about Paul's mission to this city in a general way without knowing the details.[25] On the other hand, the "god-fearing Greeks" (σεβομένων Ἑλλήνων) in Acts 17:4 may not have been strictly monotheists when Paul first meets them. Rather than being proselytes or Gentile monotheists, they may have been sympathetic towards the Jewish God and certain Jewish practices without entirely abandoning polytheism.[26]

The emerging Christians in Thessalonica were probably seen as subversive to family, government, and local religion.[27] Although there is evidence of entire households converting to the early Christ communities,[28] the gospel message at times set family members against each other when some members believed and other did not (cf. Luke 12:49–51; Matt 10:34–39; Origen, *Cels.* 3.55). This also may have been the case in certain Thessalonian households. It probably surprised and disturbed friends and family members that loved ones were converting to this new and strange religious group that encouraged its practitioners to shun the traditional worship and customs associated with local deities. Their peculiar behavior of holy living caused them to decline from certain social activities and pleasures, and this likewise may

24. Gaventa, *Thessalonians*, 3, suggests that "the harsh polemic of 2:14–16 against the Jews (or Judeans) is difficult to imagine if Paul is addressing a group of Jewish Christians or even a group consisting of both Gentile and Jewish Christians." Paul, however, is Jewish Christian himself, and he obviously does not think that such language offends his colleagues Silas, who is also Jewish Christian (cf. Gillman, "Silas," 6.22–23), and Timothy, who may be half-Jewish (Acts 16:1), even though they assist him in writing this letter (1 Thess 1:1). The Thessalonians probably already agreed with Paul's view.

25. Ehrman, *New Testament*, 303. Differently, Merk, "1 Thessalonians 2:1–12," 112, denies altogether the situation in Acts 17 as a backdrop for this letter. For a discussion see Donfried, "1 Thessalonians, Acts," 3–26.

26. See argument further in Woyke, *Götter*, 132–57, who reads from Philo three groups of Gentiles attracted to ancient Diaspora Judaism: circumcised proselytes, monotheists in thought and practice ("Gesinnungsproselyten"), and sympathizers who in some sense acknowledged a creator and yet still believed in other gods (cf. Philo, *QE* 2.2; *Spec.* 2.165; *Ebr.* 33–40).

27. See Barclay, "Conflict in Thessalonica," 512–30; and Still, *Conflict at Thessalonica*, 226–67, from where the threefold subversion is derived. Interestingly, Tacitus brings up that Christians are haters of humanity (Tacitus, *Annals* 15.44). On the Christians as politically subversive, see Pliny, *Letters* 10.96. For outsider perceptions of early Christians, see Wilken, *Christians*. Other reasons why non-Christians persecuted Christians are explored by De Ste. Croix, "Early Christians," 7–38.

28. E.g., 1 Cor 1:16; 16:15; Acts 10:24–48; 16:15, 31–34. This was not always the case: 1 Cor 7:12–16; 1 Pet 2:18–25; 3:1–7.

have troubled their compatriots (cf. 1 Thess 5:23; 1 Pet 4:3–4). Beyond alienation of close relationships, the emerging Christians could be viewed as social deviants upsetting the status quo of the *Pax Romana* by abandoning political and religious customs. The Thessalonian believers are accused of rebelling against the decrees of Caesar and civic deities (cf. Acts 17:7–8), and the persecution they experience in Paul's letter may reflect such accusations.[29] In later decades the Christians' exclusive claims about Christ and one true God were interpreted negatively as atheism by outsiders (cf. *Mart. Pol.* 3.2; 9.2; 12.2; *Diognetus* 2.6; Justin, *1 Apol.* 4–6, 13; Tertullian, *Nat.* 1.1–3). Such factors as these seem to have contributed to the persecution of the Thessalonian church.

The persecution they face, however, should not be misunderstood in terms of later decades and centuries when Rome imprisoned, tortured, and killed Christians. The Thessalonians do not face an official pogrom of this sort but local mistreatment characterized by social discrimination and harassment; in addition, they may have also experienced mob action and criminal accusations (cf. Acts 17:5–10). Some of them may have experienced physical harm also, but there is not enough evidence from Paul's letters or Acts to suggest that the death of some of the church members in Thessalonica involved martyrdom (1 Thess 4:14–18).[30] If such were the case, we might expect Paul to praise these martyrs much the same way he celebrates others who have risked their lives for the gospel's sake (cf. Phil 2:25–30; Rom 16:3–4).[31] To be sure, Paul compares this congregation's affliction to the Lord's (1 Thess 1:6), but the central point of comparison is their shared affliction, not necessarily death. Paul and his colleagues, all who are still alive, also participate in this affliction.

Malina and Pilch think the believers in this community are experiencing a conflict with Thessalonian Israelites.[32] In Acts some Jews from Thessalonica oppose Paul and instigate a conflict in the city (Acts 17:5–7). In Luke's narrative, however, it seems to be a mob of Gentile riffraff that becomes the focal point of oppression for the local congregation (17:5). There is no mention in 1 Thessalonians that the congregation was suffering affliction because of Jewish oppressors. Rather, the Thessalonians suffer persecution from their compatriots (συμφυλέτης) in a manner similar to the Judean Christ-followers who suffer at the hands of their own countrymen (1 Thess 2:14–16). Paul writes that the persecutors of these Judeans will not escape divine

29. See Judge, "Decrees of Caesar," 1–7; Donfried, "Cults of Thessalonica," 336–56.

30. Contrast Donfried, "Cults of Thessalonica," 349–50, who suggests the persecution led to death, and for support he points out persecution by the "sword" in Rom 8:35–36. In Romans, to be sure, Paul may be referring to early martyrs even prior to the persecution of Nero (e.g., Acts 7:54–60; 12:1–4), but this does not necessarily mean that any occurred in Thessalonica during Paul's travels.

31. Rightly on this point is Barclay, "Conflict in Thessalonica," 514.

32. Malina and Pilch, *Letters of Paul*, 41.

judgment; God's wrath in fact has finally come upon them (2:16c: ἔφθασεν δὲ ἐπ᾽ αὐτοὺς ἡ ὀργὴ εἰς τέλος).[33] There is no substantial reason to support 1 Thess 2:13–16 as an interpolation;[34] God's wrath (2:16) does not refer to the temple's destruction but possibly to the slaughter of Jerusalemites that happened around 49 CE, and perhaps Claudius's expulsion of Jews from Rome which occurred that same year.[35] Paul's harsh tone, in any case, is not against all Jews but only unbelieving Judeans hostile toward Judean Christ-followers, including himself (1 Thess 2:15–16). In this manner the language is not much different than Jewish condemnations against other Jews who are perceived as apostates and traitors (e.g., 2 Macc 6:1–17; *T. Levi* 6.5–11; 1QH 10[2].21–29). Nevertheless, such calamities as a general slaughter in Jerusalem or expulsion from Rome seem to be far too sweeping as types of judgment and would not seem to target only the persecutors. Hence, there remains a possibility that 2:16 finds it ultimate fulfillment on judgment day when, from Paul's perspective, those who persecuted the Christ-followers will experience divine wrath (cf. Rom 12:14, 18; Phil 1:28)

PAUL'S OPPONENTS? (1 THESS 2:1–12)

Relevant to the situation in Thessalonica is the question of whether Paul is defending himself against accusations from church members or other Christians in 1 Thess 2:1–12.[36] Some interpreters suggest his words reflect an apologetic against internal criticisms over his leadership in this congregation or his lack of demonstrating spirituality.[37] John Frame suggests that Paul is refuting accusations against being deluded, deceptive, immoral, and flattering the congregation to cover his greed (2:1–6; cf.

33. On the aorist of φθάνω as "arrived" and εἰς τέλος as "finally" or "at last," see esp. Green, *Thessalonians,* 148–49.

34. Some scholars believe 2:14–16 to be a post-Pauline interpolation due both to its anti-Jewish tone and a postulation that the wrath which has already arrived refers to the destruction of the temple in Jerusalem in 70 CE, an event that took place several years after Paul's death. On the interpolation view see Pearson, "1 Thessalonians 2,13–16," 79–94; Richard, *Thessalonians,* 125–27. See criticisms of this view in Schlueter, *Filling Up the Measure.*

35. Suetonius, *Claud.* 25.4; Acts 18:1; Josephus, *Ant.* 20.112; *J.W.* 2.227). See Still, *Conflict at Thessalonica,* 36.

36. On the apologetics view of this passage see, e.g., Weima, "Function of 1 Thessalonians 2:1–12," 114–31.

37. E.g., Schmithals, *Paul and the Gnostics,* 140, who sees the opponents as Gnostics; Jewett, *Thessalonian Correspondence,* 102–4, 149–57, 176–78, who views the opponents as millenarian radicals. Sumney, *Servants of Satan,* 214–52, concludes that for both 1 and 2 Thessalonians no opponents are in view. See also Rigaux, *Thessaloniciens,* 59, 72; and Best, *Thessalonians,* 22, who considers the enemy to be "vague." For an overview of various positions see Sumney, "Studying Paul's Opponents," 33–38.

1:5).[38] This perspective, however, is a mirror reading of the text in which Paul's words are assumed to be a denial of accusations posed by opponents.[39] To be sure, some resistance between certain members and their local leaders is evident in 5:12–13,[40] but this problem may have little to do with accusations against Paul's own character or style of leadership. The apostle and his colleagues were successful in their founding mission to the Thessalonians as evinced by the fruitful behavior of the converts (1 Thess 1:4–8, 9; cf. 2:1–2, 4, 9).[41] The letter stresses the Thessalonians' salvific well-being, confirmation as believers, and exemplary conduct and continuance of walking in faith, hope, and love despite opposition. If they persevere through affliction, then his missionary efforts among them would not be in vain (1:2–3; 2:1, 13–14; 3:5–9).[42] Rather than presenting a self-apologetic in 2:1–12, Paul may be highlighting his own exemplary conduct as an imitative model for the Thessalonians to emulate (cf. 1:6; 2:14). As Paul and coworkers endure suffering, so do they; and as Paul's behavior is gentle, blameless, and dedicated to laboring among them, so also they must be gentle and labor before others if they are to stand blameless before God at the *parousia* (2:2, 7, 9–10; cf. 4:11–12; 5:23).

Abraham Malherbe argues for a paraenetic emphasis in 1 Thess 2. If we compare the apostle's words with those of Dio Chrysostom against Cynic philosophers, the apostle makes statements similar to Chrysostom's "ideal philosopher" (e.g., *Or.* 32). Paul, wanting to "firm up" his relationship with the Thessalonians, distinguishes himself from philosophers and charlatans of bad repute.[43] This letter nonetheless gives high approbations of the Thessalonians in the first three chapters, and so we question the extent to which the early sections function as paraenetic.[44] The rhetorical arrangement of 1 Thess 1–3 combines *narratio* with an emphasis on thanksgiving (cf. 1:2–3; 2:13; 3:9–13). Indeed, as certain scholars have argued, the letter resembles epideictic rhetoric, which demonstrates a pattern of praiseworthy and blameworthy

---

38. Frame, *Thessalonians*, 90. Morris, *First and Second Thessalonians*, 70–71, is also similar.

39. On this interpretative error see Barclay, "Mirror-Reading," 73–93.

40. So Marshall, *Thessalonians*, 149.

41. See Merk, "1 Thessalonians 2:1–12," 98–99, who connects this thought with confidence in the Thessalonians' divine election. This view nonetheless must be tempered with Paul's lack of confidence in them prior to Timothy's report (1 Thess 3:5).

42. Differently, Marshall, *Thessalonians*, 62–63, interprets "in vain" (2:1) as "lacking in content" rather than "lacking in effect," but even so he claims that a Greek thinker would not make this either/or distinction.

43. Malherbe, "Gentle as a Nurse," 203–17; *Thessalonians*, 153–63.

44. For criticism of Malherbe's view see Mitchell, Review of *Letters*, 1–12; Witherington, *Thessalonians*, 17–20.

conduct.[45] Our view is that epideictic rhetoric in chapters 1–3 alters to a combination of epideictic and deliberative in chapters 4–5, so that praise turns into persuasive speech by the end of the letter. Paul's ultimate concern at any rate is not to present himself as a stellar rhetorician who orchestrates an impressively composed epistle that is built entirely on one species of rhetoric. Rather, as a pastor-missionary, he is more concerned about his audience's well-being than whether or not his rhetoric is perfectly composed. Thus he praises their behavior in the early part of the letter and attempts to correct sexual misconduct, bad work ethics, and misconceptions about death and the end times in the latter part of it.

Whatever else 2:1–12 might mean, Paul refers to his past friendship with the Thessalonians, sets apart his gospel from delusional and idolatrous teachings of non-believers, and presents himself as a model for the Thessalonians.[46] If he seems to protest too much against being a bad servant and leader, it may be his way of discouraging the Thessalonians from such a track. Then again, it is just possible that Paul's intention includes some preventative maintenance against this congregation buying into false accusations against his ministry from *outsiders* (esp. 2:3–5), namely, those who came against his ministry in Thessalonica (cf. Acts 17:5–8). To offset such accusations, he may be reinforcing his excellent conduct before the Thessalonians, telling them what they already know and affirm to be true. *The only opponents in Thessalonica are outsiders, non-Christian neighbors of the Thessalonian congregation that have been harassing its members.*[47] It is rather doubtful that Paul faces personal opposition from within the congregation itself.

COMFORTING CONGREGATION MEMBERS AND WARNING THE ἌTAKTOI: PREVENTATIVE MAINTENANCE AGAINST APOSTASY (1 THESS 5:14; CF. 2 THESS 3:6–15)

Paul urges the Thessalonian church to warn the ἄτακτοι congregants, cheer up the faint-hearted, and help the weak members (1 Thess 5:14).[48] The need to instruct, nurture, and warn these congregation members is necessary, no doubt, because such

45. E.g., Hughes, "Rhetoric of 1 Thessalonians," 94–116. For a synopsis of rhetorical arrangements for the letter, see Jewett, *Thessalonian Correspondence*, 216–21; cf. 72–78.

46. In agreement with Donfried, "Epistolary and Rhetorical Context," 60.

47. It is possible that these neighbors include non-Christian Jews who instigate the non-Christian Gentiles. On this view see, e.g., Holtz, *Thessalonicher*, 92–95. Differently, Horbury, "1 Thessalonians ii.3," 492–508, considers Paul's words in light of the Jews charging Paul with false prophecy.

48. The language and thoughts of 5:14 make it seem likely that Paul is addressing the entire congregation (cf. 1 Thess 3:7; 2 Thess 3:15; Rom 15:14; Col 3:16; Gal 6:1), not just leaders (5:12); contrast Black, "Weak in Thessalonica," 312.

individuals may be susceptible to disturbing the welfare of the entire congregation, and they could abandon their faith.

The faint-hearted members (ὀλιγόψυχος) need encouragement and consolation perhaps due to their worry and fear of being persecuted (e.g., 2:12–14) and anxiety about dying before Christ returns (e.g., 4:13–18; cf. 2 Thess 2:1–2). They likely harbor doubts about their salvation, which is one reason why Paul emphasizes the Thessalonians' election and safekeeping as God's people (1 Thess 1:4–5; 2:13; 5:9; 5:23–24; cf. 2 Thess 2:13–14). Malherbe rightly suggests the problem with these congregants is psychological.[49] Without proper consolation and instruction, it is not difficult to draw the inference that these believers might end up denying their faith and becoming apostates.

Support for the weak members (ἀσθενής) may be assuming those with a weak conscience and high scruples against certain foods; elsewhere Paul claims that this type of parish member is prone to fall away by eating idol meats or foods that are not kosher (1 Cor 8–10; Rom 14).[50] But there is no indication of conflicts over table fellowship in 1 Thessalonians, and since this letter was written before Romans and 1 Corinthians, a less specific identity for the weak may be in view. The "weak" in this letter perhaps identifies those who are physically and economically challenged,[51] or the term's ambiguity in this context may be inclusive of both the spiritually and physically frail congregation members. The former, at least, are susceptible to apostasy—these weak members might be growing weary of being watchful for the time of the end and tempted to give up hope.[52]

The Thessalonians also are to warn the ἄτακτοι among their members (1 Thess 5:14). The term refers to either idlers/loafers or unruly/disorderly.[53] Examples from early Jewish and Greco-Roman literature suggest the latter,[54] but both senses may be implied in the Thessalonian correspondence. The unruly members may be disrupting congregational fellowship as a result of their behavior, which is exemplified by their refusal to earn their pay by working. They "walk" in an insubordinate way,

---

49. Malherbe, *Thessalonians*, 318.

50. On this identity for the weak see Friedrich, *Thessalonicher*, 248; Best, *Thessalonians*, 230–31.

51. Cf. Wanamaker, *Thessalonians*, 197–98.

52. On this view see Black, "Weak in Thessalonica," 318–20.

53. For the former view see, e.g., Ellingworth and Nida, *Thessalonians*, 118–19; Best, *Thessalonians*, 229–30; the latter view includes, e.g., Yeo, "Rhetoric of Election," 535, 537; Richard, *Thessalonians*, 269–70.

54. 3 Macc 1:19; Josephus, *Ant.* 15.152; *J.W.* 2.517; Philo, *Creation* 20; *T. Naph.* 2.9; Herodotus, *Histories* 6.93; Thucydides, *Hist.* 8.10. See further Delling, "ἄτακτος," 8.48, who writes that, apart from Christian use, when the verb form is "applied to work, [it] does not in the first instance lay emphasis on sloth but rather on an irresponsible attitude to the obligation to work."

meddling in other people's affairs (2 Thess 3:6–12; cf. 1 Thess 4:11).[55] This behavior may be seen in contrast to Paul's exhortation for the believers to walk worthy of God's calling (1 Thess 2:12; cf. Phil 1:27; Col 1:10; Eph 4:1).

One possible scenario suggests that a group within this church espoused to a type of realized eschatology that embraced rebelliousness or idleness (cf. ἄτακτοι: 1 Thess 5:14), libertinism in sexual ethics (4:1–8), dualism of spirit and body (contrast 5:23), and a view that the resurrection had already taken place; hence, persecution took them by surprise because they thought such a thing could not happen in the new age (4:13–18). Paul instructs them about death in relation to Christ's second coming as an imminent event (4:13–5:10), but this teaching was interpreted to support the ἄτακτοι in their radical millennialism. This is one of the reasons Paul had to write 2 Thessalonians—to respond to their realized view of the eschaton and sternly warn against the ἄτακτοι members (2 Thess 2:1–12; 3:6–13).[56] It is questionable, however, to what extent the Thessalonians held to a realized eschatology in the first letter. Paul teaches them about the coming Day of the Lord by way of *reminder* (1 Thess 5:1–2), and their eager expectation of Christ's *future* return may have led them to wrongly believe that no one from their congregation would die before he returned.

Their view of eschatology nevertheless appears to move from imminent in the first letter (1 Thess 4–5) to realized in the second (2 Thess 2:2). Connections between the ἄτακτοι (1 Thess 5:14; 2 Thess 3:6, 7, 11), those who are not working (1 Thess 4:11; 2 Thess 3:6–13), and those who are having sexual affairs (1 Thess 4:1–8) may be related if this group had a lot of extra time on their hands by wrongly thinking the end was so near.[57] Perhaps one of their favorite pastimes involved pursuing sexual relationships with other congregation members. Regardless of our knowing details about the situation, *the ἄτακτοι are disturbing the cohesion within the community and not pleasing God by their conduct.* Moreover, if the ἄτακτοι disobey Paul's instructions and do not yield to the congregation's warnings, the other members should disassociate with such individuals (2 Thess 3:14–15).[58] The exact nature of this separation is not specified, but it does not appear to be a complete expulsion from the

55. Barclay, "Conflict in Thessalonica," 525n46, suggests that Paul may have the unruly of 5:14 in mind in 4:11–12, and the two passages were connected in 2 Thess 3:6–13.

56. Holding to the ἄτακτοι as radical millenarians is Jewett, *Thessalonian Correspondence*, esp. 176–78. See also similar views in Friedrich, *Thessalonicher*, 205, 225; Lütgert, *Volkommenen*.

57. The term ἄτακτος in 1 Thess 5:14 is closely related to the adverbial ἀτάκτως in 2 Thess 3:6, 11 and the verb ἀτακτέω in 3:7 (cf. Delling, "ἄτακτος," 8.47). The thought of manual labor (cf. 1 Thess 4:11–12) is not part of Paul's stock paraenesis, *pace* Hock, *Social Context of Paul's Ministry*, 43–47, but entirely relevant to the Thessalonian situation, as argued by De Vos, *Church and Community Conflicts*, 160–70.

58. Witherington, *Thessalonians*, 254, rightly notices the offender is isolated here, that is, individualized from the corporate community.

church on the level of the man committing fornication with his stepmother in 1 Cor 5:1–5.[59] The Thessalonians are not to consider the unruly person as an enemy but warn him as a "brother" (2 Thess 3:15), a term often used by Paul for identifying fellow believers.[60] As recent converts to the gospel, the Thessalonians are no longer idolaters but take on a new identity as a familial community "in Christ" (1 Thess 1:1; 2:14; 4:16) with God as their heavenly Father (1:1, 3; 3:11, 13; cf. 2:11) and they all as brothers and sisters (1:4; 4:1, 6, 9–13; 5:14, 26). This designation of ἀδελφός may suggest that the idler is not completely banished from the church; he is not banished from Christ's *community*, and hence, he is not cut off from *Christ*. Moreover, unlike the fornicator in 1 Cor 5, there is no mention that the disobedient person in Thessalonica is delivered over to Satan or that a destruction of his "flesh" must take place for the remedial purpose of saving him.

The punishment in 2 Thess 3:14, then, seems to be a further elaboration of Paul's imperative to keep away from such individuals (3:6).[61] The nature of this disassociation, even so, probably involves more than merely ignoring the person or looking the other way when that person is at church; it probably involves some sort of disciplinary action. *The unruly idler who refuses correction may be excluded from table fellowship and partaking of the Lord's Supper.*[62] The concept of not mingling or associating (συναναμίγνυμι) is found elsewhere in Paul only in 1 Cor 5:9–11, which involves table fellowship, and this view dovetails nicely with an earlier admonition against the rebellious idler: "if anyone is not willing to work, let him not eat" (2 Thess 3:10). Fellow believers could still admonish this idler whenever they talk with the person apart from church gatherings or presumably even at the gathering so long as food is not being served. This sort of discipline against the erring believer is remedial: "that he may be ashamed" (2 Thess 3:14) and hopefully repent of unruly and idle behavior. There is hope, then, for his complete restoration. His period of discipline, however, would seem to be a delicate time in which he could be hardened further and so decide to leave the community in Christ. If that were the case, then Paul and his followers would undoubtedly consider him an apostate and no longer a "brother" (2 Thess 3:15; cf. Phil 3:18).

---

59. Contrast Wanamaker, *Thessalonians*, 289, who thinks the disassociation involves excommunication.

60. See ἀδελφός in 1 Thess 1:4; 2:1, 9, 17; 3:2, 7; 4:1; 5:4; 2 Thess 1:3; 2:13, 15; 3:1 cf. Rom 8:29; 1 Cor 1:1, 26.

61. Frame, *Thessalonians*, 310, perceptively connects the dots between 3:6 and 3:14.

62. See 1 Cor 5:9, 11; 1QS 6.24–7.25; 8.16–18; and Best, *Thessalonians*, 343. Marshall, *Thessalonians*, 228, adds the interesting nuance that the discipline includes a discouraging of hospitality towards such individuals in the various homes of the believers; this would "prevent the idlers from sponging on the other members of the church."

WALKING IN HOLINESS AND THE WORK OF FAITH
(1 THESS 4:1–2; CF. 1:3; 2:12; 3:11–13; 2 THESS 1:11)

The central paraenesis in the letter comes by way of reminder for the Thessalonians—
they are to walk in holiness and in a manner that pleases God (1 Thess 4:1–2; cf.
2:12).[63] The exhortation material in 4:1–12 is grounded for the most part in earlier
Jewish thoughts. The ideas of receiving instruction (Thess 4:1–2), of walking in moral conduct (4:1, 12), of pleasing God (4:1), of following God's will (4:3), of holiness
(4:3–4, 7), of "brother" as originally Jewish terminology (4:6, 9), of concern about
outsider perceptions (4:11–12),[64] and of possible echoes from Israel's scriptures[65] all
point to Jewish influence.[66]

Paul exhorts the Thessalonians to "walk" (περιπατέω) in sanctification (4:1, 3,
12). This manner of advancement is similar to ancient *halakah*; it involves following
a moral pattern for conducting one's life. Faithful Israelites "walked" before God by
living in a way compatible with the Torah and godly wisdom (Deut 8:6; 10:12; 11:22;
13:5; 30:6; 1 Kgs 3:3, 6, 14; 8:23, 25; 2 Kgs 20:3; Ps 85[86]:11; Prov 6:20–22; 8:20;
28:6; Isa 33:15; 59:9; 1QS 3.21; 4.11, 24; CD 19.4). Paul in a similar manner instructs
his churches to "walk" in a way that pleases God, requiring spiritual sensitivity and
righteous conduct (cf. Gal 5:16; 1 Cor 7:17; Rom 6:4; Phil 1:27; 3:17–18; Col 1:10;
2:6; Eph. 4:1).[67] The apostle seems to be influenced here by his earlier training as a
Pharisee, which required him to conduct himself on a daily basis in accordance with
the Law in order to be righteous before God. Sometime after becoming a Christ-
follower he reconfigured the moral principle of walking according to the commands
of the Law and began to teach that believers exhibit personal righteousness by walking according to the example of Christ.

He stresses in his letters the importance of walking in the Spirit (Gal 5:16, 25;
Rom 8:4, 14), which becomes a source of guidance in place of the works of the Law
and produces virtuous conduct such as love and self-control among believers (Gal
5:22–23). This type of walking may be contrasted with unrighteous strides associated with the "flesh" (Gal 5:16–17; Rom 8:4–5), unbelievers (Col 3:7–8; Eph 4:12;

---

63. See Collins, "Function of Paraenesis," 398–414. On the centrality of holiness in the letter see
Weima, "How You Must Walk," 98–119.

64. Cf. Exod 32:12, 25; Num 14:14–16; Deut 9:25–29.

65. 1 Thess 4:6/Ps 94:1; 1 Thess 4:8/1 Sam 8:7; 1 Thess 4:9/Isa 54:13.

66. For Jewish elements, see further Carras, "Jewish Ethics and Gentile Converts," 306–15.

67. Stressing the influence of Proverbs on this metaphor is Steinmann and Eschelbach, "Walk This
Way," 43–62, who rightly criticize NT translations (e.g., NIV) that render "walk" (περιπατέω) as "live"
(ζάω) and thus overlook the significant nuance of the former term. The former centers on "activity and
movement, which suggests purpose and destination" (52).

5:8), carnal believers (1 Thess 3:6, 11; 1 Cor 3:3), and apostates (Phil 3:18). The contrast between these oppositional ways of walking may be influenced in part by Jesus' teaching on two paths, one leading to life and the other to destruction (Matt 7:13–14; cf. Luke 13:24). As well, Paul may be influenced by the prominent two-ways motif stressed by the Law and Proverbs (e.g., Deut 30:6, 15–16; Prov. 15:9; 16:25). If so, he shifts an earlier emphasis on language about the "way" (ὁδός) to the more active περιπατέω and other verbs related to advancement in a forward motion.

The Thessalonians' walk includes their receiving and actualizing godly instructions that originate from the Lord Jesus and have been passed on from his immediate apostles to Paul and his colleagues (1 Thess 4:1–2). Christ's command to love one another no doubt would be at the forefront of these instructions (4:9 cf. Mark 12:28–34; Matt 22:36–40; Luke 10:25–28; John 13:34–35). In a very deep sense, to follow Christ is to walk in love, which includes sacrificing for the sake of others (cf. Rom 14:15; Eph 5:2) and behaving properly towards outsiders (1 Thess 4:12; cf. Rom 13:13; Col 4:5; Eph. 5:15) even though the Christ community is to be distinct from the society (1 Thess 4:3, 5). *This love reflects God's love for Christ's followers, and they are to reciprocate by conducting their life in a holy manner that pleases God, obeys the Lord's teachings, and perseveres in faithfulness and God's word* (1 Thess 2:12–14; 4:1–3; cf. 2 Thess 3:5; 2 Cor 5:7; Col 1:10).

In the Thessalonian correspondence, "work" is not set in contrast to "faith," but involves obedience and service to God exemplified by a new lifestyle that embraces the virtues of faithfulness, love, and hope (1 Thess 1:3 cf. Gal 5:6; 1 Cor 13:13).[68] Paul uses the singular "work" in 1:3, not "works" as in "works of the Law," which in Galatians and Romans is set in contrast to faith.[69] The singular is unattached to the Law here and indeed can have positive connotations elsewhere in Paul (cf. Rom 2:7; 13:3; 14:20; 1 Cor 3:14). The congregation's "work of faith" (1 Thess 1:3; cf. 2 Thess 1:11)[70] is virtually synonymous with the "obedience of faith" that Paul mentions in Rom 1:5 and 16:16. For Paul sanctification is essential for the Thessalonians if they are to be considered blameless at the second coming of Christ (1 Thess 3:11–13; 5:23; cf. 1:3; 2:19; 4:6).[71] Paul hopes they will indeed live up to this expectation (2:19). As

---

68. Harink, *Paul among the Postliberals*, 32–38, rightly argues against an oppositional view between faith and works in 1 Thessalonians.

69. See Best, *Thessalonians*, 67–68.

70. On 2 Thess 1:11, Menken, *2 Thessalonians*, 93, identifies the verse as a prayer wish for salvation in which "one might speak of double causality: both the Christians themselves *and* God's Spirit are working" (cf. Phil 2:12–13; Rom 8:4).

71. On 1 Thess 3:11–13, Mitchell, "1 and 2 Thessalonians," 56, writes, "Here, as elsewhere, he reminds the Thessalonians rather pointedly that what is at stake now, as always, is their eschatological salvation at the parousia." Schnelle, *Einleitung*, 52, may be correct when suggesting through 1 Thess. 4:6

Pieter De Villiers affirms, "They must live up to the salvation that has been granted to them in Christ. If they do not do so, they are lost and fall under the judgment of God."[72] Until the end takes place, then, the congregation must continue in holiness and both encourage and warn its members (5:14).

ABSTAINING FROM *PORNEIA* (1 THESS 4:3-9)

Paul claims that the will of God for the Thessalonians is to abstain from πορνεία (1 Thess 4:3; cf. 5:22). In this case God's will (θέλημα) refers to God's desire, which is something they must obey; to do God's will is to please God (2:4, 12; 4:1, 3).[73] In a broad sense the word πορνεία, sometimes translated as "fornication," may be defined as "illegitimate sexual activities."[74] Paul uses the word or its derivatives to identify a form of incest (1 Cor 5:1–5), cultic prostitution (1 Cor 6:13–18; 10:8), adulterous relationships (1 Cor 7:1–2), and frequently sexual vice that could prevent its practitioners from inheriting God's kingdom (1 Cor 6:9–11; 10:8; Gal 5:19–21; Col 3:5).[75] Paul is responding to sexual misconduct as most Jews would who read the Septuagint; he condemns *porneia* in its various forms (e.g., Gen 38:24; Num 25:1; Prov 7; Sir 23:16; 41:17–22; Wis 3:16–19; 14:26).

The term, moreover, reflects sexual deviance as found in the sex codes of Deuteronomic and Levitical traditions (Deut 22; Lev 18–21). He considers this kind of prohibition against Gentile believers to be binding, even though in Jewish thinking these codes originate from Mosaic Law. Obviously such rules do not constitute the "works of the Law" that he condemns in Galatians; there πορνεία is considered one of the "works of the flesh" contrary to walking in the Spirit (Gal 5:19–25). Such works reflect the unregenerate behavior of outsiders who live in the old, fallen era. These works are also committed socially and thus violate the solidarity of the community in Christ and the command to love others (Gal 1:4; 5:14). Perhaps this is the

---

and 5:9 that the future judgment will be according to a person's works.

72. De Villiers, "Life Worthy of God," 353; cf. 345.

73. Cf. Donfried and Marshall, *Shorter Pauline Letters*, 30.

74. On this definition and activities identified by the term, see Oropeza, "What Is Sex?," 27–63. Malina, "Does *Porneia* mean Fornication?," 17, identifies πορνεία as "unlawful sexual conduct." For Jensen, "Does *Porneia* Mean Fornication?," 165–66, this would include premarital sexual activities (e.g., Lev 19:29 LXX; 21:7–14 LXX; Deut 22:13–21; Sir 42:9–11). For Gaca, *Making of Fornication*, 19–20, 124, 151, the LXX emphasizes πορνεία as sexual activities that digress from the norm of worshiping the one true God. Religious endogamy is also stressed by its usage. Glancy, "Obstacles to Slaves' Participation," 493, 497, 501, more specifically defines Paul's use of the term narrowly as prostitution (1 Cor 6) and more widely as "sexual irregularity." Henceforth, the term will be transliterated *porneia* in this chapter.

75. See further 1 Cor 5:9–11; 2 Cor 12:21; Rom 1:24–32; Eph. 5:3, 5; 1 Tim 1:10.

basis for Paul's thinking in 1 Thess 4 even though he does not mention the works of the flesh in this letter. Then again, even though the Law does not bring about righteousness in Paul's view (Gal 3:19–25), he could still maintain the Levitical codes against πορνεία in agreement with the decision of the Jerusalem meeting that prohibited such activities among the Gentile converts (Acts 15:19–20, 28–29). We will see in 1 Corinthians and Romans, however, that even though Paul agrees with the prohibition against fornication he is not entirely in agreement with the Jerusalem church on its dietary prohibitions, including the ban on idol foods. Paul, in any case, mentions nothing about the Jerusalem verdict in his correspondence to the Thessalonians. A better explanation of his prohibition in this letter rests on internal evidence.

The Thessalonians are to refrain from *porneia*, and each one of them is to possess or guard his "vessel" (σκεῦος) in honor and holiness (1 Thess 4:3–5). In all probability the "vessel" is not referring to a wife despite its being used this way in 1 Pet 3:7.[76] If the Thessalonians are to take a wife without having lustful passion (1 Thess 4:4–5), this would tend to contradict what Paul writes in 1 Cor 7:9: the Corinthians are allowed to take a wife for the very purpose of relieving their lustful passion![77] We do not need to argue that Paul changed his view from passionless marital sex in 1 Thessalonians to passionate sex in 1 Corinthians. The vessel in the former correspondence (1 Thess 4:4), as certain scholars rightly argue, is a euphemism for the penis in which σκεῦος can be translated back into כלי, a Semitic euphemism for the genitalia (cf.4Q416[4QInstructionᴮ] 2.2.21; 1 Sam. 21:4–6).[78] Paul exhorts the Thessalonian men to control their sexual organ. Alternatively, Paul may understand the penis as a kind of synecdoche for the whole body (cf. 2 Cor 4:7).[79] The driving issue for Paul in either case rests not on his meaning behind the word "vessel," but on his urging the Thessalonians to abstain from *porneia*. Beverly Gaventa is instructive

---

76. Supporting the vessel="wife" view are, e.g., Kondradt, "*Eidenai ekaston hymōn*," 128–35; Yarbrough, *Not Like the Gentiles*, 68–76; Witherington, *Thessalonians*, 113–14.

77. See further Oropeza, "What Is Sex?," 31–32. Ellis, *Paul and Ancient Views of Sexual Desire*, rightly affirms that Paul argues for self-control over sexual desire rather than the elimination of such desire, and sex within marriage seems intended for pleasure (cf. 1 Cor 7)—it is not passionless. His view contends against Martin, "Paul without Passion," 201–15; and Fredrickson, "Passionless Sex," 23–30. Assuming that the "vessel" means a wife, Ellis suggests that Paul may be advocating for self-control of sex within marriage (161). As we argue, however, 1 Thess 4:4 does not support the vessel=wife view.

78. Smith, "Another Look at 4Q416 2 ii.21," 499–504; Elgvin, "Master His Own Vessel," 604–19; Donfried, "Cults of Thessalonica," 342.

79. Cf. Oropeza, "What Is Sex?," 32. On the vessel as the human "body," see especially Carras, "Jewish Ethics and Gentile Converts," 308–11, who concentrates on undermining the vessel="wife" view. For discussions on the meaning of 1 Thess 4:4, see further Ellis, *Paul and Ancient Views of Sexual Desire*, 5–14; Still, "Interpretive Ambiguities," 209, 214; Weima, "Walk to Please God," 107–8.

here: "Whatever Paul means in this particular text, it is certain both that Paul was opposed to adultery and that Paul was opposed to all sexual expression outside of monogamous marriage (see 1 Cor 6:15–20; 7:1–2)."[80]

The Thessalonians should not mimic non-believing Gentiles in their sexual practices (1 Thess 4:5), since they were often thought by Jews and emergent Christians to be promiscuous.[81] Paul warns that they must not trespass and take advantage (πλεονεκτέω) of a "brother" in this matter; in other words, they should not cheat fellow believers in reference to sexual matters (4:6–7).[82] It is quite possible that some of the unruly idlers in the congregation occupied a good portion of their time pursuing sexual affairs. They tried to woo the wives, daughters, sons, or servants that belonged to the households of other male believers. This view would be in keeping with the ancient patriarchal assumption that illegitimate sexual relations with the members of another man's household violates that man's rightful "property" (cf. Exod 20:14–15).[83] As such, *porneia* may have been understood by Paul as infringement on the reciprocal ethic to love one another (cf. 1 Thess 4:9): it involved cheating the rightful "owner" of his possession by taking or using what was his without proper consent, whether that "owner" was the father, master, male kinsman, spouse, or future spouse. In this sense, Paul's assumption is that those who engage in *porneia* are violating bodies that belong to another male believer, and so they are not walking in a manner that loves their male neighbor as themselves. *Ultimately, then, Paul's ground for prohibiting porneia in 1 Thessalonians centers not on its being a work of the flesh, nor on the Jerusalem church's decision against it; he forbids it because it violates the law of love by which all Christ-followers must conduct themselves* (cf. Gal 5:14; 6:2; Rom 13:8–10).

The potential for congregation members to commit apostasy is evident in 1 Thess 4:8—the one who rejects Paul's exhortation concerning sexual conduct rejects

---

80. Gaventa, *Thessalonians*, 53.

81. On sexual promiscuity in the ancient Greco-Roman world see, e.g., Richlin, *Pornography and Representation*; Hallett and Skinner, *Roman Sexualities*; Varona, *Eroticism in Pompeii*; Ford, "Bookshelf on Prostitution," 128–34.

82. Alternatively, ἀδελφός might be understood as "brother or sister" (cf. NRSV), hence a "fellow Christian" (Ellingworth and Nida, *1 Thessalonians*, 82). If so, Paul may be exhorting male congregants (i.e., those who must control the penis) more generally against exploiting both male and female congregation members. In reference to the "matter" (πρᾶγμα) at hand, Paul is not changing the subject to business ventures in 1 Thess 4:6, as argued by Holtz, *Thessalonicher*, 161–62. This verse is still referring to sexual practices: cf. ἀκαθαρσία in 4:7, which often refers to sexual impurity in Paul's letters (2 Cor 12:21; Gal 5:19; Col 3:5; Eph 5:3). See further Weima, "Walk to Please God," 109; Wanamaker, *Thessalonians*, 154–55.

83. On sex and property see further Countryman, *Dirt, Greed & Sex*, 147–220; Oropeza, "What Is Sex?," 33–34.

God who gives them the Holy Spirit to work sanctification in their lives and help them resist vices such as *porneia* (1 Thess 4:8; cf. Gal 5:19–23; 1 Cor 6:15–20; Eph 4:30; Luke 10:16; Acts 7:51; CD 5.11; 7.2).[84] The Thessalonians are being spiritually cleansed as God's eschatological people via the work of God's Spirit (1 Thess 1:9; cf. Ezek 11:18–20; 36:25–29; 37:14, 23). Hence, to resist this work and not turn away from *porneia* is to reject the Holy Spirit and, in the words of Frank Thielman, "opt out of the eschatological era."[85] Paul affirms the Lord as the avenger of those who are cheated, implying divine punishment on the believers who defraud others and commit *porneia* (1 Thess 4:6). This probably assumes the typical consequence of divine judgment on sexual offenders as was prevalent in Israel's scriptures.[86] Yet for Paul God's judgment will be fully manifest at the eschaton. When Paul was still in their city he apparently taught the Thessalonians about the future judgment and gave them a solemn warning (διαμαρτύρομαι) not to practice immorality if they wished to escape that judgment (4:6c–8). Now he adds that if they continue practicing sexual vice and reject his words they are rejecting God and his Spirit. *Their immorality, if unchecked, will thus lead to apostasy, which in turn will bring on them divine wrath at the parousia.* The recalcitrant sexual offenders in the church would seem to suffer a final punishment similar to those who do not know God (1 Thess 1:10; 5:3, 9; 2 Thess 1:8–9; 2:10–12).

THE COMING APOSTASY AND *PAROUSIA* (1 THESS 5:1–11; 2 THESS 2:1–12)

The Thessalonians seem to have expected Christ to return before death could claim any members of their church, but when some of their faithful had died, they became disturbed about end-time events and the fate of the dead in Christ (1 Thess 4:13–5:10; cf. 3:13). In order to instruct them about the eschaton, Paul reconfigures apocalyptic traditions, especially those originating from the "Little Apocalypse" in the Synoptic Gospels (Mark 13; Matt 24). Paul's words about the Day of the Lord coming as a "thief in the night" (5:1–2) are reminiscent of Jesus' warnings to his disciples to be watchful and morally prepared, lest they face divine punishment at the *parousia* (Mark 13:33–37; Matt 24:45–51; Luke 12:41–48). Although 1 Thessalonians was written earlier than the canonical gospels, the Thief in the Night sayings were

---

84. Cf. Wanamaker, *Thessalonians*, 158.

85. Thielman, *Paul & the Law*, 77.

86. Gen 19:1–29; Lev 20:10; Num 25; Deut 22:20–24; Job 24:15–24; Prov 7; Wis 3:16–19; 14:26–31; cf. Rom 1:27, 32.

probably well-known orally by the time Paul wrote to this congregation.[87] His spin on these sayings is that, rather than stressing them as warnings to the Christ-followers as do the Synoptic texts, he is more interested in encouraging his audience and highlighting distinctions between their behavior and that of their unbelieving neighbors (1 Thess 5:4–11). The believers belong to the "day"; the outsiders belong to the "night." And whereas the Thessalonians are "sons of light," the outsiders are in "darkness," not being alert and morally self-controlled. They are not prepared for the *parousia* (1 Thess 5:4–8).[88]

Paul's mention of the specious peace and safety claimed by the outsiders echoes a slogan of imperial Rome (5:3),[89] and it may be an indirect slam against the false sense of security provided by the *Pax Romana*. Paul's words also sound similar to Dan 8:24–25 and 11:6–7, in which destruction comes upon those who are "at ease." Regardless of whether the false peace betrays a political or prophetic voice or both, the outsiders are led astray by false security, and this itself is reminiscent of the proclamations of false prophets who wrongly speak of peace when impending doom lurks around the corner (cf. Jer 6:14; Ezek 13:16).[90] The oppressors of the Thessalonian church will suffer eschatological destruction on the Day of the Lord (1 Thess 5:3; cf. 1:10; 2 Thess 1:6–9; 2:10–12). Differently, the faithful congregation will be rewarded when the Lord returns, and its members are to comfort one another with the assurance of this salvation (1 Thess 5:9–11; cf. 1:10; 2:19; 3:13; 4:16–18; 5:23; 2 Thess 1:7).

The contrast between the people of light and darkness resembles Qumran literature (e.g., 1QS 1.9–11; 2.16; 1QM 1.1), but perhaps ultimately the contrast recalls Israel as God's elect people protected against the plagues that God sent on Egypt. In the Thessalonian correspondence Paul identifies Gentile believers as the holy people of God set apart from other Gentiles (e.g., 1 Thess 4:3, 7; 5:23; 2 Thess 2:13–14), which is similar to Israel being called out of Egypt. In this sense the community in Thessalonica may be patterned after Israel.[91] Even so, it would be inaccurate for us to say that that Paul merely consoles the Thessalonians when referring to the *parousia*. More in keeping with the gospel traditions, *Paul exhorts his audience to remain vigi-*

87. On the possibility of Paul echoing Jesus sayings or Q, see Plevnik, "1 Thess 5,1–11," 81–82; Witherington, *Jesus, Paul and the End*, 160f.

88. The metaphor of sleep in 5:6–7 is negative and connotes the outsiders' lack of watchfulness. In 5:10, however, being asleep refers to believers who have already died (5:10; cf. 4:13–16), and so the negative connotation is removed in the latter verse.

89. So Green, *Thessalonians*, 233–34. Gaventa, *Thessalonians*, 70, cites an example from Velleius Paterculus, *Compendium of Roman History*, 2.103.5.

90. See examples in Löverstam, *Spiritual Wakefulness*, 104–5.

91. See further Thielman, *Paul & the Law*, 75.

lant and morally self-controlled until the Lord returns (1 Thess 5:6, 8; cf. 1 Cor 16:13). If he is informed by the Thief in the Night traditions, he probably knows about the eternal consequences against the spiritually lethargic followers of Jesus (e.g., Matt 24:48–51); albeit, he does not warn the Thessalonians against committing apostasy in this regard.

Spiritual apostasy related to the end times surfaces instead in 2 Thess 2:1–12 when Paul is forced to clarify his view of the eschaton. Here he must affirm to the congregation that prior to Christ's second coming a great apostasy (ἀποστασία) will take place, and the "man of lawlessness" will be revealed (2:3–4).[92] This massive falling away does not seem to be merely political or social, but it involves moral and spiritual dimensions that were in some sense already manifest as the "mystery of lawlessness" (2:7).[93] Predictions of apostasy and deception that would occur towards the close of the eschaton seem to be prevalent in early Jewish traditions,[94] and the early Christians tend to adopt this theme in their own predictions (e.g., 1 Tim 4:1–3; 2 Tim 3:1–5; Rev 12:3–4; *Did.* 16:1–5). Paul's view is thus held in common with Jews and Christians of antiquity.

More specifically, Paul is still being informed by sayings attributed to Jesus and found in the "Little Apocalypse" of the Synoptic Gospels; this time he echoes words that warn of a coming apostasy among the Christ-followers (e.g., Mark 13:5–22; Matt 24:5–13; Luke 17:30–33; 18:8; 21:34–36).[95] If these sayings originate with Jesus or the Twelve, they would seem to have been known, at least orally, prior to Paul writing to the Thessalonians. Paul is certainly not unfamiliar with teachings attributed to Jesus that were later included in the gospels.[96] He also seems familiar with the tradition of Daniel in terms of a coming apostasy in the eschaton and a leader who exalts himself above every god (cf. Dan 8:10, 24–25; 11:23, 30–31, 34–36; 12:11). Perhaps his view blends ideas attributed to Daniel and Jesus, especially in relation to predictions about an "abomination" standing in the temple in Jerusalem (Mark 13:14–22; Matt 24:15–24; Dan 9:27; 11:31, 36; 12:11; cf. Luke 21:16–20).[97] If so, Paul may have

---

92. On ἀποστασία as defection see further sources in Giblin, *Threat to Faith*, 245; cf. 81–88; Schlier, "ἀφίστημι, ἀποστασία, διχοστασία," 1.513.

93. Cf. Hughes, *Early Christian Rhetoric*, 58–59.

94. E.g., *4 Ezra* 5.1–13; *Jub.* 23.14–21; *1 En.* 91.5–7; 1QHab 2.1–10.

95. On comparisons between apocalyptic/prophet material in the gospels and Thessalonians, see further Hartman, *Prophecy Interpreted*, 178–205; Beasley-Murray, *Jesus and the Future*, 226–30.

96. E.g., 1 Cor 7:10/Mark 10:1–12; 1 Cor 11:23–25/Luke 22:14–20; Rom 12:14, 19–21/Matt 5:10–11, 39–44.

97. In Matt 24:15 the "holy place" almost certainly refers to the temple in Jerusalem: cf. Matt 23:38; Luz, *Matthew*, 3.195–96. If this is Paul's backdrop, then he did not intend the temple in 2 Thess 2:4 to be a reference to the seat of the body or "temple of the Holy Spirit" (cf. 1 Cor 3:16–17; Giblin, *Threat*

taken seriously an exhortation to study Daniel (cf. Matt 24:15) and interpreted the man of lawlessness as the "abomination" mentioned in the gospels. For Paul, this person will sit in the temple in Jerusalem and proclaim or display (ἀποδείκνυμι) himself as God. The followers of this Lawless One will be deceived and worship him as God—namely, they will turn from God by committing this ultimate act of idolatry (2 Thess 2:3–4). For Paul, this person's designation as "the man of lawlessness" (2:3: ὁ ἄνθρωπος τῆς ἀνομίας) and "the lawless one" (2:8: ὁ ἄνομος) does not center on his violation of the works of the Law but on his opposition to the will of God (cf. 1 John 3:4; John 17:12).[98] He sets himself up as God and leads others into apostasy.[99]

Whereas Antiochus IV (Epiphanes) setting up an image of Zeus in the temple of Jerusalem[100] seems to be closer to the meaning of Daniel's abomination (cf. 164–67 BCE), the Thessalonians may have been more familiar with the attempt of Emperor Caligula (c. 40 CE) to set up an image of himself in the guise of Zeus in Jerusalem's temple. Paul, however, is referring to a future event from his vantage point. While it is possible that the apostates in 2 Thess 2 will fall away through persecutions, he does not mention this as the reason.[101] Paul has idolatry and deceptive miracles as the points of leading the masses away from God, not persecution.

He does not reveal the identity of those who will commit the future apostasy, perhaps because his audience already knew these details from previous instructions (cf. 2 Thess 2:5). To this we may add an observation by Menken that the definite articles appearing before "apostasy" (ἡ ἀποστασία) and "man of lawlessness" (ὁ ἄνθρωπος τῆς ἀνομίας) assume the original readers were already familiar with these subjects.[102] The followers of the Lawless One who are destroyed in 2:10–12 would seem to include those who commit apostasy in 2:3. Unless Paul changes his thinking by the time he writes Rom 9–11, these followers of the Lawless One do not appear

---

to Faith, 76–80). This also suggests a pre-70 CE date for 2 Thessalonians, when the temple was still standing.

98. In 2:3 the older reading is ἀνομίας (e.g., ℵ, B, 81) and is preferred over ἁμαρτίας (e.g., A D, G): cf. 2:8 and Metzger, *Textual Commentary,* 567; Wanamaker, *Thessalonians,* 251. In essence, however, that this man is lawlessness is not much different than claiming him an ultimate sinner or evildoer: see Trilling, *Zweite Brief,* 83. For ἀνομία and ἄνομος in early Jewish and Christian sources see Gutbrod, "ἀνομία," 4.1085–87.

99. Similarly in emergent Judaism, Malherbe, *Thessalonians,* 419, writes that "lawlessness came to describe the influence of paganism on Jews (*Pss Sol* 1:8; 2:3; 3:13), especially as it was embodied in a person like Pompey (*Pss Sol* 17:13 cf. 20)."

100. 1 Macc 1:54–59; 6:7; 2 Macc 8:17.

101. Nevertheless, if he has Daniel in mind, then persecution and idolatry may be related, for, similar to Antiochus Epiphanes, the Lawless One may persecute or discriminate against those who refuse to submit to worshipping him.

102. Menken, *2 Thessalonians,* 102.

to be non-Christian Jews who have never accepted Paul's gospel. The fate of those who follow the Lawless One is eternal destruction at the second coming of Christ (2 Thess 2:8–12); differently, the unbelieving Israelites who reject the gospel will still be saved in the future (cf. Rom 11:26). *The apostates who worship the Lawless One are probably former Christ-followers.*[103] If this phenomenon is to take place at the temple in Jerusalem (2:4), then apostate Jewish Christians seem to be primarily in view. Nevertheless, if Paul is borrowing ideas found in the canonical gospels and Daniel, the latter dealing with all humanity and kingdoms, then it is quite possible that the apostasy not only points to Jewish but also Gentile Christians, and even a more general rebellion against God involving the entire world (cf. Mark 13:8, 10; Matt 24:7, 14, 21; Luke 21:34–35). In terms of worldwide chaos, Malherbe's words are instructive: "If Paul had taught the Thessalonians the apocalyptic view of apostasy, they would not have thought that only a part of humanity would be deceived but that the whole world would be in jeopardy (cf. Rev 13:3)."[104]

The fate of the apostates and followers of the Lawless One would seem to be the same as that of the Lawless One. He is called the "son of perdition" (2 Thess 2:3; cf. John 17:12), pointing to his ultimate destruction and condemnation, and those who follow him will suffer God's wrath on the day of the Lord (2 Thess 2:8–13; cf. 1 Thess 1:10; 5:3; 2 Thess 1:6–10). Paul claims that God sends them delusion so that they believe a lie because they did not receive the "love of the truth" and so be saved (2 Thess 2:10–11).[105] They are excluded from salvation and God confirms them in their spiritual obduracy[106] after they reject the truth (2:10–11).

Excursus: Evil Spirits and God's Strong Delusion (2 Thess 2:10–11)

The thought in 2:10–11 shows that God is sometimes directly or indirectly involved in deluding or otherwise hardening his enemies. In Israel's scriptures, the means by which God hardens hearts or stirs up calamity is sometimes attributed to evil spirits. While the Pentateuch affirms divine hardening (e.g., Exod 4:21; 7:3; Num 21:23; Deut 2:30; Josh 11:20; cf. Isa 29:10; Sir 16:15), it mentions nothing about evil spirits that work

103. Some suggest the apostates may be related to the disorderly/idle members among the Thessalonians (1 Thess 5:14): e.g., Holland, *Tradition that You Received*. There is no clear connection, however, between the apostates in 2 Thess 2 and the disorderly members.

104. Malherbe, *Thessalonians*, 431.

105. The unusual phrase τὴν ἀγάπην τῆς ἀληθείας perhaps refers to the gospel message that has love as its object (Wanamaker, *Thessalonians*, 261). Either this or it refers to the gospel message about the true God who is the source of genuine love, as opposed to the Lawless One, who is a false deity they worship (2 Thess 2:4; cf. 1 Thess 1:9).

106. See Beale, *Thessalonians*, 222; Witherington, *Thessalonians*, 224.

for God to accomplish this end. The Book of Judges, however, mentions God sending an evil spirit between Abimelech and the people of Shechem in order to avenge the murder of Gideon's seventy sons (Judg 9:23). God also sends an evil spirit to deceive King Ahab (1 Kgs 22:1–40). God incites David to take the census in 2 Sam 24:1, but 1 Chr 21:1 has Satan inciting David. Whereas God may be viewed as a destroyer of the wicked (Deut 32.39; 1 Sam 2.6; Isa 45.6-7), the "Destroyer" sometimes appears to be an angelic being sent by God (Exod 12:23; cf. 1 Cor 10:10; Heb 11:28; Rev 9:11).[107]

Sometimes the spirits are not necessarily benevolent even though God carries out God's plan either through or despite these beings. King Saul in his disobedience to God is plagued by an evil spirit (1 Sam 16:14; cf. 15:22–26). Then while under the influence of this spirit sent by God, Saul attempts to kill David (1 Sam 19:9 cf. 26:17–19). In Job's story the accusing messenger or "Satan" works in permission with God's purposes even though Job is innocent of wrong-doing (Job 1–2).

In later traditions Mastema, the leader of evil spirits, aids Pharaoh's magicians and hardens the hearts of the Egyptians to pursue the Israelites after they had left Egypt, and yet God conceives of the idea to overthrow the Egyptians in the midst of the sea (*Jub.* 48.9, 15–17; 49.2). Unclean spirits also lead astray the sons of Noah, causing them to become spiritually blind (10.1–3). In the *Testament of Solomon* the king interrogates a malevolent spirit coming out of the Red Sea who claims to have hardened Pharaoh and opposed Moses by aiding the magicians Jannes and Jambres (*T. Sol.* 25.1–7). *Pseudo-Philo* claims that the calamities that befell apostate Israel in the wilderness are the work of destroying angels (e.g., *L.A.B.* 15.5–7; cf. Num 10–16).[108]

Qumran literature possesses accounts of angels who bring calamity on deceitful and obdurate humans (1QS 4.9–14; cf. CD 2.6).[109] According to this community's version of Abraham's sojourn in Egypt, Pharaoh Zoan takes Sarai as his bride and intends to kill Abraham, but Sarai claims to be Abraham's sister. Pharaoh Zoan cannot have sexual

---

107. See other angels of destruction sent by God in 2 Sam 24:15–17; 2 Kgs 19:35; 1 Chr 21:14–27; 2 Chr 32:21; Isa 37:36; cf. Gen 19:10–13.

108. For Targums and other sources along these lines see Perrot, "Les examples du desert," 440; Str.B. 3.413–16.

109. For the Qumran group, stubbornness and hardness of heart are associated with blind eyes and dull ears, and these are often attributed to outsiders, apostates, and those expelled from the community (1QS 2.3, 14, 25–26; 4.9–14; 5.4–5; 7.18–25; CD 8.3–8; cf. 1QS 1:2–3; 1QH 7[15].3; 11.25–29; 1Q26 5). Early Jewish literature often attribute obduracy to human sin or demonic activity and tend to stress forgiveness (Philo, *Spec.* 1.54–55; *L.A.B.* 10.2; *Jub.* 10:1–3; *b. Megillah* 17b; *b. Rosh Hashannah* 17b; *b. Abodah Zarah* 5a; *S. Eli. Rab.* 16; *Lev. Rab.* 27.8; *Lam. Rab.* 1.22 §57; *Pesiq. Rab.* 8.3; 33.13). Israel, however, is not always the exclusive target of spiritual obduracy. Some early Christian sources use this motif to warn against Christian apostasy (*1 Clem.* 3.1; 51.3; *Herm. Vis.* 3.7.6). See further Evans, *To See and Not Perceive,* 138–62.

relations with Sarai because God sent an evil spirit to plague his household in response to Abraham's prayer. After Pharaoh returns the patriarch's wife, Abraham lays hands on him and the spirit departs, enabling the monarch to recover from illness (1QapGen ar 20.8–29).[110]

In 2 Thess 2:9–12 Satan is at work performing lying wonders before the apostates who follow the Lawless One. God sends them a "working of delusion" (2:11: ἐνέργειαν πλάνης), implying perhaps that God uses some sort of malevolent activity or spirit as the instrumental means of punishment to bring judgment against those who rebel against God. This act may be similar to God delivering rebels over to anti-God powers (cf. Rom 1:24, 26, 28), but in 2 Thessalonians the divine role is more active: God "sends" (πέμπει) them this working of delusion.

Paul does not elaborate on how God goes about doing this. Since the followers of the Lawless One refuse to accept the gospel (2 Thess 2:10b), Paul believes it is God's prerogative to have them completely deceived and consequently destroyed (2:8–10). They already rejected God's message of salvation prior to God sending the delusion; hence their punishment is a consequence of their prior rejection.[111] Perhaps God reciprocates *lex talionis* their acceptance of delusion with more delusion. God recompenses their refusal to follow the truth with more spiritual blindness.[112]

THE ELECTION AND FINAL SALVATION OF THE COMMUNITY (2 THESS 2:13–14; CF. 1 THESS 1:4–5; 2:13; 5:9; 5:23–24)

One of the primary aims of 1 Thessalonians is to commend and encourage the congregation for its steadfast faith and love despite persecution. Among other things, and especially in the opening chapters, the letter reaffirms, reinforces, reminds, amplifies, and consoles the audience, which is typical epideictic rhetoric (cf. Aristotle, *Rhetoric* 2.18.1391b[17]; Quintilian, *Inst.* 3.7.6).[113]

With this aim in mind Paul reassures the Thessalonians that their election (ἐκλογή) is from God and they are "beloved by God," a phrase used of elect Israel (1 Thess 1:4; cf. Deut 32:15; 33:12; Isa 44:2).[114] The apostle and his missionary col-

---

110. Here the evil spirit brings pestilence and is also called a "pestilent spirit": see Fitzmyer, *Genesis Apocryphon*, 116–17, 121. Also see Knibb, *Qumran Community*, 193, and similar examples in *Jub.* 10.9–13; 13.13; Josephus, *Ant.* 1.8.1[164]; Philo, *Abr.* 96; *Tg. Onq.* on Deut 28:60.

111. Malherbe, *Thessalonians*, 426, says it well: "God's action is thus in consequence of theirs."

112. See a similar example in Mark 4:10–12 (vol. 1 of this work).

113. See further Witherington, *Thessalonians*, 21–29, 63–64.

114. So Marshall, "Election and Calling," 262. On election in 1 Thessalonians see further Roetzel, "Election/Calling," 554–58; Witherington, *Thessalonians*, 65–70.

leagues confirm the congregation's status by recollecting their original preaching to the Thessalonians, which was presented with confidence, deep conviction, and substantiated with powerful signs and wonders in the Spirit (1 Thess 1:5).[115] God's choice of the Thessalonians was prior to any decision of theirs, and the actualizing of that choice resulted in their calling.[116] The gospel message became the instrument God used to reach the Thessalonians—they received the divine word that was spoken by Paul and works effectually in them (2:13). Paul's prayer wish[117] is that God will watch over the Thessalonians, and on account of God's faithfulness he will see to it that their sanctification is made complete (5:23–24).[118]

In relation to final salvation the Thessalonians are delivered from the coming wrath directed against the unbelieving outsiders who afflict them (1 Thess 1:10; 2:14–16; 3:13; 5:9; 2 Thess 1:6–12; 2:8–12). They are not appointed for wrath but will obtain (περιποίησις) salvation on the Day of the Lord through the believers' watchfulness (1 Thess 5:9; cf. vv. 4–8).[119] God is the one who destines (ἔθετο) them to salvation. By implication the unbelievers also seem destined, but they for God's wrath. Both destinies will be finally realized at the culmination of the eschaton. Even so, whether to salvation or wrath, these destinies are general categories that do not appear to be fixed when speaking of particulars. Paul does not guarantee that every Thessalonian who is presently a believer will remain so until Day of the Lord regardless of his or her lack of watchfulness and sanctification.[120] Nor does Paul affirm

---

115. Here πληροφορία can mean "full conviction" (Holtz, *Thessalonicher,* 47); "deep conviction" (NET); "full assurance" (BDAG, 827); or possibly "fullness of divine working" (Delling, "πληροφορία," 6.311): cf. Col 2:2; Heb 6:11; 10:22; *1 Clem.* 42.3. Whichever is the case, this conviction in 1:5 refers to the manner of Paul's preaching (cf. Malherbe, *Thessalonians,* 112), not its effect on the Thessalonian audience, which will come in 1 Thess 1:6.

116. Cf. Donfried and Marshall, *Shorter Pauline Letters,* 29. Donfried associates the term with the Hebrew בחר indicating divine choice (cf. 1 Chron. 16:13; Ps 89:3; Isa 42:1; 43:20; 45:5; 65:9, 15, 22).

117. As the prayer wish in 3:11–13 concludes 2:17–3:10, so 5:23–24 concludes 4:1–5:22: cf. Bruce, *Thessalonians,* 128. Such invocations are appropriate in epideictic rhetorical discourses (cf. Quintilian, *Inst.* 3.7.3–4).

118. Such words need to be qualified, however. Marshall, "Election and Calling," 276, is correct when he writes: "we have not found any clear evidence in these epistles to support the view that the elect are a body of specific individuals chosen before the foundation of the world to be effectually called and to attain final salvation without any possibility of their falling away."

119. περιποίησις probably does not convey here the notion of "preserving," as suggested by Rigaux, *Thessaloniciens,* 570–71; and Holtz, *Thessalonicher,* 228–29, because salvation and wrath are still in the future (cf. 1:10; Malherbe, *Thessalonians,* 299).

120. On 1 Thess 5:9 Marshall, *Thessalonians,* 139–40, writes that the plan of God is not fulfilled "independently" of human actions; otherwise, "Paul's exhortations to vigilance would be nonsensical if vigilance was the product of some inward causation in the believer by God or if there was no possibility of disobeying the exhortation." To this statement we would qualify that vigilance is not *solely* the product of divine inward causation.

that every person who is presently an unbeliever must remain in this state until the time of the end. Repentance is always possible for the unbelieving neighbors of the Thessalonian faithful, and salvation can be forfeited if a believing Thessalonian is not watchful and lives immorally.

In 2 Thess 2:13–14 the believers are chosen by God for salvation through sanctification of the Spirit and belief of the truth. Their election is either "from the beginning" (απ' αρχης: e.g., ℵ, D), or as "firstfruit" (ἀπαρχὴν: e.g., p³⁰, B). If we assume "firstfruit" as the correct term,[121] then Paul may be understanding ἀπαρχήν in terms of the new creation, the reception of the Spirit, or the general harvest of Gentiles in the eschatological scheme of events (Rom 8:23; cf. Rev 14:4; Jas 1:18). The Thessalonians may be just one of many communities Paul would consider to be the "firstfruit." If we assume the original text is "from the beginning," the meaning of this verse is still not clear. The "beginning" may refer to: 1) the beginning of Paul's mission to that region (cf. Phil 4:15), 2) the beginning of the new era of the good news predicted through the prophets and related to Gentiles' salvation (cf. Acts 13:47–48), 3) the beginning of Israel's tradition history starting with Abraham or the creation story in Genesis (cf. Luke 11:50; *Mek. Exod.* 14.15), or 4) pretemporal history, as from the beginning of time (cf. John 17:24). The last of these is perhaps the most often held position of the four.[122] When combined with God's calling, election, and "eternal comfort" (2 Thess 2:13–16), the fourth option would stress salvific encouragement and the Thessalonians' predestination.[123] If we assume the beginning of time as the correct nuance, then this passage may be compared with Rom 8:29–31 and Eph 1:3–14, in which God's prior choice of his people involves their corporate election via God's choice of Christ, through whom the entire plan of salvation would eventually unfold to the Gentiles, including the Thessalonians. For Paul, God's desire has always been to bless Israelites and Gentiles who have faith (Gen 12; cf. Gal 3:6–14; Rom 4), and God will see to it that his collective people will be finally saved (Rom 11).[124]

121. Metzger, *Textual Commentary*, 568, favors this reading because: 1) nowhere in Paul's letters do we find the phrase ἀπ' ἀρχῆς, unless here (but see 1 Cor 2:7; Col 1:26); 2) ἀρχή is normally interpreted as "power" in Paul's letters (except Phil 4:15); 3) Paul uses ἀπαρχή six other times in his letters (but five times with a genitive); and 4) there is early evidence that ἀπαρχήν was changed to ἀπ' ἀρχῆς in other texts (e.g., Rev 14:4 [ℵ]; Rom 16:5 [D]).

122. E.g., Marshall, *Thessalonians*, 207; Gundry Volf, *Paul and Perseverance*, 16; Trilling, *Zweite Brief* 121; Rigaux, *Thessaloniciens*, 570; Davidson, *Pauline Predestination*, 10–11.

123. Eternal comfort or encouragement (παράκλησις) in 2 Thess 2:16 perhaps means that this comfort will last from the present age through to eternity. Malherbe, *Thessalonians*, 442, writes that "the expression has the ring of prayer to it."

124. If we assume this alternative to be the correct one for 2 Thess 2:13–14, then the words of Menken, *2 Thessalonians*, 121, are in order: though the passage is "redolent of predestination . . . it

In either case this passage is no denial of the Thessalonians' own responsibility to continue walking in a worthy and holy manner before God (1 Thess 2:12; 4:1–2; 2 Thess 1:11). Despite passages on encouragement in the correspondence, the Thessalonians still must take action in the process of their sanctification (cf. 1 Thess 4:3),[125] and they are to stand firm and hold the traditions they have been taught (2 Thess 2:15).[126] Persecution, rebellion, and immoral sexual acts are still struggles that threaten the spiritual well-being of the Thessalonians. If their faith is in some sense passive involving God at work in them (1 Thess 2:13; 5:24; 2 Thess 2:13), it is also active—they exercise faithfulness towards God (1 Thess 1:8), and this is demonstrated by their activities manifested through love (1 Thess 1:3; 3:6; 4:9; 5:8) and their decision to turn away from idols to serve God (1 Thess 1:9). Faith that leads to salvation is two-sided, involving both God's work in humans and human responsibility to be obedient.[127] The Thessalonians' faith is to be understood as continual loyalty to God, similar to the Hebrew scriptural terms related to אמן or "faithfulness" (Deut 32:20; 1 Sam 26:23; Psa 32[33]:4; cf. Rom 1:5, 17). Karl Donfried correctly distills this aspect of faith: "The Old Testament theme of faithfulness is dominant. Since God has called the Thessalonians they are no longer to be involved in idolatry and must avoid the continuous temptation to apostasy."[128]

From Paul's perspective, if the future apostasy among the Christ-followers seemed inevitable because it was predicted by Paul and the Jesus tradition (2 Thess 2:3–4; cf. Matt 24:6–14; Mark 13:7–13), then Paul could at least affirm also that the same tradition promised that the elect community would be preserved by God during the eschatological crisis (e.g., Matt 24:21–24; Mark 13:20–23). In his Thessalonian correspondence, Paul believes the elect community will persevere to final salvation even if all its members do not (1 Thess 5:9, 23–24 contrast 3:5; 4:8; 5:14). This view is entirely consistent with what he teaches in other letters also (e.g., 1 Cor 1:5–9 vs. 10:1–13; Rom 11:20–22 vs. 11:26–32; Phil 1:6 vs. 2:12–14; 3:18–19).

---

serves the goal of convincing the addressees that it is indeed the eternal God who is active in the preaching and the accepting of the gospel, and it does not exclude human responsibility and human effort."

125. Cf. Marshall, "Election and Calling," 271.

126. Krentz, "Theology and Fidelity in 2 Thessalonians," 61–62, rightly views their holding on to tradition as indication of their fidelity, which the Pauline writer attempts to rouse with "steadfast waiting as the apocalyptic calendar unfolds."

127. Contrast Nicholl, *From Hope to Despair*, 64–66; and Gundry Volf, *Paul and Perseverance*, 20–27, who both want to emphasize God's salvific work in the Thessalonians independent of human effort but then run into difficulties with Paul's other statements involving human obedience (e.g., Nicholl, 98n37; Gundry Volf, 27n120). The working together of both divine initiative and human obedience involves a form of compatibilism. See further Barclay, "By the Grace of God," 156–57.

128. Donfried and Marshall, *Shorter Pauline Letters*, 54.

Namely, there is no indication that Paul is nullifying any real potential for members to commit apostasy by using salvific assurances and elective language to encourage the congregation.[129] His comforting words to them serve a rhetorical strategy to suppress any temptations they might have of returning to their former lifestyle as idolaters. *They are constantly reminded of their new identity as God's people to help them differentiate themselves from outsiders and remain a separate community unassimilated with the immoral practices of the host society.* His words likewise intend to bolster the confidence of members who may still be disturbed or confused about end-time events (2 Thess 2:1–2; cf. 1 Thess 4:13–14; 5:9–11). In particular Paul hopes to comfort those members with weak consciences and still prone to fear of death and final judgment despite their conversion (2 Thess 2:13–16). He is doing no less than what he charges the congregation to do: he is consoling the faint-hearted members and supporting the weak (1 Thess 5:14). Thus, Paul both affirms the election of frail members and warns of the potential apostasy of unruly ones (1 Thess 4:8; cf. 2 Thess 3:6–15), all of whom he calls "brothers and sisters," that is, fellow believers in Christ.

CONCLUSION

We have posited that 1 and 2 Thessalonians were written by Paul. His letters to the Thessalonians aim at encouraging and instructing a congregation that has been experiencing persecution from Gentile compatriots. As former Gentile polytheists, they recently turned away from idols to serve God, and have continued to operate in faith, love, and hope despite afflictions. Paul commends their faithfulness and encourages the congregation to continue walking in a manner that pleases God. His words of praise and comfort, however, are mixed with exhortations showing that he believed congregation members faced the danger of committing apostasy. First, he fears that during his absence they had turned away from God as a result of persecution (1 Thess 3:5). Second, he must exhort them to "walk" or conduct their lives in holiness and not commit sexual immorality with other members of the congregation. To do so is to violate a fellow believer's possession and reject the command to love one another (4:1–9). Those who refuse to receive his instruction on this matter are said to reject God's Spirit who works sanctification among them. Third, even though God has not destined them for eschatological wrath, they must still be vigilant and self-controlled until Christ returns (5:1–9). This watchfulness is in keeping with prophesy from Daniel and oral sayings attributed to Jesus that are found in the Synoptic Gospels—prior to the *parousia* there will be a great apostasy that will claim the spiritual lives of many saints (2 Thess 2:3–4). Those who fol-

129. Contrast Gundry Volf, *Paul and Perseverance*, 15–27.

low the Lawless One instead of God will be destroyed when the Lord Jesus returns (2:8–12). Another conflict in the congregation centers on the chastisement of unruly idlers among them. If they refuse instruction, they should be excluded from table fellowship (1 Thess 5:14; cf. 2 Thess 3:6–15). This form of discipline aims to get these idlers to be ashamed of their conduct and repent.

The future apostasy among Christ-followers and also their safekeeping until the end are both affirmed by Paul in unison with the Jesus traditions he echoes (1 Thess 5:9, 23–24; 2 Thess 2:3; cf. 1 Cor 1:4–9; 10:1–12; Matt 24:6–14, 21–24; Mark 13:7–13). He gives us no indication that he sees a tension between the apostasy and preservation of believers. His assumption is that God will keep the elect people safe, and the Gentile believers in Thessalonica belong to the elect people. This assumption, however, breaks down on the level of particulars. Namely, when individuals from among the elect community refuse to walk in a manner worthy of God, they might forfeit the salvific assurance and benefits promised to the elect community as a whole. If they continue to commit *porneia*, fail to be vigilant, or turn away from God to serve the Lawless One, then such individuals cannot presume upon receiving the final salvation promised to the elect community. In all this there is also a rhetorical strategy for Paul that aims at keeping all members persevering in faith: for the weak and faint-hearted members he stresses the comfort of salvific hope, but for the unruly idlers he warns of potential judgment. He comforts and warns with the same objective in mind—that all the believers in Thessalonica would continue to walk in holiness and please God (1 Thess 4:1–3).

Unlike his letter to the Galatians, Paul is not concerned about the Thessalonians falling away on account of the works of the Law. External pressures for the latter do not come by way of Jewish Christian opponents who are attempting to lead astray Gentiles converts to get circumcised. Rather, the Thessalonians face opposition in the form of harassment from Gentile neighbors who do not believe the gospel message at all. Paul will maintain throughout his letters a generally positive attitude towards such persecution as beneficial for the believer's status in Christ (e.g., Rom 8:18–39). His anxiety over the Thessalonians committing apostasy as a result of external mistreatment (1 Thess 3:5) is more the exception than the rule. His optimism contrasts sharply with Matthew and Mark, who emphasize the danger of apostasy through persecution. Spiritual dangers for the Thessalonians come more by way of vice in 1 Thessalonians, and in 2 Thessalonians it will come through idolatrous deception brought about by a person who, unlike Paul's typical opponents, violates the Torah's first commandment to have no other gods beside the one true God.

3

1 Corinthians: Vices and False Security in a Divisive Congregation

Paul's message in 1 Corinthians centers on congregational division (1:10–17). In keeping with the thesis or *propositio* of the letter (1:10), he wants to maintain group solidarity among the Corinthians and discourage factions.[1] The letter is not his first to this congregation (5:9); it is a response both to their previous correspondence to him[2] and his hearing of a recent report about their conduct (1:11; 5:1). As the apostle who led this congregation to Christ,[3] Paul writes to them in a personal manner, using bluntness and sarcasm to rebuke their misbehavior (e.g., 4:8–10; 11:17; 15:34). His rhetoric is deliberative; he is attempting to persuade the Corinthians to turn from their factions.[4] In the opening chapter of this letter, Paul counters division by exhorting the Corinthians to live in unity and humility in light of the message of the cross (cf. 1:10, 18–31). Unless the names have been used by Paul for the sake of his argument against their divisions,[5] certain congregation members were claiming Peter, Apollos, Paul, or Christ as their leader (1:12). These members preferred the authority of one leader above another, but they are probably not organized parties.[6]

1. Cf. Mitchell, *Rhetoric of Reconciliation*, 225.

2. Cf. 7:1, 25; 8:1; 12:1; 16:1, 12: "now concerning" (περὶ δὲ) is Paul's response to the Corinthians' correspondence to him. See Hurd, *Origin*, 63–71.

3. Cf. 4:14–15; Acts 18:1–18.

4. On the deliberative rhetoric and arrangement of the letter in general, see Mitchell, *Rhetoric of Reconciliation*.

5. As proposed by certain scholars such as Dahl, *Studies in Paul*, 40–61.

6. Contrast recently Malina and Pilch, *Letters of Paul*, 62–63, who identify the Corinthian situation in terms of "cliques," which they define (in the singular) as "a type of coalition, defined as a collection of people within some larger, encapsulating structure, consisting of distinct parties in temporary alliances

There remains no scholarly resolution on the identity and teachings of these various groups or clusters of members.[7] As we shall observe, the divisions in Corinth cannot be reduced to one cause alone. More relevant for our purposes is the interface between the divisions and Paul's warnings to the congregation against committing apostasy. The Corinthian congregation was mostly comprised of Gentiles who were formerly idolaters but had converted to Paul's message several years earlier (1 Cor 12:2 cf. 8:7; Acts 18:1–18).[8]

FACTIONS IN CORINTH (1:10–17; CF. 1:18—2:16; 12:3)

Paul does not elaborate on the beliefs of those who claim him as their leader (1:12). He may have thought this allegiance was negative because he did not desire loyalty at the expense of congregational division (1:10–11). He did not want the Corinthians comparing him in a competitive way with his colleagues and other church leaders.

He mentions those who are for Peter (1:12), but this should not be interpreted to mean that Paul's own relationship with Peter was estranged at this point in his ministry. There is no evidence in 1 Corinthians that Peter and Paul are set at odds against each other (theologically or otherwise), as in Galatians 2. The viewpoint of a Pauline versus Petrine Christianity, famously championed by F. C. Baur and others, should be laid to rest, at least in 1 Corinthians.[9] This congregation is not struggling over the works of the Law, and although table fellowship is an issue for them the problem is not related to Jew-Gentile relationships (see below). In the letter nothing else is said about those who prefer Peter's leadership (3:22; 9:5; 15:5). The letter's brief references to this apostle sometimes have been construed to mean that Peter and his wife visited the Corinthians and received financial support from them, and that the impact of his teachings left its mark on certain congregation members, so that those members claimed him as their leader.[10] This scenario is possible, but even if we assume it the nature of Peter's teachings is not disclosed, nor the motive behind why some Corinthians favor his authority. In 2 Corinthians Paul will encounter a Jewish

---

for some limited purpose." This view may be reading into the situation more than what was actually happening. Strüder, "Preferences Not Parties," 431–455, criticizes the position that Paul is dealing with various parties. He is perhaps correct in identifying the divisions as congregational *preferences*. He also thinks it better to translate ἐγὼ . . . εἰμι in 1:12 as "I am for" rather than "I belong to."

7. For discussions on the various factional identities, see Sumney, *Servants of Satan*, 34–78; Merklein, *erste Brief*, 134–52; Schrage, *erste Brief*, 1.142–48; Hurd, *Origin*, 75–142; Thistelton, *1 Corinthians*, 122–33; Allo, *Saint Paul*, 80–87.

8. Paul writes to this congregation roughly around the mid-50s CE, as many scholars agree.

9. Contrast Goulder, *Paul and the Competing Mission*.

10. E.g., Barrett, "Cephas and Corinth," 57.

group he calls "super apostles," which might be associated with Palestinian Christ-followers,[11] but in 1 Corinthians he seems to be indifferent about Peter's influence.

Even more oblique in 1:12 is the reference to those who claim allegiance to Christ. Speculations have run the gamut regarding their identity as Judaizers, spiritual elitists, libertarians, or merely a rhetorical device used by Paul to emphasize the seriousness or absurdity of group divisions.[12] The reference to those who are "of Christ," however, may be nothing more than Paul's way of identifying independent members in the congregation who reject all forms of human leadership, including Paul's authority.[13] In other words, and regardless of their level of spiritual enthusiasm, they refuse to be accountable to anyone but Christ.[14]

Paul's references to Apollos may suggest that Apollos's eloquent speaking captivated the Corinthians (3:4–6, 22; 4:6; 16:12; cf. Acts 18:24–28). Given Paul's emphasis on speech and wisdom in chapters 1–4, perhaps certain members were comparing Apollos' rhetoric and style of preaching with Paul's.[15] The Corinthians' attitude of competitiveness, especially in relation to comparing their teachers, would seem to be derived from secular conventions associated with their upbringing in Roman Corinth.[16] Paul, at any rate, still speaks positively before the Corinthians about Apollos as his fellow colleague (e.g., 3:4–6), and so we can surmise that

11. See Thrall, *2 Corinthians*, 2.940–42.

12. Favoring the Judaizers is Robertson and Plummer, *1 Corinthians*, 12. Lüdemann, *Opposition to Paul*, 69–80, opts for the Cephas party (rather than the Christ party) as a group associated with missionaries from Jerusalem. Fee, *1 Corinthians*, 59, suggests the Christ-party may have been spiritual elitists who did not boast in mere humans. Barrett, *First Epistle*, 45 suggests the group may have emphasized philosophical monotheism, freedom, and immortality. Compare and contrast also 1 Cor 3:23; 2 Cor 10:7. On the rhetorical view, see Collins, *1 Corinthians*, 73; Mitchell, *Rhetoric of Reconciliation*, 83n101.

13. Witherington, *Conflict and Community*, 95, questions the reality of this faction by saying, "Could there really have been a Christ party, since all were claiming to be Christians? If there had been a group that said simply, 'we are of Christ and are above all mere human bickering and name calling,' it is hard to see why Paul would not side with them." But if these were independent members who did not respect any authority but Christ, they also would not seem to respect Paul's instructions and exhortations (i.e., "Paul, I listen to Christ, not you"), and their view would seem to perpetuate more divisions. Hence, the apostle could not approve of such individuals.

14. How they listened to "the voice" of Christ may not have been necessarily through tongues or prophecy (or at least not through these means alone), but they may have relied on wisdom and knowledge or some other means to come to the belief that Christ was speaking to them.

15. Highlighting the Apollos/Paul problem in Corinth are Smit, "What Is Apollos?," 231–51; Ker, "Paul and Apollos," 75–97. Pogoloff, *Logos and Sophia*, stresses the point of Paul and Apollos as rhetoricians. Pearson, *Pneumatikos*, extends the influence of Apollos in Corinth to the subjects of wisdom, spirit, and mystery.

16. Winter, *After Paul Left Corinth*, 31–43, goes further: "they had replicated in the Christian community the secular élitist educational model which was promoted by the sophists" (43).

Apollos neither instigated nor encouraged the divided allegiances in this congregation. Nevertheless, Paul may be insinuating that the Corinthians be less critical about him and more critical about Apollos (16:12).[17]

Paul informs the Corinthians that God has chosen them, the "foolish things" of the world, to confound the wise, and he uses this and similar ideas as arsenal against the Corinthians finding any ground for boasting and competitive attitudes related to human speeches (1:26–31; 4:7).[18] He combats the boasting and overconfidence of some members in the congregation by addressing spiritual knowledge and wisdom in view of the cross of Christ (1:18—2:16). He cites Isa 29:14 and relates that God will destroy the wisdom of the wise (1:19). The original setting for these words in Isaianic context betrays an abundance of divine criticisms against the counselors of Judah who depended on the wisdom of the Egyptians (Isa 28–33). Yet God will turn their societal norms upside down by uplifting the humble and humbling the proud, and the Spirit will provide restoration (e.g., Isa 27:1; 29:1–8, 18–20; 31:1–9; 32:6–20; cf. 58:4–7; 59:4, 15).[19]

This backdrop to Isa 29:14 influenced Paul's thoughts. Perhaps it suggested for him that the proper way to combat human boasting would be to stress to his audience the importance of humility, which he associates with the cross of Christ. And for him the way to contest worldly wisdom and speaking would be through God's Spirit as the eschatological source behind true wisdom. The former type of wisdom, void of the Spirit, does not recognize Christ; the rulers of this age who exemplify such wisdom had Jesus crucified (1 Cor 2:1–16).[20] Paul claims that the instrumental means by which God saves is through the "foolishness of preaching" (1:21), a message proclaimed by the apostle that demolishes human arrogance because this message finds meaning in the humiliating event of Christ crucified. Outsiders (whether Jew or Gentile) who reject this message are in the process of perishing, whereas insiders (the believers) consider it "the power of God" and are in the process of salvation (1:18–31). For Paul the crucified Christ has become the eschatological event that has invaded and overturned the earlier age of human wisdom.[21]

---

17. See Ker, "Paul and Apollos," 93–97.

18. Even so, this does not mean that God does the salvific work entirely by himself (cf. 1 Cor 3:5–9).

19. For elaboration on the Isaianic background in this section, see Oropeza, "Echoes of Isaiah," 87–112.

20. In 2:7 the "mystery" (i.e., Christ crucified: Schrage, *erste Brief*, 1.250) was ordained or "predestined" (προώρισεν) by God "before the ages" or very long ago. This probably refers to God ordaining this event from the beginning of time itself, or there is a possibility that Paul has in mind the Isaianic prophecy as the starting point (1 Cor 2:9 cf. Isa 64:4; 65:17).

21. On this aspect see Hays, "Conversion of the Imagination," 403–4.

The message in this section probably suggests not only a problem with the Corinthians' view of eloquent speech but also their view of the gospel. They are not properly identifying with humility related to the cross. They boast in status, wisdom, and rhetorical speeches not rooted in Christ or the Spirit. Sigurd Grindheim writes that if the congregation pursues these worldly activities they run the risk of "defining themselves among those for whom the gospel is hidden and thus forfeiting the divine gift. The divisions are therefore indicative of the fact that the Corinthians are jeopardizing their salvation."[22]

Several observations are in order regarding the factions in Corinth. First, their preferences for leaders may be influenced, in part, by the person who baptized them, and this may be one reason why Paul plays down the number of people he himself baptized among them (1:13–17).[23] They may have held to magical presuppositions regarding the importance of names (cf. 1:13; 10:2).[24] We can speculate further that the congregation accentuated the importance of baptism, both in water and Spirit (10:2; cf. 15:29). In 1:13–17 water baptism seems to be foremost in view if the meaning of "in the name of Paul" hints at the ancient baptismal words "in the name of Jesus" (cf. Acts 2:38b). Even so, for Paul, Spirit baptism is also part of conversion-initiation (1 Cor 12:13; cf. Acts 2:38c). Perhaps baptism was being embraced to the extent that it provided for the Corinthians a sense of security and spiritual boasting, especially when coupled with prominent leaders performing their initiation ceremony (1:13–17; cf. 1:29–31; 3:21; 4:7; 12:1–14:40). Although Paul considers the proclamation of the gospel to be more important than baptism (1:17), elsewhere he links the latter with conversion-initiation into the "body of Christ," which he identifies as the church, the collective body of believers "in Christ" who operate in God's Spirit.[25] *The Corinthians' factions threaten to "part out" Christ by fragmenting the solidarity of this community of believers in Christ* (1:13).

Second, our problem with identifying the four divisions in 1:12 is eclipsed by the later factions we find related to sexual mores in chapters 5–7, the "strong/*gnosis*" and "weak" in chapters 8–10, social dissimilarities in 11:17–34, and misperceptions

22. Grindheim, "Wisdom for the Perfect," 709.

23. Chester, *Conversion* at *Corinth*, and others suggest a special bonding taking place between the baptizer and baptized, and this aspect inadvertently carried over into the congregation via their previous involvement with mystery cults (290, 303). More primary sources need to be cited that directly support this view if it is to be taken seriously. Apuleius, *Metam.* 11, is one possible source: cf. Garland, *1 Corinthians*, 52.

24. On this possibility, see further Oropeza, *Paul and Apostasy*, 79–82, 88–89.

25. See 1 Cor 12:13; cf. 1:1–9, 30; 6:11, 15, 17, 19; 10:16–17; 2 Cor 5:17; Rom 6:11; 8:1, 9–16; Gal 3:2; 2 Thess 2:13; Eph 1:1–14, 22–23; Titus 3:5.

about the resurrection, eschatology, or both in chapter 15.[26] Scholars are sometimes interested in positing a situation in Corinth that highlights one opponent or faction that comes by way of Jewish Gnosticism, wisdom traditions, disparity between rich and poor, Roman elitist customs and ethics, or something else.[27] While certain reconstructions seem more plausible than others, interpretative attempts to reduce the later factions in the letter to specific groups behind the four leaders in 1:12 frequently veer off into unconvincing speculations.[28] We will address the divisions relevant for apostasy without presupposing any of these groups are pure loyalists to Peter, Paul, Apollos, or "Christ."

Third, *we do not gain much insight into 1 Corinthians by comparing it with the conflicts in 2 Corinthians.* Paul's apostolic authority is at stake in the second letter, but in the first it is only initially challenged (e.g., 1 Cor 10:10; 14:37). Moreover, chapter 9 does not function as an apologetic against the Corinthians' charges against him.[29] In this section Paul presents himself as an exemplar. He is able to relinquish his "authority" or freedom for the sake of others; something the *gnosis* believers in Corinth must do for the sake of weak believers (ch. 8).

Finally, the divisions and potential apostasies in 1 Corinthians are not related directly to persecution (contrast 1 Thessalonians) or misperceptions about the Law (contrast Galatians). It is sometimes argued that utterance of the "Jesus curse" (Ἀνάθεμα Ἰησοῦς: 1 Cor 12:3) evinces Christians renouncing faith in Christ due to persecutions (Pliny, *Letters* 10.96–97; *Mart. Pol.* 9.3; Rev 2:13; 3:8).[30] A curse against Christ may be considered the antipode of "Jesus is Lord," a confession made at baptismal conversion (Rom 10:9–13; Acts 2:38; 22:16). Paul, however, mentions the

26. On the last of these see especially Wire, *Corinthian Women Prophets.*

27. Horrell and Adams, *Christianity at Corinth*, collect a good compilation of scholarly sources (mostly late twentieth century) addressing possible situations in Corinth. Recently, for the Corinthians as elitists and influenced by the conventions and mores of *Romanitas*, see Winter, *After Paul Left Corinth.* For criticisms see Horrell, Review of *After Paul Left Corinth*, 660–65.

28. It could be misconstrued, for example, in 1 Cor 8–10 that the "strong" share an affinity with Paul because they all have loose boundaries related to table fellowship (like Paul); whereas Peter would be associated with the "weak" believers that have strong boundaries. The wrong assumption here is that the "weak" are associated with Jews or those who still hold to Jewish food laws. But the Corinthian problem is not a Jew/Gentile conflict, nor is it centered on kosher/non-kosher food regulations based on the Mosaic Law (see below).

29. Contrast the apologetic/defense view in Horsley, *1 Corinthians*, 124; Conzelmann, *1 Corinthians*, 151–52.

30. On this view see Cullmann, *Christology*, 218–20. The elusive verb in the phrase may be understood as either imperative ("Let Jesus be cursed") or indicative ("Jesus is cursed"). In favor of the latter is that the contrasting phrase, "Jesus is Lord," is indicative. Differently, Winter, *After Paul Left Corinth*, 164–83, argues from curse tablets in Roman Corinth as well as other sources that the phrase is requesting that Jesus curse one's enemy (i.e., "Jesus [grants] a curse"). This view, however, does not make a good symmetrical parallel with "Jesus is Lord."

curse in passing, and no doubt he would have elaborated on something as serious as falling away on account of persecution if it were an actual problem in the congregation. Local mistreatment or harassment of congregation is not a major concern in the letter, and Paul is writing prior to the time of imperial persecutions of the church (c. 55 CE). The phrase, then, could hardly be referring to Corinthian believers reviling or renouncing Jesus in this manner.

Quite possibly a curse on Jesus may have been something the pre-Christian Paul would have uttered.[31] Then again, it may have been something the pre-Christian Paul would have forced the Christ-followers to say (Acts 26:11; cf. Gal 3:13; 1 Tim 1:13). But if so, why would Paul resurface this negative memory as he begins to address the subject of spiritual gifts? It seems more plausible to surmise that the Jesus curse reflects something idolaters may have expressed in a cultic setting (1 Cor 12:2),[32] or that it was something uttered by non-Christian Jews in the synagogue (cf. Justin, *Dial.* 47.4; 96.2; 137.2). The Corinthians' experience in worship would then be set in contrast to other cultic experiences that deny the Lordship of Jesus.

THE ELECT COMMUNITY "IN CHRIST" (1:1–9; 12:4–31)

The opening of the letter stresses the congregation's election and final salvation at the *parousia* of Christ. The plethora of concepts attributed to the Corinthians, as "called," "saints," "sanctified," "empowered," "sustained" to the end, and preserved "blameless" on the day of judgment, argues forcefully that their final salvation is in some sense secured (1:1–9). Paul unmistakably considers them to be part of God's elect community. They have accepted the witness of the cross, they confess Jesus as Lord, and they possess spiritual gifts. Moreover, as believers "in Christ," they have fellowship or intimate communion with him (1:2, 4–5, 9), and God has graciously called them to this type of fellowship (1:9).[33] The Corinthians, though primarily Gentile believers, are confirmed in their new identity as God's people because of God's faithfulness. He loves them and will be faithful to his promises for them.

31. On this view see Bassler, "Curse and Confession," 415–18. Also noteworthy is Derrett, "Cursing Jesus," 544–54, who posits the renunciation caused by a situation in which Christians face expulsion from the Jewish synagogue.

32. On this option as well as others, see Thiselton, *1 Corinthians*, 918–27. Another option (e.g., Hays, *First Corinthians*, 209) is along the lines of Paul creating the Jesus curse as a literary device to highlight the counter phrase "Jesus is Lord," or to point out the Corinthians' spiritual ignorance, or both.

33. Chester, *Conversion at Corinth*, 105, distinguishes Paul's call as one of "task," and the call of his converts that "grants them a new identity understood primarily in terms of who they have become rather than what they are to do." Although Chester stresses Pauline language of calling in terms of individuals (e.g., 1 Cor 7:21), he admits that the calling in 1:9 is "collective" rather than individualistic (91).

In terms of rhetorical arrangement, however, these words of assurance are found in the *proem* of this letter.[34] We do well to temper thoughts about their final perseverance with the fact that Paul's rhetorical intention via the *proem* at the beginning of his letters is to build rapport with his readers by praising and complementing them (cf. Phil 1:6). As is conventional in deliberative discourses, his strategy at the beginning of the letter is to rally the audience on his side before attempting to persuade them against what he perceives as their problems. The many warnings throughout the letter clearly suggest that final perseverance in an unqualified sense is not what Paul is teaching in 1:1–9. In fact in the final passage of the letter, as in the opening pericope, Paul again mentions Christ's second coming, this time through the Aramaic phrase *maranatha* ("Our Lord come!"). But in this instance Paul gives a warning and anathema that almost seems to be the counterpart to 1:8—the Corinthians who do not love the Lord will be accursed (16:22). The salvific assurances given in the opening verses, then, do not nullify the potential ways the Corinthians' salvation might be undermined in later portions of the letter.

Moreover, apart from Paul's rhetorical strategy, *the assurances of 1:1–9 typify how Paul is able to confirm believers of eschatological salvation in terms of their participation "in Christ," while at the same time infer through his many warnings that such assurances do not guarantee that every individual member within the community will persevere to final salvation.* A message that we will hear over and again in the letter is that authentic members of the community in Christ are susceptible to apostasy and could miss out on inheriting God's kingdom. The promise of God's future deliverance in the present time rests on the community itself rather than all the individuals that presently make up the community. Paul describes the Corinthians in corporate terms as the "temple of God" (3:16–17) and "body of Christ" (12:4–31; cf. 6:15). The words of J. Louis Martyn on the community in Christ are instructive here: "Nothing less than God's new creation, this new human agent contains individuals, but, as was the case with ancient Israel, this agent is the new community *itself* (12.4–31), typically addressed by Paul with plural verbs, a pattern quite infrequent in Hellenistic paraenesis."[35]

TWO DIFFERENT JUDGMENTS (3:10–17)

Paul cannot talk to the Corinthians as mature believers but must speak to them as "babes" in Christ on account of their divisive behavior (3:1–3; cf. 2:6). In his

---

34. See 1:4–9, e.g., in Mitchell, *Rhetoric of Reconciliation*, 194–97.

35. Martyn, "Pauline Meta-Ethics," 180–81.

view they are not spiritual but "fleshly" (σάρκινος/σαρκικός);[36] their conduct is not derived from God's Spirit but a human point of view motivated by self-interest. They are not properly walking in the Spirit but "walk as mere humans" (3:3b: κατὰ ἄνθρωπον περιπατεῖτε).

Two different judgments are discussed in 3:10–17: a judgment on the labors of Christian workers (3:9–15), and another judgment on congregation members that cause division or otherwise ruin the church (3:16–17). The laborer must build on the foundation of Christ (3:11)—a thought that recalls Jesus as the metaphoric cornerstone of a building, a structure referring to the church (Rom 9:32–33/Isa 8:14; 28:16; Eph 2:20–22; cf. Matt 16:16–18; Mark 12:10–11; 1 Pet 2:4–6). Paul's own proclamations about Jesus became the Corinthian congregation's foundation and the paradigm for future service (1 Cor 2:2).[37]

The six materials used for the building (3:12) are sometimes compared with those used for the Feast of Tabernacles or Solomon's temple.[38] Another proposal relates the passage to the language of a legal agreement involving workers and contractors building a temple or some other structure. Such projects needed to pass a final inspection, and penalties could be imposed on the workers if the building did not meet proper specifications.[39] Even so, the quality of these materials seems to be Paul's main point of mentioning them. Some materials can be easily destroyed by fire (wood, hay, straw) while others cannot (gold, silver, precious stones). The testing of the work is related to the "day," which refers to the eschatological judgment that will take place when Christ returns (3:13). At that time the inner motives of everyone will be revealed (1:8; 4:4–5; 5:5; 2 Cor 5:10; Phil 2:16; Rom 2:15–16; cf. *T. Abr.* 13.9–14).

The fiery test, which seems related to the destruction that occurs on the Day of the Lord,[40] exposes the flaws of the Christian laborer's work and burns it up. Despite this loss the laborer will still be saved (1 Cor 3:14–15).[41] The scene envisions a last moment escape from a burning house (cf. Amos 4:11; Zech 3:2; Jude 23; *Sib. Or.* 2.252–54).[42] The third-person future passive of ζημιόω in 1 Cor 3:15 can refer to the worker's own chastisement ("he will suffer punishment") or, more likely, the worker will be penalized of the wages he was to get for his labor ("he will be mulcted of his

---

36. Thiselton, *1 Corinthians*, 289, distinguishes the two words: "σάρκινος means moved by entirely human drives, while σαρκικός means moved by self-interest."

37. Cf. Derrett, "Paul as Master Builder," 129–37.

38. See e.g., Kuck, *Judgment and Community*, 177–78; Ford, "You are God's '*sukkah*,'" 139–42.

39. Cf. Shanor, "Paul as Master Builder," 461–71; Watson, *Corinthians*, 35.

40. Cf. 2 Thess 1:7–8; 2 Pet 3:12; Isa 66:10–11, 24.

41. This passage has sometimes been interpreted as evidence supporting the doctrine of purgatory: see examples in Gnilka, *1 Kor. 3.10–15*.

42. See further references in Townsend, "1 Corinthians 3.15," 500–504; Schrage, *erste Brief*, 1.304.

pay").[43] In other words, he is deprived of an unspecified eschatological reward (3:15; cf. 3:8).[44] This loss may be similar to Paul's anxiety over his own labors among his congregations being "in vain" (15:58; Phil 2:16).[45]

Ronald Herms would add to this loss of reward a conceptual link between 1 Cor 3:10–15 and *1 Enoch* 50.1–5, because the latter refers to "other" individuals that are "saved" during eschatological judgment but "have no honor before the Lord of Spirits."[46] Paul's words may be similar to this text in that he envisions the builders as saved but losing honor at the eschaton. This is possible if we consider that the reward gained or lost has to do with honor and shame. Paul does mention a reward in this context (3:8, 14–15), but he does so without explicitly mentioning an honor/shame concept until 4:14. Our passage, in any case, teaches that certain believers will receive some sort of reward at final judgment while others will not, even though both groups will be saved. Though Paul speaks generically of any Christian worker in 3:12, the passage takes a special interest in the labors of leaders such as Paul and Apollos (3:5–10). Paul is not disclosing implicitly that he is the one who will receive an eschatological reward while Apollos's efforts will be burned up.[47] Instead his implication for the congregation in general and its leaders in particular is for them to avoid building on the foundation of Christ with wrong motives, self-interests, and void of the Spirit's guidance; everything done in the Lord's service must be centered on the crucified Christ.[48]

A second judgment mentioned in 3:16–17 is more severe than a worker's loss of eschatological reward. The Corinthians are considered to be the temple of God, with God's Spirit dwelling in them. Paul states in reciprocal style that anyone who destroys the temple of God will be destroyed by God. The concept for destruction here (φθείρω) is that of eternal ruin that God will bring upon such a person on judgment day (cf. Jude 10; 2 Pet 2:12).[49]

What is at stake here is the corporate well-being of the entire congregation as God's temple (contrast the Corinthians as individual temples in 1 Cor 6:19–20). Their unity in the Spirit is being threatened by the congregants who are causing division, whether through boastful and selfish attitudes, insensitivity towards weaker

43. So Barrett, *First Epistle*, 89.

44. This reward is not concerned, at least primarily, with rates of pay: cf. Konradt, *Gericht und Gemeinde*, 222–58.

45. Cf. Kuck, *Judgment and Community*, 182–83.

46. Herms, "Being Saved without Honor," 187–210. On the shaming aspect of this judgment see also Konradt, *Gericht und Gemeinde*, 272.

47. Contrast Horsley, *1 Corinthians*, 34.

48. See especially Kuck, *Judgment and Community*, 172; Thiselton, *1 Corinthians*, 312.

49. See BDAG, 1054.

members, practicing vices, or something else. If they persist in ruining the congregation, they will be excluded from God's temple, and God will destroy them at the eschaton. Anthony Thiselton perceptively writes regarding this passage, "to damage the church [so] that the work of the Spirit becomes impeded is *thereby* to cut oneself off from the Spirit as one's own source of life."[50] Rhetorically speaking, Paul is appealing to the *pathos* of fear. In an effort to dissuade them from their divisions, he tries to "scare the hell out of them"! Even so, his words are more than hypothetical warnings with no substance behind them. He firmly believes that those who commit divisive activities, such as strife and jealousy (3:1–3), or endanger the congregation in some other way may be excluded from God's kingdom on judgment day (10:9–10; 2 Cor 12:20; Gal 5:20–21; Rom 1:29; 13:13; cf. 1 Tim 6:3–4; Titus 3:9).

The first type of judgment in 1 Cor 3:10–15 involves building God's house in a faulty manner. It does not entail a loss of salvation. The second judgment in 3:16–17 involves a person destroying God's house and does result in loss of salvation.[51] *Congregation members who destroy other members—that is, influence them to engage in destructive vices or otherwise get them to commit apostasy—will themselves be punished by God as apostates.*

PORNEIA AND EXPULSION (1 COR 5)

A major section of 1 Corinthians addresses the threat of defilement from outside sources (5:1—11:1). The first problem Paul addresses in this section involves sexual immorality (πορνεία). A man in the congregation is committing fornication with his father's wife, and the congregation has become "puffed up" (φυσιόω) over the incident instead of mournful (5:1–2). The son decided "to have" (ἔχειν) sexual relations with his stepmother,[52] and the present infinitive of ἔχω suggests the problem was not a one-time event—the man is having an ongoing sexual relationship either by cohabiting with her or by marrying her (cf. 7:2).[53] Since Paul calls on the congregation to punish only the man, the stepmother most likely did not attend the church or profess to be a Christ-follower.[54]

---

50. Thiselton, *1 Corinthians*, 318.

51. Watson, *Corinthians*, 36, rightly affirms of 3:16–17 that "the punishment will fit the crime."

52. Paul uses "father's wife" (5:1), not "mother," to identify the stepmother (cf. Lev 18:7–8). It is not evident from the passage whether the father was still alive. The sexual act here can be identified as incest or incest-like because it occurs between family members. Technically speaking, however, the woman is not a blood relative of the man. While I recognize this complexity, for brevity's sake I will sometimes identify him as the "incestuous man."

53. See Fee, *1 Corinthians*, 200.

54. See e.g., Schrage, *erste Brief*, 1.371.

Paul's judgment seems informed by the Mosaic Law, as it condemned incest, and his expulsion of the man is based on Deuteronomic tradition (1 Cor 5:2, 13/ Deut 17:17; cf. 23:1; 27:20; Lev 18:7–8; *m. Sanhedrin* 7.4). It appears to be rather odd at first to hear Paul proclaiming in Galatians and Romans that the Law is insufficient to deal with sin, and yet his argument in 1 Cor 5 presupposes the sexual codes of the Law. More generally Paul considers sexual immorality to be a breach of the grand law to love one's neighbor as oneself (see 1 Thess 4), but this approach is not mentioned in 1 Cor 5 and he in fact refers to the Law here in relation to sexual misconduct. In this case perhaps his view of sexual violations of the Law has been filtered through the decision of the apostolic meeting from Jerusalem, which determined that *porniea* should not be practiced by Gentile Christians (Acts 15:19–29).[55] Paul agrees with the Jerusalem church's decision on prohibiting fornication, but as we will notice in 1 Cor 8–10 and Rom 14 he deviates from the church's decision on Gentiles abstaining from certain foods, including idol meats. He does not explain his rejection of Jerusalem's dietary prohibitions for Gentile converts. In Antioch, maybe his observation of Peter and the followers of James refraining from table fellowship with Gentile believers played a major role in his rejection (cf. Gal 2:11–14). Be that as it may, he expects that his condemnation of the sexual act should be self-evident to the Corinthians—not even the unbelieving Gentiles practice such a thing (1 Cor 5:1). Outsider sentiments against incest probably should be understood only in a general everyman sort of way. Boris Paschke shows many examples from Greco-Roman and ancient Jewish literature on the subject of incest to argue that Paul's evaluation in 5:1 is too positive on the sexual ethics of Greco-Romans. Although ancient writers mostly view incest negatively, some rulers and philosophers practiced or promoted it. The apostle thus uses "rhetorical exaggeration" to make his point about fornication in 5:1, and other sources make similar rhetorical moves (e.g., Seneca, *Phaedra* 165–72; Cicero, *Cluentio* 5.15; *Ligario* 1.1; Andocides 128; 1 Macc 7:23; *Pss. Sol.* 8.13).[56]

The congregation's boasting in the context of this situation seems highly presumptuous given the strict Jewish and Christian sexual ethics of the time. Were the members relishing in the man's freedom (cf. 1 Cor 6:12; 10:23) and thumbing their

---

55. For the connection between Acts 15 and the earlier sex codes, see e.g., Hays, *Moral Vision*, 383.

56. Paschke, "Ambiguity in Paul's References," 169–92. Winter, *After Paul Left Corinth*, however, argues from Roman law (*The Digest* 48.30–40) that extramarital incest was condemned, but the law was more lenient toward incestuous marriage. He suggests the father may still be alive as the son had sexual relations with his stepmother, which constitutes adulterous incest (45–49). But if Paschke is correct and rhetoric colors our text, then 5:1 should be understood only in a general sense. There may be no need to speculate on which aspect of Roman law best fits Paul's words.

noses at prohibitions against sexual misconduct?[57] This is one possibility. Another view is that their boasting is related to the man's social status.[58] One possible scenario in this regard is that a lucrative dowry would have been lost if the woman remarried outside the family after her husband had died, and so to prevent this loss the son married his stepmother. If the son were a patron of some of the congregation members, those members may have boasted about the relationship. This may help explain why "greed" is mentioned as a vice in 5:10–11.[59] A third option is that the congregants were boasting despite the man's activities. This view is weakened, however, by their boasting in 5:6, which points back to 5:2. The first two options seem more possible than the last, but we simply do not know enough details to take a firm stand on any choice.

Paul calls on the congregation to expel the man from their community; this is to preserve the well-being and purity of the church (5:6–13), which is the temple of the Holy Spirit.[60] Brian Rosner writes perceptively: "In calling for the incestuous man to be removed Paul effectually cleanses the temple, calling for his destruction (5:5), for 'if any one destroys God's temple, God will destroy him' (3:17)."[61] The man's expulsion from the community implies more than his being ostracized from the church in Corinth. If Paul understands the congregation as the body of Christ in this letter (6:11, 15–19; 12:13), and all members belong to this one body, then for a member to be expelled from the congregation means that that member is cut off from Christ. In first-century communities it is not uncommon for individuals to be banished for the sake of the whole group.[62] Dale Martin posits that Paul is assuming an ancient concept of invasion etiology in which diseases must be expunged from the body; in this case, the man operates as a disguised pollutant that threatens to contaminate the body of Christ. The proper procedure, then, is to cast the man "outside" the body of Christ into the world or *cosmos* associated with the fallen age.[63] If this view has some merit, then Paul does not own a hotline to Satan in 5:5 in which he gets him

---

57. The congregation's abuse of freedom is suggested by Collins, "Function of Excommunication," 253.

58. See Chow, *Power and Patronage*, 130–41; Clarke, *Secular and Christian Leadership*, 80–81.

59. Cf. Chow, 137–40; Witherington, *Conflict and Community*, 156.

60. Pascuzzi, *Ethics, Ecclesiology and Church Discipline*, 12, 97–146, 180–81, rightly contests the perspective that Paul is using this incident to reassert his authority. Paul's concerns are not defensive or polemical in 1 Cor 5 but motivated by Christology, ecclesiology, and ethics. The apostle's main concern is to protect the community's well-being.

61. Rosner, "Drive Out the Wicked Person," 29.

62. Cf. Malina and Neyrey, "First-Century Personality," 77. On excommunication in Second Temple Judaism see Horbury, "Extirpation and Excommunication," 13–38.

63. Cf. Martin, *Corinthian Body*, 139–74, esp. 163–70.

to attack whomever he wills. Rather, once the man is expelled from the believers "in Christ," the only community left for him to join is with non-believers and apostates in a realm where Satan and anti-God powers reign supreme (cf. 2 Cor 4:4).

The expulsion of the fornicator echoes richly the Deuteronomic tradition that warns against being cut off from the community of God as a result of heinous sins (1 Cor 5:13; cf. Deut 13:1–5; 17:2–7; 19:16–19; 21:18–21; 22:21–24, 30).[64] In the society of ancient Israel this type of expulsion often involved the physical death of the offender.[65] Paul's judgment on the incestuous man that he be handed over to Satan seems to be similar to the expulsion of gross sinners and apostates in ancient Israel; albeit, the apostle is not officially sentencing the violator to a form of ancient capital punishment.[66] Instead that man is cut off from the community of Christ for the "destruction of the flesh" (1 Cor 5:5). This is variously interpreted by scholars as the physical suffering/death of the man, the destruction of his sinful nature, the eradication of fleshly works in the congregation, or a combination of these.[67] The "spirit" that might be saved could refer to the man's human spirit, the "spirit" in the congregation, or both.[68]

Unless this is the only exception in his writings, Paul does not use the verb σῴζω ("save") to speak of the salvation of a congregational "spirit," let alone a church or God's Spirit being kept safe. He consistently uses σῴζω to speak of *humans* being saved in relation to the eschaton (1:18, 21; 3:15; 9:22; 10:33; 15:2; 2 Cor 2:15; Rom 5:9–10; 10:9–13; etc.). The fact that a definite article ("the") rather than a possessive pronoun ("his") appears before "flesh" and "spirit" does not necessarily strengthen the case that these terms are referring to the congregation. Definite articles sometimes function as possessives,[69] and the definite articles before "flesh" and "spirit" can

---

64. Rosner, *Paul, Scripture and Ethics,* 61–93; idem, "Deuteronomy in 1 and 2 Corinthians," 122–23, helpfully elaborates on relevant Deuteronomic passages in our text.

65. e.g., Exod 31:14–15; Forkman, *Limits of the Religious Community,* 17–20, 36.

66. Contrast Derrett, "Handing Over to Satan," 11–30, who holds that Paul hands over the man to civil authorities for physical punishment and execution. Roman law forbade such incest (Gaius, *Institutes* 1.63; Cicero, *Cluentio* 5.27). Similarly, Gaca, *Making of Fornication,* 139–40, holds that Paul sentences the man to the death penalty. But a weakness with this view is that Paul does not actually mention civil authorities, only Satan.

67. See the scholarly spectrum of options in Pascuzzi, *Ethics, Ecclesiology,* 114–17. Martin, *Corinthian Body,* 174, adds the church to the concept of the "flesh": he suggests that the "sarx" of the man is what invades the church, so that the "sarx" of both the man and the church needs to be destroyed, and the "pneuma" that must be saved is both that of the man and the church.

68. For the first option see, e.g., Gundry Volf, *Paul and Perseverance,* 114n67; for the second, e.g., Collins, "Function of Excommunication," 259–60; for the third, e.g., Martin, *Corinthian Body,* 174.

69. E.g., "the faith" as "their faith" in 1 Tim 1:19.

be rendered "his flesh" and "his spirit" (e.g., NASB).[70] Moreover, Paul normally refers to the "flesh" (σάρξ) in an anthropological sense in the Corinthian correspondence (e.g., 1 Cor 6:16; 15:39, 50; 2 Cor 4:11; 7:1, 5; 12:3). Also, he sometimes uses the word "spirit" (πνεῦμα) to refer to the human spirit or human spirit as empowered by God's Spirit (e.g., 1 Cor 2:11; 7:34; 14:14; 16:18). More pointedly, this is in fact how he uses πνεῦμα in the same context (5:3–4). Without further qualification, his parallelism of "flesh" and "spirit" likely would have been read by the Corinthians as either both referring to the man or both referring to the church, but since both σῴζω and σάρξ are normally used by Paul in an anthropological rather than ecclesiastical sense, the man's flesh and spirit/spiritual life is the more plausible meaning here.

If we compare the way Paul uses "flesh" in Romans and Galatians, the "flesh" as sinful nature is a possible option (e.g., Gal 5:16–21; Rom 8:3–9); however, there are a few weaknesses with this position. First, Paul does not clearly use the term "flesh" (σάρξ) to refer to the sinful nature in 1 Corinthians.[71] The word is relatively synonymous with the mortal/material body[72] or is understood in terms of being outwardly human, involving human standards, human life, and similar things (1 Cor 1:26, 29; 7:28; 10:18; 2 Cor 1:17; 5:16; 10:2–3; 11:18). Even in 1 Cor 3:1–3, when Paul connotes the immaturity of the Corinthians, he does not use σάρξ but σαρκικός (and σάρκινος), which means "human," "material," or "fleshly" (cf. 1 Cor 9:11; 2 Cor 10:4).[73] Second, Paul's word for "destruction" in 5:5 (ὄλεθρος) normally means "ruin" or "destruction" (cf. 3 Kgs[1 Kgs] 13:34; Jer 28[51]:55–56; *T. Reu.* 6:3; Josephus, *Ant,* 17.38).[74] This word speaks to the eschatological demolition of wicked humans, not merely their sinful nature. Brian Rosner compares the "destruction" (ὄλεθρος) in 1 Cor 5:5 with "put to death" (Rom 8:13) and "crucify" (Gal 5:24) to support that the "flesh" should be understood as the sinful nature in this passage.[75] However, in Romans and Galatians the *believers* are the ones who put to death or crucify *their own* "flesh." Paul does not use ὄλεθρος this way—he uses the term

70. See also Ellingworth and Hatton, *1 Corinthians*, 114: "for the destruction of his flesh, that his spirit . . ."

71. Some understand that Israel according to the "flesh" in 10:18 recalls sinful Israel or Israel trapped under sin's power. Cf. Gardner, *Gifts of God*, 165–72. Admittedly there may be some negative connotation here, but still it is not clear that "flesh" should be equated with "sinful nature" in this verse, and the most natural meaning for the "flesh" would be Israel according to their "earthly descent" (cf. Rom 4:1; 9:3; Collins, *First Corinthians*, 380).

72. 1 Cor 6:16; 15:39, 50; cf. 2 Cor 4:11; 7:1, 5; 12:3.

73. See BDAG, 913–914.

74. We notice also the concepts of destruction and flesh in Gen 17:14; Lev 17:14; Jdt 2:3; 4Q268; 1QHa 16.31–33; 1QS 4.12–27; Heb 11:28.

75. Rosner, "Drive Out the Wicked Person," 32–33.

against unbelievers or apostates, and a different entity (rather than the unbelievers themselves) brings about their physical calamity, whether God, Christ, or vice (1 Thess 5:3; 2 Thess 1:9; cf. 1 Tim 6:9). Perhaps the closest parallel to the word in 1 Corinthians is ὀλοθρευτής (10:10): the "destroyer" is an angelic being that kills grumblers among the Israelites in the wilderness. Here the meaning refers to the destruction of human lives, which Paul uses as a warning to the Corinthians against their falling away. Third and finally, it makes little sense to hand over the person to Satan if the destruction of the sinful nature is meant; Satan as the tempter works to incite sinful activities, not destroy them (e.g., 1 Cor 7:5; 1 Thess 3:5; cf. Matt 4:3; *1 En.* 19.1; *Jub.* 11.4–5; *T. Dan.* 1.6–8; 1QS 3.21–24; *Herm. Mand.* 4.3.4–6).[76] Both the devil and sinful nature are anti-God powers that can work together rather than against each other in order to undermine human relationships with God and Christ.

These observations regarding the "flesh" in 5:5, then, point us to the fornicator's physical body as the appropriate meaning here. Interestingly, Paul sometimes uses "flesh" to refer to the penis (Gal 6:12–13; Phil 3:2–3; Rom 2:28; Col 2:11, 13; cf. Gen 17:11–14). Such a meaning here would not be impossible given that he also mentions the penis when speaking against fornication in 1 Thess 4:4. With this view in mind the incestuous man's "spirit" might be saved if his penis, the physical instrument of his vice, is destroyed. But if this is the intended meaning, we are not told the details of how this destruction of his penis could take place, whether through disease, accident, or something else. Then again, neither are we told exactly how his body could be destroyed if this is what is meant by the "flesh." Paul's words in 5:5 are vague enough to allow for both meanings: the flesh represents the man's physical body in general and genitals in particular. Whatever the precise nuance might be, the primary meaning for the "flesh" and "spirit" in this context is anthropological rather than ethical or ecclesiastical.

Nothing in the passage suggests the destruction must be instantaneous, and so the man's immediate death is probably not the point, despite any alleged similarities between this incident and the death of Ananias and Sapphira (Acts 5:1–11). Likewise, there is no reason for us to assume that the man's death will make atonement for his sin. Paul does not think this way in the Corinthian correspondence; Christ is seen as the one who atones for sin (2 Cor 5:14–21; cf. 1 Cor 1:18, 30; 6:11, 20). Rather, *the man's fate seems based on the reciprocating notion that those who defile or destroy the "temple of God," the community in Christ, will be destroyed by God* (cf. 1 Cor 3:16–17). *The destruction in 5:5, however, is not intended to be eternal. Paul hopes the punishment will be remedial and the man will be saved.*[77] There is the

76. Cf. Kondradt, *Gericht und Gemeinde*, 319; Lampe, "Church Discipline," 351.

77. The *hina* clause in 5:5b (ἵνα τὸ πνεῦμα σωθῇ) probably indicates the purpose of the expulsion

possibility of restoration from sin and apostasy (cf. Gal 6:1; Rom 9–11; Jude 23–24; Jas 5:19–20). Presumably, the man could repent of his fornication and so be saved after he has physically suffered or faced misfortune for an undisclosed amount of time in the realm of Satan.[78]

If he does repent, his "spirit" or inner person will be saved even though his natural body and genitals perish, and when the Day of the Lord comes he will have a resurrected and glorified body (cf. 1 Cor 15:42–46). Despite the dichotomy between inner person ("spirit") and outer person ("flesh") creating an apparent tension with the hope of the resurrected body, Paul embraces both views. He could affirm without qualification that the inward person is spiritually strengthened on a daily basis, while the outward person is gradually perishing (2 Cor 4:7, 16; 5:1, 6–8). Moreover, he holds to the existence of a human inner self or "spirit" in the very context under examination, as well as elsewhere,[79] and he seems to believe that the inner self survives death *prior* to Christ's second coming, even if disembodied (cf. Phil 1:21–23; 2 Cor 5:1–8). This view likewise seems supported in other New Testament passages (e.g., Luke 16:19–31; 23:43, 46; Rev 6:9–11). To be sure, this transitory state is not the goal of salvation; in fact, it may be seen as being metaphorically "naked" (2 Cor 5:3f). But even if the goal for Christ-followers in the eschaton is the resurrection of the body (Rom 8; 1 Cor 15) we should not make the wrong inference that Paul does not believe the human spirit could ever be separated from the human body (cf. 1 Cor 5:3–4; 2 Cor 5:6, 8; 12:2–3). Alternatively, since the man's restoration is in view in 5:5, the "spirit" may refer to his spiritual life revived by God's Spirit.[80] This life nevertheless may take place via the human spirit.

Does Paul think that the man was never truly converted? The term ὀνομαζόμενος in 5:11 has been translated "so-called brother," possibly suggesting the incestuous man is an inauthentic believer.[81] The middle/passive participle of ὀνομάζω, however, is more commonly rendered "calls himself" (middle) or "is called" (passive). Presumably, if the middle voice is preferred, the man considered himself a believer, as did the congregation members, despite his sexual immorality. Nevertheless, Paul's focus in 5:11 is no longer centered on the incestuous man but on anyone (τις) who calls himself a "brother" (i.e., a believer) yet engages in the vices that are mentioned.

---

rather than a necessary result.

78. Satan can inflict suffering and physical punishment according to Paul, but God is still able to fulfill his own purposes through such attacks (2 Cor 12:7–10; cf. Luke 13:11–16; Job 1–2; *Jub.* 11:11–12; 48:2–3; *T. Ben.* 3.3; 1QS 4.14).

79. 1 Cor 5:3–4; cf. 2:11; 14:14; 16:18; 2 Cor 2:13; 7:1, 13; Rom 8:16.

80. For a similar view see Kondrat, *Gericht und Gemeinde*, 321.

81. So Gundry Volf, *Paul and Perseverance*, 124–25; BDAG, 573–74.

Paul is not saying that all vicedoers are inauthentic believers; he is clarifying something he already taught them in a previous letter (5:9). To paraphrase 5:9–11, he wrote them in a previous letter not to associate with "fornicators" (5:9), but he did not at all mean for them not to associate with the fornicators and vicedoers of the world . . . (5:10); what he meant to say when he wrote to them was that they should not associate with a person who calls himself a "brother" but is a fornicator or vicedoer. Paul is requesting the Corinthians to exercise more discernment. Not every individual should be accepted into the Corinthian fellowship automatically just because the person claims to be a believer. The person's lifestyle should be compatible with the person's self-proclaimed faith in Christ. If it obviously is not, then the congregation is told not to fellowship with such a person. Perhaps the assumption is that such a "brother" is blatant and unrepentant about his vicedoing. We wonder about the ramifications of this exclusion from fellowship if the Corinthians were to take to heart Paul's words and apply them to all the drunkards and sexually immoral persons in the congregation (cf. 6:12–20; 11:21)!

In any case, *it makes more sense to view the incestuous man as a believer at one time whose vice has caused or will cause him to be cut off from fellowship with Christ.* Otherwise, it would seem rather odd for Paul to expel a non-believer from the realm of believers (i.e., the body of Christ) so that in the realm of non-believers (i.e., the *cosmos*) the man might convert into a believer.[82] Similar to other members of the congregation, the man was probably baptized, received the Spirit, and converted in the name of Jesus (1 Cor 6:11; cf. 1:13–14; 10:2; 12:13; Acts 2:38; 19:1–5). Paul's authoritative use of the name of Jesus when expelling the fornicator suggests a kind of status reversal of his conversion-initiation (5:4–5). In relation to the limits of purity in the thought of Paul, Jerome Neyrey discusses entrance and exit rituals that mark boundaries—baptism is the most notable example of an entrance ritual, and the circumcision of Gentile believers would exemplify an exit ritual (cf. Gal 5:2–4). The early form of excommunication in 1 Cor 5 would be another example of an exit ritual.[83] This man will now be officially cut off from the community in Christ via Paul's authority and the congregation's decision to expel the man (5:3–5). Once this takes place, the man will be like a fish out of water in the *cosmos* and hopefully he will see the error of his ways, repent, and return to the believers' fold. If this view is correct, then the expulsion of the fornicator from the congregation would seem to indicate the man's loss of status as a Christ-follower. He is no longer to be considered a member of the body of Christ, the elect community in Christ. His new associates will be the outsiders who do not know Christ. In short, he will become an apostate,

---

82. Cf. Oropeza, *Paul and Apostasy*, 194.

83. Neyrey, *Paul*, 72, 79–80, 87–92, 190–92.

cut off from Christ, not saved, and along with other fornicators and vicedoers he will not inherit God's kingdom unless he repents (5:9–11; 6:9–10).

Paul's decision to expel the man exposes the culprit's sin as an act of apostasy. The man has rejected the moral precepts of the Christ-community (1 Thess 4:1–8; Acts 15:21–29), and by doing so he essentially rejects Christ, who guides the community by God's Spirit. The expulsion makes the man "officially" apostate even though he apparently considered himself a believer, at least up to the time of the community's verdict. The significance in this case, as in Matt 18, is that spiritual leaders are given authority to determine when sanctions need to be taken against congregation members who are sinning. Even so, in both 1 Cor 5:3–5 and Matt 18:15–20 Christ is said to be present in the community's decision making. The apostle never explains the quantity of sins that must be committed by a believer in order to consider the person an apostate. His abhorrence against this man's vice is clearly seen by his determination to expel the culprit and others like him: in 5:5a "such a one" (τὸν τοιοῦτον) suggests a similar punishment for others who would commit similar acts. Yet Paul does not expel the men who are having sex with prostitutes (1 Cor 6), nor does he ostracize the fornicators in 1 Thess 4. Perhaps he feels that the incestuous man's sin would greatly harm congregation members, especially those who are boasting in the man's activities. Also, if there were legal sanctions in Roman Corinth at the time against a person committing incest (cf. 5:1) this act could have been more damaging to the congregation's reputation with outsiders than other cases of sexual misconduct.

VICEDOERS AND SEX WITH PROSTITUTES (1 COR 6)

The second case of *porneia* in Corinth implicates some of the men in the congregation who are having sex with prostitutes (πόρνη: 6:15–16).[84] The men apparently justified their activities, claiming that "all things" are "permissible" for them.[85] The satisfying of their sexual urges is seen as similar to satisfying their appetite for food (6:12–13).[86] Paul qualifies their slogans by claiming that not all things are beneficial

---

84. cf. Prov 29:3; Isa 1:21; Ezek 16:30–35; *T. Lev.* 14.5–6; *Pss. Sol.* 2.11[13]; Matt 21:31–32; Luke 15:30; Rev 17:15.

85. On Corinthian slogans in the letter see Murphy-O'Connor, "Corinthian Slogans," 391–96. These slogans were perhaps included in their rejoinder to his previous letter, which warned them not to associate with fornicators (cf. 5:9). Differently, Garland, *1 Corinthians*, 228, thinks that "Paul cites a familiar notion about freedom found in the Corinthian culture and recasts it in Christian terms."

86. Κοιλία sometimes is sexual in meaning (cf. Sir. 23:6) such as when it refers to the womb (cf. 2 Sam[2 Kings LXX] 7:12; Luke 23:29; John 3:4; Behm, "κοιλία," 3.786–88).

for their community, and some things are capable of enslaving them.[87] He does not cite for them a passage from the Levitical codes that condemns sexual immorality, nor does he mention the Jerusalem meeting's decision that Gentiles must keep the Law in reference to fornication (Acts 15:21–29). Such reasons may not have provided adequate rationale *for them* on why their fornication is wrong. Paul must come against their ideology in which all things are permissible for them, including sexual relations with prostitutes.

Bruce Winter suggests that the saying "all things are permissible" resembles conventional prerogatives of the socially elite in the Greco-Roman world (Dio Chrysostom, *Or.* 3.10; 14.13; 62.2; Polybius, *Histories* 3.24.12). Their feasts include sexual license, gluttony, and drunkenness—"the possible *Sitz im Leben* for 1 Corinthians 6:12–20; 8:1–11:1, and 15:32–32."[88] For Winter, these sexual encounters with prostitutes take place in banquets rather than brothels.[89] Paul does not seem to be concerned about the location of these sexual liaisons; his goal is to persuade the Corinthians to abandon these encounters wherever they might be taking place. The Corinthians must "flee" from *porneia* (6:18), not banquets.

Imagery related to marriage and bodily ownership is used by Paul to dissuade his audience from committing fornication. He cites the joining together of Adam and Eve as "one flesh" (1 Cor 6:16/Gen 2:24) to highlight the audacity of a Corinthian believer becoming one with a prostitute.[90] This mock marriage is set in contrast to the true spiritual union of the person who is joined to Christ and becomes one with him through the Spirit (6:16–17). The assumptions for Paul are that Christ has become the metaphoric husband of the believer, and the believer's body is joined with other members to become one body in Christ (cf. 1 Cor 12:13, 27; 2 Cor 11:2–3; Rom 7:4; Eph 5:21–23; Isa 54:5; Hos 3:1–3). Authentic solidarity for the believers involves their being joined to Christ, who then, as the heavenly spouse, becomes the proper owner of their bodies (1 Cor 6:13b; cf. 7:4). The congregation members thus

87. This appears to be an implication derived from ἐγὼ ἐξουσιασθήσομαι ὑπό τινος: "I will not be brought under the power of anything" in 6:12d.

88. Winter, *When Paul Left Corinth*, 85; cf. 81–84.

89. Ibid., 88. He also thinks that sexual license in the congregation may have centered on young men receiving the *toga virilis* and thus now allowed to participate in the banquets (89–93). On Corinthian women in relation to prostitution and sexual promiscuity, see Strabo, *Geography* 8.6.20c; Athenaeus, *Deipnosophists* 13.573c–574e; Plato, *Republic* 404C; Philetaerus, 13.559E. Temple prostitution is related to Greek rather than Roman Corinth, according to Winter (87).

90. Heil, *Rhetorical Role of Scripture*, 103–5, rightly affirms that the passage relies on the implied audience's understanding of Gen 2:21 as establishing the basic unity "between a man and his wife by the institution of marriage as created by God" (104). This union becomes analogous to the union between the Corinthian members and Christ (116).

have no authority over their own bodies; they belong to Christ.[91] Marital possession collides with thoughts about slave ownership when Paul continues that Christ has "purchased" (ἀγοράζω) the Corinthians through his atoning death (6:19c–20). Moreover, their bodies are sanctified as holy temples in which God's Spirit dwells, and these bodies are destined for heavenly perfection at the eschaton when they will be raised from the dead (6:11, 14, 19 cf. 15:44–49).

By committing *porneia* with prostitutes, outsiders who are not connected with the body of Christ, the Corinthians show themselves unfaithful to Christ their spouse. They violate his rightful possession of their bodies by surrendering them to the possession of another. Victor Furnish expresses the correct sentiment here: "Whatever actions threaten to exercise their own control over the believer's life are thereby subversive of this relationship [with the Lord], and therefore not permissible."[92] There is probably a double meaning to Paul's use of the word "body" in 6:18–19: the Christian fornicators not only sin against their own bodies but also against the social body of Christ (cf. 3:16–17; 6:14–16; Eph 1:22–23).[93] To be joined with a prostitute is to be in union with someone who belongs to the fallen *cosmos*, the realm of Satan and forces hostile to Christ. This introduces confusion and a blurring of body boundaries so that the collective body of Christ, via the fornicator, becomes one, as it were, with a fallen world via the prostitute.[94]

Paul's understanding of sexual unions may presuppose a Jewish perspective that considers sexual mingling with outsiders as a defilement of both the individual and community (*Jub.* 30:7–17; Josephus, *Ant.* 4.126–158; cf. Deut 23:17–18; Lev 18; Num 25). In this case, the Corinthian believers are God's community and the outsiders are non-believing prostitutes. To avoid fornication the Corinthians are to "flee" from it, similar to the patriarch Joseph fleeing from Potiphar's wife, an Egyptian and outsider who wanted to have sex with him (Gen 39:7–13). The Corinthians, moreover, are to take on the positive incentive of honoring God with their bodies (1 Cor 6:18, 20).[95]

In this passage there are strong implications that the Corinthian's sexual union with prostitutes leads to apostasy and divine judgment. *The believers' fornication is*

91. Here the body means more than simply the outward, physical flesh of humans but the self or whole person, "which, precisely in its corporeality and creatureliness, is capable of communicating with and therefore relating to other selves": Furnish, *Theology of the First Letter*, 56.

92. Furnish, *Theology of the First Letter*, 57.

93. Paul's statement that every sin a person commits is outside the body (6:18) probably represents a Corinthian slogan. For options, see Fisk, "Πορνεύειν as Body Violation," 540–58.

94. Martin, *Corinthian Body*, 176–78, describes this general idea more graphically as sexual penetration.

95. Cf. Oropeza, "What Is Sex?," 43–48.

compared with taking away (ἄρας) members from the body of Christ to become members of a prostitute (6:15).[96] Furnish relates this incompatible union to defection: "Anyone who goes to a prostitute has deserted the realm where Christ is Lord for the death-dealing chaos of a realm that is ruled by many 'so-called' gods and lords (cf. 8.5)."[97] Paul warns the Corinthians that *porneia* was one of the causes of apostasy for many Israelites who were destroyed in the wilderness, and the Corinthians should take heed that they do not fall away and be eschatologically destroyed as a result of their vices and fornication (10:8, 11–12).

Moreover, sexual immorality is among the vices that prevent a person from inheriting God's kingdom (1 Cor 6:9–10; cf. 5:11; Gal 5:19–21). The Corinthians once practiced the vices mentioned in 1 Cor 6:9–10 but escaped them as a result of their conversion. This passage, unlike Gal 5:19–21, does not list a catalogue of vices but *vicedoers.* Even though members from the church commit vices, Paul creates a distance between the vicedoers and his congregants. It is as though he wanted to say, "This is not who you are any more, even though this is what you still practice." His rhetorical strategy in contrasting vicedoers and believers would help them recognize that unrighteous behavior characteristic of unbelievers should not be *their* behavior as converted and sanctified followers of Christ.[98] Stephen Chester says it well: "His anxiety reflects not simply the possibility of fresh sins requiring forgiveness, but the fact that in his view their conversion ought to have alienated them from sin."[99]

The list in 6:9–10 (cf. 5:9–11) is not entirely random or conventional.[100] The vices Paul infers were being committed by the Corinthians before their conversion, and ironically most of the vices were *still* being committed by them, including sexual immorality (cf. 6:12–20; 5:1–5; 10:7), idolatry (cf. 10:1–22), drunkenness (cf. 11:21), and greed, theft, and swindling, which are unrighteous activities implied in 6:1–8, where the idea of believer taking believer to court is rebuked.[101] The full impact of 6:9–11 for the original audience is that their lives should not be characterized by

---

96. Cf. Robertson and Plummer, *1 Corinthians*, 125.

97. Furnish, *Theology of the First Letter*, 59.

98. Lopez, "Vice List in 1 Corinthians 6:9–10," 59–73, esp. 71, rightly sees this point but incorrectly thinks the passage does not address that believers could lose salvation because, among other things, "it does not harmonize with passages that teach unconditional inheritance or eternal security . . . John 10:28–29; Rom 3:21–4:25 . . ." (60). The main problem with this view is that the other passages do not teach systematic notions of "eternal security" (for John see vol. 1 of this work). Moreover, non-Pauline texts do not need to "harmonize" with 1 Corinthians if my thesis for this three-volume study is correct.

99. Chester, *Conversion at Corinth*, 139.

100. See Oropeza, "Situational Immorality," 9–10.

101. On 6:1–8 as a warning against exclusion from God's kingdom, see further Kondradt, *Gericht und Gemeinde*, 329–45.

vices associated with their pre-converted status. *It follows from this that if unbelieving vicedoers will not inherit God's kingdom then neither will the Corinthian converts inherit it if their lifestyle is virtually indistinguishable from the vicedoers. Both will be excluded from the salvific inheritance promised to the righteous.* The Corinthians are thus warned against eternal loss that could happen as a result of the various activities that are leading them to apostasy.

THE PROBLEM OF MEAT SACRIFICED TO IDOLS (1 COR 8–10)

In his effort to help maintain the community's purity and solidarity, Paul also addresses problems related to meat sacrificed to idols (8:1—11:1).[102] His instructions arise out of a conflict between Corinthians of prominent social standing in the congregation who are "strong" or *gnosis* (knowledgeable) and the lower-class members who are "weak." The strong/*gnosis* members have knowledge that idols are not really gods, and so for them eating idol meat is not spiritually harmful.[103] The weak do not know that idols are not gods, and their "conscience" (συνείδησις) can be defiled if they eat idol meats (8:1–13).[104] The severity of Paul's warnings in this section of the letter moves us to favor an actual division in the congregation over this issue. He is not fabricating the positions of the strong and weak for the sake of persuading the congregation to abstain from idol foods.[105] The Corinthian situation does not center on disagreements between those who adhere to dietary laws related to the Torah, unlike Rom 14. And whereas it could be argued that Jewish Christ-followers are among the weak and Gentiles among the strong members in Rome, both the strong

102. Here εἰδωλόθυτος means that which is "idol offered" or "offered to an idol." The word may have been coined by Christians: cf. Horrell, "Idol-Food," 121–22. More specifically the concept may refer to idol "meat" (κρέα: 8:13). I will be using "idol meats" and "idol foods" interchangeably. For a recent overview of scholarly positions on 1 Cor 8–10, see Willis, "1 Corinthians 8–10," 103–12.

103. Fee, *1 Corinthians*, 372–73, thinks 1 Cor 8:5b affirms that Greco-Roman deities "exist," but only subjectively in so far as "they are believed in." They should not be identified objectively or ontologically as actual "gods" because for Paul and the strong believers, there is no such thing as other deities beside the one true God (8:5; cf. 12:2; Gal 4:8). On the view that demons are "gods," see Phua, *Idolatry and Authority*, 144–45; Fotopoulos, *Food Offered to Idols*, 249, 262.

104. Συνείδησις probably refers to self-awareness or moral consciousness: cf. Horrell, *Social Ethos*, 147. Alternatively, Garland, *1 Corinthians*, 383, understands it in 8:7–13 as a "moral compass . . . [that] comprises the depository of an individual's moral beliefs and principles that makes judgments about what is right and wrong." A person with a weak conscience has a propensity to make bad moral judgments "based on faulty criteria" (384; cf. Epictetus, *Discourses* 2.15.20). In 10:29, however, Garland interprets the term as "consciousness" (496). For discussions on the word see, e.g., Eckstein, *Begriff Syneides*; Gooch, "Conscience," 244–54.

105. Although I recognize the situation involves *gnosis* members, for the sake of brevity I will use the term "strong" (rather than always with the more specific strong/*gnosis*).

and weak are primarily Gentiles in Corinth.[106] The weak members were formerly idolaters (cf. 1 Cor 8:7; 12:2), making it implausible for us to consider them Jewish, especially given that a distinction is made between "Jews" and "the weak" in 1 Cor 9:20, 22 (see on Rom 14 below for further comparisons of the two passages).

In an affirmation of the *Shema*, altered to include Christ as Lord, Paul sets the tone for this entire section of the letter by making a contrast between worship of God and the potential idolatry threatening the Corinthian strong members (1 Cor 8:4–6/Deut 6:4–5). The congregation's unity, it seems, is based on the unity and love of the one true God as expressed in the *Shema* and Deuteronomic tradition. This tradition permeates the text and will resurface again towards the end of Paul's discussion on idol meats, when he alludes to the Song of Moses in an effort to warn them against idolatry and demons (1 Cor 10:20–22; cf. Deut 32:16–21, 37–39).[107] Both Deuteronomy and Psalms reserve an idea similar to Paul that idols are lifeless vessels and yet a connection exists between demons and idols (Deut 29:17: 32:17–21; Ps 105[106]: 28–37). The Deuteronomic text stands as a witness against the wilderness generation committing apostasy through idolatry, and Paul compares the Corinthians with the wilderness generation in order to warn them against idolatry and apostasy (1 Cor 10:1–22).

The consumption of idol meats, however, does not necessarily fall into the category of idolatry. *For Paul the main problem with the strong members' consumption of idol meats is that it might cause the weak members to fall away from their faith in Christ and worship of God.* The weak cannot grasp in a consistent way the idea that idols do not represent actual (ontological) deities. Their consumption of idol meats might then lead them back to their former worship of these deities, whom they believe to be real. In terms of gods and lords, they apparently see things in black and white (no doubt encouraged by Paul!): they must either serve God and Christ or the deities and lords they formerly venerated prior to their conversion.[108] For the sake of the spiritual well-being of weaker brothers and sisters, Paul warns the strong members against eating idol foods (8:7–13). Their authority or "right" (ἐξουσία) to eat these foods must not become a stumbling block by which weaker members turn away from Christ to serve idols (8:9).[109] Instead they should follow Paul's example of relinquishing personal rights and freedoms so that others might be saved (9:1–23).

106. Contrast the all-Jewish perspective of Phua, *Idolatry and Authority*, 27.

107. On the influence of Deuteronomic tradition in 1 Cor 8–10, see further in Oropeza, "Laying to Rest the Midrash," 57–68; Hays, *Echoes*, 94–102.

108. Interestingly, Caesar may have been venerated already as an earthly deity, but if so no hostility towards Christ-followers who refused such veneration appears to be evident in Paul's time. For evidence of the cult and its relevance to first-century Corinth, see Winter, *After Paul Left Corinth*, 269–86.

109. The stumbling block here (πρόσκομμα/מִכְשׁוֹל) is associated with serving idols or other gods

Again in 10:23—11:1 Paul recapitulates his view of one's refraining from idol meats for the sake of others, but this time the focus centers on one's buying idol meat in the marketplace and eating in a non-Christian setting.[110] If Paul's primary objective was to save people (e.g., 9:19–22), he may have thought that invitations from non-believers provided opportunities for sharing the gospel message. He approves of congregants accepting such invitations. If they are told by someone at the dinner that the food set before them has been offered to an idol, they are to refrain from eating it being mindful of the "conscience" of another person (10:28–29). The informing person is probably non-Christian. Rather than using the Christian term for idol meats (εἰδωλόθυτος), this individual uses the more reverential ἱερόθυτος ("sacrificed to a deity"), something a non-Christian Gentile might say. If this person were the host, it would be odd that Paul would not clarify this. More likely it is another guest. Why would a non-Christian's "conscience" be troubled by what a Christian eats? Some propose that a weak Christian guest or slave is imagined to be present at the meal.[111] This is certainly possible if we assume that the person invited may not necessarily come by himself to the dinner. Did he bring his own guest, family members, or a household slave? Or was another guest at the table a Christ-follower?

The unnamed informant (τις . . . ἐκεῖνον τὸν μηνύσαντα) is not necessarily the "other" (ἕτερος) whose "conscience" is affected. It is possible that, despite any close connections in Greek, the καὶ between τὸν μηνύσαντα and τὴν συνείδησιν . . . τοῦ ἑτέρου suggests two different persons. If so, then the "other" may be a weak Christian who is not even present at the dinner.[112] Paul may be thinking of a believer who only later finds out about the incident, whether through conversation or inquiry, and this person's "conscience" is troubled to find out that a fellow believer knowingly ate meat sacrificed to idols. Paul, at any rate, charges the Corinthians to refrain from idol foods not only for the sake of the person with a troubled "conscience" but also for the sake of the non-Christian informant (10:28). In this case the reason would seem to be that the non-believers at the table, and the informant in particular, might feel confirmed in their idolatry rather than challenged to abandon it. For them, the Christian's partaking of idol food might be interpreted as an endorsement of the deity to whom the food was offered.[113]

(Exod 23:33; 34:12; cf. Ezek. 14:3–7; 1QHᵃ 12.15; 4Q430 1,3; *b. ʿAbod. Zar.* 6a; 14a; Ciampa and Rosner, "1 Corinthians," 718).

110. Collins, *First Corinthians*, 383, makes the interesting but speculative suggestion that the non-believers could be the believer's in-laws (cf. 7:12–15).

111. E.g., Hays, *First Corinthians*, 177–78.

112. My view is not entirely unique: Lang, *Korinther*, 131, for instance, raises a similar possibility.

113. On this point see Conzelmann, *Corinthians*, 178.

The most severe consequences, however, are found in 10:1–22. *In this pericope those who are primarily in danger of apostasy are not the weak believers, but the strong members whose presumptuous attitude about idols is shot down by Paul* (10:12; cf. 10:9 with 10:22). He warns this group that despite their spirituality, God-given gifts, and election in Christ they could fall away (πίπτω) through idolatry and other vices (10:12).[114] Even though idols are not really gods, Paul continues that malignant demons are a present reality associated with idolatry.[115] If the Corinthians engage in idolatrous activities they will be partnering with demons (10:14–21). Such a union would be entirely incompatible for those who believe; it would amount to their joining the body of Christ with the demonic world.

Is Paul condemning the consumption of idol meats as idolatry here? If so, how is that the strong members are apparently free to eat idol foods in a temple setting in 8:10 so long as they do not offend the weak? Perhaps the best solution to these questions is to posit that Paul did not categorically condemn the consumption of idol meats. His Jewish heritage does not prevent him from claiming that no food is unclean (1 Cor 8:8; Rom 14:14). It is even quite possible that he himself ate such foods on occasions (1 Cor 9:4; cf. 9:21–22). The strong Corinthians who originally read and heard this letter probably would have associated Paul's words in 9:4 with his authority to consume any food he wants, including idol meats, which he discusses only a few sentences earlier in chapter 8.[116] He agrees with them that Greco-Roman deities do not exist, and he will agree with their freedom to eat idol foods as he recapitulates his instructions in 10:29b—11:1. To be sure, 9:4 is related to his reception of free meals when he preaches or is on his missionary travels, but such meals were offered to him not only by hospitable Jews and Christians but also by non-Christian Gentiles, who might have offered him idol foods (cf. 9:21). His main point, nonetheless, is that even though he has the right to receive free meals he does not insist on such liberties. In a similar way, chapter 9 assumes the strong congregants have similar rights; otherwise the argument from chapter 8 tends to break down.[117] One of those rights is their freedom to eat idol meats provided that they do not offend weaker believers.

---

114. On πίπτω in relation to apostasy see, e.g., Rom 11:11, 22; 14:4; Heb. 4:11; Rev 2:5.

115. Presumably, these entities would be no different than the evil spirits found in other places in the New Testament. They possessed people and were associated with Satan. Luke portrays Paul as having the authority to cast out demons (Acts 16:16–18; 19:12).

116. That he adds the word "drink" to 9:4 is not a compelling argument against the probability that he is still thinking about idol foods. He in fact mentions eating and drinking in relation to idolatry later on in this section (cf. 1 Cor 10:7).

117. Cf. Still, "Paul's Aims Regarding εἰδωλόθυτος," 335.

We notice also that Luke, Paul's colleague, has Jesus commissioning his disciples to preach in various towns. Their travels will include lodging at various homes and eating and drinking whatever is set before them (Luke 10:7–8; cf. 1 Tim 5:18).[118] The Lukan version seems to reflect Paul's sentiments that no food is intrinsically unclean (1 Cor 8:8 cf. Rom 14:17, 20–22). We are safe to assume that if Paul and his colleagues were guests in a non-believer's home and idol meat was set before them, they would eat it as long as no one found offense in their liberty to do so.[119]

The view that Paul comes against all acknowledged forms of idol meats is sometimes held by scholars due to a reluctance in admitting that the early church fathers misinterpret Paul's view on idol meats, even though it is quite likely that some of the very problems in Paul's churches, Corinth included, arise from congregants who misinterpret Paul's earlier teachings to them (e.g., Gal 1:10; Rom 3:8; 6:1; 1 Cor 6:12; 2 Thess 2:2). It seems to be common knowledge among early Christians that Paul's letters are difficult to understand and frequently misread (cf. 2 Pet 3:15–16).[120] The church fathers would be no exception to this. It is quite possible, even likely, that they did not entirely comprehend Paul's view on idol meats, especially when other Christian scriptures prohibited idol foods without having to reply back to intellectual arguments of knowledgeable Gentile Christians who resented such a prohibitions.

Likewise, a very restrictive view of Paul on idol meats is sometimes supported in an effort to make his position conform to the apostolic decree in Jerusalem (Acts 15:21–29), which prohibited the consumption of idol foods by Gentile Christians.[121] There is no evidence, however, that Paul entirely agreed with all the decisions in Jerusalem—he never explicitly mentions the decree in any of his letters. A point often overlooked by scholars is that in his letters Paul repeats fornication as a destructive vice that can undermine a believer's inheritance in God's kingdom (1 Cor 5:11; 6:9; Gal 5:19; Col 3:5; Eph 5:3, 5; cf. Rom 1:26–27; 1 Tim 1:10), but nowhere does he affirm the consumption of idol foods as a vice. This omission is especially significant for the Corinthian letters because the vices that he does mention are not merely conventional, but have special relevance to the Corinthian situation. Idolatry (εἰδωλολατρία) is condemned as a vice (1 Cor 10:7, 14) but not the consumption of idol meats (εἰδωλόθυτος).[122] Apart from the prohibition against sexual immo-

118. Interestingly, the more Jewish Matthean version of this saying omits this aspect (Matt 10:10).

119. Notice also that the second gospel, traditionally written by Mark, another colleague of Paul's, also seems to reflect freedom to eat any food (Mark 7:1–23).

120. Contrast Cheung, *Idol Food*, 165–295, who does not address the evidence in 2 Pet 3 when examining early Christian interpreters of Paul. In favor of Paul being misunderstood by the church fathers on idol meats, see Brunt, "Rejected, Ignored," 113–24, esp. 120–21.

121. E.g., Cheung; Witherington, *Conflict and Community*, 190.

122. Contrast Fotopoulos, *Food Offered to Idols*, 234, 250, who thinks that the idolatry in 10:14

rality, he does not seem to adhere to the food restrictions.[123] The decisions from the meeting in Jerusalem are motivated by a need to foster a breach in fellowship between Jewish Christ-followers, who still practiced ancient Jewish customs, and Gentile Christians, who were not familiar with such customs and laws. Differently, the problem in 1 Cor 8–10 focuses on conflict between weak Gentile Christians and strong Gentile Christians. Regarding idol meats, Paul is not motivated by a concern that they maintain the decision from Jerusalem. On this point he does not seem to be entirely in agreement with the decision. Moreover, their fellowship with Jewish Christians is not at stake.

If we stop expecting Paul to conform to other early Christian and Jewish writers on every issue, it becomes quite evident that he maintains loose boundaries regarding the consumption of idol meats; he does not always prohibit it (cf. 1 Cor 8:8–9; Rom 14:14).[124] He grants the strong members their right to eat idol meats in 8:8–9 (cf. 10:29b–30), which could hardly be the case if he condemned wholesale every instance of eating such food, whether at home, in a guest's house, or even in a pagan precinct.[125]

When 8:1—11:1 is taken as a whole, Paul's position is not contradictory,[126] nor is it that Paul condemns all consumption of idol meats unless such knowledge of the food remains unknown.[127] Neither the conscious nor unconscious eating of idol meat is at stake. Moreover, Paul is not necessarily condemning all consumption of idol meats in idol precincts.[128] The complexity of the situations in the Greco-Roman world related to the eating of idols foods in temples and other locations warrants that a monolithic answer is not the best answer.[129] Paul seems to hold to a continuum

---

concerns idol food consumption.

123. What would make him agree with sexual rules but not food laws? A partial answer may rest in his belief that sexual sin violates the body (6:18) and the ethical code to love one's neighbor as oneself (1 Thess 4), whereas foods do not violate these principles, as long as weaker believers are not offended.

124. While it is possible that 8:8 is a slogan of the Corinthians, there seems to be no good reason for our denying that Paul shares their sentiments in this verse. See Fee, *1 Corinthians*, 383–84. The idea is similar to Paul's own in Rom 14:14, and even though this verse is not related to idol meats it demonstrates Paul's radical view on eating, which would not have been shared by many Jews and Jewish Christians of his day.

125. Hence Still, "Paul's Aims Regarding εἰδωλόθυτος," 335, is correct in stressing that Paul affirms "this authority of yours" to the strong in 1 Cor 8:9, "without suggesting that it is inauthentic or that the act in which it is exercised inherently defiles the knower."

126. Contrast, e.g., Cope, "First Corinthians 8–10," 114–23.

127. Contrast, e.g., Cheung, *Idol Food*, esp. 162; Tomson, *Paul and the Jewish Law*, 202–3.

128. Contrast, e.g., Witherington, "Not So Idle Thoughts," 246–51; Fee, "Εἰδωλόθυτα Once Again," 172–97. See the perceptive but often overlooked response to Fee by Fisk, "Eating Meat Offered to Idols," 49–70.

129. Examples of such eating from various Greco-Roman sources may be found in Klauck,

of situations regarding idol meats; some situations can lead to idolatry while others may not.[130] *The strong members' consumption of idol meats can, but not necessarily will, lead to idolatry on every occasion.* Paul believes that God is ultimately in control of the earth, and praying and giving thanks over any food would seem to make it acceptable for consumption provided that eating it would not be a stumbling block to others (10:23, 26, 30–31; cf. 1 Tim 4:4–5). It seems that one's praying for God's blessing over food is more powerful than any possible demonic presence.

Idolatry, on the other hand, leads to fellowship with demons, and it would be incompatible for the Corinthians to partake of both a demonic table and the Lord's Supper (1 Cor 10:14–22). The believer's eating and reclining at a temple precinct (8:10) may or may not include sacrificial acts and participating at the table of demons (10:20–21).[131] *If there is any line that a believer can step over from the acceptable eating of idol meats to idolatry, it may be at a pagan alter table as the devotees perform their sacrifices.*[132] Paul is not concerned, however, about giving precise boundaries for discerning when the boundary line of idolatry is crossed.[133] This is probably because even though he affirms the freedom of the stronger Corinthians to eat idol meats, in practice his argument allows very few opportunities for them to do so.[134] Unless they prepare their own food and eat alone in their homes, there is almost always the potential for offending weaker believers who might see them eat idol foods.

Herrenmahl Und Hellenistischer Kult, 91–163; Willis, *Idol Meat in Corinth*, 17–62; Gooch, *Dangerous Food*, 1–46; Fotopoulos, *Food Offered to Idols*, 49–157.

130. My position stands in general agreement with Fisk, "Eating Meat Offered to Idols," 62–63, 69; Horrell, "Theological Principle," 99–100; Newton, *Deity and Diet*, 338.

131. Horrell, "Idol-Food," 124, makes the important observation that in numerous cases of meals or dining related to sanctuaries (e.g., Asklepeion, Demeter, Kore), imperial cult, and funerary and athletic events, "only a small group of worshippers or cultic officials took part in the sacrificial act and ate of the sacrificial offerings; others might eat food, and might do so in adjacent rooms, or in the open air, or in other settings which evinced no close connection with the cultic act itself."

132. For general support of this view see Sanders, "Paul between Jews and Gentiles," 70; Borgen, "'Yes,' 'No,'" 56.

133. Contrast *m. Sanhedrin* 7.6 and *m. 'Abod. Zar.* 1.3—4.7, which attempt to determine such boundaries.

134. Still, "Paul's Aims Regarding εἰδωλόθυτος," 339, 341–42, goes a bit further and opines that Paul's argument, though affirming the strong's viewpoint, amounts to complete abstinence.

APOSTASY AMONG THE STRONG AND WEAK AND DISCERNING WHEN IT TAKES PLACE (8:7–13; 9:24—10:13; CF. 5:1–13; 16:13)

In 8:1—11:1 the Corinthian congregation faces several potential dangers of committing apostasy, and Paul also mentions a way that even his own faith could be undermined.

First, if the weak members eat idol meats their "conscience" could be damaged and they might fall away, which in 8:7–13 is conveyed by words such as σκανδαλίζω (cf. 2 Cor 11:29) and πρόσκομμα (cf. Rom 9:32–33; 14:20–21; 2 Cor 6:3: προσκοπή). In this predicament the end result for them would be eternal destruction (ἀπόλλυμι: 8:11; cf. 1 Cor 10:9–12; Rom 14:15; Matt 10:28; Jas 4:12; Mark 8:35; *Herm. Sim.* 9.26.3). His warnings against the weak members falling away is not without substance—he generally recollects instances of apostasy taking place with weak members in mind in 2 Cor 11:29. It is possible that Paul equates the wounded "conscience" of the weak with their eating in doubt (cf. Rom 14:23). For Paul, where there is doubt there is lack of faith; and where there is lack of faith there is the possibility of losing faith altogether. Their falling away, however, is not merely caused by a subjective experience of having guilty feelings about eating idol meats. Rather, *the weak members' consumption of idol meats could draw them back to committing idolatry because, unlike the strong believers, they are not aware that the consumption of such foods does not entail a worship of the deities they formerly served.* They would interpret this consumption as idolatry and a repudiation of the Christian claim to worship God alone. As a result, they may decide to give up their faith altogether and fall back into old patterns of worshipping the gods they once served before their conversion. Another possibility is that they might worship many gods along with the God of Israel,[135] a position that Paul would consider unacceptable for the emerging Christians, who are to worship one God, the Father of all, and one Lord, Jesus Christ (1 Cor 8:6).

A second potential danger is related to the strong members who, due to their eating of idol meats, become the cause of the weak believers falling away. If the strong members' inconsiderate behavior of consuming such food results in the destruction of their fellow Christians, they would be sinning against Christ who died for all believers (1 Cor 8:11–12). The penalty is severe for those who destroy members of the body of Christ: they themselves will be cut off from Christ and destroyed (3:16–17). The implication seems clear: *to destroy a weak believer is to destroy God's holy temple, and the consequences of such destruction will be reciprocated—the strong members will be punished by God if they cause others to fall away.* Perhaps Paul is recalling the

---

135. Jerry Sumney (personal correspondence).

words of Jesus that if anyone causes his "little ones" to apostatize from belief in him, it would be better if a millstone were placed around that person's neck and he or she be cast into the sea (Mark 9:42; Matt 18:6; Luke 17:2). At the eschaton, it seems that those who turn from God to serve idols (the weak) and those who were the cause of their stumbling (the strong) would both face final destruction.

Another danger involves the possibility of Paul jeopardizing his own salvation, which indirectly undermines a false sense of spiritual security possessed by the strong members (1 Cor 9:24–27). He presents himself as an example of one who exercises self-control by comparing himself to an athlete competing in a footrace in order to win the victor's wreath at the end of the competition.[136] Even an apostle of God must discipline his body or else he could lose out on eternal life at the eschaton when his earthly "race" is finally over. The *Sibylline Oracles* claim that idol foods can defile someone who "enters the contest of receiving a crown of life and immortality" (*Sib. Or.* 2.39–55; 149–153).[137] Paul, however, does not seem to be indicating his own potential to commit idolatry. Nor is the possibility of being "disqualified" (ἀδόκιμος) only referring to the rejection of his apostolic commission.[138] His commission and salvation are bound up together, so that he would consider himself accursed ("woe is me") if he did not preach the gospel (1 Cor 9:16; cf. Mark 14:21; Luke 22:22). Gordon Fee is therefore correct in saying that the "woe" (οὐαί) in 9:16 "is not to be understood in terms of common parlance, as if he would experience some kind of inner distress if he were to fail to preach. Since this is his divinely appointed destiny, he thereby would stand under divine judgment if he were to fail to fulfill that destiny."[139]

His potential disqualification in 9:27 immediately precedes his warnings against the Corinthians being rejected and divinely punished (10:1–12). He is referring to the possibility of being disqualified from eschatological salvation. *Paul includes his own potential to become an apostate as a way to deflate the overconfidence and presumptuous attitude of the strong believers.* If even a missionary who has dedicated his life for the advancement of the gospel could fall away, how is it that they deem themselves beyond spiritual harm when carelessly eating idol meats? *He attacks their perspective of spiritual security that divorces self-control and moral obligation from their salvation.* No doubt this is a rhetorical maneuver that does not reflect an inner

136. Unlike Paul's prophetic running as a courier in Gal 2:2, his metaphor in 1 Cor 9:24–27 is related to the *agon motif* and possibly colored by the Isthmian games. See Brändl, *Agon bei Paulus*, 186–244.

137. Oropeza, *Paul and Apostasy*, 143. See also 1QS 4.2–14; cf. 2.7–8; CD 2.6 for the idea of practicing virtues in relation to receiving a crown.

138. A view held by Gundry Volf, *Paul and Perseverance*, 237.

139. Fee, *1 Corinthians*, 419.

anxiety Paul was experiencing in relation to the process of his own salvation. Even so, his message in 9:24–27 does not seem to be for rhetorical effect alone; he believes that it is possible for an apostle like himself to fall away.

A final danger related to apostasy in this section is directed again at the strong congregants. Paul's thoughts on self-control, rejection, movement, and completion in 9:24–27 spill over to the next pericope, in which the Israelites advance through the wilderness attempting to complete their journey, but many are destroyed along the way (10:1–11). Paul also expands on the aspect that "all" enter the footrace in 9:24–27 but only "one" obtains the prize. In the exodus-wilderness episodes, "all" the Israelites were under the sea, under the cloud, baptized "into Moses," and received spiritual food and drink (10:1–4: πάντες is repeated five times in the passage). But God was displeased with "many" of them, and they were "strewn out" (κατεστρώθησα) in the desert, unable to complete the journey (1 Cor 10:5; cf. Num 14:16, 29, 32).[140] God's displeasure with them is the reverse of his taking pleasure with his elect children (Hab 2:4 LXX; Heb 10:38; cf. Exod 4:22; Deut 1:31; Hos 11:1). God rejected the majority of the wilderness generation for committing vices, and they suffered divine judgment. Paul repeats the phrase "some of them" (τινες αὐτῶν) four times in 1 Cor 10:7–10 to highlight the ways that various factions among them rebelled. Some became idolaters by worshipping the golden calf,[141] some committed fornication and twenty-three thousand were destroyed in one day,[142] some tempted "Christ" and were destroyed by serpents,[143] and some grumbled and were destroyed by the angelic Destroyer.[144]

Paul depicts these wilderness episodes as a way to warn the strong that their presumptuous eating, overconfidence, vicedoing, and discordant behavior may lead them to apostasy and divine judgment (10:12).[145] Especially relevant to the idol meat situation is 10:7 because the golden calf incident involves eating and drinking. Paul implies that the strong members' consumption of idol foods could easily turn into

140. The term κατεστρώννυμι is commonly used in reference to a mass destruction of life (cf. Judith 7:4; 14:4; 2 Macc 5:26[A]; 11:11; 12:28; 15:27).

141. Exod 32:6; cf. 1 Cor 10:14–22. For examples of idolatry from Israel's scriptures and early Jewish traditions, see Phua, *Idolatry and Authority*, 29–125.

142. Cf. Num 25:9. On the discrepancy between 24,000 killed in Num 25:9 and 23,000 in 1 Cor 10:8, see Oropeza, *Paul and Apostasy*, 156–57.

143. Cf. Num 21:4–9; Ps 77[78]: 17–19, 40–41, 56–58.

144. Num 16:11, 41–50; Wis 18:20–25; cf. Num 11:1; 14:27–29; 17:5, 10; Jude 11, 16. For intertextual allusions in this passage relevant to the stories in Exodus and Numbers (e.g., Baal-Peor, Bronze Serpent, and Korah incidents), see Oropeza, *Paul and Apostasy*, 123–28, 133–45, 149–53, 157–77. Also on the Baal-Peor incident (Num 25) as apostasy, see Josephus, *Ant.* 4.126–58; Borgan, "'Yes,' 'No,'" 33–36.

145. For a refutation of perspectives that attempt to mitigate the meaning of apostasy in 10:12, see Oropeza, *Paul and Apostasy*, 192–204.

idolatry. They must therefore "flee" idolatrous situations and avoid partnering with demons (10:14–22). He also implies that apostasy and judgment may result from their committing fornication (10:8 cf. 5:1–5; 6:9–20), tempting Christ with their presumptuous and selfish behavior (10:9 cf. 10:21–22), and their grumbling (10:10), presumably against Paul. If the Corinthians do not recognize Paul's Spirit-guided instructions, they will not be recognized by God (cf. 14:38), and this would result in severe eschatological ramifications.[146] Similar reciprocation is found in 1 Cor 3:16–17; 8:2–3; and 1 Thess 4:8, and seems to evoke the thought of Christ rejecting apostates on judgment day by saying "I do not know you" (cf. Matt 7:22–23; Mark 8:38; Luke 12:9).

The judgments inflicted on the wilderness generation happened as "types" (τύποι), that is, hypothetical prefigurations for the Corinthians, so that they would *not* follow the rebellious ways of their predecessors (1 Cor 10:6, 11).[147] Here we find Paul using exodus/wilderness stories in a negative way to warn the Corinthians against fulfilling these prefigurations. To do so would result in new plagues and judgments from God that would destroy the Corinthians and prevent them from completing their spiritual journey to final salvation at the eschaton. Similar to Paul potentially failing to finish his footrace in 9:27, the Corinthians would be eternally lost if they did not finish their metaphoric expedition. Like Israel, they have become God's people, and they venture on a new exodus/wilderness trek that intersects with the old and new ages (10:11). The completion of their journey, no doubt, will end when Christ returns to raise the dead and finalize God's kingdom (cf. 15:20–28). If they continue in their vices, however, they will not finish the journey and will be unable to participate in God's fully realized kingdom. By persisting in their vices, the Corinthians are following in the steps of the apostate Israelites of old. They are being unfaithful to the faithful God, who requires those who participate in his new creation to shun sinful living associated with the old era. They must therefore abandon vices associated with their pre-converted status (cf. 6:9–10), or else God will punish them just as he will the vicedoers who belong to the cosmos ruled by anti-God powers and Satan.

If some of the Corinthians were to fall away, this would not indicate that they had been inauthentic Christ-followers throughout the metaphoric journey to final

---

146. See further Hays, *First Corinthians*, 244–45; Garland, *1 Corinthians*, 674. My interpretation of 14:38 accepts the present passive indicative ἀγνοεῖται. The alternative reading is the imperative ἀγνοείτω. On textual variations see Metzger, *Textual Commentary*, 500.

147. On the meaning of types in this passage see Goppelt, *Typos*, esp. 176; Bandstra, "Interpretation in 1 Corinthians 10:1–11," 15–16.

salvation.[148] Moreover, Paul's warnings to them do not necessitate that elect individuals who hear the warnings will take heed to them and persevere.[149] To be sure, biblical exhortations sometimes become a means to final perseverance when congregants consistently take heed to the warnings, but this is not always the case and there is no support from the Corinthian correspondence, let alone Paul's other letters, that such perseverance is based on a person's election or non-election.[150] Congregational problems in 2 Corinthians show that some of the Corinthians whom Paul considers elect (1 Cor 1:26–28; cf. 1:2, 4, 9; 10:1–6), did *not* pay attention to his warnings (e.g., 2 Cor 12:20–21).[151] Some of the weak, in fact, fall away despite Paul's warnings, and without any implication that they were not elect (cf. 2 Cor 11:29). The clear inference we can adduce from the letters is that the apostle's authoritative warnings were not always accepted by the congregation members who heard them, even though the apostle considers these members to be part of the elect community. The normative pattern in Paul is clear enough: his warnings are not necessarily efficacious for the hearers, and their acceptance or rejection of the warnings are not predetermined by their elect status. This was no less true of God's people in the scriptures that informed Paul's thought world. Ancient Israel's tradition-history shows a repetitive pattern of God's elect people who fall into sin, are warned by God's prophets, and yet commit apostasy despite the warnings and suffer curses and exile as result (e.g., Deut 27–32; Lev 26; Judg 1–13; 2 Kgs 21–25; 2 Chr 24–25, 36).

Our view is confirmed in 1 Cor 10. The stress on Israel's "baptism," spiritual experiences, and gifts of sustenance in the wilderness show that even though they were God's elect people who experienced God's grace (10:1–4), such experiences did not prevent them from rejecting God's gifts and committing apostasy in the wilderness (10:5). The comparison between Israel and the Corinthians is inescapable (cf.

---

148. Contrast Gundry Volf, *Paul and Perseverance*, 120–30.

149. Along these lines contrast ibid., 215; Schreiner and Caneday, *Race*, esp. 38–45, 207, 212–13. Such a view often assumes an individualistic emphasis on election rather than the elect as God's community.

150. Likewise, in later Pauline tradition the Ephesians' previous knowledge of a hymn that warns against falling away did not prevent everyone who heard or sang it from committing apostasy (2 Tim 2:11–14; cf. 2:25–26; 1 Tim 1:19–20); and if the Pastoral Letters portray the apostasy warned against in Acts 20, then such warnings to the leaders in Ephesus did not prevent some of them from turning away from the faith. Although it can be surmised without proper support that such examples only prove to show the individual apostate's faith was always invalid and the person was never elect, what is often missing with such a position is a consistent and persuasive way to test the hypothesis that elect individuals will necessarily persevere via the biblical messages and warnings. Such a view does not seem to be derived from the Pauline texts themselves but systematic-theological presuppositions read into the texts.

151. Likewise, congregational problems are still seen in the Corinthian church when Clement writes to them a generation later (e.g., *1 Clem.* 1.1; 44.6; 47.6–7).

10:6, 11–12). The "all" or entire Christian community in Corinth is chosen by God and given grace, just as the wilderness generation of Israel was elect. Baptism in the name of Moses through the sea and "cloud" points to the Corinthians' baptism in the name of Jesus and Spirit baptism (1:13c; 12:13). The passage confirms salvific gifts the Corinthians currently benefit from and experience as God's chosen people. Paul considers the Corinthians to be genuinely converted, operating in the Spirit, and sustained by grace and communion through the Lord's Supper. *Despite their salvation and election, "some" of the believers are in danger of apostasy and divine judgment because of committing vices, similar to the "many" Israelites who fell in the desert* (10:6–11).

A backward glance at 1:8–9 does not pose a contradiction here. Just as a remnant of the elect community of Israel survived the wilderness journey, so Paul could assure the Corinthian "body of Christ" that at the end of its eschatological journey final salvation will be experienced. "Some" of the elect may fall away, perhaps even the majority, but not "all." As in Paul's other letters, the language of election in Corinth is focused on the community rather than individuals, and yet the warnings against apostasy and divine judgment are frequently directed at individuals or groups within the greater community in Christ. For individuals among the community in Christ, see 3:17 ("if any one destroys the temple of God . . .)"; 5:5, 17 ("cast out such a one"); 8:13 ("so that my brother or sister does not fall"); 9:27 ("lest I myself might be disqualified"); 10:12 ("the one who thinks he stands should take heed, lest he fall"); 11:29 ("he . . . eats and drinks judgment to himself"); 14:38 ("if anyone does not recognize this, he is not recognized"); 16:22 ("if anyone loves not the Lord, let him be *anathema*"). For subgroups/factions among the community in Christ, see 8:7–13 ("some . . . being accustomed . . . are defiled . . . destroyed"); 10:7–10 ("some of them . . . were destroyed"); 11:30 ("a number [of you] sleep"); 15:12 ("how say some of you that there is no resurrection from the dead?").

Paul does not specifically indicate all the limits that must be crossed in order for the church to determine when a strong member who is committing vices has officially become an apostate. Such congregants are not publically renouncing their faith in Christ. They show themselves to be apostates by their actions and lifestyle, despite any claims they might make regarding their faith or adherence to the gospel message. The boundary between Christ-follower and apostate, however, is blurry. A clear example of *boundary crossing is seen by the status degradation of the incestuous church member being expelled from the community in Christ* (1 Cor 5). Other cases, however, are not as clear unless we are to assume that Paul must step in and make an official pronouncement or ritual of some sort every time he thinks a believer has committed apostasy. Possibly there is a normative procedure that the local church community itself is expected to take in order to determine apostasy on a case-by-case basis (cf. Matt 18:15–20). In fact, the church community must take on the responsibility of ostracizing the incestuous man, and the community again will step in to confront another rebellious member in 2 Cor 2:4–11.

The only status degradation from believer to apostate that we can discern in 1 Cor 10:1–11 takes place at the moment God decides to punish the vicedoers with destruction. This may take place at some unspecified time in the present era, or it could be reserved for the time of final judgment. If we press the analogy far enough, the former would seem to be the case because the wilderness travelers never make it to the culmination of their journey. The problem here is that we do not know if Paul intended to press the comparison this far. He may believe in any case that *God himself will determine when the Corinthian vicedoers have become apostates.* Still this does not explain how Paul could determine the incestuous man as apostate and yet leave it up to God to decide the fate of the strong members and other vicedoers. Is it that the incestuous man's influence over the congregation threatens the spiritual life and unity of the congregation in a more immediate way than those who practice other vices? This option gains some credibility if the man were a patron to the church. Ultimately Paul's concern is for the greater good of the congregation as a whole. It seems that some practices that threaten the spiritual life of many congregants must be dealt with swiftly and severely. If 1 Cor 5 can be used as our paradigm, Paul seems to rely on the Spirit's guidance as well as his God-given authority for discerning apostasy.

After the stern warnings in 10:5–12, Paul gives his audience some comfort and assurance, perhaps to offset the possibility that some members, especially weak ones, might feel overwhelmed with anxiety after hearing the warnings. God will not permit them to be tempted beyond what they can handle (10:13); the temptation to commit vices is not irresistible.[152] In this letter Paul occasionally speaks words of comfort after giving discomfiting information (cf. 3:17, 21–23; 6:9–10; 11:30–32; 15:12, 58). In 10:13 he agrees with the Deuteronomic affirmation that God is faithful despite his people's unfaithfulness (Deut 7:9; 32:4). God will be faithful to give grace to the Corinthians when they are tempted, but this does not guarantee final perseverance of individuals irrespective of their moral behavior, and it does not erase their personal responsibility to flee from idolatry (cf. 10:14). Paul's encouragement to the congregation does not mitigate the real possibility of their committing apostasy. God works through those who obey him and persevere in faith (cf. Rom

152. So Ciampa and Rosner, "1 Corinthians," 727.

1:5; Phil 2:12–13; 1 Thess 1:3). The Corinthians are to honor God and imitate Paul's behavior, giving up their authority and freedom if insistence on such things poses a stumbling block for others (1 Cor 10:31—11:1). Moreover, in 16:13 they are to stand firm in faith and be spirituality alert;[153] being strong and brave may be set in contrast to cowardice and apostasy (cf. *Mart. Pol.* 9.1; contrast Rev 21:8; *Mart. Pol.* 4.1). Here is the only place in the letter where it could be implied that persecution may lead to apostasy if the exhortation is not taken seriously. The exhortation, however, is quite general and does not reflect a belief that the Corinthians are facing some sort of ancient pogrom. Their problem in fact is one of assimilation—they are running *to* the host society rather than away from it, and they fail to be separated from the attitudes and mores of outsiders.

DIVISION AND JUDGMENT AT THE LORD'S SUPPER (11:19-34)

Another problem in the congregation centers on social disparities related to the Corinthians partaking of the Lord's Supper. The passage assumes that the sacred breaking of bread and drinking of wine took place as part of a full meal or love feast. Perhaps the members' sharing from a common loaf initiated the dinner and their drinking from one cup ended it.[154] The problem at these gatherings may have been instigated by inequality between wealthy or prestigious members eating most of the food at the meeting, and overdrinking, while other members received hardly any food at all and went away hungry (1 Cor 11:20–22). The poorer members were thus being neglected. The conflict is primarily between two groups: the "well-to-do" (those who have houses: 11:22a, 34) and the "have-nots" (11:22b).[155] From what we know about ancient homes in that area, the well-to-do members may have been seated in the *triclinium,* having the best dining place in the house, while the poorer members ate in the *atrium* or some other place.[156]

Paul claims that αἱρέσεις (often translated as "factions") are necessary in order that those who are οἱ δόκιμοι may be manifest among them (11:19). Do the factions reveal inauthentic believers as opposed to those "approved" by God, as the NIV suggests? This meaning is possible given that charlatans are often found in congregational settings (e.g., 1 John 2:19; Matt 7:15–20). The alleged necessity of factions in 1 Cor 11:19, however, creates tensions with what is said earlier in 1:10–17. Is Paul

---

153. The latter word recalls the eschatological language of 1 Thess 5:6. Cf. Schrage, *Erste Brief,* 4.450.

154. So Hofius, "Lord's Supper Tradition," 80–88; Furnish, *Theology of the First Letter,* 79.

155. Cf. Theissen, "Social Integration," 145–74; Meeks, *First Urban Christians,* 67–68.

156. See further, O'Connor, *St. Paul's Corinth,* 153–61. On first and second tables related to Greco-Roman dinners, see further Lampe, "korinthisches Herrenmahl," 198–203.

now conceding with the thought of Christ's body being divided?[157] The verse also does not fit well with the immediate context—Paul does not suggest that the sick and dying members were inauthentic believers (11:27–32). R. A. Campbell suggests that δόκιμοι in 11:19 may be understood as "dignitaries" (cf. Philo, *Jos.* 34[210]), which is intended to describe the Corinthians' overestimation of themselves, and the word αἱρέσεις may convey a sense of choosing (cf. Philo, *Gig.* 18.6; Josephus, *Ant.* 7.321).[158] He translates 11:19 thusly: "For there actually has to be discrimination [αἱρέσεις] in your meetings, so that . . . the elite [οἱ δόκιμοι] may stand out from the rest."[159] Such a reading suggests that Paul does not consider these divisions to be inevitable or something good, which are thoughts that would rub the wrong way against his thesis in 1:10–17. The verse betrays sarcasm similar to 4:8.

For Paul, those who partake of the Lord's Supper in an inappropriate manner (ἀναξίως) are held accountable (ἔνοχος) to the body and blood of Christ (11:27–34).[160] Garland makes sense of Paul's thinking here: "The Lord's Supper proclaims the Lord's death. Those whose behavior at the Lord's Supper does not conform to what that death entails effectively shift sides. They leave the Lord's side and align themselves with the rulers of this present age who crucified the Lord (1 Cor 2:8 cf. Heb. 6:5)."[161] More than this, there may be a mystical connection between Christ and his community via the Lord's Supper (cf. 10:16–17). If so, the Corinthians are to be discerning about the reality of Christ behind this meal, and so they must examine themselves before partaking of it.

Although divine punishment is assumed as the explanation of why some of the congregants are getting sick and dying (11:30), we are told that the Lord's chastisement does not lead to eternal destruction. Congregation members are thus disciplined so that they may not be condemned with the world (11:32).[162] Some

---

157. Garland, *1 Corinthians*, 538, rightly raises this question. One alternative is to interpret 11:19 as end-time prophecy—that as the Christians head toward the eschaton more and more divisions and heresies will inevitably arise (cf. Matt 10:35–37; Justin, *Dial.* 35.3; Schrage, *erste Brief*, 3.21–22). Garland, however, responds that γάρ in 11:19 "provides the evidence for Paul's dismay in the previous verse. It explains *why* he cannot praise them" (538).

158. Campbell, "Does Paul Acquiesce in Divisions?," 65–70.

159. Ibid., 70. See also Horsley, *1 Corinthians*, 159, who translates 11:19 to read: "For of course there must be 'discriminations' among you so that it will become clear who among you are the 'distinguished ones.'"

160. On the former Greek term see Klauck, *Herrenmahl*, 324; on the latter see Thiselton, *1 Corinthians*, 889–90. For judgment terms in this passage see also Roetzel, *Judgement in the Community*, 136–37, who considers the sicknesses and death as divinely inflicted rather than magical, and Moule, "Judgement Theme in the Sacraments," 472.

161. Garland, *1 Corinthians*, 550.

162. This lesser judgment probably should not be read back into 5:5 to suggest that the fornicator's

Jews, Gentiles, and the Opponents of Paul

interpreters affirm a condition in 11:32. The congregants who are judged and disciplined must repent so that they will not be condemned.[163] If so, then Paul would be thinking more about the ones who are sick rather than those who have already died, unless his assumption is that the ones who died are given another chance to repent after death. He mentions nothing directly about repentance in either case. Perhaps a more plausible interpretation of 11:32 is that the sin of those who died was not heinous enough to exclude them from salvation.[164] Paul does not seem to believe that every sin or shortcoming leads to the same kind of judgment. Some do not lead to condemnation (3:10–15), while others do (3:16–17; 6:9–10; 10:1–12). One tension with this view is that some members are getting intoxicated with wine at the Lord's Supper (11:21), and this is considered a vice serious enough to exclude drunkards from God's kingdom (6:10). Yet in 11:32 there is no final condemnation for abusers of the Lord's Supper, which would seem to include those who were getting drunk at the meal. There is no way of knowing, however, that some of the members who were getting drunk should also be numbered among those who had died. Also, 6:9–10 identifies those who belong to the realm of the fallen cosmos and Satan, and it mentions vicedoers rather than vices. The passage stresses sinful dispositions more than sinful acts. The errors and vices in 11:22–30, on the other hand, are committed by believers in Christ and may have involved some sporadic acts of inebriation rather than a lifestyle of drunkenness. Such a view goes along with the common-sense notion that even though Paul warns that sinning can lead to apostasy and damnation, he would not automatically condemn believers in this manner who fall into occasional sin (cf. 1 Cor 15:34; Gal 6:1). One's lifestyle must be *characterized* by sin if one is to be eternally condemned (cf. Gal 5:19–21). If this interpretation of 1 Cor 11:32 is correct, then Paul's view shows us that some errors and sins may lead to a lesser type of judgment than final condemnation.

Unless he is being purely rhetorical in 11:31–32, Paul includes himself ("we") among those who must examine themselves or be chastised by the Lord. In 11:30, however, he addresses the result of the congregation's misconduct at the Lord's Supper without including himself. Verses 31–32, then, may function as a general statement relevant for the entire body of Christ, including Paul. It is the responsibil-

---

only punishment will be physical death or affliction, regardless of whether or not he repents. The problem at the Lord's Supper occurs within the congregation, not in the realm of Satan as a result of being expelled from the community in Christ. Apparently, Paul does not think the divisions at the Lord's table are on the same level as the incestuous vice of the fornicator.

163. Cf. Allo, *Saint Paul*, 283.

164. Cf. Gundry Volf, *Paul and Perseverance*, 106; Fee, *1 Corinthians*, 566. The former claims that the death of these members shows no indication that they repented before dying, and yet they are still exempt from final condemnation.

ity of all believers to make sure they are not partaking of the Lord's Supper inappropriately, but they can also know that if they are chastised by the Lord the purpose of the chastisement is intended to be remedial.

DENYING THE RESURRECTION FROM THE DEAD (1 COR 15; 16:22)

The factions in this congregation may also be related to Corinthian misunderstandings about the nature of the resurrection of the body (e.g., 1 Cor 15). Although they believe the message of Christ's resurrection (15:1, 11), some of them apparently claim there is no general resurrection from the dead in which the bodies of believers will be transformed (15:12; cf. 15:35).[165] Did they believe that death simply meant an abandonment of the body? If so, this view does not have to presuppose Gnosticism as some interpreters have argued.[166] Bodily resurrection is a Jewish belief, and so for a Greek audience this idea may have sounded quite foreign. It seems that the Corinthians did not believe in their own future resurrection.

Possibly, the Corinthians' overrealized view of the eschaton plays into their misperception (cf. Cor 4:7–8, 20).[167] If so, they may have felt no need to anticipate a future resurrection since the age to come in some sense had already arrived for them, manifesting itself by their operating in the Spirit's power that was promised for the new era.[168] Paul finds it necessary to teach them that without love their spiritual gifts are rather meaningless, and that love is the antipode of their divisive behavior: it is not jealous, boastful, arrogant, selfish, or rude (13:1–7; cf. 8:1). Unlike Galatians and Romans, the central ethic of love is stressed by Paul in 1 Corinthians not as fulfilling the requirements of the Law but as countering vices and boastful attitudes about one's spirituality in the present era. In the present time, or "now," the new era has not completely arrived. Its perfection and full realization will not take place until the Lord returns, and "then" such things as tongues, prophecy, and spiritual knowledge will come to an end (13:8–13). Paul may be arguing that the Corinthians' spiritual exploits are no indication that the eschaton has fully arrived,

---

165. A comparison between our text and 2 Tim 2:18 does not enlighten us much. The latter passage has apostates claiming that the resurrection has *already past*. The Corinthian faction does not seem to believe in any resurrection at all, except for Christ's.

166. E.g., Schmithals, *Gnosticism in Corinth*, a view that is now becoming outdated.

167. For other options on 4:8 see Paige, "Stoicism, ἐλευθερία and Community," 180–93; Martin, *Slavery as Salvation*, 210; Kuck, *Judgment and Community*, 216–28. The issues do not necessarily have to be either/or (contrast Garland, *1 Corinthians*, 138).

168. On overrealized eschatology in Corinth see Thiselton, "Realized Eschatology," 510–26; Schrage, *Erste Brief*, 1.338–40; Fee, *1 Corinthians*, 12–13, 172.

and their divisive behavior exposes them not as spiritually mature but as immature and not walking properly in love (cf. 3:1–3).

It remains unclear, however, to what extent their overrealized eschatological view and denial of the resurrection are to blame for the congregational problems. Their low regard for the physical body, social dissimilarities, and excessive spirituality, to name a few issues, also contribute to the congregation's divisions.[169] Such aspects interact with eschatological misperceptions, but exactly how they do remains a mystery. The situation in Corinth is complex, and we should not attempt to pigeonhole the congregation's multifaceted divisions into one overarching framework related to eschatology. At best, we can affirm that confusion about the nature of the resurrection and eschaton do play a role in the situation at Corinth; otherwise Paul would not spend large portions of his letter discussing and responding to these issues. Beyond this, we devolve into too much speculation.

Whatever the reason might be for their misperception in 1 Cor 15, their view on the resurrection seems to be another cause for dissensions with others in the congregation who affirm the resurrection from the dead: only "some" of them deny the resurrection (15:12). Paul's inclusive language of "all" of them partaking of the resurrection (15:22–23, 28, 51) may be set in contrast to the "some," and it rallies unity of beliefs about the resurrection and eschaton. Perhaps Paul's language of affirming their future victory over death via the resurrection has the intention of showing them the pettiness of their present divisions.[170] He writes to the Corinthians about the gospel tradition delivered to them, a gospel that centers on the resurrection of Christ and by which they are being saved "unless they believed in vain" (15:2). When communicating to his congregations that their salvation is in jeopardy or called into question, Paul somewhat frequently uses εἰκῇ ("in vain") along with the synonyms κενός and μάταιος (1 Cor 15:10, 14, 17, 58; 2 Cor 6:1; Gal 2:2; 3:4; 4:11; 1 Thess 2:1; 3:5; Phil 2:16).[171] If the Corinthians do not hold to the gospel that Paul proclaims, their faith will be useless and ineffectual; they will not saved.[172]

Anders Eriksson argues that Paul is appealing to pathos by attempting to stir the emotions of fear and hope among his audience. He uses variations of the term

169. E.g., Thiselton, *1 Corinthians*, 40, affirms that doctrinal misperceptions in Corinth are combined with non-Christian "cultural attitudes" derived from the area. See further discussion in Horrell and Adams, "Scholarly Quest for Paul's Church," 23–26.

170. Along these lines see Mitchell, *Rhetoric of Reconciliation*, 175–77.

171. In some of these passages, Paul claims his own work among the believers might be in vain, but this too implies a concern that the believers have not properly received his gospel or they are abandoning it.

172. Contrast Thiselton, *1 Corinthians*, 1186, who mitigates the meaning of "in vain" in 15:2 to "incoherent."

"in vain" a number of times in the ending or *peroratio* of his message (1 Cor 15:2, 10, 14, 17, 32, 58). Paul ends on a positive note, hoping to persuade the Corinthians to believe his view of the gospel; the negative consequence is that if they do not believe they risk the forfeiture of their salvation.[173]

His anathema on those who do not love the Lord reflects the *Shema* commandment to love God (16:22a; cf. 8:3, 4c–6), suggesting covenant loyalty and a curse upon those who break it.[174] When the Lord Christ returns (16:22b) he will judge "those who are not loyal to the covenant and its long-awaited Savior rewarding 'those who have loved his appearing' (2 Tim 4:8)."[175] Amidst Paul's final instructions in the letter, then, *there is an implicit warning for the Corinthians to stay connected to the gospel that Paul preaches; if they do not, they might jeopardize salvation, which will result in eschatological judgment.*[176]

Paul argues that if there is no resurrection, then Christ is not raised, and if Christ is not raised, then: 1) the gospel is false and void of salvific benefits (1 Cor 15:14a); 2) the Corinthians' own faith is worthless (15:14b, 17); 3) the apostles are demonstrated as liars, being false witnesses (15:15); 4) the believers are still enslaved to sin (15:17; cf. Rom 4:25; 6:5); 5) the dead in Christ are perished and will not be raised (15:18); and 6) the believers are "pathetic dupes," suffering for the sake of Christ to no purpose (15:19; cf. Phil 3:7–11).[177] Moreover, if Christ is not raised, the perils that Paul and his colleagues face in Ephesus are also worthless (15:30–32). They and the Corinthians might as well party it up, because this life is all that there is (15:33).[178] "Let us eat and drink, for tomorrow we die" is derived from Isa 22:13. The original context is instructive. Jerusalem as the "valley of vision" faced an impending Assyrian onslaught. Instead of repenting, the people decide to live it up by eating meat and drinking wine knowing that their time was limited (Isa 22:12–13). This sin will remain unforgiven until they die (22:14). In a similar way, if Christ is not risen, the Corinthians' sins also remain unforgiven (1 Cor 15:17). And if they are still in their sins, they can go ahead and "eat and drink" (cf. 10:7), that is, consume idol meats and the Lord's Supper inconsiderately of others in the church, get drunk (11:18–22), and indulge in idolatrous and sexual misbehavior with outsiders (1 Cor

173. Eriksson, "Fear of Eternal Damnation," 115–26.

174. This language relates similarly to the curse upon the opponents in Galatia that were teaching the congregation a different gospel (Gal 1:8–9).

175. Eriksson, "Fear of Eternal Damnation," 124.

176. Konradt, *Gericht und Gemeinde*, 455, relates judgment in 16:22 with a person rejecting Paul's instructions. Such an individual will have no place in God's kingdom.

177. Quote and idea from Garland, *1 Corinthians*, 703; cf. 701–2.

178. Cf. Hays, *First Corinthians*, 268.

6; 8, 10; cf. 2 Cor 6:14–18). Paul's sarcasm ends on this note. Not wanting his audience to understand him literally about eating and drinking, he warns them not to go astray by their misconceptions but respect the maxim that bad social company corrupts good moral habits (1 Cor 15:33/Menander, *Thais* frag. 187[218]; cf. Plutarch, *Moralia* 491E; Philo, *Worse* 38).[179] Their interactions with idolaters and prostitutes would be two examples of this.[180] *They are to sober up from their drunken revelries (ἐκνήψατε)*[181] *and stop "sinning," especially practicing fornication and inconsiderate eating and drinking* (15:34).

CONCLUSION

Paul writes to a predominately Gentile congregation in Corinth that is facing various types of divisions that could lead the members to apostasy and divine judgment. In the early chapters of his correspondence, their competitive and boasting attitude about spiritual knowledge and wisdom prompts Paul to stress humility exemplified by the message of the crucified Christ and authentic wisdom as generated by the Spirit of God (1 Cor 1:18–2:16). Those who labor on building God's house, the community in Christ, in a faulty manner will suffer eschatological loss or shame, but they will be saved (3:10–15). Later on in the letter, the members who are partaking of the Lord's Supper inappropriately, and are being inconsiderate toward poorer members who went away from dinner still hungry, suffer from illness and death, but they will not be eschatologically condemned by the Lord (11:17–32). Divine judgment in these two cases does not entail a loss of salvation or final condemnation of the congregation members.

The same cannot be said, however, for other cases. God will bring eschatological destruction on believers who destroy his church, the temple of the Holy Spirit (3:16–17). The Corinthians' divisive attitude jeopardizes their salvation. Another threat comes by way of *porneia*. The incestuous man is treated as an apostate. Similar to ancient apostate Israelites, he is cut off from God's community, but in this case the man is expelled from the body of Christ into the realm of Satan so that an unspeci-

179. Winter, *After Paul Left Corinth*, 98, is perhaps correct in suggesting their problem of deception has to do with thinking that "their future was not spiritually affected by their present actions." This view, I would add, is not necessarily distinct from their overrealized eschatological misperceptions.

180. Ibid., 99–100, perceptively adds that the context of the quote from Menander involves prostitution, and he suggest the behavior in 15:33 replicates "the behaviour of their non-Christian compatriots." Differently, Mitchell, *Rhetoric of Reconciliation*, 175–77, suggests that the maxim in 15:33 may be referring to bad associations in relation to "Corinthian party politics" (176); and Martin, *Corinthian Body*, 107, relates the problem to the accompanying of the "strong" in the congregation.

181. On this meaning of ἐκνήφω see BDAG, 307.

fied destruction of his physical body or penis might take place (1 Cor 5). The punishment is nonetheless remedial; Paul hopes the individual will be restored to Christ by repenting of his fornication. Other members are in danger of being excluded from God's kingdom through their sexual relationships with prostitutes (6:10–20). Through such unions these members act unfaithfully to Christ, their true marital partner, and as members of the body of Christ their sexual unions with outsiders are compared with the incompatible notion of joining Christ to the anti-God cosmos.

Paul then addresses another division, this time between weak and strong/*gnosis* members over the issue of the latter's consumption of idol meats (1 Cor 8–10). The strong members have knowledge that the Greco-Roman deities do not exist: there is one God and one Lord alone. The weak members believe that other deities do exist, and they could fall away to idolatry if they are encouraged by the strong members to eat idol meats. Paul warns the strong to be mindful of the weak members and refrain from their right to eat idol foods when the weak are present. If they became the cause of a weak member turning away from God to serve idols once again, they would be sinning against Christ and destroying a fellow believer. Paul warns them that they, too, could fall away to idolatry and other vices despite their salvation and election, just as the wilderness generation was divinely chosen, delivered, and yet destroyed by God (10:1–12). Paul attempts to shake the Corinthians' presumptuous confidence by suggesting that even he, an apostle of Christ, could be rejected by God if he failed to be self-disciplined (9:24–27). The Corinthians must love the Lord, stop sinning, and recognize Paul's spiritual instruction, or face the threat of not being recognized by the Lord on judgment day (14:38; 15:34; 16:22). In essence, if they continue with their vices the Lord may say to them on judgment day, "I do not know you." They must also stay connected with the gospel of the resurrection of Christ, or else their faith would be in vain (1 Cor 15).

We see in the Corinthian correspondence, then, that all vices are not treated alike. For Paul, some acts can lead to apostasy and eschatological condemnation, and others apparently result in only a mitigated form of divine punishment. The distinction between the two remains unclear. Perhaps it can be answered, in part, by the potential threat a particular vice or action poses to the spiritual well-being of the community in Christ. A person who labors in ministry but does so with wrong motives (e.g., 3:10–15) would not seem to pose an immediate threat to the salvation of other believers, as would the one who causes other congregation members to fall away. Paul considers the man's incestuous marriage an immediate threat that must be judged quickly, lest the influence of his action contaminate many congregation members to boast in his fornication, a vice that could result in exclusion from God's kingdom (cf. 6:9–10). The inconsiderate members at the Lord's Supper, on the other hand, may pose less of a threat to the salvation of the other congregants. The "have-nots" went away from dinner humiliated and hungry, but not influenced to practice the same selfishness they experienced from the "haves." Of course, we could ask whether such treatment, if left unchecked, would ultimately discourage the "have-nots" from attending fellowship altogether, and so this answer is not completely satisfying. There are too many variables relevant to the situation in Corinth that are left unanswered, and perhaps they can never be answered, given that we are missing important correspondence between Paul and the Corinthians.

Divisions are a problem in both 1 Corinthians and Galatians, and both letters tend to associate congregational factions with vices. Unlike the Galatians, however, the Corinthians' faith is not threatened by the works of the Law. Their danger of committing apostasy turns primarily on their committing vices. Their moral boundaries compromised their walk with Christ. If the Galatians needed to realize their freedom in Christ, Paul argues almost the opposite for the Corinthians. They exercise too much freedom and assimilation with Greco-Roman culture and social status, which has manifested itself in presumption and loose boundaries related to fornication, idolatry, drunkenness, and other immoral actions. Paul's own boundary regarding idol meats betrays his disagreement with James and the Jerusalem meeting's decision to prohibit such foods from Gentile Christ-followers (Acts 15). For Paul the consumption of idol meats is not the issue. He grants the Corinthians the right to eat such foods as long as they do not become a stumbling block to weaker church members by what they eat. He condemns idolatry, however, and believes the consumption of idol meats can lead to idolatry in certain cases. Interestingly, however, Paul is in agreement with Jerusalem's decision against the Gentile Christians committing fornication. This is most evident by his echoing of the Law in relation to the incestuous man. Paul's rejection of the Jerusalem church's dietary prohibitions may rest on his bad experience in Antioch, in which he saw firsthand the hypocrisy of the Jerusalem members refraining from fellowship with Gentiles at mealtime (Gal 2:11–14). Be that as it may, the reasons he gives his congregants for abstaining from *porneia* stem from maintaining church unity, keeping the body of Christ separate from the cosmos (1 Cor), and loving one's neighbor as oneself (1 Thess).

The Thessalonian congregants separated themselves from Gentile outsiders, and as result they suffered a persecution that Paul feared would cause them to commit apostasy. Similar to the Corinthians, they practiced fornication, but this vice was kept "in-house," within the community of believers in Christ. The Corinthians, on the other hand, fail to separate themselves from outsiders. They commit fornication with prostitutes and eat idol meats in pagan precincts. Their assimilation with the host society threatens to blur distinctions between Christ and the cosmos ruled by Satan and anti-God forces. They are in danger of committing apostasy, not on account of persecution, but by practicing vices associated with their pre-converted status as idolatrous Gentiles. Paul's congregations face unique challenges, and his warnings against apostasy and judgment are relative to the situations in the respective communities.

4

2 Corinthians: In Danger of Apostasy Once Again: The Corinthians and Paul's Opponents

Rather than correcting internal divisions within the congregation as he did in 1 Corinthians, Paul defends his reputation against those who are coming against his authority in 2 Corinthians. He cannot take for granted any longer that the Corinthians will obey him. Intruders have penetrated the congregation and seem to be instigators of the conflict (2 Cor 10:12–16; 11:4–5). They apparently found audience with divisive church members who remained dissatisfied with Paul's responses to them in previous letters.[1] The historical development behind this opposition in relation to the Corinthian correspondences remains tedious and unresolved. Whereas many scholars agree that 2 Corinthians was written after 1 Corinthians,[2] they disagree on the unitary integrity of the letter. Some maintain 2 Corinthians as a single letter, but many others suggest it is a compilation originally made up of two (2 Cor 1–9; 10–13), three (1–8; 9; and 10–13), or more Pauline letters.[3] Complicating matters further, later portions of the canonical letter may have been written before

---

1. Murphy-O'Connor, *Theology of the Second Letter*, suggests the *pneumatic* people who were bent toward Philonic-Apollos influence sought revenge when Paul humiliated them through his earlier correspondence, and so they joined the Judaizing intruders in order to spite Paul. The Judaizers adopted some Hellenistic conventions in order to maintain influence at Corinth (12–15). But if so, Paul fails to mention anything about the Jewish customs they are promulgating in 2 Corinthians.

2. It was written about 56 CE. Possible chronologies of events and correspondences between Paul the Corinthians are reconstructed in, e.g., Young and Ford, *Meaning and Truth*, 144–48; Thrall, *2 Corinthians*, 1.74–77.

3. For discussions on various partition theories, see Mitchell, "Paul's Letters to Corinth," 317–24; Bieringer, "Gegner des Paulus," 181–221; Betz, *2 Corinthians*, 1–25. On its unity see, e.g., Bieringer, "Plädoyer für die Einheitlichkeit," 137–79; Long, *Ancient Rhetoric and Paul's Apology*.

earlier portions, especially if 2 Cor 10–13 is part of the "tearful letter" mentioned in 2:4.[4] Whether 2 Corinthians was originally one letter or several, there seems to be no major change of opponents in its final form; albeit, Paul targets his rivals in a far more pronounced fashion in chapters 10–13. Jerry Sumney shows convincingly that the opponents in chapters 1–9 and 10–13 are the same.[5] We will proceed with this understanding in mind.

THE OPPONENTS: JEWISH MISSIONARIES BUT NOT JUDAIZING (2:14—4:6; CF. CHS. 10-11)

We learn very little information about the opponents in 2 Corinthians by reexamining 1 Corinthians. This does not mean that influences on the congregation in the earlier letter are not present in the latter. Some *pneumatic* sway and loose moral boundaries, problems related to the first letter, are present in the second letter also (cf. 2 Cor 12:12, 21). The latter correspondence, however, centers on adversaries who claim a Jewish heritage and are persuading members of the congregation to abandon respect for Paul's authority (2 Cor 11:22). Even so, these opponents are neither the same agitators Paul encounters in Galatians nor another group that would be considered "Judaizers."[6] We find no evidence that their agenda is to persuade the Gentile believers in Corinth to conform to Jewish customs, let alone circumcision. If a conflict related to the works of the Law were at stake, then, similar to Galatians, we might expect the apostle to warn the Corinthians in a clear way about the grave dangers related to their embracing the works of the Law.[7] Paul's designation of the opponents as false ministers of "righteousness" probably does not suggest they are teaching the Corinthians a different interpretation of the Law (11:15).[8] This is perhaps a self-designation by the opponents, much like the term, "ministers of Christ" (cf. 11:23). It does not inform us about their promulgations of Jewish customs or interpretation of the Torah. Moreover, Paul's discussion about the ministry of Moses

4. See opposing viewpoints in, e.g., Aejmelaeus, *Schwachheit als Waffe* (pro); and Schnelle, *Einleitung*, 79–87 (con). Another option is that chs. 1–9 were originally one unit, and chs. 10–13 were written after Paul learned about some new and negative developments in the congregation (e.g., Martin, *2 Corinthians*, 298).

5. Sumney, *Servants of Satan*, 130–33; idem, *Identifying Paul's Opponents*.

6. For discussions on the identity of the opponents in 2 Corinthians see, e.g., Sumney, *Identifying Paul's Opponents*, 15–67; Bieringer, "Gegner des Paulus," 181–221; Harris, *Second Corinthians*, 67–87; Georgi, *Gegner des Paulus*.

7. Interestingly, Paul mentions a different set of "false brothers" in relation to his past hardships (2 Cor 11:26). We wonder if he has the Galatian opponents in mind among these predecessors.

8. Barrett, *Second Corinthians*, 287, rightly considers the genitive of righteousness in 11:15 to be descriptive rather than objective, suggesting Paul is speaking in moral rather than legal terms.

in 3:1—4:6 tells us virtually nothing specifically about the opponents' view of Law or their alleged Judaizing tendencies.[9] To read the opponents' agenda into Paul's words in this pericope would be to mirror-read the text.[10]

The apostle uses *qal wahomer* (*a fortiori*) to show that the new era of ministry in the Spirit has greater glory than the ministry of Moses and the Sinai covenant (3:7–11). Paul considers his ministry greater than that of Moses because the apostle participates in the epoch of the new covenant. An allusion to Exod 4:10 may be felt in 2 Cor 2:16b, when the apostle asks about competency in relation to proclaiming God's word. Moses considered himself incompetent for such a task. But Paul, inclusive of his colleagues, affirms himself to be sufficient for his assignment through the Spirit's enablement (cf. 3:12). The letter in stone (3:7), alluding to the Ten Commandments, is the written word of the Sinai covenant. It "kills" if it has not the Spirit.[11] Jeremiah 31:31–34 and Ezekiel 11:19–20; 36:25–26 may be assumed in the background of the passage with their emphasis on the coming era of the Spirit in which a new covenant would be written on the hearts of God's people.[12]

Paul's words about Moses in 2 Cor 3:13–16 recall the story of Moses veiling the glory of the presence of God that shined on his face in order to protect the Israelites who, in their hardened condition after worshipping the golden calf, would have died if they had seen the unmediated glory of God (Exod 32–34; esp. 33:3, 5).[13] Paul seems to have adopted the language of this tradition to address Israel's presently hardened state (2 Cor 3:14; cf. Rom 9–11). Israel is hardened and fails to grasp the temporal character of the era Moses represented. In the words of Dunn, "presumably it is this shortfall in understanding which gives the 'letter' its killing character, in contrast to the writing of the Spirit in the human heart" (3:3, 6–7; cf. Rom 2:28–29; 7:6).[14] Whenever Moses is read in the synagogues, a veil covers the hearts of the hearers unless they "turn" (ἐπιστρέφω) to the Lord.[15] Here not only does Paul loosely recall the words of Exod 34:34, but also Isaianic influence seems

---

9. Contrast Oostendorp, *Another Jesus*, 35–37.

10. Sumney, *Servants of Satan*, 28–31, is a helpful corrective in sorting through unclear, implicit, and explicit statements about the opponents.

11. Cf. Hafemann, *Paul, Moses*, 131f, 147–49.

12. Incidentally, the gospel also kills without the Spirit (cf. 2 Cor 2:15–16) as Hafemann, "Paul's Use of the Old Testament," 247, rightly notices.

13. In 3:7, 11, 13, καταργέω may be interpreted as "abolish," "nullify," or "render inoperative" (Hafemann, *Paul, Moses*, 147–49, 301–9; Hays, *Echoes*, 134–36), but some versions (e.g., NASB, NIV) use the less dramatic "fade away."

14. Dunn, *Theology of Paul*, 149.

15. The term ἐπιστρέφω is used by Paul to refer to both conversion (1 Thess 1:9) and apostasy (Gal 4:9). In the passage in 2 Corinthians the veil has moved from Moses' face to the people's hearts!

clear in that the spiritual blindness of Israel will be removed when they turn to God (Isa 6:10 LXX; cf. 19:12; 31:6; 44:22; 55:7).[16] In Paul's reconfiguration, the veil is removed for those who are in Christ (2 Cor 3:14–16), and the "Lord" to whom the people must turn refers to the Divine name in Israel's scriptures, but for Paul it may suggest Christ (3:14c) or the Spirit (3:17–18) or both. The people who are "veiled" from the new era are thus unbelieving Israelites, not the opponents who claim to be followers of Christ (e.g., 11:23). Should they convert to Paul's message, they would participate in a new creation that sets them on a spiritual exodus guided by the "light" of spiritual knowledge and the glory of God's presence in Christ through the Spirit (2 Cor 4:4, 6/Isa 9:1 LXX; cf. 2 Cor 5:17; Acts 26:16–18).

This section of Paul's letter, then, contrasts the old covenant with the new covenant and era in Christ in which moral righteousness that sums up the Law is etched on the hearts of those who are guided by the Spirit. Similar thoughts contrasting the Law with walking in the Spirit are expressed in Gal 5:14–26 and Rom 8:2–16, but here in 2 Cor 3–4 Paul focuses on the validity of his own message as a minister of God rather than giving ethical imperatives for his audience to follow (cf. 3:1–6; 4:1–6). In essence Paul is establishing his authority as a minister of the new covenant, which is more glorious than the temporal covenant and era related to Moses. Moses' unveiled entering into the presence of God and reflecting God's glory is held as a paradigm or prefiguration for Paul and the believers' experience with the Spirit.[17] It is quite possible that the Corinthians held Moses in high esteem (cf. 1 Cor 10:2).[18] Perhaps they interpreted the glory on Moses' face as authentication of his ministry and wondered why Paul did not reflect a similar glory if he is truly God's messenger. Their accusation perhaps centers on the weakness of Paul's outward appearance. Paul sets the record straight by suggesting that authority in the new era is not based on outward appearances or one's relation to Moses; it comes through the Spirit of God to which Moses and the old covenant pointed. In 2 Cor 4:1–3 it is quite possible that Paul is accusing the opponents of craftiness and exploitation of God's word (cf. 2:17; 11:3), or he may be responding to accusations about his own alleged craftiness (cf. 12:16). In either case, it seems that his message of the gospel is accused of being obscure or veiled (4:3; cf. 1:13). Perhaps the power behind Paul's message was said to be ineffective, especially in relation to Israelites;[19] or maybe his teachings were thought to be confusing and contradictory. *His response in this section of the letter, then, does not appear to be a rebuttal of the opponents' interpretation*

---

16. Here ἐπιστρέφω is used in Isa 6:10 as in 2 Cor 3:16 rather than εἰσπορεύομαι as in Exod 34:34.

17. So Hays, *Echoes*, 144 cf. 143, 151. See also Matera, *II Corinthians*, 86.

18. See further Oropeza, *Paul and Apostasy*, 82–89.

19. Cf. Thrall, *2 Corinthians*, 1.304.

of the Law, circumcision, or other Jewish customs, but a response to accusations against his ministry. This same ministry he argues is more glorious than that of Moses on account of the Spirit and new era.

Paul concedes that to an extent his gospel is in fact veiled, but only to unbelievers. This is not because his message lacks power or coherency but because Satan as "the god of this age" has blinded their minds, lest they should see the light of "the gospel of the glory of Christ" (4:3–4).[20] In 3:4—4:6 spiritual obduracy and blindness pertain to Israelites and Gentiles who do not believe the new covenant message.

The opponents, on the other hand, first implicated in 2:17,[21] are Jewish Christ-followers rather than unbelievers (cf. 10:7; 11:4, 13, 22–23). They come to the foreground by way of contrast to Paul's ministry. The apostle and his colleagues are not like "many" (opponents included) who are dishonest exploiters of God's word. We may be able to draw some inferences from the apostle's words to help gain an incomplete sketch of them.

First, they are ministers of Christ and confident of their belonging to him (10:7; 11:22–23).[22] Paul calls them "super-apostles" (11:5), not necessarily because they are genuine apostles of the churches or Jewish Christ-followers who come from Jerusalem, such as James or Peter. If the opponents were in fact these or similar leaders, Paul would likely mention them by name as he normally does in other letters (Gal 2:6–13; 1 Cor 1:12; 9:5–6; 15:5–7). He seems to be using the term "apostle" in a sarcastic manner.[23] These workers have too high an estimation about their own spirituality, authority, and importance as itinerant preachers. According to Paul they have a high-minded, boastful attitude (cf. 2 Cor 10:3–4, 12–18; 11:17–18).

Second, they are probably missionaries as suggested by the term "workers" (2 Cor 11:13; cf. Matt 10:10; *Did.* 13:2).[24] Paul also calls them "false apostles" (2 Cor 11:13). They have come to Corinth (11:4) masquerading as "servants of righteousness," but Paul considers them "deceitful workers" who lead astray their followers.

20. They remain in spiritual darkness as his pawns unless they turn to the gospel message (2 Cor 4:4–6 cf. Acts 15:19; 26:20), and yet Satan's blindness over them prevents them from understanding Paul's message and being transformed. The apostle does not attempt to resolve this catch-22 dilemma; his concern is with defending why his message is not always accepted by those who hear him.

21. On 2:17 as the thesis of the letter, see Kennedy, *New Testament Interpretation*, 87–89.

22. The term διάκονος in this case probably is intended to mean an apostle: cf. Georgi, *Gegner des Paul*, 31.

23. With Sumney, *Servants of Satan*, 113. Contrast Käsemann, "Legitimität des Apostels," 44; and Barrett, *Second Corinthians*, 31, 277–78, who both suggest Paul is referring to apostles from Jerusalem. See discussions and arguments in Penna, *Paul the Apostle*, 1.273–75.

24. Cf. Furnish, *2 Corinthians*, 494; 510; Georgi, *Gegner des Paulus*, 49–50.

They are compared with Satan, who masquerades as an angel of light (2 Cor 11:13–15; cf. *Apoc. Mos.* 17.1; *L.A.E.* 9.1).

Third, to support their legitimacy as ministers they present the Corinthians with letters of recommendation that are apparently from other apostles (2 Cor 2:17; 3:1–3; 4:2; 5:12; 6:4; 10:12–18; 11:7–11, 20; 12:11–12). Paul feels no need to come to the Corinthians with such recommendations, claiming instead that the proof of his apostleship rests with the fact that he is the one God used to convert the Corinthians (3:1–3).

Fourth, they proclaim a gospel message similar to Paul, but they do so with insincere motives and for financial gain. They are by implication "peddlers" (καπηλεύοντες) of God's word, presumably being financially supported for their preaching by the Corinthians and others (2:17; cf. 11:20).[25] Perhaps by their stressing Jewish heritage and apostleship, they found an audience with some of the Peter loyalists in the congregation (cf. 1 Cor 1:12). Likewise, wealthier members at Corinth, eager to pay Christian leaders for preaching, may have been susceptible targets for these rivals.[26] Unlike his opponents, Paul refuses payment from the Corinthians.

Fifth, the opponents (or the Corinthians or both) question Paul's authority by saying that he and his colleagues are unspiritual, walking according to the "flesh" or worldly standards (2 Cor 10:2). His speaking is unimpressive (10:10; 11:5–6), and his reasons for rejecting financial support from the Corinthians are a mark of duplicity (11:7–11; 12:14–18).

When Paul associates these opponents with someone coming to the Corinthians and preaching "another Jesus," and their receiving a "different" gospel and Spirit (2 Cor 11:4), the accusations seem recycled from Gal 1:7–9, but this is not because he faces the Galatian opponents again or a similar group in Corinth.[27] The differences between the viewpoints of Paul and his opponents center on ethics and methods rather than doctrine.[28] For Paul the rivals are immoral not only because of their insincere motives and financial practices, but also because they possess a haughty attitude and come against his ministry. They do not abide in the message of suffering

---

25. Hafemann, *Suffering and Ministry*, 106–25, says that dishonesty was often associated with retailers and peddlers in Paul's world (e.g., Isa 1:22; Sir 26:29; Philo, *Giants* 39; Josephus, *Ant.* 3.276; Lucian, *Hermotimus* 59; Philostratus, *Apoll.* 1.13f).

26. Perhaps the affluent members wanted to be patrons to Paul. On patron-client perspectives between the Corinthians and Paul, see Marshall, *Enmity in Corinth*, 172–74; but see also criticisms in Grindheim, *Crux of Election*, 80–82.

27. The term "recycled" is adopted from Sampley, *2 Corinthians*, 17–18.

28. Contrast Oostendorp, *Another Jesus*, 7–9, as an example of pneumatological and christological differences between Paul and the opponents.

and humility related to the cross.[29] The gospel of Jesus held by the opponents seems to be one in which the offense of the cross and suffering related to ministry is greatly diminished. These rivals do not preach or live by the same gospel message Paul does, and the proof of this is that they discredit his apostolic authority.[30] Hence, from Paul's perspective, their gospel does not lead to the same Jesus that he preaches, and the Corinthians are in danger of being led astray by his opponents (2 Cor 11:1–15).

Since we are reading only Paul's loaded description of these opponents, which is motivated by his effort to get the Corinthians to side with his ministry and reject theirs, we must wonder whether they were truly deceitful and immoral. It is rather likely that they would see themselves as authentic ministers of Christ. *We could only determine that they are false Christian workers as perceived by Paul.* In any event they seem to reject or at least highly question Paul's apostolic authority, and it may be the case that they have capitalized on what seemed to be Paul's wavering decisions related to visiting the Corinthians (cf. 1:15–19). In sociological studies one of the primary reasons defections take place in contemporary religious groups is due to a leader's inconsistencies or the disaffection that occurs between group members and their leader.[31] A similar crisis may be brewing among members of the Corinthian congregation over Paul's leadership.

In contrast to the behavior of his opponents, Paul defends his ministry by affirming his sincerity and that he works for the Corinthians' benefit. He does not extend his preaching to another minister's area, perhaps implying this as something the opponents have done by encroaching on the Corinthians (2:17; 10:8–18; 12:19).[32] Unlike his opponents, he denies using trickery or seduction (4:2; 12:16). The proof of his apostolic authority involves his operating through signs and wonders (12:12–13), and his "boasting" in hardships is intended to show that the true display of apostleship is power working through weakness, which is patterned after Christ and his crucifixion (2 Cor 4:10–11; 8:9; 10:1; 11:30; 13:4; cf. 1 Cor 1:18).[33] God's grace is operating through the apostle's weakness, which shows all the more

---

29. Notice Matera, *II Corinthians*, 244: "If . . . the intruding apostles focused attention on their powerful deeds, eloquent speech, and ecstatic experiences, it is unlikely that the cross of the crucified Christ played as central a role in their preaching."

30. In Gal 1:6–7 Paul believes there is only one gospel—the one he preaches: cf. Bultmann, *2 Korinther*, 202. While this may be correct, Phil 1:17–18 suggests that Paul could agree it is possible for preachers to spite him and yet still be preaching the correct Christ, which is not the case in 2 Cor 11. Interestingly in other respects the opponents are somewhat similar to the rivals in Philippians 1:15–18: they preach out of selfish ambition.

31. See sample studies in Wilson, *Leaving the Fold*, 122–23.

32. See Sampley, *2 Corinthians*, 16–17.

33. See Grindheim, *Crux of Election*, 99–105.

that his authority does not originate from his own human words or efforts but from Christ and God (2 Cor 13:3; cf. 5:20).[34] Paul's threefold denial, "We have wronged no one, we have ruined no one, we have exploited no one" (7:2), is probably in response to accusations against him. Paul and his colleagues have neither treated the Corinthians unfairly nor been a stumbling block that causes them to fall away from God or Christ, nor have they taken advantage of them through financial gain or other self-interests. The middle denial (οὐδένα ἐφθείραμεν) may be a response to an accusation that Paul ruined the salvific hope of some congregants through his disciplinary actions (e.g., 1 Cor 5).[35] By claiming such members as apostate and kicking them out of the church, he destroys their faith. If this is what is meant, then *Paul denies any blame for the apostasy of church members.* He reaffirms his love for them (cf. 2 Cor 2:4; 6:6, 11; 8:7; 11:11; 12:15) and assures them that his purpose, even in his present response, is not to bring about their condemnation (7:3).

FOLLOWING THE OPPONENTS TO APOSTASY AND FINAL JUDGMENT (5:9–11; 11:1–15)

Paul fears for the Corinthians, whom he has betrothed to Christ as a pure virgin. They are in danger of being deceived by his opponents, and this deception could lead to their acceptance of another Jesus and Spirit (2 Cor 11:2–4; cf. Rom 7:11; 16:18; 2 Thess 2:3; 1 Tim 2:14).[36] As the Serpent deceived Eve by his craftiness (πανουργία: 2 Cor 11:3; cf. 2:17; 4:2; 11:13–14; Eph 4:14), so also their thoughts could be "seduced" from the "singleness of purpose" and purity of devotion to Christ.[37] The passage refers to the primordial story from the Garden of Eden (cf. Gen 3:1, 13 LXX), and Paul seems to equate the antagonist in this story with Satan (2 Cor 11:2; cf. 11:14; Wis 2:24; Rev 12:9). Likewise, echoes of Israel's apostasy in terms of marital unfaithfulness to God resonate in Paul's words about the Corinthians' relationship

34. Cf. Court, "Controversy with the Adversaries," 101–2, 105.

35. On this possibility, see Thrall, *2 Corinthians*, 1.481. Other options include moral ruin or financial ruin.

36. Harris, *Second Corinthians*, 739, notices the construction φοβοῦμαι μή πως + subjunctive occurs in 2 Cor 11:3 and 12:20. In both passages Paul fears for the spiritual safety of the Corinthians. Barrett, *Second Corinthians*, 273, rightly says regarding this passage that there is a "real danger that his [Paul's] work in Corinth may be lost." On the serpent's deception of Eve in early Jewish traditions, see *1 En.* 69:6; *Jub.* 3:17–35; *Apoc. Ab.* 23; *L.A.E.* 9–11 [44].

37. The word φθείρω could mean "to corrupt," "ruin," or "destroy" (cf. 1 Cor 3:17; 2 Cor 7:2), but in 11:3 the passive φθαρῇ probably means "seduced" (cf. Josephus, *Ant.* 4.252; Justin, *Apol* 1.9.4; *Diognetus* 12.8). The word ἁπλότης may mean "sincerity" or "simplicity," but with devotion as its object, I have adopted the translation "singleness of purpose" (cf. Omanson and Ellington, *2 Corinthians*, 193) and prefer to add "purity" based on the longer reading of 11:3 included in P⁴⁶ ℵ* B, etc.

with Christ (e.g., Ezek 16; Hos 1–2).[38] *The upshot of Paul's apprehension is that the Corinthians are once again in danger of committing apostasy, this time by following false apostles.*

A hint of divine judgment that might await the Corinthians who follow the opponents is inferred by the eschatological fate of the latter. In a somewhat abrupt manner Paul says that their "end" will be according to their works (2 Cor 11:15b). If he is referring to judgment day, his assumption is that the works of his adversaries are thoroughly "bad" (cf. 2 Cor 5:10; 2 Tim 4:14). His rivals are boastful, encroach on Paul's evangelistic territory, and oppose his ministry. From his perspective, they are false missionaries who serve another Jesus and work on the side of Satan (2 Cor 11:13–15). Hence, the opponents' deeds in 11:15b could hardly result in anything else besides their condemnation (cf. Phil 3:18–19; 2 Thess 2:8–12). Ralph Martin says it rather cogently: "They have done Satan's work; to Satan's fate they will go."[39] The Corinthians would seem to be able to draw this kind of inference from the correspondence and be warned that they too might suffer a similar fate by following these ministers of Satan. When the counterfeit apostles stand before the real Christ on judgment day, stripped bare of all façade and hypocrisy,[40] their "end" will involve eternal punishment.

This judgment in 2 Cor 11:15 recalls 5:10 where Paul claims that all will stand before the tribunal of Christ. Paul sometimes considers God to be the judge of humanity (Rom 2:3, 5, 11; 3:6; 14:10; 1 Thess 3:13) and other times it is Christ (1 Cor 4:5; 5:5; 1 Thess 2:19; 2 Thess 2:8) or God through Christ (Rom 2:16). In 2 Cor 5:10 Christ will be the judge, and each individual will receive recompense (ἵνα κομίσηται ἕκαστος) from the Lord for the things he or she did in the mortal body whether morally good or bad (2 Cor 5:10; cf. Rom 2:6; 14:10, 12; Col 3:22–25; Eph 6:8).[41] The thought of reciprocity is stressed—a person's punishment or reward will correspond to that person's works that were done during his or her earthly existence.[42] The na-

---

38. Along these lines, see Klauck, *2 Korintherbrief*, 82. There are some similarities between 2 Cor 11:2–4 and ancient Jewish writings that connect sexual seduction or lust with the story of Eve and the serpent (4 Macc 18:7–8; *b. Yebamot* 103b; *b. ʿAbod. Zar.* 22b; *b. Shabbat* 146b). Paul, however, seems to be referring to spiritual unfaithfulness.

39. Martin, *2 Corinthians*, 353.

40. This idea is adopted from Hughes, *Second Corinthians*, 180.

41. The body here relates to their earthly existence (cf. 5:1). In 5:10 "bad," κακός in the Greek texts (p[46], B, D, *Byz*, etc.), has strong ancient support and is probably to be preferred over φαῦλος (ℵ, C, 81 etc.), which also means "bad" but could be interpreted as "worthless." The nuance of "bad" or perhaps "evil" seems to be the appropriate word to use in the context of final judgment and in contrast with "good" (cf. John 5:28–29).

42. In Jewish texts of that time, this kind of reciprocity could lead to punishment that would include damnation: cf. VanLandingham, *Judgment and Justification*, 200–202.

ture of this judgment should not be mitigated to one in which the believer's deeds are merely burned up if they are found to be worthless.[43] Such a judgment may be true in 1 Cor 3:10–15, where those who work for the sake of the gospel are in view, but not in 2 Corinthians. The judgment in 5:10 includes "all of us" (πάντας ἡμᾶς)—Paul, his colleagues, the Corinthian and Achaian recipients of the letter—and it may also implicate his opponents because he defends himself against them in this context (cf. 5:11–13). Even though the Christ-followers are primarily in view, this time of reckoning is most likely referring to judgment day, when the righteous will be rewarded and the unrighteous condemned (Rom 2:6, 16; 14:10, 12; 1 Cor 4:4–5; cf. Matt 7:21–23; 16:27; Rev 2:23; 20:12–13; 22:2).[44]

Human deeds are bound up with righteous or unrighteous living, and those who walk in the Spirit will receive eternal reward, but if believers walk according to their sinful nature and commit heinous vices, they will reap eternal consequences (Gal 5:19–21; 6:6–7; Rom 8:13; 1 Cor 5:1–5; 10:5–12; 2 Cor 7:1). Obedience to God and Christ includes shunning the practice of vices. It becomes important, then, for the Corinthians and everyone else to live in a manner that pleases God (2 Cor 5:9). They must know the "fear of the Lord" (5:11; 7:1) not merely because he might take away some of their heavenly rewards, but because he could condemn them to eternal punishment if their lifestyle exemplifies bad deeds (2 Cor 5:9–11; cf. Phil 2:12; Matt 10:28; Heb 4:1).[45] *We can adduce from Paul's words that the Christ-followers will all be judged according to their works.*

Paul is anxious about his upcoming visit because it might reveal that the Corinthians still practice strife, jealousy, rivalries, disorders, and similar deeds. He might also find out that those who sinned in the past remain unrepentant of their divisions and sensuous vices (2 Cor 12:20–21; cf. 1 Cor 6:9–20). If he is consistent in his letters, then those who participate in these activities face a danger of being cut off from God's kingdom (cf. 1 Cor 6:9; Gal 5:21). Consequently, Paul would probably consider the Corinthians who follow the false apostles to be among those who destroy the church of Christ through division,[46] and the culprits of such factions will themselves be destroyed on the day of judgment (cf. 1 Cor 3:16–17).

43. Contrast Hughes, *Second Corinthians*, 182, who supports a judgment like this based on 1 Cor 3:15; and Barnett, *Second Corinthians*, 276, who thinks that believers will face "evaluation" at this tribunal but not potential condemnation.

44. Whether or not the judgment of believers and unbelievers takes place at the same time or at different times (cf. 1 Thess 4:17–19; 1 Cor 15:20–26) is left unspecified in 2 Cor 5:10. Paul's point is not on the timing of this judgment but the fact that everyone will be judged. For discussion see Thrall, *2 Corinthians*, 1.395–400.

45. Although Paul's knowing about the fear of Lord in 2 Cor 5:11 sets up the next thought, it also points back to knowing about Christ's judgment in 5:10.

46. See Barrett, *2 Corinthians*, 287.

"BE RECONCILED TO GOD" (5:17–6:3; CF. 6:11–7:3)

The new era of salvation proclaimed through the Isaianic prophet has come upon the Corinthians and the rest of the world through Christ's sacrificial death (2 Cor 6:1–2/Isa 49:8; cf. 2 Cor 5:17, 21). This is the message of reconciliation Paul and his colleagues proclaim (2 Cor 5:18–20), and those who accept it become members of the community "in Christ," participating in the salvation and righteousness that this relationship brings (5:17). Paul views himself as one who proclaims salvation to Israel and the Gentiles in the era of the new creation and new exodus (2 Cor 6:2/ Isa 49:8 cf. 42:9; 43:18; Acts 13:47). He believes himself a servant or herald of the Isaianic Servant.[47] In the Isaianic pericope, the exiles of Israel are to "come out" of Babylon similar to how Israel came out of Egypt, and they are to be sustained by water from the rock in the wilderness (cf. Isa 48:20–21; 49:9–10).

Even so, the Isaianic Servant is apprehensive that his work before God has been "in vain" (Isa 49:4), and Paul picks up on this language. Similar to the exiles who would not accept the message given by the Isaianic Servant, the Corinthians are in danger of receiving God's grace to no effect (2 Cor 6:1; cf. 1 Cor 15:2, 10, 14, 58; Gal 4:11; Phil 2:16; 1 Thess 2:1; 3:5).[48] The aorist infinitive of "receive" (δέχομαι) may be understood as past tense, referring to the Corinthians' initial reception of Paul's gospel in the past (2 Cor 11:4; 1 Thess 1:6; 2:13; 2 Thess 2:10).[49] The Corinthians, however, are already saints and have accepted the message of reconciliation in relation to Christ.[50] More likely, then, the aorist is timeless, a sense used elsewhere when Paul makes an appeal.[51] The Corinthians are not to receive God's grace in vain, now or

47. See Gignilliat, *Paul and Isaiah's Servants*, esp. 53–54, 132–42, 159. Isaiah 49:1–8 segues from Israel as the servant to an individual (72–73).

48. Reinmuth, "Nicht vergeblich," 97–123, draws our attention to the importance of election in relation to the phrase "in vain" by comparing its use in *Pseudo-Philo* with Pauline passages. A reading of the former unfolds the phrase in terms of a hopeful outcome—that God will not forsake his elect people so that his work would turn out to be in vain (cf. Ps.-Philo 9:4; 12:6, 9; 18:11; 23:12). To what extent Paul conveys a hopeful attitude for the Corinthians, however, seems to be clouded over by his rhetorical agenda to scare them into accepting his point of view in this letter. Elsewhere he has confidence that God's corporate elect will persevere (e.g., Rom 8:28–39); God's election will therefore not be in vain. But as we have already argued in 1 Corinthians, divine election provides no present guarantee of final salvation to every individual or splinter group belonging to the chosen community (e.g., 1 Cor 10:1–12).

49. So Collange, *Enigmes*, 281.

50. Balla, "2 Corinthians," 768 agrees.

51. Cf. παρακαλέω + aor. infinitive in 2 Cor 2:8; Rom 12:1; 15:30; Eph 4:1; Plummer, *II Corinthians*, 190. Alternatively Bultmann, *2 Korinthierbrief*, 166 views the receiving as ingressive (inceptive), that the Corinthians do not start receiving the grace of God in vain. He asserts that δέχομαι is "never a thing in the past, but as genuine decision must always be carried out anew" (164), and is related to the eschatological now (6:2); hence, the command to be reconciled is correctly addressing the Corinthian congregation.

ever.[52] This type of grace may be understood, partially if not primarily, as Paul's proclamation of reconciliation, which involves redemption and salvation in Christ during the present era (2 Cor 5:20–21; cf. 5:14–15; 6:13; 7:2; 13:9, 11).[53] The Corinthians must not take God's grace for granted; they are in danger of receiving this grace "in vain" if they respond with ingratitude towards Paul, the minister whom God used to bring them the message of salvation (6:1–2). *The implication is that if they reject Paul's message of reconciliation they will fall away from the undeserved favor of salvation God is granting them—to reject Paul's words is to reject the grace of God.*[54] This admonition is not for the purpose of showing that the Corinthians' salvation might be proven false but that it might be forfeited.

The rhetorical agenda of scaring an audience to embrace correct behavior seems to be Paul's objective not only as he exhorts the Corinthians about the possibility of their rejecting grace but also as he implores them to be reconciled, or reconcile themselves, to God (Cor 5:20).[55] The aorist imperative καταλλάγητε is not merely generic or kerygmatic in 5:20, as though Paul and his colleagues are only proclaiming to the lost the need to be reconciled to God.[56] Rather, as both the context and letter suggests, Paul is also addressing a deficit among the Corinthian congregants (cf. 6:11–13; 7:2; 13:9, 11).[57] His appeal goes out to *them* (cf. παρακαλέω:

52. With Harris, *Second Corinthians*, 458.

53. For the effect of grace on the Corinthians' action as distinct from self-achievement, see Schmidt, *Nicht vergeblich empfangen*, esp. 248–49. In whatever sense we interpret the reception of grace 2 Cor 6:1, it could hardly be denied that this involves human responsibility. Barrett, *Second Corinthians*, 183, places well the balance between grace and responsibility: "Nothing the Corinthians can now do, or fail to do, can alter the fact that Christ died for all, and that potentially all men died in his death ([2 Cor 5] v. 14); it is no forgone conclusion that all will cease to live to themselves and live henceforth for Christ ([2 Cor 5] v. 15). If they fail to do this, as far as they are concerned God's free favour will have been bestowed upon them in vain."

54. See Wilk, "Isaiah in 1 and 2 Corinthians," 152; Hofius, "'Gott hat unter uns aufgerichtet,'" 18.

55. If a passive voice is used here for the aorist imperative καταλλάγητε, this may suggest something the Corinthians receive from God ("be reconciled to God by God"), but if so, an active response is still required on their part (cf. 1 Cor 7:11; Matt 5:24; Garland, *2 Corinthians*, 299). If it is a middle reflexive, then the Corinthians are called to reconcile themselves to God, but if so, as Reimand Bieringer, "Reconcile Yourselves to God," 36, writes: "in 2 Cor 5:14–21 as elsewhere Paul does not speak about human activity without having stated God's initiative."

56. Contrast Porter, "Reconciliation and 2 Cor 5,18–21," 703–4, who thinks the ambassadors are Paul and the Corinthians; they are calling to reconciliation those in the world who are still unconverted. Contrast also Harris, *Second Corinthians*, 147–49. To be sure, the message of reconciliation includes the lost (cf. "the world" in 5:19), but Paul is not being exclusive here—this message is also directly relevant for the Corinthians.

57. Hence it is not entirely correct to see this reconciliation merely as a normal, ongoing process in the Corinthians' salvific life as believers. The present tense of καταλλάσσω would have been a better choice for Paul to use had he wished to suggest this (albeit, the aorist imperative may be used here to highlight the imperatival nuance as a request/entreaty: Wallace, *Greek Grammar*, 487–88). More

5:20; 6:1)—they are the ones who must be reconciled. He embellishes the need for the Corinthians' reconciliation with pathos,[58] wanting to stir them up with a little bit of godly fear (cf. 5:10–11; 7:1) so that they might come back to a proper relationship with himself. To be reconciled with Paul is to be reconciled with God, for God speaks through Paul and his colleagues.

Paul also urges the Corinthians to open up their hearts to him even as he has opened up his heart to them (6:11–13; 7:2–3). He desires reciprocation in which they would love return love for him.[59] He does not desire that any spiritual harm come to them or that the gospel ministry be discredited on his account. On the contrary, he insists that he has not cast any stumbling block[60] before them so as to instigate their falling away or ruin their faith so as to exclude them from eternal life (6:3; 7:2–3). He has not hindered anyone, whether inside or outside the church,[61] from being reconciled to God. Garland is perceptive here regarding Paul's relationship with the Corinthians: "if they have accepted God's grace in vain [6:1], it is not because of anything he has done."[62]

Vestiges of thoughts from 5:18—6:13 are carried over into 6:14—7:1, which seems to convey how complete reconciliation with God can take place for the Corinthians.[63] The catena of scriptural citations and allusions that appear in 6:16–18 fortify the Corinthians as the new exodus and new covenant children of God. Like Israel of old, they are called out from the midst of unbelievers to serve God, and because God dwells among them they are to become a holy people.[64] The Corinthians

importantly, 5:20 is followed up by 6:1, suggesting the Corinthians are not fully reconciled to God.

58. Keener, *1–2 Corinthians*, 187, views this need for the Corinthians to be reconciled with God in the colorful words of a "rhetorical shock attack."

59. Cf. Barrett, *Second Corinthians*, 203. Notice Garland, *2 Corinthians*, 329: "Their love has grown cold, while he professes that he still loves them with heated passion. He has opened his heart to them; they have closed theirs and, in effect, squeezed him out of their hearts by treating him with distrust and suspicion. If they do love him, that love is best shown by their obedience. If they refuse to accept his teaching and reproof, they have closed their hearts not only to him, but also to the Spirit."

60. προσκοπή is used by Paul only 6:3. In other sources, see LSJ, 1517. Related terms for Paul are πρόσκομμα (1 Cor 8:9; Rom 9:32–33; 14:13, 20); προσκόπτω (Rom 9:32; 14:21); and ἀπρόσκοπος (1 Cor 10:32; Phil 1:10).

61. This is implied by his emphatic "μηδεμίαν ἐν μηδενὶ" in 6:3. A desire not to cause salvific hindrance to either insiders or outsiders is seen more clearly in 1 Cor 10:32–33.

62. Garland, *2 Corinthians*, 306.

63. This pericope is problematic, in part, due to its having a high content of non-Pauline words and its apparent asymmetry with the larger context. For discussions, see Webb, *Returning Home*, 16–30; Bieringer, "2 Korinther 6,14–7,1," 551–70. Whether the passage originates with Paul or not, the message of reconciliation seems to be a thread that runs through the larger context.

64. Cf. Exod 25:8; 29:45; Lev 26:12; Deut 11:16; Isa 43:6; 52:11; Jer 32:38; Ezek 20:34, 41; 37:27; 2 Sam 7:14.

are called to be separated from the idolatry and practices of outsiders. They must cleanse themselves from all spiritual defilement (μολυσμός), thus "perfecting holiness in the fear of God" (2 Cor 7:1; cf. 1 Thess 3:13; 5:23).[65] Sanctification is necessary for them because they will stand before Christ on judgment day and give an account for everything they did when living in their mortal bodies (cf. 2 Cor 5:10–11). And Paul has apprehensions that some of the members are still flirting with idolatry, committing fornication and other practices that yoke them together with unbelievers who do not participate in the new creation (cf. 6:14–16; 12:20–21). An appeal against assimilation with Greco-Roman culture is therefore pronounced in both canonical letters to the Corinthians. Whereas temple imagery is used by Paul to stress in 1 Corinthians a need for the congregation to be a consecrated community standing over against factional behavior with other insiders and sexual immorality with outsiders (1 Cor 3:6–17; 6:19–20), in 2 Corinthians temple imagery is used to discourage church members from partnering with and being defiled by unbelievers and worldly standards.

SELF-EXAMINATION AND PUNISHMENT BY EXPULSION (13:1–11; CF. 1:22; 5:5; 2:5–11; 7:8–12)

Paul's emphatic "examine yourselves" may be his response to some Corinthians who were examining *him* and questioning his authority (2 Cor 13:5). This is a significant reason why he repeats the concepts of being approved (δόκιμος) or unapproved (ἀδόκιμος) in 13:5–7. Some members, probably instigated by the opponents, think that he might be unqualified as an apostle. They possibly turned around his previous words about his own potential to become ἀδόκιμος (cf. 1 Cor 9:27) and used them against him. Instead of scrutinizing him, the apostle wants the Corinthians to point the finger back at themselves and test whether or not they are genuinely "in the faith."[66] They must determine if they are living in faithful obedience to Christ and following the guidance of God's Spirit. As well, they must make sure that they are

---

65. Harris, *Second Corinthians*, 512, notices μολυσμός as a *hapax legomena* in the NT (cf. cognate in 1 Cor 8:7). References to the word in the LXX involve defilement by means of idolatry (cf. Jer 23:15; 2 Macc 5:27; 1 Esdr 8:80[83]). On the possibility of idol meats in 2 Corinthians, see Fee, "II Corinthians VI.14–VII," 140–61. We probably should not read too much into the concept of defilement and idolatry in 6:14—7:1 because Paul includes himself ("us"/"ourselves") among those who need cleansing (7:1).

66. Héring, *Second Corinthians*, 100–101, views this examination in terms of self-criticism and examining their conscience. To this may be added their need to test whether they have an authentic spiritual relationship with Christ.

"in Christ" with the Lord working in and among them (2 Cor 13:5 cf. 1:24; 5:17; 1 Cor 16:13).[67]

The words of this closing exhortation are grounded more on reaction and rhetoric than acute doubts about the congregation's authentic Christian experiences. The Corinthians in this letter are affirmed as genuine believers—they are "saints" (1:1), "brothers and sisters" (13:11), they stand in the faith (1:24), and they are metaphorically Paul's "letter" of recommendation (3:2). At times Paul has confidence in them (1:7; 7:4, 16), but he may be using rhetoric related to frank speech in this letter (παρρησία: 7:4; cf. 6:11; 7:2) which can convey rebuke and harsh language on one end of the continuum (cf. 2 Cor 10–13) and praise and commendation on the other (cf. 7:4–16).[68] If Paul's "us" 1:22 and 5:5 includes the Corinthians, then he considers them "sealed" or owned by God (σφραγίζω cf. 1 Cor 9:2; Rom 4:11; 15:28; esp. Eph 1:13; 4:30) and given the "first installment" (ἀρραβών) of the Spirit. The word ἀρραβών may be translated as "pledge," "down payment," or "first installment."[69] Overconfidence in the security of one's spiritual relationship with Christ is a perspective Paul argues *against* in his earlier correspondence (cf. 1 Cor 10:1–12). In 2 Corinthians, at any rate, it is doubtful that he would be encouraging the carnal Corinthians to believe that their final salvation is secured in an unqualified sense via their spirituality gained from their Spirit baptism.[70] Rather, the Spirit is evidence of their future hope of final salvation and glory *if* they persevere in Christ and the new creation through faith and righteous living. This letter as a whole affirms that the Corinthians are truly part of God's new creation *and* they are truly in danger of being ostracized from it.

Hence, if some of the Corinthians were to fail the self-examination in 13:5, this would not mean that they never possessed authentic faith.[71] *Given his affirmations about their identity as Christ-confessors, Paul would more likely consider the disapproved members as apostates whose faith had been destroyed via their acceptance of the different gospel and Jesus preached by the opponents.* Perhaps since he is anxious that some of them are causing division and remain unrepentant of past sins (12:20–21),

---

67. See options in Thrall, *2 Corinthians*, 2.888–89.

68. On the frank speeches in Greco-Roman sources, see Sampley, "Paul and Frank Speech," 293–99.

69. See NASB, NET, NRSV, respectively. *Contra* "guarantee" (NKJV, NIV), which tends to support the misleading implication that being given the Spirit secures final perseverance for all individuals who have it.

70. See similar thought in 1 Cor 1:1–9.

71. Contrast Gundry Volf, *Paul and Perseverance*, 217–21. For criticisms of her interpretation here, see VanLandingham, *Judgment and Justification*, 204. Notice Martin, *2 Corinthians*, 478, who correctly sees the possibility of loss of salvation by the self-test, "Are we really Christians or have we lost that position?" Similarly, Sampley, *2 Corinthians*, 176, writes: "Are you *still* in the faith, and is Christ really in/among you?" (emphasis added).

Paul's questioning of their faith has as its primary aim a desire to get them to change their ethical behavior. His hope is for them to realize both his authenticity and their own, and by doing so they would turn to right behavior and shun the opponents' false gospel (13:6–7).[72]

He both defends his authenticity as a minister and exhorts the Corinthians in hope of their complete restoration to the apostle, one another (due to divisions), and God (13:9, 11; cf. 5:20).[73] In this passage the noun καταρτισις and the passive verb of καταρτίζω do not convey so much the thought of becoming mature or perfect as they do the notion of restoring something that has gone wrong (cf. Gal 6:1; 1 Pet 5:10; Mark 1:19).[74] The idea of the Corinthians' restoration connotes the proper meaning here: "Your restoration is what we pray for . . . Aim for restoration . . ." (2 Cor 13:9b, 11b ESV). Paul's prayer for their restoration may be a rhetorical ploy to scare them back into fully accepting his authority. If they continue following the opponents this would mean complete alienation from God. *The apostle wants them to realize how quickly they are sliding down the hazardous slope to apostasy—so quick in fact that they already must be restored to God.*

Paul threatens to punish the troublemakers in the congregation the next time he visits the church (13:1–2). His reference to Deut 17:6–7 and 19:15 recalls judicial punishment against wrongdoers by the testimony of two or three witnesses. The numbers from Deuteronomy are reconfigured so that they no longer refer to different human witnesses; Paul alone is the witness, but his witness has been multiplied on account of his two visits to Corinth and his upcoming third visit. In the Deuteronomic passages the wrongdoer's punishment normally resulted in that person being cut off from the community through expulsion or execution.[75] When Paul sees the Corinthians again he will punish those who sinned "beforehand," that is, those who opposed him at some earlier time or visit. This group may include the unrepentant fornicators and vicedoers he fears that he might find during his upcoming visit (2 Cor 12:20–21). These are apparently the same members who were causing divisions and having sex with prostitutes in 1 Cor 1:10–17 and 6:12–20 (see above). He will also confront "all the rest" (2 Cor 13:2), that is, those members not included with the first group but who follow the opponents. Of course it is quite likely that many in the first group have also now followed the opponents. The main distinction,

72. Court, "Controversy with the Adversaries," 99, rightly sees the self-test involving ethical behavior. Oostendorp, *Another Jesus*, 23, considers the unrepentant vicedoers and the Corinthians who praise the super-apostles as having some kind of "unholy alliance."

73. Cf. Martin, *2 Corinthians*, 484.

74. See further LSJ, 910.

75. See especially Paul's reference to the same Deuteronomic setting when expelling the incestuous man from the Corinthian community (1 Cor 5:1–13/Deut 13:5; 17:7, 12).

it seems, is that the second group had not been previously forerunners in opposition towards Paul or committing vices. The idea of Paul not sparing (οὐ + φείδομαι) the members reflects Deuteronomic language of showing no pity when punishing wrongdoers within the community (Deut 13:9; 19:13, 21; 25:12). *Presumably, he will expel troublemakers from the congregation in a manner similar to the fornicator in 1 Corinthians 5* (2 Cor 13:2; cf. 10:6; 13:10).

Alternatively, the punishment Paul enforces in 2 Cor 2:5–11 (cf. 7:8–12) might resemble his upcoming judgment in 13:1–2. A comparison between this account and the discipline in Qumran literature (e.g., 1QS 7.15–18) suggests for some that the punishment involves temporary exclusion from the community, perhaps from the celebration of the Eucharist.[76] If so, this would be more along the lines of 2 Thess 3:6–15. Problematic with this view is that Paul claims to be severe the next time he visits the church (2 Cor 13:2). We do not know the precise nature of the punishment related to Paul's earlier visit in 2:5–11. A certain individual in the congregation had committed an offense in an earlier incident. Most scholars today have abandoned the position of earlier church fathers who connected this situation with incestuous man in 1 Cor 5 (e.g., John Chrysostom, *Hom. 2 Cor.* 1).[77] Unlike the incestuous man, the person in 2 Corinthians specifically came against *Paul* (2:5; cf. 7:12).[78] His offense may have involved slander or possibly a misappropriation of the collection funds.[79] Paul claims the man has been inflicted enough. He forgives this individual, and the Corinthians should forgive and comfort the offender, lest he be overwhelmed with grief (2:6–10). The apostle is concerned that Satan could take advantage of the situation (2:11), but he does not specify how. One option is that if no reconciliation were to take place Satan would instigate the offender to join Paul's opponents. Another possibility is that Satan would use the overwhelming predicament to discourage the offender to the point of his leaving the church permanently and falling away. If so, the possibility of the Corinthians suffering "loss" (7:9) may suggest their losing the offender to "the god of this world" as a result of disciplinary action initiated by Paul.

76. E.g., Meurer, *Recht im Dienst der Versöhnung*, 135–39; Furnish, *2 Corinthians*, 161.

77. See further supporters in Bray, *1–2 Corinthians*, 205. Modern supporters include, e.g., Kruse, "Offender and the Offence," 129–39; Hughes, *Second Corinthians*, 59–65. Kruse posits a scenario that developed beyond 1 Cor 5 in which the man who committed incest came against Paul's decision. But this would suggest the man committed two major offenses by the time Paul wrote 2 Corinthians, in which only one is mentioned (7:12), as Harris, *Second Corinthians*, 226 rightly responds. For discussion and refutation of the older viewpoint, see Furnish, *2 Corinthians*, 163–68.

78. Even though in 7:12 Paul speaks of the offended party as if this person were someone other than himself, this verse may be similar to Paul's circumlocution of self-reference in 2 Cor 12:3–5; cf. 12:7–9.

79. For the former view see Furnish, *2 Corinthians*, 164, 168; for the latter see Thrall, *2 Corinthians*, 1.68–69, 171–72.

One clear implication is that if the individual had not repented of his misdeed, his salvation would seem to be jeopardized. Had the Corinthians not responded by disciplining the offender, they would have further alienated themselves from Paul, and in so doing they would have alienated themselves from the work God is doing through Paul. The congregation's sorrow, however, showed true repentance over the situation, and such repentance leads to final salvation. Worldly sorrow, on the other hand, leads to "death" or eternal condemnation (7:10).[80] The distinction between the two types of repentance centers not on the grief they may produce but on whether or not a positive change of mind and action results from the grief. Paul's "soul care" in this case mimics Greco-Roman traditions that contrast the grief God inflicts with the grief humans inflict. The latter simply involves punishment, but the former brings about moral improvement.[81] The Corinthians show godly repentance by the majority of them taking action and disciplining the offender (2:6).

The majority of the congregation, however, seems to be against Paul in 2 Cor 10–13, and C. K. Barrett raises the possibility that Paul would find himself excommunicated from their congregation before gaining a backing to expel the troublemakers during his third visit (13:1–2).[82] Nevertheless, Paul does not seem too concerned about this potential problem. His hope is that the majority will be reconciled with him, so that he will not have to act severely when he comes to them (13:10). Regardless of whether many or few of them will back up his judgment when he visits them, he is determined to stand in the truth (2 Cor 13:8), having sincere motives and preaching the correct gospel message. From his perspective, the Corinthians who will side with him side with the Lord, and those who will side with the opponents side with Satan.

THE HARDSHIPS OF PAUL (2 COR 11–12)

Typical of Paul in his letters, he considers his hardships and persecutions as beneficial for salvation rather than as a danger leading to apostasy. Afflictions are said to produce empathy and endurance (2 Cor 1:4–7), and his "thorn in the flesh,"[83]

---

80. Barnett, *2 Corinthians*, 377, contrasts the two forms of repentance with David as an example of godly repentance (Ps 51) and Esau as worldly repentance (Gen 27:38–41).

81. Plutarch, *Sera* 551C–E; 549F–50A; cf. Philo, *Worse* 144–46; *Dreams* 1.91; Heb 12:10–11; Rev 3:19; cf. Fredrickson, "Paul, Hardships, and Suffering," 182–83 (cf. 194), who adds that God causes "no damage" (Philo, *Conf.* 171), and Paul asserts that godly sorrow caused by his letter did no damage (2 Cor 7:9).

82. Barrett, *Second Corinthians*, 334.

83. The identity of Paul's thorn in the flesh will not be decided here. For discussion on the identity see, e.g., Minn, *Thorn that Remained*; Powers, "Thorn in the Flesh," 85–100.

whether referring to persecution, illness, demonic oppression, or something else, becomes exemplary of Christ's power in spiritual gifts and gracious enablement being manifest through human weakness (12:1–9).[84] Personal hardships are viewed by Paul christologically in light of the cross of Christ, and eschatologically in view of the believers' future hope.[85] They are evidence of his authentication as a minister of the faith as well as beneficial for encouraging the community of believers.[86] As a partaker of Christ's sufferings Paul could rejoice in his various afflictions (2 Cor 1:5–7; 4:17–18; 7:4; cf. 1 Thess 1:6; Rom 5:3–5; 8:18; Col 1:24).[87] Frequently when Paul mentions suffering and afflictions it seems that he has in mind persecutions and things related to the hardships he faces as a missionary. Although persecution is emphasized, labor, hunger, thirst, and enduring cold nights are among the more general sufferings he experiences as a missionary (2 Cor 11:27).

Paul mentions an affliction that overtook his group in Asia Minor. His affliction in this region is sometimes associated with a dire illness (cf. Acts 13:13–14; Gal 4:13–14; 2 Cor 12:1–9).[88] But if this were so the illness would seem to have plagued his colleagues also: the apostle speaks of "our affliction" (τῆς θλίψεως ἡμῶν: 2 Cor 1:8). He is more likely referring to the persecution his party faced in Ephesus, a hardship that came by way of hostile opponents physically harming him or imprisoning him or both (2 Cor 1:8–11; cf. 1 Cor 16:8–9; Act 19:23–41). Paul's fighting with "wild animals" in Ephesus (cf. 1 Cor 15:32), no doubt, is metaphoric language of the conflict he faced in the area. If it were literal he obviously would have included a forced battle with beasts in the arena as one of the crowning achievements among his list of hardships in 2 Cor 11. Moreover, if traditional descriptions of Paul as a small, bow-legged man have any merit (e.g., *Acts of Paul and Thecla* 1.7) he probably would not have been a competent enough gladiator to survive such deadly combat! He is confident that the persecutions he encounters do not mean that God has forsaken him (2 Cor 4:8),[89] and being physically struck down by opponents does not mean that he is destroyed (4:9). Here καταβάλλω probably refers to being struck

---

84. On δύναμις as virtually synonymous with χάρις in 12:19, we notice Harris, *Second Corinthians*, 863: "Both denote divine gifts of enablement, the power for Paul to fulfill his apostolic calling of service and suffering (4:7; 6:7; 13:4; 1 Cor 15:10)."

85. On the theological motifs, see Davids, "Why Do We Suffer?," 450–51.

86. 2 Cor 1:3–10; 4:8–11, 17; 6:4–10; 7:4–6; 8:2; 11:23–33; 12:7, 10; cf. 1 Cor 4:8–16; 12:26; 15:30–32; 16:9; Gal 5:11; 6:12, 17; Rom 8:18–39; 15:30–31; Phil 1:29–30; 3:10; 4:14; Col 1:24; see also 1 Thess above. For elaboration on Paul's list of hardships, see Fitzgerald, *Cracks in an Earthen Vessel*.

87. See Dunn, *Theology of Paul*, 482–87, esp. 486.

88. E.g., Harris, *Second Corinthians*, 170–72.

89. cf. Gen 28:15; Deut 31:6, 8; Ps 15[16]:10; 36[37]:25; Sir 2.10.

down by a weapon or perhaps even slain.[90] If the former is correct, then physical death is probably meant by ἀπόλλυμι (i.e., the destruction of the physical body as a metaphoric jar of clay in 4:7). If the latter, then eschatological condemnation would seem to make more sense of ἀπόλλυμι (cf. 2:15; 4:3)—the physical death of the faithful does not lead to eternal punishment. In either case, the apostle's confidence rests on God's faithfulness to never abandon those who show themselves faithful to God.

Although Paul is aware of the possibility of believers falling away through persecution (e.g., 1 Thess 3:3–5), we do not find this aspect emphasized in his writings, and he is not in the habit of warning believers against denying faith when suffering. Nevertheless, *he mentions in his own list of personal hardships believers who do fall away from faith, a phenomenon that makes him "burn" emotionally as a minister (τίς σκανδαλίζεται καὶ οὐκ ἐγὼ πυροῦμαι: 2 Cor 11:29b).*[91] He may be using σκανδαλίζω to identify the weak believers who finally commit apostasy and are eternally lost as a result (2 Cor 11:29; 1 Cor 8:10–13; Rom 14:21; cf. Rom 14:13).[92] The apostle does not say, however, that being "weak" is tantamount to committing apostasy, nor that his own weakness is leading him to doubt his faith (2 Cor 11:29a). Rather, as a minister sensitive to the potential of weaker believers defecting as a result of their observing his own freedom to eat what he pleases, he refrains from such privileges to become one with these individuals (cf. 1 Cor 8:11, 13; 9:22; Rom 14:21). Paul's anger and grief may be aroused whenever such members end up committing apostasy anyway because of the insensitivity of the other congregation members who do not follow Paul's example of abstinence.[93] In those cases not only does another believer leave the church, but Paul's labor and role modeling among them would be in vain. If this falling away is related to the strong and weak believers, then the apostasy of the weak that he has in mind may be idolatry. The thought, however, is not unpacked in this pericope, and it is possible that the falling away of congregation members could

90. Cf. LSJ, 884.

91. Alternative explanations that the burning refers to a fiery eschatological ordeal (Barré, "Paul as 'Eschatologic Person,'" 500–526), or a fire associated with 1 Cor 3:15 (Andrews, "Too Weak Not to Lead," 263–76) are not convincing. See criticisms in Lambrecht, "Strength in Weakness," 285–90; Thrall, *2 Corinthians*, 2.752–54.

92. Giesen, "σκανδαλίζω," 3.248, perceptively writes regarding 2 Cori 11:29: "Because Paul also understands σκανδαλίζομαι in the sense of a falling away from faith, he cannot feel solidarity with the person taking offense, as he does with the 'weak,' but can only express his concern." On the concept of σκάνδαλον in Paul see further Rom 9:33; 11:9; 14:13; 16:17; Gal 5:11; 1 Cor 1:23; Müller, *Anstoss und Gericht*.

93. Matera, *II Corinthians*, 270–71, suggests the super-apostles are the ones who are the stumbling block to the weak. In 11:29 Paul is speaking primarily about his *past* experiences, however, and so it is more likely that he has the strong/*gnosis* believers in mind from 1 Cor 8–10 as the ones who cause the weak to fall.

be more general than simply isolating the weak. The main reason why apostasy is even mentioned in this case is because such experiences are among the various hardships the apostle must cope with as a minister. For Paul, these hardships strengthen his own hope and endurance. The power of Christ becomes more evident through the apostle's weaknesses. He does not believe that personal sufferings will lead to his own downfall as a minister. Implicit through his robust spirit is for the Corinthians to likewise be armed with the same attitude, knowing that suffering is to be expected for following a savior who suffered and died for them and now expects them to live for him (2 Cor 5:14; cf. 4:10). They can be assured that suffering produces a greater eschatological glory in comparison to momentary afflictions (4:17).

CONCLUSION

The second canonical letter of Paul to the Corinthians was written about a year after the first, and although there is evidence that this letter is actually a compilation of the letters or sources written at different intervals, the opponents of Paul are the same throughout. These adversaries are not belligerent members of the congregation but Jewish-Christian missionaries (2 Cor 11:13, 22–23). Unlike Paul's rivals in Galatians, however, they are not teaching about the works of the Law. There is no evidence that circumcision, dietary rules, Sabbath keeping, or similar observations are being taught by them to the Gentile Christ-followers in Corinth. The reason Paul stresses the Spirit's glory exceeding that of Moses and the old covenant (3:1–4:6) may center on accusations against the credibility of Paul's ministry, which from the Corinthians' perspective fails to show outward signs of God's endorsement. From what we can adduce through Paul's words, the opponents' strategy is to discredit Paul's apostolic authority rather than insist that the Gentile Christ-confessors keep the Mosaic Law. Paul considers them to be false apostles and servants of Satan (11:2–14). They do not appear to be among the original apostles from Jerusalem; they are perceived by Paul as apostolic charlatans because they claim to be ministers for Christ, yet they discredit Paul and influence the Corinthians to reject his authority (e.g., 4:2–3; 10:2, 10; 11:5–11; 12:14–18). It is also evident that Paul thinks they are exploiting the Corinthians financially (e.g., 2:17). In reality the opponents may have thought themselves to be authentic Christ-followers, and the problem in this letter centers on a question of Christian leadership roles rather than doctrinal issues related to the Law.

For Paul all believers and everyone else will be judged according to their works on judgment day when they stand before Christ (5:10; 11:15), and the apostle assumes that the opponents' judgment will turn out to be negative. Likewise, the

Corinthians could expect their fate to be similar to the opponents on judgment day if they continue to follow them. Hence, it behooves the Corinthians to reject the seductive influence of the false apostles that is leading them to apostasy (11:2–3). If they reject Paul's gospel, they will be disapproved by God and will have received saving grace in vain (6:1–2; 13:5). Paul describes them as already in the process of backsliding—they must examine themselves to make sure that they have not already become apostates (13:5), and they must be reconciled to God and Paul's ministry (5:20; 13:9, 11). In Paul's upcoming third visit to this congregation, those who are sinning by rejecting Paul's authority, or committing divisive and sexual vices that he warned against in earlier correspondence will be punished by the apostle (13:1–2; cf. 6:14–7:1; 12:20–21). They apparently will be cast out of the church similar to the incestuous member that he handed over to Satan in a previous letter (2 Cor 13:1–2; cf. 1 Cor 5). The Corinthians must be reconciled and restored back to God and Paul (2 Cor 5:20; 13:9, 11). Paul's message, while severe, holds out the hope of their restoration. Likewise a previous visit and punishment on a man who offended Paul has brought about this person's repentance (2:5–11; cf. 7:8–12). The hardships Paul faces in 2 Corinthians provide a way to demonstrate Christ's power is at work in Paul (12:1–9; cf. 1:3–10; 4:8–11; 11:23–33). He stands firm in the midst of his suffering, which exemplifies power through weakness. Although he does not think that the hardships he suffers will lead to his own defection from faith, the apostasy of weak congregation members is listed as one of the hardships that burden him as a minister (2 Cor 11:29).

Paul maintains a positive attitude throughout his letters regarding suffering and affliction, and when it comes to persecution he appears to have more confidence in his own ability to persevere than in his congregations' ability (cf. 1 Thess 3:5). Sufferings related to persecution and problems related to travelling as a missionary characterize the list of hardships he faces beginning in 2 Cor 11:23. The Corinthians, however, are not experiencing persecution but division and vices. In 1 Corinthians the divisions are mostly internal factions, and the vices are more pronounced. In 2 Corinthians the vices and divisions are not as explicit, but now a much greater rift has occurred between the congregation and Paul. Whereas apostasy is repeatedly warned against in the earlier correspondence and reconciliation needs to take place among congregation members, in the latter correspondence Paul views the members as already in the process of backsliding, and so he appeals for their reconciliation to God and himself.

Although we do not know what happened on his third visit to this church, he does not appear to have been entirely rejected by the Corinthians or banished from the congregation if, as is often surmised, he wrote his letter to the Romans while staying in Corinth during this visit (cf. Rom 15:25–26; Acts 20:1–3). Perhaps the crisis was generally corrected on the third visit, with the opponents shunned and their main advocates expelled from the community. Whatever might have transpired, we see in 2 Corinthians a different set of Jewish Christ-followers opposed to the Pauline message than those in Galatia. Their opposition seems to be centered more on his shortcomings as a leader than his version of the gospel, and we should rightly ask if they otherwise agreed with his message. If they are not apostles from Jerusalem, then we have several different Jewish-Christian groups in contact with the Pauline churches, and Paul does not entirely agree with any of them. The list of rival teachers who confess Christ will continue to expand as we examine more of Paul's letters.

5

Romans: Jews, Gentiles, and the Obedience of Faith

Paul's letter to Romans was probably written during his so-called third mission somewhere about 57 CE.[1] It may have originated from Corinth or somewhere in Macedonia before the apostle travelled to Jerusalem (Rom 15:25–26; Acts 20:3).[2] At that time he had never visited the congregation in Rome before writing to them (Rom 1:10–15; cf. 15:15; 16:19). He writes to them for more than one reason, not the least of which would be his intention to visit this community on his way to Spain, hoping to be encouraged and supported by them (1:11–12; 15:24–28).[3] Another motivation behind this letter involves the apostle's explanation of his gospel to an audience who had only heard about his teaching secondhand. Bad rumors about Paul's view of the Law probably reached Rome, and so he thought it appropriate to clarify his message to them before his visit. His purpose for this letter, however, is not to argue a specific rejoinder against hostile congregation members, nor is it a polemic against opponents who may be perverting the message of the gospel.[4] If there is any problem in this community, Paul may be addressing it by way of cultural differences

1. The majority of scholars support that 1 Corinthians was written before Romans; the former is normally dated somewhere around 55/56 CE, and the latter about a year or two later in c. 57 CE: see, e.g., Brown, *Introduction*, 512, 560.

2. See e.g., Dunn, *Romans*, 1.xliv.

3. On various positions regarding the purpose of Paul's letter to the Romans, see Donfried, *Romans Debate*; Esler, *Conflict and Identity in Romans*, 109–34; Miller, *Obedience of Faith*; Jervis, *Purpose of Romans*; Minear, *Obedience of Faith*.

4. Porter, "Did Paul Have Opponents in Rome," 167 seems to agree.

between Jewish and Gentile Christ-followers; the interplay between the two groups seems central to the letter.

OPPONENTS AND A SITUATION IN ROME? TABLE FELLOWSHIP AMONG JEWS AND GENTILES (1:13–16; 14:1–23; 15:15–16; 16:17–18)

Paul opens the letter by affirming his dedication to preach to both Jews and Gentiles, and this commitment itself has the potential to create cultural conflicts spilling over to religious beliefs and practices. In Rome his audience seems to be primarily Gentiles (1:7, 13–16), but it can be adduced from the letter that this congregation also includes some Jewish believers (Rom 2:17; 16:3–4, 7, 11; cf. 1:16; Acts 18:2). Although Paul warns the Romans to stay away from those who cause dissensions and bring about occasions for stumbling contrary to the teaching they have received (Rom 16:17–18),[5] this advice seems to be given as precaution rather than conveyance of an actual anti-Pauline group within their midst.[6] Paul is cautioning the congregation in a general way against false teachers who can potentially lead them astray into apostasy through deceptive doctrines. To be sure, Paul writes that certain individuals had been slandering the apostle and his colleagues (cf. 3:8), but their location is not mentioned. Their accusation against the apostle's alleged antinominanism resembles his Jewish-Christian opponents in general (e.g., Acts 21:20–21), not specific opponents from Rome.

The letter to the Romans is argumentative in terms of diatribe and use of an interlocutor, but it lacks the severe tone one finds in Galatians where his opponents are endangering the congregations. The warning in Rom 16:17–18 bears a similarity with Phil 3:18–19—in both cases those who do not really serve Christ are governed by their own "belly" (κοιλία). This does not necessarily mean that he is referring to the same group in both passages; the similarity may reflect conventional language denouncing groups that Paul is attempting to discourage the faithful from following. The group mentioned to the Philippians is nonetheless discerned as apostates (see Philippians below), and the Romans are warned against deceivers who could lead

5. 16:7: "... σκοπεῖν τοὺς τὰς διχοστασίας καὶ τὰ σκάνδαλα ..." On dissensions (διχοστασία) see Gal 5:20; cf. Hermas *Sim.* 8.7.5; 8.10.2; Hermas *Vis.* 3.9.9; *Sib. Or.* 4.68. On σκάνδαλον as related to apostasy/stumbling in Romans see 9:33; 11:9; 14:13. The combination of σκάνδαλον and διχοστασία may be seen in *T. Sol.* 18.6; Cratinus, *Frag.* 457–59; Aristophanes, *Acharnenses* 687: cf. Jewett, *Romans*, 989–90. See also the notion of deception (ἐξαπατάω: Rom 16:18) in 1 Cor 3:18; 2 Cor 11:3; 2 Thess 2:3; cf. 1 Tim 2:14; Oepke, "ἀπατάω," 1.384–85.

6. Contrast, e.g., Tobin, *Paul's Rhetoric*, who argues that Paul wrote Romans to deter distrust and hostility towards himself. They were troubled by how he previously wrote against the Mosaic Law in Galatians, and they knew about the excesses of the Corinthian congregation. See also Wedderburn, *Reasons for Romans*; Moo, *Romans*, 20–21.

them into apostasy. Then again, Paul warns against other groups that lead astray as well. A similarity may be drawn between this warning in Romans and the dissenters in Corinth who deceive by virtue of smooth talking (cf. 2 Cor 10–13; esp. 11:3). This danger would become all the more apparent in Paul's mind if he is stationed in Corinth while writing to the Romans. *Paul, in any case, seems to be forewarning the church in Rome about a potential threat that may come their way, a threat that had not already disseminated among their ranks but one he has personally experienced.*

The major topics we find in Romans appear to be written as a result of Paul surmising potential conflicts in a congregation he does not know personally. As such, his instructions to the Romans about the Law, Abraham, table fellowship, and living in the Spirit seem derived and developed from previous conflicts he experienced with other congregations with which he was more familiar. His discussion about the Law and Abraham (Rom 1–5), for example, resembles what he writes to the Galatians even though these topics are argued differently. Unlike his correspondence to the Galatians, however, we do not find warnings directed to the Romans about a current danger of apostasy they face if they embrace the works of the Law. Doubtless, one reason for the lack of admonitions on the subject is because he heard no reports from others that the Romans were in danger of succumbing to a position on the Law that militated against his own. The most extended discussion of apostasy in this letter centers on Israel's current rebellion according to Paul's eschatological scheme of salvific history (see on Rom 9–11 below).

More relevant for the Roman congregation are his exhortations related to their table fellowship involving "weak" and "strong" members (14:1–23). The auditors of the letter must welcome weak believers and not pass judgment on them (14:1–13a), which is followed up by a warning directed at the strong members—their careless eating and drinking could inadvertently cause the weak members to fall away (14:13, 20–21: σκάνδαλον, πρόσκομμα, προσκόπτω), be destroyed (14:15, 20: ἀπόλλυμι, καταλύω), and condemned to eternal death (14:23: κατακρίνω). Albrecht Oepke graphically portrays the word ἀπόλλυμι in Pauline thought: "ἀπόλλυσθαι is definitive destruction, not merely in the sense of the extinction of physical existence, but rather of an eternal plunge into Hades and a hopeless destiny of death."[7] This section of the letter is comparable with 1 Cor 8–10. *Both passages are concerned primarily about the potential for weaker believers to fall away and be eschatologically ruined as result of what the stronger members consume* (1 Cor 8:9–13; cf. Rom 2:12;

---

7. Oepke, "ἀπόλλυμι," 1.396. Schreiner, *Romans*, 733–34, lists various Greek words in Rom 14 indicating destruction, stumbling, condemnation, and grief and correctly concludes that these "terms reveal that the danger spoken of here is nothing less than eschatological judgment."

2 Cor 11:29). A closer look at some comparisons between the letters of Romans and Corinthians on table fellowship is in order.

First, in relation to apostasy, both texts use the binary concepts of "stand" and "fall," the latter referring to apostasy or the condemnation it entails or both. In 1 Cor 8:1–11:1, falling away is in view when Paul warns the strong or *gnosis* believers against causing weak believers to fall ("πρόσκομμα γένηται . . . σκανδαλίζει . . . σκανδαλίσω") and be destroyed because of eating idol meats (8:10–13). The strong are also susceptible to apostasy: if the strong think they confidently "stand" (ἵστημι) in grace, they too could "fall" (πίπτω) and be destroyed similar to the wilderness generation who became idolaters as they ate and drank before the golden calf (10:12; cf. 10:5–11). In Romans Paul comes against the idea of believers passing judgment on one another over eating and drinking: they "stand" (στήκω) or "fall" (πίπτω) to their own Lord and will give account of themselves before God on judgment day. The Lord will either approve ("stand") or reject ("fall") them at that time (Rom 14:4 cf. vv. 10–12). Using imagery related to the concept of falling, Paul asserts that the "strong" must avoid creating an obstacle[8] or stumbling block[9] for the "weak" so as to "destroy" (ἀπόλλυμι) such a person (14:13);[10] namely, the weak might fall away and be condemned on judgment day (14:15). The binary terms of "standing" and "falling" have a slightly more positive ring in Romans than in 1 Corinthians because both the strong and weak are to realize that God accepts both groups regardless of what they eat or drink; hence, they should not pass judgment on one another (Rom 14:17–18; cf. vv. 3–6, 14).

A second comparison between these passages involves early Christian ethics and suggests that their operating in love becomes a preventative against causing the weak to fall away (Rom 14:15/1 Cor 8:1, 3). In 1 Cor 8 the concept of love opposes a boastful attitude that flaunts one's freedom or authority to eat idol meats. A proper attitude of loving one's fellow believers would thus mean relinquishing one's authority to eat idol foods. This is done for the sake of others who might equate such eating with the worshipping other gods. Paul refers to himself as an example of restraint and self-control for the sake of others in 1 Cor 9 and ends the discussion by challenging the Corinthians to imitate his behavior (1 Cor 11:1). If the strong are to love the weak, they must not insist on their right or freedom to eat whatever they want when in the presence of the weak. In Rom 14 the notion of walking in love is placed in the context of a paraenesis beginning in 12:1 emphasizing proper conduct in con-

8. πρόσκομμα: Rom 14:13b, 20; cf. 9:32–33.

9. σκάνδαλον: Rom 14:13b; cf. 9:33; 11:9; 16:17; 2 Cor 11:29; 1 Pet 2:8.

10. Stählin, "προσκόπτω," 6.753, remarks that "προσκόπτω in R. 14:21 is almost synon. with ἀπόλλυμαι in 1 C. 8:11." See further on the word family in Stählin, 6.744–58.

gregational and societal settings. Love is considered the central virtue for ethical living (12:9–10; 13:8–10), and for the strong believers this means that they should be concerned for the salvific welfare of others, including welcoming in fellowship and accommodating weaker believers (Rom 14:1, 3; 15:1–13; cf. Acts 28:2; Phlm 17).[11] The principle of loving one's neighbor is assumed prominently here (Rom 14:15; 15:2).

A third parallel centers on the food that is eaten. The food in 1 Corinthians is specifically idol meat (8:1 εἰδωλόθυτος; cf. 8:13: κρέας), and because the Corinthians are formerly idolaters (8:7; 12:2) eating idol meats presumably would lead the weak members back into idolatry, roughly similar to the way that drinking wine might lead a former alcoholic back to a lifestyle of drunkenness. In Romans, although "meat" is mentioned in 14:21, there is no direct mention of idol foods or εἰδωλόθυτος, and so we are left to surmise that Paul's exhortation assumes either Mosaic dietary laws, or at least they tend to predominate in this context. In favor of this view is that Paul also mentions observing special days (Rom 14:5–6), which are almost certainly related to special Jewish calendar days. Idol foods, however, may be assumed in a different sense in Rom 14:2. A diet of "vegetables" in 14:2 is not a Mosaic edict (cf. Lev 11; Deut 14); it perhaps recalls early Jewish stories such as Daniel and his colleagues eating vegetables or seed products and refusing to eat King Nebuchadnezzar's food because the Babylonians (i.e., Gentiles) may have dedicated such foods to their deities (Dan 1:8–16; cf. Exod 34:15; Tob 1:10–11; Jdt 12:2; Josephus, *Life* 13–14).[12] The assumed problem between strong and weak in Rom 14 seems to rest on potential conflicts with Jewish food laws and remotely with idol foods that may be assumed in 14:2 or at least in the "anything" in 14:21. Possibly, Paul's reluctance to address idol foods more specifically in Romans may have been due to his not wanting to arouse a conflict in the Roman church where there was none. Nevertheless, in Romans the potential for apostasy through eating does not seem to rest on intrinsic properties within the food itself nor on its potential to lead former idolaters back to worshipping other gods. Paul personally considers all foods to be clean (14:6, 14, 17, 20b)—

11. On the aspect of welcoming (προσλαμβάνω), see further, Jewett, *Romans*, 835–36.

12. Goldingay, *Daniel*, suggests from Dan 1 that these Hebrew boys refused to assimilate with the Babylonians by eating their food. He raises Bel 3 as evidence that even vegetarian-type products may have been dedicated to Babylonian deities (18–19). Even so, it is not clear that the food in the latter passage was intended to be consumed by humans, let alone at the king's table, nor are the foods in both cases the same in the LXX (Dan 1:12: σπέρμα/Bel 3: σεμίδαλις). Non-assimilation with pagan neighbors definitely plays a major role among Diaspora Jews, but the *reason* for the Jews not wanting to assimilate with Gentiles included the food's relation with idolatry, and hence, food that would be sacrificed to foreign deities became a major factor for Jewish refusal of Gentile foods. An alternative viewpoint is that there may have been actual vegetarian groups that Paul has in mind, though not necessarily in the Roman congregation. For examples in the Greco-Roman world see, e.g., Jewett, *Romans*, 837–38.

contrary, it seems, to the Jerusalem church's decision to prohibit Gentile believers from eating certain foods (cf. Acts 15:20, 29).[13] The real problem, at all events, seems to be that those who observe Jewish food regulations might decide to break fellowship with the strong who eat anything, including foods banned by the Torah and idol foods. Perhaps the weak congregants' desire to stay away from such foods and those who eat them might eventually cause them to break fellowship altogether, leave the church, and turn back to doing all the works of the Law instead of practicing righteousness by faith. Paul would consider this to be apostasy.

A fourth comparison involves the self-perception of weak believers. Eating idol meats can defile their conscience (συνείδησις) in 1 Cor 8:10–11, and this could lead to their spiritual destruction. Presumably, if they were to eat idol meats while still believing in the existence of the gods the idols represent, they would feel an inner guilt about being unfaithful to God and Christ. This might actually lead to their abandoning the one true God altogether to serve the deities they once did prior to their conversion. In Romans the weak members who eat in "doubt" bring condemnation on themselves because their eating does not arise from faith (Rom 14:23). This might occur as a result of the weak feeling pressured to eat against their inner convictions due to their being despised by the strong (Rom 14:3).[14] Exactly how this condemnation (κατακρίνω) takes place is not made clear, but it seems to be referring to divine judgment rather than merely self-condemnation (cf. Rom 2:1; 8:3, 34; 1 Cor 11:32; Sir 14:1–2).[15] Paul claims that the reason for the condemnation is because doubt does not come from faith, and he then adds the universal maxim, "whatever is not from faith is sin" (Rom 14:23b). The words bear some resemblance to Heb 11:6, in which the author states that without faith it is impossible to please God.[16] Perhaps the passage is intended to show that the absence of faith in some sense involves a denial of Christ's lordship and trusting him for every aspect of one's life (cf. Rom 14:6–8). It may also suggest that doubt takes away from one's operating by the "law of faith," the *modus operandi* for the new era "in Christ," and so doubt can eventually cause a person to revert back to operating in the realm of sin and death (3:27; 8:2–4).[17] Paul seems to be taking his argument to its logical conclusion: if the weak regularly eat in doubt because they do not possess the kind of faith the strong have,

---

13. See Gal 2; 1 Cor 5, 8–10 above.

14. Cf. Barclay, "Do We Undermine the Law?," 302.

15. The idea of self-judgment, however, may be present in 14:14, 20: cf. Gundry Volf, *Paul and Perseverance*, 91f. On condemnation in this passage see further Moo, *Romans*, 863.

16. Conversely, Paul uses Abraham as an example of unwavering faith in Romans 4:19–20.

17. Obviously a one-time event of doubting would not be able to do this! See Marshall, *Kept by the Power*, 113.

they could find themselves losing whatever faith they do have. If so, this too may end up turning them from faith in Christ to the works of the Law. The end result would be that *doubt leads to losing faith and losing faith leads to apostasy and divine condemnation.* It seems that even though συνείδησις is not actually mentioned in Rom 14, the thought is lurking in the background of 14:23. Paul tightens the loose chord between doubt and damnation in his rhetorical flare to persuade the congregation to eat with a good conscience.

The "work of God" that is torn down in 14:20a may be referring to the congregation or individuals such as the weak.[18] Perhaps both ideas are present because the context refers to the destruction of the weak in a similar way in 14:15, and yet the overarching concern of the pericope involves the congregation members maintaining unity in relation to table fellowship. Paul's word on doubting in 14:23 may be vague enough to support both readings.[19]

These observations from Rom 14 and 1 Cor 8:1—11:1 on eating and apostasy drive us to conclude that Rom 14 is the more general of the two exhortations. Paul does not even bother to specify exactly which food contention is causing a problem. As we have observed, Rom 14 mimics concepts found in 1 Cor 8:1—11:1, and since his letter to the Corinthians was written first, he is no doubt borrowing information from this letter and adapting it to Romans. This view makes all the more sense if we are correct in suggesting Corinth as the place Paul writes Romans. Problems over table fellowship at Corinth would be fresh in his memory and perhaps still an issue. Paul probably borrowed the term "weak" in Rom 14–15 from 1 Cor 8.

The upper-class Gentiles would seem to be among the strong members if meat rather than vegetables is an item on the menu (cf. Rom 14:2), and Jews who follow their ethnic customs might gravitate toward the weak members due to dietary observations, but the differences between the strong and weak groups in Romans do not appear to be consistently drawn along the lines of ethnicity or social standing.[20]

18. For the former view see Jewett, *Romans*, 866; for the latter see Fitzmyer, *Romans*, 698. Romans 14:20b may be addressed to the strong (Schreiner, *Romans*, 737) or the weak (Wilckens, *Römer*, 3.95). Then again, perhaps both are in view.

19. See also Barrett, *Romans*, 244–45.

20. For a survey of viewpoints related to the situation and identities in Rom 14 see Gäckle, *Starken und die Schwachen*, 3–35; Reasoner, *Strong and the Weak*, 1–23; and Toney, *Paul's Inclusive Ethic*, 1–38. Both Gäckle, 437–49; and Toney, 46–47, are supportive of the view that Romans borrowed information from 1 Corinthians on the subject. Das, *Solving the Romans Debate*, determining an all-Gentile congregation in Rome, argues that the conflict centers on Gentile God-fearers who hold to Jewish customs and other Gentiles who did not discriminate between foods. On Romans as a Gentile congregation see also Stowers, *Rereading of Romans*; Elliot, *Rhetoric of Romans*. An exclusively Gentile congregation, however, is hard to defend not only in Rom 2 (see below) but also because Paul mentions others in Rome who seem to share his ethnicity (i.e., Jews: Rom 16:7, 11).

Paul is a prime example of this—he places himself among the strong even though he is a Jewish believer of the artisan class who was once zealous for the Law (Rom 15:1; cf. 14:14; 1 Cor 9:4).[21] At most, then, we could surmise that the majority of the weak are Jewish Christ-followers and the majority of the strong are Gentile Christ-followers, but perhaps it may be more accurate to say that the weak tend to follow Jewish food regulations while the strong do not. Romans 14 seems to center on the assumption that the strong members believe they are free to eat and drink whatever they want, whereas the weak discriminate between foods. The same is essentially true about the identity of the strong and weak in the Corinthian congregation also, even though this letter's situation centers squarely on idol meats (see ch. 3 above on 1 Corinthians). Likewise, in both letters, if the weak are in danger of committing apostasy due to their conscience or self-perception when eating, then the weak members in both cases seem to be Christ-followers, for Paul considers Jews who are not followers of Christ to be *already* apostate (see on Rom 9–11 below).[22]

The specificity in which Paul deals with the Corinthian congregation is due to his familiarity with the members; he speaks more generally in Romans as result of unfamiliarity with this community. More than this, *his generalities may suggest that no major crisis exists between weak and strong members in Rome.* Paul seems to be continuing a set of exhortations he started at Rom 12:1, and chapters 14–15 stress welcoming the weak and others in the congregation for the sake of walking in unity and love (cf. 14:1, 3, 15; 15:7). It is even possible that his discussion on table fellowship may be no more a problem than his writing about spiritual gifts and civil authorities reveal this congregation has issues with charismatic excesses or paying taxes to Caesar (cf. 12:3–8; 13:1–7). His generalities (e.g., 14:5, 15, 21, 23) are precisely what one might expect from Paul when he is *not* responding to a major crisis but is nevertheless passionate about his communication and insists that his viewpoint is to be taken as the correct one. A plausible reason for Paul's message in Rom 14–15 is that, based on his earlier experiences that shaped his ministry and churches (e.g., 1 Cor 8–10; Gal 2:1–15), he often considered divisions related to table fellowship to be a potential problem in emerging Christian congregations. This

21. We wonder if Paul would place James and Peter among the "weak" in Rom 14 (cf. Gal 2).

22. Nanos, *Mystery of Romans*, argues that the strong are Christ-following believers and the weak are Jewish non-believers (esp. 85–165). The churches related to the Roman community of believers, however, seem to have met in houses that functioned as churches, not synagogues (Rom 16:5; 1 Cor 16:19; cf. Phlm 2). The meals would seem to be served at these church homes, and thus it would seem odd that non-Christian Jews would be attending Christian church homes on a regular basis. See further problems with this viewpoint in Gagnon, "Why the Weak at Rome," 64–82; Das, *Paul and the Jews*, 69–74. On the household as the context of Pauline congregations, see the discussion in Ascough, *Formation of Pauline Churches*, 5–9.

should come as no surprise seeing that at least three of the four commands from the apostolic decree in Acts 15 focused on table fellowship issues between Jewish and Gentile Christians. Perhaps Paul is simply trying to offset potential problems he anticipates might happen when he eventually eats with this congregation. If so, then he may be doing some preventative maintenance on an issue that he sometimes faced when visiting churches that may or may not have shared his own convictions about eating and drinking. As such, Rom 14–15 may be a general paraenesis combining Paul's assumptions about divisions over table fellowship.[23]

A distinction, however, can be made regarding the issue of table fellowship when compared with other topics in Rom 12–15: it stands as the longest topic in this section, and if combined with 15:1–13 its appearance is at the climactic end of it. Why emphasize this subject and use such strong words of warning related to apostasy and eschatological destruction? Perhaps some differences of opinion on table fellowship did exist among members of this church. It would be naïve for us to assume this congregation, let alone others, always acted like one big happy family when it came to celebrating love feasts. Paul had good reason to suspect potential problems based on his previous experiences with other churches, and it may have even been the case that some of his friends or colleagues (cf. Rom 16) reported that the Roman congregants had questions or disagreements over food matters. Maybe they witnessed an incident or two in which a person who had scruples over food was slighted or made to feel unwelcomed. It is also possible that Paul had some general knowledge about the nature of the problem being related to Jewish food laws rather than idol meats; hence the former is stressed in this letter. Be that as it may, there is simply not enough evidence from what we find in the letter to develop a full-blown conflict over table fellowship, let alone make claims that this is the purpose of Paul writing the letter.

If Paul were addressing a crucial problem in Rome, it seems rather odd that he overtly commends the Roman congregation—"full of goodness" "filled with all knowledge," "empowered to admonish one another," and having a reputation of obedience (1:8; 15:14–15; 16:19)—and claims the only reason he was writing boldly to them on some points (ἀπὸ μέρους) was by way of *reminder* (15:15). The bold points of reminder likely center on his exhortational material beginning in 12:1 and especially the division and potential apostasy that could arise in relation to table fellowship (e.g., 14:4, 10, 13, 15, 20–21, 23).[24] While it is possible that the generali-

23. Skeptical of a situation in Rome over the strong and weak are Karris, "Romans 14:1—15:13," 65–84; and Sandy and Headlam, *Romans*, 384–86, 401–3. Contrast, e.g., Donfried, "False Presuppositions," 102–25. My view stands in tension with those who propose a full-going situation behind the weak and strong in Rom 14.

24. Witherington, *Romans*, 354, rightly affirms that Paul probably did not intend everything in

143

ties in Rom 14 and the reminder in 15:14–15 are rhetorical and diplomatic, hiding the fact that Paul knows more about the situation than he chooses to reveal,[25] it is more plausible to suggest that Paul would not be commending this congregation in light of its divisions, given that he explicitly refuses to praise the Corinthians over a similar issue due to their divisions (cf. 1 Cor 11:17). And this sharp difference in Paul's attitude does not seem to be explained entirely on the ground that he knew the Corinthians but not the Romans.

Therefore we find no compelling reason to affirm that Paul is responding to a major crisis or division between the weak and strong in the Roman congregation, or that one of the main purposes for his writing the letter was to correct such a situation. At very most there may have been a soft problem between congregation members over table fellowship and Paul is attempting to offset *potential* escalations over the issue.

GOD'S RIGHTEOUSNESS AND THE OBEDIENCE OF FAITH
(1:5, 16–17; 16:26)

In Romans the first and last references to faith combine this concept with obedience to make the phrase "obedience of faith" (ὑπακοὴν πίστεως: 1:5; 16:26), with faith and obedience used almost interchangeably throughout the letter (cf. 10:16; 15:18; 11:23, 30–31). The genitive πίστεως can be appositional ("obedience which consists in faith"), objective ("obedience to the faith"), subjective ("obedience that springs from faith"), or adjectival/attributive ("believing obedience"). The last of these options is quite attractive in keeping with the almost synonymous nature of faith and obedience in this letter, but it must be admitted that ultimately the phrase may be deliberately ambiguous.[26] Whatever else "obedience" might mean for Paul, it almost certainly refers to a positive human response when hearing the spoken word, namely the gospel message and instructions derived from it (cf. 2:8; 6:16–17; 10:16–17; 15:18; cf. 1:16). Paul's view seems to be in keeping with the Septuagint, which often uses the concept of obeying (ὑπακούω) to translate the Hebrew idea of hearing (שָׁמַע), and its meaning may include answering or taking heed to some-

---

his letter to be a reminder if he was teaching them something new at least about the destiny of Israel in Rom 9–11. The word for remembering in 15:15 (ἐπαναμιμνῄσκω) is unique in the NT, but related words are found in 1 Cor 4:17; 2 Tim 1:6; 2 Pet 1:12. See further Dunn, *Romans* 2.858–59.

25. So Barclay, "Do We Undermine the Law?," 289.

26. See the discussion in Garlington, *Faith, Obedience*, 10–31.

thing.[27] In short, *human obedience requires conformity to God's will.*[28] Among other things Paul's message makes prominent that humans have a responsibility to operate on the principle of faith, to reject the deeds of the "flesh," and to love their neighbors (e.g., 3:21–30; 8:2–14; 13:8–10).

In Romans, faith is not merely needed to receive initial righteousness or justification at the inception of the believers' conversion; it is ongoing for those who are in Christ. They must continue in trust and obedience throughout the course of their lives until the consummation of all things. For Paul faith includes the notion of faithfulness.[29] Sometimes he stresses faith as a gift God graciously bestows on those who are in Christ (e.g., Rom 12:3, 6; cf. 1 Cor 12:9; Phil 1:29), but *more frequently faith functions as a virtue Paul's congregations are expected to exercise and are held responsible for if they do not* (Rom 1:5; 3:26; 4:3–5, 17–18; 9:32; 10:9–10, 17; 14:23; 16:26).[30] It involves hearing and responding to the spoken word that proclaims Christ (Rom 10:17; cf. Gal 3:2, 5; Luke 17:5–6).[31] Even when the thought of grace is stressed regarding faith, and the granting of favors gift giving in the ancient world of Paul normally had the expectation that the recipient was to return an appropriate response: some sort of reciprocity was expected (e.g., Prov 18:16; 21:14; Gen 43:22–34).[32] Paul is no stranger to this way of thinking when he expects the

27. Cf. Dunn, *Romans*, 1.17; LSJ, 1851. Obedience for Dunn, *Theology of Paul*, 635, involves "responsive hearing. 'The obedience of faith,' then, characterizes faith as not merely receptive but also responsive." Nanos, *Mystery of Romans*, 222–37, argues that the obedience of faith is tied into the apostolic decree to the Gentiles in Acts 15 (cf. Rom 6:17–19). This view is certainly possible, but strikingly Paul neither mentions nor seems to follow this decree when addressing table fellowship; contrast Acts 15:19–20 with Rom 14:14; 1 Cor 9:4.

28. See Yinger, *Paul, Judaism*, 181–82, 202. In addition, Yinger believes that obedience in ancient Judaism "evidences" or "manifests" one's covenantal position rather than "maintains" it, since "obedience is ultimately credited to God's mercy" (95). Even so, for Paul, human responsibility is not nullified if obedience ultimately rests in divine grace and mercy. Both the divine and human sides of the equation are affirmed, and so it is not incorrect to assert that personal obedience must be maintained, especially in the context of perseverance.

29. On the concept of πίστις as "faithfulness" in the LXX, see πίστις *ad loc* in LEH; cf. Ps 32[33]:4. Paul's use of πίστις shares similarities with the Hebrew אֱמוּנָה, which is understood as "firmness," "steadfastness," or "fidelity"; cf. BDB, 53; Dunn, *Theology of Paul*, 373.

30. See further Gal 5:6, 22; 1 Cor 3:5; 16:13; 2 Cor 1:24; 8:7; 1 Thess 1:3, 8–9; 3:2; 2 Thess 1:11; Eph 6:16; 1 Tim 6:11; 2 Tim 3:14; cf. Mark 11:22. A helpful synopsis of faith in Pauline theology is found in Donfried and Marshall, *Shorter Pauline Letters*, 54–56. Faith may be viewed as an activity and is dynamic rather than static (cf. Phil 1:25, 27; 2 Cor 10:15).

31. On the "word of Christ" (10:17) see Moo, *Romans*, 666. Nolland, *Luke*, 2.838, is perceptive on the disciples' request in Luke 17:5 and Jesus' response: "What is needed is not *increase* of faith, but the *exercise* of faith" (emphases in the original). The thought is relevant to Paul's view of faith as well.

32. On grace in terms of reciprocity and benefaction in the ancient world of the NT, see further Harrison, *Paul's Language of Grace*. On gift giving and reciprocity in anthropological studies and ancient Israel, see Stansell, "Gift in Ancient Israel," 65–90; Matthews, "Unwanted Gift," 91–104. On show-

Gentiles in Macedonia to reciprocate for blessings they have received from the saints in Jerusalem (Rom 15:27) and anticipates a returned favor from Philemon (Phlm 14, 17, 19–21). In Romans the gift of Christ brings the recipients under obligation. Now that they are "under grace" the appropriate response is the enactment of obedience (cf. Rom 6:15–23), and as John Barclay affirms, "obedience in service to God has its proper expression in ἁγιασμός [sanctification], whose τέλος [appropriate end] is eternal life (6.22)."[33]

An understanding of faith as requiring obedience is confirmed by the *propositio* of the letter in Rom 1:16–17.[34] Paul declares that he is not ashamed of the gospel, for it is God's power for salvation to everyone who believes, to the Jew first, then Gentile; for in it God's righteousness is revealed "from faith to faith" (ἐκ πίστεως εἰς πίστιν), as it is written in Hab 2:4, "and the righteous one by faith(fulness) will live" (ὁ δὲ δίκαιος ἐκ πίστεως ζήσεται). The Masoretic version of Hab 2:4 reads, "the righteous (one) by his faith(fulness) shall live" (וצדיק באמונתו יחיה), which seems to imply continual trust and faithfulness. Paul's version of Hab 2:4, unlike the MT, omits the pronoun "his." It also does not include the possessive "my," which is found in the best versions of the LXX: "and the righteous one by my faith(fulness) will live" (ὁ δὲ δίκαιος ἐκ πίστεώς μου ζήσεται).[35] The omissions of "his" and "my" make Paul's version ambiguous, probably intentionally so, in order that the phrase be more inclusive.[36]

Habakkuk raises the question of theodicy in relation to God's mysterious ways with Israel,[37] and this provides a "scriptural matrix" for Paul justifying his gospel. In view of the invaders from Babylon oppressing Judah, God declares that the righteous Judahite will live by his own fidelity.[38] The "righteous one" in the context of Habakkuk probably does not refer to a messianic figure. This individual is warned not to "draw back" in unfaithfulness (Hab 2:4 LXX), which could hardly be true of the Messiah. More importantly for the Roman congregation, Paul has already mentioned human faith relevant to them (Rom 1:5–6), and so they would have most

---

ing ingratitude (ἀχάριστέω and variants) see sources in LSJ, 295; Conzelmann, "χάρις," 9.375.

33. Barclay, "Believers and the 'Last Judgment,'" 5.

34. Most scholars accept the thesis or at least significance of 1:16–17 in Romans: e.g., Jewett, *Romans*, esp. 23–24, 29–30, 135–47; Tobin, *Paul's Rhetoric*, 1–15, 87–88.

35. See LXX S, B, Q, V. Another significant variant is A, C: ὁ δὲ δίκαιος μου ἐκ πίστεως ζήσεται ("and my righteous one will live by faith[fulness]"). See further variants in Fitzmyer, *Romans*, 264–65.

36. See Dunn, *Romans*, 1.48: "[Paul] wants to read *as much meaning* into the verse as possible—just what we would expect a Jewish exegete, especially a Pharisee, to do with a text of Scripture."

37. Among other themes, theodicy is addressed in Habakkuk by Watts, "For I Am Not Ashamed," 3–25.

38. Cf. Fitzmyer, *Romans*, 264.

naturally understood the righteous one living by faith in 1:17 as referring to them.[39] This meaning also seems to be the way Hab 2:4 is used when cited elsewhere by Paul and the author of Hebrews (cf. Gal 3:11; Heb 10:38). Such an understanding steers away from our leaning too hard on Rom 1:17 as stressing a righteous person living by God or messiah's faithfulness.[40] The omission implies that Paul is not thinking solely in terms of a faith given or effected by God to believers; otherwise it would have been more expedient for Paul to keep the "my." He wanted to include that believers find righteousness through faith in and faithfulness to Christ and the gospel message (cf. Rom 6:23; 10:5–6). Ultimately, perhaps there is no either/or to Paul's words here: *those rectified by God live by divine faithfulness and their own faith(fulness).*

The thought of living by one's own faith(fulness) involves both trust and obedience inclusive of activity fostering righteous living. The Qumran community interpreted Habakkuk in a somewhat similar manner to Paul, promising life for those who toil and are faithful to the Teacher of Righteousness (1QpHab 7.5—8.3).[41] Conversely, the Wicked Priest exemplifies unfaithfulness; he deserted God and betrayed the Law for riches (1QpHab 8.4–11). Paul's idea of living in believing obedience (cf. Rom 1:5) becomes all the more evident in the context of Hab 2, which affirms God's displeasure with the arrogant, scorners, boastful persons, and the one who "draws back." Punishments and woe await vicedoers among the Gentiles (Chaldeans) who engage in activities related to exploitation, bloodshed, drunkenness, and idolatry. These thoughts from Habakkuk may have influenced Paul to turn from the faithfulness of believers in Rom 1:16–17 to the next topic addressing unrighteousness of Gentiles who commit heinous vices in 1:18–32.

It is quite possible that Paul's affirmation "I am not ashamed of the gospel" (Rom 1:16) echoes the words of the servant in Isaiah, a role he sees himself bound up with by his spreading of the good news to the nations (cf. Isa 50:7 LXX; Gal 1:15–16/ Isa 49:1–6). If so, Paul may be adapting thoughts about the servant's ability to remain loyal to the Lord despite persecutions, knowing that the Lord will justify him (Isa 50:6–9). The thought of not being ashamed of the gospel likewise recalls the words of Jesus (cf. Mark 8:38; Matt 10:33; Luke 12:9): "For whoever is ashamed of me and my

39. In agreement with Taylor, "Faith to Faith," 338–41. Contrast the righteous one as messianic in Campbell, "Romans 1.17," 265–85.

40. Jewett, *Romans*, 145 is instructive: "That πίστις here refers to the faithfulness of God or Christ would more easily have been achieved by citing one of the LXX versions of Hab 2:4, which Paul obviously chose not to do."

41. See Fitzmyer, *Romans*, 264. Watts, "For I Am Not Ashamed," 3–25, examines Habakkuk and observes that both Habakkuk and Romans share in common views that set the righteous/righteousness in contrast with the arrogant and boasters, the Law as weak in restraining sin, and judgment falling on the Jew (Judah) first, then Gentile (Chaldeans).

words in this adulterous and sinful generation, the Son of Man will also be ashamed of him when he comes in the glory of his Father with the holy angels."[42] As we have seen already through the Synoptic Gospels (see Volume 1 of this study), this saying of Jesus refers to confessing him publically. To deny him before others will constitute Jesus denying such a person belongs to him. A future fate of divine judgment awaits the disciple who denies Christ when facing persecution. Paul may be fusing this saying with the Isaianic servant's to express a positive affirmation that the apostle has remained faithful to his commission to preach the gospel of salvation in Christ, despite his many hardships caused by opposition and persecution (e.g., Rom 3:8; 5:1–5; 8:17–39; cf. 1 Cor 4:9–13; 2 Cor 11:23–33; Acts 14:19; 16:22–26). His gospel continues to spread from the Jews to Gentiles by the power of God (Rom 1:8, 14, 16–17),[43] and *his bold affirmation functions as a confession, the antipode of repudiating Christ and committing apostasy* (cf. Phil 1:20; 2 Tim 1:6–8, 12; 1 Pet 4:16).

His echo of Jesus, however, suggests neither a systematic persecution of the Christ-followers in Rome, nor a concentrated effort made by local residents to physically harm the believers. There is no evidence of such persecution when Paul writes this letter (c. 57 CE). He also seems to commend the Roman government's judicial system (Rom 13:1–4), which would become in the final years of Nero something quite difficult for Christians to do. It would have been rather unwise for Paul to choose Rome of all cities for future lodging if the Christians were presently facing persecution there. No doubt he wished to visit them not only because it was expedient but also because it was safe for him do so. He does mention hardships that require perseverance (e.g., 8:17–18, 28–39), but these are generalized and probably inclusive of his past sufferings as a missionary (cf. 2 Cor 11:23–33).

If Paul cites Hab 2:4 in Rom 1:17, he may already have this verse in mind in 1:16. Habakkuk 2:4 LXX adds that if a righteous individual draws back (ὑποστέλλω), God will not take pleasure in that person; i.e., God will reject the person. The author of Hebrews would later use the same passage to contrast faith and apostasy (Heb 10:37–38/Hab 2:4). A major distinction between Rom 1:16–17 and Hebrews, however, is that the former never explicitly addresses ὑποστέλλω from Habakkuk.[44] In any case Paul's gospel centers on his proclamation that the righteous live by faith, and as a result of this message he frequently experiences conflicts with others who

---

42. On this reading of Rom 1:16 see Barrett, "I Am Not Ashamed," 19–50. On "not ashamed" as a formulaic affirmation of one's confession of Christ, see e.g, Stuhlmacher, *Romans*, 28 ; Wilckens, *Römer*, 1.82. Contrast Watts, "For I Am Not Ashamed," 21–22.

43. Stowers, *Rereading of Romans*, 306 rightly observes that the gospel in Romans is Paul's *own* gospel; cf. Rom 2:16.

44. On this reading there is also an assumption that Paul's version of Habakkuk relies on the Septuagint variation; the Masoretic text omits the sentence related to ὑποστέλλω.

reject that message. Despite opposition, he remains steadfast with a firm conviction that his gospel has transforming power to save lives and to restore God's righteousness throughout the world.

Whereas faith(fulness) addresses the human side of the equation in Rom 1:16–17, the concept of righteousness stresses God's activity. God's righteousness is manifested through his act of bestowing upon his people a correct standing with himself.[45] This righteousness is now being revealed to both Jews and Gentiles with the goal of delivering his people and the entire creation from bondage and oppression. It involves an entire scheme of salvific history that spans from the beginning of God's dealing with humans[46] to the future event when "all Israel" will be saved (Rom 11:25–26; cf. Isa 46:13; Ps 97[98]:2). Although Paul considers believers to be righteous in 1:17 (cf. 3:24–26), he stresses a theodicy that God is righteousness in God's activities towards his creatures.[47] God's righteousness is also imparted to believers in terms of both status and ethical living.[48] Without our denying individualistic aspects related to the "righteous one," the salvific thought in 1:16–17 centers more specifically on corporate righteousness. Robert Jewett correctly highlights this emphasis: "the question of life should be understood as a matter of living together in faith communities rather than in the traditional theological sense of gaining eternal life on an individualistic basis. The proper question to be posed on the basis of Paul's argument in Romans is not, 'Are you [sg.] saved?' but, 'Are you all living together righteously in faith communities?'"[49]

The phrase "from faith to faith" (ἐκ πίστεως εἰς πίστιν) in 1:17 has been understood in different ways, among the most prominent include: 1) a progression of personal faith from one degree to the next ("from initial to final faith" cf. 2 Cor 2:16; 3:18); 2) from the subject to the object (i.e., from the faithfulness of God/Christ to

---

45. The statement of Sanders, *Paul and Palestinian Judaism*, 447, is directed at Paul's readers: "the main theme of Paul's gospel was the saving action of God in Jesus Christ and how his hearers could participate in that action." Wright, *Romans*, 426, includes the entire human race and *cosmos* being restored to harmony by God's righteousness. For various interpretations of the righteousness of God in Paul, see e.g., Käsemann, "Righteousness of God," 168–82; Ziesler, *Meaning of Righteousness in Paul*; Seifrid, "Paul's Use of Righteousness," 2.39–74. For discussions in relation to the New Perspective, see Koperski, *Paul and the Law*; Westerholm, "New Perspective at Twenty-Five," 2.1–38; and in relation to judgment, see discussions in Konradt, *Gericht und Gemeinde*, 1–22; Donfried, "Justification and Last Judgment," 90–99.

46. Cf. Rom 1:18–32; 5:11–21.

47. The point of theodicy in Romans is emphasized in Oropeza, "Paul and Theodicy," 57–80, an article from which the research on Rom 9–11 in this book is derived.

48. Ziesler, *Meaning of Righteousness*, 43, affirms that status and ethical behavior in relation to righteousness are often inseparable. See also Yinger, *Paul, Judaism*, 63.

49. Jewett, *Romans*, 146.

the faith of the believer); and 3) the scope of salvific history (e.g., from the faith of "Old Testament" believers to the faith of the New Testament believers).[50] Differently, John Taylor, examining primarily the LXX, suggests instead that the construction ἐκ + A + εἰς + A in Rom 1:17 has the primary functions of "movement, extended time, and progression or increase," and he favors an interpretation that stresses an eschatological event with quantitative growth involving the advancement of the gospel to Gentiles: "If the righteousness of God is revealed by the faith of the Gentiles, then Paul is taking their response as a confirmation that the eschatological salvation has indeed arrived. Gentile faith in Israel's Messiah fulfills Isaianic predictions that the nations will come to Zion" (Cf. Isa 51:4–8; 52:10; 56:1; cf. Isa 52:15; 53:1; Ps 97[98]:2).[51]

If we carry this view one step further, the growth of the gospel is for everyone—to Jews first, then Gentiles (Rom 1:16). The proper reading of "from faith to faith" in 1:17 would then be "from faith" first preached and received by Jews "to faith" extending to the Gentiles. This interpretation complements the way Romans constantly interacts with righteousness and faith in relation to both Jews (e.g., 1:16; 2:1–4:25; 9:1–11:29) and Gentiles (e.g., 1:13, 16; 1:18–32; 3:20–31; 5:12–21; 11:20–25).[52] Righteousness that is attributed to individuals is primarily viewed in terms of their respective social locations as Jews, Gentiles, and the elect remnant. As such, *the salvation and righteousness they experience is an ongoing process culminating to a future point in salvific history when God will reveal the extent of his mercy on both Jews and Gentiles (Rom 11). Until then, precisely which individuals are justified in a final sense is not irrevocable.* In Paul's view, and especially in Rom 9–11, many Israelites are presently not righteous before God, and the Gentiles who have been made righteous in the present era may still be severed from Christ prior to the culmination of all things (cf. 11:20–22).[53] In Romans, as in Galatians, those who believe the gospel message are initially made righteous/justified (δικαιοσύνη: Rom 1:17), but their final righteousness/justification will not take place until the second coming of Christ. Moreover, the righteousness in which they participate during the present era does not guarantee their final righteousness at the eschaton. They must persevere and not reject faith.

50. For various interpretations of the phrase, see further Quarles, "Fresh Examination," 1–21.

51. Taylor, "Faith to Faith," 337–48; citations from 342, 346 respectively.

52. Ibid., 347 tentatively recognizes this interpretation of Rom 1:17.

53. Equally, Gentiles who are not believers are subject to God's wrath, rejecting the revelation God has given them and becoming more obdurate as they continue to practice vices (Rom 1:18–32/Wis 12–14).

This understanding of Romans leads us to the perspective that *righteousness and faith are not merely relevant for believers at the inception of their conversion in order to "get in" Christ, but they must remain faithful and righteous despite suffering and opposition so as to "stay in" Christ until the culmination of all things.*[54] To be sure, Paul's view of salvation involves divine grace and election, and grace works in believers throughout their salvific journey (cf. 1 Cor 10:13; 2 Cor 1:21; Phil 2:13). However, this is not the same thing as Paul claiming that every individual who comes to faith and is made righteous will necessarily persevere to the end and finally be saved, and hence preclude the potential for genuine believers to commit apostasy.[55] Such an idea, as we have already observed elsewhere in Paul and will see again in Romans, is not supported by the texts. He teaches instead that "staying in" salvation involves an ongoing union with Christ requiring believing obedience and perseverance; believing obedience is characterized by one's implementing Christ's love commandment and being guided by the Spirit instead of the "flesh" (e.g., Rom 1:5; 6:16–23; 8:1–18; 13:8–14; cf. Gal 5:14–16; 1 Thess 4:9).[56]

---

54. Garlington, *Faith, Obedience*, 145, says it differently as the "initial, intermediate, and ultimate phases" of faith. For Sanders, *Paul and Palestinian Judaism*, Paul believes that "salvation is by grace but judgment is according to works; works are the condition of remaining 'in', but they do not earn salvation . . . In Paul's usage, 'be made righteous' ('be justified') is a term indicating getting in, not staying in the body of the saved" (544). But Paul emphasizes perseverance for final justification, a point Garlington attempts to remedy. As well, Paul's "works" involve a faith exemplified by obedience to God (Rom 6) and love in action (Rom 13).

55. A position generally supported by Gundry Volf, *Paul and Perseverance*. See further critique of this position in Oropeza, *Paul and Apostasy*, 28–33, 193–204. O'Brien, "Was Paul a Covenantal Nomist?," 2.265, writes regarding "staying in" and Paul's perspective: "it is the activity of God, not the effort of the *fallen* human being, that is the *ground* of one's perseverance in salvation. Human effort is the effect rather than the cause." If so, then Paul would seem to believe that, despite God's activity, negative human effort (disobedience) is able to undermine perseverance to the point of apostasy (e.g., Gal 5:4; Rom 8:13; 1 Cor 10:12).

56. The notions of "getting in" and "staying in" are popularized by the New Perspective and Sanders (e.g., *Paul and Palestinian Judaism*, 543). Although these aspects are often associated with covenant faithfulness, I view them more in relation to the believers' experience of being "in Christ." Although I think the notions of "getting in" and "staying in" may be helpful tools for understanding Pauline soteriology in a broad sense, I do not consider Sanders' study of covenant nomism to be entirely accurate. Gathercole, *Where is Boasting?*, finds an emphasis from Second Temple literature on confidence before God in both election and obedience to the Law so that a person is able to boast at the final judgment. For Gathercole, both early Judaism and Christians "share an elective grace and also assign a determinative role to works at final judgment" (135; cf. 33, 90, 111, 159–160, 194). VanLandingham, *Judgment & Justification*, contests Sanders' connection between grace and election for Second Temple Judaism. In ancient Judaism, election is a "reward for obedience to God's will, not the unmerited gift of God's grace" (333). Second Temple Judaism appears to be more variegated on grace, election, and obedience than Sanders presents. See also Carson et al., *Justification and Variegated Nomism*.

JUDGMENT ACCORDING TO WORKS FOR BOTH JEWS AND GENTILES
(1:18—2:16; 4:2-8)

Paul writes that God's wrath is against the unrighteous Gentiles who do not honor God but commit vices such as idolatry and sexual immorality (Rom 1:18-32). *An apostasy is implied by Paul's words. The Gentiles originally knew about the invisible God but have suppressed the truth and exchanged the Creator for idols* (1:18-25; cf. Jer. 2:11; Ps 105[106]:20).[57] Their progressive turning away from God is reciprocated with progressive spiritual obduracy: God delivers them over (παρέδωκεν αὐτοὺς),[58] that is, he abandons or consigns them to impurity, dishonorable passions, and a reprobate or "unfit" mind (ἀδόκιμος: cf. 1 Cor 9:27; 13:5-7) as a form of punishment (Rom 1:24, 26, 28). The end result is that they indulge in further perversions (Rom 1:23-28; cf. Wis 4:12; 18:30-31), and their final recompense will involve death and divine wrath (Rom 1:18, 32). Exactly how this delivering over takes place is not clear. This may involve God no longer constraining them to moral principles, and so they are completely at the mercy of their sinful desires, which inevitably leads to disastrous consequences and eternal judgment. God's privation in this sense is an absence of grace that consigns them to spiritual imprisonment with the jailors as their own desires. Robert Jewett comes close to this idea:

> Paul insists that God became directly involved in the process of moral retribution in the period before the enactment of the final wrath, whereby the distorting and darkening of the heart (v. 21) result in God's confining the heart within the twisted circle of its desires (v. 24). Those who choose a dishonest heart are required to live out the life imposed by its twisted desires . . . They are released from God's control and handed over to the control of their own desires . . . Such wicked desires of the heart are the punitive custody into which God consigns sinners.[59]

Beverly Gaventa, on the other hand, argues that in this passage God hands over humanity to a third party.[60] This may be compared to Paul handing over the incestuous man to Satan (1 Cor 5:5). Romans betrays apocalyptic characteristics in which

---

57. The echo from Ps 105[106] in Rom 1:23 refers to Israel's apostasy through the golden calf incident. Romans 1:18-32, however, associates idolatry with acts committed by unrighteous Gentiles. The appropriate backdrop for this passage is Wis 12-14, where idolatry, fornication, and other vices are viewed as characteristic of the things the nations/Gentiles do. On the Gentiles/nations committing apostasy see, e.g., *T. Naph.* 3-4; *T. Ash.* 7; *T. Ben.* 9.1. Paul does not have Israel in mind in Rom 1:18-32 unless through the "backdoor" in Adam (cf. Rom 5:12-20). The sinful activities in Rom 3:9-12, on the other hand, apply to all humanity whether Jews or Gentiles.

58. On the use of παραδίδωμι in Paul see Popkes, "Aufbau und Charakter," 490-501.

59. Jewett, *Romans*, 167-68. See also Wis 11:15-16; *T. Gad* 5.10; Rev 13:10.

60. See e.g., παραδίδωμι in LXX Deut 2:24-30; 28:7; Josh 2:14; 6:2; Jer 21:10; Ezek 7:21.

the people are handed over to cosmic "anti-God" powers: "When, three times in Romans 1, God is said to have 'handed over' humanity to the powers of uncleanness, dishonourable passions and a deformed mind, that action places humankind in the power of Sin."[61] Release from this handing over takes place through the redemption of Christ, who defeats the anti-God powers on the cross (cf. Rom 1:16–17; 3:24; 8:3, 32).[62] In this case the cosmic powers, especially sin, are seen as the forces that enslave and imprison humanity. This adds an important dimension to the passage, especially given that in 6:11–21 Paul exhorts against the people becoming sin's slave. The power of sin, it seems, works in and through wrongheaded human desires. They may have started out as competent human beings, but through acts of disobedience and being delivered to the anti-God powers their incompetency was deepened.[63]

At all events the progression of human rebellion against God and the divine retribution that follows provides a pattern consistent elsewhere in Paul—God initiates grace, and humans initiate rebellion against God; and when humans rebel, it becomes God's prerogative to punish them. One way God does this is by obduracy (cf. Rom 9–11; 2 Thess 2:10–12). Similar to the gospels that have God reciprocating human callousness with spiritual blindness (e.g., Mark 4:10–12; John 12:37–40), Paul's assumption may be that God reciprocates in some sort of *lex talionis* manner for the Gentile's hardness of heart. The threefold "exchange" (ἀλλάσσω) of God's image, truth, and human sexual urges for something wrong in Romans 1:23, 25, 27, is matched by further hardening that intensifies and results in divine judgment that is considered well-deserved (1:32).[64]

An important corollary follows from this. The Gentile's predicament in 1:18–32 is a rejection of the Creator's gracious gifts to them. Such rejection results in falling away from God and incurring divine wrath. The interplay between God's grace and apostasy in this passage says something important about the way Paul thinks about the relationship between the two. It is common knowledge that grace may be viewed as a gift from God, including salvific grace (e.g., Rom 3:24; 5:15; 8:32; Phil 1:29; 2:9; Gal 3:18; 1 Cor 2:12; cf. 2 Cor 9:15; Eph 2:8–9). God's gifts are initiated by God and freely bestowed on humans, including unworthy recipients (e.g., Rom 5:8), but the

---

61. Gaventa, "God Handed Them Over," 51f. For a similar view on sin and death see de Boer, *Defeat of Death.*

62. Gaventa, "God Handed Them Over," 52.

63. Cf. Martyn, "Pauline Meta-Ethics," 179.

64. This may be roughly similar to the intensifying disobedient acts of Israel that result in punishment in Lev 27:14–25. In Romans, however, Paul claims that Israel's hardening is partial and will end when they finally turn to Christ (11:1–26). This is because, among other things, they are still God's elect and their scriptures have predicted their ultimate salvation as a people.

recipients are free to reject those gifts.[65] Such thoughts would resonate well with ancient Jews whose tradition-history provides various examples of gift and favor rejection.[66] Along these lines is the wilderness generation's rejection of God and his provisions for them in the wilderness,[67] a thought not unnoticed by Paul who is quick to implicate such gifts in the wilderness as God's grace and then warn the Corinthians against apostasy through examples from the wilderness episodes (1 Cor 10:1–11).[68] Gifts may be unearned in the ancient Mediterranean world, but as John Barclay rightly affirms, they "may be rejected or repudiated: it is always possible for a potential donee to refuse a gift or, having received it, to repudiate it by refusing to acknowledge the gift as a gift; the forgetful or ungrateful recipient of gifts is, in fact, a much-discussed phenomenon in ancient discussion of gift."[69] It follows from this that *in Romans, Paul could both affirm the unmerited aspect of divine grace bestowed on humans and yet at the same time affirm that humans could reject gifts of grace, commit apostasy, and suffer divine judgment.* Romans 1 has set the stage for this way of thinking.

Paul comes against a hypothetical interlocutor in Rom 2. The identity of the interlocutor in 2:17 seems to be Jewish and presumably a representative for Israel; albeit, both Jews and Gentiles ultimately will be declared sinners by Paul (e.g., 2:17, 25, 27; 3:1, 3:9–20, 23).[70] The identity of the person in 2:1 is not as clear; it could be either a Jew or a God-fearing Gentile.[71] Several observations, however, suggest that Paul has the same person in mind in both 2:1 and 2:17: 1) the interlocutor is appalled at vices associated with Gentiles, in particular idolatry and sexual vice (2:1; cf. 1:18–28), which is typical of Jewish attitudes;[72] 2) "we" in 2:2 assumes someone familiar with Israel's scriptures, which makes proper sense if a Jewish interlocutor is assumed; 3) Paul's stress on repentance in 2:4–5 is an important aspect of Jewish

---

65. Cf. Barclay, "Believers and the 'Last Judgment,'" 1–9.

66. E.g., 1 Sam 25:2–14, 21, 39; 2 Sam 11:8–9; 23:15–17; 1 Kgs 13; 2 Kgs 5:15–16; Dan 5:16–17; Gen 33:8–9; cf. 32:13–21; Josephus, *Ant.* 10.11.3.

67. Cf. Num 11:4–6; Deut 8:3; Neh 9:18–21, 26; 2 Esdr [4 Ezra] 1:12–24.

68. See further Oropeza, *Paul and Apostasy.*

69. Barclay, "Believers and the 'Last Judgment,'" 5.

70. Contrast Thorsteinsson, *Paul's Interlocutor in Romans*, who thinks the interlocutor is a Judaizing Gentile. The weakness with this position is evident by Paul's use of Ἰουδαῖος in Rom 2:17 (cf. vv. 25, 27) and in that 1:16 sets the stage for discussion of both Jews and Gentiles in the letter.

71. Advocates of different interlocutors at 2:1 and 2:17 include, e.g., Stowers, *Rereading Romans*, 101–4; Elliot, *Rhetoric of Romans*, 127.

72. E.g., Wis 12:23–14:31.

soteriology;[73] and 4) the hardened heart of this person (2:5) resembles Israel's status in an unrepentant mode,[74] a subject Paul will revisit again in Rom 9–11.[75]

The interlocutor remains unrepentant, obdurate, and prideful, storing up wrath for himself on judgment day (2:4–5; cf. 9:22–23). Paul considers this person a self-righteous hypocrite who essentially does the same things he finds fault with in others (2:1–3, 21–23).[76] He attempts to get this interlocutor who thinks himself better than the Gentile sinners to realize that he also is unrighteous and subject God's wrath if he does not repent. Paul drives home the goal of undermining Jewish overconfidence and boasting in their election by asserting that, among other things, God shows no favoritism between Jews and Gentiles. Both will be judged by God according to their deeds, and both are under the power of sin (2:6—3:20).[77] Simon Gathercole understands the interlocutor as an apostate and that Paul is opposing "confidence at the final judgment that is based on election in conjunction with obedient fulfillment of Torah. Paul is trying to persuade his interlocutor that his sin runs much deeper than he thought, and so the interlocutor's obedience to Torah is by no means comprehensive enough for his justification."[78] In the sense of being a transgressor of the Law and unrepentant, *the Jewish interlocutor is an apostate* (cf. 2:4, 23) and, true enough, Paul is attempting to undermine this person's self-confidence. More than this, it is almost as though Paul is accusing the interlocutor of losing the true meaning of the Law as love one's neighbor as oneself, which sums up "you shall not steal," "you shall not commit adultery," and other commands (2:21–22; cf. 13:9–10). We wonder if, via this interlocutor, Paul has his own previous attitude as a Pharisee in mind. There is also a hint in 2:29 that Paul has the "law of the Spirit of life in Christ Jesus" in view (cf. 8:2), and so he may be examining this person in light of the new age in Christ.[79]

73. E.g., Sir 17:25–32; Wis 12:10, 19; *1 En.* 50.2; CD-A 2.5.

74. E.g., Deut 10:16; Isa 6:9–10; Jer 4:4.

75. See further, Dunn, *Romans* 1.79–93.

76. Dunn, *Romans*, 1.80, notices that "pride and presumption" are included in the vice list mentioned by Paul in 1:29–31 so that Paul may have already had the interlocutor in mind before 2:1. Unlike 1:18–28, the vices in 1:29–32 are not necessarily committed by Gentiles alone.

77. Regarding Israel, O'Brien, "Was Paul a Covenantal Nomist?," rightly discerns, "Election-based privileges will not protect the unfaithful in Israel," and refers to Isa 48:1–2; Jer 5:12; 6:14; 7:4; 8:11; Ezek 33:24; Amos 6:1; 9:10; Mic 3:11.

78. Gathercole, *Where Is Boasting?*, 206–9; citation from 214–15.

79. Along these lines, Garlington, *Studies in the New Perspective*, 298–99, argues that the Jewish interlocutor "has refused to submit to God's righteousness which has now been localized in Christ (10:3–4). Given the premise that Chris is the 'end' (*telos*) of the law (Rom 10:4), both as the law's goal and its termination, not to believe in him is to prove unfaithful to God's eschatological purposes," and so this person has renounced God's "plan for the end of the ages in his Son. It is in this sense that the interlocutor may be regarded as apostate."

For Paul, at the culmination of the eschaton everyone will be judged according to their works, including the believers (Rom 2:6–16; cf. 14:4, 7–12; 1 Cor 4:1–4; 2 Cor 5:10). It is also in the eschatological future that God's wrath will be revealed (Rom 1:18).[80] Here Paul is very much in keeping with other early Jewish and Christian authors who inform their readers that God will judge everyone according to their deeds.[81] The names and deeds of individuals are recorded in "books" that will be read on judgment day.[82] For Paul, *these works are not weighed on a scale or given a tit-for-tat comparison between good and bad deeds; rather, these works are probably considered holistically, exposing a person's entire character, motives, and lifestyle.*[83] Romans 2:6–16 shows that judgment according to works applies to everyone, both Jews and Gentiles. The argument is probably not hypothetical or referring only to non-believers.[84] The final judgment in 2:6, 16 seems to be inclusive of Gentiles who have already been initially made righteous by faith and are not under the auspices of the Mosaic Law. Human works, at least those of the Gentiles, are not strictly centered on their keeping the Law; they refer instead to a lifestyle of obedience or disobedience to God. The perspective of believing obedience must exemplify the Christ-follower's life—works and obedience are not being set at odds here. Paul will speak later on of God reckoning people righteous "without" or "apart from" works (4:2, 6), but differently in that case the works are "works of the Law," works specifically related to the Mosaic Law in contrast to the righteous redemption that has come about through Christ in the new era (cf. 3:28).[85]

80. Cf. Eckstein, "Gottes Zorn," 74–87. VanLandingham, *Judgment & Justification*, esp. 222–41; and Gathercole, "Law unto Themselves," 27–49, both see final judgment determining eternal destinies, and the importance of works in relation to those destinies. For VanLandingham this includes the possibility of God rejecting Christians because of their moral failure.

81. Cf. Prov 24:12; Ps 27[28]:4; *Pss. Sol.* 9:5; *T. Lev.* 3:2; Rev 2:23; Jas 2:19–22; Matt 25:31–46; 2 Pet 3:8–9, 15.

82. Phil 4:3; Rev 20:15–20 cf. Luke 10:20; Isa 65:6; Mal 3:16; Dan 7:10; *4 Ezra* 6.20; *Jub.* 30.22; 36.10; *1 En.* 81.4; 98.7; 104.7.

83. Yinger, *Paul, Judaism*, 95–96, 181–82, 284, affirms that judgment by works in Paul is not some sort of atomizing task but involves one's entire "way." Final judgment will be "according to one's deeds, and will not so much determine as *reveal* one's character and status as righteous or wicked" (16; cf. 286). Works are seen as a necessary confirmation of salvation rather than its cause (288–90).

84. See further the various interpretations in Snodgrass, "Justification by Grace," 73–74; Schreiner, *Romans*, 113–15. The hypothetical view suggests that doing the Law leads to righteousness, but no one can really "do" the Law: e.g., Bell, *No One Seeks for God*. This view assumes more than the text seems to deliver. The view of Snodgrass, 81–82, is that Rom 2 depicts a pre-gospel era, but in both eras obedient response is required and judgment according to works is on "the basis of the amount of light received" (82).

85. Righteousness in 4:6, then, centers on God initially justifying the ungodly rather than their receiving final justification on judgment day. It is probably not the case that Paul is thoroughly inconsistent when we compare 2:6, 13 with 4:4–6; *pace* Räisänen, *Jesus, Paul, and the Torah*; Kuula, *Law*.

Even though not explicitly mentioned as such, the "doers of the Law" (2:13) who will be justified on judgment day seem to be Christ-following Gentiles, and they are contrasted with those who "hear" the Law only but do not live in obedience to God.[86] Rather than referring to Mosaic commands or "works of the Law," Paul seems to anticipate his later discussions on believers operating through the "law" of the Spirit, faith, and love (cf. 2:29; 3:27; 8:2–4; 13:9–10). Those who are Gentiles "by nature" (φύσει) do not have the Law, but they do what the Law requires by having it "written in their hearts" (2:13–15).[87] This recalls the words of Jeremiah when referring to the new era when God will write his commands on the heart of his people, a thought which Paul seems to apply to believers, as does the author of Hebrews (Jer 31:31–34; 38:33 LXX; cf. Heb 8:8–12; 10:16–17).

In Rom 3 Paul continues that a righteousness independent of the works of the Law has come about by the death of Jesus Christ, so that those who trust in Christ are now made righteous. As a result, Jewish confidence in election and the works of the Law might be shaken, and their misplaced boasting stifled (3:21–28). If Christ functions as the τέλος of the Law, which probably refers to his being both the "goal" and "end" of the Law (10:4),[88] this does not mean that one's dependence on grace and faith foster antinomianism, as Paul is wrongly accused of teaching in the past (3:8; cf. 6:1). Rather, *the new era that is characterized by faith transforms and renews the Law not on the basis of a written code, but by imprinting moral requirements in the hearts of the believers so that they in principle fulfill the Law's requirements by walking in the Spirit and loving their neighbors as themselves* (8:2–4; 13:8–12). This is how believing Gentiles who do not have the Law can nevertheless do what the Law requires (2:14–16)—they operate under the "law of faith" (3:27–31; 9:30–10:8) and the "law of the Spirit of life" (Rom 8:2, 14; cf. Gal 5:16), and fulfill Mosaic law by loving their neighbors (Rom 13:8–10; cf. Gal 5:14; 6:2).[89] In short, they walk in the obedience

86. Cf. Jas 1:22, 25; 2:8; Luke 6:46–49; *m. Abot* 1.17; Josephus, *Ant.* 20.44; Philo, *Praem.* 79; Str.B. 3.84–88.

87. Alternatively φύσει has as its referent the Law so that Gentiles do "by nature" the Law. On φύσει as qualifying the Gentiles see Achtemeier, *Romans*, 45; Gathercole, "Law unto Themselves," esp. 31–39, who also notices parallels with 2:14–15 in 2:25–29 and 8:3–4, and sees similarities between 2:14 and 9:30 to suggest that, in principle, believing Gentiles are contrasted with unbelieving Israel.

88. For the both/and position see Wilckens, *Römer*, 2.221–23; Moo, *Romans*, 637–42. Contrast Fitzmyer, *Romans*, 584–85.

89. The tension between the "doers of the law" who are being made righteous (2:13) and Paul's insisting that by the "works of the Law" no one will be made righteous (3:20) is thus alleviated by this interpretation. Only the latter refers strictly to Mosaic Law as prescribed in the old era. Similarly, the "commandments of God" in 1 Cor 7:19 is probably not referring to the Mosaic commandments unless we introduce a Corinthian slogan at this point. Instead it refers to either Paul's own instructions (ἐντολή) related to the gospel message and inspired by God/Christ (cf. 1 Cor 14:37; Col 4:10; 1 Tim 6:14) or something similar to the love command (cf. Rom 13:9). If the latter, it is peculiar that he uses a

of faith (Rom 1:5).[90] In Romans, the Law is more distanced from apostasy than in Galatians, but it is implicated as a culprit related to Israel's rejecting Paul's gospel message and faith in Christ (Rom 9:31—10:13); likewise, as we have suggested, the danger the weak members seem to face is an apostasy to fall back to thoroughgoing adherence of the Law. The Law is also exploited by the power of sin.

As in Galatians, Paul brings up the example of Abraham as one who had faith in God and was reckoned as righteous before God on that basis of faith rather than works of the Law (Rom 4:2–5; cf. Gen 15:6). But unlike Galatians, among other things, Paul claims that God considered Abraham righteous before he was circumcised (Rom 4:9–13; cf. Gen 17:10–11), and the purpose of this was to make the ancient patriarch a father to both the uncircumcised Gentiles as well as the circumcised Jews.[91] Perhaps due to his idolatrous upbringing, Abraham is viewed here as "ungodly" (ἀσεβής: 4:5), similar to the uncircumcised and non-Torah observing Gentiles who are made righteous independent of the Law.

Likewise, in relation to the ἀσεβής, Paul also cites from Ps 31[32]:1–2 to affirm that a person is blessed whose lawless deeds are forgiven and sins covered (Rom 4:7–8).[92] Psalm 31[32] is a penitent song attributed to David that recalls the divine forgiveness he received after committing adultery with Bathsheba (2 Sam 11–12).[93] Several key words from this psalm may have influenced Paul.

First, the word λογίζομαι (to "reckon," "consider," or "take into account") becomes his referent that connects Gen 15:6 with Ps 31[32]. Abraham is reckoned by God to be righteous through faith; in the latter text the blessed individual's sin is forgiven and *not* reckoned or taken into account by God. Both cases for Paul exemplify God considering a person righteous apart from Mosaic works of the Law. Second, the concepts of righteousness and boasting may recall the "righteous ones" (δίκαιοι) in Ps 31[32]:11 who are encouraged to "boast" (καυχᾶσθε) "in the Lord." Third, the concept of the forgiven person hoping in the Lord is similar to Paul's discussion about Abraham hoping "against hope" regarding God's promise that he

---

plural in 1 Cor 7:19; hence, the former view seems more likely (cf. also 1 Cor 7:10, 25, where Paul uses synonymous words for "command"). Paul's brief statement about the Law in 1 Cor 15:56b assumes the Corinthians are already familiar with his interpretation of the Mosaic Law as revealing and exacerbating sin.

90. On Rom 1:5 in relation to 2:13 see Garlington, *Faith, Obedience*, 59.

91. Genesis 15:6, then, is not Abraham's "conversion"; he is a "believer" from Gen 12 onward (cf. Heb 11:8). Rightly, Don Garlington, personal correspondence.

92. Paul's citation follows the LXX: cf. Wilckens, *Römer*, 1.263.

93. In agreement with me is Aletti, "Romains 4 et Genèse 17," 318. On the motif of David's forgiveness in ancient Jewish literature, see Sir 47:2, 11; Josephus, *Ant.* 7.153; CD 5.5–6; 4QMMT C25–32; Str.B. 4.177–78. The LXX attributes this psalm Τῷ Δαυιδ.

would produce many descendants and be father to many nations (Rom 4:18). The triple combination of the believers being made "righteous" and encouraged to "boast in hope of the glory of God" in Rom 5:1–2 seems linked with Ps 31[32]. The ideas that stand out are that sinners can be made righteous through the Lord and receive forgiveness. This includes the privilege of making one's boast not in the Law or in one's own works (Rom 3:27; 4:2–4) but in Christ, who died for sinners, and in God, who is able to transform the ungodly into righteous persons (5:2, 6, 11; cf. 4:5).

Finally, Paul's inclusion of God making righteous the "ungodly" (ἀσεβής: Rom 4:5) seems derived from Ps 31[32]:5, in which the psalmist declares that the Lord forgave the ungodliness (ἀσέβεια) of David's heart. David is also compared to a person outside the covenant, similar to a Gentile.[94] David's sin with Bathsheba involved both adultery and the murder of her husband Uriah; and yet the forgiveness he received after confessing his sins emphasizes the extent of God's mercy to the repentant sinner. Paul's argument would seem to presuppose that crimes of adultery and murder are in direct violation of the Ten Commandments, and crimes like these are so heinous in Israel's community that such violators should be punished by death (e.g., Lev 20:10; Deut 19:11–13; 22:22; Num 35:16–34; Gen 9:5–6). In other words it would be expected that David could not be forgiven, at least not without the penalty of his death, and this assumption perhaps highlights the surprise of Nathan's declaration to David after his repentance: "The LORD has taken away your sin; you will not die" (2 Sam 12:13; cf. 12:5).[95]

Paul references Ps 31[32] in this regard to demonstrate forgiveness and righteousness apart from any works done in adherence to the Law, or for that matter any works done *against* the Law, as David committed. David did not deserve God's mercy, but he received forgiveness anyway. He stands as an example of an ungodly individual who receives forgiveness from God despite the terrible sins this person has committed (Rom 4:5–8). On this line of thought for Paul, God's righteousness and mercy is capable of forgiving even the most despicable sins committed by the unrighteous who practice deeds worthy of death (1:32). The reception of divine righteousness and mercy becomes a possibility for sinners *independent* of the works of the Law; it happens through Christ's atoning death and one's placing faith in him (3:20–26).[96] *We see, then, in Rom 4 that righteousness is not only characterized by a*

94. Cf. Garlington, *Studies in the New Perspective*, 303–4.

95. The story goes on to say, however, that calamity will befall David and his household as a result of this sin (2 Sam 12:14–18). Hence, forgiveness was granted David, but negative consequences happened because of his sin, and it may be that in some sense the atonement for his sin was transferred to his posterity. So Anderson, *2 Samuel*, 163. For Paul, Christ's atoning death removes sin.

96. God's former redemption of the Israelites from Egypt provides the backdrop for the new redemption in Christ (ἀπολύτρωσις: Rom 3:24; cf. Deut 7:8; 9:26; 13:5 [6]; Ps 25[24]:22; Isa 41:14;

person having faith like Abraham's, the father of both Jews and faithful Gentiles, but it is also characterized by a person receiving the forgiveness of sins, like David. This point on the remedy for sin in Rom 4 paves the way for further discussions about sin in relation to the "flesh" and Spirit.

SIN, APOSTASY, AND NEW LIFE IN THE SPIRIT
(3:10–12; 5:3–5; 6:11–16; 8:1–16)

The culprits that lead to apostasy in Romans are sin and being in the "flesh," the sinful nature of human beings void of the Spirit and related to the old age prior to God's righteousness being manifested through Christ. Paul affirms that all humanity, *Jews and Gentiles,* are unrighteous and have "turned aside" (ἐκκλίνω) from God and his ways, that is, they *have committed apostasy* (Rom 3:10–12/Ps 13[14]:1–3; 52[53]:1–3).[97] Their forsaking God comes as no surprise to the auditors given that Paul has already explicated that the Gentiles once knew the Creator but exchanged his gifts for idolatry and vices (Rom 1), and the Jews, represented by the interlocutor, have become unrepentant transgressors of the Law (Rom 2).

In this letter sin is universalized, functioning as a contagious, hostile force affecting everyone (5:12–21).[98] The Mosaic Law is powerless to defeat it—the ineffectiveness of the Law is stressed to the point in which it has been co-opted by sin.[99] The Law only exacerbates the problem by identifying sin and not giving its adherents the power to defeat it (Rom 5:20; cf. 3:20; 4:15; 7:5–25; Gal 3:19, 22; 1 Cor 15:56). It is in the present age, through Christ's atoning death, that righteousness can be properly attributed to faithful Jews and Gentiles (Rom 3:21–26). The new era has arrived, and the "now" (3:21, 26; 7:6; 8:1) supersedes the "then" (cf. 6:20–22) that assumes the sinful state of humanity in 5:6–21 and 1:18—3:21. The complete eradication of sin, however, has not yet taken place; sin and death will not be completely defeated until the future resurrection of believers (Rom 8:18–25; cf. 2:7; 6:21–22; 1 Cor 15:20–28, 54–57). Their salvation still has a futuristic element to it that needs

---

43:1, 14; 44:22–24; 52:3; 63:9), and Christ's "blood" becomes the atoning sacrifice or "mercy seat" (ἱλαστήριον) for sin (Rom 3:25; cf. Exod 24–25; Lev 16; Heb. 9:5; Stuhlmacher, *Romans,* 57–65).

97. See further ἐκκλίνω as apostasy in Deut 5:32; 17:11; 29:18; 31:29; Josh 1:7; 23:6; Judg 2:17; 1 Sam 12:20; 1 Kgs 11:2–9; Neh 13:26; Ps 118[119]:21–22; Jer 5:23; Dan 9:5, 11; Zeph 1:1–6; Mal 2:8; Sir 2:7; Bar 4:12; Sus 1:9. Conversely, see its use in 1 Kgs 15:5; 22:43; 2 Chr 20:32; 34:2, 33; Ps 32[33]:15; Rom 16:17; 1 Pet 3:11; *1 Clem.* 22.4; Ign. *Eph.* 7.1.

98. Garlington, *Faith, Obedience,* 87, 95, 98, relates sin to apostasy in Rom 5:12–14 by claiming Adam's sin against God as the first instance of apostasy. Adam's act of disobedience indeed infects the human race with sin and condemnation, making possible the ability to commit apostasy, and yet neither Paul nor Gen 3 mentions that Adam rejected God to serve idols or commit vices.

99. See Snodgrass, "Spheres of Influence," 93–113 (esp. 98–99); Sloan, "Paul and the Law," 35–60.

realization (5:9–10; 13:11). The present era of "now" and "not yet" undergirds Paul's assumption that *believers are being saved but have not yet received final salvation, and they are dead to the sinful nature but not finally dead to it.* They face conflicts and struggles in the process of being saved and sanctified until the redemption of their mortal bodies takes place at the culmination of the age (8:18, 23–25; 15:13). Until then they must persevere and not be conformed to the evil power of the present age (Rom 12:1–2; cf. Gal 1:4; 1 Cor 2:6; 10:11; 2 Cor 4:4). This requires believing obedience. Karl Donfried is apropos regarding this process: "Sanctification (6_{19} εἰς ἁγιασμόν), the development and maturation of the Christian life in Christ is an integral part of justification and can only be accomplished in obedience to the will of God (παριστάνετε ἑαυτοὺς δούλους εἰς ὑπακοήν, 6_{16}). Sanctification serves both to elucidate and to preserve what has taken place in justification. Only when this is carried out in obedience will God fulfill what he has begun."[100]

The sufferings Paul and other believers may experience in the present age will amount to an inexpressible future glory, and until then the believers are to rejoice in suffering, knowing that the trials they face produce perseverance (ὑπομονή), the virtue of patient endurance that functions as a preventative against falling away (Rom 5:1–3; cf. 2:7; 12:12; 15:4–5; 2 Cor 1:6; 6:4; 1 Thess 1:3; 2 Thess 1:4; Col 1:11; 1 Tim 6:11; 2 Tim 3:10; Titus 2:2).[101] Perseverance also produces character, which in turn produces a confident hope in their future glory that is fully realized at the end of the age (Rom 5:3–5). Paul's attitude toward suffering, hardships, and persecution in the present era is strikingly positive—such challenges experienced by the faithful provide further grounds for their "boasting" and assurance of the eschatological prize up ahead. His rhetorical strategy is to encourage the Romans to remain confident in Christ rather than give up faith. Secondhand stories about Paul's own hardships as a missionary may have been heard by this congregation, and *he now presents himself to them as a model of perseverance.* Despite all his setbacks, he is not ashamed of the gospel he preaches and will not succumb to discouragement or apostasy (cf. 1:16).

For Paul the danger of apostasy in the present age rests not on succumbing to suffering and persecution, but on the potential for the faithful to be enslaved by the power of sin related to the "flesh." Christ-followers are not necessarily exempt from divine judgment: to live according to the "flesh" is to live according to vice, and if a believer's deeds characterize such a lifestyle the inevitable outcome for that person would spell death and divine wrath concomitant with the idolatrous rebels of the

---

100. Donfried, "Justification and Last Judgment," 98.

101. In 15:4–5 the "God of perseverance" is probably a genitive of source; God is viewed here as the one who gives the believers the scriptures where they can find perseverance and encouragement: cf. Robertson, *Word Pictures*, §Rom 15:5.

past and unconverted Gentiles in the present (Rom 6:16, 21, 23; 8:13; cf. 2:6, 14–16; Gal 5:19–21; 1 Cor 6:9–10). The way the emerging Christians are to overcome sin is not through the enfeebled works of the Law but through their being "in Christ." Namely, they overcome sin through their participating in a faith-based relationship with Christ—initiated by their baptism-conversion—and their continual "walk" in the Spirit and remaining in the community of the faithful. They are to take on the mindset true to their experience and consider themselves "dead" to sin and alive "in Christ" now that they have crucified and buried the old sinful self at the waters of conversion, and have risen to a new spiritual life (Rom 6:1–11). The power of sin must loosen its stronghold on those who have faith because they are not under the auspices of the Law, which can only exacerbate sin (6:14).

Their new life, however, does not mean that their struggle against sin is completely over, and so Paul gives the believers a set of imperatives: 1) they are to consider (λογίζεσθε) themselves to be "dead" to sin and alive to God in Christ (6:11);[102] 2) they are not to allow sin to rule in their bodies so as to obey its lusts (6:12); 3) they are not to "offer" (παριστάνω) the members of their body to sin as weapons of unrighteousness (6:13a); and 4) they are to offer themselves to God as though rising again from the dead and their members to God as weapons of righteousness (6:13b; cf. 6:19). The imperatives anticipate Paul's paraenetic section beginning in 12:1–3 (μὴ συσχηματίζεσθε . . . ἀλλὰ μεταμορφοῦσθε) where he exhorts the Roman believers to "offer" (παριστάνω) themselves, this time as living sacrifices to God.[103] Paul informs the Romans that they will become slaves to that which they offer themselves, whether the power of sin which leads to spiritual death or obedience which leads to righteousness (6:16; cf. 1:5; 6:21–23; 8:13). We see here obedience in action—those who become righteous die to the old self and are given new life, but they must become more and more what they are meant to become in Christ. "Become what you are" is an insufficient prescription here. Due to the eschatological tension of the present age in Christ, "become what you are becoming" captures better the imperative language.[104] Whatever else the individual struggle Paul brings up in Rom 7:7–25

102. Contrast Jewett, *Romans*, 408, who thinks λογίζεσθε in 6:11 is indicative and suggests the imperative "would imply that some congregations are falling short of proper life with Christ." But this very reason seems to be the problem why Paul needs to write some of his letters, especially Galatians and 1, 2 Corinthians: the congregations do *not* always live up to proper standards of life in Christ. Hence, knowing that human weakness affects many believers, it would seem perfectly natural for Paul to use an imperative here in Romans even without knowing the congregation personally.

103. For other imperatives in Paul's paraenetic section see Rom 12:14, 16; 13:14, 18; 14:1.

104. With Dunn, *Romans* 1.337, who adds that the thought "would retain the note of an active cooperation with and living out of the grace which precedes and makes possible all moral effort" and that the real possibility of "defection to sin" gives the believers' "decision for God the character of freedom," something they did not have when still under the reign of sin.

might mean, he appears to be speaking as a representative for humanity under the Law in the old era void of the Spirit and prior to being "in Christ."[105]

Another major key to the struggle against sin and the "flesh" is for the believers to operate in the Spirit (Rom 7:5–6; 8:1–16; cf. Gal 5:16, 22–25). The "law of the Spirit of life" contrasts the "law of sin and death" (8:2). The second instance of the "law" (νόμος) refers the Torah, which, because of its weakness against sin leads to death, whereas the "law" in the new era that is associated with God's Spirit allows those who are "in Christ" to obey and fulfill in principle the righteous requirements (δικαίωμα) expected in the Mosaic Law (Rom 8:2–4; cf. 2:13, 15, 26; 13:8–10; Gal 5:14–16; Jer 31:31–34; Ezek 36:26–37).[106] This new era of living in the Spirit is made possible by Christ's death as an offering "for sin,"[107] an event that condemned to destruction sin's stronghold over human weakness.[108] Through this sacrifice death now becomes sin's destruction rather than its alley, and this brings the epoch of sin's reign to an end.[109] Freedom from the "flesh" and sinful living nonetheless seem contingent on being governed by the Spirit, which allows for divine intervention into the decisions of the community in Christ (Rom 8:4, 14).[110] Presumably, the faithful community's encounters with the Spirit also involve some sort of personal and subjective intimacy left unexplained (cf. 8:16). With the aspects of walking according to and being lead by the Spirit, we are probably dealing with a *halakah*, or ethical pattern of living (cf. Gal 5:16–25; 1 Thess 4:1–8; Phil 1:27; 3:17–19).[111] As Israel's abiding in the Law meant keeping God's commandments (e.g., Josh 22:5; Deut 8:6), so those who are "in Christ" must obey God and operate in and with the Spirit's guidance.

Did Paul believe that such direction manifested itself through spiritual gifts and ecstatic experiences? If so, then the formula for power over sinful living would have amounted to a precept that the more "charismatic" the congregation, the more holy the people. The sinful behavior of the Corinthian congregation, however, contradicts this notion. Even so, Paul is still more mystical than contemporary Western

---

105. See the various interpretations of Rom 7:7–25 in Cranfield, *Romans* 1.342–47; Moo, *Romans*, 423–31.

106. This new and transformed law may be contrasted with the Mosaic Law in 7:4–6. Dunn, *Romans*, 1.422, rightly observes that Paul's thought here is not much different than Matt 5:17.

107. περὶ ἁμαρτίας: 8:3; cf. LXX Lev 4:3; 5:6–13; 9:2; 14:31; Num 6:16; Isa 53:10; Heb 10:6–8.

108. On Christ as the sin offering, see further Wright, *Christian Origins*, 220–25; Wilckens, *Römer*, 2.126–28.

109. Cf. Dunn, *Romans*, 1.422. Witherington, *Romans*, 214, is instructive regarding Rom 8:1–3: "The declaration of no condemnation on those in Christ (v. 1) is based on the judgment of condemnation on sinfulness exercised on Christ on the cross (v. 3)."

110. On the corporate dimension of the passage see Jewett, *Romans*, 496.

111. In agreement with Grieb, *Story of Romans*, 77.

sensibilities sometimes allow.[112] The manifestation of the Spirit appeared to Paul and his churches in rather overt and supernatural ways not far removed from the spiritual phenomena described in the early chapters of Acts in which we see believers filled with the Spirit, proclaiming the gospel boldly, operating with signs and wonders, maintaining united fellowship and selfless giving, and seeking God's will through prayer and fasting (e.g., Acts 2:1–4, 42–47; 4:24–31; 13:1–3; Luke 4:1; cf. Rom 15:18–19; Gal 3:5; 1 Cor 2:4–5; Eph 5:18–21).

We see similarities between such phenomena and the conduct Paul requires in Rom 12–13—the Roman Christians are not to be assimilated with the attitudes of the present fallen age;[113] they are to live in selflessness, unity, and humility in the church or "body of Christ," and serve one another with spiritual gifts and love (12:1–10; cf. 14:1–23), being zealous in Spirit and service to the Lord (12:11), rejoicing in hope, persevering in tribulation, persistent in prayer (12:12), giving to the needs of the saints, avoiding pride and conceit, and attempting to live peacefully with everyone including outsiders such as their persecutors and civil authorities (12:14—13:7). The Mosaic Law and its commandments are fulfilled by them when they love their neighbors as themselves (Rom 13:8–10; cf. Gal 5:14; Lev 19:18; Matt 22:37–40), and rather than gratifying the "flesh" and practice vices they are to conduct themselves in ways that characterize Christ (Rom 13:11–14). By practicing such activities, it is not difficult to see how the congregation would be accomplishing what Paul meant by *walking according to the Spirit*.

Moreover, Paul no doubt refers to the same kind of walking and being lead by the Spirit as in Gal 5:16–25. Those who operate in the Spirit bear righteous "fruit" exemplified by love and other virtuous deeds (5:22), and these are set in contrast to vices or "works of the flesh" that lead to exclusion from God's kingdom (5:19–21). For Paul in Romans, to walk according to the "flesh" leads to sin and death, but to walk according to the Spirit leads to life and peace (Rom 8:4–6). *If the believers live according to the flesh and its deeds—that is, if they operate in the sinful ways of the old era and succumb to the practices of the old self concomitant with unbelievers who are not "in Christ"—they will fall away into eternal death rather than receive eternal life* (8:13; cf. 6:21–23; 1:18–32; 13:12–13). As in Paul's other letters, then, Romans shares the perspective that a believer's constant succumbing to the desires of the sinful nature and practicing vices can lead to apostasy and condemnation.[114] Oppositely, believers who walk in the Spirit and remain in Christ face no condemnation (8:1, 6, 9).

112. Cf. Christoph, *Pneuma und das neue Sein.*

113. Perhaps this is another hint that Paul is writing from Corinth and is seeing first-hand what he perceives as sinful depravity of non-believing culture in that city.

114. We notice that ζῆτε in 8:13 is in the present tense perhaps supporting the notion that living

For Paul "justification/righteousness by faith" and "judgment by works" are not contradictory notions. *Righteousness by faith requires faithfulness and ongoing obedience to the purpose of God in the eschatological era marked by the Christ's advent and atoning death. In such a context the "works" of the believer are not works of the Law, but obedient behavior prompted by the Spirit's guidance that manifests itself in ways comparable with the paraenetic acts Paul describes in Rom 12–15,* such as not conforming to or assimilating with the mindset of the fallen age nor its haughty values and vices (12:2–3; 13:13–14), not retaliating evil for evil when persecuted by outsiders (12:14–21), and loving one's neighbor, which in a practical sense would be inclusive of welcoming weak believers to one's fellowship at the dinner table (13:8–11; cf. 14:1–15:1–3, 7). Through Romans, as in Paul's other letters and the gospels likewise, we see the preeminence of love for early Christian ethics.[115] Such types of behaviors as in Rom 12–15 should characterize the believers' lifestyle; they are so vital that, if not practiced, such "works" would count *against* believers on judgment day. An expectation may be that the love and forgiveness God has shown to the believers in Christ is to be reciprocated with the obligation that believers are to love and forgive others. Paul seems to share this conviction in common with other emerging Christian groups, and the idea was in fact taught by Jesus (e.g., Matt 18:21–35; Luke 11:4; John 13:34; 1 John 4:11).

SUFFERING, FOREKNOWLEDGE, AND THE FINAL PERSEVERANCE OF THE ELECT (8:14–39; 11:2–6)

Romans shares in common with Galatians imagery from Israel's exodus, especially in 8:14–17 in which the early Christ-followers, like the Israelites before them, have been adopted as sons, freed from slavery, and experience the presence of God's Spirit. The concept of fearless believers has as its negative counterpart recollections of Israel's fear of enemies in the wilderness that prompted their wanting to return back to Egypt (Rom 8:15; cf. Exod 14:10–12; Num 14). In the new exodus described in Isa 41:8–16; 43:1–7; 44:1–15 God affirms his faithfulness to Israel in bringing about salvation after divine judgment.[116] In this eschatological journey God guides his people, and together with those whom God has gathered among the nations/

---

in the "flesh" is not merely a one time event but a lifestyle. Paul does not hold to a legalistic idea found in later church fathers who believed that if Christians were to commit a single sin after baptism, this would be enough to jeopardize their hope for eternal life.

115. Contrast Hays, *Moral Vision*, who does not highlight the prominence of love for NT ethics.

116. See further Conrad, "'Fear Not' Oracles," 129–52; Wright, "New Exodus, New Inheritance," 26–35.

Gentiles they make their journey through the wilderness and experience a final deliverance by the Redeemer from Zion (cf. Isa 59:20–21).

These vestiges from Israel's traditions seem to have informed Paul's view of salvation as both "now" and "not yet." The believers have been redeemed from slavery to sin and death through Christ (Rom 3:21–25; 8:1–4), and yet their final redemption awaits them at the culmination of the eschaton. For Paul the end takes place when righteousness is restored to the cosmos and the believers' bodies are transformed by the future resurrection (8:19–25; 11:15, 26–27). Until then, they must persevere through sufferings and struggles against the "flesh" as they make their way through the spiritual wilderness of the salvific "now" and "not yet." Even so, the community in Christ are not alone on their mission and have no reason to fear because as the Divine Presence guided, fed, and sustained Israel throughout her journey so the Spirit guides God's people in the new era, warring against the "flesh" and making intercession for them (Rom 8:4–14, 26 cf. Isa 44:1–3; 63:9–14).[117]

Unlike the letters to the Galatians and Corinthians, Paul gives no warnings about the Roman congregation's potential to apostatize in the metaphoric wilderness. Instead of arousing godly fear in them, he encourages them not to fear but to be confident that no external forces have the power to overcome God's love for them (Rom 8:16, 28–39). Despite potential hardships, God is faithful and the love that God and Christ have for believers remains constant (Rom 8:35, 37, 39; cf. 1:7; 5:5; 2 Cor 5:14; 13:13).[118] This congregation escapes the warnings we find in some other letters due perhaps in part to Paul's lack of familiarity with the congregation and that no major crisis in this church is at stake (see above). Paul is not writing to a "fleshly" congregation like the Corinthians, or a church that he cannot even give a customary thanksgiving to God for, like the Galatians; the Romans reportedly have a reputation of being "full of goodness" and obedience (Rom 15:14–15; 16:19). His encouraging words likewise betray a context in which Christian suffering is the issue, not congregational factions or immorality. The audience is "us" (8:28, 31–32, 35–37, 39), inclusive of Paul, spiritual brothers and sisters (8:29), the "elect" (8:33), and "those who love God" (8:28). The last of these phrases has a rich Jewish background, possibly presupposing the Deuteronomic tradition in which the community of Israel are those who love God and keep his commandments (Deut 5:10; 7:9).[119]

117. The Spirit is viewed metaphorically as water poured out in the desert (Isa 32:15–16; 35:6–10; 41:17–20; etc.), and God's Spirit became associated with the renewed eschatological era (Isa 59:21).

118. In Rom 8:39 τῆς ἀγάπης τοῦ θεοῦ is a subjective genitive; cf. Wallace, *Greek Grammar*, 114 (cf. Rom 8:35). The longer phrase "the love of God, which is in Christ Jesus" perhaps suggests that God's love for "us" is known via Christ's love for "us."

119. See also Sir 2:15–16; *T. Iss.* 5.1–2; CD 19.1–2.

Paul has reconfigured this thought to refer to the Christ-followers, and his assumption is that they love and obey God. They are the community "in Christ" and identified as "children of God" that are led by the Spirit (Rom 8:1, 14–17). A reciprocating relationship exists between God's love for this people (8:35, 37, 39) and their love for God (8:28); albeit it is certainly God who first initiated his love for them (Rom 5:5, 8; cf. 1 John 4:10, 19).

With these assumptions in mind Paul affirms that the community in Christ will be finally saved in the eschaton. No creature is able to separate the believers from God's love (8:39), and they will be "glorified," a concept referring to the eschatological blessing related to the final salvation (8:18–19, 23–24a, 30). Paul assures the Romans that God works out all things,[120] even bad things, for the "good" or spiritual benefit of those who love God, to those who are called according to purpose (8:28).[121] Paul's objective is to show that persecution, other sufferings, and other external hardships as well as demonic powers (8:38: οὔτε ἄγγελοι οὔτε ἀρχαὶ ... οὔτε δυνάμεις) cannot wrench those who are "in Christ" from the love God and Christ have for them. They need not be fearful or ashamed of the gospel of Christ when such opposition comes their way. Hardships build endurance and thus confirm the believers' faith (1:16; 5:1–5), and the catalogue of hardships Paul mentions in Rom 8:31–39 resembles his "boast" of sufferings that he personally experienced and records in 2 Cor 11:21–29, which establishes his conviction that God's power is greatly manifested through human weakness.

In light of the rest of the letter, however, this confidence could hardly be saying that perseverance to final salvation is automatically guaranteed for every individual believer regardless of whether they fall into unbelief, disobedience, or immoral behavior.[122] Such a meaning can only be maintained at the expense of other Pauline

---

120. Or alternatively, "all things work together for good." The verse in fact may be interpreted several ways. For discussion see Cranfield, *Romans*, 1.425–28; BDAG, 969; Zerwick, *Grammatical Analysis*, 477.

121. Presumably, in 8:28 God's purpose is in view even though God is not mentioned: τοῖς κατὰ πρόθεσιν κλητοῖς οὖσιν (cf. 9:11). Moo, *Romans*, 529–30, associates the "good" here with a goal to final salvation that is inclusive of things in this life contributing to that goal. This understanding of "good" would include godly character building rather than selfish human desires such as personal wealth (cf. Rom 5:3–4).

122. Witherington, *Paul's Narrative Thought World*, 232–33, adds that what "Paul does not include in his listing in 8:35–39 is the individual himself or herself, who may indeed commit apostasy." This point may have some validity, but it must be stressed that Paul is not primarily concerned with individual believers in this passage but the corporate elect, and so we probably would not expect him to include language about the individual self for that reason. We must also take into consideration that no created thing (κτίσις ἑτέρα: "another created thing" [P46, D]; or τις κτίσις ἑτέρα: "any other created thing") can sever God from his elect in Rom 8:39. Either he is using τις κτίσις ἑτέρα in a qualified sense that does not go beyond the categories of external persecution, sufferings, and demonic opposition in

thoughts in Romans that suggest the possibility of believers committing sin and apostasy with spiritual death as the end result (cf. 8:13; 11:20–22; 14:10–12, 13, 15, 20–21, 23; cf. 2:6–16; 6:16). Romans 8:28–39 does not affirm that a believer can turn from faith, commit idolatry, or live according to the lusts and the "flesh" and still expect to never be separated from God and Christ. Paul focuses on conflicts related to human suffering. Hardships and hostile forces such as human persecutors of the church, hunger, nakedness, Satan, and his minions do not have the power to sever the relationship between God and his elect. Most *likely he does not wish to include vices or unbelief to the list of hardships and opposing forces in 8:35–39 because, based on what he writes elsewhere in this letter, such things can undermine salvation, and it would be rhetorically counterproductive to include caveats and conditions at this point when his objective in this passage is to encourage the congregation.*

Paul's so-called *ordo salutis* of the elect in Christ being foreknown, predestined, called, justified, and glorified in 8:29–30 likewise makes proper sense through the lens of Paul encouraging followers of Christ to persevere in times of suffering.[123] He does not bother to unpack the content of these words, and so we are left to speculate much about what he meant by these terms in this context and whether he is adopting traditional material.[124] Such observations make me wary of viewpoints that would interpret this passage as the cornerstone of Paul's soteriology.[125] The apostle wanted to comfort the congregation and encourage them in perseverance, having just mentioned that suffering belongs to the current "now" and "not yet" age of the believers (cf. 8:17–24). In the midst of the struggles experienced in the present life before the complete redemption of the cosmos is fully realized, Paul assures the church of its final salvation. God has determined that the elect community in Christ will endure to the end of the age, despite hardships and opposition. God foreknew and predestined

---

this context (cf. Rom 13:9; 1 Tim 1:10), or unqualified and hence, even other categories that he does not mention in this context, such as vices, unbelief, and human decisions are nonetheless unable to destroy the entire elect body of believers. The former is possible if Paul deliberately intended to exclude vices and unbelief, but the latter is very similar to the way in which Paul argues for the election of corporate Israel in Rom 9–11: not even the unbelief of many Israelites ruins Israel's corporate election.

123. Garlington, *Faith, Obedience, and Perseverance*, 158–61 rightly observes that there is no uniform order of salvation presented by Paul (e.g., 1 Cor 6:11) and that "sanctification" is missing from Paul's list in Romans 8:30. He prefers the term *historia salutis*.

124. Uncommon Pauline word usage and the aorist tenses of the verbs have led some scholars to believe 8:29–30 may not have originated with Paul: e.g., Tobin, *Paul's Rhetoric*, 294–96 who also notices the lack of symmetry between Pauline elements in the clauses, "to be conformed to the image of his Son, that he might be the firstborn among many brethren."

125. Gundry Volf, *Paul and Perseverance*, 9–14, makes these verses foundational for interpreting Paul's view of perseverance in relation to salvation, and so her arguments generally come against the reality of apostasy in the warning passages of the Pauline corpus. See Oropeza, *Paul and Apostasy*, 28–34, for a response to this position.

them to "be conformed to the image of God's son" (8:29–30), which anticipates their future resurrection. Like Jesus before them, they also will be raised from the dead (cf. 1 Cor 15:49; 2 Cor 3:18; Phil 3:10, 21).[126] They are "called" (κλητοῖς 8:28/ἐκάλεσεν: Rom 8:30; cf. 1:6–7; 9:12, 24–26; 11:29) according to God's divine purpose, which is to establish his children in the new creation and ultimately show mercy to all people (cf. 8:17–25; chs. 9–11). This call may imply a creative act of God calling into being "a people for himself."[127] The emphasis in this verse rests on the calling of a corporate people rather than individuals. The community is "justified"/"made righteous" (ἐδικαίωσεν) and "glorified" (ἐδόξασεν); among other implications, the use of these words suggest that the inevitable goal for them is final salvation with their bodies raised from the dead. The glorification also marks a finalized reversal of the "glory" humanity originally exchanged in their first instance of apostasy against God (1:23).[128] Paul unveils in apocalyptic fashion God's plan of salvation for them from start to finish.

The concepts of foreknowing (προγινώσκω) and predestinating (προορίζω) seem to preclude human involvement in the initiating processes of salvation. The term προορίζω is not entirely synonymous with προγινώσκω but, as Brendan Byrne affirms, it "adds the sense that God has formed a plan in respect of those who have been chosen: cf. 1 Cor 2:7 and the development of this Pauline usage in Eph 1:5, 11."[129] Although προγινώσκω can mean mere knowledge beforehand, it often means more than this (e.g., Acts 26:5; 2 Pet 3:17) and conveys a sense of God's prechoice or prior love for the object upon which God foreknows (Gen 18:19; Exod 2:25; Jer 1:5; Hos 13:5; Amos 3:1–2; Acts 2:23; 1 Pet 1:2, 20).[130] Paul emphasizes God's gracious and prior choice of the elect, and human effort or works related to the Law

126. See Dunn, *Romans*, 1.482–84, for the significance of "image" and Adam Christology of this verse.

127. Cf. Byrne, *Romans*, 269, who references Hos 11:1. On the call of God see further 1 Cor 1:2; 7:17–24; 1 Thess 5:24; 2 Thess 1:11; Phil 3:11–14; Eph 4:1. For references on the divine purpose see πρόθεσις in Rom 9:11; Eph 1:11; 3:11; 2 Tim 1:9; cf. Isa 46:10; Rengstorf, "πρόθυμος, προθυμία," 6.694–95. We are not specifically told in Rom 8:28–39 whether an individual has the freedom to reject God's calling. Paul is not centering his discussion in this passage on individuals but on the corporate elect pertaining to the universal church "in Christ." If Rom 11:29 is brought into the discussion, divine gifts and calling in relation to corporate and elect Israel are irrevocable, and yet many Israelites have committed apostasy (cf. Rom 9); thus it seems that, on the human side of this equation, the irrevocable gifts and calling of God can be rejected by individuals.

128. Along these lines see further Dunn, *Romans*, 1.485.

129. Byrne, *Romans*, 272.

130. See foreknowledge also in Sir 23:20; 42:18–21; 33:7–13; 39:16, 20, 34; Jdt 9:5–6; Wis 8:8; 19:1; *L.A.B.* 52.4; *T. Mos.* 1.12–14; 12.4–13; Jacobs and Krienke, "Foreknowledge, Providence, Predestination," 1.692–95. On God knowing the Christ-followers see also Gal 4:9; 1 Cor 8:3; 13:12. Schreiner, *Romans*, 452, uses the term "covenantal love."

are excluded so that prideful Jews and Gentiles could not boast about their election (e.g., Rom 2:17–29; 4:1–6; 9:11–12; 11:5–6, 20–22). The elect body of believers are predestined to become adopted children via the sonship of Christ,[131] and Christ is the "firstborn" child of God, beloved and chosen (cf. Rom 1:3–4; Eph 1:4–11; Acts 2:23; 10:42; Rev 2:26–27; Ps 2:7; Isa 11:4; Exod 4:22). This word about God's children recalls earlier exodus intimations from 8:14–17, but in 8:29–30 the eschatological tension of two ages and entire salvific plan of God is seen in retrospect. From a predetermined point of view, the elect people will live to see their spiritual Zion and final salvation, as did Christ their forerunner.

In Rom 9–11 a more complete understanding of election and predestination of God's people comes into view, as we will observe below.[132] At this point it will suffice to look further into divine foreknowledge. In Rom 11 God foreknows Israel and has not rejected or cast away his people (11:1–2; cf. 1 Kgs 12:22; Ps 93[94]:14–15), and here again we find the emphasis relates to the people of God rather than individuals. Paul cites from the Elijah narrative that God has a remnant of 7,000 who have not bowed the knee to Baal (Rom 11:2–4; cf. 1 Kgs 19:18; cf. 19:10). The original text seems to be altered from a future tense to the aorist in Romans, and Paul may have added "to myself" (ἐμαυτῷ) in order to emphasize God's grace in the election of this remnant, which is then used to demonstrate that God has not forsaken present-day Israel.[133] Israel's election is by grace and not by their personal merits or law keeping. Paul's reading of 1 Kings assumes God either graciously preserves or at least assists this remnant in their ability to remain faithful to God (cf. Rom 14:4c; 1 Cor 10:13). The word καταλείπω in Rom 11:4 normally means "leave behind" (Gen 14:10), but Paul seems to be using it in terms of divine preservation.[134] Whatever else Paul might

---

131. On this view see Allen, "Old Testament Background," 104–8. On predestination/foreordination see further Add Esth 11:12; 10:4, 10; *Odes Sol.* 7.9; 8.13–18; CD 2.7–18; 1QS 3.15; 1QH 7.8–21; 18.9; 20.31–32; Jacobs and Krienke, "Foreknowledge, Providence, Predestination," 1.695–96.

132. Schnelle, *Paulus*, 401–3, rightly associates calling and election in Rom 8 with 9–11 but comes to the conclusion that Paul is advocating a view of double predestination, following the lead of Maier, *Mensch und freier Wille*, 356–57. However, even if God calls and rejects whom God wills in Rom 9:16, Paul does not affirm from this that those whom God rejects in this verse and elsewhere in Rom 9 are eternally damned. Eskola, *Theodicy and Predestination*, 160, 171–75, 309, rightly denies double predestination, affirming instead that the Pauline predestination has salvation as its goal (e.g., Rom 11:32). On a corporate level, in my view, this is certainly true of Rom 9–11.

133. Among the reliable extant sources Paul may have used, the LXX reads "you will leave in Israel seven thousand . . ." but the Lucianic version of it has "I will leave from Israel seven thousand . . ." and the Masoretic reads "I will leave over in Israel seven thousand . . ."; cf. Jewett, *Romans*, 657. The word "Israel" is omitted from Paul's citation of 1 Kings perhaps to give the impression for his predominately Gentile audience that the Israelites are not the only ones who are faithful or elect.

134. The word could be translated either as the passive "left" or the more active "kept." It can also mean "forsake" or "abandon" (Deut 29:4; Sir 13:4), which makes for an interesting word play with Paul's

intend by their preservation, he does not appear to be denying human freedom and responsibility (Rom 11:14, 23) or the necessity of human faith and endurance (11:20, 22). This divine preservation, then, may be interpreted as God strengthening the 7,000 with sufficient grace to secure their refusal to commit apostasy, a result bestowed to them because of their decision to remain faithful to God; or perhaps more likely, it means that God physically protects the faithful 7,000 via their escape from Jezebel's persecutions that would attempt to force them to commit idolatry.[135]

As a former Pharisee he probably had been influenced by Pharisaic thoughts on divine determination and human freedom, and if so, he may have still believed in both divine sovereignty and human freedom (cf. Josephus, *Ant.* 13.172; 18.1; *J.W.* 2.162–63; Phil 2:12–13).[136] God's favoring of Israel in any case highlights that they have not lost their election despite their unbelief (cf. Rom 11:2, 28). And if divine foreknowledge in this case includes prescience, God may have known about Israel's apostasies before Israel committed them, and yet God chose this people anyway.[137] Hence, according to Paul, God's foreknowledge does not seem to be based on his foreseeing ahead of time the individuals who would choose him and thus elect them on that basis (Arminianism); nor does God's foreknowledge center on a seemingly arbitrary selection of individuals to final salvation and others to damnation (Calvinism); nor yet does God choose this world over a plethora of other possible worlds so that individuals who happen to believe in the world God has chosen are elect on that basis.[138] Paul's focus is not on the individual—God has chosen the people of Israel and the church "in Christ," and foreknowledge in 11:2 stresses the object of God's people as a corporate community.

This same emphasis holds true for the way Paul speaks about the elect whom God foreknows in Rom 8:28–39.[139] The "elect" in this pericope identify the com-

---

use of ἀπωθέω in Rom 11:1–2.

135. Marshall, *Kept by the Power*, 104, adds that Israel's response in Rom 11:5, 7 is not divinely predetermined, nor is God's grace "limited to the number of those who actually responded to it."

136. In Jewish tradition see also Sir 15:11–17; 4 Ezra 8.55–56; *m. Pirke Abot* 3.15; *Mekilta Exod.* 15.26; *b. Niddah* 16b, and further Witherington, *Romans*, 246–49. Sanders, *Paul and Palestinian Judaism*, 257–70, argues that even from Qumran literature both predestination and human choice are affirmed.

137. Kaminsky, *Yet Jacob I Loved*, examines mostly the Hebrew scriptures and arrives at the conclusion that, among other things, Israel's election does not depend on her failing to always live up to her given responsibilities. See also Dunn, *Romans*, 2.645.

138. The third option is a mediating philosophical position that operates within the framework of Western thought related to individualism. Of course, both Calvinist and Arminian positions have further nuances that do not always conform to the ones mentioned above. On the debate see my discussion in Oropeza, *Paul and Apostasy*, 15–21, and lists of sources in the appendix (252–54).

139. Notice Moo, *Romans*, 675, who connects foreknowledge with election in Rom 11:2 and rightly

munity of believers in Christ, not individuals per se.[140] The plural "elect" (ἐκλεκτῶν
θεοῦ), and further plurals describing "those" (τοῖς) the ones being "called" (κλητοῖς
οὖσιν), "whom" (οὓς) "many brothers" (πολλοῖς ἀδελφοῖς) and "these" (τούτους), is
language typical of Paul when referring to or addressing a group rather than singling
out individuals. When he addresses the congregation with second- and third-person
singulars, something not done in this pericope, the passages seem to have more
special relevance to individuals, and human responsibility in relation to faith comes
into view (10:6, 9–10; 11:18–24; 14:1–6, 10–12, 23; cf. 8:2).[141]

This does not mean, however, that all language about election in Romans is
corporate. It is assumed that Abraham was an individual elected by God to become
the forefather of the Israelites and faithful Gentiles. In terms of Pauline soteriology,
however, Abraham's election did not make his righteousness/justification automatic:
he exercises faith in order to be justified (cf. Rom 4:3–5; Gal 3:6–9).[142] Paul's references from the Scriptures on individuals such as Isaac, Esau, Jacob, and Pharaoh
address the issue of election (cf. Rom 9:6–19; see below), but their election or re-

affirms, "Paul reflects the common OT and Jewish corporate sense of election, according to which
God's choosing of the nation Israel guarantees blessings and benefits (as well as responsibility . . . Amos
3:2 . . .) to the people as a whole but does not guarantee salvation for every single Israelite." Moo,
however, opines that those foreknown in Rom 8 refer to individual believers rather than the "church"
or those "in Christ," claiming that nothing is said here about the latter phrase (532). But we need only
backup to 8:1 to find the believers participating "in Christ," a verse that Moo (536) uses in reference to
glorification in Rom 8:30.

140. Rightly stressing the corporate importance of election in Romans are, e.g., Tobin, *Paul's
Rhetoric*, 297; Byrne, *Romans*, 272; Fitzmyer, *Romans*, 563; Wright, *Climax of the Covenant*, 238–39.
Abasciano, "Corporate Election in Romans 9," 351–71, interacts with individual and corporate language of election in Romans and rightly concludes, "the group as primary and the individual as secondary. Such an outlook finds (1) the corporate identity and reality to transcend that of the individual on
his [sic] own; (2) that some things that are true of the group might not be true of the individual; and (3)
that the individual's experience of corporate realities depends on his [sic] participation in the group"
(170). These points are valid, but some aspects of the article are criticized by Schreiner, "Corporate and
Individual Election," 373–86, who also responds that one "cannot have a corporate group without the
individual. A corporate group of believers cannot exist if individuals do not believe, and so too corporate election cannot exist without individual election" (383–84). I would suggest that for Paul, Christ is
the elect individual in whom the corporate elect finds its identity. The individual's election stands "in
Christ" and falls if severed from this relationship.

141. Paul also addresses the interlocutor in 9:19–20 with second-person singulars.

142. Rufus is presented as an elect individual, but not much can be derived about his final salvation on that basis (Rom 16:13). Perhaps Rufus is designated for a special task or ministry, which
is sometimes how the term "election" is used by early Jewish and Christian sources; see the many
examples of this alternative in Klein, *New Chosen People*, though unfortunately not all of his examples
are convincing. Abasciano, "Corporate Election in Romans 9," 356n20, notices that Rufus' election is
"in the Lord," which attests to corporate election. For the individual election position in Rom 9–11 see
Piper, *Justification of God*, 163–86; Schreiner, "Does Romans 9 Teach?," 89–106; idem, "Corporate and
Individual Election," 373–86.

jection by God is brought out to make more relevant points to the Romans about communities such as Israel (9:23–10:3, 18–21; 11:26–32), the Gentile believers (9:24, 30; 11:13, 25), and the faithful remnant (11:1–7). Likewise in this context, Paul considers himself elect not by virtue of his own independent status with God but because he is a member of the elect remnant of Israel (11:1–7). As such, language highlighting individuality in chapters 9–11 rhetorically points to a climax at the end of chapter 11 in which Paul reveals the ultimate destinations of corporate Israel and the Gentiles.[143] For the Romans whom Paul is addressing, *the individual is elect by participating in the elect community "in Christ," and the assurances of final salvation given to that community pertain to the individual as long as that individual is identified as belonging to the elect community.* If Paul is consistent here with what he teaches elsewhere, the "no condemnation" (8:1, 29–39) the elect community will experience in the age to come does not pertain to individuals who fall away from being "in Christ" in the present age (e.g., Rom 8:13; 11:20–22; 14:15; Gal 5:2–4; 1 Cor 5:5; 10:12; etc.).

This emphasis that Paul makes on the community is not superficial but confirmed by the citation of Ps 43[44]:22 (Rom 8:36). It is introduced, no doubt, because of its relevance to *corporate suffering*. The psalm alternates between the king ("I") and his people ("we"), and is intended to be a national lament and prayer in which the psalmist requests God not to reject Israel forever (Ps 43[44]:9, 23). Israel suffers in the midst of the nations and a hostile environment, yet it has remained faithful to God (Ps 43[44]:10–16, 22; cf. vv. 17–18). Paul applies the "we" of this psalm to himself and the elect believers who for Christ's sake are the corporate sufferers.[144] As "sheep" who face death "all the day long," one could almost hear Jesus' words for his followers to take up their crosses daily (Luke 9:22; cf. 1 Cor 15:31). Paul's citation is intended to express the elect community's solidarity with the sufferings of Christ.[145] Being transformed into the image of Christ involves suffering, but those who are "in Christ" can be assured that God will never abandon them.

Moreover, if the new exodus-wilderness is still in view with the concept of predestination at Rom 8:29–30, then the remnant of God's people who make their trek across the metaphoric wilderness, together with the faithful Gentiles, are predestined for the final deliverance of the redeemer from Zion. God predicted through his prophet that such an event would take place, and from Paul's perspective God's word

143. On the importance of the climax of Rom 9–11 as ch. 11, see the rhetorical suspense model of Cosgrove, *Elusive Israel*.

144. Rom 8:36: "For your sake" refers most immediately to 8:35; hence, Paul is likely addressing Christ rather than God.

145. Cf. Luz, "Paul as Mystic," 141; Jewett, *Romans*, 548.

will inevitably be fulfilled. In this manner both Jews and Gentiles are predestined by God to experience this deliverance, signifying final salvation in which the elect people's destiny is bound up with Christ's, who is the "firstborn" among many spiritual siblings via his resurrection.[146] Such thoughts about travel would make good sense to Paul's audience. Any ancient pilgrim would know that a wilderness journey is fraught with dangers from bandits, wild beasts, and the unpredictable elements. There is the potential for sojourners to lose their lives. Yet those familiar with the exodus story knew quite well that, even though many Israelites never made it to land of Canaan, God's promise that they would inherit the land held true despite their disobedience in the wilderness. A remnant always survives. The blessing of the land that God promised to the community as a whole did not come to pass for every individual in that community. Many had fallen victims to unbelief and vice.

The upshot of all this is that even though Paul assumes the election of God's community is entirely by grace, this does not nullify the requisite for individuals to exercise the obedience of faith, and if divine grace is given for this requisite also, it does not appear to be to the extent that individual believers cannot reject Christ or that grace. *In short, the divine election, foreknowledge, predestination, and perseverance of the community in Christ does not preclude the possibility of individual believers committing apostasy and falling into spiritual death.*[147] Likewise Israel's election does not preclude that individual Israelites can and do commit apostasy. Nevertheless, each individual congregant hearing Paul's encouraging words in 8:28–39 would still be able to take comfort in God's love for them personally. Such a person could maintain confidence in final salvation so long as that individual remained "in Christ." *Individuals have no claim to the salvific promises given to the Christ-community without actually being part of it and remaining in it.*[148]

---

146. Is the starting point of predestination in 8:29 the prophetic scriptures or is it pretemporal (i.e., from before the foundation of the world)? Paul does not give us a clear answer. Romans 1:2–4 would suggest Israel's scriptures as the starting point. See similar problems in 1 Cor 2:7; 2 Tim 1:9, and contrast Eph 1:3–11; 3:8–10.

147. Contrast Moo, *Romans*, 533; Schreiner, *Romans*, 454; and Gundry Volf, *Paul and Perseverance*, who writes: "For Paul the individual Christian is always a member of the Christian community and the community is always made up of individuals. There can be no certainty for the group then without certainty for its individual members" (14). While it is correct to affirm a reciprocating relationship between elect community and individual, election pertaining to final perseverance is not individualistically based for Paul.

148. Jocz, *Theology of Election*, 191, rightly affirms: "Only in his togetherness with the fellow-man [*sic*] is the individual elected. The Kingdom of God does not consist of isolated individuals, but in the fellowship of the Saints."

THE FATE OF APOSTATE ISRAEL IN ROM 9–11 (9:1–13)

Paul's letter to the Romans comes to a climax in chapters 9–11.[149] After affirming in chapter 8 God's faithfulness to those who are his elect, the upsetting reality for Paul is that many of his kinsmen the Israelites (Ἰσραηλίτης: Rom 9:4) did not share his faith. Paul therefore sets out to explain the predicament of Israel in relation to God's eschatological plan of salvation. How is it that God is righteous if Israel does not accept the gospel Paul preaches? The inquiry assumes something both Paul and his readers seem to believe—that the Israelites' election from God has not prevented many of them from unbelief and apostasy. This is why Paul has great anguish over his kinsmen (9:1–5). He wishes or would pray that he himself were "accursed" (9:3: ἀνάθεμα), that is, brought under a religious ban and devoted to destruction (cf. Lev 27:28; Deut 13:18; Josh 7:11–13; Judg 1:17; Zech 14:11).[150] This is the same word Paul uses against his opponents in Galatia (Gal 1:8–9) as well as to pronounce a curse on those who do not love the Lord (1 Cor 16:22). The implication in this self-curse is clear: he wishes himself to be cursed because he thinks that unbelieving Israel is cursed.

The ἀνάθεμα is "from the Christ" (ἀπὸ τοῦ Χριστοῦ). This suggests at least two things. First, the ban is related to being cut off from Christ, which brings into sharper relief his previous words about perseverance for the community "in Christ" (8:1, 39) and anticipates unbelieving Israel being cut off from the metaphoric olive tree (cf. 11:17–24).[151] The Gentiles are also warned in the same passage that the same thing could happen to them. Such words evoke the warning to the Galatians not to commit apostasy and be cut off from Christ and divine grace (Gal 5:2–4). Second, the definite article before Χριστός suggests the meaning of "the Christ" rather than "Christ" (cf. Rom 9:5).[152] They do not believe Jesus is the Messiah, and their unbelief (cf. ἀπιστία: 11:20) has led to the apostle's current anguish. They lack faith and fail to see that Jesus as the Christ is both the goal and end of the Law (cf. 9:31–10:4). *For Paul the Israelites are therefore cut off from salvation in Christ—they have committed apostasy by repudiating the salvific eschatological plan of salvation that God has ushered in though the Christ.*

Romans 9–11 may be understood, then, as a theodicy focusing on the question of God's faithfulness to the people of Israel despite their predicament of unbelief.

149. Many scholars have noticed this: e.g., Wright, *Climax of the Covenant*, 234; Grieb, *Story of Romans*, 86–87; Stendahl, *Paul among Jews and Gentiles*, 4; Wilckens, *Römer*, 2.181.

150. See further sources in, e.g., Stuart, "Curse," 1.1218–19.

151. Some interpreters go further to stress the cutting off is from the community and also involves a reversing of baptism: see, e.g., Käsemann, *Romans*, 158; Jewett, *Romans*, 560–61.

152. Cf. Dunn, *Romans*, 2.525.

This theme about God's faithfulness has been carried over from the thesis of the entire letter (1:16–17). If Paul is defending this thesis in chapters 9–11 this would help explain why he cites or alludes to so many scriptures. If he considers the scriptures to be the "oracles of God" (3:1–2) and "holy scriptures" (1:2) they would help establish his arguments. When we compare all his letters, the majority of Paul's citations come from Romans, and the majority of these come from chapters 9–11.[153]

Most scholars agree that the general structure of Rom 9–11 takes specific turns or section breaks at 9:6, 9:30, 11:1, and 11:33.[154] While there is some dispute over the substructure, a familiar outline would be as follows:[155] 9:1–5, Paul's anguish over Israel; 9:6–29, God's freedom and purpose of election; 9:30—10:21, Israel's stumbling to attain righteousness by faith; 11:1–32, God's mercy on Israel and the Gentiles; 11:33–36, doxology on the unfathomable ways of God.

Romans 9:6 stands out as the main thesis of chapters 9–11: "Now it is not as though the word of God has failed" (9:6a). Paul wants to defend the view that God's word has not become invalidated despite Israel's failure to receive the same salvation mentioned in Rom 8. Does Paul give satisfying answers to the questions he posits in relation to the thesis? His supporting proof is stated in the next line: "For not all those from Israel are Israel; nor is it so that all Abraham's children are Abraham's seed" (9:6b–7a). After attempting to support his thesis, Paul raises three questions directly related to God in the remainder of the argument:

9:14 – In reference to his discussion of God choosing Jacob over Esau: "Is there not injustice with God?"

9:19 – In reference to God hardening Pharaoh's heart to manifest God's glory and name: "Why then does [God] still find fault? For who has resisted his will?"

11:1 – In reference to 9:6 (that God's word has not failed in relation to apostate Israel): "Has God rejected his people?"[156]

153. Hübner, *Vetus Testamentum*, 144–91, lists 47 pages worth of citations or possible echoes from ancient Jewish-Hebrew texts in Rom 9–11 alone. Hays, *Echoes*, 34, depending on Koch, *Schrift als Zeuge*, 21–24, posits that 51 out of 89 Pauline citations from Israel's scriptures are from Romans.

154. See Dodd, *Romans*, 150, and similar structures in Kim, *God, Israel*, 17–24, 115–21; Jewett, "Following the Argument," 382–89; Hays, *Echoes*, 64.

155. The titles for each of these sections are mine.

156. Subsequent questions that follow up on the heels of 9:19 include 9:20a, 20b, 21, 22, 23–24; 9:30a, 32a; 10:6–7, 8a, 14a, 14b, 14c, 15a, 16b, 18a, 19a. These queries, however, do not present significant breaks in Paul's thought. Most interpreters do maintain another break at the question posed in 9:30: "What then shall we say?" The phrase also introduces 9:14 and is found in other locations to mark apparently a new turn (4:1; 6:1; 7:7; 8:31; 9:14). The query in 9:30, however, does not mention a direct question about God. Instead, it builds on the previous line of thought concerning Jews and Gentiles in

The thesis or *propositio* in 9:6a (God's word has not failed) seems to echo the Isaianic tradition, the source used most often in this section of Romans. Isaiah 59:20[21] defends God's faithfulness in terms of God's words not failing in the mouth of his prophet nor his "seed." The message of Isa 59 appears to be significant for Paul because he cites a portion of it in his climactic ending to affirm "the Deliverer" who comes from Zion will take away the ungodliness of Jacob. The apostle interprets this passage eschatologically, associating the Deliverer as Christ and connecting this idea with the salvation of "all Israel" (Rom 11:26–27). Another possible echo in Rom 9:6 comes from Isa 40:8: "The word of our God abides forever." Isaiah 40 resurfaces again at the end in praise of God's unfathomable wisdom related to his divine purposes (Rom 11:34/Isa 40:13–14). While Paul may have had either Isa 40 or 59 in mind, the evidence is tipped in favor of the latter because both the concepts of "seed" and "word" play a significant part of Paul's message (cf. Rom 9:7–8; 10:6–17). Interestingly, the Isaianic tradition forms an *inclusio* in Rom 9–11; Paul echoes it at the beginning and ending of his message.

Romans 9:6b–9 claims that all those from Israel are not Israel, and all of Abraham's children are not Abraham's "seed." This becomes a catchword for Paul as he makes distinctions within Israel and refers to Gen 21:12 and 18:10–14 to support that Isaac is the true "seed" (σπέρμα) of Abraham and Sarah. The children of promise are the true seed rather than the children of flesh. Here the "promise" and "flesh" are picked up from Israel's privileges in Rom 9:4–5. The flesh also recalls in a negative sense 8:1–17, where Paul contrasted those who live according to the flesh and others who live according to the Spirit—a theme that can be traced back to Paul's opening in 1:3–4.[157] The unspoken premise is that those who live according to the Spirit in 8:1–17 are transformed into the children of "promise" and Abraham's "seed" in Rom 9–11. Paul already affirms in 8:13–17 that those who are led by God's Spirit are the children of God. On the other hand, those after the flesh in Rom 8 will be compared with the children of the "flesh" in Rom 9–11. Romans 4 already mentioned Abraham and his seed in terms of Abraham inheriting the world and becoming the father of many nations (the Gentiles). This promise comes about through righteousness and faith rather than by works or ethnic entitlement.[158]

9:24, which links us back to Paul's argument in 9:19–23. Questions after 11:1 likewise do not address God in any direct fashion (11:2b, 4a, 7a, 11), and while the inquiries in 11:34–35 do, they function in a doxology intended more for praise than debate. Thus, we will focus primarily on how Paul answers the three questions about theodicy in 9:14; 9:19; and 11:1; other questions will be addressed as they relate to this topic.

157. Cf. Lodge, *Romans 9–11*, 43. On possible allusions to Exod 32–34 in Paul's lament in Rom 9:1–5, see Abasciano, *Old Testament in Romans 9.1–9*.

158. The distinction within Israel in 9:6 thus seems to center on physical and believing Israel; it is

The promise coming through Isaac rather than Ishmael (the son of Hagar) leads the apostle to mention God's selection of Jacob over Esau (9:10–13). The latter choice was made that "the purpose of God according to election might stand, not of works but of him who calls" (9:11–12). Two references are used in support of this: Gen 25:23, "The older shall serve the younger," and Mal 1:2–3, "Jacob I have loved, Esau I have hated."[159] In its traditional setting Malachi indicates that the nation of Edom, Esau's descendants, assisted Babylon in the captivity of Jerusalem (cf. Jer 49:14–16; Obed 9–14).[160] It became almost proverbial in early traditions that Edom was a betrayer that would be punished by God for its deeds (Isa 34:9–17; 63:1; Ezek 25:12–14; Joel 3:19; Philo, *Alleg. Interp.* 3.88; *L.A.B.* 32.5). Malachi thus confirms the nation's destruction, and unlike the restoration of Israel (Jacob), God would see to it that Edom would not be restored. While Paul quotes the words of Malachi, he steers in the direction of the Genesis text by emphasizing God's sovereign election to prefer one brother over the other rather than choose on the basis of Esau's (or the Edomites') bad behavior. *Before* either brother could do good or bad deeds God had selected the younger brother over the elder (Rom 9:11–12).

Perhaps Paul understood an assumption from the macro-context of Genesis that he assumed his readers knew: God chooses to show mercy on those who are lowly and insignificant instead of those who are mighty and highly esteemed. In the eyes of society the patriarch Esau is preferred over Jacob, but in God's eyes Jacob is preferred. There is a fairly consistent pattern in Genesis demonstrating God's favor on the ones the culture least expects.[161] We find preferential treatment of the younger brother instead of the firstborn with Jacob over Esau, Abel over Cain, Joseph over

---

not a denial of Israel's election: cf. Jewett, *Romans*, 574–75. Dunn, *Romans*, 1.539–40, rightly affirms that Paul will explain how Israel's election works: "Paul's argument concerns the character and mode rather than the fact of election" (540). An alternative option includes that one Israel is the physical people of Israel and the other is the "Israel of God" comprising of Jews and Gentiles in Christ (cf. Gal 6:16; Rom 2:28–29). Still, another option is that, rhetorically speaking, in 9:6 we are made to think election refers to the second Israel group alone, but then Paul overturns this assumption in Rom 11 by maintaining that even hardened Israel is elect.

159. The idea of God hating Esau should be compared with Luke 14:26, which has Jesus instructing the disciples to hate their own parents. This seems to be a Semitic device highlighting the preference of one over the other. Compare *Jub.* 28.12–13, where Leah is "hated" by Jacob and Rachel "loved." Anyone familiar with the Genesis story (Gen 29–30) would recognize that Jacob did not literally "hate" Leah, especially if they were having sex and producing babies during the same time in which he was supposed to hate her. The language intends to show that Jacob favored Rachel over Leah. The words in Malachi reflect God's favoring Jacob over Esau, and more negatively they may also reflect Israel's own emotional animosity toward Edom.

160. Cf. Redditt, *Haggai, Zechariah, Malachi*, 162.

161. So Thielman, "Unexpected Mercy," 181; Tamez, "God's Election," 29–37.

Reuben, Perez over Zerah, Ephraim over Manasseh.[162] From the beginning of Israel's salvific history, then, God seems to select what is small and insignificant (e.g., Deut 7:6–11).[163] An election of this sort might help explain why a reversal of expectation or values became popular in Jewish and Christian circles—*God resists the proud and gives grace to the humble* (e.g., Jas 4:10; 1 Pet 5:6; Luke 14:11; 18:14; Mark 10:31; Matt 23:12).[164] Paul seems to think along these lines when affirming that God has chosen the "foolish" things of the world to confound the wise so that humans may not boast (1 Cor 1:26–29).

God's election becomes relevant for Paul because he makes a distinction between Abraham's seed according to promise and Abraham's seed according to the flesh (Rom 9:8 cf. 9:3, 5, 6b).[165] While it is possible that Paul boldly equivocates on the term "Israel" in 9:6, the first "Israel" mentioned may be somewhat synonymous with "Abraham's children," while the second "Israel" refers to the promised line continuing through Isaac and Jacob. If this sense is correct, Esau, though a child of Abraham, was rejected as a child of "promise" while Jacob was accepted. We find a similar comparison in Gal 4:21–31, where Paul considers Ishmael as a son of Abraham according to "the flesh" and Isaac through "promise." Paul compares Hagar/Ishmael with Jerusalem, and he aligns the believers in Galatia with Isaac's lineage. He then cites Isaiah, echoing the barrenness of Sarah turned to rejoicing because her children and "seed" have expanded due to inheriting the Gentiles (Isa 54:1–3/Gal 4:27). Both Galatians and Romans have Israel according to the flesh representing Ishmael or Esau instead of Isaac and Jacob—a surprising reversal of expectation!

While Esau/Jacob and Isaac/Ishmael are examples of God choosing one person over the other, they serve as illustrations for the current status of corporate "Israel," Paul's fellow kinsmen who have become apostate according to his perspective. This section does not address predestination; *neither Paul nor his immediate sources speak to the eternal destinies of the historical persons he mentions. Paul focuses on the character of election instead of predestination, and his emphasis rests on corporate rather than individual election.* To be sure, this election is not related to Esau or

---

162. This concept of election is stressed repeatedly in the Hebrews scriptures. See further Kaminsky, *Yet I Loved Jacob.*

163. For more examples of election in reference to a "reversal of values" in Israel's scriptures, see Grindheim, *Crux of Election,* 7–34.

164. Alternatively, in Jacob's case, it is also possible that God merely predicts that the older brother shall serve the younger because God foreknows that Jacob would steal Esau's birthright and be the one best suited for God's ultimate purposes; so Gooch, "Sovereignty and Freedom," 531–42. If this were the way the Genesis story was intended to be read, Paul seems to overlook it.

165. Meyer's definition of election is helpful here: "divine love sovereignly choosing its instruments for the realization of a divine plan" ("Election-Historical Thinking," 1–7).

Jacob's deeds/works, but Paul uses this language to indirectly speak against those who attempt righteousness through the works of the Law rather than faith (Rom 9:30–10:21; cf. 3:20). While he expresses that God has a purpose behind election, he has yet to unfold what that means.

IS GOD UNJUST?: THE HARDENING OF PHARAOH (9:14–18)

Paul already anticipates the readers' objection in Rom 9:14: "What then shall we say?[166] There is no injustice with God, is there?" The question seems aimed at God's preferential treatment of the promised seed apart from works; in other words, God's apparently capricious selection of one over the other. Paul answers in the negative and then cites what God had told Moses: "I will have mercy on whom I have mercy, and I will show compassion on whom I show compassion" (Rom 9:15/ Exod 33:19). In Exodus, Moses and Israel are those whom God favors and shows mercy (Exod 33:13, 14, 16–19; 34:6–9; cf. 3:14). The singular relative pronoun ὅν ("whom") in Rom 9:15, then, may have a corporate intention to it, much like the singular ὅν refers to the community of Israel in 11:2.[167] The phrase Paul selects in Exod 33:19 also mentions God's name or self-revelation of himself in the context, which is connected with his character as merciful and compassionate. For Paul, "mercy" (ἔλεος) is another key concept that will be fleshed out in the remainder of his argument. His answer to the question in Rom 9:14 is that *God elects on the basis of his own purpose, and that purpose is connected with his compassionate character and desire to show mercy* (9:15–16).[168] God does not arbitrarily select some individuals and reject others, but has a special purpose in mind.

Paul then brings up an example of how God demonstrates his purpose in relation to compassion and mercy even through Israel's enemy.[169] Paul refers in Rom

166. Paul uses this opening question in relation to false inferences that could be drawn from the argument (cf. 3:5; 6:1; 7:7; Cranfield, *Romans*, 2.481–82). Paul goes on to reject such inferences.

167. Abasciano, "Corporate Election in Romans 9," 359, raises this point and also views ὅν in 9:18 as a "collective singular relative pronoun." 9:15 has surely informed 9:18, but in the latter verse, at least, Pharaoh has just been mentioned, and so the ancient reader would have no doubt associating Pharaoh (an individual) with this "whom." Whether or not this was Paul's intention is more difficult to determine. In any case, we could speak of an *emphasis* on corporate language throughout Rom 9–11 without denying individualistic language, including such language in relation to the characters in 9:6–19.

168. Hence, Dunn *Romans*, 2.562, rightly affirms that "God's purpose is not conditioned on Israel's good will and effort . . . The additional assurance afforded by God's word to Moses is that that purpose is one of compassion, that that election is God demonstrating his character of mercy," and that "The central motivation in election is God's compassion; his purpose has the primary object of showing mercy."

169. The conjunction γάρ shows the connection of thought from God's mercy in 9:16 to the example of Pharaoh in 9:17. Cranfield, *Romans*, 2.485, connects γάρ in 9:17 with 9:15 instead, but the flow of Paul's intertextual argument seems to fit better with the former idea.

9:17 to Exod 9:16 where God, through Moses, says to Pharaoh that God raised up Pharaoh to demonstrate God's power and name. In the Exodus story God hardens Pharaoh's heart so that he will not allow the people of Israel to leave Egypt, while God uses the opportunities to display his name, glory, and power via the miracles and plagues he performs through Moses.[170]

Paul then mentions that God has mercy on whom he wills and hardens whom he wills (Rom 9:18). Exodus 4–14 has God taking the initiative to harden Pharaoh (e.g., 7:3; 9:12), but some references are not entirely clear (e.g., 7:13; 9:7), and others seem to suggest that Pharaoh hardened his own heart (e.g., 8:[11]15; 9:34).[171] What is rarely mentioned is that, prior to all this God tells Moses that he knows Pharaoh well enough to claim that Pharaoh will not let the Israelites go (3:19–20). Perhaps no coercion is mentioned here because none is needed. Pharaoh (and his immediate predecessor) is already a proud tyrant who has chosen to be cruel to God's people, abusing Israel under harsh slavery (1:8–22; cf. 2:23; 3:7-8, 19). From the Hebrews' vantage point, he already deserves divine judgment for the choices he has made prior to Moses confronting him. As Israel's oppressor, the king of Egypt becomes the enemy of God. This alone seems to justify God taking initiative to punish Pharaoh by hardening him, or at very least it suggests that God's hardening of the king is not entirely arbitrary. Paul, however, does not go in this direction rhetorically. He suggests instead God's freedom to bring about God's desired purposes and mercy despite Pharaoh's efforts.

For Paul, the result of God hardening Pharaoh serves to glorify God's power with the outcome that "all the Egyptians shall know that I am the LORD" (Exod 14:4–8, 17–18; cf. 7:5, 17; 8:6, 18; 9:14, 29; 10:2; 11:7). This phrase, no doubt, func-

170. The Greek verb for "harden" (σκληρύνω) essentially means "to make firm" or simply "to harden" in reference to unbelief. Both Jews and Christians could be hardened (Acts 19:9; Heb 3:8, 15; 4:7; cf. Schmidt, "σκληρύνω," 5.1030–31). In the Exodus story at least three distinct words are used in the Hebrew text that can mean "to be tough [strong]," "to be difficult [stubborn]," and "to be heavy"; cf. Currid, "Why Did God Harden?" 46–51.

171. Chisholm, "Divine Hardening," 410–34, argues that the LORD gave Pharaoh a "window of opportunity" to accept the LORD's word, including the initial encounter between Moses and Pharaoh (Exod 5:2); the monarch rejected these opportunities. God responded by hardening Pharaoh as a way to demonstrate his judgment and sovereignty. While the hardening in 4:21 precedes 5:2, Chisholm asserts that the former passage predicts the future hardening God would do to Pharaoh after Moses performed the signs. This hardening does not take place until Exod 7. Hence, while 4:21 is stated before 5:2, the event in 5:2 is intended to be chronologically earlier than the hardening in 4:21. For Chisholm (417–18) Exod 5:2 is best understood as an autonomous action of Pharaoh. This perspective seems akin with the rabbinic understanding that God gave Pharaoh five warnings before closing the door to repentance (*Exod. Rabbah* 13.3). While I agree with Chisholm's view of 5:2, the former verse is not as convincing. My view is that prior to 4:21 Pharaoh is already seen as a tyrant who deserves divine hardening.

tions as an ironic reversal of Pharaoh's prideful claim that he does not "know" the LORD in 5:2. The notion that even non-Israelites would come to know God attracted Paul to quote Exod 9.16: "I raised you up for this very purpose that I might display my power in you and that my name *might be proclaimed in all the earth*" (Rom 9:17). And it is precisely in this context that some of the Egyptians who believed the word of the LORD gathered in their cattle before the plague of hail struck and they were spared (Exod 9:20–21). The reason for hardening Pharaoh was not just so that God could magnify his power but so that his fame might spread to other people apart from the Israelites. For Paul, these other people are Gentiles who come to know God, and God would be glorified because of this (Rom 9:23–26, 30). *God's election and hardening of "whom he wills" is for the purpose of bringing about a greater good: to be merciful to more people.* Stowers puts it well in reference to Rom 9:17: "Paul probably suggests here that without the miracle of the Exodus and the establishment of the land of Israel, the other nations of the earth would not have heard the good news (cf. 15:9–12)."[172]

If Paul is teaching that God hardened Pharaoh for a higher purpose in 9:15–18, the exact nature of divine hardening is not made clear. The closest Paul gets to pondering the "how" of divine hardening in this letter is found in 1:18—2:5, where God delivers over rebellious Gentiles who originally knew God over to their own lusts to practice vices, and they become more recalcitrant because of it. As we have suggested earlier, their hardening may be related to their being surrendered to their own desires or anti-God powers or both (1:24, 26, 28). In 2 Cor 4:3–4 Paul seemingly believes Satan is "the god of this world" who blinds the hearts of unbelievers. Interestingly, some Jewish traditions affirm a demonic activity as hardening Pharaoh (*T. Sol.* 25.2–3; cf. *Jub.* 48.17). In any case the Gentiles' misconduct is then charged to the self-righteous interlocutor, who refuses to repent, and because of his hardened heart he is storing up God's wrath upon himself (Rom 2:1–5). The rebels make their own choices resulting in spiritual obduracy, and they are confirmed in their disobedience as a form of punishment. For Paul the hardening of Pharaoh probably assumes a pattern similar to 1:18–32 in which God punishes unrighteous Gentiles with obduracy *as a result of* their prior idolatry and vices. A distinction between Pharaoh and the apostate Gentiles is that Pharaoh claims that he does not know the LORD;[173] the Gentiles at least knew the Creator. Paul never bothers to systematize his thoughts on this issue explicitly. Sometimes hardening seems initiated by the humans, other times by Satan, and other times by God, as in 9:18 (Pharaoh) and

---

172. Stowers, *Rereading of Romans*, 300.

173. This knowledge is perhaps related to getting to know someone through experience. It does not necessitate that Pharaoh has never heard about the LORD before. See Houtman, *Exodus*, 1.462.

11:7, 25 (Israel).[174] Nevertheless, Israel's hardening came about because of a different reason than that of the idolatrous Gentiles of Rom 1. Israel strived after righteousness but did not obtain it (9:30–33; 11:7–8). Perhaps the occasion for Israel's hardening has to do with relying on works for righteousness rather than the preaching of the gospel (of Christ), which if not received by faith creates a stumbling block (Rom 9:30–33; 10:17, 20–21; cf. 1 Cor 1:18–31). If this is the case, then while Paul affirms God's freedom to harden or not harden whomever he wills, divine hardening is not altogether one-sided—God hardens those who harden themselves.

Did Paul answer in adequate fashion the question he started with in Rom 9:14: is God unjust? The reader would have to gather from Paul's argument and intertextual gleanings that God is righteous because God's purpose in election is to demonstrate his mercy and compassion for his own glory, even if he withholds judgment for a period of time so that his name could be proclaimed all the more.[175] Paul opened up another can of worms, however, by introducing the subject of divine hardening, and apparently he realizes this. His next leading question in 9:19 addresses God's freedom to show mercy on whom he wills and harden whom he wills.

WHY DOES GOD FIND FAULT, FOR "WHO HAS RESISTED HIS WILL?": THE EVASIVE ANSWER (9:19–33)

When Paul argues for God hardening Pharaoh's heart, he anticipates the response of his antagonistic interlocutor who might say that God should not hold wrongdoers such as Pharaoh responsible for their actions: "Why does he yet find fault? For who has resisted his will?" (Rom 9:19). If God is the one who is responsible for hardening Pharaoh or whomever he decides to harden, how can he blame Pharaoh and hold him or anyone else responsible for their misdeeds? Romans 9:14 is derived from Paul anticipating his interlocutor's wrong inference about God, and 9:19 follows up with a

---

174. When God is seen as the sole initiator of Pharaoh's hardening, it is also not clear how this takes place or to what extent God is actually involved in the hardening process. This perplexing issue is perhaps best left to mystery. In any case here are several explanations, some more plausible than others: 1) the Mosaic authors may use ambiguous language that merely simplifies God knowing Pharaoh well enough to foreknow that the monarch will become stubborn; 2) God becomes to Pharaoh a stumbling block *vis-à-vis* his mere confrontation against the ruler; in other words, Pharaoh in his prideful role as divine ruler of a powerful nation will not bow down to slaves and a humble shepherd's staff, at least not with any consistency; 3) God supernaturally coerces Pharaoh; 4) God uses demonic powers as the instrumental means of accomplishing Pharaoh's hardening, or God surrenders him over to them; 5) God places thoughts in Pharaoh's mind that will cause Pharaoh to become stubborn again; 6) God brings about the circumstances that he knows will cause Pharaoh to harden his own heart; 7) God withholds some means of grace to accomplish Pharaoh's hardness.

175. Along these lines see Wright, *Romans*, 640–41.

second inference resulting from Paul's answer to the first inference. Thus 9:19 begins a section that will try to alleviate foils in 9:14–18 rather than primarily address the thesis in 9:6. It is not clear whether Paul originally intended this line of reasoning or if his argument in 9:14–18 led him down a path he did not originally anticipate.

Paul responds to the question in 9:19 with more questions in 9:20–23. His initial response seems to be more an evasion than an answer: "Who are you, o man, who answers back to God?" This response is supported by scripture concerning a potter having authority over the clay he molds and the clay not having the right to question what the potter decides. The illustration buttresses the apostle's implication that the imaginary interlocutor has no right to ask the question in 9:19. The answer in 9:20a might echo Job 9:19 (though not exactly following the LXX or MT), in which contextually (Job 9:4–19) God's power is stressed and that "no one can compel God into any kind of debate of litigation."[176] The *Testament of Job* picks up the language by asserting, "Who dares to ascribe to the Lord an injustice?" (*T. Job* 37.7).[177] At the end of Job's righteous suffering, God does not answer all the questions that faithful Job posits. Instead when God appears to Job, he begins to question whether or not Job understands how God does his work in creation (Job 38–42). In essence, he answers Job by claiming that Job, a mere human, cannot attain the high knowledge of all the hows and whys of God's work. The answers given in Job and Romans are rather similar: What are mere humans that they should question the Almighty?[178]

God does affirm, however, that Job has spoken correctly, unlike his friends, who attempted to justify God and blame Job (Job 42:7–8). Although Job lacked proper understanding in his questions and complaints he raised (38:2–3), he was not condemned by God. Job is permitted to ask the tough questions about God's justice and still remain right with God. A questioning of the injustice that Job felt seemed warranted, despite God's sovereignty to do as he pleases with his creatures. What gets lost in the shuffle of Paul echoing Job on the futility of questioning God is that his original question is never directly answered. Are humans able or unable to resist God's will? Is the reader to not posit the tough questions because the reader is the creature and not the Creator? Paul's evasive answer in Rom 9:20–21 forces readers to regress back to 9:15–19 and ask again whether or not God is being fair for finding fault with the creatures he himself hardened. Both Job and Paul do not come to a clear resolution about God's justice but are apparently content to know God and accept mystery (see 11:33–36).

176. Clines, *Job 1–20*, 235.

177. *OTP* 1.857.

178. Likewise, Wis 12:12 parallels Job 9:19 and contextually stresses God's sovereignty and righteousness in executing judgment.

Paul's scriptural allusion to the potter and clay is found in at least several scriptures,[179] but the initial wording seems closest to Isa 29:16.[180] It becomes evident that Paul has not abandoned the thought of Pharaoh in all this: Isa 29–30 reads that Ariel (Jerusalem) has become proud and does not seek the LORD's wise counsel; instead, Israel consults Egypt, which is identified as "Pharaoh" in this passage. In ironic fashion Israel wrongly thinks that its Maker (the potter) does not understand what is going on, is not wise, and did not create Israel (the clay). This context may have been suitable for Paul because Pharaoh is collaborating with rebellious and blind (i.e., hardened) Israel, an Israel that from Paul's perspective is still spiritually obdurate (Rom 11:7–8, 25). Hence, it is not technically Egypt, Ramses, or a generic individual that Paul is ultimately hinting at by using the term "Pharaoh," but unbelieving Israelites. In this sense Ishmael, Esau, and Pharaoh all represent Israel "of the flesh" (9:6–9). Moreover, the Isaianic text calls rebellious Israel "Sodom" in Isa 1:10, a context Paul no doubt knew when he cites Isa 1:9 in relation to Israel's current unbelief (Rom 9:29–32). The Isaianic language reflects the earlier Deuteronomic curse, which affirms that Israel's apostasy would be characterized by Israel returning back to Egypt and its land becoming like Sodom (Deut 28:68; 29:23). Consequently, Paul seems to be following the Isaianic example of name switching whereby the name of God's people becomes associated with the name of God's enemy.[181]

While Isa 29:16 offers the closest language parallel to the potter/clay illustration Paul uses, it is quite possible that he had more than one particular Isaianic background in mind. Similar potter/clay imagery appears in Isa 45:9, and he alludes to Isa 45 in reference to the salvation of his people (Rom 11:25–26; cf. Isa 45:17, 20–24, 26). He echoes the text again in Rom 14:11 (Isa 45:23–24).[182] In this Isaianic passage God's sovereignty is stressed, and the catchwords "mercy" and "righteousness" appear in the same context (Isa 45:7–8). God has raised up the Gentile monarch Cyrus as a restorer for Israel, and the Gentiles are included in God's eschatological plan for Israel (Isa 44:28—45:6; 45:14–26). The questioning of the clay to the potter is associated with Israel's questioning of the LORD's plan to use a Gentile as Israel's liberator. The idea that a Gentile would be included in Israel's anticipated redemption and that

179. Jer 18:1–10; Sir 33:10–13; Wis 15:7; Isa 45:9; 64:8.

180. I concur with Shum, *Paul's Use of Isaiah*, 204–5, that Isa 29:16 has the closest verbal similarity with Rom 9:20–21.

181. Other early Christian writers apparently picked up on this language. Revelation 11 calls Jerusalem "Sodom" and "Egypt."

182. Cf. Hübner, *Vetus Testamentum*, 180, 202; Shum, *Isaiah in Romans*, 222–23. Also compare the idea of calling upon the Lord in Rom 10:12 with Isa 45:23–24. Echoes of Isa 28–29 appear in several Romans texts as well (Rom 1:17/Isa 28:16; Rom 9:33/Isa 28:16; Rom 10:11/Isa 28:16; Rom 11:8/Isa 29:10).

God would be acknowledged among Israel's enemies may have been interpreted as a blow to Israel's pride.[183] The message may have also been misunderstood in terms of Israel continuing its submission to the Gentiles after the Babylonians had conquered Jerusalem. The potter/clay illustration reflects a type of second-guessing of God instead of submitting to his sovereign plans. In the same passage the catchword "seed" is used to support the idea that Israel will be made righteous, a universal salvation of the world will take place, and "in God shall all the seed of the children of Israel be glorified" (Isa 45:[25]26). [184] Perhaps it is not coincidental that the goal of this text fits surprisingly well with Paul's climax in Rom 11:26, in which all Israel will be saved once the Gentiles come to faith. The Isaianic potter/clay passages enlighten our understanding of Rom 9:20–21.[185] *Israel became blind and wrongfully associated itself with God's enemies (Isa 29–30), and Israel lacked understanding when it came to God's sovereign purposes related to its eschatological deliverance, which includes the Gentiles (Isa 45).*

The "what if" questions in Rom 9:22 and 9:23 are Paul's closest attempt at answering his theodicy-bent question posed in 9:19. He asks if God, wanting to show his wrath and make his power known, endured with much patience the vessels of wrath. These vessels are in some sense prepared or ready (καταρτίζω) for destruction. God's purpose is to make known the glory of his riches on the vessels of mercy, which he has prepared for glory.[186] The perfect middle/passive of καταρτίζω (κατηρτισμένα) can mean "prepared," "fit," "ready" (cf. Ps 39:7 LXX).[187] The precise meaning is difficult to pin down in this case because elsewhere Paul uses the word or its derivatives in a positive sense, as in the case of establishing, equipping, and restoring (1 Cor 1:10; 2 Cor 13:9, 11; Gal 6:1; 2 Tim 3:17).[188] Ephesians 4:12 may be helpful because the similar καταρτισμός is used in the context of preparing or equipping the body of believers for complete maturity or perfection. The word group is used with some goal in mind (cf. Ps 39[40]:6–7; Heb 10:5). In Rom 9:22, the sense is probably something similar to "ready" "ripe," or "made ready," or it could mean that

---

183. Cf. Watts, *Isaiah 34–66*, 163.

184. Cf. Blenkinsopp, *Isaiah*, 263; Oswalt, *Isaiah*, 219–20.

185. In 9:21 Paul begins to drift close to Wis 15:7. The concepts of "mercy," "righteousness," and "glory" are found in its context (Wis 15:1, 3, 9), but the illustration breaks down rather quickly. In this tradition, while the potter is able to make vessels as he sees fit, he makes certain vessels into idols and does not know his own Maker. If this tradition is echoed here, Paul seems to pick up only the potter's ability to make the clay as he sees fit.

186. Here "destruction" and "glory" involve eternal glory or eternal destruction; cf. Dunn, *Romans*, 2.560.

187. See καταρτίζω in LEH.

188. See further Schippers, "ἄρτιος," 3.349–51.

the vessels are "tailor-made" in the sense of perfectly deserving the destruction. The middle voice might imply that vessels prepare themselves for this destruction, but since the analogy has the potter doing the work, this idea remains tentative at best.[189] In any case it does not appear that these vessels are created simply to be destroyed. Potters do not, and cannot afford to, make vessels for this purpose. G. B. Caird articulates it memorably: "A vessel may in the end have to be discarded, but the potter does not make vessels for the ghoulish delight of hurling them against a wall."[190]

Thoughts about an object of God's wrath being used to bring about glory was already illustrated by God's use of Pharaoh (Rom 9:17; cf. Exod 9:16). God can bring about his purpose of mercy even through God's enemies. The idea in 9:22–23 may be that God has every right to destroy these vessels but that he holds out in order to bring about more glory. But if God knew his wrath and glory would be manifest in a greater way by holding out on his judgment against the vessels of wrath, why would this require enduring "patience" on God's part?[191] It is difficult to imagine God hardly being able to contain himself because he so badly wants to destroy these vessels! We hear Paul's echo of Wis 12:12 in the background ("What have you done?"; "Who will resist your judgment?"), which is similar to the wording of Rom 9:19–20 and anticipates 9:21–23. The context contains the catchword "seed," mentions God's sovereignty, and, similar to God withholding judgment against Pharaoh, it refers to God withholding judgment against the Canaanites so as to give them space to repent (Wis 12:3–18).[192] Here God's patience is associated with a desire to lead them to repentance. If this backdrop to Rom 9:19–22 is anywhere in Paul's mind, then it may be that Paul introduces God's patience in this passage for the same reason he brought up earlier in 2:4–5: God's patience with those in danger of his wrath (i.e., the Jewish interlocutor representative of Israel) is for the purpose of getting them

189. Cosgrove, *Elusive Israel*, 28–29, finds enough possible nuance in the fact that Paul writes "make" rather than "pre-make" (προκαταρτίζω) for the vessels of wrath in 9:20–23 (playing on the προ- in the vessels of mercy as "prepare beforehand": προετοιμάζω) to allow for Paul's surprising twist in 11:26 that the objects of wrath end up becoming objects of mercy. Nevertheless, even if the vessels of mercy are "pre-made," they still are able to fall away and become vessels of wrath (cf. 11:22f), and it seems better to let the macro-context assist us with the interpretation of the meaning of these difficult words than to insist on a precise definitional nuance at this juncture, such as trying to get them to mean double predestination, and then have that meaning drastically overturned in Rom 11.

190. Caird, "Predestination," 324–27. See also Lodge, *Romans 9–11*, 84.

191. The interpretation of the participle θέλων in 9:22a, whether concessive ("although" God willed) or causal ("because" God willed), encumbers much debate. Contextually, if Wis 12 is one of the texts behind Paul's intertextual backdrop, the concessive meaning makes more sense.

192. That God already knows that they will not repent (Wis 12:10–11) is beside the point, and their accursedness "from the beginning" is not because God created them that way, but because of the curse Noah placed on the Canaanites in Gen 9:25; cf. Charles, *Pseudepigrapha*, 1.554.

to repent. God's patience and forbearance are intended to ultimately lead objects of wrath to repentance.[193]

If this interpretation is appropriate for 9:22–23, Paul is finally giving a roundabout answer to the question posed in 9:19: God may be responsible for hardening the enemies of his followers, but this does not preclude their ability to repent. They are not predestined to be eternally destroyed. While the wrath of God is implied in this passage, it is not finally executed in this passage.[194] It should also not be missed that *Paul probably would have considered himself as belonging with the vessels of wrath before his encounter with Jesus, when he was still presumably hardened and persecuting the Christ followers* (Phil 3:2–9; Gal 1:13; cf. Acts 9; 1 Tim 1:13–15; Eph 2:3).[195] Assuming that Acts portrays the gist of Paul's early days somewhat correctly, God used Paul's persecution of the Way as a means to advance the preaching of the gospel by spreading it to other regions outside of Jerusalem (Acts 8). Hence Paul, much like Pharaoh, was unwittingly used by God so that God's name might be glorified and proclaimed throughout the earth!

Paul already hinted through Isaiah that Israel has no right to question God's salvific plan for the Gentiles. This plan becomes his next topic in Rom 9:22–33. The passage points to the corporate problem of Israel and the Gentiles, in which Paul identifies the "vessels of mercy" as Gentile believers and the faithful remnant of Israel, Paul himself included. If corporate entities are primarily identified as the vessels of mercy, it is *not* a good idea to surmise that the "vessels of wrath" are to be identified as generic individuals.[196] And while God's hardening of Pharaoh helped spark the train of thought for Paul, the historical king of Egypt is not primarily in view.[197] Israel according to "the flesh" seems to be Paul's primary target when dis-

193. The alternative way to understand this verse would be that God's "patience" involves God postponing Pharaoh's punishment in order to make a further show of his wrath and power. Presumably this was most spectacularly accomplished at the Red Sea when God destroyed Pharaoh's army (although nowhere in the text does it mention that Pharaoh himself was killed). But given the various points brought up in the main text, at best this alternative reading may be placed along side Paul's view of patience in Rom 2:4, so that 9:22 has a both/and meaning.

194. Noteworthy is Westerholm, "Paul and the Law in Romans 9–11," 215–37, concerning the "vessels of wrath" in this passage: we do not really see God executing or determined to execute his wrath. What is affirmed is that "it is God's prerogative to do so ('What if . . . ?' implies some such apodosis as 'Do you then, as a mere creature, have any right to object?')."

195. Cf. Caird, "Predestination," 327.

196. Isaianic passages (chs. 29–30, 45 above) might enlighten us on one reason why Paul uses the language of individualism in the clay illustration of Rom 9:20 when he is ultimately using it in relation to national Israel and the Gentiles. Isaiah uses singular language to illustrate the relationship with the potter and clay even though such language points to national/corporate Israel.

197. Pharaoh's eternal destiny is not what is at stake either in the original or Pauline version. In fact the Pentateuch is not even clear in recording that Pharaoh drowns with his army. Later scripture

cussing the vessels of wrath.[198] The faithful remnant of Israel stands in contrast to this other Israel that stumbles over Christ and does not currently possess salvation (9:24–10:21).[199]

While Paul may have invented these two categories of vessels,[200] perhaps he was also influenced by his pondering of Isa 54:7–17. This passage is pregnant with words important to his argument: "sons," "children," "righteousness," "mercy," "wrath," "vessels," "destroy," and the concept of preparing/creating vessels. The passage discusses God's abandonment of Israel in his wrath, but afterward he returns to her with great mercy and compassion. Strangers will also join Israel in this second return. God assures Israel that he has not created her for destruction (Isa 54:16–17 LXX). The common denominator that resonates with Rom 9:22–33 and Paul's climax in 11:25–32 is that Israel, once the object of God's wrath, becomes the object of his mercy, and her return includes others—namely the Gentiles. That Paul was already thinking along these lines is evident in his citation of Hos 2:25 (cf. Rom 9:25–26). Complementary with Isa 54, Hos 1–2 informs readers that God abandons apostate Israel but then once again embraces her, and Paul takes some hermeneutic liberties by interpreting this episode to include Gentiles as God's "people."[201] Paul may have been attracted to this text because in it God originally has mercy on Judah but not all Israel. This reading would support his own argument that not all Israel is Israel (Rom 9:6–7; cf. Hos. 1:6–7). Afterward the rejected and disowned Israelites find God and become his people once again in Hos 2; and this text influenced Paul's argumentative climax that "all Israel" would be restored (Rom 11:26). The combined weight of Paul's use of Israel's scriptures and corporate language in Rom 9:22–33, along with his belief that God's patience is for the objects of wrath (i.e., Israelites) to repent (Rom 2:4; cf. Wis 12) and that the objects of wrath (i.e., Israelites) are not finally destroyed (Rom 11:26–32), and also that elsewhere in Pauline literature the objects of wrath can indeed become believers (e.g., Eph 2:3), argues rather pointedly against the view that

---

traditions, such as Ps 136:15, might suggest this by claiming that God overthrew/shook off Pharaoh and his army in/at the Red Sea. But even here such an interpretation is questionable due to poetic language.

198. E.g., Byrne, *Romans*, 301–2; Wright, *Romans*, 639.

199. On the stone of stumbling as Christ, see Lindars, *New Testament Apologetic*, 169–86.

200. Jeremiah 27:25 mentions vessels of wrath as weapons of destruction against Babylon, but the idea does not seem to fit well with our passage. Another possible echo comes from Isa 66:18–23, which mentions key words such as "seed" and the LORD being glorified in reference to the Gentiles. But the connection with Rom 9:22–23 is not very strong.

201. See contextual link words in Hos 2 such as "call," "righteousness," and "faithfulness." Paul appears to misapply the text to the Gentiles as God's people when the Hosea text was originally intended for Israel after God disowned the Israelites but then loved them again (cf. 1 Pet 2:9–10 for a similar application).

the objects of wrath in Rom 9:22 are individuals who are irrevocably predestined to eternal damnation.

Paul continues his argument by resonating a small catena of Isaianic texts in Rom 9:27–33.[202] The loudest echo comes from the concept of a remnant of Israel in Isa 1:9, which links us back to the thesis of Rom 9:6–7 with the catchword "seed": if the Lord of hosts had not left Israel "seed" they would have been like Sodom and Gomorrah. Isaiah 1 presents the idea of a remnant from the nation of Israel (daughter of Sion) that God had spared from destruction (Isa 1:2–9).[203] God desires righteousness rather than sacrifices, offerings, and observing special days (Isa 1:10–20). Paul may have been attracted to the language here because of the connection between "seed" and remnant. Both terms from the Isaianic passage were tied in with right doing and obedience, which are preferred by God above outward deeds of the Law, a prominent theme in Romans. Through these scriptures Paul is also able to make the claim that Israel in his day has stumbled and become apostate, lacking faith and attempting to establish her own righteousness under the Law instead of trusting in Christ, the τέλος of the Law (9:30—10:20).

Romans 9 was never intended to be read by itself; one must read on to chapter 11 to gain the full perspective of what Paul is attempting to argue and why he uses the sources he does. The contextual backdrop behind his sources is remarkably similar to his grand finale in 11:24–32. Its plot suggests that a fragmented Israel will be restored along with another set of people (Gentiles) in the future. This suggests that Paul knew all along where he was going with his argument despite the apparent disjunctions between chapters 9 and 11.[204] It is also probably safe to say at this point that, given the way Paul uses his sources, he never intended to convey human destinies as irreparably fixed by divine decree to eternal life or eternal damnation so that nothing could ever change the destinies of the individuals who happen to be in either category. God's purpose in election is a way of showing God's mercy. His concern is with Israel and Gentiles, not individualistic double predestination. Israel's

---

202. Isa 28:22/Rom 9:28; Isa 1:9 [cf. 10:22]/Rom 9:29; Isa 28:16/Rom 9:33.

203. Shum, *Isaiah in Romans*, 212. For more examples of remnant language in Isaiah, see Hasel, *Remnant*. For other ancient Jewish traditions, see Grindheim, *Crux of Election*, 29–33, 65–67,150–56, 160; Meyer, "Remnant," 5:669–71; Herntrich and Schrenk, "λεῖμμα," 4.193–214.

204. Differently, Aageson, "Scripture and Structure," 280, suggests that Paul developed his theology as he went along from chapter 9 to 11. If so, the development must have been minimal because the apostle already seems to have his sources in place and just needed to flesh them out. Nevertheless all the tensions between Rom 9 and 11 remain difficult to resolve. For me, the idea of Paul using rhetorical suspense (*sustentatio*), in which the apostle leads his readers down a wrong track in order to later surprise them, seems more plausible than saying that Paul was just a bad thinker who flatly contradicted himself. On the rhetorical concept see Cosgrove, *Elusive Israel*, 33–34.

apostasy is quite clear from what we read in chapter 9, its restoration is also quite evident in chapter 11.

HAS GOD REJECTED HIS PEOPLE?: THE HARDENED AND ELECT ISRAEL (ROM 11)

The third question about God's faithfulness finally directs our attention to the thesis Paul wanted to defend in Rom 9:6. When coupled with 11:1 the answer may be stated as follows: God's word has not failed because God has not rejected his people. Israel shares a special love relationship with God. Paul refers to himself as living proof that God has not rejected Israel. He belongs to the "seed" of Abraham and remnant of Israel who are like those who refused to worship Baal in the Elijah narrative.

It is important to see the role played by Isaianic tradition in the remnant language (Rom 11:1–10; cf. 9:29). Ronald Clements argues rather persuasively that Isa 7:3–9 is related to Rom 11:5. The former passage affirms the necessity of belief in order to establish one's share in the remnant of Israel: "If you will not believe, surely you shall not be established" (Isa 7:9; cf. 11:10).[205] This dovetails nicely with Paul's own view of the prominent role faith plays in the remnant's salvation and why Israel according to the flesh is not presently included with the remnant (Rom 9:32–33; 10:6–17; 11:20, 23). "Israel" has both an elect remnant (λεῖμμα) and "the rest" (λοιπός) that are hardened (Rom 11:5, 7). If we were to stop here we might be misled into thinking that the "rest" were not elect. This perspective is overturned in 11:11–12, 26–28. When Rom 9–11 is read as a whole, Paul seems to pour more than one meaning into the word "Israel" (9:6; 11:7), and possibly this is true of the idea of election,[206] or perhaps Paul is simply keeping his audience in suspense before unpacking all Israel's destiny later on in chapter 11. Both in Israel's scriptures and Paul's citation of the Elijah narrative (11:2–6), the prevailing thought that wins out over national apostasy is that a faithful remnant of Israelites always seem to survive the community's apostasy and the divine judgment that may ensue because of it (see 1 Kgs 19:10–18; cf. Num 14:23–24; Deut 4:23–31; Judg 2–6; Ezek 20:35–38). God graciously preserves a remnant of his people; he promised that he would never forsake all Israel (Jer 5:10, 18; 31:36–37; Mic. 7:18–20). Exactly how this preserva-

---

205. Clements, "Remnant Chosen by Grace," 106–21. Paul refers to another remnant passage in Rom 15:7–13 (Isa 11:10), and it has special reference to an eschatological remnant of God's people, Gentiles and Israel, who shall be ruled by the "root of Jesse," and that day will be similar to when Israel left Egypt (Isa 11:10–16). Through the Isaiah texts, Paul has an eschatological conception about Israel and the Gentiles in both Rom 11 and 15.

206. That Paul would use polyvalent meaning for a term is not altogether unique; compare his use of "rock" in 1 Cor 10:4.

tion takes place remains a mystery, which even Paul would probably admit (Rom 11:33–36), but certainly God would seem to be wise and powerful enough to bring it to pass without the coercion of human freedom and responsibility.

The Isaianic equivalent to Israel's hardening is the spiritual blindness and deafness that comes upon God's people in Isa 6:9–10 and 29:9–10. Romans 11:8 alludes to the latter passage.[207] In Isaianic tradition, Israel is caught up in idolatry, and so God gives the people over to spiritual obduracy as a form of punishment.[208] In ironic fashion those who trusted in their idols have become deaf and blind like their idols (Isa 42:17–20; 44:9–20; 46:5–7; 48:1–8). They also are unable to discern God's word. Israelites and the guides they rely on lack wisdom and spiritual insight (Isa 6:9–10; 19:11; 28:7, 12; 29:9–14; 30:9–11; 33:18 43:8; 44:24–25; 48:8, 18–20). During the eschatological era, however, the blindness and stupor will be removed and Israel's restoration will take place. Then the blind and deaf will see and hear again (Isa 29:18–19; 30:20–22; 32:1–5; 33:17–22 cf. 35:1–10; 42:16–19; 43:8; 61:1–11). Israel's blindness is therefore only temporary. The concepts of blindness and being hardened seemed interrelated in Isaiah when the prophet on behalf of Israel asks the Lord why he has "hardened" their hearts (Isa 63:17).

The way Paul uses the imprecatory Ps 68[69]:22–23 in Rom 11:9–10 would seem to be targeted against Israel. Even so, Paul finally unfolds the salvific hope for this people in Rom 11:11–32. Israel's hardness is only temporary (11:8, 25–26); the λοιποί have stumbled but not fallen irreparably. The eschatological dimension of falling is closely associated with the concept of apostasy or being severed from God, and here a punishment resulting in eschatological destruction is in view (Sir 1:30; 28:22–26; *Pss. Sol.* 3.9–12; cf. Gal 5:4; Rom 11:22). Paul affirms that Israel— the portion of Israel that was hardened—has not decisively fallen even though they have stumbled, but their hardness has resulted in the Gentiles coming to faith. Here Paul begins to suggest that these hardened Israelites will eventually come to faith also (Rom 11:12, 15). Paul anticipates Israel being provoked to jealousy by Gentiles (11:11, 14 cf. 10:19; Deut 32:21). Namely, as Richard Bell argues, Israel "would come to see that the Gentiles were playing *her* role in history," become jealous, and come to salvation by faith through the Christ.[209]

---

207. See also Deut 29:2–4 for a parallel passage.

208. NT writers are fond of using the motif, and they seem to place different emphases on who is ultimately responsible for the blindness: God or the people (Mark 4:12; 7:6f; John 12:40; Acts 28:26–27; 1 Cor 1:19; 14:21; 1 Pet 2:6). In Isa 6:9–10 God seems to initiate the spiritual blindness. The obduracy in any event was God's way of punishing a people who were unwilling to repent of their apostasy in Isa 1–5.

209. Cf. Bell, *Provoked to Jealousy*, 199.

Paul gives the illustration of an olive tree, apparently started from Abraham's lineage or "seed" to show that these Israelites were branches "cut off" so that Gentiles could be engrafted in the tree of fellowship with God's promised people.[210] The hardened Israelites will also be re-engrafted if they do not persist in unbelief. As the Israelites were cut off, so also Gentiles may be severed from this tree if they grow proud (ὑψηλός) of their status in comparison to Israel and do not persevere (ἐπιμένω) in God's goodness (Rom 11:17–25a). In this section the destinies of unbelieving Israel and believing Gentiles are not permanently fixed. Whatever else the olive tree might signify, salvation is to be found in connection with it and not cut off from it. Paul leaves open the possibility for ostracized Israelites, who were vessels of wrath in chapter 9, to return to the olive tree. He also warns Gentile believers, who were vessels of mercy in chapter 9, not to fall away through a boastful attitude about their election and failure to continue in God's grace (11:19–22). Their potential haughtiness perhaps recalls from the intertexts of Rom 9 Pharaoh's recalcitrance and the Genesis pattern of God favoring the humble and rejecting the proud. Such an attitude would presumably cause them to rely on themselves instead of Christ and either spurn or take for granted God's grace, similar to the original Gentiles who rejected God's gifts and committed apostasy (Rom 1:18–32; cf. 1 Cor 4:7). More than this, their attitude of superiority over the Jews would be a major step towards division, hatred, and racism.

That Rom 11:19–22 warns the Gentile believers of a real possibility that they could be "cut off" from salvation is quite evident. This is in essence what happened to Israel. Paul affirms that Israel after the flesh has become apostate and "cut off" from salvation at the present time.[211] If Paul were teaching double predestination as a permanent

210. Some see the olive tree (cf. Jer 11:16–19; Hos 14:6–7) as representing ethnic Israel (e.g., Wilckens, *Römer*, 2.246), and/or the branches not broken off as Jewish Christians (e.g., Cranfield, *Romans*, 2.567). Others suggest it refers to the people of God, both Jews and Gentiles (e.g., Schreiner, *Romans*, 605). The precise nuance of identity is vague perhaps because the notion of being broken off from the tree might seem to imply these branches are no longer part of "Israel," which is *not* what Paul wants to argue. Dunn, *Romans*, 2.661, rightly suggests that Paul "still regards even the broken-off branches as still properly part of, or at least belonging to, the tree." The olive tree may have evoked for Paul's audience imagery from one of the Jewish synagogues in Rome called "Synagogue of the Olive," and possibly is the place from where the Christ-community in Rome first emerged; see further Davies, *Jewish and Pauline Studies*, 159–60.

211. Contrast Schreiner, *Romans*, who writes regarding falling away in Rom 11:22: "When we look at it retrospectively (cf. 2 Tim 2:11–21; 1 John 2:19) we discover that those who fail to persevere thereby reveal that they were never actually part of the elect community" (609). But the references to the Pastoral and Johannine sources are not entirely relevant in Rom 11. We notice what Paul says about Israel on a corporate level: Israel's falling away cuts Israel off from salvation, and yet Israel's apostasy has *not* nullified Israel's election (cf. 11:17, 21, 23, 26–28). On an individualistic level Paul in his letters, including Romans, consistently teachers that a person's belonging to the elect community does not safeguard against that person's apostasy if he or she rejects Christ through unbelief, disobedience, vices,

or fixed state in chapter 9, this could hardly be the case in chapter 11 without contradicting himself.[212] There might be a contradiction between the two passages, but if we choose to give Paul the benefit of the doubt he clearly identifies the believing Gentiles as vessels of mercy (9:23–24). Even though he claims that these vessels are "pre-prepared" for eternal glory (9:23b), in 11:22–23 these same believers can still be cut off from the salvation associated with the olive tree. Even so, if the Christian Gentiles were to be "cut off" this would not necessarily mean that every individual Gentile believer would become apostate, anymore than Paul means that every individual Israelite is presently apostate. It appears that a fixed destiny for every individual represented by the "vessels of mercy" and "vessels of wrath" cannot be convincingly maintained throughout Rom 9–11.

The climax to Paul's question in 11:1 arrives in 11:25–32. God has not rejected his people, even if they are in some sense temporarily rejected (11:15), because the hardening is only partial or on a part ("the rest," 11:7) of Israel. The hardening, it seems, will be removed when the time of the "fullness" (πλήρωμα) of the Gentiles has come in,[213] and then "all Israel" will be saved (11:26, 28, 32).[214] This Israel includes not only the remnant but also, as inferred from the original question in 11:1 and continued by the question in 11:11, those that had been hardened. They too will be saved after the fullness of the Gentiles comes into the kingdom. Paul claims this as a "mystery" not previously understood by his audience (11:25).[215] All along,

---

and so on. Here in Rom 11:19–22 the Gentiles could fall away because pride and arrogance just as Israel fell away *despite* election.

212. This is one of the weaknesses with Piper, *Justification of God.* The monograph can sustain a relentless view of double predestination because it remains in Rom 9 without moving to the climatic ending of Rom 11.

213. Stowers, *Rereading of Romans*, 314–15, argues through Philo and other sources that the word group ἡττάομαι/ἥττημα in Rom 11:11–12 was used for failure or defeat in athletic contests: "The race imagery makes the meaning of the troublesome 11:12 transparent: If Israel's misstep (that is, tripping, stumbling) in the race resulted in wealth for the world and her loss of the race in wealth for the gentile competitor, how much more will her completion (πλήρωμα) of the race mean?" While I partially resonate with this reading, I believe the movement depicts a journey (Isaiah's new exodus-wilderness, see below) rather than a race. Other alternatives include: 1) the full number of Gentiles that Paul will reach once he gets all the way to Spain to preach over there also (cf. Bell, *Provoked to Jealousy*, 345, 361); 2) a "full restoration," or simply a very large multitude, "a quantitative comparison between a small remnant and a fullness of the saved" (cf. Witherington, *Romans*, 268–69); 3) a fixed number of elect individuals known to God but not humans (if so Rom 11 would seem to teach that individuals can fall in and out of this number until the set number is reached!); and 4) an open or foreknown number of however many Gentiles eventually choose to come to faith; the rest refuse.

214. In 11:26, καὶ οὕτως probably means "in this manner" (cf. 1 Thess 4:17; 1 Cor 11:28; 14;25); i.e., after the Gentiles come, all Israel will be saved. For options see, e.g., Köstenberger and O'Brien, *Salvation to the Ends of the Earth*, 188–91.

215. Paul frequently uses a phrase about not wanting his audience to be "ignorant" whenever he

however, we were hearing tremors of this via the intertextual background he echoes. The church has not taken on the name "Israel" or superseded it in 11:26. This view is difficult to be maintained if all along Paul has been referring to Israel in ethnic and nationalistic ways. Nor does 11:26 mean that only the elect among Israel are saved, a view that conflicts with 11:28: the same ones that are saved in 11:26 are they that are presently enemies of the gospel and yet elect and beloved.[216] Rather, *Israel as whole will be saved at the end of the eschaton. Israel's salvation is corporate, and this salvation started with the remnant of Israel, added the Gentiles, and will finish with the "rest" of Israel* (e.g., 11:7, 12, 15).

Perhaps the closest parallel to Rom 11:26a recalls Isa 45. Israel as the "seed" is saved with an everlasting salvation, made righteous, and glorified (Isa 45:17, 19, 25–26). The citations in Rom 11:26b–27 come from Isa 27:9 and 59:20[21]. The former passage is located in an apocalyptic portion of Isaiah in which the iniquity of Jacob will be taken away and people from different parts of the world will come to Zion/Jerusalem for worship. The latter passage recalls the thesis in Rom 9:6 and uses the catchterm "word": God's words would not fail in the mouth of his spokesperson nor his "seed" and "the Deliverer" will come from Zion to take away the ungodliness of Jacob (Isa 59:20–21). The Isaianic tradition is rather clear that those from other nations (i.e., the Gentiles) will worship along with the restored remnant of Israel. Israel is not equated with these nations, but the nations will be included with Israel. If we press beyond Rom 9–11, Paul quotes Isa 11:10 to support the Gentiles trusting in the "root of Jesse," and because of this God is glorified for his mercy in relation to the confirmation of the promises he gave to Israel's patriarchs (Rom 15:7–13).[217] In the Isaianic new exodus-wilderness travels, Israel (11:12) and Gentiles (11:25) will make a journey to Zion (cf. Rom 11:25–27/Isa 27, 59; Rom 15:11–12/Isa 11:1–12:6).[218] The πλήρωμα in Rom 11:25 most likely refers to the completion of this eschatological journey. In 11:28 one finds a thought similar to that of *2 Bar.* 13:9–10, where God did not spare his own sons but afflicted them as if they were his enemies. The Israel that was hardened are beloved in reference to election, though they are "enemies for

gives information not previously understood (Rom 1:13; 1 Cor 10:1; 12:1; 2 Cor 1:8; 1 Thess 4:13 cf. 1 Cor 15:51).

216. Contrast Ridderbos, *Paul*, 354–61, and see further weaknesses with this view in Köstenberger and O'Brien, *Salvation to the Ends of the Earth*, 189–90. For discussion on the identity of Israel in 11:26, see Zoccali, "And So All Israel," 289–318.

217. The eschatological renewal of Israel may have also been known to Paul apart from the Isaianic tradition (cf. Deut 30:3–5; Jer 31:7–14; Ezek 37:15–23; Hos 11:10–11; Pss 106:47; 147:2; Bar 5:5–9; *1 En.* 57; *4 Ezra* 13.12–48; *2 Bar.* 78.5–7; 1QM 2–3; *T. Jos.* 19.4; *Pss. Sol.* 11.2–7; Matt 19:28; Acts 1:6–7; Rev 7). Notice *m. Sanhedrin* 10.1: "All Israelites have a share in the world to come" (cf. *T. Benj.* 10.11). On passages where Judaism relies on God's mercy, see Cosgrove, *Elusive Israel*, 7–8.

218. See Schreiner *Romans*, 617, for more sources.

your sake"; namely, in order that an opportunity might arise for the Gentile readers to come to faith, hardened Israel has become an enemy of Paul's gospel. Paul does not attempt to unpackage the paradox of Israel as an elect enemy but lets the thought stand, much to our frustration.

Romans 11:29–32 unfolds some final aspects about the fulfillment of God's mercy. If all Israel eventually receives mercy, this idea would seem to extend to Israel according to "the flesh" (9:6–18), the "vessels of wrath" (9:19–23), unbelieving Israel (9:24–10:21), and hardened Israel (11:1–24). Israel's status took these various turns in the text to affirm ultimately in the climax that Paul's people will receive God's mercy and salvation in the end. An interesting thought related especially to 11:32 is that disobedience is assigned to all before God's mercy is given to all. In later Pauline thought, mercy normally presupposes disobedience (Eph 2:1–4; Titus 3:3–5; 1 Tim 1:13–16; cf. 1 Pet 2:10). In Rom 11:32 God confines or "delivers over" all to disobedience in order to have mercy on all, both Gentiles and Jews.[219] In Gaventa's argument (cf. Rom 1:18–32), the consignment would be to anti-God powers, but temporarily so in this case.[220] Through it all Paul maintains that however God was involved in their disobedience, God's faithfulness is not tainted because even hardened Israel will be saved.[221]

What is left unsaid, however, is the current status of hardened Israel. While the collective people called "Israel" will be saved in the eschaton, Paul says little about their salvific status if some hardened Israelite individuals in the "present time" (11:5) were to die in that hardened state. Before "all" receive mercy and salvation, what happens to such individuals? Are the ones who died prior to the end saved in some sort of retrospective sense?[222] Are they given a second chance after death? Are they lost eternally? Is "all" universal, referring to every single individual?[223] Answers to

219. The Greek word συγκλείω may reflect its use in the Pss 30:9; 77:50, 62 LXX, which has a meaning of "giving over" and recalls God handing over the Gentiles to their vices in Rom 1:24–28; cf. Moo, *Romans*, 736. "Consign," "enclosing," or "imprison" are alternative ways to translate the word (cf. Gal 3:22–23).

220. Gaventa, "God Handed Them Over," 52.

221. Kim, *God, Israel*, 126–27, writes that in Rom 9:14–18 part of the defendant's argument in this unit is that "the result of his [God's] actions is mercy on all." But this perspective is not clearly presented in Paul's words in 9:14–18; we have to wait until ch. 11 to find out the extent of God's mercy. With Cosgrove, *Elusive Israel*, I agree that text leaves tensions unaddressed until ch. 11. While the reader is left with the impression in ch. 9 that God has mercy on some and not others, it is not until ch. 11 that we read about God's mercy to all.

222. E.g., Fitzmyer, *Romans*, 623, finds a diachronic meaning to Mal 3:22 LXX [4:4]: "'all Israel' of every generation," and Paul believes ethnic Israel will be saved in the diachronic sense.

223. Bell, *Provoked to Jealousy*, 139–44; and Jewett, *Romans*, 702, side with the view that every (individual) Israelite will be saved.

these questions are not very clear. In the end, absolute universalism does not sit well with Paul's anguish over his people (9:3; 10:1). Why be filled with sorrow over Israel if all Israel will be saved anyway?[224] Equally difficult to maintain in reference to Paul's anguish is the idea of double predestination. If such were the case, then we might expect Paul to be rejoicing. According to this viewpoint's interpretation of 9:14–23, the appropriate response for Paul would be to praise God for glorifying God's name because he has chosen certain vessels for eternal life and others for eternal destruction. Instead we find Paul in anguish over his lost compatriots. Both individual universalism and individual predestination tend to mitigate the importance of Paul's despair. Most likely, since he has been referring to Israel in terms of "remnant," the "rest," and "children," and has been focusing on corporate entities such as Israel and Gentiles, the "all" in 11:26 probably does not refer to every individual Israelite, but to Israel as a whole.[225]

Perhaps Paul believed in the potential for real eschatological destruction of certain individuals despite his belief that "all Israel" will be saved. This perspective would at least seem to be true in reference to the sort of teachers he warns against in 16:17–18. If so, more questions about theodicy must be raised in relation to these individual's own responsibility if God is involved in spiritual hardening (9:18 cf. 11:7, 25c, 32a) and yet Israel seems responsible for its own unbelief (9:31–10:3; 10:11–21; 11:23). Maybe Paul realized that he did not have all the complete answers to such questions, and so the doxology in 11:33–36 stresses the mystery of God in his salvific plan related to Israel and Gentiles.[226] Paul's words in 11:35 softly echo Job 41:3[11]: "who has given beforehand to him, that it should be paid back to him?" This passage is found at the end of Job's suffering, when God reveals himself to Job and asks him questions too difficult to answer. The idea stresses God's sovereignty in relation to his wisdom, and it shows that he does not owe humans anything.[227] This thought drifts remarkably close to Rom 9:20, where Paul originally evades the question he posits in 9:19 and answers instead with another question resembling language from Job 9. Romans 11:1–32 reaches the climax of Paul's argument and connects the final theodicy question in 11:1 with his thesis in 9:6: God's word has not

224. The phrase "all Israel" was used corporately in terms of national Israel: e.g., 2 Chr 12:1; Dan 9:11; *T. Benj.* 10.11; *Jub.* 50.9. See further Bryan, *Jesus and Israel's Traditions*, 182.

225. Fitzmyer, *Romans*, 623, determines that "all Israel" occurs 148 times in the Hebrew scriptures and means "historic, ethnic Israel."

226. The idea of mystery here is thus used differently than when he uses the word in 11:25.

227. This might speak to those in Israel who thought it was their "national prerogative" to assume divine privileges; so Dunn, *Romans*, 2.703.

failed in reference to Israel because there is an Israel of promise and an Israel of flesh. The Israel of promise is associated with the faithful remnant of Israel that believes, and Paul belongs to that remnant, as do the believing Gentiles. The Israel of flesh, which seems to be ethnic Israel in a temporary state of unbelief, is also included in the eschatological plan of salvation. The answer to the third question in 11:1, then, is "No, God has not completely rejected apostate Israel." Now that Rom 11 has been unpackaged, we can look back and evaluate the apostle's answers regarding theodicy and Israel's apostasy.

Romans 9:14: Is God unjust in reference to his election? Paul would answer no to this question. God's divine purpose is expressly tied in with God's mercy, and he turns out to be merciful to all humanity, even apostate Israel.

Romans 9:19: Why does God find fault, for who has resisted his will? Paul does not immediately answer 9:19 but replies that humans have no right to pose such a question because God is free to do whatever he wants with his creatures. We do gain the idea that God is working his ultimate purposes for his own glory through his creatures in relation to their obedience and through (or despite) their disobedience. The readers must draw the inference from 11:32 that God does not ultimately find fault because he is merciful to the faithful remnant of Israel and the believing Gentiles (vessels of mercy) as well as apostate Israel (the vessels of wrath). In the immediate context a somewhat ambiguous answer arrives at 9:22–23: in God's patience, God is granting time for the vessels of wrath to repent. The dynamics of how God hardens hearts and consigns to disobedience, however, are never fully unpackaged. While Paul affirms that God hardens hearts to serve God's ultimate purposes, the paradox of how divine sovereignty and individual human freedom work themselves out in a context of corporate entities—and more specifically how this all fits into God's salvation for Israel in the present era—remains an imponderable mystery that Paul seems to acknowledge in his attestation of the incomprehensible ways of God (11:33–36).

Romans 11:1: Has God rejected his people? Paul affirms that God has not rejected Israel despite the people's unbelief and apostasy. There is some confusion in the apostle's argument because of his apparent equivocation on terms such as "Israel" and the mode of "election" that threads together Rom 9–11. Even so, his answer in chapter 11 attempts to address his thesis in 9:6: the word of God has not failed—Israel is still included in the salvific plan of God, which will (from Paul's perspective) unfold in the future. Paul is less clear, however, about the salvific status of unbelieving Israelites who die before this culmination takes place. If we follow his reasoning in chapters 9–11 and compare it with the rest of Romans, it turns out that *even though many Israelites are currently apostates—"vessels of wrath" (9:22), hard-ened (11:7–10; cf. 9:18), lack faith (9:31–32), stumble over Christ (9:32–10:4), and disobedient (10:16–21)—they are still foreknown (11:2), elect (11:28), and predestined for salvation and eternal glory (11:26). And even the Gentiles who are "in Christ," who are foreknown, predestined, elect, and bound for final salvation (cf. Rom 8:1, 29–39), can also become apostate through pride, racism, and a failure to persevere in faith (Rom 11:20–22).*

CONCLUSION

Paul never visited the congregation in Rome prior to writing his letter to this community, which consists of both Jewish and Gentile members, though the latter predominate. Although Paul warns the congregation of a potential danger related to deceptive teachers, he considers the congregation to be generally virtuous and obedient (15:14–15; 16:17–19). His letter intends to build rapport with this congregation before visiting them, and he uses this opportunity to clarify his own position on the gospel. There is no compelling reason to assume that a crisis between Jewish and Gentile members over table fellowship became the incentive for this letter (Rom 14). At best a soft problem over this issue may exist in Rome. Paul's objective through his instruction on table fellowship seems to be for the purpose of offsetting potential questions about foods and fellowship that might create heated arguments once he arrives in Rome. His motivation may be based not merely on reports of possible tensions there but on his past experiences with churches such as Antioch and Corinth. Informed by his correspondence to the Corinthians (1 Cor 8–10), Paul warns the Romans that such a division could lead to the strong members causing weak ones to fall away and be eschatologically destroyed (e.g., Rom 14:15). In this case, however, the weak members are oriented to Jewish dietary customs rather than being former idolaters. Divisions over table fellowship might cause them to leave the church or return back to following the entire works of the Law instead of practicing righteousness by faith.

For Paul faith requires loyalty to Christ and obedience in conforming to God's will (1:5). Paul himself is an exemplar of faithfulness—he is fulfilling his prophetic role of proclaiming the good news and is not ashamed of his message despite hardships, akin with the Isaianic herald (1:16). In short, he takes a popular warning from Jesus seriously by confessing Christ publically and refusing to deny him. God's righteousness includes God's saving work in setting right the entire cosmos and rectifying both Jews and Gentiles who possess faith (1:17). Their election is by God's grace, and initial righteousness is imparted to those who place faith in Jesus Christ, whose own faithfulness to God has made explicit God's ultimate plan to save the world. Final righteousness/justification, however, requires God's people to persevere in the present time and remain obedient to God and Christ, because everyone will be judged by their deeds on judgment day at the end of human history (2:5–6, 16). Such a judgment assumes that certain believers who were initially rectified may be punished on judgment day for wrongful deeds, that is, for not living in way characterized by believing obedience. In Romans the consequences of final judgment on apostates are described in terms of destruction, eternal death, and facing God's wrath. Paul finds no contradiction between the thoughts of "justification by faith" and "judgment by works." Righteousness by faith, even as a gift, requires the reciprocity of its converts to walk in believing obedience to the will of God in the new era in Christ. This new lifestyle involves "work" but not the "works of the Law"; it requires obedient behavior led by the Spirit's guidance, which manifests in practical ways such as loving one's neighbor as oneself inclusive of welcoming all believers at dinner meals, refusing to retaliate against one's persecutors, and not conforming with the pride and vices associated with the current fallen age (cf. Rom 12–15). Without such behaviors or "works" to mark out the believer's lifestyle, it is always possible that such a believer might receive an unfavorable verdict on judgment day.

Humanity, represented by Gentiles, were originally competent people who knew God the Creator. Rejecting God's gifts, they committed apostasy through idolatry, fornication, and vices so that they became progressively obdurate and incompetent (1:18–32). The Jews, likewise, represented by an apostate interlocutor, transgressed the Law (Rom 2). For Paul both Jews and Gentiles have committed sin and turned aside from following God, and the Mosaic Law was unable to defeat this power. The power of sin, however, has been dealt a massive blow by Christ Jesus' atoning death, which ushers in a new era and makes righteous living possible for those who are "in Christ" and who are led according to God's Spirit instead of the desires of the "flesh" associated with enslaving vices that lead to spiritual death (Rom 3; 6; 8:1–16). Believers who live according to the flesh will "die" and fail to inherit eternal life (8:13; cf. 6:21–23).

Paul's salvific paradigm follows a sequence of divine grace and election, which makes possible human faith(fulness), righteousness, obedience, and perseverance in the present age, which in turn make possible final righteousness/justification in the age to come. The community that loves God and remains "in Christ" may be confident that persecutions, sufferings, and hostile forces will not overpower God's love for them—the community in Christ will persevere until the end (8:1, 28–39). Paul centers on the destiny of the corporate elect, which struggles through the spiritual wilderness of "now" and "not yet" as it journeys to spiritual Zion to meet its redeemer face to face. The community is predestined by God through the scriptures of Israel to reach its final destination and will experience the glory of bodily resurrection at the eschaton. Paul's confidence of the community's final salvation in the face of opposition, however, does not preclude the possibility that vices and unbelief can undermine the faith of individual believers. His omission of vice and unbelief in 8:28–39 has to do with his rhetorical finesse to encourage his recipients of their final hope. He did not intend to suggest that individual believers could never commit apostasy, especially given that in the previous pericope he affirms this possibility (8:13) and does so again in chapters 9–11.

Israel has committed apostasy by not believing Jesus is the Messiah, and this has led to Paul's anguish over his fellow kinsmen. An intertextual reading of the sources Paul echoes in Rom 9–11 suggests that Paul already knew in chapter 9 where he was going with his argument before the climatic ending in chapter 11. The Isaianic and Hosea texts that Paul uses make distinctions between faithful and apostate Israelites who will be restored, and Isaiah uses prominently the language of a faithful remnant who will be joined with Gentiles in God's eschatological plan of salvation. These sources buttress the position that Paul is not teaching double predestination if what is meant by this is that God arbitrarily preselects some individuals to eternal life and others to eternal damnation so that their destinies remain forever fixed. Paul focuses on the election of corporate Israel rather than individualistic double predestination. Moreover, Paul never mentions that Esau and Pharaoh are irrevocably destined to eternal damnation. To be sure, God hardened Pharaoh, who represents Israel in an enemy name-switching strategy of Paul's, but obdurate Israel, included as the "vessels of wrath," will be saved at the end of the eschaton (9:14–23; cf. 11:26–28). Hardened Israel is still elect and will be restored to salvation when the Christ returns. Paul presents a theodicy by arguing for the faithfulness of God who has not rejected his people. The believing Gentiles, on the other hand, who are presently "vessels of mercy," are warned that they too could fall away and be cut off from salvation through pride, racism, and failing to persevere in Christ during the present era (11:20–23).

Similar to his other letters, Paul affirms once again in Romans that restoration from apostasy is possible. This time the certainty of a return anticipates the future salvation of Israel even though Paul thinks Israel to be currently in a state of unbelief.

The focus of restoration in this instance is both corporate and prophetic. Likewise, Paul's emphasis on hardships and persecution as incentives for believers to stand confident and persevere rather than fall away is reminiscent of his other letters. In his list of hardships he includes, beyond human persecution, some thoughts that hint at demonic oppression, and a few other hardships that might recollect things he has faces when travelling as missionary. The combination of persecution, demonic oppression, and other forms of suffering may recall his personal list of hardships from 2 Cor 11. Given his robust personality of not succumbing to denial of Christ in the face of his persecutors, his strong words on the certainty of the community "in Christ" being predestined to eternal glory despite opposition make proper sense.

Again we see in Paul that vice, not persecution, is the real danger to the believing communities. Whereas in Galatians apostasy takes place primarily by believers who get circumcised and embrace the works of the Law, in Romans sin and death are the ultimate enemies, and the Law is seen as exacerbating sin due to its powerlessness to defeat it. Sin's center of operation is "the flesh" manifesting itself through different vices. Sin contaminated both Jews and Gentiles in their turning from God, and it can threaten believers to apostasy if they are not diligent to live in accordance with faith, obedience, and the Spirit. The Gentiles are specifically warned against pride that leads to racism. In comparison to Paul's other letters, Romans says more about apostasy in general but less about it in particular. This is to be expected given that he does not know enough about the Romans personally to address their specific issues. We find a similar phenomenon in the letter to Ephesians, where the Pauline author seems unfamiliar with his audience and so not much is said specifically about apostasy. In relation to the gospels, Paul's view of righteousness clashes the most, it seems, with Matthew's; the latter finds righteousness through the Law. Even so, both see that the main objective of the Law is the love of one's neighbor, and the Sermon on the Mount affirms Jesus as fulfilling the Law and thus being its exemplary interpreter. The Matthean community reads righteousness from the Law through the lens of Jesus; Paul reads righteousness through God and Christ, and the works of the Law can be an obstruction to that righteousness. Mark's emphasis on faith and lack of emphasis on the Law, especially in relation to foods, is more at home with Paul's view. Incidentally, Mark is seen in Acts and the Deutero-Pauline letters as a colleague of Paul. It seems they are writing to the same community in Rome, but Paul's letter would have preceded Mark's gospel by about a decade. Unlike Mark's community, the environment in the Rome of Paul's day has not been distressed by

Nero's persecutions. Paul's words about suffering and persecution in his letter seem more relevant to his own experiences than that of the Roman community.

6

Philippians: Living Worthy of the Gospel— Exhortations on Opponents, Apostates, and Perseverance for the Philippians

Paul writes to the Philippians while in prison, most likely from Ephesus or Rome sometime between the mid 50s to early 60s CE (cf. Phil 1:7, 13–14, 17; 4:22).[1] The Greek names of congregation members suggest this church was comprised of Gentiles (2:25; 4:2). If Paul's original mission to Philippi in Acts 16 helps at all with their identity, these Gentiles may have been former God-fearers (Lydia), "pagans" (the fortune-telling maidservant), and Romans of low status (the jailer).[2] He thanks his friends and the congregation for a recent offering, comforts them regarding his status as a prisoner, and returns to them their emissary, Epaphroditus (2:25–30; 4:10–20).[3] Paul uses this letter as an opportunity to encourage the congregation to continue living out their heavenly citizenship in a manner worthy of the gospel in which Christ is its content (1:27; cf. 2:18; 3:20).[4] The words in 1:27 in fact may capture the thesis (*propositio*) of the letter, which combines deliberative and epideictic rhetoric.[5] The apostle hears about some friction between congregation members

1. On Rome as the provenance see Acts 28:14–31; Bockmuehl, *Philippians*, 25–32. On Ephesus, compare Acts 19–20; Reumann, *Philippians*, 14. For discussion on the various dates and provenances see, e.g., Gnilka, *Philipperbriefe*, 18–25; Collange, *Philippiens*, 30–34.

2. See Oakes, *People to Letter*, 63–65, who adds primarily from Acts a preponderance of slaves in the church.

3. For options on the various purposes of this letter see, e.g., O'Brien, *Philippians*, 35–38; Fee, *Philippians*, 24–39. The latter proposes the letter is primarily about the Philippians' affairs.

4. See Gräbe, "Citizens of Heaven," 289–302.

5. See various rhetorical options in Reumann, *Philippians*, 9–10.

through Epaphroditus (4:2–3) and that they are being persecuted by outsiders; he thus encourages them to live in unity, humility, and imitate Christ as well as follow Paul's own example (1:27—2:5, 14; 3:17; 4:9).

THE PERSECUTION OF THE PHILIPPIANS (1:27–30; 2:15)

The congregation is suffering persecution in Philippi (1:28–30). The persecutors of these believers should not be confused with Paul's opponents in 1:15–18 nor with the adversaries mentioned in Phil 3.[6] The conflict in 1:28 does not seem to originate from Jewish or Jewish Christian adversaries in the city. A number of scholars notice an insignificant population of Jews in Philippi during Paul's era.[7] Likewise, there is no mention of a synagogue in Philippi in Acts 16, and Luke typically includes Paul visiting synagogues in other cities during his missions (e.g., Acts 13:5, 14; 14:1; 17:1, 10, 17; 18:4; 19:8). The Philippian congregation's opponents in Phil 1:28 are probably non-Christian Gentiles similar to the crowd described in Acts 16:16–40 who had Paul and Silas thrown in jail after the town magistrates ordered them to be beaten with rods.[8] Perhaps Paul recalls this incident when he compares the congregation's persecution with his own—they themselves saw the "struggle" (ἀγών) he went through when he was with them (Phil 1:30; cf. 1 Thess 2:2; 2 Cor 11:25).

If the Philippians' stand firm (στήκετε) in unity, this will foster mutual encouragement through their sufferings (1:27). Such standing is the antipode of falling or committing apostasy, which in this case would mean rejecting the gospel faith as a result of persecution and so miss out on eschatological salvation (1:28; 4:1).[9] These

6. Contrast e.g., Collange, *Philippiens*, 70 who thinks they are Jewish Christians in Philippians 1:28; Hawthorne and Martin, *Philippians*, 72 who think the adversaries here are non-Christian Judaizers; and Silva, *Philippians*, 8–9 who sees the same opponents throughout the letter as Jewish Christians. Differently, Bateman, "Opponents at Philippi," 39–61 views these opponents as Gentile sympathizers to Judaism. For discussions on the identities of the opponents proposed by various scholars, see Williams, *Enemies of the Cross*, 54–60; Sumney, "Studying Paul's Opponents," 25–29. Partition theories on the letter also influence the different identities of opponents in Phil 1 and 3. For a convenient list of various partitions see Williams, 49 who rightly rejects this approach (50–54).

7. E.g., Murphy-O'Connor, *Paul: A Critical Life*, 213–14; Oakes, *People to Letter*, 58–59; cf. 84–89.

8. More specifically Fee, *Philippians*, 31–32, suggests the Romans as persecutors here (cf. Acts 16). Harink, *Paul among the Postliberals*, 112–14, interprets Philippi as a community suffering under imperial opposition, and Paul preaches against the imperial cult. But if Acts 16 has any merit for our interpretation, the persecution may be coming primarily from the townspeople who are inciting Roman officials against the Christ-followers. On ἀντίκειμαι in 1:28, cf. 1 Cor 16:9; 2 Thess 2:4; Luke 21:15, and for military language in this passage see Geoffrion, *Rhetorical Purpose*.

9. Cf. Gal 5:1; 1 Thess 3:8; 1 Cor 10:12; 15:1f; 16:13; 2 Cor 1:24; Rom 5:2; 11:20; Eph 6:10–11; 2 Thess 2:15. The gospel faith is more literally "the faith of the gospel" (τῇ πίστει τοῦ εὐαγγελίου). Loh and Nida, *Philippians*, 41, more freely translate it, "Fight for the kind of trust which results from the good news."

verses combine military and eschatological thoughts, pointing to the Day of Christ, when the believers' earthly struggles will be over and their relentless stand will result in final salvation. Their adversaries, on the other hand, will be punished with "destruction" (cf. ἀπώλεια: Phil 3:19; Rom 9:22; 2 Thess 2:3; 1 Tim 6:9).[10] *The gospel faith in which the Philippians stand functions negatively as an "omen" (ἔνδειξις) related to their opponents' upcoming demolition, but it also functions positively as evidence of the Philippians' salvation due to their persevering in faith* (Phil 1:27–28).[11]

These opponents reject the gospel faith, which is Paul's preaching of the cross, the message of Christ crucified. D. K. Williams rightly argues that cross terminology in Philippians is used polemically as a rhetorical means by which Paul, among other things, validates his mission and message.[12] Paul speaks of the message of the gospel and the message of the cross almost interchangeably (1 Cor 1:17–18). His message of the cross has a twofold effect: it becomes folly and a stumbling block for unbelievers who are eternally perishing, and yet it becomes God's saving power for believers who are being saved (1 Cor 1:18–23). Likewise similar to ἔνδειξις in Phil 1:27–28, which functions both as "evidence" for the believers' salvation and an "omen" for the unbelievers' destruction, the message about Christ in 2 Cor 2:14–17 functions simultaneously as a "fragrance" related to the believers' eternal life but an "odor" in relation to the unbelievers' eternal death.[13] The content of Paul's gospel faith, the preaching of the cross (cf. Phil 2:8; 3:18), produces both positive and negative re-

10. Understanding the term in the context of war, Loh and Nida, *Philippians*, 42, translate ἀπώλεια as losing in contrast to winning: "*And this will prove to them that they will lose.*" But the nuance of eschatological destruction is missing from this interpretation. Hawthorne and Martin, *Philippians*, 72–74, read 1:28 thusly: "In no way let your adversaries strike terror in you. For although they see your loyalty to the truth as inevitably leading to your persecution and death [ἀπωλείας], you see it as leading through persecution to the salvation of your souls [σωτηρίας]." But this interpretation makes the eschatological dimension lopsided, applying only to the salvation of the Philippians but not the destruction of opponents. The meaning of ἀπώλεια is also relegated merely to death in the physical body by their view. Fowl, *Philippians*, 65–68, tries to alleviate this difficulty by affirming that the opponents see "the Philippians' physical destruction as testimony of their eternal perdition" (68); i.e., that they are judged by the gods. But Paul is more likely referring to the *opponents'* destruction if his thought here is similar to his Corinthian letters.

11. The relative feminine singular "which" (ἥτις) in 1:28 probably refers back to the preceding feminine singular "faith" (πίστις) in 1:27 (cf. 1:25), hence, the gospel faith. Alternatively it could refer to the entire thought of the Philippians standing firm in unity and faith despite their opponents. If so, "which" refers either inclusively or exclusively to the "faith of the gospel." To be sure, it is certainly possible that ἥτις is attracted to the feminine singular ἔνδειξις in 1:28 (e.g., Fee, *Philippians*, 168–69), but even if this were the case such an attraction does not negate that 1:28 may be referring back to thoughts in 1:27 that include the gospel faith. In 1:28 αὐτοῖς may be a dative of reference; the believers, it seems, rather than the opponents, are the ones who see this ἔνδειξις.

12. Williams, *Enemies of the Cross*, 235; cf. 116–17.

13. Incidentally, both Phil 1:27–30 and 2 Cor 2:14–17 function as the thesis for their respective letters.

sults depending on whether its message is accepted or rejected, and this is what Phil 1:28 conveys. His message, in addition, determines eschatological judgment against those who reject the message—they will face divine wrath and destruction at the end of time (Phil 3:19; 1 Cor 1:17–19; 2 Cor 4:3–4; 1 Thess 2:14–16; 2 Thess 1:6–10; Rom 12:19; cf. 2:5–6, 9).

The early Philippian Christ-followers live amidst a "crooked and perverse generation" and shine as lights in the world (Phil 2:15). This "generation" recalls the Song of Moses in Deut 32:5, 20, which describes Israel's covenantal unfaithfulness to God. The song mentions Israel's apostasy through idolatry—they are a perverse and unfaithful wilderness generation because they have angered God with their worthless idols (Deut 32:21; cf. vv. 16–17, 37–39). The notion of a wicked generation is sometimes used as well in settings that contrast Jesus and his followers with non-believing Israelites (Matt 12:39–41; Luke 9:41; Acts 2:39–40). Is Paul referring to Jewish opponents here? This seems unlikely because such opponents of the early church were not idolaters, and elsewhere Paul clearly makes a connection between idolatry and the perverse generation in Deut 32 (cf. 1 Cor 10:1–22). The Jews who oppose Paul, whether Christ-followers or not, would agree with the apostle that idolatry stands out as a heinous vice that unconverted Gentiles practice. Moreover, as we have already noted, there is no evidence of a significant community of Jews in Philippi at this time. *The perverse generation opposed to the Philippians, then, is probably the same adversary as in 1:28–30: non-Christian Gentiles.*[14] The Philippians are depicted as God's children and as "lights in the world" (2:15b), which not only recalls Jesus' words to disciples who would present the gospel to outsiders (Matt 5:14–16), but also Paul's divine commission to be a light to the Gentiles (Acts 13:47; 2 Cor 6:2/Isa 42:6; 49:6).[15]

Paul is here encouraging the Philippians to conduct themselves in a manner worthy of the gospel by living righteously and blamelessly as children of light in the midst of their non-believing neighbors and magistrates. An assumption for Paul is that these neighbors practice deeds of darkness typical of Greco-Roman society (cf. 1 Thess 5:3–9 cf. 1:9–10; Rom 13:12–14; Eph 5:5–11). The Philippians must persevere in this environment despite harassment and hostility against their peculiar faith. Their suffering would seem to be similar to that of the Thessalonian congregation, which is comprised of faithful Gentiles being persecuted by their unbelieving com-

---

14. Contrast the view of Jewish opponents in this passage in, e.g., Collange, *Philippiens*, 99–100.

15. Even if the Philippians did not the connect "light of the world" with Israel's scriptures, the thought would find meaning for them as Greco-Romans, given that the societal heroes were viewed as stars and other astral phenomena (cf. Reumann, *Philippians*, 393). See examples in Bormann, *Philippi*, 219.

patriots. The nature of this persecution does not seem related to any official Roman edict; it probably comes by way of general harassment involving such things as false accusations, verbal abuse, sporadic physical violence, and social alienation that may be affecting them economically.[16] His advice to them includes their being worthy soldiers for the cause of Christ (Phil 1:27–30; cf. 2:25), their enduring hardships and suffering (1:29), and their changing their allegiances from Rome to live as heavenly citizens (πολιτεύομαι: 1:27; πολίτευμα: 3:20).[17] Paul's exhortation for the Philippians to live this way seems to be another variant of the metaphor to "walk" or live one's life in a sanctified manner (Phil 3:17; cf. 1 Thess 4:1–3; 2 Cor 4:2; Gal 5:16). In the LXX πολιτεύομαι has special relevance to living according to the Torah and being faithful to God's covenant and institutes,[18] an idea that early Christians transposed to teach believers to live according to Christ.[19] Beyond this, given the context of a city that was considered a Roman colony in which citizenship was highly prized, Paul's choice of πολιτεύομαι would seem to be a particularly relevant term to use in order to help the Philippians perceive and appreciate the value of their heavenly citizenship as a community in Christ.

PAUL'S OPPONENTS (1:15–18; 3:2; CF. 3:4–9)

The Philippians' adversaries in 1:27–28 are not Paul's adversaries in 1:15–18. Those who proclaim Christ with insincere motives, having strife, envy, selfish ambition, and rivalry towards Paul are still preaching the gospel (1:15–18). This could hardly be said of the unbelieving neighbors of the Philippians who were mistreating them (1:28–30), or the "enemies of the cross" in 3:18.[20] The identity of these opponents also seems to be different than the group Paul writes against in 3:2 who appear to be promulgating the doctrine of circumcision. The group in 1:15–18 resembles the believers who attack Paul's apostolic authority in 2 Cor; the group in Phil 3:2 resembles the missionaries he writes against in Galatians. An exact correlation, however, between the opponents in 2 Corinthians and Paul's rivals in Phil 1:15–18 would be overdrawn. Paul reserves harsher words for the Corinthian opponents; Satan works through them and they teach a "different gospel" (2 Cor 11:2–4, 13–14). In the end

16. See Oakes, *People to Letter*, 89–99, for some lucid scenarios on how societal discrimination against Christian business owners, women, and slaves might have hurt them economically and otherwise.

17. For these points, see further De Vos, *Church and Community Conflicts*, 277–86.

18. 2 Macc 11:25; 3 Macc 3:4; 4 Macc 2:8; *Letter of Aristeas* 31; Philo, *Spec.* 4.226.

19. *1 Clem.* 6.1; 21.1; 51.2; Pol. *Phil.* 5.2; cf. Acts 23:1; BDAG, 845–46.

20. Contrast Fredrickson, "Envious Enemies," 22–28, who equates the opponents in 1:15 with 3:18 primarily by associating the ancient conception of envy with enmity.

it is not clear exactly who Paul has in mind in 1:15–18, but these preachers are neither unbelieving Gentiles nor necessarily the opponents mentioned in chapter 3.[21] It should also be noted that the group in 1:15–18 is probably not the same set of Christians identified in 2:21—the former refers to "some" preachers who oppose Paul; the latter refers to "all" except Timothy, which seems to be somewhat of an exaggeration regarding believers who seek their own interests. Paul has the rhetorical aim of persuading the Philippians to emulate Timothy's sacrificial behavior rather than follow the example of believers who are motivated by self-interests (cf. 2:4).

In 3:2 Paul seems to describe another set of opponents. A number of identities are possible, including Jewish Christians, non-Christian Jews, Jewish Gnostics, Cynics, or followers of Cybele or some other cult group.[22] The apostle's preponderance with circumcision, the Law, and his Jewish identity in 3:1–9 would seem to suggest these opponents are Jewish; more specifically they are probably missionaries who claim to be Christ-followers but want to circumcise Gentile Christians and get them to become followers of Jewish Law and customs. Paul vituperatively labels them in 3:2 as "dogs," "evil workers," and the "mutilation" (κατατομή). Mark 7:27–28 and Matt15:26–27 may be examples of Jesus/the gospel writers associating "dogs" with unclean Gentiles, and it is frequently suggested that Paul is reversing this term on his Jewish opponents.[23] *Paul, however, could be associating "dogs" with either false teachers or apostates*, similar to 2 Pet 2:20–22 and Rev 22:15. If so, then he is not calling the opponents "dogs" with the intention of reversing a Jewish labeling of Gentiles; rather, he is using invective language against false teachers who have strayed from the path God intended for them. In any case Paul also calls them evil

---

21. Reumann, *Philippians*, 202–7 presents eleven options for their identity and suggests, speculatively in my opinion, that Paul's use of his Roman citizenship may have sparked the envy and resentment in 1:15–18.

22. See e.g., O'Brien, *Philippians*, 33–34, for the first view; Klijn, "Paul's Opponents," 278–84, for the second; Holladay, "Paul's Opponents in Phil 3," 77–90, for the third. Suggesting the possibility of the fourth and fifth views is Nanos, "Paul's *Reversal* of Jews," 25–33. On the view of two opponents (Jewish/Jewish Christian in 3:2 and Libertine/Gnostic in 3:18f) see Baumbach, "Frage nach den Irrlehren," 252–66; Jewett, "Conflicting Movements," 362–90.

23. E.g., O'Brien, *Philippians*, 355; Müller, *Philippians*, 106. Nanos, "Paul's *Reversal* of Jews," 1–33, however, demonstrates the scarcity of evidence in early Jewish sources associating the word "dog" with Gentiles, contra, e.g., Michel, "κύων, κυνάριον," 3.1101–2; Str.B. 1.724–25. Nanos suggests alternative opponents in Phil 3:2 such as the Cynics or Cybele cult (25–33). I am not convinced, however, that he has explained in a persuasive way why Paul brings up his boasting in his Jewish ancestry and Law observance immediately after his warning and counts such things as loss. It seems more contextually plausible to suggest either Jewish opponents or missionaries that stress Law keeping in 3:2–9. Against the Cynic view, see recently Reumann, *Philippians*, 471–72. Nanos is right, though, that even if the predominant viewpoint were correct about Paul associating "dogs" as a reversal of his Jewish opponents' claims against Gentiles, "that would not thereby make repeating this kind of malicious language toward Jews—or anyone else, for that matter—appropriate" (31).

workers, which is probably a play on their self-designation as workers or missionaries for God (cf. 2 Cor 11:13; 1 Tim 5:18; 2 Tim 2:15; Matt 9:37–38). The "mutilation" perhaps implies that these opponents' circumcision, which is not from the heart (cf. Deut 10:16; Jer 4:4; Ezek 44:7), is akin to ritualistic laceration and mutilation done by pagan groups.[24] He contrasts the Philippians, his colleagues, and himself as those who are truly circumcised—they worship by means of God's Spirit and boast in Christ instead of placing confidence in "the flesh" (Phil 3:3), which may refer to physical circumcision along with other external things that become grounds for self-boasting, whether in ethnic privileges, self achievements, or both (cf. 3:4–8). This group appears to be similar to the opponents he contends with in Galatia, and similar to Galatians he contrasts the Law over against righteousness by faith(fulness) (Phil 3:9).

Paul discusses his former role as a Pharisee who persecuted the church and was blameless concerning righteousness in Law (3:4–7).[25] He is not claiming to be sinless in his former days; his observance of the Law as a Pharisee included a sacrificial system to deal with sins that he may have committed. Even so, blameless conduct did not prevent him from self-righteous boasting in his heritage, and he considers the things he had previously gained to be "crap" for the sake of gaining the surpassing knowledge of Christ and "be found in him" on the Day of Christ (3:8–9a). As a Christ-follower Paul has abandoned confidence in his own righteousness from the Law (cf. Rom 10:3) and desires instead the righteousness that comes from God on the basis of faith and through the faithfulness of Christ (Phil 3:9). Here two forms of righteousness are set in contrast: one gained by one's ethnic heritage and self-achievements, the other by Christ's achievements, especially on the cross, and by faith in him.[26] This does not necessarily mean that Paul considers it impossible to keep the Law; he himself was an example that one *could* keep it (3:6).[27] Rather, ever

24. See De Vos, *Church and Community Conflicts*, 268; Bockmuehl, *Philippians*, 189. Both relate the term to a verb in the LXX describing pagan self-mutilation (Lev 21:5; 1 Kgs 18:28; Isa 15:2; Hos 7:14). Similar sarcasm may be found in Gal 5:12, in which Paul crudely wishes that his circumcision-promoting opponents cut off the entire penis.

25. Compare Zechariah, who is considered righteous and blameless in relation to God's commandments and requirements (Luke 1:6), and yet the song attributed to him is very nationalistic (1:67–80), implying the Gentiles or Romans as enemies (1:71, 74).

26. Righteousness in this passage is perhaps both subjective and objective: it involves "faith in Christ" and the "faithfulness of Christ," both of which bring about righteousness. Moreover, righteousness here may be both forensic and participatory, if Chester, *Conversion at Corinth*, 172–84, 203–10, is correct.

27. Of course this interpretation interacts with numerous questions and positions related to Paul and the Law. On the New Perspective view of Phil 3:7–9 see, e.g., Dunn, *Theology of Paul*, 369–71; and on the debate with special reference to Phil 3:9 see Koperski, *Paul and the Law*. Chester, *Conversion at Corinth*, 164–83, 202–4, (through 1 Cor 4:1–5; 14:20–25) argues that Paul's blamelessness in Phil

since Christ's accomplishment on the cross, other forms of making one righteous are now passé. Moreover, Paul knew firsthand that having pride in one's heritage and own achievements often becomes a stumbling block to having faith in Christ because, as a Pharisee, he himself rejected Christ and became hostile toward the followers of Jesus. The presupposition for Paul is that a new era has arrived through Christ.

More important for our purposes is whether the Philippians were in danger of apostatizing through the teachings of these opponents. *Paul's warning for the Philippians to "watch out" (βλέπετε) in 3:2 may suggest that succumbing to such teaching would lead to apostasy—* βλέπετε parallels Pauline texts that warn against falling away (1 Cor 8:9; Gal 5:15; Col 2:8; Eph 5:15; cf. Acts 13:40).[28] It is also used elsewhere in the New Testament with the same force (cf. Mark 4:24; 8:15; 13:5; Luke 21:8; Heb 3:12; 12:25; 2 John 8). The warning against these opponents nonetheless seems to come by way of precaution, as a safeguard (ὑμῖν δὲ ἀσφαλές: Phil 3:1b). Nothing in the letter clearly indicates that the congregation is actually being infiltrated by these adversaries; the Philippians are not on the verge of abandoning Paul's gospel due to such teachings. *The opponents are real, and have influenced other Pauline churches, but they do not seem to have reached the Philippian congregation when Paul writes his letter.*[29]

ENEMIES OF THE CROSS AS APOSTATES (3:17–19)

The "enemies of the cross of Christ" in 3:18–19 may not be the same group as the Christian proselytizers to Jewish customs in 3:2. Paul's exhortation for the Philippians in 3:17 is to imitate his own conduct, but he laments that many do not follow his example. Their "walk" or conduct reveals them as enemies of the cross of Christ. In language typical of polemic *topoi*, he claims that their god is their stomach (appetite), their glory is in their shame, and they set their minds on earthly things (3:19). Their "glory" and "earthly" mindset is set in contrast with Paul and the Philippians, whose citizenship is heavenly and expectation of glory anticipates their bodily resurrection at the *parousia* (3:20–21). Paul stereotypes and discredits these "enemies,"

---

3 must be understood in light of his pre-conversion when he did not recognize that persecuting the church was sinful.

28. Contrast Kilpatrick, "Βλέπετε: Philippians 3.2," 146–48, who softens the impact of βλέπετε to convey merely an observation or consideration. See criticisms of this view in Reed, *Discourse Analysis of Philippians*, 244–46; Williams, *Enemies of the Cross*, 154–56.

29. We do not have to side with Kilpatrick, "Βλέπετε: Philippians 3.2," on his interpretation of 3:2 simply because the opponents are not already influencing the Philippians.

making it difficult to determine whether any specific opponent is in mind.[30] This group is possibly a more generalized type of enemy. They reportedly oppose the "cross of Christ," not necessarily Paul.[31] The missionaries in 3:2 seem to be a smaller group than the "many" mentioned in 3:18, but it is quite possible that "many" is a rhetorical exaggeration (cf. 2:21). He does not want the Philippians mimicking their behavior. Even so, the language on 3:18–19 is not *merely* rhetoric or stereotyping; these enemies of the cross do exist for Paul. Jerry Sumney is correct in thinking that these opponents are Christians whom Paul rejects: "Paul's exclusion of them as examples for Christians implies that they are Christians."[32] The identity of this group is probably a set of Christ-followers whom Paul considers apostates on account of their immoral living.[33] They have not necessarily repudiated the cross of Christ in a public sense, but they have essentially denied Christ through their behavior. Some noteworthy observations support this perspective.

First, Paul is not indifferent towards these individuals but claims to be in sorrow over their condition, which parallel his tears and anguish over the Corinthian congregation's wrongful behavior (2 Cor 2:4), apostate Israel (Rom 9:1–3), and the Lukan Paul's warning with "many tears" to the Ephesian elders about a coming apostasy that will take place in their congregation (Acts 20:29–31).

Second, the fact that they are "enemies" resembles Paul's rhetorical question to the Galatians who are contemplating circumcision (Gal 4:17), his identification of apostate Israel (Rom 11:28), and the unruly believers whom the Thessalonians are to warn and chastise (2 Thess 3:6–15).[34]

Third, the notion of following the desires of the "belly" (Phil 3:19) may be associated with sin and apostasy, similar to certain early Jewish writings. We see Philo,

---

30. See further Williams, *Enemies of the Cross*, 247–48 (cf. 10–40), who considers the cross of Christ language in Paul as polemical; albeit, Williams thinks the same opponents are in view throughout Phil 3. Compare also the polemic language of the Pastorals in Karris, "Polemic of the Pastoral Epistles," 549–64. On options related to deciphering the denunciations in 3:19 with various views of opponents, see Reumann, *Philippians*, 571–74.

31. Hence it is questionable that "opponent" is the best term for them.

32. Sumney, *Servants of Satan*, 173, who also writes that "Paul never uses 'enemies' for unbelievers." See also Lohmeyer, *Philipper*, 153. But see Paul's theological and prophetic uses of the word "enemies" in Rom 5:10 and 1 Cor 15:25.

33. Both Williams, *Enemies of the Cross*, 225, and Jewett, "Conflicting Movements," 377, rightly see these opponents as once belonging to the church or fellowship of believers. De Vos, *Church and Community Conflicts*, 273, calls them "apostates" and "former Christians." Schneider, "σταυρός," 7.576, seems more correct than Lohmeyer, *Philipper*, 153, by stressing that the spurning of the cross relates to their "manner of life" rather than renouncing Christ due to persecution.

34. To be sure, the Thessalonians are forbidden to regard the unruly idlers as "enemies," and so apparently they are not completely ostracized from the community. If they were ostracized the implication would seem to be that they would become apostates.

for example, using such language in reference to apostate Jews: they forsake ancient Judaism for the flesh and "for luxurious food . . . and beauty of the body, thus ministering to the pleasures of the belly and the organs below it" (*Virtues* 34, 182).[35] Similarly 3 Maccabees describes those who transgress the divine command for their belly's sake (3 Macc 7:11).

Finally, the enemies' "glory in their shame" (ἡ δόξα ἐν τῇ αἰσχύνῃ αὐτῶν) may allude to Hos 4:7 (LXX), in which God turns Israel's glory into disgrace due to Israel's sins.[36] "Glory" in Hos 4:7 is probably understood in terms of an ascribed reputation (cf. Gen 45:13; Job 19:9; Sir 3:11; *T. Ash.* 5.2) and relates to the people and priesthood's greatness, splendor, and prosperity during the reign of Jeroboam II.[37] God's people, however, reveled in a state of apostasy by committing covenant violates such as cursing, lying, murder, theft, sexual sins, and false worship (e.g., Hos 4:2, 11–14). Because of this God would reject them, bringing judgment and shame their way (Hos 4:1–10). If Hos 4 is in the background of Phil 3:19, then the "glory" and "shame" in the latter would seem to imply a contrast between honor/splendor on the one hand and disgrace/divine rejection on the other.[38] The conceptual connections between Phil 3:17–19 and 3:20–21 (e.g., belly/body, earthly/heavenly, glory/glory) suggest that these texts should be read and understood together, and so "glory" and "shame" in 3:19 means more than simply their being proud of that which they should be ashamed.[39] It implies also an eschatological judgment that awaits these enemies of Christ when he returns and transforms the believers' bodies in conformity to his own body of "glory" (3:20–21). The apostates at that time will be rejected by Christ and put to shame (cf. 1 John 2:28; Mark 8:38; Luke 9:26).

Moreover, if Hos 4 is being echoed in Paul's thought then the notion of committing vices may be another one of Paul's points that is being implicated from this background. His use of "shame" is sometimes associated with committing vice,[40] and the "belly" or bodily appetite (κοιλία) is likewise used in the same manner (1 Cor 6:9–13; Titus 1:12; cf. Rom 16:18; Sir 23:6; 37:5). The upshot of this is that it

---

35. Citation from Wolfson, *Philo*, 1.73. Wolfson lists different types of apostates in Philo (72–86): those who fall away to desires of the flesh, intermarriage to "pagans," social ambition (such as wealth), and intellectualism (Hellenistic influence).

36. Cf. Bockmuehl, *Philippians*, 231–32, but he does not see a connection between shame and final judgment.

37. For the term as "reputation" here, see Kittel, "δοκέω, δόξα," 2.243. However, "glory" may also refer to God if the MT is preferred over the LXX in Hos 4:7. More likely, however, Paul refers to glory as something similar to honor and splendor in the context of 3:19–21.

38. Gnilka, *Philipperbrief*, 205 rightly affirms final judgment in relation to these terms.

39. E.g., Loh and Nida, *Philippians*, 117.

40. Rom 1:27; 6:21; 2 Cor 4:2; cf. Eph 5:12; Jude 13; *T. Ash.* 5.2.

confirms the enemies in Phil 3:18–19 to be conducting themselves immorally—they "walk" or behave in opposition to the cross of Christ. Paul normally uses the word "walk" (3:17–18: περιπατέω) to encourage moral conduct and sanctification that is diametrically opposed to living in a way that characterizes a lifestyle of committing vices frequently associated with unregenerate Gentiles (1 Thess 4:1–3; 1 Cor 3:3; 2 Cor 4:2; 5:7; 10:2–3; 12:18; Gal 5:16; Rom 8:4; 13:13; Col 3:7; Eph 2:2). This kind of behavior does not fit well with the opponents who teach circumcision based on the Law in 3:2, and it seriously weakens the view that in 3:19 Paul is referring ironically to Jewish dietary laws ("god is their belly") and circumcision ("glory in their shame").[41] Paul never speaks this way about food laws and circumcision elsewhere in his letters, but more importantly, *the enemies in 3:17–19 conduct themselves in a manner contrary to a "walk" that is normally interpreted by Paul in terms of moral living rather than the observance or non-observance of Jewish customs and rituals.*

The "enemies" do not verbally deny Christ or his atoning sacrifice; they deny him in practice and reject his sacrifice for sin by means of their sinful lifestyle. *If a believer's life is characterized by vicedoing, Paul does not hesitate to declare that such a person will be excluded from God's kingdom and suffer eternal death; in essence, such an individual has become apostate* (Gal 5:19–21; 1 Cor 10:1–12; Rom 8:13). The consequence of such behavior for the "enemies of the cross," who are concerned about earthly rather than heavenly things, will be eternal destruction (Phil 3:19; cf. Phil 1:28; Rom 9:22; 2 Thess 2:3; 2 Pet. 2:1; 3:16; cf. 1 Cor 1:18; 8;11; Rom 2:12).[42] The best interpretation of these enemies, then, is that they are apostate Christ-followers.

If our observations suggest anything, they point away from equating the enemies of the cross with the circumcision party in Phil 3:2 and lean in the direction of supposing former congregation members who from Paul's perspective have rejected Christ by practicing vices. The imitation Paul desires of the Philippians in 3:17 is for them to follow his ethical conduct, humility, and persevere through suffering, a pattern we find in other appeals also (1 Cor 4:16; 11:1; 1 Thess 1:6; 2:14; cf. Eph 5:1).

WORKING OUT SALVATION WITH FEAR AND TREMBLING BEFORE THE LORD (2:12; CF. 2:14–17)

While absent from them, Paul exhorts the congregation to continue to "work out your own salvation with fear and trembling" (2:12). This is in keeping with his exhortation that the Philippians are to conduct themselves in a manner worthy of the

41. E.g., Hawthorne and Martin, *Philippians*, 224–25. Mearns, "Paul's Opponents at Philippi," 194–204, highlights circumcision with both terms.

42. On ἀπώλεια as eternal destruction see also Mark 1:24; Matt 10:28; Gnilka, *Philipperbrief*, 205.

gospel (1:27—2:4). One issue at stake is whether the salvation in 2:12 is to be understood in Paul's normal sense of a person or group being considered righteous before God at final judgment. The alternative is that this salvation refers to the health and well-being of the Philippian congregation as a whole.[43] Several observations about the passage must be considered.

First, 2:12 should be understood within a context that echoes Israel's exodus-wilderness epoch (2:14–17). Allusions to Deut 32 in Phil 2:15 may suggest that Paul thinks the Philippians participate in a new exodus-wilderness epoch as God's people, similar to the way he perceives other churches, such as in Gal 4 and 1 Cor 10. The Philippians are to stand as blameless children of God (ἄμεμπτος . . . τέκνα θεοῦ) unlike Israel in Deut 32:5, who sinned and are blameworthy children (τέκνα μωμητά). The Philippians stand out in the midst of a "crooked perverse generation" (γενεᾶς σκολιᾶς καὶ διεστραμμένης), which in Deuteronomic tradition recalls the rebellious Israelites (Deut 32:5b). Also, they must do all things without "murmuring" and disputing (Phil 2:14), which reminiscences on the behavior of the wilderness generation (Deut 1:27; Exod 16:7; Num. 11:11; 14:27; Ps 105:25; cf. 1 Cor 10:10; John 6:41; Jude 14).[44] Here, as with the Gentile Christians who originally read Gal 4 and 1 Cor 10:1–11, the Philippians may be assumed by Paul to know about the story of the apostasy of God's children in the wilderness. The story functions as a negative example for the Philippians not to follow. Even though God promised them a land this did not make Israel exempt from being punished when disobeying God—many of them never made it to the land of Canaan due to grumbling, divisive conduct, and committing vices (e.g., Num 13–20, 25). What was true of Israel as God's community in making it to the promised land was not true of every Israelite.

With this backdrop to Paul's exhortation, the Philippians' salvation in 2:12 probably consists of more than their well-being as a corporate group; it includes perseverance on their own salvific journey that culminates with the *parousia* that takes place on the Day of Christ. *The goal of final salvation, if promised to the community of believers (1:6), may not necessarily take place for every person within the community* if they do not practice obedience and conduct themselves in a manner worthy of the gospel of Christ. No doubt Paul has been addressing the congregation as a whole, and yet he is very aware that his exhortations pertain to its individuals: "each of you" must not look to self-interests (cf. 2:4a). Salvation has both corporate and individualistic dimensions (former: 2 Cor 1:6; Rom 10:1; 11:11; latter: Phil 1:19; 2 Cor 1:6; 2 Cor 7:10; cf. 2 Tim 3:15).

---

43. For a corporate/well-being view see, e.g., Hawthorne and Martin, *Philippians*, 139–40.

44. On the notion of disputing (διαλογισμός), see Isa 59:7; Sir 40:2; Jas 2:4.

Second, present problems within the congregation at Philippi such as division, grumbling, and selfish ambition Paul normally interprets as vices: γογγυσμός (grumbling, Phil 2:14),[45] διαλογισμός (disputing, 2:14),[46] ἐριθεία (selfish ambition, 1:17; 2:3);[47] κενοδοξία (conceit, 2:3);[48] διχοστασία (divisions, cf. 4:3);[49] φυσίωσις (pride, cf. 2:3);[50] ἀπειθής (disobedient, cf. 2:12);[51] φθόνος (envy, 1:15);[52] and ἔρις (rivalry/discord, Phil 1:15).[53] Elsewhere he warns vicedoers of possible exclusion from God's kingdom (Gal 5:21; 1 Cor 6:11). The Philippian congregants would not be exempt from such judgment if they persist in vices and factional behavior. An assumption for Paul is that certain individuals could fall away from salvation if the congregation does not maintain unity (cf. 1 Cor). Hence, *an either/or distinction between salvation as "final deliverance" or "health" probably should not be maintained in Phil 2:12.* Even if "salvation" refers to the corporate well-being of the congregation as whole, certain individuals who might be the culprits behind the church's lack of well-being and unity would be in danger of being rejected by God (cf. 1 Cor 3:16–17; Gal 5:10b).

Third, *Paul highlights the necessity of perseverance for final salvation* in Phil 2:12–17. In the midst of their sufferings they are to persevere by "holding firm" (ἐπέχω)[54] the word of the gospel that leads to eternal life (2:16a) so that Paul's "running" (i.e., his travelling proclamation of the gospel) and work among them would not be "in vain" (Phil 2:16b; cf. Gal 2:2). The implication is rather clear: if the Philippians do not continue adhering to the gospel message, Paul's missionary work among them would have been useless; they would not be living in a manner worthy of the gospel, and he would not be able to boast on the Day of Christ because their salvation was

---

45. Cf. 1 Cor 10:10.

46. Cf. 1 Cor 3:20; 1 Tim 2:8; cf. Mark 7:21; Rom 14:1.

47. Cf. 2 Cor 12:20; Gal 5:20; cf. Phil 2:21, 25.

48. Cf. Gal 5:26.

49. Cf. 1 Cor 3:3; Gal 5:20; Rom 16:17.

50. Cf. 2 Cor 12:20.

51. Cf. Rom 1:29; Titus 1:16; 3:3; 2 Tim 3:2.

52. Cf. Gal 5:21; Rom 1:29.

53. Cf. 1 Cor 1:11; 3:3; 2 Cor 12:20; Gal 5:20; Rom 1:29; Titus 3:9.

54. The participle form of ἐπέχω here has an imperatival force, and means "holding firm" or "holding fast." Alternatively, the word may be understood as "holding forth" as in holding a torchlight: cf. LSJ, 619; Müller, *Philippians*, 94. On this reading, the Philippians are to share Paul's missionary task of offering the world the word of life. This meaning is attractive because it imagines an athlete holding up a torch (light) and running a course. Problematic with this view, however, is that Paul's running metaphor, at least in this passage, may be prophetic, echoing the "light" to the Gentiles motif of Isaiah (e.g., Isa 9:2; 42:6, 16; 49:6; 60:1–3).O'Brien, *Philippians*, 297, more correctly relates this word to holding fast against the attacks of external opponents.

never brought to its completion (Phil 2:12, 16, 27–28; cf. 1:6, 10; 3:19–20). Salvation is both a present reality for those who trust in Christ (cf. 2 Cor 6:2; Rom 1:16–18; 10:9–10; 11:11) and futuristic, involving a process in which believers must persevere until the time of final judgment when Christ returns (Phil 1:19; 1 Cor 1:18; 15:2; 2 Cor 2:15; Rom 5:9–10; 13:11; Eph 2:7–8; 2 Tim 2:10). The Philippians must continue in the gospel faith until the end; without doing so they might fall away and become another statistic among the "many" enemies of the cross of Christ. Paul knows very well that believers in Philippi could turn apostate not only by means of immoral living, as a number of former Christians have already done (3:18–19), but also by the possibility of abandoning Christ or Paul's gospel through persecution (1:27–28) and following false teachers (3:2).

Fourth and finally, the notion of the Philippians living in obedience and working out salvation with "fear and trembling" (2:12) carries with it a sense of trepidation when one stands before God or Christ on judgment day. The phrase is used in reference to fearing Jesus,[55] but it more normally conveys fearing God and God's presence,[56] fearing God's judgment,[57] or fearing a king or one's enemy.[58] In reference to God's judgment, Frank Thielman suggests that 2:12 recalls "the proper fear of judgment that characterizes the disobedient Israelites . . . and serves as a reminder to the Philippians not to presume upon their calling as the new people of God."[59] All the more, then, 2:12 anticipates Paul's allusions to the wilderness epoch in 2:14–17, which relate to a blending of salvific and eschatological concepts of enduring present suffering in a metaphorical wilderness where hostile forces must be resisted until final deliverance comes on the Day of Christ.

He uses "fear and trembling" elsewhere in the context of human relationships (1 Cor 2:13; 7:15; cf. Eph 6:5), and certainly the aspects of weakness and humility are involved with the members' relationships with each other (cf. Phil 2:1–4). This is what ignites the pericope related to Christ's incarnation as the exemplar of such humility (2:5–11). Philippians 2:12, however, stresses instead the idea of fearing and trembling before God or the Lord rather than humans. Whereas 2:12 looks forward to 2:14–17, there seems to be also a prominent factor influencing Paul's use of "fear and trembling" that points backward to 2:10–11. Paul's use of Isa 45:23 in Phil 2:10–11 conveys the notion of knees bowing and tongues confessing before God/the Lord,

---

55. Mark 5:3; cf. *Dialogue of the Savior* III, 120[1].

56. Ps 2:11–12; Jer 5:22; Dan 6:26–27; *1 En.* 14.13; 89.28–40; 4Q204.26; Philo, *Heir* 6[23–24]; Heb 12:21; Justin, *Dial.* 67.

57. Exod 15:16; Isa 19:16; *1 En.* 1:5; 13.3; *2 En.* 60:3; cf. Ps 119:20 MT.

58. Deut 2:25; Judg 7:3; Dan 5:19; 1 Macc 13:2; Josephus, *J.W.* 1.17.7[341]; cf. Jdt 15:2.

59. Thielman, *Paul & the Law*, 286n48.

which is directly related to the final judgment that includes the believers giving an account of themselves before God (cf. Rom 14:10–12/Isa 45:23). Either God (Rom 3:6; 1 Thess 3:13) or Christ (1 Cor 4:5; 1 Thess 2:19; 2 Thess 2:8) can be the judge. Philippians 2:10–11 portrays Christ's exaltation and lordship on the Day of Christ at his *parousia* (2:16 cf. 1:6, 10; 1 Cor 15:20–25). Thus, in 2:12 *the Philippians must fear and tremble in working out their salvation because they will have to stand before the judgment seat of Christ to be judged according to their deeds when he returns* (cf. 2 Cor 5:10–11a).

A striking parallel to Phil 2:12 is Ps 2:11–12 (LXX), a messianic psalm that charges the readers to "fear" and "tremble" before the Lord, lest he be angry and they be destroyed from the way of righteousness when his wrath is kindled. Paul is not concerned about modernistic notions of how politically incorrect he may sound when he intimates that his audience to fear God; his concern is that the members of this congregation stand blameless on judgment day, and if stirring them up with a healthy dose of godly fear helps them to this end then his missionary efforts among them would not be wasted. The salvation in 2:12, among things, most definitely includes the meaning implied in 1:28: exemption from the eternal destruction that will plague the opponents of the church on judgment day.

GOD'S GOOD WORK AND THE PHILIPPIANS' GOOD WORK (2:12–13; CF. 1:3–6)

Despite Paul's instilling godly fear among the Philippians in 2:12, he ultimately intends to encourage the congregation in this letter. They should not despair in attempting to live out the gospel as though their salvation depended purely on them; God is also at work in their congregation so that both their "willing" and "doing" is for the sake of God's own good purpose (2:13). Thus we observe in 2:12–13 a balance between the Philippians working out salvation and God also at work among them, which is typical of Paul and Pharisaic thinking that affirm both divine sovereignty and human responsibility (e.g., 1 Cor 10:12–13; 2 Thess 2:13–15; Josephus, *Ant.* 13.172–73).[60] God empowers the congregants with the Holy Spirit to the effect of transforming their conduct and desires for God's purposes (cf. Phil 3:21; 1 Cor 12:6, 11; Rom 7:6–8:14).[61] As in 2:12, Paul is thinking primarily in terms of the community of believers in Christ in 2:13: it is through the corporate community that God

60. Bockmuehl, *Philippians*, 154; cf. *m. Abot* 3.19. Notice also *Odes Sol.* 8.10: "Keep my mystery, you who are kept by it; keep my faith, you who are kept by it" (*OTP* 2.742).

61. Cf. Fee, *Philippians*, 237–38, who affirms the Holy Spirit in this text even though the Spirit is not mentioned explicitly.

fulfills his purpose. This is not a denial that God works his grace through individuals; it is merely an affirmation that Paul has the Philippian community foremost in mind.[62] This church can be encouraged that it is not left alone in working out its own salvation. God is working in and through this congregation, and this community can expect God's grace and Spirit to enable and empower it to continue in the gospel faith.

Paul has confidence that God will continue to do a work with this congregation until the Day of Christ arrives (1:6). He gives thanks to God when remembering the Philippians (1:3; cf. Phlm 4; Rom 1:9),[63] praying for them with joy because they share in the gospel and a good work is being done in the midst of the congregation (Phil 1:5–6).[64] The "good work" God began in this church and will bring to completion at the *parousia* seems directly related to the members giving a gift to Paul (1:5; cf. 4:10–19; 2 Cor 9:8). This work might include thoughts about completing an offering or collection,[65] missionary-related work,[66] good deeds or ethical well-doing,[67] a combination of these, or something else. The passage likewise resembles other Pauline verses in which the congregation's salvation at the end of the age is in view, and so it is quite possible that the "good work" will result in the community's final salvation (cf. Phil 1:9–10; 1 Cor 1:8–9; 1 Thess 5:23–24).[68] The multiple interpretations of this phrase make it difficult to side with one particular meaning.

If we suggest the single meaning of salvation behind the "good work," then Phil 1:6 probably functions in a similar way to 2:12–13 with salvation as something God works among the congregation, without a denial that human work is still necessary for this to take place. At any event Paul does not seem to suggest that every individual Philippian believer will necessarily persevere to final salvation regardless of what he or she might believe or practice in the future prior to the Day of Christ. His exhortation for congregants to conduct themselves with a lifestyle befitting the

62. Ibid., 190, rightly argues this kind of emphasis when discussing 2:4—stress on the entire Pauline paraenesis rests "primarily on the community, but obedience must begin with the individual."

63. Alternatively "of you" (ὑμῶν) may be a subjective genitive: cf. O'Brien, *Philippians*, 58–61.

64. The perfect active participle in 1:6, πεποιθὼς ("being persuaded"), seems dependent on the main verb, εὐχαριστῶ ("I give thanks"), in 1:3, and this is something that is done in Paul's prayers for the congregation (1:4).

65. 2 Cor 8:6–11; Rom 15:28.

66. Phil 1:22; 2:16, 30; 1 Cor 16:16; Gal 4:11.

67. Rom 2:7; 1 Thess 1:3; Col 1:10; Eph 2:10; 1 Tim 2:10.

68. See, e.g., Gundry Volf, *Paul and Perseverance*, 33–47, who emphasizes the salvific aspect; Hawthorne and Martin, *Philippians*, 21–25, emphasize the gift giving. Reumann, *Philippians*, 113–14, divides scholarly interpretations of the "good work" into three general categories: the "work of God," "the work of God and the Philippians," and "human activity." He lists a total of ten different interpretations.

gospel (1:27), his warning against the circumcision party (3:2), and his sorrow over apostates who were once faithful believers like the Philippians (3:18–19) directs us against such a conclusion. Moreover, as we have noticed in his other letters also, Paul affirms the reality of apostasy and repeatedly warns his congregations against it. Whatever else might be meant in 1:6, this verse does not preclude the possibility of Philippian congregation members falling away.

Nevertheless we suspect that Paul may be overloading the term "good work" in 1:6 with both salvific and material support nuances, or if he has one view in mind, the audience may have understood his words differently.[69] Another important aspect is that this verse functions rhetorically as part of the exordium of this letter; in this section Paul builds rapport with his audience and intends to secure the congregation's goodwill in his anticipation of their Christian maturity (3:3–11).[70] He no doubt wants to encourage the congregation to continue their gift giving and salvation until the *parousia* by expressing with confidence that God has initiated these things among them and will continue to work through them.

PAUL AND PERSEVERANCE (3:10–17; CF. 1:19–24)

Despite his imprisonment Paul maintains hope of his eschatological salvation (1:19).[71] Regardless of what might happen to him as a prisoner awaiting the court trial, whether he is eventually executed or released, he trusts that he will not be disgraced before God's tribunal (Phil 1:20–24; cf. Job 13:13–18 LXX; Rom 1:16; 9:33; 10:11).[72] In other words he has no intention or fears about rejecting faith on account of his sufferings, and he believes he will receive God's vindication rather than punishment on judgment day.[73] This confidence and hope is typical of Paul's expectation when experiencing persecution and hardships—such things provide opportunities to develop perseverance, character, and hope (cf. Rom 5:3–5). Now that he is in

---

69. A point perceptively adduced by Reumann, 152.

70. See Watson, "Rhetorical Analysis of Philippians," 63–64.

71. With Gnilka, *Philipperbrief*, 66; O'Brien, *Philippians*, 109–10.

72. Relevant passages from the LXX on being disgraced suggest a failure of faith (apostasy), according to Fowl, *Philippians*, 46–47; cf. Isa 50:7; Ps 33[34]:3; 34[35]:27; 39[40]:16; 56[57]:10. On LXX allusions here see further Fee, *Philippians*, 130–36. On the association between disgrace and divine judgment see Silva, *Philippians*, 71; Reumann, *Philippians*, 245.

73. Schenk, *Philipperbrief*, 143–44, 147f rightly connects the positive statement of salvation in 1:19 with the negative statement "not disgraced" in 1:20. The alternative explanation regarding salvation in 1:19 is that Paul refers to his physical "deliverance" from prison (e.g., RSV, GNB). Against this view Paul seems to expect this deliverance will take place regardless of whether he lives or dies (1:20). See Silva, *Philippians*, 69–72, for further critique.

prison and his earthly life might be over very soon, he expresses his confident hope (cf. 2 Tim 1:12; 4:7–8, 17–18).

The Philippians are to imitate Paul in relation to humility, suffering, and perseverance to perfection (3:10–17; 4:9),[74] and Paul's own humility and anticipation of resurrection follows a pattern of imitating Christ (cf. 2:5–11).[75] His ambition in the present life is not to boast of his privileged status as an Israelite or his own righteousness through the Mosaic Law, as he once did, but to know Christ in a personal and ever-increasing way that involves both suffering for Christ's sake and operating in the power that God demonstrated by raising Christ from the dead (3:10). To conform to Christ's death may suggest a possible expectation of Paul's own martyrdom (3:10; cf. 1:21–23), but more than this it suggests obedience and willingness to die for Christ, similar to Christ's humility and obedience that led to his own death (2:5–8). For Paul, being "in Christ" requires living in obedience to God and dying to selfish and sinful ways on a continual basis (cf. Rom 6:1–11; Gal 2:20; Col 3:3–5); sharing in Christ's death and resurrection involves union with him related to experiencing sufferings and God's personal power.[76]

Paul's own perseverance comes to the foreground in Phil 3:11–14. Though he once thought himself blameless in terms of righteousness related to the Law, as a follower in Christ he now sees himself as not having attained a state of perfection; apparently, he will not attain this state until the future resurrection of the saints (cf. 3:11, 20–21). The "prize" for which he hopes to gain at the end of his metaphoric footrace is the full realization of the heavenly call to eternal fellowship (3:14).[77] This will take place at the end of the age when the faithful are raised from dead (Phil 3:11, cf. 3:20–21; 1 Cor 9:24–27). Paul's seemingly hesitant "if somehow" (εἴ πως) in reference to attaining his final salvific goal (Phil 3:11) probably does not convey personal doubts about his future hope. Rather for the Philippians' sake, some of them perhaps having an attitude of perfection different than his own (3:15),[78] Paul rhetorically challenges them through his own race that they need to continue in

74. The preeminence of suffering in Philippians has been examined by a number of scholars: see esp. Bloomquist, *Function of Suffering in Philippians*; Walter, "Philipper und das Leiden," 417–34.

75. On the issue of imitation, Williams, *Enemies of the Cross*, 236–41, juxtaposes a pattern in Paul (3:5–11) and the Christ hymn (2:6–11): privileged status, suffering loss/kenosis, and exaltation/hope of resurrection.

76. Bockmuehl, *Philippians*, 214–15, describes this particular union as an "incorporation" into Christ (e.g., Col 2:12–13; Rom 6:1–11; 8:11).

77. Here the imagery of running does not center on travelling and proclaiming the gospel as in 2:16 but on the notions of attaining and endurance.

78. There is no reason to suggest that Paul's use of perfection in this context reflects something his opponents in 3:2 preached to the Philippians. Our view is that this group has not influenced this congregation by their teachings.

firmness of faith and properly appreciate their new life in Christ—their perfection is still futuristic, the metaphoric race of life is not over, and the eschatological prize has yet to be attained. In short, *their final salvation should not be taken for granted.* The Philippians are to keep in step with the standard in which they have already attained (3:16). They should continue to advance on the metaphoric course of salvific life and not retreat or fall back from what they have been taught. Markus Bockmuehl's words are a fitting end here: "Paul exhorts the Philippians not to jeopardize the progress in the Christian life which they have already made, but to continue in accordance with the same stand of striving to know Christ."[79]

CONCLUSION

One of the primary purposes of Paul's letter to the Philippians involves the apostle's response to a recent gift the Philippians gave him while he remained in prison. He uses this opportunity not only to thank and encourage them that God is at work among them (1:3–6), but also to exhort the congregation to live worthy of the gospel faith entrusted them despite their suffering persecution via harassment, accusations, abuse, and social alienation from outsiders (1:27–28). The Philippians must persevere in the midst of a "crooked and perverse generation" of Gentile non-believers (2:15). Their opponents, however, are not Paul's opponents in 1:15–18, who are Christian missionaries that preach the gospel of Christ but oppose Paul's ministry. They do not come from Philippi or influence that congregation. In a sense they resemble the opponents in 2 Corinthians, but Paul reserves much harsher words for the latter.

His opponents in Phil 1, in turn, are not the same ones he warns against in 3:2. The latter are Jewish Christ-followers and missionaries that insist on the circumcision of Gentile Christians. Although he warns the Philippians against following these false teachers, whom he labels "dogs," "evil workers," and "the mutilation," there is no evidence that this group had infiltrated the congregation. Paul speaks by way of preventative maintenance similar to his letter to the Romans. Finally, the group he labels as "enemies of the cross" (3:18–19) are not the same group as the missionaries in 3:2. These "enemies" are apostates who once belonged to local assemblies of emerging Christians, but they "walk" immorally; that is, they conduct themselves with lifestyles that for Paul repudiate Christ's atoning work on the cross to remove human sin. In a word, they deny the gospel message by committing vices; there is no evidence that they verbally renounce Christ. Their own self-reflection

---

79. Bockmuehl, *Philippians*, 228.

about their status is not given, but Paul claims they will suffer eternal destruction on the Day of Christ.

Similar to other Pauline churches, the Philippians are viewed as God's people who make their way through a metaphoric wilderness and must persevere against hostile forces until the Day of Christ (2:14–17; cf. Gal 4; 1 Cor 10). They must work out their own salvation with "fear and trembling" before the Lord (Phil 2:12/Ps 2:11–12 LXX); that is, the congregation must hold firm to the gospel message and fear God knowing that they will have to give an account of their deeds before the divine tribunal on judgment day. This work of salvation, however, does not amount to self-righteousness or boasting in human achievement; God also is at work in this congregation and will see to it that their work is brought to completion (Phil 2:13; cf. 1:6). Paul likewise needs to persevere if he will attain the prize of God's call to everlasting fellowship (3:11–14). His language indirectly exhorts the Philippians not to take their salvation for granted. They must continue to walk and live as heavenly citizens in an ethical manner acceptable to God (1:27), shunning division, grumbling, and selfish behavior. Without living in this manner they might turn into apostates similar to the enemies of the cross in 3:18–19.

The letter to the Philippians, along with Galatians and Romans, all have in common a pattern in which Paul discusses Mosaic Law and righteousness (Gal 2:16—5:15; Rom 1:17—7:24; Phil 3:2–9) before encouraging his audiences to "walk" in practical righteousness (Gal 5:16—6:10; Rom 8:1–17; Phil 3:17—4:9). Whereas Galatians and Romans stress walking in the Spirit, Philippians urges recipients to live as heavenly citizens. This term is appropriate for a community that belonged to a colony with special privileges as Roman citizens. Unlike the Galatians, the congregants are not on the verge of apostasy and there is no evidence that the circumcision party they are warned against was actually influencing them.

7

Ephesians: Walking as an Elect Community in Christ

Since 1991 scholarship is presently divided evenly on whether Paul is the actual author of Ephesians, with slightly more in favor of a Deutero-Pauline authorship if we go back to major publications on Ephesians since 1971.[1] While the verdict is still out, we will have to be content to consider the author to be "Pauline." The purported name of the letter's author is Paul (1:1), and if the apostle is not the immediate author then someone seems to be writing in the tradition of Paul to a location he once had influenced. It will be assumed that other letters attributed to Paul can inform the interpretation of this letter even though they should not govern it.

The precise community behind this letter remains ambiguous because some of the oldest manuscripts of 1:1 do not identify which city or congregation is being addressed (e.g., P^{46}, ℵ, B, Origen) and Marcion has the Laodiceans as the recipients.[2] The canonical Ephesians is possibly the letter to the Laodiceans mentioned in Col 4:16b (cf. Col 2:1; 4:13).[3] If so, then Paul or whoever wrote it wanted this correspondence to be read to a wider audience than the house churches in just one city—the Colossians are told to read the letter also (Col 4:16b). Since Ephesus, Laodicea, and Colossae are all cities from western Asia Minor, the letter may be especially relevant

---

1. See categorization of scholars and positions in Hoehner, *Ephesians*, 9–20. For Deutero-Pauline arguments see, e.g., Best, *Ephesians*, 7–36; Gnilka, *Epheserbrief*, 13–21; for Paul, e.g., Barth, *Ephesians*, 1.36–50; O'Brien, *Ephesians*, 14–47.

2. Cf. Metzger, *Textual Commentary*, 532, whose committee decided to retain "to the Ephesians" in brackets.

3. So Murphy-O'Connor, *St. Paul's Ephesus*, 231–32. Some suggest Hierapolis and Laodicea as the recipients (cf. Col 4:13): e.g., Lincoln, *Ephesians*, 3–4.

to the saints in that area. Some interpreters have suggested that Ephesians was a cyclical document, perhaps read in various churches throughout the region of Asia Minor.[4] The letter in any event does not appear to be addressed solely to one particular congregation, and yet it is quite possible that the community in Ephesus was one of its recipients.[5]

THE ELUSIVE SITUATION

Several prominent purposes have been orchestrated for this letter.[6] Some interpreters suggest the letter was used as a liturgical homily, perhaps targeting new converts or older ones who were renewing their baptismal commitment (e.g., Eph 4:4–6, 22–24).[7] Some find the author refuting an early heresy having Gnostic tendencies (e.g., 4:14–15).[8] Others read it as a polemic against the ideology of imperial Rome (e.g., 2:14; 6:10–17).[9] Still others stress a conflict between Jew and Gentile relationships in which unity and reconciliation is necessary (e.g., 2:11–22);[10] or differently, a problem with members following Torah "mysticism" has influenced the church, and the author contends against the legal validity of the Law.[11] Yet others center the conflict on Christian and non-Christian Gentile relationships—the letter counters "pagan" magical rites, and the churches do not need to be intrigued by these powers because God's power is superior.[12] The last of these situations is not incompatible with an audience in Asia Minor that is steeped in the cult of Artemis (cf. Acts 19:23–41).

While each of these views has its strengths and weaknesses, we find insufficient evidence to support with confidence a grand scheme behind the historical situation of this letter. Even so, the letter does seem to take special interest in preserving the unity of the church, both locally among the recipients, and universally among Jews and Gentiles.[13] The letter also takes interest in cosmic harmony, affirming the power of God over opposing forces whether spiritual (demonic) or human (imperial).

---

4. See Martin, *Ephesians, Colossians*, 3–5; Bruce, *Ephesians*, 240. Others suggest the possibility of the letter being written *from* Ephesus, e.g., Trebilco, *Early Christians in Ephesus*, 91.

5. See Heil, *Empowerment to Walk*, 7–8.

6. For surveys see Gnilka, *Epheserbrief*, 33–49; Hoehner, *Ephesians*, 98–106; Muddiman, *Ephesians*, 12–17.

7. E.g., Dahl, *Studies in Ephesians*, 325–27.

8. E.g., Porkorný, *Epheserbrief und die Gnosis*.

9. E.g., Long, "Paul's Political Theology."

10. E.g., Yee, *Jews, Gentiles*.

11. Moritz, *Profound Mystery*.

12. Arnold, *Ephesians*.

13. On terms related to unity in the letter see Patzia, *Ephesians*, 133–39.

Likewise, the exhortations in the later chapters suggest the importance of identity formation—the Christ-followers are to live in a way ethically consistent with their calling "in Christ" and not as the unbelieving Gentiles who are alienated from God.[14] The epistle is structured under the rubrics of bringing the readers to remembrance of the past (Eph 1–3) and then exhorting them to "walk" or conduct themselves in a worthy manner as believers in Christ (Eph 4–6). We are perhaps on safe ground to suggest that our author wished to encourage ethical behavior among his recipients because he knows the congregants live in a non-Christian society that can always influence or pressure Gentile congregation members to return to their pre-converted lifestyles. Likewise, it is quite possible that the main reason why unity is stressed in this letter is because division happens to be a recurring problem among Pauline churches, and the author knows that factions can lead to apostasy and the disruption of local congregations.

Emergent Christian communities in Ephesus can be found not only in Revelation but also in sources as diverse as Acts, the Pastoral Letters, Johannine writings, and Ignatius.[15] If Ephesians is a late first-century document, its message does not reflect the schism or false teachings of the sort that devastated the Johannine community (e.g., 1 John 2:18–19). The Pauline and Johannine communities may have remained two distinct Christian groups that both resided in Ephesus.[16] A comparison of Ephesians with the Pastoral Letters—1 and 2 Timothy purportedly written to Timothy in Ephesus—informs us that both communities are Pauline and struggle with false teachings. In the Pastoral Letters the problem centers on apostate Christian teachers who misuse the Torah to stress fables, asceticism, and an over-realized eschatology in which they denied a future resurrection. The false teachings implied in Ephesians, however, are more general (cf. Eph. 4:14).

In Acts 19 the Christ-followers are portrayed as participating in magic rituals (19:18–19), and supernatural and demonic encounters take place in the area (19:11–17). In Ephesians an emphasis is placed on power terms[17] with God and Christ as supreme over the entire cosmos including the hostile principalities and

---

14. E.g., Heil, *Empowerment to Walk*, 165–86, 318. Paul also realized that the Ephesians were starting to "forsake their first love," (Rev. 2:1–6), according to Hoehner, *Ephesians*, 102–6. This view of countering the congregation's initial steps towards apostasy would be more credible if it could be determined that the Ephesians were the only, or at least primary, recipients of the letter and that it was written during a time comparable with Revelation.

15. See Trebilco, *Early Christians in Ephesus*, for a good comparative study.

16. See ibid., 712–13. Nevertheless, on parallels between the communities see Heckel, "Einheit der Kirche," 613–40.

17. Eph 1:3–23; 2:2; 3:10; 4:8–10; 6:10–18.

powers (Eph 1:21; 2:2; 3:10; 6:12; cf. 1:20–23). [18] The recipients, it seems, need to be assured that God reigns supreme over all other powers, and so they should neither fear nor desire alternative powers and magic rituals. At any event, the community addressed is not merely from Ephesus (1:1 variants); the letter's many similarities with Colossians may suggest this larger region as the matrix for the letter. Even so, if the early Christians faced struggles in this region of Asia Minor, the struggles may have come primarily from non-Christian outsiders and the spiritual powers that work among them. Amidst this possible societal backdrop the author reaffirms the identity of his recipients who seem to be mostly Gentiles and perhaps recent converts to the faith (2:11, 13, 17, 19–20; 3:1; 4:17–18). The powers that threaten their spiritual walk, whether false doctrines, spiritual entities, Greco-Roman ideologies, or imperial cults, come by way of the local society, which is dominated by non-Christian Gentiles. *The author is set against the believers' assimilation with outsiders.* He does not want the believers to lose their place in the family of God by reverting back to their former non-Christian practices (2:1–3; 4:17–24; 5:1–12).

THE ELECT COMMUNITY IN CHRIST (1:1–14)

Ephesians 1:3–14 is perhaps best considered a eulogy or *berakah*, apparently created by the author ad hoc. Although the pericope functions as an acclamation, it also serves a didactic purpose. It may possess in seminal form the content of the letter.[19] The passage contributes to the development of the recipients' Christian identity, which has paraenetic ramifications about how they should conduct their lives.

The recipients are called the "faithful in Christ" who belong to the elect community (1:1). The opening passage repeats the phrases "in Christ" (1:1, 3, 10, 12; cf. v. 6), "in him" (1:4a, 9c), and "in whom" (1:7, 11, 13 [twice]) to suggest a binding spiritual and salvific relationship between Christ and his followers, as is typical in Pauline letters (Gal 3:27–28; 2 Cor 5:21; Rom 8:1; cf. Eph 1:20; 2:6–7; 10, 13, 21–22; 3:6, 11–12, 21; 4:21). Our author clearly stresses that the faithful community finds its identity *in Christ.* It is "in Christ" that this community can experience spiritual blessings in the heavenlies (1:3), consider itself elect (1:4), and possess favored status (1:6), redemption (1:7), special knowledge (1:9), inheritance (1:11), and a special sealing by the Spirit (1:13; cf. 4:30). The phrase "in Christ" has both locative and instrumental force.[20] It is through Christ and his redemptive act that believers are chosen and able to enjoy mystical communion and solidarity with Christ via the

18. Arnold, *Ephesians.*

19. See O'Brien, "Ephesians 1," 504–16.

20. See Best, *Ephesians,* 153–54.

Spirit. Ephesians more specifically adds that the elect in Christ is the corporate "church" (ἐκκλησία), the metaphoric and mystical body of Christ on earth (1:22–23; cf. 5:31–32). To be in Christ, then, involves not only belonging to Christ but also to the church. The believers are elect not as individuals prior to being in Christ, but as Klyne Snodgrass articulates, "they are in Christ and therefore elect."[21] Moreover, the individual believers cannot be elect and inherit the heavenly blessings without the prior election of Christ and the church community that stemmed from his immediate disciples.[22] *The individual finds his or her new identity as part of this collective community so that all the blessings bestowed to the church belong to that individual as long as he or she remains in Christ.*

The believers have also been favored "in the beloved" (ἐν τῷ ἠγαπημένῳ: 1:6); they are loved by God and elect through Christ's election (1:4, 6; 2:4). The term "beloved" recalls God's special love for Christ, and probably implies Jesus as messiah and the "elect one" of God.[23] Also, the church community is elect "before the foundation of the world" (πρὸκαταβολῆς κόσμου: 1:4).[24] Christ is the one first elected in the pretemporal past, and the community's election and predestination are bound up with Christ's. They become elect by participating in his election. The view in *1 Clem.* 64.1 is essentially the same as in Eph 1: "God . . . elected the Lord Jesus Christ and through him us for his own people."[25] If this letter shares with other Pauline writings

21. Snodgrass, *Ephesians*, 49.

22. Rightly stressing corporate community in Paul's thought is Martyn, "Pauline Meta-Ethics," 173–83. Hoehner, *Ephesians*, 176, argues from Ephesians 1:4 that a person cannot argue for "a collective election because of the plural pronoun 'us.' Paul would not have used the singular pronoun, for he was not writing to an individual but to the church as a whole." This does not prevent the Pauline author, however, from using language specifying individual members of the congregation whenever he wishes, and frequently this kind of language appears in the paraenetic section where individual members are to be responsible for their personal conduct (Eph 4:7, 16, 25; 5:33; 6:8; cf. 5:14; 6:2; Col 2:8). In the undisputed letters of Paul see the language of individualism in, e.g., Gal 6:1; Rom 8:2; 10:9; 12:3; 13:4; 14:4; 1 Cor 4:5, 7; 7:17, 21; 8:10; 10:12; 12:7, 11. The author could have used such language in 1:3–14 if he wanted to stress individual election; the reason why he does not is quite evident—election for him is centered on the body of believers "in Christ" that consists of the collective community called the church. The author seems informed by scriptures that present a corporate view of election: God's *people* are foremost the object of God's love (Eph 1:4c; cf. Deut 4:7; 7:7–13; 10:15; Ps 77:68 LXX; Hos 11:1–4; Isa 43:1–7).

23. Cf. Mark 1:11; Matt 3:17; 12:18; Luke 9:35; John 1:34; cf. Isa 42:1; Ps 2:7; *Odes Sol.* 3.5; 7.1; 8.21; *1 En.* 62.1–5; *Apoc. Ab.* 2.31; 4Q534 1.10). In the dative case, "beloved" in the LXX refers to Israel (Bar 3:[36]37) or the seed of Abraham (2 Chr 20:7; cf. Deut 33:5; Isa 5:1). Notice also 2 Chr 2:11 LXX.

24. The idea is pretemporal: here πρό- suggests something that extends further back than the beginning of human history (cf. 1 Pet 1:20; *Jos. Asen.* 8.9–11[50.1]). Contrast "from" (ἀπὸ) the foundation of the world, which points back to the creation of the world or the Genesis story (cf. Luke 11:50). For related uses of the phrases, see Hofius, "Erwählt vor Grundlegung," 123–28.

25. Cf. Barth, *Ephesians*, 1.107–9. See also Stendahl, "Called and the Chosen," 68; Klein, *New Chosen People*, 180: "Election is the corporate choice of the church 'in Christ.' Before the foundation of

a belief in Christ's preexistence,[26] then it is not difficult to imagine the author assuming a pretemporal relationship between Christ and the Father prior to the creation of the world. This relationship established the plan of salvation for humanity that would be proclaimed through the prophets of Israel and finally revealed to Jews and Gentiles as a result of the Christ event that took place in the first century CE. The pretemporal aspect of the church's election is thus grounded in Christ's preexistence.[27]

The community in Christ is also predestined to adoption through Christ (Eph 1:4–5). The goal of this divine appointment for believers is that they would receive heavenly blessings related to God's family to the praise of God's glory (cf. 1:3, 11–12). That they are chosen to be holy and blameless refers not merely to their ethical conduct in the present but also their acquittal in the future—they will be blameless before God on judgment day (cf. Col 1:22; 1 Thess 3:13; 1 Cor 1:8). The evidence of future salvific hope is confirmed to the recipients by their being "sealed" with God's Spirit, which is the first installment or down payment (ἀρραβών) of the future heavenly inheritance (Eph 1:13–14; cf. Ezek 9:4–6; Rev 7:2–8; 9:4).[28] This seal of divine ownership may be related to baptism, but more specifically it refers to the reception of the Spirit at conversion. Hence, it refers to Spirit-baptism with its spiritual manifestations evidenced in the early days of the church. The Spirit's presence in a believer's life identifies that person to be in Christ, divinely owned, and protected.[29] Although Ephesians betrays elements of a present eschatology (e.g., 1:3; 2:6), it also evinces futuristic elements (1:10, 21; 5:6, 27; 6:8, 13).[30] The church inherits God's blessings through the Spirit in the present era, but there are more blessings to come and spiritual battles to be fought (1:13–14; 2:7; 4:30; 6:10–18).

The inception of the church's predestination in 1:4 is either grounded in Christ's preexistence, similar to election, or it originates with the prophetic words of Israel's scripture which predicted the salvation of Gentiles as a people who would follow Israel's God (e.g., Isa 57–60; cf. 2:2–4; 11:10; 42:6; 49:6; Jer 3:17; Gen 12:3; 18:18; Zech 2:15; 9:9–10). This message remained veiled to the Ephesians in times past, but

---

the world God made his choice: those in Christ would be his people."

26. Cf. 1 Cor 10:4; 2 Cor 8:9; Phil 2:5–11; Col 2:9.

27. This, however, does not mean that the church preexisted ontologically. See Schnackenburg, *Ephesians*, 53.

28. If the "seal" of 2 Cor 1:22; 5:5 sheds any light on the Pauline meaning here, Ephesians does not provide an unconditional guarantee for the individual's final salvation. Paul could affirm both the hope of final salvation and the potential for individuals to commit apostasy (see on Corinthians and Romans above).

29. On the last thought, the seal of the Spirit may have functioned as a sort of amulet or talisman, as Thomas, "Seal of the Spirit," 155–66, suggests.

30. Cf. Witulski, "*Gegenwart und Zukunft,*" 211–42.

in keeping with Pauline thinking, it is finally being unveiled in the new era ushered in by Christ. The prophetic writings made possible the later elaboration and full disclosure of the "mystery"; namely, that Gentiles and Jews would become one new entity with Christ, inheriting heavenly blessings and salvation, and that God plans to bring together all things in the cosmos (Eph 1:10, 20–23; 2:13–22; 3:3–11; cf. Rom 4:16–17; 11:25–26; 16:25–26; Gal 3:22, 29). It is the purpose of God to sum up all things in Christ (1:9–10). As Lincoln says, "God achieves his purpose for all things through what he accomplishes in the one person, Christ," and in him God sums up all things in heaven and earth, restoring the cosmos to harmony.[31]

Divine predestination, in any case, marks out the community in Christ. God in his gracious love and mercy had determined long ago that Christ would be the elect one who takes on the role of saving humanity, both Jews and Gentiles, so that they could experience salvation and heavenly blessings. This predestining of believers is corporate; the destiny of the entire church in Christ receives the heavenly blessings and will stand blameless before God. In this regard Eph 1:1–14 is similar to Rom 8–11. The collective church of Christ is elect and predestined to final salvation, and a panoramic scope of life is given for those who are in Christ, which extends from God's prior plan in Christ, to the community's conversion, to its final destination (cf. Rom 8:29–30). This scheme includes the reception of God's mercy and final salvation on the basis of faith (Rom 9–11).

As in Rom 8–11, Eph 1 does not intend to uncover all the intricacies related to divine foreordination and human freedom.[32] Rather, such passages intend to show the letter's recipients that it was God's plan all along to provide salvation through Christ, and those who faithfully abide "in Christ" can be assured of salvation (cf. 1:4b, 10, 13–14). The author, however, gives no guarantee that every individual who is presently in Christ will *remain* in Christ until the *parousia* or judgment day and be declared innocent at that time. Neither predestination nor election in this letter appears to be fixed and final when it comes to individual believers. The extent to which the author exhorts the church members to conduct their lives in a way that is worthy of their calling (4:1) probably implies his belief that not every member in fact does this. Satanic and societal powers might influence some of the Christ-followers to grieve God's Spirit (cf. 4:30). Our author betrays a concern that some of these believers might revert back to their former pre-converted lifestyles; hence, he writes an extensive paraenesis to deter such a possibility. The exhortations in Eph 4–6 assume that vices, deception, and spiritual forces could undermine the believer's faith.

31. Lincoln, *Ephesians*, 34.

32. Helpful on our understanding of the balance between divine and human agency are the various articles in Barclay and Gathercole, *Divine and Human Agency*.

Conversely, the elect recipients should not assume that a child of God's wrath will always remain as such (2:1–3; 5:5–6).[33] They too were once children of God's wrath before hearing and believing the gospel message, and so there is hope for the conversion of others who presently remain objects of divine displeasure. This is one reason why the author needs their prayers—so that he might proclaim his gospel with boldness to outsiders who are still trapped in spiritual darkness (6:19–20; cf. 3:10; 6:15). As is true of other Pauline letters, faith in Christ and the gospel message is essential not only for conversion but also for perseverance to final salvation (1:1, 13, 15, 19; 2:8; 3:12, 17; 6:16).

The upshot of this is that *the author's insistence on affirming the congregations' identity as elect in Christ in the opening chapter has as one of its main objectives a desire to get them to distance themselves from their former way of living.* The more they realize all the benefits of their new identity in Christ, the less they will be tempted to fall away to their former status. They are children of God and no longer children of disobedience; they are bound for heavenly blessings and no longer destined for divine wrath. The community lived in a social order in which spiritual powers, magicians, and planetary spirits were often believed to be controlling the fates of humans. Likewise, the political power of Rome and societal customs that determined the roles of various members in a household reinforced an attitude of inevitability for many Gentiles.[34] The audience of this letter may have needed to comprehend that God was in control of their lives—not fate, planets, spiritual powers, Caesar, empire, or society. They have become citizens of a new Lord, Christ, and belong to the family of the God who loves them and has prepared heavenly blessings for them.

SALVATION AND NEW IDENTITY FOR FORMER NON-BELIEVERS (2:1–10)

The community that read this letter was once "dead" in sin and trespasses,[35] and children of disobedience who were controlled by the demonic "prince of the air"; their destiny was to experience divine wrath (2:1–3).[36] The believers have been converted,

33. Notice the similarity with Rom 9:22–23: Israel became apostate objects of God's wrath, but they will eventually be saved (Rom 11:26).

34. Cf. Faust, *Pax Christi*, 465–70, 482–83, who notices that planetary spirits were sometimes associated with Rome/Caesar.

35. Barth, *Ephesians*, 1.216, translates παράπτωμα here as "lapse," a falling out associated with Adam's sin (Rom 5:12–20). The Gentiles could not have *trespassed* the Mosaic Law because they never possessed the Law (cf. 83–84). Regardless of whether "trespass" or "lapse" is the proper translation, their misbehavior is severe enough to separate them from God and incur God's wrath.

36. God's wrath against them as individuals, however, is not unalterably predestined. If "we" in-

however, from children of wrath to the elect in Christ. They are saved not by works but by God's grace through faith (2:4–9). Our author highlights salvation as a gift rather than something earned.[37] The recipients, then, have no ground for boasting in this regard. Even so, faith is required for this salvation; they must respond with belief in the message about Christ to receive God's gracious deliverance (Eph 1:13, 15; 3:12, 17; 6:16; cf. 1 Thess 1:3; 2 Thess 1:11; Rom 1:5; 16:16).[38]

In contrast to human accomplishments that may foster pride, then, salvation comes from God, and the church ("we") is God's workmanship (ποίημα) having been created in Christ for good works, "which God prepared beforehand that we should walk in them" (Eph 2:10).The phrase probably does not mean that God fore-ordains every believer's good works so that each of them necessarily performs the works at the proper intervals.[39] Rather, the idea recalls 1:4–5.[40] The corporate church in Christ, as a collective entity, is destined pretemporally to do good works and eventually stand before God holy and blameless. In essence, God's plan from long ago included that the community would live righteously and perform good deeds similar to the way Christ lived in obedience to God when he walked the earth. Even though it seems that God will prompt the believers to do good works, it will still be necessary for them to "walk" in such works, a thought that anticipates the exhortation material beginning in 4:1 and stresses personal responsibility. Whatever else the Pauline author might mean in 2:8–10, he is not erasing the believer's personal freedom to live morally, or for that matter, immorally. He is discouraging pride via personal boasts about being saved and living morally on the basis of one's own efforts independent of God. In view of the next subject of the letter, the relationship

cludes the author and present believers who were once in a state of unbelief but now are saved, then the same hope of salvation and escape from God's wrath would seem to be possible for others.

37. Salvation in 2:8 is not so much a present process (e. g., 1 Cor 1:18) as it is a present state produced by past action (σεσῳσμένοι is a perfect passive participle).

38. The neuter "this" (τοῦτο) in Eph 2:8b does not make a good fit with the feminine "faith" (πίστις) in 2:8a. Hence, it seems that the gift is not referring to faith. Instead, τοῦτο points to the antecedent salvation expressed in 2:8a with the neuter word for salvation (σωτήριον) in mind even though only the verbal participle of σῴζω appears in the context. The verse may be translated: "For by grace you are saved [σεσῳσμένοι] through faith and this *salvation* is not of your own doing . . ." Or τοῦτο may be understood adverbially, in which case Wallace, *Greek Grammar*, 335, is correct in translating it as: "For by grace you are saved through faith *and* [you are saved] *especially* not by your own doing . . ." (emphasis original).

39. In agreement with Best, *Ephesians*, 232; Barth, *Ephesians*, 1.251.

40. Cf. Heil, *Empowerment to Walk*, 107; Lincoln, *Ephesians*, 115–16. An alternative way to interpret the sentence in 2:10 is to understand the relative pronoun "which" (οἷς) not as a dative of attraction (to its antecedent) but as a dative of reference that implies "us" as the object of the verb: "in which God prepared us in advance that we should walk . . ." This makes humans the objects of the preparation rather than works: cf. Muddiman, *Ephesians*, 113. This interpretation is certainly possible, but we wonder if it is motivated on the basis of avoiding the more difficult reading.

between Jews and Gentiles, it is not impossible that our author was primarily concerned about individuals making their boast in the works of the Law. The believers are to trust and depend on God "through faith" to live in a way that pleases God; hence, the only legitimate ground for boasting is in the Lord, not in one's own self-righteousness, observances of the Law, or ethnic privileges.

UNITY AMONG GENTILES AND JEWS (2:11-22; 4:14-19)

The author takes an interest in showing his predominately Gentile audience (those "far off") that its family roots extend back to the Israelites (those "near"), God's chosen people. Gentiles in Christ stand together in a new relationship with believing Jews as the unified body of Christ, and this corporate entity is identified as the church (2:10—3:6; cf. 1:22-23; 5:30-32). They were once alienated from the commonwealth of Israel, but Christ's crucifixion broke down the "dividing wall of partition" between Jews and Gentiles (2:14: τὸ μεσότοιχον τοῦ φραγμοῦ), thus producing one new creation from the two peoples. Our author may be reinforcing the churches in Asia Minor to maintain unity among their Jewish and Gentile ranks. There should be no ethnic factions among believers, for they have all become one body in Christ.

More than this, however, one sense in which this unity might be disrupted is through false instruction that leads astray (πλάνη) immature Gentile converts (4:14). The instruction, if pointing back to 4:13 (which stresses unity, maturity, faith, and "knowledge of the Son of God"), may suggests that the false teaching leads believers away from faith in Christ and knowing him in an ever-increasing experiential and cognizant way (cf. 1:5, 17; 3:17-19). If the deception points forward to 4:15, the false teaching might cause the faithful to wander from the path of "truth" related to the gospel message of salvation (cf. 1:13; 4:21, 24-25; 5:6, 9; 6:14).[41] In either case, the deception can lead believers away from that which is essential to their Christian faith. The deception is carried out by the use of trickery (κυβεία), cunning (πανουργία), and scheming (μεθοδεία).[42] Both cunning and scheming are attributed to Satan in Pauline writings (2 Cor 11:3; Eph 6:11), but in Eph 4:14 the deception comes from humans (τῶν ἀνθρώπων). The false teachings could refer to human-made ideologies

---

41. Cf. 1 Thess 2:3; 1 John 4:6; Jas 5:20; Jude 11; 2 Pet 2:18; 3:12.

42. Eph 4:14 is rich with colorful imagery: 1) they must no longer be immature *children* (νήπιος: cf. 1 Cor 3:1-3); 2) tossed about by waves (κλυδωνιζόμενοι: Isa 57:20; Jas 1:6; Heb 13:9; Jude 12-13; Ps 107:23-27; Philo, *Decal.* 67); 3) carried about by every wind of instruction (περιφερόμενοι: cf. Ign. *Eph.* 7.1; παραφέρω in Heb 13:9); 4) trickery (κυβεία: literally "dice playing," which often becomes associated with deception and dishonesty: Best, *Ephesians*, 405); 5) cunning (πανουργία: 1 Cor 3:19; 2 Cor 4:2; 11:3; Luke 20:23); and 6) scheming (μεθοδεία: Eph 6:11; μεθοδεύω in 2 Sam 19:28).

practiced by the non-Christian Gentiles (cf. 5:6), or more pointedly they may be addressed against Christian teachers of Jewish Law and customs.[43]

Our author is informed by the Isaianic tradition when discussing those who commit unrighteous deeds and have no understanding (Eph 4:17–19; 5:11/Isa 59:12–15).[44] Unlike the righteous, who possess peace (Isa 57:19/Eph 2:13), the unrighteous find no rest: they are "tossed to and fro by waves" (Isa 57:20; cf. Eph 4:14).[45] The verb κλυδωνίζομαι, found only in Isa 57:20 in the LXX and Eph 4:14 in the New Testament, suggests a meaning of being disturbed or troubled.[46] There is no peace for the unrighteous in Isaiah, and the implication in Ephesians may be that those who adhere to the false teachings disturb the internal peace or cohesion of the congregations (4:14–16). Our author, it seems, associates the unrighteous in Isaiah with the false teachers and their deceived followers. If he alludes to Isa 57:19–21 in Eph 2:13 (cf. 4:3) to affirm peace and solidarity among Jews and Gentiles, and then alludes to the same passage when encouraging unity and combating false teachings in 4:14–16, then it is possible that he associates the false teachings with Jewish and Gentile relationships. In other words, the doctrines the Pauline author comes against include those that would disrupt congregational peace between Jewish and Gentiles Christians. Perhaps these teachings would consist of the keeping of *Jewish customs* related to food laws, circumcision, or similar issues that create division within the Pauline churches.

Nevertheless, the primary concern of our author seems directed at external Gentile or "pagan" influences rather than Jewish customs (4:17—5:15), and even in 4:14 the idea of "every wind of doctrine" (παντὶ ἀνέμῳ τῆς διδασκαλίας) may suggest that the author has multiple deceptive teachings in mind, not just one type.[47] If Gentile outsiders are involved in deceptions that might influence believers (cf. 5:6), then such deceptions might include idolatry, magic, Hellenistic religious and Roman imperial ideologies. These can all lead astray similar to Jewish customs imposed on Gentile believers. They may all lead to unrighteousness and the disruption

43. Interestingly, Acts 19:32–34 portrays conflicts between Jews and Gentiles in Ephesus.

44. See further possible references to Isaiah in Ephesians in Qualls and Watts, "Isaiah in Ephesians," 249–59; Moritz, *Profound Mystery*, 28–52. The dominant Isaianic tradition in Ephesians is the Septuagint (Moritz, 213).

45. The LXX uses "peace" (εἰρήνη) in Isa 57:19 but "joy" (χαίρω) in 57:21; the MT uses peace in both verses.

46. Cf. LEH, *ad loc.*; Josephus, *Ant.* 9.239; *Sib. Or.* 1.289. The wind and waves in Eph 4:14 may recall seafaring imagery. Fred Long (correspondence) draws my attention to Euripides, *Iph. taur.* 1391–97; Thucydides 2.84.3; Didorus Siculus 3.44.2; Cassius Dio 41.46.3; Luke 8:24, and in relation to moral discourse, Jas 1:6.

47. See, e.g., Lincoln, *Ephesians*, 258.

of congregational peace. It is difficult for us to specify or develop the non-Jewish form of deception. Our author leaves us with just enough hints to suspect that such influence is a concern, and yet he leaves us with not enough clear markers to determine something more specific. It is always possible the he is deliberately general about the deception so as to make this letter relevant for a number of congregations. *Presumably, such deception could lead to various congregants committing apostasy.*

WALKING IN MORAL AND IMMORAL BEHAVIOR (4:1—5:21)

The concepts of election, unity, and love that are communicated to the readers in chapters 1–3 are given more specific application in chapters 4–6. The leading exhortation is for the audience to "walk" or conduct their life in a way worthy or their calling (4:1).[48] This pattern roughly follows other Pauline letters that typically open with words of thanksgiving and encouragement (except Galatians) before appealing to the audience to behave in a manner appropriate to their calling as Christ-followers and to live in unity (4:2–6, 16; cf. 1 Thess 2:12; 4:1, 7–8; Phil 1:27; Gal 5:16; Rom 8:4; Col 1:10; 2:6; 3:15). The concept of walking in a manner that pleases God is Jewish, resembling Paul's adaptation of *halakah* to accentuate the importance of moral conduct and conformity to the Spirit's guidance (1 Thess 4:1–3; Gal 5:16, 25; Rom 8:4–14; Phil 1:27; Col 1:10).[49] A comparison with Ephesians and other Pauline letters along these lines also draws our attention to the importance of the recipients' efforts to shun destructive vices[50] associated with the unbelieving Gentiles,[51] and yet they must behave properly towards these outsiders (Eph 4:12, 17–19, 22, 25–31; 5:4–8; 5:15; cf. 1 Thess 4:12; Col 4:5; Rom 13:13).

Ephesians calls the believers not only to walk worthy before God (4:1; cf. 5:8) but also to walk in love (5:2);[52] that is, their conduct is to follow the commands of Christ to love God and love one another. This is accomplished relationally involving communion and solidarity with Christ and fellow believers, and it assumes God's antecedent love (1:4; 2:4; 3:17; 4:2, 15–16; 5:28, 33). As the community in Christ the church must act in a manner consistent with its election.

The author encourages spiritual maturity so as to prevent the faithful from being swayed by false teachings that misinterpret Mosaic Law (4:11–15) and perhaps

---

48. Heil, *Empowerment to Walk*, affirms 4:1–16 forms the central component of the entire letter.

49. Differently, Perkins, *Ephesians*, 419, sees Pauline paraenesis as having strong ties with Hellenistic philosophers.

50. Cf. 1 Thess 4:1–7; Gal 5:16–21.

51. Cf. Col 3:5–8; 1 Thess 4:3–5.

52. Cf. Col 3:14; 1 Thess 4:1, 9.

deception by various "pagan" practices, beliefs, or ideologies (5:6). We are not told more specific details about the false doctrines. The author is writing to a network of churches in a region that encounters multiple religious and philosophical options contrary to the Pauline gospel. At any event, an assumption derived from this passage is that our author believes that immature Christians are susceptible to apostasy.[53] If Isa 57:20 is being echoed in Eph 4:14, the false teachings might cause the saints to fall into unrighteous living. In the immediate context, however, the Pauline writer is concerned primarily about the believers maintaining unity and growing in their maturity in Christ (4:11–16). *The false teachings, then, threaten foremost the unity and love shared among the saints. The metaphoric "winds" of deceptive doctrines in 4:14 may depict a boat being tossed about on the sea with the end result of being shipwrecked. Such a consequence would be similar to the ruined faith of Hymenaeus and Alexander,* two apostates from Ephesus who were ostracized from the community in Christ for teaching false doctrines (cf. 1 Tim 1:19–20). The community in western Asia Minor are thus encouraged to speak the truth in love and continue in the teachings of Jesus (Eph 4:15, 20–21; cf. Col 2:6–7; Rom 16:17; Phil 4:9).[54] Both correct knowledge ("truth") and moral behavior ("love") must exemplify the community's daily living.

These believers are exhorted to "put on" and exemplify virtues appropriate for their new life in Christ (Eph 4:20–24, cf. 4:2–3, 32; 5:8b–5:9). The imagery of "putting off" the old and "putting on" the new in 4:22–25 may relate to early Christian baptism-initiation. One ancient ritual involves the neophyte disrobing before baptism and then putting on a new garment afterward (cf. Col 3:8–10; *Gos. Thom.* 37; *Gos. Phil.* 101).[55] Conversion imagery reinforces their new identity in Christ. As well, instead of getting drunk with wine the believers are to be continually filled with God's Spirit. The author recalls their baptism in the Spirit that took place at conversion and ushered them into the body of Christ (cf. 1 Cor 12:13). They must be filled with the Spirit on a continual basis, and this is not merely referring to their operating of spiritual gifts or basking in ecstatic phenomena. To be filled with God's Spirit carries with it the idea of being a corporate community in unison with the divine presence and operating under the full capacity of godly virtues (Eph 4:2–3, 22–32; 5:19–21; cf. Gal 5:22). An abundance of love, gratitude, and thanksgiving that

---

53. See Bouttier, *Éphésiens*, 194.

54. They have been have been taught "in him" (Christ); hence, Christ is both the object and sphere/locus of Christian learning; see Hoehner, *Ephesians*, 595.

55. See further Cyril, *Myst. Cat.* 2; Hippolytus, *Trad. ap.*; Moule, "New Life in Colossians," 489; Smith, "Garments of Shame," 217–38; Meeks, "In One Body," 210. This view, however, must be held tentatively because the clearest evidence comes from the second century and later sources.

comes from the heart, together with edifying others by spiritual songs and submitting to one another, will countermand hurtful and venomous words that damage fellow saints and disrupt intimate fellowship (Eph 5:18–21; cf. 4:25, 29, 31–32; 5:4).

Consequently the believers must abandon their old self, namely, their preconverted life with its destructive habits and vices (4:15, 20–32; 5:3–5). The author's message discourages assimilation with outsiders. Contrary to operating in love and unity, the wrong way of walking is to conduct oneself in a manner resembling the non-Christian Gentiles who walk "in the futility of their minds," being alienated from spiritual life, darkened in their understanding, and having hardened hearts (Eph 4:17–18; cf. 2 Pet 2:18). Spiritual obduracy in Paul recalls Pharaoh and apostate Israel (cf. Rom 9, 11), but more specifically our author may have in mind the Gentiles' original apostasy. They once knew God but turned away and were delivered over to idolatry, fornication, and vice (cf. Eph 4:19; Rom 1:18–32). In Rom 1:24 God surrenders them over to the lusts of their heart; in Ephesians they surrender themselves over to licentiousness, uncleanliness, and greed (Eph 4:19; 5:3, 5). In both cases idolatry is seen as a primary culprit (Rom 1:19–23; Eph 5:5); albeit, the idolatry in Ephesians is bound up with greed. In relation to Eph 5:3–5 and Col 3:5, Brian Rosner examines the concept of greed as idolatry in early Jewish and Christian literature, and one of his perceptive conclusions is that "the way for the expression seems to have been paved by the comprehensive scope of the first commandment, by the characterization of idolatry in terms of evil desire, and above all by the association of wealth with apostasy."[56] *These exhortations may suggest that the Pauline Christians in western Asia Minor were being tempted more by the lure of wealth than worshipping local deities.* To this we can add that one of the main struggles Timothy faces with his congregation in late-first-century Ephesus centers on riches and materialism (1 Tim 2:9; 6:6–10, 17–19; cf. Acts 20:33–35), and the neighboring church in Laodicea is sharply rebuked for placing its confidence in wealth (Rev 3:14–19).

These exhortations, however, are somewhat general and probably come more by way of reminder than from the author's anxiety over an immediate situation in which the audiences' salvation is greatly jeopardized. The region he is writing to probably consisted of quite a few congregations, and even if he were to know the specific condition of each of these churches it is unlikely that he would write in a way that specified a situation in some of the congregations and not others. Even so, the Gentiles are painted rather degenerately by the author, who is no doubt attempting to distance his readers from their former lifestyles (Eph 2:1–6; cf. 5:8a). Implicit in

---

56. Rosner, *Greed as Idolatry*, 99.

the exhortations is a preventative maintenance plan to discourage Christ-followers from practicing former vices associated with their pre-conversion.

In essence *two ways* are set before the auditors. The community in Christ is to continue advancing on the path of light, that is, holiness and true knowledge.[57] They are to practice virtues and good works; this path leads to a blameless status before God and Christ at the eschaton (1:4; 2:10; 4:1–3). The path of darkness is trod by unbelievers who practice vices, and it leads to divine wrath (2:2–3; 4:17–18; 5:3–14; 6:12). These "children of disobedience" walk in darkness instead of the light, and they commit "deeds of darkness" (5:11), or immoral acts, in contrast with deeds of righteousness associated with the children of light (cf. 5:6–15). The children of light are to expose deeds of darkness (5:11), which probably means that they are to confront unbelievers with the true knowledge of the gospel (6:15; cf. 1 Cor 14:24–25).[58] If the believers succumb to vices, this would cause the Spirit that fosters sanctification, unity, fellowship, and peace among believers to be grieved (Eph 4:30; cf. 4:4; 5:18–21). For Christians to walk contrary to God's Spirit is to behave in manner incompatible with their new identity. The Pauline author never mentions what would happen if they persisted in grieving the Spirit. If a parallel thought from Isaiah is present in the background, then grieving God's Spirit might be associated with God's people committing acts of unrighteousness and apostasy (Isa 63:10). Now that the Gentile Christians have become God's people along with the Jews (Eph 2:11–22), a plausible inference derived from the Isaianic background may be that *a persistence in grieving the Spirit can lead ultimately to community divisions, apostasy, and divine rejection.* This inference is strengthened by the fact that elsewhere in Pauline literature a member's disregard for God's Spirit is tantamount to rejecting God (1 Thess 4:8). Similar to other Pauline letters, the author presents a vice list and then claims that individuals who practice such things will not inherit the heavenly kingdom (Eph 5:3–5). An unstated premise is that if the Christian recipients follow false teachings or practice vices, they may end up being excluded from God's kingdom just like the children of darkness (5:5–18).

STANDING FIRM THROUGH SPIRITUAL STRUGGLES (6:10–18)

Towards the end of the letter, the community of believers is urged to put on the whole "armor of God" (Eph 6:10–18). The metaphoric combative gear and weaponry

---

57. See Lincoln, *Ephesians*, 327, who affirms light as holiness in Eph 5. On knowledge, see Eph 1:18.

58. The alternative is that the children of light are to confront others within the church (cf. 1 Tim 5:20). Talbert, *Ephesians and Colossians*, 127–28, finds both meanings possible but opts for the believer/unbeliever.

include truth, righteousness, faith(fulness), knowledge of the God's word, empowerment by God's Spirit, confidence in salvation, and a grounding in the gospel that restores peace to the cosmos. These virtues and spiritual enablements prepare the believers to fight battles against spiritual forces (Eph 6:10–18; cf. Rom 13:12; 1 Thess 5:8). Although these forces are demonic in nature, they presumably use humans and institutes to accomplish their ends.[59] It is necessary for the saints, having made all the proper preparations, to stand firm and resist the spiritual onslaught on "the evil day" (Eph 6:13). This period of time is not purely futurist but present for the recipients (cf. 5:16).[60] *The "evil day" may suggest a special occasion of demonic visitation that would seek to undermine the believers' salvation through severe temptations* (cf. Luke 4:1, 13). They must watch and persevere in prayer (Eph 6:18; cf. Col 4:2; 1 Thess 5:6–8, 17; 2 Tim 4:5), similar to Jesus' example of watching and praying at the Garden of Gethsemane. Christ's words to his disciples are relevant here: "Continue to watch and pray that you come not into temptation" (Mark 14:37–38; cf. Matt 26:40–41).

The "schemes" of the devil (Eph 6:11) are not specified, but ἡ μεθοδεία is used also in 4:14 to denote deceptive scheming caused by humans.[61] It is quite possible for demonic powers to influence false teachers and instigate congregational divisions.[62] Hence, it would not be difficult to imagine Satan exploiting the local residents of Asia Minor to advance their views on magic, national pride, ethnic prejudice, and religious and political ideologies in an effort to confuse, discourage, divide, or destroy the faith of congregation members. Yet Satan thwarts the Pauline mission in other ways also, including tempting and persecuting the believers (1 Thess 2:18; 3:5; 1 Cor 7:5; 2 Cor 12:7; Rom 16:20; 1 Tim 3:6–7; Eph 4:26–27). *The spiritual battle the church must fight, then, includes an entourage of various schemes the Enemy might throw their way.*[63]

The believers are to "stand" against the devil (Eph 6:11, 13–14),[64] taking firm footage and not retreating, falling down, or otherwise being shaken by his attacks. In Pauline letters the converse of standing is falling, which is to commit apostasy (cf.

---

59. See Arnold, "Exorcism of Ephesians," 71–87.

60. On the "evil day" in prophetic/apocalyptic sources, see O'Brien, *Ephesians*, 471.

61. Eph 6:12 in P[46] likewise uses the word, but without further ancient witnesses this addition seem too weak to be original.

62. 2 Cor 2:11; 11:3, 13–15; 2 Thess 2:9–12; 1 Tim 4:1; 5:15; 2 Tim 2:26; cf. 1 John 4:1–6.

63. Muddiman, *Ephesians*, 288, suggests the schemes involve hostility between Jews and Gentiles, threats from the Roman state, and immoral activities (vices) of the "pagan" society (cf. Eph 4:19, 26–27, 32; 5:18). Best, *Ephesians*, 595, says that Satan threatens the "hope of salvation" through heresy, despair, doubts about God, resurrection, eternal judgment, and "belief that one can save oneself without God's help." Both may be correct.

64. Cf. 1 Cor 16:13; 2 Cor 1:24; Phil 4:1; 1 Thess 3:8; 2 Thess 2:15.

Rom 14:4; 1 Cor 10:12; cf. Rom 11:20–22; 1 Cor 15:1–2; Gal 5:1–4).[65] Even though potentially negative outcomes are not mentioned by our author, we could surmise that in virtually any war there will be casualties and defectors. It can be rightly assumed that a prominent goal of the devil is to draw believers into spiritual bondage and make them subject to his kingdom of darkness once again (cf. Eph 2:2).

CONCLUSION

The congregations that the Pauline author addresses in Ephesians seem to be located in western Asia Minor. They live among Gentile non-Christians and were themselves once children of God's wrath prior to believing the gospel message (2:1–7, 11, 13; 3:1; 4:17–18). The situation behind the letter cannot be determined with specificity, but it appears to have as its primary objectives 1) a reaffirmation of the believers' identity as the unified community in Christ (1:1–14; 4:4–6), and 2) an exhortation for the believers to "walk" or conduct themselves with the kind of moral behavior appropriate for their Christian identity (4:1—5:20). The recipients are never directly warned against apostasy, but their potential to fall away is quite evident.

First, the author underlines unity among Jewish and Gentile believers as a result of the accomplishments of Christ (2:11–22). They find a new identity in Christ as the "church," the corporate body of Christ, which is elect and predestined "in Christ." The church's election has taken place in pretemporal time, grounded in Christ's pre-existence. Its final destination is to stand blameless before God on judgment day (1:3–14). The believers have been saved by grace, not works, whether by works of the Law or self-accomplishments that may foster boasts independent of trusting in God and Christ (2:1–10). The surplus of positive affirmations related to the community in Christ suggests a rhetorical strategy the author is using to suppress the opposite effect. The more these Gentiles realize all the blessings they possess as Christ's followers, the less inclined they will be to return to their former lifestyles as unbelievers. The author strongly discourages assimilation with outsiders and their activities (2:1–3; 4:17–18; 5:6–12).

Second, they are to please God by walking worthy of their calling as Christians (4:1—5:20). They must continue to advance in the way of love, virtues, and good works, and shun the way of disobedience exemplified by false teachings, committing vices, and falling prey to the lure of wealth. The right path leads to spiritual maturity and heavenly blessings; the wrong path leads to death and divine wrath. They

---

65. Muddiman, *Ephesians*, 288, interprets the fall in Ephesians as a "lapse into sin (cf. 1 Cor 10:12) rather than to lapse from the faith." However, in 1 Cor 10:12, Paul is warning against falling away from grace and salvation, not merely sinning. See further Oropeza, *Paul and Apostasy*, 192–204.

must not be tossed by the winds of false doctrines that seek to undermine their faith (4:14), and these false teachings come significantly from adherence to Jewish customs, but there may be also a second danger of being deceived by Gentile outsiders (5:6). Such deception would seem to include a number of other persuasions, such as magic, Greco-Roman religions and philosophies, or imperial ideology, as previous scholarly studies have pursued. We have suggested that the author may be writing to more than one community, and so perhaps he has several of these influences in mind. In addition the believers must not succumb to division, for this would grieve God's Spirit, and based on Isaianic underpinnings and other Pauline texts, the act of grieving the Spirit entails apostasy and divine rejection (Eph 4:30; cf. Isa 63:10; 1 Thess 4:8). Vicedoers will not inherit Christ's kingdom (Eph 5:3–5). The readers of this letter must therefore stand in faith and godly enablements so that they will not fall away when pummeled with the various schemes Satan uses to confuse and undermine their salvation (6:10–19).

Apart from Philemon, when Ephesians is compared with other letters attributed to Paul, it turns out to be the least explicitly concerned about the subject of apostasy. The letter clearly implies, however, that if members of the community in Christ commit vices or embrace false teachings they will suffer apostasy and fail to inherit God's kingdom at the eschaton. Be that as it may, the author is more concerned about reaffirming their identity as Christ-followers than questioning it or warning against the possibility of losing it. Ephesians is somewhat similar to Romans with its stress on the church's election and predestination, and in both letters the author does not seem to be entirely familiar with the community's situation. Whereas Romans is written to a congregation Paul does not personally know, Ephesians may be written to a network of congregations that face different sorts of challenges and levels of external threat. The author's exhortations are therefore general and typical of the kind of paraenesis one finds in other Pauline letters; albeit, apostasy through greed and wealth may be a relevant problem in western Asia Minor, as several early Christian sources can attest (5:3, 5; cf. Col 3:5; 1 Tim 6:6–10; Rev 3:14–19). The letter shares in common with Colossians a warning against certain Jewish teachings, but we fail to find in this letter adequate support that the opponents are an Essene-like sect. Among other similarities, we notice the cosmic Christ motif, but whereas Ephesians stresses the church's election in Christ as a way of buttressing self-identity, Colossians emphasizes Christ's supremacy over other beings in a manner that suppresses the importance of the viewpoint held by a specific opponent who venerates angels. Both letters nonetheless advance a high Christology for congregations situated in a location where hostile spiritual forces are present, competing religious options seem to abound, and imperial ideology influences the society. In this milieu the Pauline author stresses Christ's supremacy over the anti-God cosmos.

8

Colossians: Nomian Philosophy
in the Lycus Valley

Colossians has been disputed as authentically written by Paul because of the letter's style, unique vocabulary, and unique theology.[1] Paul's authorship is, however, still maintained by a number of scholars. It is quite possible that Paul's colleague or amanuensis assisted in writing the letter when the apostle was still alive.[2] Timothy is sometimes suggested as the author (Col 1:1).[3] The letter mentions colleagues associated with Paul's correspondence to Philemon (Col 1:1; 4:9–14, 17; cf. Phlm 1–2, 9–10, 12–13, 23–24).[4] Also, Paul's mark of authentication stands at the end of this letter, which complicates matters if one wishes to posit a pseudonym (Col 4:18; cf. Gal 6:11–18; 1 Cor 16:21–24; Phlm 19; 2 Thess 3:17). Some scholars suggest that if it were written after the earthquake that devastated Colossae in 60–61 CE there would have been no Christian community remaining in the city. This lends credibility for an earlier date for the letter, when Paul was still alive. Then again, it is always possible to suggest pseudo-recipients if the letter were written after his death.[5] This chapter takes the position that Colossians was authored by

1. See discussions in Wilson, *Colossians and Philemon*, 8–35; Schnelle, *Einleitung*, 282–88. Those who hold to the pseudonym position include, e.g., Kiley, *Colossians as Pseudepigraphy*; Bujard, *Stilanalystische Untersuchungen*.

2. See e.g., Smith, *Heavenly Perspective*, 6–16; Arnold, *Colossian Syncretism*, 6–7.

3. E.g., Bevere, *Sharing in the Inheritance*, 54–59; Dunn, *Colossians*, 35–39.

4. Paul's Letter to Philemon will not be addressed in this chapter because it does not directly interact with the notion of religious apostasy.

5. E.g., Lincoln, *Colossians*, 580; Sumney, *Colossians*, 9–10.

either Paul, Paul's colleague, or both. To avoid confusion, "Paul" will be used to designate the author, which is in keeping with the prescript of the letter (Col 1:1).

THE CONFLICT IN COLOSSAE (1:23; 2:6–7, 18–20)

The main concern in the letter to the Colossians is twofold: Paul comes against a certain "philosophy" that is disturbing the congregation (2:4–23), and he desires the members to live ethically (3:1—4:6). Both ideas are encapsulated in the *partitio* of 2:6–7:[6] the recipients must continue to "walk" in Christ, that is, conduct themselves with behavior appropriate for those who live in union with Christ (cf. 1:9–10; Eph 4:1; Gal 5:16; Rom 8:4; 1 Thess 4:1). This "walk" refers not only to their practicing good moral conduct (Col 3–4), but it also includes maturity in their faith (in Christ) which is related to their ongoing adherence to gospel teachings. They are to be rooted in Christ and not follow empty philosophy (cf. 2:8–23). The audience is comprised primarily of uncircumcised Gentile believers once involved in practicing the transgressions of Gentile outsiders before conversion (1:12–13, 21–22, 27; 2:11–13; cf. 3:1–3). Paul uses "we" and "us" to identify the redeemed believers, including his colleagues, himself, and by implication all Jews and Gentiles who follow Christ (1:12–14; 2:14). He anticipates the Colossians' unity and experience of the full wisdom and spiritual knowledge that comes from being in Christ (1:24—2:3). They are encouraged in this manner so that they would not be deceived (2:4).[7]

A number of proposals have been offered attempting to identify the deceptive teachers and their philosophy. These include Gnostic Jews or Gnostic Essenes,[8] mystery cults,[9] Pythagorean syncretism,[10] Cynics,[11] folk magic and Jewish teachings,[12] imperial cultic elements,[13] Middle Platonism and Jewish teachings,[14] Jewish

6. On 2:6–7 as central to the letter see, e.g., Dunn, *Colossians*, 41; Hay, *Colossians*, 28. Differently, Sumney, "Argument of Colossians," 339–52, and others determine the thesis is 1:21–23, which emphasizes the Colossians' salvation.

7. Τοῦτο in 2:4, a demonstrative neuter singular, refers to either the content of 2:1–3 (Lightfoot, *Colossians*, 173) or it could span all the way back to 1:24 (Barth and Blanke, *Colossians*, 285). In favor of the latter, the author seems to be contrasting the "persuasive speech" (πιθανολογίᾳ) with his preaching "the word of God" (τὸν λόγον τοῦ θεοῦ) in 1:25.

8. Lightfoot, "Colossian Heresy," 13–59; Lindemann, *Kolosserbrief*, 81–86; Porkorný, *Epheserbrief und die Gnosis*.

9. Dibelius, "Isis Initiation," 61–121.

10. Schweizer, *Colossians*, 26–28; Lincoln and Wedderburn, *Later Pauline Letters*, 3–12.

11. Martin, *Philosophy and Empty Deceit*.

12. Arnold, *Colossian Syncretism*.

13. Jeal, "Rhetoric of Resistance," 1–19.

14. DeMaris, *Colossian Controversy*.

mysticism,[15] synagogue Judaism,[16] the Johannine community,[17] or no opponent at all.[18] Up till now the center of the debate has focused on whether the opponents are Jewish or syncretistic.[19]

One problem in our determining the identity of these teachers includes the unique non-Pauline words that are used, which frequently find parallels in both ancient Jewish and non-Jewish literature (e.g., φιλοσοφία, νεομηνία, καταβραβεύω, θρησκεία, συλαγωγέω). Our author may be borrowing terminology used by his opponents.[20] Another problem is that we do not know how accurately these teachers and their views are being portrayed, especially given that our author is attempting to dissuade his readers from the opponents' errors.[21] Moreover, if Paul intended this letter to be read to the Laodiceans also (2:1; 4:16), are we to assume the believers in that city faced the same deception experienced by the Colossians? This is certainly possible given the close proximity of the two cities in the Lycus Valley. Then again, it is equally possible that this is the reason why he is somewhat vague about the opponents; their influence may have been felt only in Colossae. If this were the case, though, the letter would seem to perform two opposite functions: it must be general enough to be relevant for the Laodiceans and yet specific enough for the Colossians to know what Paul is talking about in relation to their opponents. In the end we do not know if the congregations of both cities faced the same conflict, and even if they did we remain ignorant of the extent to which the false teachings had infiltrated the churches.

Other Pauline letters sent to western Asia Minor address false teachers, and it is possible that the points of contention in those letters overlap with Colossians. Although the letter to the Ephesians seems too general to be of much help, the Pastoral Letters address a problem in Ephesus similar to Colossians regarding the

15. Sappington, *Revelation and Redemption at Colossae*; Smith, *Heavenly Perspective*.

16. Bevere, *Sharing in the Inheritance*; Dunn, *Colossians*, 23–35; Stettler, "Opponents at Colossae," 169–200.

17. Royalty, "Dwelling on Visions," 329–57.

18. Hooker, "False Teachers," 315–31. Standhartinger, *Studien zur Entstehungsgeschichte*, presents a fictional situation that does not reflect Colossae at the time the letter was written. This view assumes pseudonymous authorship.

19. Helpful surveys of the various positions related to the identity of the opponents, ranking to at least 44 options in 1970s (so Gunther, *Paul's Opponents*, 3–4) and more since, are found in Smith, *Heavenly Perspective*, 19–38; DeMaris, *Colossian Controversy*, 18–40; Barclay, *Colossians*, 37–55; Schnelle, *Einleitung*, 293–96; and Barth and Blanke, *Colossians*, 21–41.

20. Or is it possible that the problem arises from a single person or "opponent"? There may be only one: cf. Col 2:18 below.

21. When considering the letter's polemic nature, Lincoln, *Colossians*, 562, perceptively asks if the philosophy is given a "straightforward description rather than negatively slanted caricature."

misuse of Torah and ascetic practices (e.g., 1 Tim 1:6–10; 4:1–5). Unlike Colossians, however, these letters do not mention a problem related to angelic worship (but see 1 Tim 5:21). Among other things they are concerned with apostate teachers denying the future resurrection (e.g., 1 Tim 1:18–19), a problem that is not apparent among the Colossians. The Johannine community in Ephesus experienced a major crisis with a group that in some sense denied Christ (e.g., 1 John 4:1–6), and like the Johannine group Colossians stresses a high Christology (Col 1:15–20; 2:9–10).[22] Then again, angelic issues do not seem to be at stake for John, and Ephesus is not Colossae. The community in Revelation, it seems, encounters a problem with angel veneration in western Asia Minor at the end of the first century (cf. Rev 19:10; 22:8–9), but the major problems in this source are related to persecution and the imperial cult. At best there may be some vestiges of continuity between elements of false teachings in these sources and those in Colossians, assuming the common locus of western Asia Minor.

Morna Hooker correctly discerns the absence of proof that some congregation members are adhering to the false teachings. Colossians 2:20 probably should not be read as "why *do* you submit yourselves to regulations?" (τί . . . δογματίζεσθε) but "why subject yourselves to regulations?"[23] Hooker, however, denies any real opponents in the letter. While it is possible that the letter is merely precautionary, the length of time Paul spends discussing the false philosophy, together with the third-person singulars in 2:18–19, suggests that members of the congregation encountered someone of a different religious persuasion, and this may have sparked Paul's response. He uses the indefinite τὶς in chapter 2 not because the person is hypothetical but because he does not know the identity of the one who is disturbing the congregation.[24] Another point raised by Hooker is that the situation in Colossae is nowhere near as bleak as the problems related to false teachers in the undisputed Pauline letters.[25] If we compare Galatians with Colossians it becomes quite evident that the latter possesses commendations and calmness in tone that escapes the former. For instance, unlike the Galatians, Paul commends the Colossians for their faith and love (1:3–8; 2:5).

---

22. Interesting but speculative is the view of Murphy-O'Connor, *St. Paul's Ephesus*, 228–29, who reads Col 1:15–20 as a hymn originally coming from the opponents, stripped of any angelic mentions and robbing Christ of "his terrestrial reality" (228). Paul, in turn, transformed the hymn by adding Christ's human death on the cross and his superiority over angels.

23. Hooker, "False Teachers," 317.

24. Lightfoot, *Colossians*, 178, claims the indefinite τὶς is used by Paul of opponents whom he "does not care to name" (cf. Gal 1:7; Ign. *Smyrn.* 5).

25. Hooker, "False Teachers," 315–31, e.g., 316.

The author nevertheless accentuates their need to persevere, perhaps primarily so because he does not want them to be seduced by the opponent.[26] They will stand before Christ on judgment day and be blameless *provided that* they continue in the faith and not be moved away from the hope of the gospel (1:22–23; cf. 1:4–5, 12, 28).[27] *The conditional "provided that" (εἴ γε) in Col 1:23 (cf. Gal 3:4) implies the possibility of the converse—namely, that if they do not continue in the faith they will not be blameless on judgment day* (cf. Rom 11:22–23; 1 Tim 4:16).[28] The Colossians will commit apostasy if they do not remain in the faith, and from Paul's perception the philosophy of the agitator is potent enough to lead the congregation members astray from the content of the gospel message (Col 2:4, 8). The author, in any case, does not seem to be personally in turmoil about the situation, and elsewhere he recognizes the Colossians' present stability of faith in Christ (cf. 2:5). He is more confident about his own suffering in prison, a hardship that, typical of Pauline letters, is not viewed as a threat to personal faith but is beneficial and in this instance possibly vicarious (1:24).[29]

DECEPTIVE PHILOSOPHY FROM A JEWISH GROUP (2:4, 8, 14–23)

The Colossians are warned to let no one deceive them through persuasive speech (2:4a: ἵνα μηδεὶς ὑμᾶς παραλογίζηται ἐν πιθανολογίᾳ). Such communication intends to fool the persons who hear it. Παραλογίζομαι suggests deluding or misleading actions similar to Laban deceiving Jacob by giving him the wrong daughter for marriage (Gen 29:25) and the Gibeonites deceiving Joshua by putting on worn-out garments and claiming to be strangers who have travelled from a far land (Josh 9:22

---

26. See Martin, *Colossians*, 59.

27. To present (παραστῆσαι: 1:22) before Christ suggests judiciary language related to standing before him at the *parousia* (cf. 1 Cor 1:8; Rom 14:10; Jude 24; O'Brien, *Colossians*, 68–69), hence, judgment day. See also parallel thoughts in 1 Thess 3:13.

28. Gundry Volf, *Paul and Perseverance*, 197n231, maintains that εἴ γε expresses Paul's confidence in the Colossians' continuation of faith, not his doubts. Dunn, *Colossians*, 110, however, provides an insightful qualification: "Εἴ γε may denote confidence more than doubt (cf. its use in 2 Cor 5:3; Eph 3:2; 4:21), but final acceptance is nevertheless dependent on remaining in the faith. The parenetic and pastoral point is that however such persistence must be and is enabled by God through his Spirit (1:11), there must be such persistence." Overstating the case on perseverance in 1:23 is O'Brien, *Colossians*, 69: "If it is true that the saints *will* persevere to the end, then it is equally true that the saints *must* persevere to the end." Melick, *Philippians, Colossians*, 234, is similar: "Paul taught that those who know the truth will continue in the truth. They will not fall away." Correct and more sobering is Garland, *Colossians*, 97: "The promise of blamelessness is, therefore, not unconditional. If the Colossians allow outsiders to dislodge them from their foundation in the gospel—what they had heard and received from Epaphras—they will find themselves removed from their hope."

29. See, e.g., Sumney, "Paul's Vicarious Suffering," 664–80.

LXX).[30] Again in Col 2:8 Paul warns them to "beware" (βλέπετε) of vain philosophy. The present imperative βλέπετε is frequently used by the author as well as other early Christians to warn the faithful against being led astray by false teachings and acts of apostasy (Gal 5:15; Phil 3:2; 1 Cor 8:9; Eph 5:15).[31] Moreover, even though συλαγωγῶν may be used by Paul as an indirect pun on the word "synagogue,"[32] its actual meaning is to rob or lead away someone as a captive (cf. Aristaenetus, *Rhetor* 2.22; Heliodorus, *Scriptor Eroticus* 10.35).[33] The Colossians might lose their faith and hope if they are carried off as booty, as it were, by the deceptive philosophy (Col 1:23). The end result of this captivity would be their transportation away from the kingdom of God's Son back into the realm of darkness where hostile forces reign supreme over humans who are ensnared by spiritual ignorance and immoral deeds (Col 1:13; cf. Eph 4:18; 5:8, 11; 6:12; 1 Thess 5:4–5; Rom 1:21; 2:19; 13:12; 2 Cor 6:14). Since we are discussing a philosophy, an emphasis may be placed on the potential for the Colossians to fall away to spiritual ignorance and confusion related to anti-God powers such as the στοιχεῖα (cf. 2:8, 20). Although the Colossians are encouraged to practice virtues and shun vices (cf. Col 3), *nothing in the letter clearly suggests that the philosophy threatening the church has as its aim an immoral lifestyle.*

What kind of philosophy might be meant in 2:8? The word φιλοσοφία is not used elsewhere in the Pauline letters. It may be the opponents' own designation for their teachings. It refers not only to Greek philosophy and oriental wisdom but also to Jewish religion, especially when it is presented to Gentiles (e.g., 4 Macc 1:1–2; 5:22–24; *Letter of Aristeas* 256; Josephus, *Ag. Ap.* 1.54; *Ant.* 18.11; *J.W.* 2.119; Philo, *Giants* 52).[34] Moses was sometimes thought to have influenced the Greek philosophers.[35] Certain teachings of the opponents related to circumcision, foods, drinks, festivals, new moon, or Sabbath days (Col 2:12–15; cf. 2:20–23) are almost certainly referring to practices in formative Judaism (Dan 1:3–16; 1 Macc 1:62–63; Add Esth

---

30. See other examples in Gen 31:41; Judges 16:10–15; 1 Sam 28:12; Barth and Blanke, *Colossians*, 285.

31. Cf. Matt 24:4; Mark 13:9; Luke 8:18; 21:8; Heb 3:12; 12:25; 2 John 8; *Herm. Sim* 9.27.5. The imperative βλέπε to Archippus (Col 4:17), however, is not necessarily a warning or chastisement (so Lindemann, *Kolosserbrief*, 77); the word is sometimes used for encouragement (cf. 2 Tim 4:5; Barth and Blanke, *Colossians*, 489).

32. So Wright, *Colossians and Philemon*, 100.

33. LSJ, 1671.

34. See further Michel, "φιλοσοφία, φιλόσοφος," 9.172–88. It likewise can refer to proponents of magic (e.g., Dan 1:20 LXX; Stobaeus, *Excerpts* 23.68).

35. E.g, Artisobulus *Frag.* 2.3–4; 3.1; 4.3–4; Artapanus, *Frag.* 3; Clement, *Miscellanies* 1.150.1–3: the fragments of Aristobulus are preserved in Eusebius, *Prep.* 8.9.38–8.10.17; *Hist. eccl.* 13.12.1–13.13.8; and Artapanus in *Prep.* 9.27.4. See *OTP* 2.837–40.

14:17; *Jos. Asen.* 1.10; 7.1; 8.5; *Jub.* 2.17–33; 50:6–13; cf. Lev 11; Deut 14).[36] It is implausible to suggest that Paul would consider a magical or pagan philosophy as a "shadow" of what is to come through Christ (Col 2:16–17; cf. Heb 10:1); he is most likely referring to Jewish customs and identity markers as a shadow pointing to the reality of Christ (cf. Gal 3:23–25; Rom 10:4; 2 Cor 3:7–16). Such customs were once useful in the old era of the Law, but that was before Christ was crucified and rose again from the dead. Eschatological life and righteous behavior now comes through abiding in Christ and following the teachings of the gospel (cf. Col 1:5, 14, 20, 23; 2:6, 12–14; 3:1–4).

As a result of Christ's crucifixion God wipes out the transgressions of Jews and Gentiles who believe. Such offenses apparently were recorded in a handwritten document (χειρόγραφον) with its ordinances (δόγματα) against them. This document, which is declared to be nailed to the cross (2:14), probably contains the book of deeds, wherein human sin is recorded,[37] and ordinances that included prescriptions from the Mosaic Law that fed this document with its "condemnatory force" (Col 2:20–23; cf. Eph 2:15).[38] Nikolaus Walter captures in sharp relief this perspective: "The general expression δόγματα may have been deliberately chosen in order to include the commandments of the Mosaic law within the prescriptions of the religious 'philosophy' of the Colossians . . . The Colossians look at these statutes with religious anxiety and regard themselves as lost before God if they do not hold strictly to them. The author assures them that such slavery is removed in Christ."[39]

The στοιχεῖα Paul mentions in 2:8, 20 have been variously interpreted as basic elements,[40] foundational principles,[41] heavenly bodies,[42] or spiritual powers in control of the movement of stars and events of the planet.[43] In Colossians the term seems closest to this last option. The στοιχεῖα seem to be personal beings rather

---

36. See further examples in Bevere, *Inheritance*, 59–90.

37. e.g., Exod 32:32–33; Ps 69:28; *1 En.* 108.3; *Apoc. Zeph.* 7.8.

38. Words in quotes are from Dunn, *Colossians*, 164. See also Aletti, *Épître aux Colossiens* 179; Martin, *Colossians*, 79–82. Nuanced differently, Bevere, "*Cheirograph* in Colossians 2:14," 199–206, argues that the Law of Moses is central to the χειρόγραφον, and the ideas of indebtedness (an ancient IOU) and book of heavenly deeds are peripheral to the concept.

39. Walter, "δόγμα," 1.340.

40. 2 Pet 3:10–12; Plutarch, *Moralia* 875C; Philo, *Cherubim* 127.

41. Heb 5:12; Xenophon, *Memorabilia* 2.1.1.

42. Diogenes Laertius 6.102; Justin, *Apology* 2.5.2.

43. Gal 4:3, 9; *Sib. Or.* 2.206. See options and further sources in Delling, "στοιχέω," 7.666–87; BDAG, 946. On the association between angels and planets/stars see, e.g., Wis 13:2; *Jub.* 2.2; 16.75; *1 En.* 60.11–22; 75:1–3; *2 En.* 4.1; *T. Abr.* 13.11; 4Q186. Notice also that angels or deities are in charge of nations: e.g., Deut 32:8–9 LXX; Dan 10:13–21.

than impersonal,[44] and they are probably associated with the malignant principalities and powers (Col. 1:16, 2:10, 15; cf. Eph 6:10–12).[45] Hence, they would seem to be included among the powers that are stripped of their authority and dignity through the death and resurrection of Christ (Col 2:13–15).[46] For Paul they are likewise connected with Jewish Torah observances.[47] As in Gal 4:1–11, observances of Jewish customs related to the Mosaic Law are analogous to following the στοιχεῖα. From Paul's perspective those who insist on the works of the Law and those who follow the στοιχεῖα are both overtly concerned about religious practices related to calendar events and the movement of stars, sun, and moon, and they become enslaved to these spiritual powers. Similar to Gal 4, the στοιχεῖα are mentioned in Col 2 as part of Paul's rhetorical strategy to dissuade the readers from adhering to teachings that are similar to their former fear of the elemental spirits they once served when still unbelieving Gentiles. They are again falling into the bondage of serving these powers by following Jewish observances related to ascetic practices, dietary rules, and calendar events (compare Col 2:20–21 with Gal 4:8–11).

The στοιχεῖα are perhaps associated with the "angels" in Col 2:18. If so, the connection between these entities may have rested on an assumption that tribal deities or various angels ruled over each nation (cf. Deut 17:17; 32:8–9 LXX; Dan 10:13–21; *Jub.* 15:31–32).[48] Then again, and perhaps more accurately, the angels may be distinct from the στοιχεῖα in the author's mind, but he makes it appear as though the στοιχεῖα and angels are in some sense connected by placing the terms close together in the same context (2:18, 20). He would do this as part of his rhetorical strategy of dissuasion so that the readers might associate a fascination with angels to their former bondage under the service of the στοιχεῖα.

The philosophy threatening the church in Colossae seem to be identified with the teachings of a Jewish group, and it is questionable endeavor to add further dimensions related to pagan, magical, or Greco-Roman philosophies so as to make the doctrine of the opponents syncretistic. A Jewish philosophy is sufficient for at least three reasons.

First, apart from the Jewish identity markers identified in Col 2, we have already mentioned that ancient Jewish writers frequently called their religion a philosophy

---

44. See Smith, *Heavenly Perspective*, 86–87; Schlier, *Principalities and Powers*, 11–14.

45. So Arnold, *Colossians Syncretism*, 193.

46. Lohse, *Colossians and Philemon*, 112, writes regarding 2:15: "In a triumphal procession God parades the powerless 'powers' and 'principalities' to manifest to all the magnitude of the victory. They are powerless figures who can neither help man [*sic*] nor demand homage and obeisance from him."

47. Cf. Bevere, *Inheritance*, 113.

48. On this interpretation, see further Longenecker, *Triumph*, 47–53.

before the Gentiles, and it stands to reason that if the Colossian church is primarily Gentile (1:21, 27; 2:13) a Jewish sect may have used such language to make inroads to these Gentiles for the purpose of persuading them to follow their teachings.[49]

Second, our proposal of a Jewish philosophy helps explain in a sufficient way how the deception could influence the congregation members. The Gentile members of the Colossian church were no doubt interested in ancient Judaism because their leaders, Paul included, were Jewish and often referred to Israel's scriptures to support their beliefs. Moreover, they could easily be intimidated by a persuasive Jewish speaker who knew the scriptures far better than they did (cf. 2:4).

Third and finally, a significant minority of Jews lived in the Lycus Valley, including Hierapolis, Laodicea, and Colossae.[50] The region may have had its own synagogues prior to the devastating earthquake (c. 61 CE). Ignatius' warnings against Jewish teachings and apostasy betray a phenomenon of early Christians defecting to Jewish beliefs in Asia Minor at the beginning of the second century (Ign. *Magn.* 8–10; Ign. *Phld.* 6.1; cf. *Phdl.* 8–9; Ign. *Smyrn.* 5.1). This phenomenon in part may be attributed to Paul's weak connection with some of the congregations that were started by his coworkers (Eph 3:2; Col 2:1) and to congregational discouragement emerging from Paul's long imprisonments (Eph 3:13). In the words of Frank Thielman, "This disillusionment seems to have led some to stray from the faith into deviant forms of Christianity, whether docetism, Jewish, antinomian or a combination of these tendencies. It may have also led some to abandon the faith altogether for the ancient and widely respected religion of the synagogue."[51]

The type of Jewish philosophy Paul warns against apparently leans toward apocalyptic/*merkabah* tendencies (cf. Col 2:16–23), and their identity as Essenes or an Essene-like sect is as good a guess as any. If Josephus's description of the Essenes in the *Jewish War* is not too distorted: 1) their doctrines[52] are considered a philosophy (2.8.2 [119]); 2) they maintain an ascetic lifestyle (2.8.2–4[120–23, 126]); 3) they travel to different cities (2.8.4[124–25])(and so why not the Lycus Valley?); 4) they have strict procedures regarding touching food (2.8.5[130–31]; 8.7[139]; 8.10[151]); 5) they have a preoccupation with angels (2.8.7[142]), and other similarities.[53] Also, if the Essenes lived in Qumran and wrote a number of the Dead Sea Scrolls, this community venerated angels (4Q400; 4Q403), observed dietary and calendar regu-

49. On the term "sect" see the Introduction in volume 1 of this study.

50. See Acts 2:9–10; 19:26; Josephus, *Ant.* 12.147–53; 14.185–267; Philo, *Alleg. Interp.* 245, 281; Feldman, *Jew and Gentile*, 69–74; Trebilco, *Jewish Communities in Asia Minor.*

51. Thielman, *Paul & the Law*, 215.

52. δόγματα: Josephus, *J.W.* 2.8.7[142].

53. E.g., see the many examples given by Lightfoot, "Colossian Heresy," 13–59.

lations, and had a preponderance for horoscopes that could have been interpreted by Paul in relation to the στοιχεῖα (e.g., 1QS 5.13; 6.16; 1QM 2.4; 4Q186).

THE "WORSHIP OF ANGELS" (2:18)

The letter mentions the opponent's fascination with angels, which remains a point of contention among interpreters: "Let no one keep disqualifying you of your prize [καταβραβευέτω], he taking pleasure [θέλων] in humility [ταπεινοφροσύνῃ] and worship of angels [θρησκείᾳ τῶν ἀγγέλων], going on in detail [ἐμβατεύων] about what he saw, vainly inflated by his fleshly mind" (Col 2:18). We notice the singular "he" in this passage that perhaps suggests one adversary in particular. Several decades ago scholars frequently interpreted the "worship of angels" as an objective genitive, and the lack of evidence for angelic cults in early Judaism led some to say that this verse contended against a mystery religion in which cosmic deities or στοιχεῖα were understood as angels.[54] In more recent years an increasing amount of scholars argue that angels are not worshipped by the opponent. Rather, the "worship of angels" should be understood as a subjective genitive conveying a worshipping *along with* the angels (cf. Josephus, *Ant.* 12.253; 4 Macc 5:7).[55] This type of phenomenon often occurs in Jewish apocalyptic literature.[56] Such texts regularly combine "humility" (i.e., ascetic practices; cf. Col 2:20–23) with experiences in which angels are observed by humans in visionary or heavenly ascents.[57] The ascetic practices may be preparatory for the visions.[58]

Against this view Clinton Arnold raises the problem that nowhere in ancient Greek literature is θρησκεία used of a divine being or objects of worship in which the genitive is understood as subjective. He argues instead that the "worship of angels" in Col 2:18 should be interpreted as an objective genitive which is related to humans invoking or venerating angels.[59] Loren Stuckenbruck, however, indicates that in some ancient Jewish texts there is evidence for both angels worshipping God and hu-

54. E.g., Dibelius, "Isis Initiation."

55. Indeed angels are commonly viewed as worshipping God (Isa 6; Dan 7:9–10; Luke 2:14; Rev 4–5; *Apoc. Ab.* 17–18; *T. Lev.* 3:4–8; *Apoc. Zeph.* 8:3–4 *Ascen. Isa.* 7–9).

56. Cf. Dan 9:3; 10:2–3; 4 *Ezra* 5:13–20; 9:23–25; 1QSb 4.25–26; 1QH 3.20–22; 2 *Bar.* 5:7–6:4; 9:2–10:1; 47:2–48:1; *Apoc. Ab.* 9:7–10.

57. See e.g., Francis, "Humility and Angelic Worship," 163–95. For more references that combine humility and worship with angels, see Stuckenbruck, *Angel Veneration*, 116; idem, "Colossians and Philemon," 131.

58. Notice, e.g., ἐμβατεύων as "entrance" combined with "what he saw" in Col 2:18.

59. Arnold, *Colossian Syncretism*, 90–95, 101. Arnold uses the Thesaurus Linguae Graecae to determine his view of occurrences of θρησκεία. Stettler, "Opponents in Colossae," 184, however, raises the issue that θρησκεία is not used for invoking angels, which weakens Arnold's view.

man veneration of angels (e.g., Tob 11:14–16; 12:16–17; 4QShirShabb[a] [400] 2.1–3; 4QShirShabb[d] [403] 1 i.32–33). Hence, "worshipping with angels" and "worshipping the angels" may not be mutually exclusive thoughts.[60] Revelation likewise provides us with examples of angels worshipping God and humans venerating angels; albeit, the latter is discouraged (Rev 4:8–11; 5:11–14; 19:9–10; 22:8–9). We may not need to decide after all between an objective or subjective meaning for the "worship of angels" in Col 2:18.

The opponent's preponderance with angels may include visionary descriptions of them, bowing down before them, communicating with them, and together with them worshipping God. These kinds of practices may be what Paul denounces as the "worship of angels." The ambiguous way he uses the phrase allows for his auditors to think about the opponent in the worst possible light—as an idolater.[61] In this manner *Paul is able vilify this person who probably thought himself to be a faithful monotheist.*

DANGER OF APOSTASY THROUGH THE TEACHINGS OF AN OUTSIDER (2:18–19)

The letter claims that the opponent is not holding on to "the head," which is Christ (2:19; cf. 1:18; 2:10). One outlook frequently suggested by these words is that the visionary person(s) is some sort of apostate claiming to be Christian, but from Paul's perspective this person has rejected Christ or has been severed from him.[62] Alternatively, the opponent is sometimes viewed as someone who is on the verge of apostasy, a loose ligament in the body of Christ.[63] On this reading the person harms the congregation from within, and he is possibly a Hellenistic Jew who joined the congregation after leaving the synagogue or a Gentile convert who had previous dealings with the synagogue. Lincoln maintains, "It would make no sense for the writer to depict someone who made no claim to a relationship to Christ in the first place as not holding fast to Christ."[64] Paul, however, regularly warns congregation

60. Stuckenbruck, *Angel Veneration*, esp. 84, 119, 154–61. See also Bevere, *Sharing in the Inheritance*, 111, 114.

61. Garland, *Colossians*, 179–80, points out contemporary examples of similar denunciation. The early church fathers railed similar accusations against Jewish opponents for their service to angels (Clement, *Miscellanies* 6.5.41[2–3]; Aristides, *Apol.*; Origen, *Comm. Jo.* 13.17; cf. *Cels.* 1.26; 5.6). For sources see further Stuckenbruck, *Angel Veneration*, 140–49.

62. E.g., Sumney, *Servants of Satan*, 191–92; idem, *Colossians*, 158; O'Brien, *Colossians*, 146, 156; Gnilka, *Kolosserbrief*, 152.

63. E.g, Lincoln, *Colossians*, 633, suggests this person is "in danger of being deprived of the essential connection with the true source of fullness (v. 10). By implication, such a person is a loose ligament out of alignment with the rest of the body."

64. Ibid., 567; cf. 632–33.

members who are on the verge of committing apostasy (e.g., Gal 5:4; 1 Cor 10:12; 2 Cor 13:5; 1 Thess 5:14); hence, if the opponent still belonged to the community in Christ then we wonder why Paul does not warn him as he does other church members. If he thinks the man is wrongly influencing the church, then why does he not discipline him or have the congregation expel him, a procedure that is normally done for such cases in the Pauline churches?[65]

It is more probable that *the opponent is an outsider who never claimed to be a Christ-follower*. First of all, Col 2:19 hints at irony. This person judges and wants to disqualify the Colossian Christians, apparently from God (cf. 2:15, 18), but Paul insinuates that this individual is really the one who is excluded from God because he does not belong to Christ, the complete representation of the invisible God in embodied form (1:15; 2:9–10).[66] Second, κρατέω in 2:19 does not need to be translated as "hold fast" but merely "hold on."[67] It is not that the opponent is holding loosely to Christ; he is not holding onto Christ at all. Third, κρατέω may be related to κοσμοκράτωρ or "world holder" (cf. Eph 6:12), which seems to be another term related to the principalities, powers, and the στοιχεῖα that allegedly "hold" the stars and course of human affairs. Indeed, there is evidence that στοιχεῖον and κοσμοκράτωρ can be used interchangeably in the ancient world (e.g., *T. Sol.* 8.2–3; 18.2). The use of κρατέω, then, may be somewhat of a pun—that by holding on to the so-called cosmic holders, the opponent was not holding on to Christ, the ultimate "holder" of the church and cosmos and its supreme ruler (cf. 1:15–20; 2:9–10). Finally, κρατέω is also used several times in Mark 7:1–23 against the scribes and Pharisees, who adhere to Jewish customs related to food laws as "human tradition" (cf. Mark 7:3–4, 8).[68] Parallel Christian thoughts against Jewish dietary regulations may be assumed in Col 2:8, 22. The opponent in Colossae does not hold on to Christ but instead holds on to a human philosophy related to Jewish customs.[69] These observations point us in the direction of discerning that this individual comes from a Jewish sect that rejects Jesus as the Christ without any indication of having previous belief in or

65. E.g., Gal 4:30; 1 Cor 5; 2 Cor 2:5–6; 13:2; 1 Thess 3:14; 1 Tim 1:19–20; Titus 3:10.

66. Similar to my view on exclusion is Wright, *Colossians and Philemon*, 124; cf. 28, 123.

67. Cf. Zerwick, *Grammatical Analysis*, 608; Bratcher and Nida, *Colossians*, 68. The former, however, assumes the person is Christian, and the latter that he stopped holding on to the head.

68. In Mark's pericope, Isa 29:13 is cited to support the argument that the Pharisees are said to neglect and invalidate the command of God by holding to human tradition. Isaiah, however, does not relate human traditions to the mitigation of dietary rules. Matt 15:1–20 is a parallel to Mark 7:1–23, but κρατέω is not used in Matthew's version.

69. Stettler, "Opponents in Colossae," 188, on a similar vein, notices from *1 Enoch* that "clinging to the Lord" (40.6; 46.7–8) is the converse of denying him (45.1; 46.6). See also Roberts, "Jewish Mystical Experience," 183.

service to him. Paul perceives him to be teaching a false philosophy, but he does not consider him to be an apostate Christian.

In Colossians, then, it is not the opponent who is in danger of apostasy; he is an outsider. It is the members of the congregation who are endangered. Even so, this threat might be actualized not so much by the Colossians adhering to ascetic practices or having visions of angels per se, but through negative consequences that might develop from such practices. *Such teachings distract from the all-sufficiency of Christ as the comic ruler and one who has forgiven them of their transgressions* (2:9–15). A falling away would take place if congregation members embraced the philosophy and joined the opponent's sect (2:4, 8). Moreover, from Paul's point of view such teachings might influence them to reject his version of the gospel and nature of Christ; at very least such aberrations would cause divisions among church members (cf. 1:23; 2:5–7, 19).

We can adduce from Colossians 2 that the opponent claims to see visions of angels, practices asceticism, and follows Jewish customs, which he puts forth as indications of being in right standing with God. He disturbs congregation members by condemning them for not practicing such things. His condemnation (καταβραβεύω: 2:18) of the believers conveys the image of an umpire giving an unfavorable decision so as to prevent someone from receiving an athletic prize.[70] The award in this case is eschatological life. Another way this condemnation has been interpreted is that Paul is threatening the Colossians: they are in danger of being disqualified from their Christian commitment if they follow the opponent.[71] However, the opponent's judging of congregation members in 2:16 makes it evident that he is the one condemning in 2:18, not Paul. His denunciations would be similar to the opponents in Galatia condemning Gentile Christians for not being circumcised (Gal 1:6–7; 4:17). Unlike the conflict in Galatia, however, the opponent in Colossae probably does not claim to be a Christ-follower. The congregation's encounter with this man may have happened when he visited one of the local house churches and confused certain members with his eloquent speaking and knowledge of Jewish traditions. Perhaps some follow-up conversations between this person and congregation members did not go as planned, and he seemed to be influencing the church members more than they were influencing him.

70. Cf. Lincoln, *Colossians*, 632.
71. So Melick, *Philippians, Colossians*, 269.

A NEW IDENTITY IN CHRIST (3:1–25)

Colossians 3:1—4:6 functions as the paraenesis of the letter and presupposes the imagery of baptismal conversion in 2:11–13. The letter's recipients were perhaps fairly new in their faith (Col 2:11–13; 3:11; cf. Gal 3:27–28; 1 Cor 12:13). The "once . . . now" distinction related to the Colossians' past and present highlights a contrast between their former lifestyle in the kingdom of darkness and their subsequent rescue from it into in the kingdom of light in Christ (Col 1:22; 2:6, 13; 3:6, 8; cf. 1:12–13).[72] Christ not only reigns supreme over the cosmos and hostile powers, but his death, burial, and resurrection provides a new life for the Gentile converts who were once "dead" in transgressions (2:9–15; cf. 1:15–20). Their old, sinful self was buried in baptism at their conversion, and they were raised again to live "in Christ," taking on the identity of "saints," "elect," "beloved," and "faithful brothers and sisters" (e.g., 1:2; 2:6, 11–12, 20; 3:1, 12; 4:7). In language recalling Israel's exodus from Egypt, they have become God's people after being redeemed from enslavement. Yet their inheritance is not the land of Canaan but the entire renovated creation—Christ as their leader is the "firstborn" son over the entire cosmos and he is the head of the church via his resurrection from the dead (Col 1:12–18).[73] His resurrection and supremacy marks the defeat of the anti-God powers and their deceptive influence on human opponents who attempt to lead the believers astray.

Be that as it may, Paul's paraenesis in the last half of the letter is more concerned about believers living a moral life than their potential to be deceived by vain philosophies.[74] Vices such as sexual immorality, greed (idolatry), wrath, slander, abusive language, and lying once made the Colossians subject to God's coming wrath (Col 3:5–11; cf. Eph 2:3; 5:5–8). This section is typical of Pauline letters that are addressed to Christian Gentiles whose former lifestyle as unbelievers included practices he condemns. Similar to the letter addressed to the Ephesians, the vice list in Colossians contains conventional elements, more so than in most other Pauline letters because it will be read to more than one congregation (4:16). The vices portray what might be typical of a Jewish author writing against Gentile immorality.[75] Consequently, *there is no evidence in Colossians that the opponent's philosophy nurtures unethical living.*

72. Along these lines see especially Witherington and Wessels, "Ethics and Ethos," 304–5.

73. Cf. Exod 4:22; 6:8; Deut 10:9; 12:12; 14:27–29; 32:9; 18:1; Rom 4:13; 8:17–25. See Cannon, *Use of Traditional Materials*, 17–19; Bevere, *Sharing in the Inheritance*, 143–46; Wright, *Colossians and Philemon*, 60–63.

74. Even the vice of lying (3:9) does not seem directly related to the opponent's deception. Paul's concern is that the members do not lie *to one another*.

75. In agreement with Bevere, *Sharing in the Inheritance*, 199.

The Colossians' moral conduct should reflect their new life in Christ. They received the gospel tradition with its central message on the lordship of Christ, and now they are to continue their "walk" in spiritual communion with Christ (2:6; cf. 1:10, 27; 4:5 contrast 3:7).[76] The Colossians must set their minds on "things above" (3:1–4), live virtuously, and not succumb to self-indulgence (Col 3). One of the functions of this prohibition is to prevent the congregation from interpreting the author's rejection of the opponent's asceticism as warranting lax morals.[77] In imagery that recalls putting off one's clothes at a baptismal ceremony and putting on a new robe (cf. Eph 4:20–24), the Colossians must put on virtues and put off (and put to death) vices related to their pre-converted status. Behind the clothing metaphors may also rest a faint allusion to the Genesis story in which the "image" of God in Col 3:10 recalls Adam and Eve created in God's image (Gen 1:26–27). Their attempt to cover their nakedness with figs implies improper clothing that is removed and replaced with garments that God made for them (Gen 3:7–11, 21). The Colossians are to strip off the sinful self or "old man," representing Adam, and be clothed with the new "man," representing the Second Adam (Christ), and so be ushered into a new creation (Col 3:9–10).[78]

As new persons in Christ the Colossians should put on virtues such as love, unity, forgiveness, and peace, making sure to do everything in the "name" of the Lord Jesus, that is, acknowledging his lordship over everything and submitting to his commissioning and enablement (3:10–17). In essence, to do something in the name of the Lord Jesus is to walk in him (Col 2:6; 3:23; cf. Eph 5:20; 1 Cor 10:31; Sir 47:8).[79] The virtue of love is no doubt intended to be "Christ-shaped," as Wedderburn affirms, cementing together the members of the church under the headship of Christ: "it is with the formation and holding together of the Church that the writer is concerned when the qualities are selected that are to be mentioned, for they are all ones which would serve to unite the Church, just as the vices that are to be 'put off' in 3.8–9 are ones that would tear it apart."[80] Another virtue we encounter is humility (ταπεινοφροσύνη: Col 3:12), which can be set in contrast with the false humility of

76. Dunn, *Colossians*, 140: "This combination of 'receiving tradition of Christ Jesus as Lord' and 'walking in him' is thus a neat summary of the mutual check and balance between outward guideline and inward motivation which was a feature of the Pauline ethic."

77. So Witherington and Wessels, "Ethics and Ethos," 308.

78. See further Kim, *Significance of Clothing Imagery*; Beale, "Colossians," 866–68.

79. We notice Dunn, *Colossians*, 240–241: "The 'name' was one of the chief ways in the ancient world by which a person could be known, by which her or his character could be disclosed, by which one could (as we might say) 'get a handle' on another . . . To identify oneself by reference to the Lord Jesus was therefore to stake all on his reputation and power" (240).

80. Lincoln and Wedderburn, *Later Pauline Letters*, 56.

the opponent (2:18, 23). Humility practiced by the latter is associated with conceit and having a "puffed up" attitude. True humility, on the other hand, works toward love and unity.

The Colossians' new conduct is to spill over into their household behavior as wives, husbands, children, slaves and masters (3:18–25). The Christian slave who serves Christ, in particular, is to be rewarded at the eschaton with the inheritance of God's kingdom (Col 3:24; cf. 1:12; Eph 5:5; 1 Cor 6:9–11; Matt 5:5; 19:29). The unrighteous, however, will be punished (Col 3:25). Some interpreters identify this person as a slave who practices unrighteousness (cf. Phlm 18); others think it refers to the master who abuses the slave (cf. Eph 6:9), or both master and slave as wrong-doers.[81] However we may interpret Col 3:25, it addresses Christian recipients. The passage has special relevance to judgment by works in relation to the way Christ's followers treat others. Every believer will receive a recompense for their deeds, and if faithful servants are rewarded with eternal inheritance then it follows that Christians who are wrongdoers will be deprived of it. If salvific inheritance finds its full realization in the future (Col 1:5, 22–23; 3:4) then *the author leaves open the possibility of that some believers might not inherit Christ's kingdom due to immoral behavior* (Col 3:25; cf. Rom 2:6–16; 1 Cor 4:5; 2 Cor 5:10). The Colossians have been qualified to share in the inheritance of the saints (1:12–13), but disqualification is always possible (1:23; 2:4, 8; 3:25).

CONCLUSION

The community our author addresses in his letter resided in the Lycus Valley in Asia Minor and was comprised of mostly Gentiles, many of whom were relatively new believers. They are charged to maintain their commitment both to their relationship in Christ and their loyalty to the gospel message. The Colossians will be blameless before Christ on judgment day provided that they continue in the faith (1:22–23). In the worst-case scenario they could be robbed of their faith, that is, commit apostasy by embracing a deceptive philosophy (2:4, 8) that comes from a Jewish outsider who belongs to a sect that holds to beliefs similar to the Essenes. The false teaching includes a fascinating with angels, which Paul uses to vilify the opponent as a worshipper of angels and thus insinuate this person as an idolater who is controlled by forces of darkness such as the στοιχεῖα (2:8, 18, 20; cf. 1:13). The opponent, however, probably considered himself to be a monotheist. He confused some congregation members through his deceptive speaking and knowledge of Jewish scriptures and traditions. He does not hold on to Christ but holds to Jewish calendar observances

81. For a list of scholars supporting these positions see Barth and Blanke, *Colossians*, 449.

and ordinances. He also practices ascetic devotion (2:8–23). The believers must walk as new people in Christ by doing good works, knowing that they will stand before Christ on judgment day and give account for their behavior towards others, and it is possible for them to be excluded from God's kingdom (cf. 3:24–25). The letter does not go into details about this final judgment, nor does it discuss restoration from apostasy.

Colossians affirms with the other Pauline letters an eschatological judgment according to works in which believers might lose out on final salvation via their acceptance of false teachings and practice of immoral conduct. The vices mentioned in Col 3, unlike in some of Paul's earlier letters, are not related in any direct manner to the opponent's conduct or known congregational misbehavior. Thus the paraenetic section of this letter fits more the stock of vices that generally discourage Gentile converts from turning back to pre-converted deeds. The deceiver in Colossae centers his teachings on Torah observances, similar to the opponents in Paul's letters to Galatians and Philippians. Among this person's beliefs, a mystical fascination with angels sets him apart from previous opponents. The all-sufficiency of Christ as redeemer and the cosmic ruler of all things renders other spiritual powers unworthy of the believers' preoccupation and veneration. The cosmic Christ motif is shared in common with Ephesians. Philippians also emphasizes a high Christology, but rather than arming the recipients with a perspective that refutes competing viewpoints or reinforces the community's identity, Philippians uses Christology with an ethical aim that instructs the congregation to walk with humility and godly fear.

9

1, 2 Timothy and Titus: The Influence of False Teachers in the Pastoral Letters

Many scholars today doubt or deny that the Pastoral Epistles of 1 and 2 Timothy and Titus are genuinely written by Paul.[1] Among the various tensions these letters demonstrate when compared with Paul's other letters are, for instance, that its historical situation cannot be placed within Paul's undisputed letters or Acts, and there are differences related to vocabulary, style of writing and theology.[2] The evidence against Paul's authorship cannot be easily dismissed. Although our surmising on the identity of the author would detract us from our main objective, it will be maintained throughout this chapter, and in agreement with many scholars, that these letters remain in the Pauline tradition even if they are not actually written by Paul.[3] It will be assumed that these letters were written or completed in the latter part of the first century CE, perhaps by a colleague of Paul's not long after Paul was martyred.[4] Because these letters seem to be written by the same person and maintain

1. For the pseudonym perspective see, e.g., Roloff, *Timotheus*, 23–39; Ehrman *New Testament*, 388–93; Kümmel, *Introduction*, 370–87. Supporters of Paul's authorship include, e.g., Fee, *1 and 2 Timothy*; Knight, *Pastoral Epistles*, 21–52; Johnson, *Timothy*, 55–99. A mediating position is favored by Miller, *Pastoral Letters*, 11, 18, 138, 144–58, who opts for an authentic Pauline "core." See discussion in Harding, *About the Pastoral Letters*, 10–27.

2. E.g., different use of prepositions, stress on terms such as "godliness," "sound teaching," etc. See fuller discussions on these and other problems in Marshall, *Pastoral Epistles*, 57–92; Trebilco, *Early Christians in Ephesus*, 197–206.

3. E.g., Trummer, *Paulustradition*; Harding, *About the Pastoral Epistles*, 28–45.

4. My view is that the authentic voice of Paul may be heard behind these writings even though someone else may have reworked or finalized that voice, presumably after Paul's death. This would be somewhat similar to Luke working over the speeches attributed to Paul in Acts. Sometime after the first century, the identity of the author behind these letters was forgotten. Bauckham, "Pseudo-Apostolic

similar themes, they can be read together.[5] In addition to using the cumbersome "Pauline author," we will use "AP" (author of the Pastorals). We can also use "Paul" to identify this author. The letters are attributed to "Paul" and so it is not wrong for us to call the author by this name (1 Tim 1:1; 2 Tim 1:1; Titus 1:1). One of the primary purposes of the Pastoral Letters is to combat a growing problem of false teachings that are influencing the churches in Ephesus and Crete (1 Tim 1:3; Titus 1:5). There is no compelling reason to deny that the problems facing the Pauline churches may reflect those in Ephesus and Crete in the late first century.[6] Strikingly, colleagues of Paul in 1–2 Timothy are those we find in Ephesus in the Book of Acts and 1 Corinthians (1 Tim 1:1; 2 Tim 4:12, 19–20/Acts 18:18–19; 19:22; 20:4; 21:29; 1 Cor 16:19).

APOSTASY AND OPPONENTS AS FALSE TEACHERS IN THE PASTORAL LETTERS: (1 TIM 1:3–7; 2 TIM 2:16–18; 4:4; TITUS 1:10–14)

The vast amount of passages in these letters that are related to the opponents can be highlighted as follows:[7] 1 Timothy alternates between the author's instructions to the young pastor in relation to his opponents (1 Tim 1:3–20; 3:14–4:16; 6:3–21) and in relation to various groups within the congregation (2:1–3:13; 5:1–6:2); the entire middle section of 2 Timothy deals with the congregation's opponents (2 Tim 2:14–3:9); and the letter of Titus alternates between the church's opponents (Titus 1:10–16; 3:9–11) and the perpetration of sound doctrines (2:1–15; 3:1–14).

These opponents are generally described as false teachers and apostates who lead astray others from the emergent Christian message of faith as taught by Paul. In 1 Timothy the author instructs Timothy to forbid certain individuals in Ephesus from teaching a "different doctrine" (ἑτεροδιδασκαλεῖν) and from paying attention

---

Letters," 492–94, suggests Timothy as the author; Marshall, *Pastoral Epistles*, 92, suggests a group that may have included Timothy and Titus; others have argued for Luke (cf. 2 Tim 4:11): e.g., Wilson, *Luke and the Pastoral Epistles*; Quinn, "Last Volume of Luke," 62–75; Strobel, "Schreiben des Lukas?" 191–210; contrast Marshall, *Pastoral Epistles*, 88.

5. Cf. Marshall, *Pastoral Epistles*, 1–2.

6. For evidence see Trebilco, *Early Christians in Ephesus*, 206–9. Some scholars in fact consider this topic as the *main* purpose of these letters. Marshall, "Orthodoxy and Heresy," 5–14, for example, considers that these letters were composed "in a situation of false teaching threatening the truth, and that their basic purpose is to deal with this situation." I do agree that 1 Timothy and Titus are primarily written for this purpose, but 2 Timothy functions somewhat differently as a type of final testament for Paul as prisoner awaiting his impending trial.

7. See Van Neste, *Cohesion and Structure*, 141–44, 224–32, 273–82. Although Van Neste's topics are helpful in distilling these passages, there is definite overlap, for example, between the widows and Timothy's opponents who are influencing them in 1 Tim 5. Also, in my view, Titus 3:9–10 centers on the opponents more than on sound doctrines.

to myths and genealogies. Rather, they are to adhere to divine training (οἰκονομία).[8] Such preparation aims at fostering love that finds its source in a pure heart, a good conscience, and sincere faith (1 Tim 1:3–5). Those who perpetrate the different doctrine are considered deviants from divine training and the virtues pertaining to it. They have turned away to foolish talking (1:6–7, cf. vv. 19–20). The *false teachers deviate (ἀστοχέω) from faith* and embrace "falsely-called knowledge" (6:20–21).[9] In 1 Timothy faith can be understood both as an initial and ongoing relationship of trusting God that also maintains a moral quality of living (1:2, 4–6, 14; 2:15; 3:11; 4:12; 6:11–12).[10] An immoral lifestyle, such as the opponents are implicated as having, thus indicates faithlessness. Apostasy is typically viewed in this letter as a defection from faith (cf. 1:6; 1:19; 5:8; 6:10, 21). The false teacher's followers turn away (ἐκτρέπω) to Satan (1 Tim 5:15; cf. 2 Tim 4:4).[11] Such language suggests that the opponents' departure from correct training was not a minor error but severe enough to expel its main perpetrators from the congregation (1 Tim 1:19–20). In the Book of Acts, Paul seems to anticipate this upcoming crisis in the church of Ephesus when he predicts that some of its leaders would become apostates and lead astray congregation members (Acts 20:28–30; see volume one of this study).

In the second letter, Timothy must hold to "sound" doctrines and guard the truth entrusted to him (2 Tim 1:13–14; cf. 4:3; 1 Tim 6:3; Titus 1:9–13; 2:1–2, 8), which may be set in contrast to unhealthy teachings of the opponents (2 Tim 2:17; cf. 1 Tim 6:4). Sound teaching embraces the message of the gospel and beliefs related to it held by the Pauline churches (2 Tim 4:2–3; Titus 1:9, 13).[12] Hymenaeus and Philetus are named as two perpetrators of false teachings (cf. 2 Tim 2:16–18). Those who follow false teachings are described as turning away (ἀποστρέφω) from the truth (2 Tim 4:4; cf. Titus 1:14), which here denotes committing apostasy in terms of rejecting the truth of the gospel.[13] Timothy is nonetheless commissioned to be a

8. Οἰκονομία is a multifaceted concept, which may be understood here as "the outworking, administration, or stewardship of God's plan of salvation through the gospel and its communication" (Knight, *Pastoral Epistles*, 75–76).

9. On ἀστοχέω (to deviate, go astray, or miss the mark) see also 2 Tim 2:18; Titus 1:6; 2 *Clem.* 17.7.

10. See De Villiers, "Heroes at Home," 367–68. On faith in relation to conversion in the Pastorals, see 1 Tim 1:14; 5:12; 2 Tim 1:5; 3:15. Various uses of "faith" in the Pastorals are discussed in Collins, *1 and 2 Timothy*, 93–95; Mounce, *Pastoral Epistles*, cxxx–xxxii.

11. On ἐκτρέπω see also 1 Tim 1:6; Josephus, *Ant.* 6.34; 8.251; Philo, *Spec.* 2.23; LSJ, 523.

12. Sound teachings (ὑγιαινόντων λόγων) are presented in the Pastorals to help maintain a healthy community: MacDonald, *Pauline Churches*, 172.

13. See also how ἀποστρέφω is used similarly to convey apostasy in 2 Tim 4:4; Heb 12:25; Acts 7:39; 20:30; Ezek 3:18–20; Hos 8:3; Jer 15:6; 3 Macc 3:23; Josephus, *Ant.* 2.48; cf. Luke 23:14; Bertram, "ἀποστρέφω," 7.719–22; BDAG, 122.

faithful "soldier" for the cause of Christ and a patient teacher willing to correct the false teachers of their errors (2 Tim 2:23–26).

Titus is charged by the author to set things right in Crete and appoint elders who are sound in doctrine and able to refute the rebellious, deceivers, and "windbags" (1:5–10).[14] *Such individuals turn away from the truth of the early Christian message* (Titus 1:10, 14; cf. Matt 15:9), and they ruin entire households by teaching for shameful gain (Titus 1:11; contrast 2:8, 12–14).[15] The correct procedure for confronting these erring congregation members is for Titus to rebuke them severely in order that they may be sound in the faith. If they do not receive correction he is to reject them (1:13; cf. 3:10). The rebuke is possibly more directed at the followers and the expulsion to the leaders, but the Pauline author does not make very clear distinctions between the two. A circumcision group is closely associated with the Cretans (1:10, 12–14) in this faction, and some of the false teachings in the Pastorals are Jewish-oriented.

The threat in Ephesus and Crete has come about from insiders rather than outsiders. The fact that expulsion from the community is discussed in relation to the false teachers in both 1 Timothy and Titus verifies this. The teachings come from some who are (or were) recognized as leaders (1 Tim 1:7; Titus 1:11). This may be one reason why these letters give detailed instruction about the qualities of leader (cf. 1 Tim 3:1–13; 5:17–25; Titus 1:5–9).[16] The overseer must be able to exhort with sound doctrine and refute opponents who oppose it (Titus 1:9). The opponents' mode of operation is through local households (2 Tim 3:6; Titus 1:11), which here might represent house churches (1 Tim 3:15; 2 Tim 1:16; 2:20; 4:19), but it is also possible that the houses are referring to family households (1 Tim 3:4–5, 12; 5:4, 8, 13–14).[17] Perhaps both thoughts are intended if the teachers enter into family homes that also function as churches. In any case the consequence is dire. *The false teachers are Christians who are still influencing the churches in these regions. They are perceived by the author as apostates who are leading other church members to fall away from faith and truth.*

The AP upholds the importance of reading Israel's scriptures (2 Tim 3:16–17; cf. 1 Tim 4:13).[18] He uses Israel's sacred texts consistently with what he claims about

14. Cf. Zerwick, *Grammatical Analysis*, 648, for the last term (ματαιολόγοι). Barrett, *Pastoral Epistles*, 130–31, translates it as "talk wildly."

15. Here "ruin" (ἀνατρέπω) could also mean "destroy," "overturn," "upset," or "cause to fail": cf. 2 Tim 2:18; BDAG, 174; see further meanings in LSJ, 124.

16. Rightly, Trebilco, *Early Christians in Ephesus*, 212.

17. On οἶκος as house churches here see, e.g., Quinn, *Titus*, 99. On οἶκος as families see, e.g., Arichea and Hatton, *Titus*, 275–76.

18. Some interpreters have argued, however, that the Pastoral Letters virtually ignore Israel's writ-

the use of "scripture" in 2 Tim 3:16: 1) it is useful for instruction; 2) correction; 3) improvement; and 4) discipline in righteousness.[19] The author instructs Timothy about the value of Israel's scriptures (2 Tim 3:14–17), and so his use of these traditions becomes significant for these letters, and also in relation to the false teachers, as we will notice below.

TORAH AND VICEDOERS
(1 TIM 1:3–11; CF. 5:18; 2 TIM 1:5; 3:5, 14–17)

The Pauline writer claims the opponents misuse Mosaic Law (1 Tim 1:3–11). They have turned aside to senseless talking related to Torah and desire to be "teachers of the law" (νομοδιδάσκαλος), but they do not know what they are talking about (1:6–9).[20] The Law is intended to regulate the lives of vicedoers, restrain evil, and obviate against the violation of specific rules.[21] The list that follows recalls the sins mentioned in the Decalogue (1:9–10). The vicedoers sin against God, dishonor parents, commit murder and sexual sin, steal, and tell lies—violations that are all found in the Decalogue (cf. Exod 20:1–16; Deut 5:1–20). The appropriate use of the Law stands in contrast to the inappropriate way the false teachers use it: for wrangling on about speculations, genealogies, and fables (1 Tim 1:4).

The righteous, on the other hand, operate under the principles of love, purity of heart, and sincere faith (1:5, 8–9a). The author mentions love as a requisite for the godly, and this may be presupposing the thought of loving one's neighbor, which, in Pauline thought, fulfills the Law (Gal 5:14; Rom 13:8). Paul makes a similar move

ings. The "scriptures" to which they refer are mainly Paul's letters. In this view the AP refers to the Paul's "scriptures" in 1 Tim 5:18a (cf. 1 Cor 9:9) and 2 Tim 3:15–16 (cf. Rom 15:4): e.g., Nielsen, "Scripture in the Pastoral Epistles," 4–23 who thinks that Marcion of Sinope (2nd c.) probably came from and was influenced by a Pauline church. One major weakness with this view is that Timothy has learned the sacred scriptures since very early childhood (2 Tim 3:15–16), which may be too early to be referring to Paul's writings as sacred. This argument stands even if we date the Pastoral Letters at c. 100 CE, although it is probably closer to 70 CE (Quinn and Wacker, *First and Second Letters*, 19). Timothy's mother and grandmother presumably taught him the scriptures, and they already knew these writings before he did (2 Tim 1:5; 3:15; cf. Acts 16:1–2). Also, Deut 25:4 is being echoed in 1 Tim 5:18a. The next verse (5:19) refers to Deut 19:15: "upon two or three witnesses," which is not found in the context of 1 Cor 9:9.

19. Hanson, "Old Testament," 217, correctly adduces from these comparisons that even though the Pastoral author is an inferior expounder of the "Old Testament" than Paul, "he is still in touch with Jewish exegesis; he can go to the scriptures directly for his material when he chooses to."

20. The term νομοδιδάσκαλος seems to be coined by early Christians. It refers to teachers of Mosaic Law rather than some generic or societal use of the law (cf. Luke 5:17; Acts 5:34). The anarthrous use of "law" in 1 Tim 1:9, though perhaps having wider societal implication than "the law" in 1:7–8, should still be understood under the rubric of Mosaic Law.

21. In agreement with McEleney, "Vice Lists," 204–5.

when setting up the ethical principles of loving one's neighbor and walking in the Spirit in opposition to vicedoing in Gal 5:13—6:2. The Law's restraining character does not apply to those who love their neighbor, walk in the Spirit, and practice virtues (cf. Gal 5:23b). The AP elsewhere associates the work of the Spirit with love and moral behavior (2 Tim 1:7, 14; cf. Gal 5:22).[22] In both Galatians and the Pastorals, then, those who practice love and moral spirituality are exempt from the Law's punishment, unlike the vicedoers. Yet in the Pastoral Letters the ethic of love is overshadowed by the concept of εὐσέβεια: behavior and conduct that pleases God and appropriate for his elect (cf. 1 Tim 2:2; 4:7–8; 6:3–11; 2 Tim 3:5; Titus 1:1).

It is probably correct to say that our author wishes to implicate the false teachers with the vicedoers even though the former do not appear to be committing the heinous crimes of the latter (1 Tim 1:9–10; cf. 1:4–5).[23] Perhaps *the author insinuates a common guilt attributed to the false teachers and vicedoers because, as errant teachers of the Torah, the former remove the restraints holding back the latter.* In this sense, for our author both the false teachers and the vicedoers would be considered Torah despisers. The false teachers are mentioned in the other vice lists as conceited, envious, coveting wealth, and full of dissension and disobedience (1 Tim 6:3–5, 9–10; Titus 1:10, 15–16; cf. 1 Tim 3:6–7).[24] They are also implicated with the hypocritical pleasure seekers who commit numerous vices in the last days (2 Tim 3:1–9). But we read too much into the last passage if we claim that every vice on the list is committed by the opponents. Some of the overindulgent vices contradict the ascetic practices of the false teachers in 1 Tim 4:1–4. The author's polemical use of language and imprecision gets in the way of our deciphering exactly which vices the false

---

22. See Fee, *1 and 2 Timothy*, 227, on 2 Tim 1:7: "For when God gave us his Spirit, it was not timidity that we received, but power, love, and self-discipline."

23. So McEleney, "Vice Lists," 205.

24. Timothy's selection of a leader must not include a novice, lest he be filled with conceit (τυφόω) and fall into condemnation (κρίμα) of the devil (1 Tim 3:6). This verse is not claiming that Satan became prideful or conceited, and this led to his original apostasy in primeval times (Contrast Witherington, *Hellenized Christians*, 1.239; Barrett, *Pastoral Epistles*, 59–60). The devil's downfall may be supported elsewhere in the NT, but it is eschatological and not directly associated with pride or conceit (e.g., Rev 12:7–10; 20:7–10; Matt 25:41), and passages in the Hebrew scriptures, such as Isa 14 and Ezek 28, are not referring to the devil but the rulers of Babylon and Tyre. First Tim 3:6 is likely suggesting an unspecified judgment the devil is able to bring on a conceited novice leader. We notice that in the next verse (3:7), the devil plays an active role by ensnaring leaders who do not have a good public reputation. Perhaps 1 Tim 3:6–7 portrays the devil as a plaintiff standing before God and finding accusation against flawed Christian leaders (Rev 12:10; see Roloff, *Timotheusbriefe*, 161). The author assumes that a prideful novice placed in a position of church leadership has real potential to become a victim of Satan, as was the case with the false teachers in Ephesus.

teachers commit as opposed to those committed by the stereotyped, fallen humanity in 2 Tim 3:1–5.[25]

Oskar Skarsaune notices that some early Christians who write against their opponents, the AP included, seem to borrow language from early Jewish polemics against the *minim*: they disdain those who blaspheme the Creator, deny bodily resurrection, and do not employ the use of the Law and Prophets (e.g., 1 Tim 1:3–11; 4:1–5; 2 Tim 2:18).[26] To be sure, this association seems more than coincidental, but the polemics found in the Pastorals are not purely Jewish. Robert Karris argues persuasively that the Pastoral Letters adopt a polemical schema held in common with ancient philosophers writing against the Sophists. Topics in the schema of the Pastorals include deceivers (2 Tim 3:13), greed (e.g., 1 Tim 6:5), verbal disputations (1 Tim 1:4–6), not practicing what one preaches (2 Tim 3:5), and success among women (2 Tim 3:6). With this perspective in mind, *the vice lists function as a polemic to help vilify the opponents and encourage the reader to disassociate with them* (e.g., 2 Tim 3:5).[27] Even so, these lists still have some paraenetic force; Timothy is charged not only to avoid vicedoers but also flee from the vices himself (1 Tim 6:11; 2 Tim 2:22; cf. 1 Cor 6:18; 10:14). The opponents and some of the vices may be real threats to the community even though colored with polemical stereotyping.

THE SHIPWRECKED FAITH OF HYMENAEUS AND ALEXANDER (1 TIM 1:19)

Two individuals are singled out as opponents in 1 Timothy. Hymenaeus and Alexander have "thrust away from themselves" (ἀπωθέω) a good conscience and suffered shipwreck as a result (1:18–20).[28] The metaphor of being shipwrecked conveys the imagery of steering off course and coming to ruin; in this case the opponents have ruined their faith (1 Tim 1:19; cf. *Barn.* 3.6; implied in Jude 12).[29] Some interpreters emphasize the Greek article "the" (τὴν) before "faith" (πίστιν) to pro-

25. Some other vice lists in these letters recollect the pre-converted lifestyles of early Christians (1 Tim 1:13–14; Titus 3:3) or qualities a minister should *not* have (1 Tim 3:1, 3, 6–8, 11; 2 Tim 2:22–23; Titus 1:7).

26. Cf. *Syr. Didascalia Apostolorum* 23–24 [VI.10–12]; Justin, *1 Apology* 16.6; *Dial.* 35.2–5; cf. *Did.* 1.2; *Herm. Mand.* 1.1; *Barn.* 19.2. Skarsaune, "Heresy and the Pastoral Epistles," 9–14. On Jewish sources for the *minim* in this light see, e.g., Moore, *Judaism*, 3.68–69.

27. Karris, "Polemic of the Pastoral Epistles," 554.

28. Here the middle participle ἀπωσάμενοι conveys "thrust away from oneself": cf. Arichea and Hatton, *Handbook*, 41. On the verb's relation to apostasy, see Acts 7:39; 13:46; Hos 4:6; Jer 23:17; Ps 118[119]:10; *T. Ash.* 1.8.

29. For the metaphoric use of shipwreck (ναυαγέω) see *Cebitus Tabula* 24.2; Philo, *Dreams* 2.143, 147; *Names* 215; Plutarch, *Quaest. conv.* 1.4622B; Diogenes Laertius 5.55.

pose that the shipwreck involves the *content* of faith, in other words, the Christian faith or body of teachings related to Christian truths rather than Hymenaeus and Alexander's own faith.[30] If this were the case, the gospel or church itself was damaged by these individuals, and a case could be made that they never had authentic personal faith. Even on this view, however, whatever damage was done would seem to include the infiltration of false teachings that lead astray congregants from the true gospel, and this type of deception causes those who do possess authentic faith to fall away (1 Tim 4:1; 5:15; 2 Tim 4:4; 2 Tim 2:17–18; Titus 1:10–11, 14).[31]

The loss of Hymenaeus and Alexander's *personal faith*, however, appears to be the correct meaning. Earlier in the same chapter those who are adhering to false teaching have turned away from love, faith, and a good conscience (1 Tim 1:5–6).[32] Though not yet named at this point, Hymenaeus and Alexander would no doubt be included among this party of false teachers. Moreover, Timothy is supposed to be "holding faith and a good conscience" (1:19a), which almost certainly concerns personal faith here. In the next sentence (1:19b) "faith" is again paired with "conscience," and the meaning of "conscience" remains the same. Hence, in 1:19b it would seem awkward for us to read the nuance of "faith" as suddenly changed to the content of faith (i.e., "the Christian faith").[33] The definite article before "faith" probably functions as a pronoun of possession to indicate "their faith" rather than "the faith."[34]

30. See e.g., Gundry Volf, "Apostasy," 44; Fee, *1 and 2 Timothy*, 58; Fee, however, affirms their own faith or "complete trust in God's grace," was ruined as well.

31. If faith is objective and creedal in 1:19b it could still be argued that Hymenaeus and Alexander fell away in terms of rejecting or thrusting away their personal faith in 1:19a. If so, then the opponents have fallen away from personal faith (1:19a) and damage the teaching of the church as a result (1:19b). Mounce, *Pastoral Epistles*, 67 (cf. cxxx), holds to such a view and finds parallels to "the faith" with περί in 1 Tim 6:21; 2 Tim 3:8. In his view, the feminine singular relative pronoun ἥν refers back the feminine nouns that precede it: "ἥν, 'which,' is the direct object of the participle ἀπωσάμενοι, 'rejecting,' and refers to both πίστιν, 'faith,' and ἀγαθὴν συνείδησιν, 'good conscience'" (67). But it seems better to connect the singular feminine accusative ἥν with only the singular feminine accusative συνείδησιν, the most immediate noun that precedes it. They are thrusting aside the voice of their conscience, as Marshall, *Pastoral Epistles*, 411–12, affirms.

32. On ἐκτρέπω ("turn away") see also 1 Tim 5:15; 2 Tim 4:4.

33. A chiastic structuring of the passage lends support to this interpretation. Ellis, "Apostasy and Perseverance," 69–70, writes that a simple chiasm appears in 1 Tim 1:19 with "Keeping Faith" and "Shipwrecking Faith" at points A and A₁ and "Good Conscience" and "Which (Conscience) some have rejected" at points B and B₁, showing close symmetry between faith in 1:19a and 1:19b. In his view, among other reasons, the apostates were once genuine believers because child training (1:20 "that they learn not to blaspheme") was an act performed on God's children for the purpose of preserving them from condemnation.

34. On the use of the Greek article here, see Knight, *Pastoral Epistles*, 109–10. My colleague Kenneth Waters has drawn to my attention a quote from Gilliard, "Paul and the Killing of the Prophets," 260: "It is well known that ancient Greek, both classical and koine, often used a definite article instead of the possessive adjective that would regularly be explicit in modern English." Marshall, *Pastoral Epistles*, 412,

This interpretation also makes better sense of the thought of being shipwrecked (ναυαγέω), which often seems to convey utter ruin in ancient traditions.[35] The metaphoric use of the word also conveys a complete loss of the ship: Philo describes ναυαγέω in terms of the loss of an entire vessel (*Names* 215) and with being overthrown and "sent to the bottom" (*Embassy* 371).[36] The Pauline author could hardly be talking about minor damage done to part of a ship; he is referring to a sunken vessel rendered totally inoperable (cf. 2 Cor 11:25; Acts 27:14–44). *As such, the term makes very little sense if attributed to the ruin of the Christian faith*, especially when the author claims elsewhere that God faithfully preserves the Christian message (2 Tim 1:12; 2:14, 19–20). *The shipwreck is referring to Hymenaeus and Alexander's own faith; they had personal faith comparable to Timothy's* (1:18–19a)*, but that faith was destroyed*. What Timothy currently has, they have lost.[37]

For the Pauline author, apostasy is also associated with their rendering their consciences ineffective (1:19a), and this is typified with behavior that runs contrary to godliness (cf. 1 Tim 4:1–3; Titus 1:14). Philip Towner correctly suggests that the apostates have ruined the "capacity of their consciences" to make trustworthy decisions.[38] Oppositely, a good conscience is committed to the faith of the apostles as the ground for godly living.[39]

EXPELLING APOSTATES FROM THE CHURCH
(1 TIM 1:19–20; CF. 2 TIM 2:24–26; TITUS 3:10)

It is possible to read the deliverance of Hymenaeus and Alexander to Satan (1 Tim 1:19–20) as a magical curse resulting in physical ailments, similar to Paul's confrontation with the false prophet Elymas resulting in his physical blindness in Acts 13:8–11. A closer parallel to the Pastoral incident, however, is found in Paul's judgment on the incestuous man in 1 Cor 5. He delivers him to Satan, which means

suggests that "the intransitive ναυαγέω, the fact that it is the opponents who suffer, and the preposition περί ('with respect to'; cf. 6.21; 2 Tim 2.18; 3.8; Titus 2.7)" all make the reference to "the faith" indirect.

35. Herodotus, *Histories* 7.236, writes about a loss of 300 vessels to shipwreck; Xenophon, *Cyropaedia* 3.1.24 mentions seafarers fearing shipwreck; Demosthenes, *C. Phorm.* 34.10 equates shipwreck to the loss of a vessel.

36. See Yonge's translation.

37. Or in the words of Quinn and Wacker, *First and Second Letters*, 154: "What Timothy has and keeps (*erchōn*), others have lost."

38. Towner, *Timothy and Titus*, 118–19.

39. Ibid., 119. Following Eckstein, *Begriff*, 314, Towner adds: "the conscience acts as a neutral judge of behavior, according to a norm that brings its judgment, either positive or negative, to the awareness of the individual by criticism or affirmation" (117). Marshall, *Pastoral Epistles*, 224–25, notices a similarity between Paul's use of "mind" in Rom 12:2 and "conscience" in the Pastoral Letters.

that the fornicator is expelled from the auspices of the church into the cosmos, the fallen world run by Satan (see on 1 Corinthians above). Some of the major differences between the expulsions in 1 Corinthians and 1 Timothy are as follows: 1) In 1 Timothy 1 the culprits are delivered to Satan for teaching false doctrine rather than for committing sexual sin (albeit the teachers are associated with committing vices also); 2) the culprits are mentioned by name in 1 Tim 1, but neither the man nor his stepmother are mentioned by name in 1 Cor 5, and only the man is expelled from the congregation (presumably the stepmother is not part of the congregation); 3) "Paul" expels the members himself in 1 Tim 1, but he orders the congregation to do so in 1 Cor 5; 4) the expulsion in 1 Tim 1 has already taken place when the author writes the letter, but in 1 Cor 5 the expulsion has not yet taken place; and 5) both 1 Tim 1 and 1 Cor 5 mention a formulaic "hand over to Satan" related to the expulsion,[40] but in the latter Paul also invokes some sort of exit ritual ("in the name of Jesus"). These differences between the two passages are not crucial enough for us to suggest they are not describing the same type of phenomenon. Thus, despite differences between 1 Tim 1:19–20 and 1 Cor 5, Hymenaeus and Alexander's "deliverance to Satan" most likely refers to their expulsion from the Ephesian congregation to hostile demonic forces prevalent outside of it.

In both 1 Corinthians and 1 Timothy, *the culprits are banished to protect the congregation while at the same time providing those who are expelled a chance to repent.* They are ostracized so that they "*learn* not to blaspheme" (1 Tim 1:20).[41] As outsiders they should find it difficult to persuade church members to embrace their false teachings. The author in 1 Timothy is presumably thinking that some demonic-related calamity will befall the ostracized individuals now that they are no longer under the spiritual protection of the church.[42] Satan already influenced their minds while they were in the church; now that they are out of the church he will have full access to their bodies. After they have been ravaged by the devil for awhile they might come to their senses, turn away from their false teachings, and seek to be restored. In 2 Timothy, Hymenaeus' words are considered unhealthy and eat like

---

40. For parallel sources related to the formula, see Quinn and Wacker, *First and Second Letters,* 156–58.

41. The Pauline author is seen here as disciplining disobedient children in hope of getting them to learn from their errors (1 Tim 1:20; cf. 2 Tim 2:25; Titus 2:12; Heb 12:6–10; 1 Cor 11:32): cf. Johnson, *Timothy,* 186. Incidentally the false teachers' blasphemy seems related to their slandering or misrepresenting the true teachings of the Pauline church (2 Tim 3:2; Titus 3:2; cf. 1 Tim 6:1).

42. Ellis, "Apostasy and Perseverance," 70, assumes that someone cannot be "delivered over to Satan" who is already in his control (cf. 1 John 5:18; 2 Thess 3:3). But the focus of the passage is ecclesiastical, referring to expelling individuals from the protection of the church into the realm of Satan even though the church is not mentioned as the "body of Christ" in the Pastorals.

gangrene. His teachings, along with those of another teacher named Philetus, ruin or overthrow (ἀνατρέπω) the faith of some (2 Tim 2:18–19; cf. Titus 1:11; 2 Tim 3:13).[43] The Pauline author names Philetus as a false teacher with Hymenaeus, but it is Alexander whom Paul expels with Hymenaeus (1 Tim 1:19–20).[44] We hear nothing more about these individuals in this letter (but see on 2 Tim 2:14–15 below). The AP in the second letter instructs Timothy to confront the false teachers in hope of their recovering themselves from being entrapped by the devil (2 Tim 2:24–26; cf. 1 Tim 4:1–2). *Such teachers are seen as Satan's pawns who will suffer calamity unless they recover themselves out of his clutches* (cf. 1 Tim 3:6–7; 5:15). Titus is likewise instructed to confront the false teachers in his community in hope that they will return again to sound teachings (Titus 1:13; cf. 3:10). They are not associated with the devil in that letter, however.

Justification for expelling the false teachers may be based on Deuteronomy, in which we read that the purpose of cutting off wrongdoers is to cleanse the community from evil influences. In Deuteronomy the false prophets and those who lead astray others to serve foreign gods are to be put to death so that evil might be removed from the midst of Israel's community (Deut 13:1–11; 17:2–7; cf. 18:20). Paul cites Deut 17:6–7 when expelling the Corinthian fornicator (cf. 1 Cor 5:13). The Deuteronomic tradition is evident behind the procedure for dealing with false teachers in the letter to Titus. Titus is to reject them if they refuse to be corrected after given a few chances (Titus 3:10), an idea that pays homage to the Deuteronomic teaching that establishes every judgment against an accused person on the word of two or three witnesses (Deut 17:6–7; 19:15). That our author was familiar with this tradition is rather clear: on evidence of two or three witnesses, Timothy can determine the validity of accusations against an elder (1 Tim 5:19–20/Deut 19:15–20). And that Paul, at least, would transform the Deuteronomic idea of the testimony of two or three witnesses into the idea of giving rebellious church members two or three chances to alter their behavior is likewise clearly seen (2 Cor 13:1).

Titus is to make one or two attempts of admonition before expelling an incorrigible person from the religious community in Crete. In Titus 3:10 the nuance of "reject" (παραιτέομαι) with an accusative of person(s) suggests dismissing or driving

43. To "upset" the faith of some, as some translators render the word, is not a strong enough connotation for ἀνατρέπω. The word refers to breaking down doors (*P.Oxy.* 1.69.2) and sinking ships (cf. LSJ, 124); Ellis, "Apostasy and Perseverance," 86, correctly notices the parallel between this passage and being shipwrecked in 1 Tim 1:19.

44. Hymenaeus appears to be an unusual name according to Quinn and Wacker, *First and Second Letters*, 155, and so we are safe in equating the two names as referring to the same false teacher in 1 Tim 1:19 and 2 Tim 2:17.

out the person.[45] The verb is also used in a less severe sense of avoiding false teachers and their teachings (1 Tim 4:7; 2 Tim 2:23). In this sense breaking fellowship would be less severe, perhaps closer to 2 Thes 3:14–15 than 1 Cor 5:1–5.[46] But given the larger context of Titus (esp. 1:9–15; 3:11), the more severe meaning is preferred. We notice also that church expulsion in Matthew involves an individual who refuses to receive correction after bringing the matter before the church (Matt 18:17–18). This involves a two- or three-step process that finds parallels within the Qumran community (1QS 5.23—6.1; cf. CD 7.2–3; 9.2–8, 16; 10:3), but we are not given specific details of the procedure in Titus. For one thing we are not told if Titus is to provide witnesses against the person or bring this issue up before his community. The action in Titus is defended by the AP echoing Deut 32:20 (LXX) in relation to Israel's apostasy (Titus 3:10–11). Titus should reject the rebellious person because such individuals show themselves to be perverted or to have "turned aside" (ἐκστρέφω) and gone the wrong way.[47] They keep on sinning and stand self-condemned (3:11).[48] In short, *they can be expelled because they already show themselves to be apostates through their behavior.* For the AP such a person is a hardened reprobate, and his refusal to receive authoritative correction makes his condemnation evident for all to see. This self-condemnation is related to some sort of judgment the rebel inadvertently brings upon himself or herself (cf. Luke 19:22; Gal 2:11). In this case it may suggest the judgment Titus would bring on such a person through expulsion. Context and rarity of terminology used here prevent us from affirming eternal judgment.[49]

The author's instructions to Titus may assist us in unlocking an otherwise peculiar aspect about the Pastoral Letters. The AP encourages Timothy to confront false teachers in some passages (1 Tim 1:3; 2 Tim 2:23–26), yet he wants him to disassociate from them in others (2 Tim 3:5).[50] How is Timothy to cleanse himself of these false teachers if he is supposed to instruct them in hope of their restoration? Perhaps the tension is alleviated in part by suggesting Titus 3:10 as a model in dealing with false teachers within the community. Titus's initial admonitions involve rebuking

---

45. See BDAG, 764.

46. Quinn, *Titus*, 251, notices that Titus is the one who is instructed to disassociate with the person; the congregation is not told to disassociate with him also.

47. Knight, *Pastoral Epistles*, 355, writes on this verb: "ἐξέστραπται (perfect middle or passive of ἐκστρέφω, a NT hapax legomenon), which means either that he 'has turned himself aside/perverted himself' (middle) or that he 'is turned aside/is perverted' (passive). In either case the person has moved away from the apostolic message by choice." See also Ezek 13:20; Amos 6:12; Zech 11:16; BDAG, 309.

48. The present tense ἁμαρτάνει may suggest continuous action.

49. The term self-condemned (αὐτοκατάκριτος) is rare and not found in the LXX or elsewhere in the NT; see Dibelius and Conzelmann, *Pastoral Epistles*, 151.

50. An observation wisely noticed by Cranford, "Encountering Heresy," 35–36.

sharply the false teachers and keeping them silent at church (1:11a, 13b). Perhaps this would be similar to the AP's charge for Timothy to publically rebuke an elder who continues to sin (1 Tim 5:20).[51] If the persons causing factions refuse to change after these admonitions, Titus should expel them (Titus 3:10–11).[52] If the same notions hold true for Timothy, then maybe the confrontation imagined between Timothy and the opponents is a similar one: if they do not repent after Timothy confronts them then he has every right to expel them from the congregation much the same way the AP has expelled Hymenaeus and Alexander.

EVE DECEIVED: GENESIS AND THE WOMEN IN EPHESUS (1 TIM 2:9–15; CF. 5:5–15; 6:2–10, 17)

Another Torah tradition relevant to the infiltration of false teachings in Ephesus is related to the Serpent deceiving Eve in the Garden of Eden (1 Tim 2:9–15; Gen 3). According to the author this deception stands as the basis for why women should be quiet in Timothy's church.[53] To be in a state of quietness (ἐν ἡσυχίᾳ) probably does not convey absolute silence, but an attitude of listening attentively and not disturbing others (cf. 2 Thess 3:12; Acts 21:40; 22:40). The idea of learning in quietness is captured nicely by the Lukan story of Mary sitting at the feet of Jesus and listening to his words (Luke 10:38–42). The pericope on the woman's prohibition to teach begins with 1 Tim 2:11 and closes at 2:15. In between the opening and closing, the passage follows the structure of a chiasm:

A. Prohibition 1: I permit not a woman to teach (2:12a)

    B. Prohibition 2: I permit not a woman to have full authority over a man (2:12b)

        C. Rule: She is to be in a state of quietness (2:12c)

51. In this case, however, it is not clear that the elder is teaching false doctrines, and his rebuke before others is so that they might be fearful of sinning in a similar way as the one who is rebuked.

52. The fact that expulsion seems futuristic in Titus and that the false teachers are still in the church might lend to the possibility that this letter was written before 1 and 2 Timothy. It might be possible to suggest the cleansing in 2 Tim 2:21 implies an expelling of members who are teaching falsely in Timothy's church. E.g., Lea and Griffin, *1, 2 Timothy*, 219, say that Timothy is urged to break all contact with them in this verse.

53. Of course this is not the only point in this passage that the author brings up about women congregants; he supports women submitting to men because, in his patriarchal view, Adam takes some sort of precedence over Eve since he was created first. For perspectives on Pauline passages related to feminine roles see, e.g., Baumert, *Woman and Man*; Kroeger, *Rethinking 1 Timothy 2:11–15*; Keener, *Paul, Women, and Wives*.

B. Reason for Prohibition 2: Adam was first formed, then Eve [Adam's priority is due to the created order] (2:13)

A. Reason for Prohibition 1: Adam was not deceived, but the woman [Eve] was deceived [by the Serpent] and has come into transgression (2:14)

This way of reading the text highlights the aspect of the woman learning in quietness (level C) while at the same time stressing a relationship between her not being permitted to teach (A1) with her being deceived by the Serpent (A2). The Pauline author's male bias and ancient Mediterranean assumption is probably that women are especially susceptible to deception, and the Genesis story attests to this as well as the situation in Ephesus.

The connection between levels A and C is strengthened when we compare this passage with the way Gen 3 is used in the Corinthian letters. In 2 Cor 11:2–5 Paul mentions the Serpent deceiving Eve and fears the Corinthians will be led astray by his opponents just as Eve was deceived by the Serpent. In Paul's view, the point of deception in the story is related to the opponents teaching a different gospel.[54] In relation to male/female roles in 1 Cor 11:2–16, Paul affirms male authority or headship over the female because Adam was first formed, then Eve (11:7–9). This passage does not mention anything about the Serpent deceiving Eve, and correspondingly no word is mentioned about women not being allowed to teach; on the contrary, they could prophesy in church (11:5). The upshot of these observations is this: in Pauline thinking, a male sense of priority over the woman is supported by God creating Adam first, and the prohibition against women teachers is supported by Eve being deceived by the Serpent.

Nevertheless, the author's instructions to Timothy could hardly mean that all women should never be permitted to teach; otherwise, this would seem to be in conflict with what he writes elsewhere. The author affirms Timothy's knowledge of Israel's scriptures from his earliest childhood (2 Tim 3:14–16).[55] He apparently learned these scriptures from his mother and grandmother when growing up because his father is not mentioned (cf. 1 Tim 1:5). We might suppose that the father is not a believer. According to Luke, who is Paul's close colleague, Timothy's father was a Greek non-believer (cf. Acts 16:1). Evidently, righteous women were allowed

54. Genesis 3 aside, the serpent's deception or seduction of Eve appears in a number of ancient Jewish sources; most notably for Paul are traditions that have the devil disguised as an angel of light (e.g., *L.A.E.* 9–11; *Apoc. Mos.* 22), an image he uses against false teachers in 2 Cor 11:13–15. For other ancient sources see, e.g., Collins, "Before the Fall," 293–308; Hanson, "Eve's Transgression," 65–77.

55. The word βρέφος used here refers to a baby, infant, or a very small child (cf. 2 Macc 6:10; Luke 2:12, 16), an age that was undoubtedly too young for the tot to be formally trained in the scriptures by a rabbi.

to teach males without the Pauline author's disapproval. Paul also allowed women to instruct in terms of prophesying (1 Cor 11:5; cf. Gal 3:28) and his colleague Priscilla taught Apollos the way of the emergent Christian faith (Acts 18:24–26). Women, it seems, could also be deacons (1 Tim 3:11).[56]

Perhaps the author's prohibition against women teachers, then, should be interpreted in light of the letter's primary topic and situation—false teachers are influencing Timothy's congregation. The Serpent's deception of Eve reflects the false teachers deceiving the women in Timothy's congregation. Our passage in 1 Tim 2 combines two streams of thought argued earlier by Paul and derived from the creation story: 1) the priority of Adam due to God creating him before Eve (1 Cor 11:8–9, 12); and 2) the serpent's deception of Eve in relation to false teaching (2 Cor 11:2–5). *As Eve was deceived by the Serpent, so the women in the Ephesian congregation are being deceived by the false teachers who are inspired by Satan* (cf. 1 Tim 4:1–3; 5:13–15). Therefore, they should not be allowed to teach.

Some other observations about the uniqueness of this situation in the Pastoral Letters support this view. The Pauline author wants the women to dress in modest apparel without gold, pearls, or costly array (1 Tim 2:9–10). This charge would be rather meaningless unless some of the women he refers to come from the affluent end of society.[57] It is also clearly evident that the false teachers hoped to gain wealth (cf. 1 Tim 1:4–7, 19–20; 4:1–7; 6:3–10; 2 Tim 2:17; Titus 1:11). An important corollary follows from this: the false teachers seem to have preyed on wealthy women in the congregation. They enter into households captivating and misleading "idle women" (2 Tim 3:6–7).[58] Certain widows in particular seem influenced by false teachings (1 Tim 5:5–15). Apparently some of the widows were wealthy, and the author mentions their self-indulgence (σπαταλάω) referring to living luxuriously (1 Tim 5:6 cf. Ezek 16:49; Jas 5:5; 1 Tim 2:9–10). This type of widow is described as spiritually dead, not possessing the Spirit of God (1 Tim 5:6). Moreover, there are widows depicted as idlers going from house to house, babbling on and saying things they ought not (1 Tim 5:13; cf. 4:7; 2 Tim 2:16).[59] Gordon Fee rightly argues that the language de-

56. On 3:11 see argument in Trebilco, *Early Christians in Ephesus*, 520–23.

57. That women in Ephesus could be wealthy at this time; see evidence in Witherington, *Hellenized Christians*, 1.218–21.

58. The actual term is "little women" (γυναικάριον), which is derogatory and refers to women as weak, foolish, or idle (2 Tim 3:7; cf. Jdt 16:9; *T. Reub.* 5:3; Ign. *Phil.* 2:2; BDAG, 208). No doubt, the idea is more polemical than realistic, and it seems that our author holds to a negative stereotype. That these women are ever learning but never coming to the knowledge of the truth may suggest they are not truly converted (cf. similar wording in 1 Tim 2:4). But we should not read too much into this polemically charged passage. It will suffice to say that some of the women were in fact deceived by these false teachers and others in the congregation would also be deceived unless Timothy puts a stop to these teachers.

59. They also may be considered "meddlesome" or "busybodies" (περίεργος: 1 Tim 5;13), but a

scribing these widows resembles what is said about the false teachers (1 Tim 1:6–7; 4:7; 6:3–4, 20; Titus 1:11).[60] The women or widows say things that they should not be saying (1 Tim 5:13; cf. Titus 1:11), need to be silenced (1 Tim 2:11–12; cf. Titus 1:11), and have turned away after Satan (1 Tim 5:15). The same concept of turning away describes those who follow false teachings and meaningless talk (1 Tim 1:6; 2 Tim 4:4), and following Satan resonates with demonic influence associated with the false teachers (1 Tim 4:1–2; 2 Tim 2:26).

The younger widow's violation of her "first faith" and resulting condemnation (1 Tim 5:11–12) may be interpreted as breaking faith with Christ, hence apostasy. But this interpretation is not clear. She may be only breaking some pledge to remain a widow that allowed her to receive some form of assistance from the church. Her condemnation may refer to divine punishment if apostasy is in view, but then again, censorship or public disapproval would be the meaning if she has only broken a church pledge. Another alternative is that her condemnation involves her decision to marry an unbeliever, which would be a violation of Pauline instruction for widows to marry someone "only in the Lord" (cf. 1 Cor 7:39). This violation would be all the more apparent if such widows had to abandon their faith in Christ as a precondition for marrying unbelievers, a view suggested by Bruce Winter.[61] In any case she is not condemned for remarriage so long as it is to another Christian; in fact, getting remarried is precisely what the author instructs her to do—younger widows are to get married, bear children, and rule their household (1 Tim 5:14).[62]

A special connection is present between the women mentioned in 1 Tim 2 and 5. Both passages have in common congregants making supplications and prayers (2:1, 8–9; 5:5), the women's role in doing "good works" (2:10; 5:10; Titus 2:14; cf. Acts 9:36, 41), a deception on the women caused by Satan/the Serpent (1 Tim 2:14 [implied]; 5:15), and bearing children as a remedy to the problem (2:14; 5:14). In the Pastorals, especially Titus, good works are not related to "getting in" salvation (cf.

---

rather different view of this term relates it to problems with practicing magic in Ephesus (cf. Acts 19:19; 2 Tim 3:6–9). On this reading see Pietersen, "Women as Gossips," 18–35, who in 5:13 interprets περίεργος as "related to magic" rather than "meddlesome." If so, then the term is still relevant to deception and apostasy because the Pauline author may be warning "his congregation concerning the dangers of falling back into magical practices from which they have escaped" (Pietersen, 31).

60. Fee, *1 and 2 Timothy*, 122. Other supporters of connecting the woman's silence in 1 Tim 2 with the problem of false teachers include, e.g., Bassler, "Adam, Eve, and the Pastor," 43–65; Trebilco, *Early Christians in Ephesus*, 507–28.

61. Winter, *Roman Wives*, 136–37; Towner, *Timothy and Titus*, 352.

62. Our author claims that the younger widows will want to remarry (1 Tim 5:12), an odd notion given that the false teachers denounce marriage (1 Tim 4:1–3)! No doubt, all the Ephesian widows cannot be lumped together with the false teachers. It may be the case that some of the younger widows were not wealthy and not as prime a target as the older widows.

Titus 3:5) but are to be demonstrated in the process of salvation; hence, they are vital to Christian conduct. They appear in visible ways such as rearing children, service, and hospitality (1 Tim 5:10), meeting the needs of others, and sharing one's wealth (1 Tim 6:18; Titus 3:14).[63] With the situation related to widows in mind, the author's exhortation for women to be in a state of quietness and not teach and boss[64] around men may be directed at least partially, if not primarily, at widows in the congregation who are going from house to house spreading erroneous ideas learned from the false teachers (cf. 1 Tim 5:13–15).

Much debated is the perspective that the woman's salvation through "bearing children" (τεκνογονία) echoes Gen 3:15–16 and infers Eve's ultimate descendent (Christ) as the seed of the woman who would bruise the head of the Serpent (1 Tim 2:15).[65] This messianic interpretation does not fit well with the context. The author uses the same term again as a verb (τεκνογονέω) in relation to having the younger widows remarry and "bear children" (5:14), and as we have already observed there is a definite connection between the women in chapter 2 and the widows in chapter 5. Likewise, the uniqueness of the terms for childbearing, found nowhere else in the New Testament or in Genesis (LXX) except in these two verses,[66] would seem to point us away from interpreting childbirth in 1 Tim 2:15 differently than in 5:14—both seem to be literal in meaning.

The contradiction this interpretation creates with Paul's view that emphasizes singleness, celibacy, and receiving salvation by faith instead of works is more imaginary than real given the situation in the Pastoral Letters. The AP wants the widows—at least the younger ones—to get married and bear children, thinking this a remedy to their being led astray (5:13–15). In the ancient patriarchal mindset, males play the dominant role and females the domestic role (cf. 5:14). Apparently the Pauline author believes that through marriage and childbearing the energy of the widows in Ephesus would be redirected toward managing their homes, and they would not be as susceptible to idleness and engaging in foolish talking, and hence, less likely to fall victims of the false teachers (5:13–15 cf. 3:11–14; 2 Tim 3:6–7). Moreover, from the author's perspective, these women would hopefully marry a man who (like Adam!) is not deceived (1 Tim 2:14; cf. 5:15). Matrimony and children bearing would also be a way to fight against the influence of the false teachers, who had been instructing

63. Service may be also for the benefit of outsiders, as the church's reputation is seen by such (cf. Rom 12:17; 13:1-3; 1 Thess 4:12; 1 Pet 2:12).

64. On translation for αὐθεντέω in 2:12 see Quinn and Wacker, *First and Second Letters*, 200–201; albeit they interpret the man as "husband."

65. A view that has been challenged again, this time by Waters, "Saved through Childbearing," 703–35.

66. The word in fact appears nowhere in the LXX, but see other ancient sources in, e.g., BDAG, 994.

congregation members to abstain from marriage (4:1–3). The woman's salvation in 2:15 is bound together with marriage and motherhood because this verse assumes the situation of false teachers who denied marriage. *From the author's perspective, if these women do not get married and bear children, the alternative would be to let them be tempted and possibly succumb to Satanic deception via the false teachers, and then suffer the same fate as the false teachers: the ruining of their faith and resulting loss of salvation* (2:15 5:14–15; cf. 1:17–19). Moreover, our author seems to be reversing, as it were, the curse of childbirth in the Eden story (Gen 3:16) by making it a blessing related to salvation for the women in the church who get married. Perhaps he is motivated to interpret the Genesis story this way because the false teachers may have manipulated the story to claim that marriage and childbirth are a result of the curse of Eden.[67]

The idea of salvation as a future rather than merely present reality is nothing new in Pauline literature (e.g., Phil 2:12). *It is, rather, normative for the apostle to stress final salvation as progressive and not yet completed when that salvation is being threatened by vices and false teachings* (cf. 1 Cor 1:18; 15:2; 2 Cor 2:15). This nuance becomes all the more visible when congregation members hold to an overrealized eschatology, perceiving themselves as already obtaining the full benefits of resurrected life, a problem not only in the Corinthian community but seemingly also in the Ephesus congregation of the Pastoral Letters (cf. 2 Tim 2:17–19; 1 Cor 4:8; 15:12–20).[68] It should be mentioned here that the AP deals with the false view of the resurrection more severely than Paul in 1 Cor 15. Whereas Paul merely corrects the false view held by the Corinthians, the AP expels two congregants for teaching it. This distinction might be explained on the ground that the false doctrine addressed in the Pastorals is more advanced than what was taught at Corinth. On the other hand, we may be looking at two similar yet distinct sets of false teachings with overlap in some areas related to eschatology. At any rate the Pastoral writer, while not denying present salvation (1 Tim 1:15; 2 Tim 1:9; Titus 3:5), presents final salvation as futuristic and achieved only by those who persevere in the present time (1 Tim 4:16; 2 Tim 2:10). When congregants have an overinflated view of salvific assurance and believe that the eschaton is completed, Paul is quick to deflate them by warning

67. Cf. Along these lines is Bassler, "Adam, Eve, and the Pastor," 55–56, who adds that salvation in 2:15 may operate on two levels: salvation *from* the false teachings, and salvation in the ultimate sense by continuing in faith, etc.

68. See Towner, "Gnosis," 95–124; Lane, "1 Tim IV 1–3," 164–67. Weiser, *Zwiete Briefe*, 224–25, sees in 2 Tim 2:18 a "Tendenz" going in the direction of Nag-Hammadi writings. Towner, *Timothy and Titus*, 527, notices a Pauline teaching reshaped by Gnostics in *The Treatise on the Resurrection*, but he believes Gnosticism is an unlikely source behind this teaching in the first-century milieu.

that they may *not* achieve final salvation if they persist in ways that displease God (e.g., 1 Cor 10:1–12).

Even so, bearing children is not a necessary condition for women to be saved in 1 Tim 2:15. The author would no doubt affirm that the older widows may achieve salvation even if they never had children or got remarried (cf. 1 Tim 5:5). Nor is motherhood even a sufficient condition for salvation because the notions of remaining in faith, love, and other virtues are also required for those who wish to be saved (2:15b). What is more, this verse is not necessarily addressing women alone. The conditional phrase "if they remain" (ἐὰν μείνωσιν) may refer not only to women but also married women and their husbands, women and their children, Adam and Eve, or some sort of combination of all of the above. In all probability *"they" in 2:15 includes males, and so both men and women are to practice virtues as part of the process of salvation.* This thought would be similar to Paul's idea of believers bearing fruits of the Spirit related to virtues in Gal 5:22; the alternative would be to practice works of the flesh and miss out on God's eschatological kingdom (Gal 5:19–21).

Perhaps the false teachers misinterpreted the early Christian view of baptism associated with the inception of salvation in terms of rising to a new life that leads to spirituality and a new creation (e.g., Rom 6:1–6; 1 Cor 12:13; 2 Cor 5:17; Gal 6:15). In some early Christian traditions the belief was that in the resurrected life men and women no longer marry (cf. Mark 12:25; Luke 20:34–36). What is probably denied by the false teachers is the future resurrection of believers because, from their perspective, the believers are already experiencing the resurrected life in the present (2 Tim 2:18). The false teachers may have understood such conceptions in a way that promoted what Egbert Schlarb argues as a *"back to Eden" way of life*: prior to the fall, Adam and Eve had no sex and ate vegetables—and the false teachers did the same (1 Tim 4:1–5).[69] If the false teachings rest somewhere within these assumptions, then 1 Tim 2:10–15 is not directed at silencing women congregation members because they happen to be women instead of men, but because they are being influenced by false teachers who themselves must be silenced (cf. Titus 1:11).

DENIAL, FAITHLESSNESS, AND APOSTASY
(2 TIM 2:11–13; CF. 1 TIM 4:1)

The potential for apostasy among individuals within Timothy's church is clearly evident in the hymn found in 2 Tim 2:11–13. The hymn was apparently known before these writings, and it may have originated within the Pauline churches.[70] This peri-

---

69. Cf. Schlarb, *Gesunde Lehre*, 132–33; cf. 86–93.

70. Cf. Hanson, *Pastoral Epistles*, 132. The trustworthy λόγος (2:11a) looks forward to 2:11b–13 (on

cope begins with a comforting statement: if we died with him (Christ), we will also live with him (2:11b). The aorist tense of dying suggests the believer's past burial of the old self at baptism (cf. Rom 6:3–4, 8). The hymn opens with conversion and the spiritual life it brings.[71] The second line of the hymn states that if we endure, we will also reign with Christ (2 Tim 2:12a). The line may recall the Lukan words of Jesus to his disciples who stood by him during his sufferings and would reign with him in the eschaton (Luke 22:30; cf. 21:19; Matt 10:22). Perseverance is related to suffering and persecution. This is something the author himself risks for the sake of the elect (2 Tim 2:8–10). "Paul" remains a good example of endurance for his followers. If he were to defect, a negative corollary to this would seem to be that many of his followers ("the elect") would also fall away.[72] The first two lines may also hint at martyrdom in relation to persecution given that the author is in prison and expects to be put to death (4:6–8, 9–18). The thought of these may also parallel Jesus' exhortation for his followers to take up their crosses daily, and in the context of Jesus' upcoming death and martyrdom he claims to his disciples that those who lose their life will save it (Luke 9:23–24; 17:33; Matt 10:38–39; 16:24–25; Mark 8:34–35). This backdrop to the hymn suggests a present reality that culminates in the future—for the Pauline writer, salvation and perseverance are both now and not yet. Final salvation has not yet been obtained by the elect (1 Tim 2:15; 4:16; 2 Tim 1:18; 3:15).[73]

A connection between the Pastoral hymn and specific Jesus sayings becomes all the more evident with the next line: "If we deny him, he also will deny us" (2 Tim 2:12b). These words almost certainly recollect Jesus' warning that if his followers deny him publically before outsiders he will deny them before his Father at the eschatological judgment (cf. Matt 10:33; Mark 8:38; Luke 9:36). This type of denial (ἀρνέομαι) refers to apostasy resulting from persecution, and this is almost certainly what it means here in 2 Tim 2:12: to deny Christ is to fall away from Christ.[74] For the

---

the trustworthy sayings in the Pastorals, see Marshall, *Pastoral Epistles*, 326–30). Differently, Mounce, *Pastoral Letters*, 502, believes this pericope could be written by Paul. In his view it is not a hymn and it is surely Pauline. However, as we will notice, this passage reflects more the sayings of Jesus than Paul.

71. A baptism ceremony may have been the appropriate setting for this hymn: cf. Quinn and Wacker, *First and Second Letters*, 654. If so, this would not seem to suggest that the church in Ephesus is filled only with new converts. The hymn may have been sung for many years in the congregation prior to its mention here.

72. See Witherington, *Hellenized Christians*, 1.334.

73. Young, *Pastoral Letters*, 71, rightly notes that such futuristic passages argue against the idea that the Pastoral Letters have lost a sense of urgency due to the delayed second coming.

74. The meaning is so evident for Loh, *Early Christian Hymn*, 201–16, 250, that he considers the proper translation of the phrase to be, "If we should apostatize, he also will disown us." The symmetry of the hymn, in my opinion, is best retained by the simple translation, "If we deny him, he also will deny us." It recalls Jesus' warnings to his disciples.

AP, denying Christ may be seen as reversing one's confession of Christ at baptism (cf. 2 Tim 2:19; Titus 2:12–13; Rom 10:9–10; Acts 22:16). *Such denial reverses conversion so that Christ disowns the person who denies him, and as with the Synoptic sayings this leads to eternal judgment.* Apart from those who deny Christ through persecution, our author would no doubt include among the deniers both the false teachers and those whose actions contradict the message of the gospel as taught in Pauline tradition. The opponents deny godly power, and though they profess to know God they deny him by their actions (2 Tim 3:5; Titus 1:16). Harald Riesenfeld's study on the biblical concept of denial interprets 2 Tim 3:5 as "having the outward mark of piety but (in reality) being apostates." This rendition assumes that those who deny the power of godliness were once believers, which may in fact be true of the false teachers.[75] What gets lost in this rendition, however, is the concept of power, which becomes important for our understanding of the deceptive magicians, Jannes and Jambres, who confront Moses in the verses that follow (see below). In domestic settings those who are considered the heads of their homes who do not provide for their own families are said to be worse than unbelievers. Their actions show that they have denied the faith (5:8).[76] These passages demonstrate that those who fail to put faith to practice, in essence, deny Christ. Presumably, as Heinrich Schlier affirms, denial in this case "consists in a failure to do justice to the claims of one's neighbours."[77] Even so, the sharp rebuke is probably intended more as a corrective against negligent Christian heads of homes than an official declaration of their apostasy.

The final line of the hymn reads, "If we are faithless, he remains faithful, for he is not able to deny himself" (2:13).[78] Some interpreters understand this line in a positive sense: he is faithful to the believers even when they lack faith.[79] But given that the previous line was a negative warning (2:12) and that what contextually follows after this verse involves the false teachers (2:14–26), this interpretation may be incorrect. The Pauline author has suffered persecution and is now in prison awaiting his foreboding sentence. He endures such things so that the elect church might

75. Riesenfeld, "Meaning of ἀρνεῖσθαι," 216.

76. More specifically, they have denied both the Christian faith in general and their own faith in particular. The objective and subjective aspects of faith probably should not be separated here.

77. Schlier, "ἀρνέομαι," 1.470.

78. Loh, *Early Christian Hymn*, 232, 247, notices that the ending in 2:13c, "he is not able to deny himself," does not properly fit the one to one ratio of protasis/apodosis symmetry in lines 1–4. It may function as a conclusion or climax to the hymn. To be "faithless" (ἀπιστέω) could alternatively mean a refusal to believe (cf. Luke 24:11; Acts 28:24). But given that the word is paired with the adjectival πιστός attributed to Christ, and Christ does not need to "believe," the ideas of faithlessness and faithfulness are what seem to be contrasted.

79. E.g., Kelly, *Commentary*, 180, who denies this line refers to apostasy.

persevere to final salvation (2:9–10; cf. 3:10–12; 4:6, 9–17). The thought of endurance in the face of suffering in 2:10 is insinuated in the first two lines of the hymn (2:11–12a). The next two lines (2:12b–13) look forward and speak to the apostasy related to false teachers that bring other hearers to ruin in 2:14.[80] Even so, the hymn uses "we" instead of "they" in reference to faithlessness, which clearly suggests that the hymn's lines applied to those who sang it; i.e., members of the Christian church. Given the hymn's context, *"if we are faithless" refers to believers losing faith.* In light of this meaning for 2:13a, how does Christ remain faithful and not deny himself (2:13b)? Some understand 2:13b as Christ being faithful to his warnings—he is faithful to carry out his punishments to those who would deny him.[81] God's faithfulness in the Pauline Epistles, however, normally refers to his comforting and protecting his people rather than making sure he condemns unbelievers and wrongdoers among them (cf. 1 Cor 1:10; 10:13; 2 Cor 1:18–20; 1 Thess 5:24; 2 Thess 3:3).[82] Another view is that this unfaithfulness in 2 Tim 2:13 is less severe than the apostasy in 2:12a. On this view Mounce writes that 2:13 is "a promise of assurance to believers who have failed to endure (line 2) but not to the point of apostasy (line 3). Peter's denial of Christ (Matt 26:69–75; Mark 14:66–72; Luke 22:54–62; John 18:15–17, 25–27.) and his repentance and forgiveness (John 21:15–19) are often used as an illustration."[83] This is certainly possible, but it is not clear how a boundary can be drawn between a believer's faithlessness to Christ, which receives divine mercy, and a believer's denying Christ, which does not. Unless a distinction similar to the Johannine "sin leading to death" and "sin not leading to death" is defensible here (cf. 1 John 5:16–17), this meaning remains tenuous at best.

A more convincing view suggests that *Christ is faithful despite the unfaithfulness or apostasies that occur among his elect church.* This outlook parallels thoughts about God's faithfulness to his own nature, purposes, and covenant despite the unfaithful-

---

80. In the Pastoral Letters unbelief can refer to the practices of people outside the faith (1 Tim 1:13; 5:8; Titus 1:15); cf. Bassler, "He Remains Faithful," 176. Bassler argues that this final line of the hymn points to the false teachers as faithless (180–83). In this context it does. Nevertheless I doubt if the original intention of this hymn, which predates the letter, was directed at false teachers. Probably it was originally intended to uplift Christ or God's faithfulness to his covenant or promises despite his people's unfaithfulness.

81. Cf. Oberlinner, *Zweiten Timotheusbrief*, 88.

82. Cf. Knight, *Pastoral Epistles*, 407: "This faithfulness is God's fidelity to his promises, and those promises relate to the positive outcome of human salvation (cf. 1 Cor 1:9). Paul does not mention God's faithfulness as a basis for the certainty that the faithless will be punished, but as the basis for the assurance of the gospel promises (2 Cor 1:18–20), for safety in temptation (1 Cor 10:13), for protection from the evil one (2 Thess 3:3), and for the sanctification and preservation of God's people (1 Thess 5:24; cf. also Heb. 10:23; 11:11; 1 Pet 4:19; 1 Jn. 1:9 [note πιστός]; Rev 1:5; 3:14; 19:11)."

83. Mounce, *Pastoral Epistles*, 518.

ness of his people (Rom 3:3–4; cf. Deut 32; 7:9; 23:19; 1QS 9.11). That Christ is faithful could mean that his purpose as savior will not be thwarted simply because some of his followers turn out to be unfaithful.[84] Or it could mean that Christ will be faithful to preserve the elect community despite individual members who ruin their own faith, as did Hymenaeus and Alexander. It could also suggest both nuances. The final words in 2 Tim 2:13 ensure the believer that Christ is faithful to his divine mission of saving people and giving them eternal life. He cannot be untrue to his purpose (2 Tim 1:9; Titus 1:2) or himself since God commissioned him and Christ himself appears to be God (Titus 2:13; cf. 1:3–4). Thus no amount of suffering (2 Tim 2:9), apostasy (2:12), or deception (2:14–26) the Christian church may face will ever change the fact that Christ will continue to save people. The elect church as a whole will survive to final salvation and inheriting God's eschatological kingdom despite "some" defections that will take place in its midst before the culmination of the age comes (1 Tim 4:1). Put differently, the unfaithfulness of the Christians who apostatize does not nullify Christ's faithfulness and dependability to saving his church and adding to their number.[85] Persecution from without and false teachings from within will not ultimately prevail against the elect community; the gospel of Christ and his church will prevail.

The AP thus seems to believe that whereas the elect community of believers will prevail because of Christ's faithfulness, not every individual within that community necessarily perseveres to final salvation. In fact "some" (τινες) will indeed fall away in the last days, according to 1 Tim 4:1 (cf. the plural τὶς in 1 Tim 1:6, 19; 5:15, 24; 6:10, 21; 2 Tim 2:18).[86] Such an onslaught of apostasy at the end of the age is well documented in ancient Jewish and Christian sources.[87] More specifically, since the Spirit is speaking lucidly about the upcoming defection (1 Tim 4:1a), this might suggest that the author's knowledge came to the author and community through prophecy (1:18; 4:14). Even so, the prophecy would seem to confirm what the author may have already known through earlier Pauline predictions of apostasy and deception that would take place before the end, Ephesus included (Acts 20:22–31; cf.

84. E.g., Arichea and Hatton, *Handbook*, 203: "Christ cannot turn his back on his true nature as the Savior who remains faithful to those who trust in him." Focusing more on the anthropological dimension are Quinn and Wacker, *First and Second Letters to Timothy*, 653: "Men [sic] can and do freely destroy their own personal relationship with the faithful Christ. God always remains a savior: men refuse to be saved."

85. On the aspect of Christ's dependability see Loh, *Early Christina Hymn*, 241.

86. Quinn, "Holy Spirit," 357, suggests "some" as a "discreet way of saying 'many'" (cf. Titus 1:10; 1 Tim 1:3, 6, 19). If such a view is correct, this still does not mean "all" will defect.

87. *1 En.* 80.2–8; 100.1–3; *4 Ezra* 5.1–12; *2 Bar.* 25–27; *Apoc. Ab.* 31.4–6; *Apoc El.* 1.13–15; 1QS 3:19–21; CD 12.2–3; 1QH 1.21–23; 4:9; 1QpHab 2.5–10; Jude 17–18; 1 John 2:18; 2 Pet 3:3–7; *Did.* 16.3–5.

2 Thess 2:3–4, 9–12). Likewise, the author may have known the predictions of Jesus that in the last days many would fall away and follow false prophets (Mark 13:5–6, 12–13, 21–23; Matt 24:10–13).

Although the defection in 1 Tim 4:1 is to take place in "later times," the author views this event as already taking place in his own time (cf. 2 Tim 3:1–9; 4:3–4).[88] The apostasy in 1 Tim 4:1 is not necessarily "from the faith"; the literal translation is, "some of the faith will fall away" (ἀποστήσονταί τινες τῆς πίστεως). The verb ἀφίστημι may be translated in an absolute sense here (cf. Luke 8:13).[89] As Mounce shows through examining New Testament occurrences of ἀφίστημι, "in the vast majority of cases if there is a recipient of the verb's action, it will most likely be indicated by a preposition and will immediately follow the verb."[90] Hence, in 1 Tim 4:1, which has no preposition following ἀφίστημι, "the faith" would seem to modify the indefinite pronoun "some" rather the verb "fall away." If so, then *the "some" who will fall away are identified as faithful church members. These ones who apostatize are not fake believers but real Christians.*[91] The nature of their apostasy involves devoting themselves to deceitful spirits and demonic teachings.[92] These teachings are no

88. See further Mounce, *Pastoral Epistles*, 234.

89. Here ἀφίστημι may be translated as "apostatize" (Mounce), "fall away" (NASB), or "desert" (NET). Others translate it as "forsake" (REB), "renounce" (NRSV), "abandon" (NIV). "Depart" (KJV, ESV) is too mild, but since these translators connect the departure with "from the faith," an idea of apostasy is still retained. The verb often conveys apostasy: Deut 13:10, 13; 32:15; Josh 22:18; Jer 3:14; Wis 3:10; 1 Macc 11:43; *1 En.* 5.4; Josephus, *Life* 158; Heb 3:12; *Herm. Vis* 6.2.3; BDAG, 157–58. On ἀφίστημι + genitive parallels, see Marshall, *Pastoral Epistles*, 538 (n. 22).

90. Mounce, *Pastoral Epistles*, 235: "ἀφιστάναι, 'to apostatize,'" occurs fourteen times in the NT. In ten of those times the verb is followed by the ablative ἀπό, 'from,' with the object of the preposition describing what they fell away from (Luke 4:13; 13:27; Acts 5:38; 12:10; 15:38; 19:9; 22:29; 2 Cor 12:8; 2 Tim 2:19; Heb 3:12). In every one of these instances, except in Acts 12:10, the preposition follows immediately after the verb. Of the other four instances (including 1 Tim 4:1), the verb is used absolutely with no object in Luke 8:13 (the seeds take root but in a time of temptation fall away [ἐν καιρῷ πειρασμοῦ ἀφίστανται]), with the ablative without a preposition in Luke 2:37 (Anna did not depart from the temple [ἀφίστατο τοῦ ἱεροῦ]), and with the accusative and a different preposition in Acts 5:37 (Judas the Galilean drew people away with him [ἀπέστησεν λαὸν ὀπίσω αὐτοῦ])." Although some instances in Pauline tradition may be found in which πίστις may be understood as "faithful" (e.g., 2 Thess 1:4), the AP is fond of using πιστός for such cases (e.g., 1 Tim 1:12, 15; 2:13; 4:3, 12).

91. Cf. 2 Cor 11:13–15; 2 Thess 2:3–12; 1 John 4:1–6; Rev 13:4, 11–14; *Apoc. Mos.* 22; 1QS 3.20–22; CD 2.16–18; *T. Dan* 5.5. Contrast Lea and Griffin, *1, 2 Timothy*, 129: "A mere profession of faith does not guarantee the actual possession of eternal life. The emptiness of mere profession would become clear by the departure from Christianity of some of the Ephesians (see 1 John 2:19 for the same idea)." But Johannine tradition is not Pauline tradition, and in any case, even if we assume the proper translation as "some will fall away/depart from the faith," more than a mere profession of faith is involved (see 1 Tim 1:19; 2 Tim 2:12–13 above). If this translation of 4:1 were accepted, then the words of Knight, *Pastoral Epistles*, 188, would seem apropos when he suggests that "the faith" in 1 Tim 4:1 can be both objective (e.g., the Christian faith) and subjective (e.g., personal/relational faith).

92. See further sources in Collins, *1 and 2 Timothy*, 113.

doubt promulgated by the false teachers (4:2–5). Satanic spiritual forces are viewed as being the inspiration of their false teachings, and these powers are mentioned as a way to vilify the teachers (1 Tim 5:15; 2 Tim 2:25–26). Some of the believers will fall away by following the opponents' teachings that have been influenced by anti-god powers (1 Tim 4:1–3). It is affirmed here that more apostasies of those who possessed faith will take place similar to the defections of Hymenaeus and Alexander (1 Tim 1:19; cf. 1:6). In the Pastoral Letters, then, *final salvation is futuristic, with the real potential to have one's faith undermined, making it all the more important for these Christians to take seriously the need to endure through potential deception.* Nevertheless, believers can take comfort in the fact that, no matter how many individuals fall away, the church will continue to exist as the community of God and the false teachings will not finally undermine the authentic gospel message. *Some* but not *all* believing Christians will fall away.

Excursus: Election in the Pastoral Letters (2 Tim 1:8–12; 2:8–10; cf. 1 Tim 5:21; Titus 1:1–2: 2:14)

The elect (τοὺς ἐκλεκτούς) in the Pastoral Letters refers to the collective community of God. More specifically, they are the people who have faith in Christ Jesus and hold to the truth of the gospel, at least as identified by the Pauline tradition (2 Tim 2:10; Titus 1:1; 2:14). This identity, then, excludes the false teachers and those who practice unrighteousness (2 Tim 2:19). The elect are already saved initially, but they must persevere in the present to obtain final salvation at the completion of the eschaton (2 Tim 2:10, 12a; 1 Tim 3:16; 6:11; 2 Tim 4:5; Titus 2:13 cf. Rom 8:18–21; Phil 3:21; Luke 20:35; Heb 11:35). Regardless of the Pastoral Letters' stress on this type of progressive salvation, the author emphasizes God's purpose and grace in saving Christ-followers (2 Tim 1:8–10).[93] These benefits were given to them in Christ Jesus "before times of ages" and are now made manifest through the appearing of Christ.[94] The Pauline author has been appointed as an instructor, and he suffers for the gospel's sake but is persuaded that God is able to guard his "deposit" (i.e., the Pauline gospel of sound teaching) until the second

---

93. Paul is not merely referring to himself and Timothy by using "us." This word is inclusive of the entire body of believers, who would sing or recite these words in 2 Tim 1:9–10 in a congregational setting. The rhythmic parallels in 1:9–10 suggest these verses may have been part of a hymn or liturgical piece; see Hanson, *Pastoral Epistles*, 122.

94. The conceptual unity of "purpose and grace" (2 Tim 1:9) is suggested by the singular feminine article and verb that follows the phrase (τὴν δοθεῖσαν ἡμῖν). The phrase may be understood as a hendiadys: "gracious purpose"; cf. Quinn and Wacker, *First and Second Letters*, 598. The "holy calling" either refers to God as holy or the believers living out a holy life.

coming (2 Tim 1:11–12). In keeping with Pauline tradition, the author is "not ashamed" of his beliefs (1:12; cf. 1:8; Rom 1:16), which suggests confidence in God and looking back at Paul's past faithfulness despite his hardships and sufferings as a missionary for Christ. His affirmation is the antipode of Jesus' warning to his disciples that at his second coming he will be ashamed of the one who is ashamed of him (Luke 12:9; Mark 8:38). The passage in 2 Timothy exemplifies God's initiative in calling and saving on the basis of his own gracious purpose, and it is God who will ultimately preserve the veracity of Paul's gospel message.

A question arises on whether "before times of ages" (πρὸ χρόνων αἰωνίων) is to be understood as "before eternal times" or simply as "ages ago" (2 Tim 1:9; cf. Titus 1:2–3). If the former is preferred, then God's purpose "in Christ" involves an eternal plan prior to creation, and the calling of the Christian church would seem to be included in this plan (cf. Eph 1:4–11).[95] If this meaning is correct then along such lines Marshall suggests that the early Christians adopted the idea from Jewish tradition—the Israelites developed the concept of salvation being rooted in God's prior decision "as an antidote to insecurity" (Matt 25:34; Acts 3:20; 1 Pet 1:20; cf. 1QS 3–4; 2*Bar* 57).[96] In the Christian view exemplified in the Pastorals, the gift of salvation rests in the preexistent Christ and is given to believers by his agency so that "we only gain it through union with Him."[97]

On the other hand, if "ages ago" is the correct meaning then this would tend to support the idea that the church's calling was predicted via prophetic promises found in Israel's scriptures given long ago (e.g., Rom 1:1–4; 9:4, 7;16:25).[98] In this case their calling goes back as far as the prophetic promises related to God raising up a messianic figure to save Israel and the nations (e.g., Isa 53).[99] The Pastoral Letters in either case hold the idea of God's gracious calling of Christians which seems to have nothing to do with their own merit, and this calling remains inseparable from salvation (2 Tim 1:9; 1 Tim 1:13–16; 6:12; Titus 3:5; cf. 2 Thess 2:13–14). Regardless of whether the starting point is pretemporal or temporal, saving grace in these letters addresses only how the believers are called and eventually "get in" a right relationship with God and Christ.

---

95. For a similar view see Nielsen, "Scripture in the Pastoral Epistles," 9–15.

96. Marshall, *Pastoral Epistles*, 126.

97. Locke, *Pastoral Epistles*, 87. Marshall, *Pastoral Epistles*, 706, connects the thought of preexistence with John 17:24.

98. Along these lines see Locke, *Pastoral Epistles*, 126; Brox, *Pastoralbriefe*, 280–81.

99. Since many scholars affirm that 2 Tim 1:9–10 was originally a hymn or liturgical piece already known by the church, we must ask whether this was already an old rather than new hymn in the church by the time the author penned 2 Timothy. If it had already been known for decades, a case could be made that the earlier meaning of Christ as the predicted Messiah would make more sense than a cosmic, preexistent Christ. But time does not permit us to pursue this venue here.

Although they are in union with Christ and saved though this connection, this does not guarantee that every one of them will "stay in" this relationship perpetually. Some in fact do not stay in it, as amply demonstrated by those who fell away (1 Tim 1:19–20; 2 Tim 2:17–18; cf. 1 Tim 4:1).

The Pauline author mentions his own suffering related to imprisonment (2 Tim 2:8–10). He endures all things for the elect's sake that they too may be able to obtain the salvation in Christ Jesus with "eternal glory." He compares his own persevering (ὑπομένω) in relation to the elect's salvation that is futuristic here, anticipating an eschatological life reigning with Christ. The hope for the elect in 2:10 is not referring to the salvation of those among humankind who, though presently not saved, have been preselected by God and will eventually obtain salvation whenever God decides to call them.[100] For our author, those whom he considers elect already believe, but they must persevere in hope until the eschaton takes place. At the very end of his life, "Paul" anticipates his own final salvation (4:18), and he desires that the elect would also persevere until the end of their lives and obtain final salvation (2:10).[101]

The meaning of the "elect angels" (1 Tim 5:21) poses some difficulties for interpreters because the term does not appear anywhere else in the Pastoral Letters or Pauline writings. It does appear in other ancient sources (*1 En.* 39.1; *Apoc. Adam & Eve* 32.2; *Odes Sol.* 4.8). Our author assumes Timothy already knows what is meant by the term. The "elect angels" may be understood as "choice" or "pure" angels (cf. ἐκλεκτός in Exod 30:23 LXX). If so, then the concept of the "elect" in 5:21 may be inclusive of all angels that serve God. Alternatively, God has selected certain angels for a specific role in his "heavenly court," perhaps as witnesses to the coming eschatological judgment (Rev 14:10; Matt 18:10; 24:31; 25:31; Luke 9:26; 1 Thess 3:13; 2 Thess 1:7). The term was added by our author to emphasize the seriousness of the charge he gives Timothy.[102] This interpretation makes sense if the Pauline author has been instructing Timothy to stay pure and not share in the sins of others (1 Tim 5:22); God and the holy angels are witnesses of what the youthful pastor does.

---

100. Contrast Knight, *Pastoral Epistles*, 399.

101. The alternative explanation would be to understand "they" with the adverbial καὶ to mean that "they as well as I ["Paul"]" may obtain salvation; cf. ibid. If so, it may be more appropriate for the author to include Timothy along with himself as hoping to obtain final salvation along with the rest of the body of believers.

102. The seriousness of the charge also warns Timothy not to commit the act of abjuration. See Huther, *Epistles to Timothy and Titus*, 174.

POINTING OUT THE FALSE TEACHERS IN LIGHT OF KORAH'S REBELLION (2 TIM 2:18–21; CF. 1 TIM 5:24)

When speaking of the false teachers who deny future resurrection, the Pauline author affirms that God's foundation related to the church's stability has this seal: "The Lord knows those who are his" and "Let every one who names the name of the Lord depart from unrighteousness" (2 Tim 2:19).[103]

We find the first saying uttered by Moses to Korah and his followers when they came against Aaron and Moses in the exodus-wilderness narrative (Num 16:5 LXX). We find an interesting parallel to Korah and the second saying of naming "the name" in the *Mishnah*. The party of Korah will be among those who do not have a share in the world to come. They are not destined for the resurrection because the earth swallowed them up and they perished among the assembly (*m. Sanhedrin* 10.3). Others who do not share a portion of the age to come include those who claim that the teaching of resurrection does not derive from the Torah, those who read heretical books, and those who pronounce the divine name (*m. Sanhedrin* 10.1; cf. Lev 24:16). That both the Pastorals and *Mishnah* include vestiges of the story of Korah, naming God, and a false view of the resurrection in the same context may suggest that an association between Korah's apostasy and false teachings was fairly common in early Christian and Jewish circles (e.g., Jude 11; 1 Cor 10:10; Irenaeus, *Haer.* 1.31:1). The Pastoral version of naming "the name" of the Lord, however, turns thoughts from the *Mishnah* upside down by suggesting that those who name the name are not the blasphemers but the elect! This point of departure from the *Mishnah* probably highlights the Christian claim that Jesus is Lord.

The concept of naming the name of the Lord in 2 Tim 2:19 also finds parallels in Isa 26:13 and Jer 20:9, in which naming the name seems virtually synonymous with the idea of calling on the name.[104] Although the wording is different, the thought also drifts close to Joel 3:5 LXX [2:32], which uses the nuance of "calling on the name" (ἐπικαλέσηται τὸ ὄνομα) instead of "naming the name" (ὀνομάζων τὸ ὄνομα). Such passages may have influenced the AP to interpret the aspect of "naming the name" with the thought of "calling on the name" of the Lord at baptism. If so, then this phrase refers to the early Christians' conversion-initiation (cf. Acts 2:21; 22:16; Rom 10:9–13).[105] In this sense 2 Tim 2:18–20 means that all baptized converts

---

103. On God's foundation in relation to the church, see 1 Cor 3:11; Eph 2:20.

104. Hence BDAG, 714, correctly associates the concept of naming in 2 Tim 2:19 as "almost" to "call on."

105. Similarly, Hanson, "Apostates," 40 cf. 34, connects the "seal" (σφραγίς) in this passage with baptism to argue that the context denotes both "the responsibilities ('depart from iniquity') and privileges ('naming the name of the Lord') of Christians conferred in baptism."

to the Christian faith must make sure their allegiance to Christ is compatible with a belief and lifestyle that exemplifies departing from wickedness. The assumption does not so much relate to a false confession as it does an incentive for them to adhere to Paul's teaching that those who are baptized into Christ have put to death the old, disobedient self to be raised from the "dead" and become servants of righteousness (cf. Rom 6). If the AP is being faithful to the Pauline tradition here, then for him, the idea of being raised to a new life through baptism does not involve denying a future resurrection (as the opponents teach; 2 Tim 2:18); rather, baptism is intended to encourage converts to live a new life of godliness. Such individuals do not encourage dissensions and disobedience, as do the false teachers.

The first saying, "The Lord knows those who are his" (2 Tim 2:19), recalls Korah's attempt to usurp the role of priesthood reserved for Aaron (Num 16). In response to the uprising, Moses has Aaron and Korah's party present censers with incense before the LORD so that God might expose once and for all the one whom God has truly chosen for the priesthood. Moses affirms that God knows those who are holy and chosen; he knows who really serves him and who does not, and he will not be fooled when separating and judging between the followers of Korah and Aaron (Num 16:5, 8–18). In the end God causes the earth to swallow up Korah and his men are consumed by fire (16:19–35). The Pauline writer chooses this relevant story from the Pentateuch to distinguish the true leaders in Ephesus from false teachers such as Hymenaeus and Philetus. Apart from parallel wording between Num 16:5 and 2 Tim 2:19, the following thoughts are relevant for our study.

First, the Pastoral Letters seem to share in common with certain Jewish traditions a stress on God's distinction between true and false community members. Right before the judgment takes place, Moses commands the congregation to depart from the company of Korah so that they would not be punished with him (Num 16:24–26). This aspect of the story is picked up by certain Jewish traditions roughly contemporaneous with the Pastoral Letters. In the Pseudo-Philo the seven sons of Korah refuse to abandon the Law and join their father in his plot (*L.A.B.* 16.4–5). Josephus records Moses' prayer for the multitude; he requests they be unharmed by Korah's sedition (Josephus, *Ant.* 4.3.2[50]). The separation of the assembly from Korah resonates with 2 Tim 2:20: every one who names the name of the Lord must depart from unrighteousness. In the Pastoral Letters *a disassociation between the congregants and the false teachers is to take place* (e.g., 1 Tim 6:20; 2 Tim 3:5; Titus 1:10–11; 3:10).

Secondly, Korah suffers divine judgment. Sirach affirms the Lord's displeasure with Korah, Dathan, and Abiram—God destroyed them in his anger (Sir 45:18–19).

The author of the Wisdom of Solomon attributes the destruction of the rebels to the angelic being called the "Destroyer" (Wis 18:20–25). Josephus emphasizes the complete annihilation of Korah's men, who are swallowed by the earth; nothing remains of them (*Ant.* 4.3.3–4[52, 56]). Philo associates Korah's judgment with the loss of priesthood (*Fug.* 26[145–46]), and Qumran literature uses the judgment against Korah as a warning for the community (4Q423 frag. 5). Earliest Christian sources associate Korah with apostasy and likewise mention the destruction of Korah's rebels (Jude 11; 1 Cor 10:10). *The Pastoral Letters have in common with these traditions an assumption that divine judgment awaits those who rebel within God's chosen community, and such punishment will be made evident for all its members to see* (e.g., 2 Tim 3:9; cf. 1 Tim 1:20).

Third and lastly, Korah and the men who follow him are chief princes (ἀρχηγοὶ συναγωγῆς), chosen counselors, and men of renown among the community (Num 16:2). Korah was no riffraff prior to his rebellion, but like Moses and Aaron he is a prominent Levite among God's people.[106] This made his sedition all the worse because of his influence within the community. Although God makes his divine appointment of Moses and Aaron known to the community by consuming Korah and his men, there is no indication that Korah was always a false leader within the ranks of Israel. Such background may inform our interpretation of 2 Tim 2:20–21. The Pauline writer claims that in a great house (i.e., the church; cf. 1 Tim 3:15) there are vessels used for noble and ignoble purposes. The pericope may hint at the vessels of mercy and wrath mentioned in Rom 9:18–33.[107] Unlike the Romans text, however, the Pastoral controversy is not contrasting Gentile and Jewish believers against Jewish non-believers, but Pauline Christians against Christian false teachers.[108] The ignoble vessels no doubt refer to the false teachers, but similar to Korah in the book of Numbers *there is no indication that these opponents were always false believers,* non-elect, or predestined for apostasy and destruction. That the false teachers have gone astray from the truth (e.g., 2 Tim 2:18) might assume that they at one time followed the truth. One reason for the AP having Timothy correct them is so that God may grant them repentance (2:24–26). These ideas run contrary to a belief that the false teachers were always false teachers and have a fixed destiny with eternal destruction. At the same time they complement the notion that it takes both human effort (Timothy correcting them) and divine grace (God's granting them repentance) to win them back to sound doctrine.

106. Other leaders in the uprising were Reubenites (Num 16:1).

107. See Barrett, *Pastoral Epistles*, 107–8, who compares the two passages and asserts that 2 Tim 2 is not referring to predestination but Rom 9 is (but see above on Rom 9–11).

108. Hanson, "Apostates," 31–32, seems to agree.

Similar to Korah and his followers, Timothy's opponents were probably once leaders. They taught certain members in the Ephesian congregation, but they went astray via false teachings. By the time the Pastoral Letters were written the author no longer considered them fellow Christians. From his perspective somewhere along their salvific journey they went off course and became false teachers attempting to lead astray others (2 Tim 2:18; cf. 2 Tim 3:13; Titus 1:11; Acts 20:28–31). It does not appear to be the case that Hymenaeus and Philetus made an insincere confession at their baptism that affirms they were always false believers. The combined evidence of scriptural echoes from Korah's rebellion, the possibility of their restoration (2 Tim 2:23–26), the perspective of apostates as once authentic believers (1 Tim 1:18–20; 2 Tim 2:18; Hymenaeus in both cases), and the emphasis on naming the name of the Lord in terms of ethical conduct all work against such a view. Indeed 2 Tim 2:20–21 affirms the church as a mixed community made up of authentic (honorable vessels) and inauthentic members (ignoble vessels), and God is not fooled—God knows who are the true and false members even though it may not always be evident to the congregation members or Timothy (cf. 1 Tim 5:6; 6:5; 2 Tim 3:5–8, 13).[109] But unlike the Johannine author, who also addresses a believing community in Ephesus, the Pauline writer does not claim that the agitators of this community were never true believers. The faithful do fall away (cf. 1 Tim 4:1), and even false teachers such as Hymenaeus and Alexander once had genuine faith (cf. 1:18–19).

Akin to those who separated themselves from Korah, Timothy and his congregation are now to cleanse themselves from these false teachers and their deviant doctrines (2 Tim 2:19–21). Yet if the hope of restoration is made possible for these teachers (2:23–26), we may surmise that the author's appeal for the community to depart from unrighteousness is also instruction for the false teachers and their followers to turn away from their deceptive ways.[110] If so, a comparison between the false teachers and Korah breaks down at this juncture. The Pauline author believes their restoration is possible, whereas divine judgment seems to be the only option for Korah.

---

109. Schreiner and Caneday, *Race*, 234, deny the cognitive sense of "knows" in 2 Tim 2:19 in favor of it signifying "God's elective love for his own, a committed relationship to save his people." But a distinction between God's cognitive knowledge and relational love for his people here is not convincing. The cognitive dimension is present in both the Korah rebellion and the false teachers: the errors of the latter will be exposed and made known for all to see (2 Tim 3:9), just as Korah's error became evident to the community (Num 16). This occurs because God knows and can distinguish in a cognitive way between the rebels and righteous. The Mosaic and Pauline authors perhaps assume that God knows all things including human hearts.

110. See Bassler, "'He Remains Faithful,'" 182–83.

Somewhat similar to 2 Tim 2:19–21 is 1 Tim 5:24. This passage combines the notion of sin being exposed with an echo from Numbers. The sins of some individuals are evident while those of others "follow after" (ἐπακολουθοῦσιν), suggesting that some sins are hid for a while but are eventually exposed. The words recollect Moses' warning to the Israelite tribes that split off from the others—Gad, Reuben, and the half-tribe of Manasseh—before entering the promised land. They promise to assist the other tribes in battling the Canaanites. Moses responds that if they do not end up helping their brothers, their sin would find them out (Num 32:23).[111] Namely, their sins would eventually be exposed and they would suffer divine punishment as a consequence.[112] The saying assured Timothy that even though some sins and deceptions related to the congregants and false teachers go unnoticed in the congregation, they will eventually be exposed.[113] Whereas Paul believes that all good and bad deeds will eventually be addressed by the Lord at the eschaton (cf. 1 Cor 4:5; 2 Cor 5:10), the thought is probably closer to some form of public exposure and punishment related to the false teachers, as in 2 Tim 3:9. What may be assumed by the author's use of Numbers is that *God will not permit the church to become entirely contaminated with the false teachings*. Timothy's opponents will not ultimately win the day. The Pauline author is confident that God will protect the sound teachings of the apostolic message (cf. 2 Tim 1:12–14; 1 Tim 6:20).[114] He believes the veracity of his gospel will stand the test of time until the second coming; the false teachers' message will not succeed in the long run.

JANNES, JAMBRES, AND THE FALSE TEACHERS (2 TIM 3:9–10)

The AP also associates the false teachers with the Exodus story of the magicians from Pharaoh's court who opposed Moses and attempted to duplicate his miracles with their secret arts (cf. Exod 7:11–12, 22; 8:7, 18–19; 19:11). They are viewed as

---

111. Here the MT is more forceful than the LXX when it uses מָצָא in relation to finding out the sin. The LXX emphasizes the evil that comes as a result of the sin. See also Isa 58:8. *Barnabas* 4 has similar wording. Both 1 Timothy and the author of *Barnabas* seem concerned with the Numbers tradition, the exposure of sin, and the possibility of divine judgment and apostasy taking place as a result of sin. Other parallels to 1 Tim 2:19–20 may include Lev 26:11, 16; Isa 26:13, 16; Amos 6:10; Ps 6:9; Sir 17:26.

112. Ashley, *Book of Numbers*, 613, views the result of the sin as part of the covenantal curse formula (cf. Deut 28–32).

113. The saying may have also served a secondary function as warrant for Timothy not ordaining a novice into a leadership role; time needs to expose the true character of a person (1 Tim 3:6–7); cf. Merkel, *Pastoralbriefe*, 46; Knight, *Pastoral Epistles*, 241.

114. The word for "deposit" (παραθήκη) in these verses refers not merely to the gospel, but the gospel in relation to its correct or sound teachings. The deposit in 1 Tim 6:20 stands in contrast to the unsound teachings of the false teachers, and it is related to Pauline-sounding words in 2 Tim 1:13–14.

men who oppose the truth, have depraved minds, and are disqualified or rejected concerning their faith (2 Tim 3:8).[115] The false teachers will not get very far; their folly will become evident to all as was the folly of the magicians who opposed Moses (3:9). The author goes beyond the original Exodus narrative by naming Moses' opponents as Jannes and Jambres, presumably intending his readers to make a connection between the two magicians and his own opponents, Hymenaeus and Philetus. The magicians' names appear in various ancient sources.[116] According to the Qumran community Jannes and his brother (apparently Jambres) are raised up against Moses by the hand of Belial (CD 5.17–21). Other legends also associate Jannes and Jambres with demons.[117] In later traditions they become apostate Israelites or assistants of Balaam. They lose their competition against Moses, and their folly catches up with them either by their suffering pains and sores or their being put to death either at the golden calf rebellion or with Balaam.[118] In common with some of these sources, the Pauline author considers false teachers to be inspired by demons (1 Tim 4:1).[119]

Origen claimed the information used in 2 Tim 3:8–9 comes from the book of *Jannes and Jambres* (*Comm. Matt.* 27:9), a document that exists only in fragments today and must have been written in the first or second century CE.[120] It states that Jannes was afflicted with a painful ulcer. He apparently dies, goes to hell, and is unable to receive forgiveness (*Jannes and Jambres* 16.23–24, 26a).[121] Both 2 Tim 3:8 and this document use the verb "to withstand" (ἀνθίστανται) in relation to these

---

115. Here again as in 1 Tim 1:19 the definite article before "faith" may be taken as a possessive pronoun. Some translate ἀδόκιμοι here as "counterfeit" faith, e.g., Hanson, *Pastoral Epistles*, 147. The word suggests being tested and found unfit, worthless, or disapproved (cf. Titus 1:16). Apparently God is the one who rejects them. See the converse in which Timothy is to be approved before God by correctly teaching the word of truth (2 Tim 2:15).

116. On Jewish aspects of the earliest Jannes and Jambres sources, see *OTP* 2.427–28, 433.

117. *T. Sol.* 25:4; *Gos. Bart.*, *Lat.* 2, 4:50; Palladius, *Laus. Hist.* 17. Hanson, "Use of the Old Testament," 209–10, connects their "folly" (ἄνοια) with Wis 15:16—16:1 to suggest that the magicians were senseless because when they attempted to rival Moses with their supernatural feats, "they failed when they were unable to manufacture vermin." But this allusion to Wisdom is not altogether clear in the Pastoral passage.

118. E.g., *Tg. Ps.-J.* Exod 7.11. For an overview of legends and sources, see Pietersma, "Jannes and Jambres," 3.638–39; Pietersma and Lutz, "Jannes and Jambres," 2.427–36; Quinn and Wacker, *First and Second Letters*, 727–31.

119. Their seared conscience (1 Tim 4:2) is sometimes understood as their having been branded in the conscience by Satan; cf. Kelly, *Commentary*, 94. The meaning is more likely that they are unable to be sensitive to moral issues; cf. Hanson, *Pastoral Letters*, 87. Oppositely, those who follow the truth have a clear conscience (e.g., 1 Tim 1:5, 19a).

120. Pietersma and Lutz, "Jannes and Jambres," 2.427, date it within the range of first to third centuries CE. The earliest extant reference to the names of the magicians comes from Qumran (c. 100 BCE)

121. Fragment in *OTP* 2.440.

magicians opposing Moses.[122] If 2 Tim 3:9 is following this tradition or a similar one, it would help confirm that some form of divine punishment awaits the false teachers. But without further evidence we cannot say with any confidence that the author of 2 Timothy knew this version of the book of *Jannes and Jambres*. It may be the case that the "folly" our author implies for Jannes and Jambres is simply alluding to the boils the magicians received when contending with Moses. God favored Moses and punished the magicians with a physical ailment. This was one of many confrontations in which God showed himself to be more powerful than the gods of Egypt (Exod 9:10–11). With this background in mind, perhaps the AP is saying that *the false teachers harassing Timothy's church will suffer some form of punishment or humiliation endorsed by God, and this will be made evident for all to see* (2 Tim 3:9). What this entails is not known. It may possibly involve something similar to the mysterious "destruction of the flesh" awaiting the ostracized apostate in Corinth (1 Cor 5:5).

THE IDENTITY OF THE OPPONENTS
(1 TIM 4:1–5; 6:20; 2 TIM 4:4; TITUS 1:10)

We notice some relevant observations related to the Pauline author's use of the Torah. The author repeatedly alludes or refers to the Pentateuch when dealing with the false teachers and their influence. The opponents and their followers are viewed as being deceived by the Serpent (Gen 3), encouraging people to violate the Law (Decalogue: Exod 20; Deut 5), are singled out by God (Num 16), expelled (Deuteronomy), will suffer divine disapproval (Exodus and Numbers). This brings us back to the standpoint of the teachers erring in their interpretation of the Torah. The Pauline author counters their viewpoints with his own elucidations from the Torah, and by doing so he demonstrates one way in which emergent Christians adopted a Jewish method of dealing with the precursors that would in later decades and centuries be identified as "heretics"—the false teachers and apostates are identified as Torah breakers.[123] The Pauline author's arguments are aimed at demonstrating how the Torah can be used "lawfully," unlike its interpretation given by the false teachers (e.g., 1 Tim 1:8). The combination of their teaching Jewish myths, genealogies, and desiring to be teachers of the Law suggest they were reading from the Torah or possibly Jewish traditions that interpreted the Torah (1 Tim 1:4–11; 4:7; 2 Tim 4:4; Titus 1:10, 14–16; 3:9).[124]

122. Cf. Pietersma and Lutz, 2.433.

123. Cf. Skarsaune, "Heresy," 9–14.

124. Karris, "Polemic," 557, considers the myths (μῦθος) as part of the "stock charge" that may not reflect the teachings of the opponents. However, the word is found in the leading descriptions of the

For the AP, the results of their teaching devolved into quarrels (1 Tim 6:3–5; 2 Tim 2:14, 23) and meaningless talk (1 Tim 1:6; 6:20; 2 Tim 2:16; 3:17). The promulgation of creation stories, speculations, and various pedigrees is fairly common in ancient Jewish literature,[125] and there remains a strong possibility that our author is contesting some speculation the opponents believed about Adam and Eve in 1 Tim 2.[126]

The opponents might be Jewish Christians if one interprets "those of the circumcision" in Titus 1:10 as referencing this group's ethnicity.[127] But they are also closely associated with the Cretans in 1:10–14, and so we must ask whether these are Cretan Jews, Cretans holding to circumcision, Christian Cretans who were originally proselytes from a Jewish group, or something else. The least preferable option is that this group is insisting on the doctrine of circumcision similar to the opponents disturbing Paul's churches in Galatia.[128] If such were the case we might expect the author to use this term as he does the myths and genealogies when referring to commandments and the Law (Titus 1:14; 3:9). The AP in fact does not repeat the term "circumcision" elsewhere in the Pastorals, but he does repeat the opponents' use of "myths" and "genealogies" (cf. 1 Tim 1:4; 4:7; 2 Tim 4:4). We can surmise from these observations that the conflict centers in part on myths and genealogies; the opponents' view of circumcision does not seem to play a major role in the conflict.[129] In support of the Jewish Christians as opponents, a considerable Jewish population does seem to be present in Crete at the time (cf. Acts 2:11; Josephus, *Ant.* 17.327; *Vita* 427; Philo, *Embassy* 282),[130] but it is still quite possible that our author is identifying Cretans as former proselytes from a Jewish synagogue or sect. Then again, both Jewish Christians and former Gentile proselytes from a Jewish group might be

---

opponents of both 1 Timothy (1:4) and Titus (1:14), and the author gives a charge for the reader to avoid these myths in both cases (see also 1 Tim 4:7; 2 Tim 4:4). This tends to suggest that the perpetration of myths is an actual problem in these churches. The word μῦθος is probably understood as some human-made legendary story that virtually forces its readers to suspend their disbelief. On the term see further Quinn, *Titus*, 100–101; Stählin, "μῦθος," 4.762–95. On sources related to genealogies see further Spicq, *Épistres Pastorales*, 1.101–3.

125. E.g., *Jub.*, 1QapGen; Pseudo-Philo; Philo, *QG*; *Moses* 2.46–47; *Rewards* 1–2.

126. Cf. Schlarb, *Gesunde Lehre*, 86–93.

127. They are Christians because they are insiders who attend Titus's church. For the circumcision in Titus 1:10 as referencing Jewish Christians see, e.g., Quinn, *Titus*, 110–11, 115–16. For the term as usually identifying Jews in the ancient world see, e.g., Feldman, *Jew and Gentile*, 153–58; Cohen, *Beginnings of Jewishness*, 156–74.

128. Contrast Bassler, *1 Timothy*, 188–90; Witherington, *Hellenized Christians*, 1.121–22.

129. It is possible to argue that, in keeping with Pauline tradition, if circumcision were an issue the author would refute false teachings about circumcision much the way Paul does in Galatians. Although the author may not always directly engage the opponents' teachings (so Barrett, *Pastoral Epistles*, 12), see 1 Tim 1:8–11; 4:1–5; 6:6–8.

130. See further sources in Marshall, *Pastoral Epistles*, 192.

view. Moreover, even if the circumcision group were definitely identified as Jewish Christians, it is quite possible that they are a subset among the entire rebellious faction in Titus 1:10. If we interpret the word μάλιστα as "especially" then the verse indicates that the circumcision group is prominent among other rebels who also participate in the false teaching.[131] We must also question whether the identity of the group in Crete is precisely the same as the opponents in Ephesus.[132] Hence, *whereas some of the opponents' false teachings arise from their interpretation of Jewish traditions, a Jewish identity for the opponents as a whole in these letters is not entirely clear.*

One challenge to the false teachings as coming from Jewish traditions centers on the polemical nature of the Pastoral Letters. We have noted that these letters share in common with Hellenistic writings a stereotyped polemic against false teachers. It can be argued that an attempt to identify the opponents and their false doctrines amounts to futility because these are imaginary characters.[133] As both Karris and Johnson maintain, however, a polemical reading of the Pastorals does not preclude the opponents' actual existence.[134]

Perhaps the most recognized alternative for the opponents' identity has been the standpoint that these rivals are early Gnostics or Jewish Gnostics.[135] One passage often cited in support of this position is 1 Tim 6:20, in which the author charges Timothy to guard what has been entrusted him, turning away from foolish talk and the "opposition of the falsely-called knowledge" (ἀντιθέσεις τῆς ψευδωνύμου γνώσεως). The "opposition" (ἀντιθέσεις) has sometimes been understood as a reference to the Marcionite *Antithesis*, and knowledge/*gnosis* in this verse has been

131. Some interpret μάλιστα as "in other words," and this would point to the circumcision group in particular. On this interpretation is Fee, *1 and 2 Timothy*, 178: "Make sure your appointees are qualified people, because there are already many insubordinates at work with their deceptions; I am referring in particular, as you know, to the converts from Judaism."

132. Sumney, *Servants of Satan*, 253–302, argues for distinct groups in the three Pastoral Letters. A more refined nuance, however, is given by Trebilco, *Early Christians in Ephesus*, who says there are minor differences between 1–2 Timothy and Titus (e.g., a problem with women in the congregation comes from 1 Timothy and an overrealized eschatology comes from 2 Timothy, but Titus does not reflect these issues).

133. Along these lines see the view of Barrett, "Pauline Controversies," 240.

134. Johnson, "Polemic against False Teachers," 1–26; Karris, "Polemic," 562–63. Johnson holds that the false teachers contrast the "ideal Christian teacher," but they are nevertheless real opponents. Karris believes the opponents are "Jewish Christians who are teachers of the Law" (562–63).

135. E.g., Haufe, "Gnostische Irrlehre," 332–33; Oberlinner, *Ersten Timotheusbrief*, 52–73; Brox, *Pastoralbriefe*, 33–42. An interesting variation is that the opponents are Christian Jewish visionaries of the charismatic sort with Docetist beliefs about Jesus; cf. Goulder, "Pastor's Wolves," 242–56. For discussions and various viewpoints related to the opponents in the Pastoral Letters see, e.g., Schlarb, *Gesunde Lehre*, 59–141; Sumney, *Servants of Satan*, 253–302; Wolter, *Pastoralbriefe als Paulustradition*, 256–70; Spicq, *Épistres Pastorales*, 1.85–119; Witherington, *Hellenized Christians*, 1.341–47.

associated with Gnosticism.[136] Likewise, it is sometimes said that the opponents have in common with Gnostic beliefs the practice of asceticism (1 Tim 4:1–5) and the denial of the resurrection (2 Tim 2:16–18). This identification of the false teachers is not without its weaknesses.

First, concerning 1 Tim 6:20, ἀντιθέσεις probably refers to the false teachers' opposition to the true faith and apostolic mission, not the Marcion *Antithesis*.[137] Second, *gnosis* need not have a special reference to Gnosticism when it can just as easily refer to doctrinal beliefs related to early Jewish traditions and sects (e.g., 1QS 10.9–12; 11:6–15; 1QH 2.18; 11.24; 4 Macc 1:16–17; Hos 4:6). The concept of knowledge functions in a similar way related to the misdirected teachings in the Corinthian and Colossian congregations, and both situations are without direct relation to early Gnosticism.[138] Ultimately there is no compelling reason to associate *gnosis* in this verse with Gnosticism.[139] Finally, this position became popular under the assumption that the Pastoral Letters were written at a time contemporaneous with Gnosticism and Marcionism. Walter Bauer's influential *Orthodoxy and Heresy in Earliest Christianity* dated the letters in the middle of the second century, a position now abandoned by the majority of biblical scholars, who date the letters at about 100 CE or earlier.[140] The date of 150 CE becomes extremely difficult to maintain if church fathers in the late first and early to mid-second centuries, such as Clement of Rome, Ignatius, and Polycarp, are already alluding to the Pastoral Letters in their own writings.[141] At best the Pastoral Letters might be instructing against proto-Gnostic teachings, but they were written too early to be attacking Gnosticism as a unified belief system.[142]

The ascetic practices of Timothy's opponents also do not have to be associated with Gnosticism (1 Tim 4:1–5). The letters to the Corinthians and Colossians de-

136. Cf. Bauer, *Orthodoxy and Heresy*, 226. For discussion see Roloff, *Timotheus*, 374. The term "falsely-called knowledge" is used later on by certain Christians when teaching against heretics (e.g., Eusebius, *Hist. eccl.* 1.1.1; 5.7.1); cf. Pearson, "Eusebius and Gnosticism," 295–305.

137. Cf. Schlarb, *Gesunde Lehre*, 62–66, 120–22, 357; see also Towner, *Timothy and Titus*, 432, who translates ἀντιθέσεις as "opposing ideas" and suggests that the heresy has a self-refuting nature.

138. Cf. Towner, *Timothy and Titus*, 433.

139. See the similar argument of Dubois, "Pastorals," 41–48.

140. See, e.g., Roloff, *Timotheus*, 45–46; Wolter, *Pastoralbriefe*, 22; Hanson, *Pastoral Letters*, 13; Merkel, *Pastoralbriefe*, 10. Contrast Koester, *Ephesos*, 124, who maintains the end of the first century as the *earliest* point; the Pastorals may have been written as late as about 150 CE.

141. *1 Clem.* 2:7/Titus 3.1; *1 Clem.* 29.1; *1 Clem.* 55.3/2 Tim 2:1; *1 Clem.* 60.4/1 Tim 2:7–8; *1 Clem.* 61:2 /1 Tim 1:17; Ign. *Poly.* 3:1; Ign. *Magn.* 8:1; Ign. *Eph.* 14:1/1 Tim 1:3–5; Polycarp, *Phil.* 4:1/1 Tim 6:7–10; *Phil.* 5/1 Tim 3:8; *Phil.* 12/1 Tim 2:2; Irenaeus, *Haer.* 1.23.4/1 Tim 6:20. See further Spicq, *Épistres Pastorales*, 1.160–70.

142. See Yamauchi, *Pre-Christian Gnosticism*, 169–74.

scribe individuals who abstain from marriage (1 Cor 7:1–2) and certain foods (Col 2:22 cf. 2:11–14), and both letters are written earlier than the Pastoral Letters—much too early for their dissenters to embrace a Gnostic system.[143] Moreover, the binary categories of pure/impure in Titus 1:15 are probably speaking against ritual purity in relation to foods, and this passage is contextually referring to false teachings related to Jewish writings (1:10, 14). For the Pauline author, purity comes through the sacrifice of Christ and involves faith and ethical living (1:15b–16; 2:14). That all things are unclean to these false teachers either refers to their overstringent tenets or, more likely, the fact that they themselves are inwardly defiled and contaminate everything around them. The idea may be related to a Jewish conception that whatever a defiled person touches becomes defiled (Hag 2:10–14; Philo, *Spec.* 3.208–9).[144] Although food laws were commonly found in the Torah and later Jewish traditions, they were not accepted in the Pauline churches (e.g., Gal 2; Col 2:13–23; cf. Rom 14).

Abstinence from marriage (1 Tim 4:3), unlike food laws, could hardly be a teaching from the Torah if God commands Adam and Noah to be "fruitful and multiply," and Moses charges the Hebrew men to carry out Levirate duties for deceased brothers. On the other hand, some early Christians familiar with Jewish traditions did see value in celibacy (e.g., Matt 19:12; Rev 14:4). In any case the promotion of celibacy by the Pastoral opponents may be related to their having an overrealized view of eschatology or a "back to Eden" approach to food and sex, and this ties in with their view of the resurrection having already taken place, as we have already noted (2 Tim 2:17–18). No doubt the false teachers had misconceptions about Jewish teachings, some of which, such as denying the resurrection, were held in common with later Gnosticism.[145] But the Pastoral opponents seem to reject the resurrection primarily because it is futuristic (2 Tim 2:18), not necessarily because it involves the physical body.

Therefore we find no compelling reason to assert the false teachers were Gnostics or direct descendants of the Gnostics. Moreover it is probably inaccurate to associate the opponents with any clearly known sect, such as the Sadducees, who denied the resurrection. *The false teachers are most likely Hellenistic Christians who*

143. A different approach on the identity of the false teachers is to associate them with an ascetic movement akin to what is described in *Acts of Paul and Thecla*; cf. MacDonald, *Pauline Churches*, 181–83; Young, *Pastoral Letters*, 13–20. This argument works better if one holds to an early second- or very late first-century date for the Pastoral Letters. I do not hold to such a date but tend to agree with Quinn and Wacker, *First and Second Letters*, 19, that the date of composition is closer to 70 than 100 CE.

144. Cf. Fee, *1 and 2 Timothy*, 181.

145. Indeed there seems to be a connection between Judaism and the inception of Gnosticism; e.g., Pearson, "Eusebius and Gnosticism," 293.

seem to use the Torah and Jewish traditions to support their speculative teachings and ascetic practices, and perhaps combine these with a misdirected development of authentic Christian teachings on resurrection. In the Pastoral Letters, then, we have one Christian calling another group of Christians apostates. Although these letters find apostates primarily in reference to the opponents teaching false doctrines, their denial of Christ cannot be verified. From the author's point of view they deny God in deeds but not by confession (Titus 1:16). Apart from teaching what the author perceives as false doctrine, are there any other deeds by which these opponents deny God? The opponents are perceived as immoral by committing or encouraging vices (1 Tim 1:3–10; 2 Tim 3:1–9; Titus 1:12), but since the vice lists are influenced by polemic material it is not very clear which vices they may be committing. Their ascetic practices are not the same thing as vices, and even though the opponents are accused of being deceptive, liars, and hypocrites, these seem related to their false teachings (1 Tim 4:2–3; cf. 2 Tim 3:13). Vices related to greed, conceit, envy, and factional behavior may be among the sins they commit (1 Tim 6:3–10; cf. Titus 3:10–11); albeit, problems related to wealth may be a more general temptation plaguing the community (1 Tim 6:17–19).[146] The opponents obviously did not think of themselves as false teachers—from their perspective the other believers they teach need enlightenment about Jewish scriptures, especially in relation to creation and resurrection. They seem committed to instruct others even if this creates division within the Pauline community. Here perhaps is the most crucial area in which the AP may have felt justified in considering them as vicedoers—they are committed to factionalism.

Could these opponents be the Johannine community that also resided in Ephesus? The two communities may have known each other if, as we maintain, the Pastoral Letters were written not too long after Paul's death, perhaps in the late 60s or very early 70s CE, and the Johannine community probably moved from Palestine to Ephesus at about the same time (see Johannine writings in volume one of this study). At least four views are possible.

The first view is that the two groups merged, similar to what is depicted in John 21. However, if we assume a two-level reading of that passage, the communities that are joined together are the Johannine and Petrine communities, not the Johannine and Pauline communities. Still, it is possible to suggest some sort of overlap between Petrine and Pauline communities—at least some congregations accepted both Paul and Peter's authority (e.g., 1 Cor 1:12; 9:5; 2 Pet 3:15). It can be surmised that the

---

146. See Bénétreau, "La Richesse," 49–60, who distinguishes 6:6–10 as a polemic against the opponents and 6:17–19 as instructing the church. In both passages the basic message is the same in communicating that the desire of possessions ensnares everyone. On greed as not merely part of the polemic schema in the letters, see Trebilco, *Early Christians in Ephesus*, 226–27.

Petrine community might have included a number of Pauline churches after both leaders were martyred. But even if this were correct we do not know if Ephesus was one of those churches. Paul Trebilco examines both the Johannine and Pauline communities in Ephesus and finds a number of distinctions between them. Among these are their attitudes towards the world, group structures, concepts about authority, and lack of a shared vocabulary.[147]

A second view is that the two communities were unaware of each other.[148] This is possible but unlikely given that Christians seem to have a strong network of communities early on.[149] Moreover, in Asia Minor we see church communities in different cities linking together in Col 4:13; 1 Pet 1:1; and Rev 2–3. Likewise, in the region of Galatia we find a similar network of churches (Gal 1:2). The Johannine community also seems to have church homes in neighboring regions outside of Ephesus (cf. 3 John). Such alliances make it difficult to maintain that the Pauline and Johannine communities would not be aware of each other.

A third view, which is provocative for our study, is that the two communities were hostile towards one another. As we have argued, however, the Johannine opponents deny Jesus as Messiah and do not seem to believe in his deity and preexistence. The earlier Johannine opponents seem to come from a Jewish synagogue. Neither of these groups reflect the Pauline community. Conversely, the opponents in the Pastoral Letters hold to Jewish myths and genealogical speculations, deny future resurrection, and practice asceticism. Such beliefs and practices do not reflect the Johannine community. Trebilco arrives at a similar conclusion when comparing the two groups and affirms that neither group fails the other's "litmus test."[150] He thus argues for another (fourth) viewpoint: the communities knew about each other and had "non-hostile" relations, but they remained separate communities.[151] The first or fourth options seem to be more plausible than the second or third. If the two communities remained separate, what is not clear is why they chose to remain separate.

For our purposes, anyway, *the opponents in the Pastoral Letters do not appear to be the Johannine community.* Moreover, the differences we have mentioned between the opponents also suggest for us that the opponents in each of these communities are not the same opponents. We have at least two Christian groups in Ephesus, possibly three: the Pauline community, their opponents, and the Johannine community. And if the Johannine opponents still hold to an allegiance to Jesus (e.g., they confess

147. See Trebilco, *Early Christians in Ephesus*, chs. 8–12.
148. E.g., Schnackenburg, "Ephesus," 41–64.
149. Cf. Trebilco, *Early Christians in Ephesus*, 591–92.
150. Ibid., 593.
151. Ibid., 589–627.

him as messiah but deny his deity and preexistence), which in fact they seem to do at least in 2 John, then we have four groups in Ephesus. Most of those who hold to false teachings in the Ephesus of Pastoral Letters, however, still seem to operate within the Pauline church homes, and so the limits of this community are not properly marked. Did Hymenaeus and Alexander form their own group? We do not know.

THE OPPONENTS AS "HERETICS"? (TITUS 3:10)

The AP instructs Titus to give an individual whom the author calls αἱρετικός one or two chances before rejecting the person (Titus 3:10). This is the only time the word appears in the New Testament, but the related αἵρεσις appears in a negative sense in Pauline writings. Its connotation relates to discrimination or dissension (1 Cor 11:19; Gal 5:20).[152] The Darby version translates it as "heretical man." The term originates in the political sphere and in group loyalties, and this older meaning is preferred in the New Testament,[153] where it is sometimes understood as "sect" and identifies the Sadducees,[154] the Pharisees,[155] and the early Christians who were known as the Nazarene sect (Acts 24:5). The emerging Christian movement was understood by others as a subgroup from among emergent Judaism. The Lukan Paul noticeably does not prefer to call his own group by the term αἵρεσις; it is a name given to a group by those outside it (Acts 24:14; cf. 24:5; 28:22). Here perhaps seeds of a negative connotation with the word seem present. We notice at the end of the first century that the Book of Revelation considers the Nicolaitans to be a deviant group, presumably coming out of a more normative brand of the emerging Christians (Rev 2:6, 15). The terms αἱρετικός or αἵρεσις, however, are not used to define this group.

In Titus 3:10 the term αἱρετικός is too premature here to be translated by its later use as "heretic," which would reflect the writings of Irenaeus and other apologists beginning in the middle of the second century.[156] The use of this term in Titus does not exclusively mean a doctrinal heretic opposed to a set standard of Christian beliefs or "orthodoxy," as commonly defined in later centuries.[157] It is referring to factious or "divisive" individuals who attend Titus' church in Crete. The division nonetheless centers on false teachings (Titus 3:9), and so what we have in Titus is *a*

152. Cf. BDAG, 27.

153. See Schlier, "αἱρέομαι," 1.180–84.

154. Acts 5:17; Josephus, *Ant.* 13.171.

155. Acts 15:5; 26:5; Josephus, *Life* 10.

156. E.g., Irenaeus, *Haer.* 3.3.4; 5.13.2; cf. 1.16.3; 3.1.2; Justin, *Apol.* 36; *Dial.* 35.3. See further examples of term in Quinn, *Titus*, 238, 248–49.

157. Cf. Bauer, *Orthodoxy and Heresy*; Desjardins, "Bauer and Beyond," 65–82.

word beginning to develop into a technical term. Likewise, we may see an emerging term in Ignatius's use of the related αἵρεσις when dealing with false teachings in Ephesus in the early second century (Ign. *Eph.* 6.2; cf. *Trall.* 6.1).[158] By the time 2 Pet 2:1 was written the term is still distinguishable from the later Christian concept of heresy because even though αἵρεσις is associated with false teachings, the focus of the letter condemns the opponents' immoral lifestyle, and the idea of "faction" is still present in the passage. Stephen Wilson may be correct in distilling the way Christians thought about heresy in the second century: "*hairesis* is established as a technical term for heresy—false teaching or practice, by individuals or groups (mostly gnostic), who are inspired by the devil but show human ancestry can be traced to particular founding figures (Simon Magus) or the influence of paganism."[159] Exactly who becomes a heretic depends on the group that is labeling the other as heretic. The so-called heretical group normally believes itself to be holding to correct religious beliefs and practices.

PAUL'S FINAL PERSEVERANCE AND HIS GRIEF OVER DEMAS AND OTHER DESERTERS (2 TIM 4:6–8, 17–18; CF. 2 TIM 1:15–16; 4:14–15; 1 TIM 6:9–10, 17)

The author presents himself as an example of perseverance and fulfilling his ministry as he awaits his trial and execution. He has fought the good fight, finished the race, and kept the faith. As a result he will receive a "crown of righteousness" on the Day of the Lord (2 Tim 4:6–8; cf. Acts 20:24). The imagery here depicts his receiving an athletic victor's crown for winning a footrace, which probably refers to a heavenly reward related to final salvation or a reward for righteous living, or both.[160] The author believes he will persevere to the end; he is assured of his own final salvation (2 Tim 4:17–18).[161] This assurance of final salvation, however, must be understood in context of the letter's intention as a type of farewell discourse. If the letter intends to portray Paul's final days in prison, it is not surprising that Paul would have such confidence after persevering for so many years in ministry and seeing how God had helped him all the way. He was prepared to die for his faith and was not about to

158. See Schoedel, *Ignatius*, 58 cf. 12. On the opponents in Ephesus during the time of Ignatius, see Trebilco, *Early Christians in Ephesus*, 690–99.

159. Wilson, *Leaving the Fold*, 14.

160. Here the three metaphors that are used relate to endurance and patience: military ("fight"), athletics ("race/course"), and stewardship ("kept"; entrusted with a pledge or deposit). Alternatively, the last of these may refer to an athlete's pledge to abide by the rules or the militant's oath of loyalty.

161. Schreiner, *Paul*, 278–79, is correct when he writes, "Second Timothy 4:18 certainly does not mean that God will rescue Paul from death in the future since Paul knew death was imminent."

abandon the ministry during the final days of his life. Earlier in his ministerial career Paul did not talk with such confidence about his final salvation but communicates the possibility of his own defection (cf. 1 Cor 9:24–27). Moreover, if the Pastoral Letters are written or finalized by one of Paul's colleagues after the apostle's death, as we have suggested, then the author could surely speak with this type of confidence about Paul because he knew firsthand that Paul never renounced his faith but died a martyr.[162] Furthermore, in farewell speeches of antiquity the hero knows he is going to die and is able to make predictions. It was commonly believed that when one approaches death one is given power to prophesy (e.g., Gen 49; 50:24; Deut 32; Josh 23; Mark 13; Luke 22:31–34; Acts 20; Homer, *Iliad* 22.355–60; Diodorus Siculus 18.1; Diogenes Laertius 1.117–18).[163] Hence, in the manner of a farewell discourse, *it may have been assumed by the ancient auditors of 2 Timothy that Paul can have absolute confidence about his final salvation because, as a man on the verge of death, he can predict the future.*

The Pastoral author does not communicate the same level of assurance about Timothy's final salvation when he charges him to "take heed to yourself . . . in doing so you will both save yourself and your hearers" (1 Tim 4:16). Timothy must continue to fight a spiritual battle and "take hold" (ἐπιλαβοῦ) of eternal life as both a present and future goal (1 Tim 6:11–12; cf. 1:16; Titus 1:2; 3:7). Not fighting a good fight of faith could lead to spiritual shipwreck, and so Timothy must continue in the instructions he has learned[164] and persevere through suffering and ministering (2 Tim 2:1–6; 4:5). Be that as it may, there is no indication that AP believed Timothy's salvation was in grave jeopardy. The same could not be said, however, for former colleagues such as Demas, Phygelus, and Hermogenes (1:15; 4:10). Some consider Alexander the coppersmith to be one of Paul's former colleagues, and since he vigorously opposes Pauline teaching he might be a hardened apostate (4:14–15). Along this line he is sometimes equated with the Alexander who was expelled from the church in 1 Tim 1:19.[165] But the two distinct occurrences of the name may easily suggest the commonality of the name without equating the persons. The name appears again in Mark 15:21, Acts 4:6, and Acts 19:33–34, where it refers to three unrelated

162. Interestingly, Psalm 21[22] LXX may be playing in the background of this passage (cf. 2 Tim 4:16/Ps 21:2[22:1]; 2 Tim 4:17c/Ps 21:22[22:21]; 2 Tim 4:17–18/Ps 21:5–6, 9, 21). On an intertextual level one may be reminded of the passion of Jesus through Paul's suffering, death, and experience of being abandoned.

163. See further examples in Talbert, *Reading Acts*, 180.

164. 2 Tim 3:14; cf. 2 Tim 1:13; 1 Tim 1:18–19; 6:14; Titus 1:9.

165. E.g., Knight, *Pastoral Epistles*, 467, who suggests the same person is intended in both passages and is also the one mentioned as "Alexander" in Acts 19:33–34.

individuals.[166] A more likely identity for Alexander the coppersmith is that of an outsider who is troubling the Pauline church in Ephesus; hence, Timothy is to be on guard against him (2 Tim 4:15). Demetrius the silversmith came against the Pauline mission in Ephesus in Acts 19:24–31, and it is said that he gathered other craftsmen and those of similar trade to come against the Christians (Acts 19:24–25). Their business of creating religious images was being threatened by the Christian message of one God who condemns idolatry. Alexander the coppersmith is probably one of those workmen whom Demetrius convinced that Paul was a threat to their business. If so, then this particular Alexander is not a recalcitrant apostate but a hostile non-Christian Gentile.

The Pauline author claims that in Asia Minor "all" turned away from him (2 Tim 1:15). This could hardly mean that all the Christians in that region deserted him or committed apostasy.[167] Timothy and Onesiphorus lived in this area and are obvious exceptions (cf. 1 Tim 1:3; 2 Tim 1:16). The "all" probably should be understood as an overstatement expressed with great emotion. Kelly suggests that the apostle's language is an exaggeration to be expected when someone is depressed.[168] No one stood by or helped "Paul" at his arrest (cf. 2 Tim 1:8, 16), which presumably took place somewhere in western Asia Minor.[169] He now feels abandoned in prison as he awaits his impending trial. Phygelus and Hermogenes are mentioned by name among the deserters (1:15). They were probably colleagues who abandoned Paul for fear of imprisonment or persecution, or possibly they left him to join his opponents. Marshall suggests this abandonment included a rejection of the Pauline Christian message, but we cannot be sure, and there is no more information about them.[170] Even if we assume that they did abandon the Pauline message this would not necessarily make them apostates in the eyes of other Christians. We wonder whether other early communities would consider defectors from Paul's churches to be apostates, especially given that those who claimed allegiance to Paul's message were sometimes considered apostates by other Christian groups (e.g., 2 Pet 3:15–17). Here again we must admit that the nature of defection is relative to who is claiming that someone has defected.

166. Spicq, *Épitres Pastorales*, 2.816, wisely questions the equating of Pauline Alexanders.

167. Despite the same word for "turn away" (ἀποστρέφω) is understood as an apostasy in Titus 1:14 (cf. also 2 Tim 4:4; Heb 12:25), this more severe nuance does not make much sense in 2 Tim 1:15.

168. Kelly, *Commentary*, 169. See also Johnson, *First and Second Letters*, 360.

169. The alternative is to understand "in" Asia as an idiom for "from" or "out of" and then suggest that the Asian Christians in Rome abandoned Paul; cf. Spicq, *Épistres Pastorales*, 2.722. But there is no evidence for this construction in any of the Pauline epistles according to Quinn and Wacker, *First and Second Letters*, 613.

170. Marshall, *Pastoral Epistles*, 717.

The author also claims that another close colleague named Demas had deserted Paul (2 Tim 4:10; cf. Phlm 24; Col 4:14). Demas' abandonment includes his having "loved this present age." Quinn and Wacker suggest that loving the present age relates to wealth (1 Tim 6:17), and the "precarious poverty of the apostolate" led to Demas' downfall—he may have even ran off with Paul's purse.[171] For emerging Christians, the temptation of possessing riches was sometimes associated with apostasy (see Luke-Acts in volume one of this study), and this type of defection remained a problem for the church in the second century (e.g., Herm. *Sim.* 1.4–6; 6.2.3–4; 8.8.2; 8.9.1–3; Herm. *Vis.* 3.6.5). Certain Jewish communities connected the love of money with apostasy or idolatry (e.g., Philo, *Mos.* 1.30–31; *T. Jud.* 19.1). In 1 Timothy the problem of wealth leads to haughtiness (ὑψηλοφρονέω)[172] and placing confidence in riches (6:17). The allurement of wealth is viewed as a problem that leads to apostasy in 6:10b.[173] People who are thus ensnared are then described as piercing themselves with many agonies. Witherington describes this most graphically: "They have become like a creature that has impaled itself on a split over an open fire, causing itself no end of agony. Once again the theme of apostasy surfaces, possibly even with an allusion here to hell and eternal destruction."[174] Contextually speaking, divine judgment is confirmed in 6:9: the person who desires to be rich falls into a snare that eventually results in ruin (ὄλεθρος) and destruction (ἀπώλεια). Both terms in Pauline tradition are used to refer to eschatological destruction.[175] The combined force of the terms seems to emphasize the greatness of this devastation—this means eternal condemnation.[176] *Greed and the lure of wealth lead to apostasy and eternal destruction.* Temptations related to wealth will apparently persist in certain churches of western Asia Minor (e.g., Rev 3:14–18), and perhaps complacency related to a

171. Quinn and Wacker, *First and Second Letters*, 800–801. The thought is also conceptually close to 1 John 2:15–16.

172. Compare the sin of haughtiness as ὑψηλοφροσύνη in *Herm. Mand.* 8.3; 9.22.3; ὑψηλόφρων in *Herm. Sim.* 8.9.1; and arrogance (ὑψηλός) in Rom 11:20; 12:16; *Barn.* 19.6 (cf. 20.1); *Did.* 3.9 (cf. 5.1).

173. On ἀποπλανάω as leading astray/committing apostasy, see Mark 13:22; Jer 27[50]:6; 2 Chr 21:11; Prov 7:21; Sir 4:19; 13:6; 2 Macc 2:2; *1 En.* 8.2; *Herm. Mand* 5.2.1; *Herm. Sim.* 6.3.3; Polycarp, *Phil.* 6.3; Braun, ""πλανάω," 6.228–53. On parallel condemnations or warnings against money, see Luke 12:15; *Sib. Or.* 2.111; Philo, *Spec.* 4.65; *Ahiqar* 137; Plato, *Laws.* 9.870A; Dibelius and Conzelmann, *Pastoral Epistles*, 85–86; Marshall, *Pastoral Epistles*, 652.

174. Witherington, *Hellenized Christians*, 1.289. On ὀδύνη compare the verb ὀδυνάω in Luke 16:24–25.

175. ὄλεθρος: 2 Thess 1:9; ἀπώλεια: Rom 9:22; Phil 1:28; 3:19; 2 Thess 2:3.

176. The other way to interpret this passage is to claim that the first term leads to physical or present ruin and the second to spiritual or future ruin; e.g., Kelly, *Commentary*, 137. But even if this interpretation were preferred, eternal ruin would still be evident in the final term.

lifestyle of luxury had something to do with the Ephesians losing their love for God (cf. Rev 2:4).

While this explanation for Demas' failure cannot be ruled out, a more probable cause for his disloyalty involved his fear of persecution. Polycarp contrasts the idea of loving the present age over against a willingness to be martyred (Polycarp, *Phil.* 9:1–2). A similar thought may rest behind the Pauline words about Demas. Perhaps we can suggest from the text that Demas was with Paul when he was arrested but fear of imprisonment caused Demas to run away. The author interprets this as abandonment similar to the way the disciples fled from Jesus at his arrest. The verb used for Demas' departure (ἐγκαταλείπω) is repeatedly found in the LXX to describe Israel forsaking God.[177] The connotation in 2 Tim 4:10 may be more mild since the author uses the word again in the same context when claiming that "all deserted" him at his defense; i.e., no one stood by Paul when he went to his first court trial (4:16). He was probably not intending to say that all the unnamed no-shows committed apostasy; rather, those who did not stand by Paul at his trial lacked courage or concern for their imprisoned brother in the Lord.[178] The author gives a prayer wish that those who deserted Paul not be punished by God (4:16b). The author's mercy here stands in stark contrast to his decision to deliver Hymenaeus and Alexander to Satan after their apostasy (1:18f). We are obviously not dealing with the same type of disloyalty. *Demas was not a false teacher leading others astray; his fault rested with failing to be brave and steadfast in the midst of persecution.*

In between "Demas" and "all" forsaking Paul, the author claims that Crescens and Titus departed from him to Galatia and Dalmatia, respectively, and Demas departed to Thessalonica. Luke alone remained with Paul (2 Tim 4:10–12). *Their departure into various cities probably suggests they decided to leave Paul or the ministry, at least temporarily; they did not abandon their faith in Christ.* It is rather probable that they, as well as Demas, joined the churches in the cities the author tags with their names. These examples of colleagues forsaking Paul remind us of John Mark's departure from Paul's missionary journey in Acts 13:13. Later on, Paul did not permit Mark to join his second mission despite Barnabas insisting that Mark join them (15:36–40). There is no indication that Paul considered Mark an apostate; rather, he may have thought him unreliable for the purpose of the apostle's ministry. In 2 Timothy Paul is portrayed as accepting Mark for his ministry and is satisfied with his performance (2 Tim 4:11; cf. Col 4:10–11; Phlm 24). If this is referring to the

177. E.g., Deut 28:20; 32:15, 18; Josh 24:20; Judg 2:13; 10:6; 1 Sam 8:8; 1 Kgs 9:9; 2 Chr 24:18; Isa 1:4; Jer 2:13; Sir 41:8. Conversely, the word was used of God's faithfulness in not forsaking his people (Heb 13:5; Deut 31:6, 8; Ps 37:22; Sir 2:10; Bel 1:38; cf. Matt 27:46; Mark 15:34; Acts 2:27, 31).

178. Cf. Marshall, *Pastoral Epistles*, 823.

same colleague who deserted Paul in Acts 13, then the AP is probably implying that Paul finally conceded with Barnabas that unfaithful workers should be given second chances. The disagreement between Paul and Barnabbas demonstrates that even apostolic leaders and close colleagues did not always agree on what constituted desertion and what should be done to restore a deserter. We can only surmise how the desertions in 2 Timothy might have sounded differently had the letter been penned by Barnabbas, or better yet by those who are said to have deserted Paul.

From what we have observed, *it is not clear that Demas apostatized from his faith.* Historically speaking, there is no evidence that he denied Christ—he forsook Paul, and we have no testimony from Demas himself, only the word of the author in 2 Timothy. For the author such abandonment was probably tantamount to abandoning Christ. Perhaps it was not easy for the author to separate the truth of gospel as taught by Jesus (and the Twelve) and the gospel as preached by Paul. For him disloyalty from one probably included the other.[179] Perhaps Demas' abandonment of Paul functions as a rhetorical strategy for making it appear as though Demas has turned apostate, and his example would be one that Timothy is discouraged from following: Timothy should not turn out to be cowardly and disloyal like some of Paul's former companions (cf. 2 Tim 1:7; 2:1, 3). Timothy is to be a strong soldier, enduring hardships for the sake of the gospel, much like his mentor, and remain faithful to Christ.

CONCLUSION

The Pastoral Letters are addressed to communities in Ephesus and Crete and may have been written by a colleague of Paul's shortly after the apostle's death. All three letters seem to portray the same type of danger facing the church homes of that region. Apparently some of the congregation members have interpreted the Torah and Jewish traditions to support beliefs related to fables, speculations, asceticism, and a view of eschatology that caused them to deny any future resurrection (e.g., 1 Tim 1:3–7; 4:1–5; 2 Tim 2:16–18; Titus 1:5–14). Their mode of operation is to teach their beliefs in the Pauline church homes, and wealthy widows seem to be one of their primary targets. Their strategy has been quite successful—they persuaded entire households in Crete and have influenced a number of women in Ephesus (1 Tim 5:5–15; cf. 1 Tim 2:9–15; 2 Tim 3:6–7; Titus 1:10–11). Two apostates, Hymenaeus and Alexander, were once leaders in the congregation, but they ruined their own faith through false teachings (1 Tim 1:19–20). They are expelled from the church, and more expulsions may be necessary for those who are straying if they do not turn from their errors. The author instructs Timothy and Titus, as the pastors of the

179. On this view see Meade, *Pseudonymity*, 127; Weiser, *Zweite Briefe*, 137.

churches, to confront these teachers and put a silence to their errors. The women in Ephesus likewise are not to teach. The author echoes stories from the Torah as he instructs his ministers against the false teachers. As Eve was deceived by the Serpent, so these women have been deceived by the false teachers who are inspired by Satan (2 Tim 2:9–15). As Korah and Jannes and Jambres were exposed by God and punished in the exodus-wilderness narratives, so the opponents will be exposed as deceivers and suffer the consequences (2 Tim 2:18–21; 3:8–9). The opponents are stereotyped in polemical fashion as Torah violators and vicedoers (e.g., 1 Tim 1:6–11; 2 Tim 3:1–5). Among the most prominent vices are greed and instigating factions. Eternal judgment is most clearly seen in those who fall away through the allurement of wealth (1 Tim 6:2–10).

While false doctrines are the primary threat to the congregations' salvation in these letters, suffering and persecution is a secondary cause of apostasy, exemplified most clearly in the hymn line, "If we deny him, he also will deny us" (1 Tim 2:11–13). Certain ministers such as Demas, Hermogenes, and Phygelus deserted Paul's ministry, presumably out of fear of persecution, but it is not clear that they defected from Christ (2 Tim 1:15; 4:10). The author is nevertheless confident that God will never let the church as a whole be entirely subdued by opposition, whether the opposition arises internally through deceptive teachings or externally through persecution. A prophetic word from the author confirms that "some," but not all, believers will fall away (1 Tim 4:1; cf. 2 Tim 1:19–20). Whereas the author in the name of Paul possesses confidence of his own final salvation at the very end of his life (2 Tim 4:6–8, 17–18), he informs his leaders and their congregations that salvation is not only present but also futuristic. If they wish to obtain final salvation they must persevere in the present and not be deceived before the end takes place.

The Pastoral Letters share in common with the Pauline letters the threat of apostasy among the faithful through deception and vice. Likewise, similar to Paul in 1 Corinthians, the consequence of apostasy results in expulsion from the church and this punishment is intended to be remedial. In 1 Timothy, however, the ground for expulsion is not related to the vice of sexual sin but to teaching false doctrines. It is hoped that Hymenaeus and Alexander will learn from their errors and forsake their false teachings, and Timothy is instructed to teach the opponents so that they can recover themselves out of the snare of the devil (2 Tim 2:24–26). The author of the Pastoral Letters speaks of coming judgment on the false teachers, but he is not as clear in determining their final condemnation. The clearest example of eternal destruction on the apostates relates more to their succumbing to greed and the lure of wealth than to false teachings (1 Tim 6:9–10). A problem related to eschatology and misperception about the resurrection plays a factor in both the church of Corinth and Ephesus; albeit, the Pastoral author is less tolerant of the error than Paul. He considers such a teaching to be demonically inspired and contributing to apostasy.

The Pauline community in Ephesus may have known the Johannine community, but as we have suggested, it is not clear that they merged. These communities do not appear to be hostile towards one another if separate, and the opponents in both communities seem to be different. In the Pastoral Letters false teaching centers on misinterpretations of scripture and denial of the resurrection; in the Johannine group false teaching centers on a denial of Jesus as the Christ and his divinity. Similar to the Johannine community, the Pauline church in Ephesus is said to be a community that has deceivers influencing the congregation, and both communities view deception in the context of the last days. Unlike the Johannine writer, however, the Pastoral author does not claim that the defectors, Hymenaeus and Alexander, were never genuine believers. They in fact believed, but they ruined their personal faith. Another distinction is that the Johannine defectors left on their own accord; Hymenaeus and Philetus were kicked out of the church. Both communities perceive the threat as present and imminent. In the Pauline church, however, the threat is still pervasive among insiders, and more expulsions might be necessary (Titus 3:10). These observations suggest that in the last decades of the first century the city of Ephesus had more than one community that claimed to follow Jesus.

Conclusion

The Christ *communities* in the Pauline letters come from Asia Minor (Galatians, Colossians, Ephesians, Pastoral Letters), Greece-Macedonia (Thessalonians, Corinthians, Philippians), Rome (Romans), and Syrian Antioch (Galatians 2). They are mostly comprised of Gentile converts to the Christ message, but Jewish influence and leadership prevails in some of these churches (e.g., Galatians, 2 Corinthians, Romans). The opponents in these letters vary. Some are Jewish-Christian missionaries who insist on the circumcision of Gentile converts (Galatians, Philippians 3) or persuade congregation members to reject Paul's authority (Corinthians). Others are unbelieving Gentiles who harass the community in Christ (Thessalonians, Philippians 1). The Pauline congregations also encounter an opposing Jewish sect (Colossians) and apostate believers whose false teachings are still being felt in the congregations (Pastoral Letters). Some warnings in the letters come more by way of preventative maintenance than by false teachers penetrating the congregations or finding receptive audiences among the members (Romans, Philippians 3, Ephesians).

Regarding the *nature of apostasy*, these letters warn repeatedly against *false teachings* and deceptive influences that can lead astray the congregation members. Paul warns the Galatians against being cut off from Christ by their embracing the "works of the Law," which among other things concerns Gentile congregations being pressured into accepting that circumcision makes a person righteous before God. The hallmark of Paul's gospel for the new era, which has been ushered in through the atoning death of Jesus, is that his congregations are rectified by their faithfulness to Christ rather than by circumcision and other Jewish customs. Likewise, Paul warns the Roman and Philippian churches against similar teachings. Differently, the Corinthians have been influenced by emergent Christian opponents whom Paul dubs as "servants of Satan." They influence the congregation to reject his apostolic authority. Paul instructs the Thessalonians about a coming man of lawlessness who will claim to be God and lead astray many. The letter to the Ephesians warns against false doctrines from both Jewish and "pagan" sectors of society, and the Christ-communities in the Lycus valley are disturbed by a Jewish sect with Essene-like beliefs (Colossians). Finally, misinterpreters of Israel's Scriptures influence the congregations in Ephesus and Crete to practice asceticism, speculate about fables, and hold to distorted beliefs about the resurrection (Pastoral Letters).

Another prominent venue for apostasy in these letters takes place through congregation members either committing or being tempted to commit various types of *vices*. These are perceived by Paul as "works of the flesh"—unrighteous behavior and practices associated with the pre-converted status of his Gentile congregants who once belonged to the fallen world of anti-god powers prior to being "in Christ." Certain vices affect his congregations more than others. In a significant way factionalism threatens the Galatians, Corinthians, and table fellowship in Rome. Fornication disrupts the spiritual well-being of the churches in Thessalonica and Corinth, and Paul is apprehensive about members of these churches falling away to idolatry, especially the strong-*gnosis* believers in Corinth. The vice lists in Colossians, Ephesians, and the Pastoral letters seem to be more conventional than addressing specific problems in the congregations, and the apostates are caricatured as heinous vice-doers (e.g., 1 Timothy; Philippians 3). These later writings reflect a general concern about the dangers of assimilation with outsiders who do not know Christ. Even so, for these communities, which are mostly from Western Asia Minor, the vice of greed and problems related to wealth stand out. As preventatives against vice-doing Paul encourages the recipients of his letters to "walk in the Spirit" and be proactive in love.

In Romans apostasy is perceived from primeval times as humanity (the Gentiles) turning away from its Creator to worship idols and commit sexual immorality, and Israel has largely become apostate due to its *unbelief* in the Christ-message. The Gentile Christ-followers are susceptible to being cut off from Christ through pride and prejudice against the Jews, and Paul informs his audience that Israel will be saved at the culmination of the present age.

One other source of defection worth mentioning arises from *persecution*. Paul admits that he was afraid the Thessalonians had fallen away from faith as a result of external pressures after he had left their city (1 Thess 3:5). The apostle, however, normally mitigates spiritual dangers related to this treat. He presents himself as the exemplar of perseverance through afflictions, and for him suffering authenticates his ministry as sanctioned by God. He considers persecution and hardships to be venues in which the character of believers in Christ are built up and confirmed (2 Corinthians, Romans, Philippians, Pastoral letters).

The immediate *consequences* of apostasy include expulsion from the community in Christ and a handing over to the anti-god powers (1 Corinthians 5; 2 Corinthians 13; Galatians 4; 1 Timothy 1). Paul's hope is that the apostate will repent and be restored to the community, and he encourages his churches to be proactive in helping restore backslidden members (Galatians 6). Likewise, he believes that apostate Israel has not lost its election; Israel will be restored and saved (Romans 9–11). Final consequences for falling away will take place at the *parousia.* Those who are not restored to the community in Christ will be excluded from God's kingdom and destroyed along with outsiders from the fallen world (e.g., Galatians; Corinthians; Thessalonians; Philippians 3).

Paul's conflicts in Antioch and Galatia uncover that Jewish Christ-followers from Judea maintained that Gentile converts needed to be circumcised and keep other teachings from the Law. Paul opposed such impositions, and his encounters with James, Peter, and John did not resolve this division among believers (Gal 2; cf. Acts 15; 21). Such events, along with the repeated confrontations we find in his letters over opponents and issues directly relevant to the Mosaic Law, point to a heated, first-century debate between Jewish and Gentile Christ-communities over the interpretation of the Torah. A number of Paul's opponents, whom he labels as apostates and warns his congregations against, confessed Jesus as the Christ (Galatians, 2 Corinthians, Philippians, Pastoral Letters). We clearly see that serious *disputes existed between emergent Christian communities* over the interpretation of Israel's scriptures, the nature of salvation, and exactly who should be identified as apostate. We do not know the beliefs of Paul's opponents from their own point of view; we only hear about them through Paul's responses in his letters. It is rather likely that at least some of the opponents would have considered Paul to be an apostate. Even James and Peter would tend to disagree with Paul's warning that if the Galatians embrace the works of the Law, they would fall from grace and be cut off from Christ.

Diverse perspectives among Christ-communities over this issue deepen when we compare Paul's letters with the Gospel writers (see Volume 1). Unlike Paul, Matthew's community stresses the importance of keeping the Torah; albeit, both Matthew and Paul affirm the command to love one's neighbor is the epitome of Law observance. Mark's community experiences angst over persecution and the possibility of repudiating Christ through afflictions. Paul, on the other hand, welcomes hardships as proof of Christian vocation. His perspective is more in line with Luke-Acts, which incidentally portrays Paul as a faithful missionary and champion of such suffering. Similar to Paul, the Johannine author struggles with emergent Christian opponents, but unlike Paul the conflict centers on the nature of Christ rather than the

Law. Moreover, Paul considers apostates to be one-time faithful followers of Christ and hopes for their restoration, but this is not the way the Johannine author views defectors from his community. Such contrasts help to confirm our suspicions that the emergent Christian communities did not all believe and act in the same manner. They did not always agree on who should be identified as apostate. Further nuances on both the unity and diversity of these groups will be explored in Volume 3.

Bibliography

Aageson, James W. "Scripture and Structure in the Development of the Argument in Romans 9–11." *CBQ* 48 (1986) 265–89.

Abasciano, Brian J. "Corporate Election in Romans 9: A Reply to Thomas Schreiner." *JETS* 49 (2006) 351–71.

———. *Paul's Use of the Old Testament in Romans 9.1–9: An Intertextual and Theological Exegesis.* LNTS 301. London: T. & T. Clark, 2005.

Abbott, Thomas K. *A Critical and Exegetical Commentary on the Epistles to the Ephesians and to the Colossians.* ICC. Edinburgh: T. & T. Clark, 1991.

Achtemeier, Paul J. *Romans.* Interpretation. Atlanta: John Knox, 1985.

Aejmelaeus, L. *Schwachheit als Waffe: Die Argumentation des Paulus im Tränenbrief (2 Kor. 10–13).* SESJ 78. Helsinki: Finish Exegetical Society; Göttingen: Vandenhoeck & Ruprecht, 2000.

Aletti, Jean-Noël. "Romains 4 et Genèse 17: quelle énigme et quelle solution?" *Biblica* 84 (2003) 305–25.

———. *Saint Paul: épître aux Colossiens.* EBib, n.s., 20. Paris: J. Gabalda, 1993.

Alexander, Loveday. "Chronology of Paul." In *DPL*, 115–233.

Allen, Leslie C. "The Old Testament Background of (PRO)ʿORIZEIN in the New Testament." *NTS* 17 (1970) 104–8.

Allo, E. Bernard. *Saint Paul: Première épître aux Corinthiens.* 2nd ed. EBib. Paris: J. Gabalda, 1956.

Andrews, Scott B. "Too Weak Not to Lead: The Form and Function of 2 Cor 11.23b–33." *NTS* 41 (1994–95) 263–76.

Arichea, D. C., and H. A. Hatton. *A Handbook on Paul's Letters to Timothy and to Titus.* UBSHS. New York: United Bible Societies, 1995.

Arnold, Clinton E. *The Colossian Syncretism: The Interface between Christianity and Folk Belief at Colossae.* WUNT 2/77. Grand Rapids: Baker, 1996.

———. *Ephesians: Power and Magic. The Concept of Power in Ephesians in Light of Its Historical Setting.* SNTSMS 63. Cambridge: Cambridge University Press, 1989.

———. "The Exorcism of Ephesians 6.12 in Recent Research: A Critique of Wesley Carr's View of the Role of Evil Powers in First-Century AD Belief." *JSNT* 30 (1987) 71–87.

Ascough, Richard S. *What Are They Saying about the Formation of Pauline Churches?* New York: Paulist, 1998.

Ashley, Timothy R. *The Book of Numbers.* NICOT. Grand Rapids: Eerdmans, 1993.

Balla, Peter. "2 Corinthians." In *CNTOT*, 753–83.

Bammel, Ernst. "Preparation for the Perils of the Last Days: 1 Thessalonians 3:3." In *Suffering and Martyrdom in the New Testament: Studies Presented to G. M. Styler*, edited by Willaim Horbury and B. McNeil, 91–100. Cambridge: Cambridge University Press, 1981.

Bandstra, Andrew J. "Interpretation in 1 Corinthians 10:1–11." *CTJ* 6 (1971) 5–21.

Barclay, John M. G. "Believers and the "Last Judgment' in Paul." Paper presented at the Durham-Tübingen Kolloquium; Thema: Eschatologie. Tübingen, 2009.

———. "By the Grace of God I Am What I Am." In *Divine and Human Agency in Paul and His Cultural Environment*, edited by John M. G. Barclay and Simon J. Gathercole, 140–57. LNTS 335. London: T. & T. Clark, 2006.

———. *Colossians and Philemon*. New Testament Guides. Sheffield: Sheffield Academic, 1997.

———. "Conflict in Thessalonica." *CBQ* 55.3 (1993) 512–30.

———. "Do We Undermine the Law?: A Study of Romans 14.1—15.6." In *Paul and the Mosaic Law*, edited by James D. G. Dunn, 287–308. WUNT 89. Tübingen: Mohr/Siebeck, 1996.

———. "Mirror-Reading a Polemical Letter: Galatians as a Test Case." *JSNT* 31 (1997) 73–93.

———. *Obeying the Truth: Paul's Ethics in Galatians*. Minneapolis: Fortress, 1991.

———. "Paul among Diaspora Jews: Anomaly or Apostate?" *JSNT* 60 (1995) 89–120.

Barclay, John M. G., and Simon J. Gathercole, editors. *Divine and Human Agency in Paul and His Cultural Environment*. LNTS 335. London: T. & T. Clark, 2006.

Barnett, Paul W. *The Second Epistle to the Corinthians*. NICNT. Grand Rapids: Eerdmans, 1997.

Barré, M. L. "Paul as 'Eschatologic Person': A New Look at 2 Cor 11:29." *CBQ* 37 (1975) 500–526.

Barrett, C. K. "Cephas and Corinth." In *Essays on Paul*, 28–39. London: SPCK, 1982.

———. *A Commentary on the First Epistle to the Corinthians*. HNTC. New York: Harper & Row, 1968.

———. *A Commentary on the Second Epistle to the Corinthians*. BNTC. London: A. & C. Black, 1973.

———. *A Critical and Exegetical Commentary on the Acts of the Apostles*. ICC. Edinburgh: T. & T. Clark, 1994.

———. *The Epistle to the Romans*. BNTC. London: Hendrickson, 1991.

———. *Freedom and Obligation*. London: SPCK, 1985.

———. "I Am Not Ashamed of the Gospel." In *Foi et Salut Selon S. Paul (Épître aux Romains 1,16)*, by Markus Barth and C. K. Barrett et al., 19–50. AnBib 42. Rome: Pontifical Biblical Institute, 1970.

———. *The Pastoral Epistles*. Oxford: Oxford University Press, 1963.

———. "Pauline Controversies in the Post-Pauline Period." *NTS* 20 (1973) 229–45.

Barth, Markus, and Helmut Blanke. *Colossians: A New Translation with Introduction and Commentary*. Translated by Astrid B. Beck. AB 34B. New York: Doubleday, 1994.

Bassler, Jouette M. "Adam, Eve, and the Pastor: The Use of Genesis 2–3 in the Pastoral Epistles." In *Genesis 1–3 in the History of Exegesis: Intrigue in the Garden*, edited by G. A. Robbins, 43–65. Studies in Women and Religion 27. Lewiston: E. Mellen, 1988.

———. "1 Cor. 12:3—Curse and Confession in Context." *JBL* 101 (1982) 415–18.

———. *1 Timothy, 2 Timothy, Titus*. ANTC. Nashville: Abingdon, 1996

———. "'He Remains Faithful' (2 Tim 2:13a)." In *Theology and Ethics in Paul and His Interpreters: Essays in Honor of Victor Paul Furnish*, edited by Eugene H. Lovering Jr. and Jerry L. Sumney, 173–83. Nashville: Abingdon, 1996.

Bateman, Herbert W. "Were the Opponents at Philippi Necessarily Jewish?" *BSac* 155 (1998) 39–61.

Bauckham, Richard. "Pseudo-Apostolic Letters." *JBL* 107 (1988) 469–94.

Bauer, Walter. *Orthodoxy and Heresy in Earliest Christianity*. Reprint, Philadelphia: Fortress, 1977.

Baumbach, Günther. "Die Frage nach den Irrlehren in Philippi." *Kairos* 13 (1971) 252–66.

Baumert, Norbert. *Woman and Man in Paul: Overcoming a Misunderstanding*. Translated by Patrick Madigan and Linda M. Maloney. Collegeville, MN: Liturgical, 1996.

Beale, G. K. "Colossians." In *CNTOT*, 841–70.

———. *1–2 Thessalonians*. IVPNTC 13. Downers Grove, IL: InterVarsity, 2003.

———. "The Old Testament Background of Reconciliation in 2 Corinthians 5–7 and Its Bearing on the Literary Problem of 2 Corinthians 6:14—7:1." In *The Right Doctrine from the Wrong Texts?: Essays on the Use of the Old Testament in the New*, edited by G. K. Beale, 217–47. Grand Rapids: Baker, 1994.

Beasley-Murray, G. R. *Jesus and the Future: An Examination of the Criticism of the Eschatological Discourse, Mark 13, with Special Reference to the Little Apocalypse Theory*. London: Macmillan, 1954.

Behm, Johannes. "κοιλία." In *TDNT* 3.786–88.

Bell, Richard H. *No One Seeks for God*. WUNT 106. Tübingen: Mohr/Siebeck, 1998.

———. *Provoked to Jealousy: The Origin and Purpose of the Jealousy Motif in Romans 9–11*. WUNT 2/63. Tübingen: Mohr/Siebeck, 1994.

Bénétreau, Samuel. "La Richesse Selon 1 Timothée 6,6–10 et 6,17–19." *ETR* 83 (2008) 49–60.

Bertram, Georg. "ἀποστρέφω." In *TDNT* 7.719–22.

Best, Ernest. *Ephesians*. ICC. London: T. & T. Clark, 2001.

Betz, Hans Dieter. *2 Corinthians 8 and 9: A Commentary on Two Administrative Letters of the Apostle Paul*. Hermeneia. Philadelphia: Fortress, 1985.

———. *Galatians: A Commentary on Paul's Letter to the Churches in Galatia*. Hermeneia. Philadelphia: Fortress, 1979.

Bevere, Allan R. "The *Cheirograph* in Colossians 2:14 and the Ephesian Connection." In *Jesus and Paul: Global Perspectives in Honor of James D. G. Dunn for his 70th Birthday*, edited by B. J. Oropeza, C. K. Robertson, and Douglas C. Mohrmann, 199–206. LNTS 414. London: T. & T. Clark, 2009.

———. *Sharing in the Inheritance: Identity and the Moral Life in Colossians*. JSNTSup 226. Sheffield: Sheffield Academic, 2003.

Bieringer, Reimand. "Die Gegner des Paulus im 2. Korintherbrief." In *Studies on 2 Corinthians*, edited by Reimand Bieringer and Jan Lambrecht, 181–221. BETL 112. Leuven: Leuven University Press, 1994.

———. "Plädoyer für die Einheitlichkeit des 2. Korintherbriefes: Literarkritische und inhaltliche Argumente." In *Studies on 2 Corinthians*, edited by Reimand Bierginer and Jan Lambrecht, 137–79. BETL 112. Louvain: Leuven University Press, 1994.

———. "'Reconcile Yourselves to God.' An Unusual Interpretation of 2 Corinthians 5:20 in its Context." In *Jesus, Paul, and Early Christianity: Studies in Honour of Henk Jan de Jonge*, edited by Rieuwerd Buitenwerf et al., 11–38. NovTSup 130. Leiden: Brill, 2008.

———. "2 Korinther 6,14—7,1 im Kontext des 2. Korintherbriefes: Forschungsüberblick und Versuch eines eigenen Zugangs." In *Studies on 2 Corinthians*, edited by Reimand Bierginer and Jan Lambrecht, 551–70. BETL 112. Leuven: Leuven University Press, 1994.

Bjerkelund, Carl J. "<<Vergeblich>> als Missionsergebnis bei Paulus." In *God's Christ and His People: Studies in Honour of Nils Alstrup Dahl*, edited by Jacob Jervell and Wayne A. Meeks, 175–91. Oslo: Universitetsforglaget, 1977.

Black, David Alan. "The Weak in Thessalonica: A Study in Pauline Lexicography." *JETS* 25 (1982) 307–21.

Blenkinsopp, Joseph. *Isaiah 40–55: A New Translation with Introduction and Commentary.* AB 19A. New York: Doubleday, 2002.

Bloomquist, L. Greg. *The Function of Suffering in Philippians.* JSNTSup 78. Sheffield: JSOT Press, 1993.

Bockmuehl, Markus N. A. *A Commentary on the Epistle to the Philippians.* BNTC. London: A. & C. Black, 1997.

Boer, Martinus C. de. *The Defeat of Death.* Sheffield: JSOT Press, 1988.

Borgen, Peter. " 'Yes,' 'No,' 'How Far?': The Participation of Jews and Christians in Pagan Cults." In *Paul in his Hellenistic Context*, edited by Troels Engberg-Pedersen, 30–59. Edinburgh: T. & T. Clark, 1994.

Bormann, L. *Philippi: Stadt und Christusgemeinde zur Zeit des Paulus* NovTSup 78. Leiden: Brill, 1995.

Bouttier, Michel. *En Christ: Étude d'exégèse et de théologie pauliniennes.* EHPR 54. Paris: Presses Universitaires de France, 1962.

———. *L'épître de saint Paul aux Ephésiens.* CNT 9b. Geneva: Labor et Fides, 1991.

Boyarin, Daniel. *A Radical Jew: Paul and the Politics of Identity.* Contraversions 1. Berkeley: University of California Press, 1994.

Brändl, Martin. *Der Agon bei Paulus: Herkunft und Profil paulinischer Agonmetaphorik.* WUNT 2/222. Tübingen: Mohr/Siebeck, 2006.

Bratcher, Robert G., and Eugene Albert Nida. *A Handbook on Paul's Letters to the Colossians and to Philemon.* UBSHS. New York: United Bible Societies, 1993.

Braun, Herbert. "πλανάω, πλανάομαι, ἀποπλανάω, ἀποπλανάομαι, πλάνη, πλάνος, πλανήτης, πλάνης." In *TDNT* 6.228–53.

Bray, Gerald, editor. *1–2 Corinthians.* ACCS 7. Downers Grove, IL: InterVarsity, 1999.

Brown, Raymond E. *An Introduction to the New Testament.* ABRL. New York: Doubleday, 1997.

Brox, Norbert. *Die Pastoralbriefe: Uebersetzt und erklaert.* RNT 7.2. Regensburg: F. Pustet, 1969.

Bruce, F. F. *The Epistle of Paul to the Galatians: A Commentary on the Greek Text.* NIGTC. Exeter: Paternoster, 1982.

———. *The Epistles to the Colossians, to Philemon, and to the Ephesians.* NICNT. Grand Rapids: Eerdmans, 1984.

———. *1 & 2 Thessalonians.* WBC 45. Waco, TX: Word, 1985.

Brunt, John C. "Rejected, Ignored, or Misunderstood: The Fate of Paul's Approach to the Problem of Food Offered to Idols in Early Christianity." *NTS* 31 (1985) 113–24.

Bryan, Steven M. *Jesus and Israel's Traditions of Judgment and Restoration.* SNTSMS 117. Cambridge: Cambridge University Press, 2002.

Bujard, W. *Stilanalystische Untersuchungen zum Kolosserbrief als Beitrag zur Methodik von Sprachvergleichen.* SUNT 11. Göttingen: Vandehoeck & Ruprecht, 1973.

Bultmann, Rudolf. *Der zweite Brief an die Korinther.* KEK 6. Göttingen : Vandenhoeck & Ruprecht, 1976.

Burton, Ernest DeWitt. *A Critical and Exegetical Commentary on the Epistle to the Galatians.* ICC 35. Edinburgh: T. & T. Clark, 1921.

Byrne, Brendan. *Romans.* SP 6. Collegeville, MN: Liturgical, 1996.

Caird, George B. "Predestination—Romans ix–xi." *ExpTim* 68 (1957) 324–27.

Calvert-Koyzis, Nancy. *Paul, Monotheism and the People of God: The Significance of Abraham Traditions for Early Judaism and Christianity.* JSNTSup 273. London: T. & T. Clark, 2005.

Campbell, Douglas A. "Romans 1.17—A *Crux Interpretum* for the PISTIS XRISTOU Debate." *JBL* 113 (1994) 265–85.

Campbell, R. Alistair. "Does Paul Acquiesce in Divisions at the Lord's Supper? *NovT* 33 (1991) 61–70.

Cannon, George E. *The Use of Traditional Materials in Colossians.* Macon, GA: Mercer University Press, 1983.

Carras, George P. "Jewish Ethics and Gentile Converts: Remarks on 1 Thes 4,3–8." In *The Thessalonian Correspondence,* edited by Raymond F. Collins, 306–15. BETL 87. Leuven: Leuven University Press/Peeters, 1990.

Carson, D. A., Peter T. O'Brien, and Mark A. Seifrid, editors. *Justification and Variegated Nomism.* 2 vols. WUNT 140, 181. Tübingen: Mohr/Siebeck; Grand Rapids: Baker Academic, 2001, 2004.

Charles, R. H., editor. *Pseudepigrapha of the Old Testament.* 2 vols. Electronic file. Reprint, Bellingham, WA: Logos Research Systems, 2004.

Chester, Stephen J. *Conversion at Corinth: Perspectives on Conversion in Paul's Theology and the Corinthian Church.* SNTW. London: T. & T. Clark, 2003.

Cheung, Alex T. *Idol Food in Corinth: Jewish Background and Pauline Legacy.* JSNTSup 176. Sheffield: Sheffield Academic, 1999.

Chisholm, Robert B., Jr., "Divine Hardening in the Old Testament." *BSac* 153 (1996) 410–34.

Chow, J. K. *Patronage and Power: A Study of Social Networks in Corinth.* JSNTSup 75. Sheffield: Sheffield Academic, 1992.

Christoph, Monika. *Pneuma und das neue Sein der Glaubenden: Studien zur Semantik und Pragmatik der Rede von Pneuma in Röm 8.* EH 23/813. Frankfurt: P. Lang, 2005.

Ciampa, Roy E. *The Presence and Function of Scripture in Galatians 1 and 2.* WUNT 2/102. Tübingen: Mohr/Siebeck, 1998.

Ciampa, Roy E. and Brian S. Rosner. "1 Corinthians." In *CNTOT,* 695–752.

Clarke, Andrew D. *Secular and Christian Leadership in Corinth: A Socio-Historical and Exegetical Study of 1 Corinthians 1–6.* AGJU 18. Leiden: Brill, 1993.

Clements, Ronald E. "'A Remnant Chosen by Grace' (Romans 11:5): The Old Testament Background and Origin of the Remnant Concept." In *Pauline Studies: Essays Presented to Professor F. F. Bruce on his 70th Birthday,* edited by D. A. Hagner and Murray J. Harris, 106–21. Grand Rapids: Eerdmans, 1980.

Clines, David J. A. *Job 1–20.* WBC 17. Waco, TX: Word, 1989.

Cohen, Shaye J. D. *The Beginning of Jewishness: Boundaries, Varieties, Uncertainties.* HCS 31. Berkeley: University of California Press, 1999.

Collange, Jean-François. *Enigmes de la deuxième épître de Paul aux Corinthiens. Étude exégétique de 2 Cor. 2:14—7:4.* SNTSMS 18. Cambridge: Cambridge University Press, 1972.

———. *L'épître de Saint Paul aux Philippiens.* CNT 10a. Neuchâtel: Delachaux & Niestlé, 1973.

Collins, Adela Yarbro. "The Function of Excommunication in Paul." *HTR* 73 (1980) 251–63.

Collins, John J. "Before the Fall: The Earliest Interpretations of Adam of Eve." In *The Idea of Biblical Interpretation: Essays in Honor of James L. Kugel*, edited by Hindy Najman and Judith H. Newman, 293–308. JSJSup 83. Leiden: Brill, 2004.

Collins, Raymond F. "The Function of Paraenesis in 1 Thess 4,1–12; 5,12–22." *ETL* 74 (1998) 398–414.

———. *1 & 2 Timothy and Titus: A Commentary*. NTL. Louisville: Westminster John Knox, 2002.

———. *First Corinthians*. SP 7. Collegeville, MN: Liturgical, 1999.

Conrad, Edgar W. "The 'Fear Not' Oracles in Second Isaiah." *VT* 34 (1984) 129–52.

Conzelmann, Hans. *Acts of the Apostles*. Hermenia. Philadelphia: Fortress, 1987.

———. *1 Corinthians*. Hermeneia. Philadelphia: Fortress, 1975.

———. "χάρις, χαρίζομαι, χαριτόω, ἀχάριστος." In *TDNT* 9.372–76.

Cope, Lamar. "First Corinthians 8–10: Continuity or Contradiction?" In *Christ and His Communities: Essays in Honor of Reginald H. Fuller*, edited by Arland J. Hultgren and Barbara Hall, 114–23. AThRSup 11. Evanston, IL: Anglican Theological Review, 1990.

Cosby, Michael R. "Galatians: Red-Hot Rhetoric." In *Rhetorical Argumentation in Biblical Texts: Essays from the Lund 2000 Conference*, edited by Anders Eriksson et al., 296–309. Harrisburg, PA: Trinity, 2002.

Cosgrove, Charles H. *Elusive Israel: The Puzzle of Election in Romans*. Louisville: Westminster John Knox, 1997.

Countryman, L. William. *Dirt, Greed & Sex: Sexual Ethics in the New Testament and their Implications for Today*. London: SCM, 1989.

Court, John M. "The Controversy with the Adversaries of Paul's Apostolate in the Context of his Relations to the Corinthian Congregation." In *Verteidigung und Begründung des apostolischen Amtes (2 Kor 10–13)*, edited by Eduard Lohse, Bruno Corsani, and Savvas Agourides, 87–105. Benedictina 11. Rome: Abbazia San Paulo fuori le mura, 1992.

Cranfield, C. E. B. *A Critical and Exegetical Commentary on the Epistle to the Romans*. ICC. Edinburgh: T. & T. Clark, 1975.

Cranford, Loren L. "Encountering Heresy: Insight from the Pastoral Epistles." *SwJT* 22 (1980) 23–40.

Cullmann, Oscar. *Christology of the New Testament*. Translated by Shirley C. Guthrie and Charles A. M. Hall. 2nd ed. NTL. London: SCM, 1963.

Currid, John E. "Why Did God Harden Pharaoh's Heart?" *BRev* 9 (December 1993) 46–51.

Dahl, Nils Alstrup. *Studies in Ephesians: Introductory Questions, Text- and Edition-Critical Issues, Interpretation of Tests and Themes*. Edited by David Hellholm, Vemund Blomkvist, and Tord Fornberg. WUNT 131. Tübingen: Mohr/Siebeck, 2000.

———. *Studies in Paul: Theology for the Early Christian Mission*. Minneapolis: Augsburg, 1977.

Das, A. Andrew. *Paul and the Jews*. LPS. Peabody, MA: Hendrickson, 2003.

———. *Solving the Romans Debate*. Minneapolis: Fortress, 2007.

Davids, Peter H. "Why Do We Suffer? Suffering in James and Paul." In *The Missions of James, Peter, and Paul: Tensions in Early Christianity*, edited by Bruce Chilton and Craig Evans, 435–66. NovTSup 115. Leiden: Brill, 2005.

Davidson, Francis. *Pauline Predestination*. The Tyndale New Testament Lecture, 1945. London: Tyndale Press, 1946.

Davies, W. D. *Jewish and Pauline Studies*. Philadelphia: Fortress, 1984.

De Ste. Croix, G. E. M. Why Were the Early Christians Persecuted?" *P&P* 26 (1963) 7–38.

De Villiers, Pieter G. R. "Heroes at Home: Identity, Ethos, and Ethics in 1 Timothy within the Context of the Pastoral Epistles." In *Identity, Ethics, and Ethos in the New Testament*, edited by Jan G. van der Watt and François S. Malan, 357–86. BZNW 141. Berlin: de Gruyter, 2006.

———. "'A Life Worthy of God': Identity and Ethics in the Thessalonian Correspondence." In *Identity, Ethics, and Ethos in the New Testament*, edited by Jan G. van der Watt and Franç[<cedilla]ois S. Malan, 335–55. BZNW 141. Berlin: de Gruyter, 2006.

De Vos, Craig Stephen. *Church and Community Conflicts: The Relationships of the Thessalonian, Corinthian, and Philippian Churches with their Wider Civic Communities.* SBLDS 168. Atlanta: Scholars, 1999.

Delling, Gerhard. "ἀργός, ἀργέω, καταργέω." In *TDNT* 1.451–54.

———. "ἄτακτος (ἀτάκτως), ἀτακτέω." In TDNT 8.47–48.

———. "πληροφορία." In *TDNT* 6.310–11.

———. "στοιχέω, συστοιχέω, στοιχεῖον." In *TDNT* 7.666–87.

DeMaris, R. E., *The Colossian Controversy: Wisdom in Dispute at Colossae.* JSNTSup 96. Sheffield: JSOT Press, 1994.

Denton, D. R. "Hope and Perseverance." *STJ* 34 (1981) 313–20.

Derrett, J. Duncan M. "Cursing Jesus (1 Cor. xii.3) the Jews as Religious 'Persecutors.'" *NTS* 21 (1975) 544–54.

———. "'Handing Over to Satan': An Explanation of 1 Cor 5:1–7." *RIDA* 26 (1979) 11–30.

———. "Paul as Master Builder." *EvQ* 69 (1997) 129–37.

Desjardins, Michel. "Bauer and Beyond: On Recent Scholarly Discussions of αἵρεσιν in the Early Christian Era." *SC* 8 (1991) 65–82.

Dibelius, Martin. "The Isis Initiation in Apuleius and Related Initiatory Rites." In *Conflict at Colossae: A Problem in the Interpretation of Early Christianity, Illustrated by Selected Modern Studies*, edited by Fred O. Francis and Wayne A. Meeks, 61–121. Rev. ed. SBS 4. Missoula, MT: SBL/Scholars, 1975.

———. *An die Thessalonicher I, II, An die Philipper.* HNT 11. Tübingen: Mohr/Siebeck 1925.

Dibelius, Martin, and Hans Conzelmann. *The Pastoral Epistles.* Hermeneia. Philadelphia: Fortress, 1972.

Dobschütz, Ernst von. *Die Thessalonicher-Briefe.* KEK. Göttingen: Vandenhoeck & Ruprecht, 1909.

Dodd, C. H. *The Epistle of Paul to the Romans.* London: Hodder & Stoughton, 1932.

Donaldson, Terence L. *Paul and the Gentiles: Remapping the Apostle's Convictional World.* Minneapolis: Fortress, 1997.

Donfried, Karl P. "Chronology: New Testament." In *ABD* 1.1011–22.

———. "The Cults of Thessalonica and The Thessalonian Correspondence." *NTS* 31 (1985) 336–56.

———. "The Epistolary and Rhetorical Context of 1 Thessalonians 2:1–12." In *The Thessalonians Debate: Methodological Discord or Methodological Synthesis?*, edited by Karl P. Donfried and Johannes Beutler, 31–60. Grand Rapids: Eerdmans, 2000.

———. "False Presuppositions in the Study of Romans." In *The Romans Debate*, edited by Karl P. Donfried, 102–25. Rev. ed. Edinburgh: T. & T. Clark, 1991.

———. "1 Thessalonians, Acts, and the Early Paul." In *The Thessalonian Correspondence*, edited by Raymond F. Collins, 3–26. BETL 87. Leuven: Leuven University Press/Peeters, 1990.

———. "Justification and Last Judgment in Paul." *ZNW* 67 (1976) 90–110.

Donfried, Karl P., and I. Howard Marshall. *The Theology of the Shorter Pauline Letters.* Cambridge: Cambridge University Press, 1999.

Dubois, Jean-Daniel. "Les pastorals, la gnose et l'héréie." *Foi et vie* 94 (1995) 41–48.

Dunn, James D. G. *The Epistles to the Colossians and to Philemon: A Commentary on the Greek Text.* NIGTC. Grand Rapids: Eerdmans, 1996.

———. "Paul: Apostate or Apostle of Israel?" *ZNW* 89 (1998) 256–71.

———. *Romans.* 2 vols. WBC 38A, B. Dallas: Word, 1988.

———. *The Theology of Paul the Apostle.* Grand Rapids: Eerdmans, 1998.

Eckstein, Hans-Joachim. "'Denn Gottes Zorn wird vom Himmel her offenbar warden.': Exegetische Erwägungen zu Röm 1:18." *ZNW* 78 (1987) 74–87.

———. *Der Begriff Syneidesis bei Paulus: Eine neutestamentlich-exegetische Untersuchung zum Gewissensbegriff.* WUNT 2/10. Tübingen: Mohr/Siebeck, 1983.

Ehrman, Bart D. *The New Testament: A Historical Introduction to the Early Christian Writings.* 2nd ed. New York: Oxford University Press, 2000.

Elgvin, Torleif. "'To Master His Own Vessel': 1 Thess 4:4 in Light of New Qumran Evidence." *NTS* 43 (1997) 604–19.

Ellingworth, Paul, and Eugene Albert Nida. *A Handbook on Paul's Letters to the Thessalonians.* UBSHS. New York: United Bible Societies, 1994.

Ellingworth, Paul, and Howard Hatton. *A Handbook on Paul's First Letter to the Corinthians.* UBSHS. New York: United Bible Societies, 1995.

Elliot, N. *The Rhetoric of Romans: Argumentative Constraint and Strategy in Paul's Dialogue with Judaism.* JSNTSup 45. Sheffield: Sheffield Academic, 1990.

Ellis, J. Edward. *Paul and Ancient Views of Sexual Desire: Paul's Sexual Ethics in 1 Thessalonians 4, 1 Corinthians 7 and Romans 1.* LNTS 354. London: T. & T. Clark, 2007.

Ellis, Mark A. "Apostasy and Perseverance in the Pastoral Epistles." ThM thesis, Dallas Theological Seminary, 1988.

Engberg-Pedersen, Troels. "Paul, Virtues, and Vices." In *Paul and the Greco-Roman World: A Handbook*, edited J. Paul Sampley, 608–33. Harrisburg, PA: Trinity, 2003.

Eriksson, Anders. "Fear of Eternal Damnation: *Pathos* Appeal in 1 Corinthians 15 and 16." In *Paul and Pathos*, edited by Thomas H. Olbricht and Jerry L. Sumney, 115–26. SBLSymS 16. Atlanta: SBL, 2001.

Eskola, Timo. *Theodicy and Predestination in Pauline Soteriology.* WUNT 2/100. Tübingen: Mohr/Siebeck, 1998.

Esler, Philip Francis. *Conflict and Identity in Romans: The Social Setting of Paul's Letter.* Minneapolis: Fortress, 2003.

———. *Galatians.* New Testament Readings. London: Routledge, 1998.

Evans, Craig A. *To See and Not Perceive: Isaiah 6.9–10 in Early Jewish and Christian Interpretation.* JSOTSup 64. Sheffield: JSOT Press, 1989.

Fascher, Erich, and Christian Wolff. *Der erste Brief des Paulus an die Korinther.* 2 vols. THKNT 7. Berlin: Evangelische Verlagsanstalt, 1975, 1982.

Faust, Eberhard. *Pax Christi et Pax Caesaris: Religionsgeschichtliche, traditionsgeschichtliche und sozialgeschichtliche Studien zum Epheserbrief.* NovTOA 24. Göttingen: Vandenhoeck & Ruprecht, 1993.

Fee, Gordon D. "Εἰδωλόθυτα Once Again: An Interpretation of 1 Corinthians 8–10." *Biblica* 61 (1980) 172–97.

———. *1 and 2 Timothy, Titus.* NIBCNT 13. Peabody, MA: Hendrickson, 1988.

———. *The First Epistle to the Corinthians.* Grand Rapids: Eerdmans, 1987.

———. *Paul's Letter to the Philippians.* NICNT. Grand Rapids: Eerdmans, 1995.

———. "II Corinthians VI.14—VII.1 and Food Offered to Idols." *NTS* 23 (1977) 140–61.

Feldman, Louis H. *Jew and Gentile in the Ancient World: Attitudes and Interactions from Alexander to Justinian.* Princeton: Princeton University Press, 1993.

Finlan, Stephen. *Problems with Atonement: The Origins of, and Controversy about, the Atonement Doctrine.* Collegeville, MN: Liturgical, 2005.

Fisk, Bruce N. "Eating Meat Offered to Idols: Corinthian Behavior and Pauline Response in 1 Corinthians 8–10 (A Response to Gordon Fee)." *TJ* 10 (1989) 49–70.

———. "Πορνεύειν as Body Violation: The Unique Nature of the Sexual Sin in 1 Corinthians 6.18." *NTS* 42 (1996) 540–58.

Fitzgerald, John T. *Cracks in an Earthen Vessel: An Examination of the Catalogues of Hardships in the Corinthian Correspondence.* SBLDS 99. Atlanta: Scholars, 1988.

Fitzmyer, Joseph A. *The Genesis Apocryphon of Qumran Cave I: A Commentary.* BibOr 18. Rome: Pontifical Biblical Institute, 1966.

———. *Romans: A New Translation with Introduction and Commentary.* AB 33. New York: Doubleday, 1993.

Ford, J. Massyngberde. "Bookshelf on Prostitution," *BTB* 23 (1993) 128–34.

———. "You are God's 'sukkah' (1 Cor. 3.10–17)." *NTS* 21 (1974–75) 139–42.

Forkman, Göran. *The Limits of the Religious Community: Expulsion from the Religious Community within the Qumran Sect, within Rabbinic Judaism, and within Primitive Christianity.* ConBNT 5. Lund: Gleerup, 1972.

Fotopoulos, John. *Food Offered to Idols in Roman Corinth: A Socio-Rhetorical Reconsideration of 1 Corinthians 8:1—11:1.* WUNT 2/151. Tübingen: Mohr/Siebeck, 2003.

Fowl, Stephen E. *Philippians.* THNTC. Grand Rapids: Eerdmans, 2005.

Frame, James Everett. *A Critical and Exegetical Commentary on the Epistles of St. Paul to the Thessalonians.* ICC. Edinburgh: T. & T. Clark, 1979.

Francis, Fred O. "Humility and Angelic Worship in Col 2:18." In *Conflict at Colossae: A Problem in the Interpretation of Early Christianity, Illustrated by Selected Modern Studies,* edited by Fred O. Francis and Wayne A. Meeks, 163–95. Rev. ed. SBS 4. Missoula, MT: SBL/Scholars, 1975.

Fredrickson, David E. "Envious Enemies of the Cross of Christ (Philippians 3:18)." *WW* 28 (2008) 22–28.

———. "Passionless Sex in 1 Thessalonians 4:4–5." *WW* 23 (2003) 23–30.

———. "Paul, Hardships, and Suffering." In *Paul in the Greco-Roman World: A Handbook,* edited by J. Paul Sampley, 172–97. Harrisburg, PA: Trinity, 2003.

Friedrich, Gerhard, Jürgen Becker, and Hans Conzelmann. *Die Briefe an die Galater, Epheser, Philipper, Kolosser, Thessalonicher und Philemon.* NTD 8. Göttingen: Vandenhoeck & Ruprecht, 1990.

Furnish, Victor Paul. *1 Thessalonians, 2 Thessalonians.* ANTC. Nashville: Abingdon, 2007.

———. *II Corinthians.* AB 32A. Garden City, NY: Doubleday, 1984.

Gaca, Kathy L. *The Making of Fornication: Eros, Ethics, and Political Reform in Greek Philosophy and Early Christianity.* HCS 40. Berkeley: University of California Press, 2003.

Gäckle, Volker. *Die Starken und die Schwachen in Korinth und in Rom: Zu Herkunft und Funktion der Antithese in 1 Kor 8,1—11,1 und in Röm 14,1—15,13.* WUNT 2/200. Tübingen: Mohr/Siebeck, 2004.

Gagnon, Robert. "Why the 'Weak' at Rome Cannot Be Non-Christian Jews." *CBQ* 62 (2000) 64–82.

Gallas, Sven. "'Fünfmal vierzig weniger einen...': Die an Paulus vollzogenen Synagogalstrafen nach 2 Kor 11,24." *ZNW* 81 (1990) 178–91.

Gardner, Paul Douglas. *The Gifts of God and the Authentication of a Christian: An Exegetical Study of 1 Corinthians 8—11:1.* Lanham, MD: University Press of America, 1994.

Garland, David E. *Colossians and Philemon.* NIVAC. Grand Rapids: Zondervan, 1998.

———. *1 Corinthians.* BECNT. Grand Rapids: Baker Academic, 2003.

———. *2 Corinthians.* NAC 29. Nashville: Broadman & Holman, 1999.

Garlington, Don B. *Faith, Obedience, and Perseverance: Aspects of Paul's Letter to the Romans.* WUNT 79. Tübingen: Mohr/Siebeck, 1994.

———. *The Obedience of Faith: A Pauline Phrase in Historical Context.* WUNT 2/38. Tübingen: Mohr/Siebeck, 1991.

———. "Role Reversal and Paul's Use of Scripture in Galatians 3.10–13." *JSNT* 65 (1997) 85–121.

———. *Studies in the New Perspective on Paul: Essays and Reviews.* Eugene, OR: Wipf & Stock, 2008.

Gathercole, Simon J. "A Law unto Themselves: The Gentiles in Romans 2.14–15 Revisited." *JSNT* 85 (2002) 27–49.

———. *Where Is Boasting? Early Jewish Soteriology and Paul's Response in Romans 1–5.* Grand Rapids: Eerdmans, 2002.

Gaventa, Beverly Roberts. *First and Second Thessalonians.* Interpretation. Louisville: John Knox, 1998.

———. *From Darkness to Light: Aspects of Conversion in the New Testament.* Philadelphia: Fortress, 1986.

———. "God Handed Them Over: Reading Romans 1:18–32 Apocalyptically." *ABR* 53 (2005) 42–53.

Geoffrion, Timothy C. *The Rhetorical Purpose and the Political and Military Character of Philippians: A Call to Stand Firm.* Lewiston, NY: E. Mellen, 1993.

Georgi, Dieter. *Die Gegner des Paulus im 2: Korintherbrief: Studien zur religiösen Propaganda in der Spätantike.* WMANT 11. Neukischen-Vluyn: Neukierchener, 1964. ET: *The Opponents of Paul in Second Corinthians: A Study of Religious Propoganda in Late Antiquity.* Translated by Harold Attridge et al. Philadelphia: Fortress, 1986.

Giblin, C. H. *The Threat to Faith: An Exegetical and Theological Reexamination of 2 Thessalonians 2.* AnBib 31. Rome: Pontifical Biblical Institute, 1967.

Giesen, H. "σκανδαλίζω *skandalizō*/ σκάνδαλον, ου, τό *skandalon.*" In *EDNT* 3.248–50.

Gignilliat, Mark. *Paul and Isaiah's Servants: Paul's Theological Reading of Isaiah 40–66 in 2 Corinthians 5.14—6.10.* LNTS 330. London: T. & T. Clark, 2007.

Gilliard, Frank D. "Paul and the Killing of the Prophets in 1 Thess 2:15." *NovT* 36 (1994) 259–70.

Gillman, John. "Silas." In *ABD* 6.22–23.

Glancy, Jennifer A. "Obstacles to Slaves' Participation in the Corinthian Church." *JBL* 117 (1998) 481–501.

Gnilka, Joachim. *Der Epheserbrief.* HTKNT. Freiburg: Herder, 1971.

———. *1 Kor. 3.10–15: Ein Schriftzeugnis für das Fegfeuer?: Eine exegetische-historische Untersuchung.* Düsseldor: M. Triltsch, 1955.

———. *Der Kolosserbrief: Auslegung.* HTKNT. Freiburg: Herder, 1991.

———. *Der Philipperbrief: Auslegung.* HTKNT. Freiburg: Herder, 1987.

Goldingay, John E. *Daniel.* WBC 30. Dallas: Word, 1989.

Gooch, Paul W. "'Conscience' in the New Testament." *NTS* 33 (1987) 244–54.

Gooch, Peter D. *Dangerous Food: 1 Corinthians 8–10 in Its Context*. SCJ. Ontario: Wilfrid Laurier University Press, 1993.

———. "Sovereignty and Freedom: Some Pauline Compatibilisms." *SJT* 40 (1987) 531–42.

Goppelt, Leonard. *Typos: Die Typologische Deutung des Alten Testaments im Neuen Anhang Apokalyptik und Typologie bei Paulus*. 2nd ed. Darmstadt: Wissenschaftliche Buchgesellschaft,1969.

Goulder, Michael. "The Pastor's Wolves: Jewish Christian Visionaries behind the Pastoral Epistles." *NovT* 38 (1996) 242–56.

———. *Paul and the Competing Mission in Corinth*. LPS. Peabody, MA: Hendrickson, 2002.

———. *St. Paul versus St. Peter: A Tale of Two Missions*. Louisville: Westminster John Knox, 1995.

Gräbe, Petrus J. "…As Citizens of Heaven Live in a Manner Worthy of the Gospel of Christ." In *Identity, Ethics, and Ethos in the New Testament*, edited by Jan G. van der Watt and François S. Malan, 289–302. BZNW 141. Berlin: de Gruyter, 2006.

Green, Gene L. *The Letters to the Thessalonians*. PNTC. Grand Rapids: Eerdmans, 2002.

Grieb, A. Katherine. *The Story of Romans: A Narrative Defense of God's Righteousness*. Louisville: Westminster John Knox, 2002.

Grindheim, Sigurd. "Apostate Turned Prophet: Paul's Prophetic Self-Understanding and Prophetic Hermeneutic with Special Reference to Galatians 3.10–12." *NTS* 53 (2007) 545–65.

———. "Wisdom for the Perfect: Paul's Challenge to the Corinthian Church (1 Corinthians 2:6–16)." *JBL* 121.4 (2002) 689–709.

Grindheim, Sigurd. *The Crux of Election: Paul's Critique of the Jewish Confidence in the Election of Israel*. WUNT 2/202. Tübingen: Mohr/Siebeck, 2005.

Gundry Volf, Judith M. "Apostasy, Falling Away, Perseverance." In *DPL*, 39–45.

———. *Paul and Perseverance: Staying in and Falling Away*. WUNT 2/37. Louisville: Westminster John Knox, 1990.

Gunther, J. J. *St. Paul's Opponents and Their Background: A Study of Apocalyptic and Jewish Sectarian Teachings*. NovTSup 35. Leiden: Brill, 1973.

Gutbrod, Walter. "ἀνομία." In *TDNT* 4.1085–87.

Hafemann, Scott J. *Paul, Moses and the History of Israel: The Letter/Spirit Contrast and the Argument from Scripture in 2 Corinthians 3*. WUNT 81. Tübingen: Mohr/Siebeck, 1995.

———. "Paul's Use of the Old Testament in 2 Corinthians." *Interpretation* 52 (1998) 246–57.

———. *2 Corinthians*. NIVAC. London: Hodder & Stoughton, 2000.

———. *Suffering and Ministry in the Spirit: Paul's Defense of His Ministry in 2 Corinthians 2:14—3:3*. Grand Rapids: Eerdmans, 1990. Reprint, Carlisle: Paternoster, 2000.

Hallett, Judith P., and Marilyn B. Skinner, editors. *Roman Sexualities*. Princeton: Princeton University Press, 1997.

Hanson, Anthony Tyrrell. "The Apostates: 2 Timothy 2.19–21." In *Studies in the Pastoral Epistles*, 29–41. London: SPCK, 1968.

———. "Eve's Transgression: 1 Timothy 2:13–15." In *Studies in the Pastoral Epistles*, 65–77. London: SPCK, 1968.

———. *The Pastoral Letters: Commentary on the First and Second Letters to Timothy and the Letter to Titus*. Cambridge Bible Commentary: New English Bible. Cambridge: Cambridge University Press, 1966.

———. *Studies in the Pastoral Epistles*. London: SPCK, 1968.

―――. "The Use of the Old Testament in the Pastoral Letters." *IBS* 3 (1981) 203–19.

Harink, Douglas. *Paul among the Postliberals: Pauline Theology beyond Christendom and Modernity.* Grand Rapids: Brazos, 2003.

Harris, Murray J. *Colossians & Philemon.* EGGNT. Grand Rapids: Eerdmans, 1991.

―――. *The Second Epistle to the Corinthians: A Commentary on the Greek Text.* NIGTC. Grand Rapids: Eerdmans; Milton Keynes: Paternoster, 2005.

Harrison, James R. *Paul's Language of Grace in Its Greco-Roman Context.* WUNT 2/172. Tübingen: Mohr/Siebeck, 2003.

Hartman, Lars. *Prophecy Interpreted: The Formation of Some Jewish Apocalyptic Texts and of the Eschatological Discourse in Mark 13 Par.* ConBNT 1. Lund: Gleerup, 1966.

Harvey, A. E. "Forty Strokes Save One: Social Aspects of Judaizing and Apostasy." In *Alternative Approaches to New Testament Study,* edited by A. E. Harvey, 79–96. London: SPCK, 1985.

―――. "The Opposition to Paul." In *The Galatians Debate: Contemporary Issues in Rhetorical and Historical Interpretation,* edited by Mark D. Nanos, 321–33. Peabody, MA: Hendrickson, 2002.

Hasel, Gerhard F. *The Remnant: The History and Theology of the Remnant Idea from Genesis to Isaiah.* Andrews University Monographs 5. Berrien Springs, MI: Andrews University Press, 1972.

Haufe, G. "Gnostische Irrlehre und ihre Abwehr in den Pastoralbriefen." In *Gnosis und Neues Testament,* edited by Karl-Wolfgang Tröger, 325–39. Gütersloh: Mohn, 1973.

Hawthorne, Gerald F., and Ralph P. Martin. *Philippians.* WBC 43. Waco, TX: Word, 2004.

Hay, David M. *Colossians.* ANTC. Nashville: Abingdon, 2000.

Hays, Richard B. "The Conversion of the Imagination: Scripture and Eschatology in 1 Corinthians." *NTS* 45 (1999) 391–412.

―――. *Echoes of Scripture in the Letters of Paul.* New Haven, CT: Yale University Press, 1989.

―――. *The Faith of Jesus Christ: The Narrative Substructure of Galatians 3:1—4:11.* Grand Rapids: Eerdmans, 2002.

―――. *First Corinthians.* Interpretation. Louisville: John Knox, 1997.

―――. *The Moral Vision of the New Testament: Community, Cross, New Creation: A Contemporary Introduction to New Testament Ethics.* San Francisco: HarperSanFrancisco, 1996.

Heckel, Ulrich. "Die Einheit der Kirche im Johannesevangelium und im Epheserbrief: ein Vergleich der ekklesiologischen Strukturen." In *Kontexte des Johannesevangeliums: Das vierte Evangelium in religions- und traditionsgeschichtlicher Perspektive,* edited by Jörg Frey and Udo Schnelle, 613–40. WUNT 175. Tübingen: Mohr/Siebeck, 2004.

Heil, John Paul. *Ephesians: Empowerment to Walk in Love for the Unity of All in Christ.* SBibL 13. Atlanta: SBL, 2007.

―――. *The Rhetorical Role of Scripture in 1 Corinthians.* SBibL 15. Atlanta: SBL, 2005.

Hengel, Martin. *The Zealots: Investigations into the Jewish Freedom Movement in the Period from Herod I until 70 A.D.* Edinburgh: T. & T. Clark, 1976.

Hengel, Martin, and Anna Maria Schwemer. *Paul between Damascus and Antioch: The Unknown Years.* Louisville: Westminster John Knox, 1997.

Héring, Jean. *The Second Epistle of Saint Paul to the Corinthians.* Translated by A. W. Heathcote and P. J. Allcock. London: Epworth, 1967.

Herms, Ronald. "'Being Saved without Honor': A Conceptual Link between 1 Corinthians 3 and 1 Enoch 50?" *JSNT* 29.2 (2006) 187–210.

Herntrich, Volkmar, and Gottlob Schrenk, "λεῖμμα, ὑπόλειμμα, καταλείπω (κατά-, περί-, διάλειμμα).» In *TDNT* 4.193–214.

Hock, Roland F. *The Social Context of Paul's Ministry: Tentmaking and Apostleship.* Philadelphia: Fortress, 1980.

Hoehner, Harold W. *Ephesians: An Exegetical Commentary.* Grand Rapids: Baker Academic, 2002.

Hofius, Otfried. "'Erwählt vor Grundlegung der Welt' (Eph 1, 4)." *ZNW* 62 (1971) 123–28.

———. "'Gott hat unter uns aufgerichtet das Wort von der Versöhnung' (2 Kor 5₁₉)." *ZNW* 71 (1980) 3–20.

———. "The Lord's Supper and the Lord's Supper Tradition: Reflection on 1 Corintians 11:23b–25." In *One Loaf, One Cup: Ecumenical Studies of 1 Cor 11 and Other Eucharistic Texts,* edited by Otto Knoch and Ben F. Meyer, 75–115. NGS 6. Macon: Mercer University Press, 1993.

Holladay, C. R. "Paul's Opponents in Phil. 3." *ResQ* 3 (1969) 77–90.

Holland, Glenn S. *The Tradition that You Received from Us: 2 Thessalonians in the Pauline Tradition.* HUT 24. Tübingen: Mohr/Siebeck, 1988.

Holmberg, Bengt. "Jewish *versus* Christian Identity in the Early Church?" *RB* 105 (1998) 397–425.

Holtz, Traugott. *Der Erste Brief an die Thessalonicher.* EKKNT 13. Zürich: Benziger, 1986.

Hooker, Morna D. "Were There False Teachers in Colossae?" In *Christ and Spirit in the New Testament: In Honor of C.F.D. Moule,* edited by Barnabas Lindars and Stephen S. Smalley, 315–31. Cambridge: Cambridge University Press, 1973.

Horbury, William. "Extirpation and Excommunication." *VT* 35 (1985) 13–38.

———. "1 Thessalonians ii.3 as Rebutting the Charge of False Prophecy." *JTS* 33 (1982) 492–508.

Horrell, David G. "Idol-Food, Idolatry and Ethics in Paul." In *Idolatry: False Worship in the Bible: Early Judaism and Christianity,* edited by Stephen C. Barton, 120–40. London: T. & T. Clark, 2007.

———. *An Introduction to the Study of Paul.* 2nd ed. London: T. & T. Clark, 2006.

———. Review of *After Paul Left Corinth* by Bruce Winter. *JTS* 53 (2002) 660–65.

———. *The Social Ethos of the Corinthian Correspondence: Interests and Ideology from 1 Corinthians to 1 Clement.* SNTW. Edinburgh: T. & T. Clark, 1996.

———. "Theological Principle or Christological Praxis? Pauline Ethics in 1 Corinthians 8.1—11.1." *JSNT* 6 7 (1997) 83–114.

Horrell, David G., and Edward Adams. "The Scholarly Quest for Paul's Church at Corinth: A Critical Survey." In *Christianity at Corinth: The Quest for the Pauline Church,* edited by Horrell and Adams, 1–43. Louisville: Westminster John Knox, 2004.

Horsley, Richard A. *1 Corinthians.* ANTC. Nashville: Abingdon, 1998.

Houtman, Cornelius. *Exodus.* 4 Vols. HCOT. Kampen: Kok, 1993–2002.

Hübner, Hans. *An Philemon, an die Kolosser, an die Epheser.* HNT 12. Tübingen: Mohr/Siebeck, 1997.

———. *Vetus Testamentum,* vol. 2: *Corpus Paulinum.* Göttingen: Vandenhoeck & Ruprecht, 1997.

Hughes, Frank W. *Early Christian Rhetoric and 2 Thessalonians.* JSNTSup 30. Sheffield: JSOT Press, 1989.

———. "The Rhetoric of 1 Thessalonians," In *The Thessalonian Correspondence,* edited by Raymond F. Collins, 94–116. BETL 87. Leuven: Leuven University Press/Peeters, 1990.

Hughes, Philip E. *Paul's Second Epistle to the Corinthians: The English Text with Introduction, Exposition and Notes.* NICNT. Grand Rapids: Eerdmans, 1967.

Hurd, John Coolidge. *The Origin of 1 Corinthians.* London: SPCK; New York: Seabury, 1965.

Hurtado, Larry W. "Pre-70 Jewish Opposition to Christ-Devotion." *JTS* 50 (1999) 35–58.

Huther, Joh. Ed, Gottlieb Lünemann, David Hunter, Maurice J. Evans, and Timothy Dwight. *Critical and Exegetical Handbook to the Epistles to Timothy and Titus.* Peabody, MA: Hendrickson, 1983.

Jacobs, Paul, and Hartmut Krienke. "Foreknowledge, Providence, Predestination." In *NIDNTT* 1.692–97.

Jeal, Roy. R. "The Rhetoric of Resistance: Opposition to the Irrelevant Imperial Powers in Colossians." Paper presented at the annual Society of Biblical Literature conference, Boston, November 23, 2008.

Jensen, Joseph. "Does *Porneia* Mean Fornication? A Critique of Bruce Malina," *NovT* 20 (1978) 165–66.

Jervis, L. Ann. *At the Heart of the Gospel: Suffering in the Earliest Christian Message.* Grand Rapids: Eerdmans, 2007.

———. *The Purpose of Romans: A Comparative Letter Structure Investigation.* JSNTSup 55. Sheffield: JSOT Press, 1991.

Jewett, Robert K. "The Agitators and the Galatian Congregation." In *The Galatians Debate: Contemporary Issues in Rhetorical and Historical Interpretation,* edited by Mark D. Nanos, 334–47. Peabody, MA: Hendrickson, 2002.

———. *A Chronology of Paul's Life.* Philadelphia: Fortress, 1979.

———. "Conflicting Movements in the Early Church as Reflected in Philippians." *NovT* 12 (1970) 362–90.

———. "Following the Argument of Romans." *WW* 6 (1986) 382–89.

———. *Romans.* Hermeneia. Philadelphia: Fortress, 2006.

———. *The Thessalonian Correspondence: Pauline Rhetoric and Millenarian Piety.* FF. Philadelphia: Fortress, 1986.

Jocz, Jakób. *A Theology of Election: Israel and the Church.* London: SPCK, 1958.

Johnson, Luke Timothy. "II Timothy and the Polemic against False Teachers." *JRelS* 6–7 (1978–79) 1–26.

Judge, E. A. "The Decrees of Caesar at Thessalonica." *RTR* 30 (1971) 1–7.

Kaminsky, Joel S. *Yet I Loved Jacob: Reclaiming the Biblical Concept of Election.* Nashville: Abingdon, 2007.

Karris, Robert J. "The Background and Significance of the Polemic of the Pastoral Epistles." *JBL* 92 (1973) 549–64.

———. "Romans 14:1—15:13 and the Occasion of Romans." In *The Romans Debate,* edited by Karl P. Donfried, 102–25. Rev. ed. Edinburgh: T. & T. Clark, 1991.

Käsemann, Ernst. *Commentary on Romans.* Translated and edited by Geoffrey W. Bromiley. Grand Rapids: Eerdmans, 1980.

———. "Die Legitimität des Apostels." *ZNW* 41 (1942) 33–71.

———. "The Righteousness of God in Paul." In *New Testament Questions for Today,* 168–82. NTL. London: SCM, 1969.

Keener, Craig S. *1–2 Corinthians.* NCBC. Cambridge: Cambridge University Press, 2005.

———. *Paul, Women & Wives: Marriage and Women's Ministry in the Letters of Paul.* Peabody, MA: Hendrickson, 1992.

Kennedy, George Alexander. *New Testament Interpretation through Rhetorical Criticism.* SR. Chapel Hill: University of North Carolina Press, 1984.

Ker, Donald P. "Paul and Apollos—Colleagues or Rivals?" *JSNT* 77 (2000) 75–97.

Kiley, Mark. *Colossians as Pseudepigraphy.* The Biblical Seminar 4. Sheffield: JSOT Press, 1986.

Kilpatrick, G. D. "Βλέπετε: Philippians 3.2." In *In Memoriam Paul Kahle,* edited by Matthew Black and Georg Fohrer, 146–48. FZAW 103. Berlin: Topelmann, 1968.

Kim, J. H. *The Significance of Clothing Imagery in the Pauline Corpus.* JSNTSup 268. London: T. & T. Clark, 2004.

Kim, Johann D. *God, Israel, and the Gentiles: Rhetoric and Situation in Romans 9–11.* SBLDS 176. Atlanta: SBL, 2000.

Kim, Seyoon. *The Origin of Paul's Gospel.* WUNT 2/4. 2nd ed. Tübingen: Mohr/Siebeck, 1984.

Kittel, Gerhard. "δοκέω, δόξα, δοξάζω, συνδοξάζω, ἔνδοξος, ἐνδοξάζω, παράδοξος." In *TDNT* 2.232–55.

Klauck, Hans-Josef. *Herrenmahl Und Hellenistischer Kult: Eine religionsgeschichtliche Untersuchung zum ersten Korinthebrief.* NA 15. Münster: Aschendorff, 1982.

———. *2 Korintherbrief.* NEchtB 8. Würzburg: Echter, 1994.

Klein, William W. *The New Chosen People: A Corporate View of Election.* Grand Rapids: Zondervan, 1990.

Klijn, A. F. J. "Paul's Opponents in Philippians iii." *NovT* 7 (1964) 278–84.

Knibb, Michael A. *The Qumran Community.* Cambridge Commentaries on Writings of the Jewish and Christian World, 200 BC to AD 200, vol. 2. Cambridge: Cambridge University Press, 1987.

Knight, George W. *The Pastoral Epistles: A Commentary on the Greek Text.* NIGTC. Grand Rapids: Eerdmans, 1992.

Koch, Dietrich-Alex. *Die Schrift als Zeuge des Evangeliums: Untersuchungen zur Verwendung und zum Verständnis der Schrift bei Paulus.* BHT 69. Tübingen: Mohr/Siebeck, 1986.

Koester, Helmut. *Ephesos: Metropolis of Asia.* HTS 41. Valley Forge, PA: Trinity, 1995.

Kondradt, Matthias. "'Eidenai ekaston hymōn to eautou skeuos ktasthai...': zu Paulus' sexualethischer Weisung in 1 Thess 4,4f." *ZNW* 92 (2001) 128–35.

———. *Gericht und Gemeinde: Eine Studie zur Bedeutung und Funktion von Gerichtsaussagen im Rahmen der paulinischen Ekklesiologie und Ethik im 1 Thess und 1 Kor.* BZNW 117. Berlin: de Gruyter, 2003.

Koperski, Veronica. *What Are They Saying about Paul and the Law?* New York: Paulist, 2001.

Köstenberger, Andreas J., and Peter T. O'Brien. *Salvation to the Ends of the Earth: A Biblical Theology of Mission.* NSBT 11. Downers Grove, IL: InterVarsity, 2001.

Krentz, Edgar. "Through a Lens: Theology and Fidelity in 2 Thessalonians." In *Pauline Theology,* edited by Jouette M. Bassler, 1.52–62. SBLSymS 4. Minneapolis: Fortress, 1991.

Kroeger, Richard Clark, and Catherine Clark Kroeger. *I Suffer Not a Woman: Rethinking 1 Timothy 2:11–15 in Light of Ancient Evidence.* Grand Rapids: Baker, 1992.

Kruse, C. G. "The Offender and the Offence in 2 Corinthians 2:5 and 7:12." *EvQ* 60 (1988) 129–39.

Kuck, David W. *Judgment and Community Conflict: Paul's Use of Apocalyptic Judgment Language in 1 Corinthians 3:5—4:5.* NovTSup 66. Leiden: Brill, 1992.

Kümmel, Werner Georg. *Introduction to the New Testament.* NTL. London: SCM, 1977.

Kuula, Kari. *Paul's Polemical Treatment of the Law in Galatians*. Vol. 1 of *The Law, the Covenant and God's Plan*. SESJ 72. Helsinki: Finnish Exegetical Society; Göttingen: Vandenhoeck & Ruprecht, 1999.

Lambrecht, Jan. *Second Corinthians*. SP 8. Collegeville, MN: Liturgical, 1999.

———. "'Strength in Weakness': A Reply to Scott B. Andrews' Exegesis of 2 Cor 11.23b–33." *NTS* 43 (1997) 285–90.

Lampe, G. W. H. "Church Discipline and the Epistles to the Corinthians." In *Christian History and Interpretation: Studies Presented to John Knox*, edited W. R. Farmer, C. F. D. Moule, and Richard R. Niebuhr, 337–61. Cambridge: Cambridge University Press, 1967.

Lampe, Peter. "Das korinthisches Herrenmahl im Schnittpunkt hellenistisch Mahl-praxis und paulinischer Theologia Crucis (1 Kor 11.17–34)." *ZNW* 82 (1991) 183–213.

Lane, William L. "1 Tim. IV 1–3. An Early Instance of Over-Realized Eschatology?" *NTS* 11 (1965) 164–67.

Lang, Friedrich. *Die Briefe an die Korinther*. NTD 7. Göttingen: Vandenhoeck & Ruprecht, 1986.

Lea, Thomas D., and Hayne P. Griffin Jr. *1, 2 Timothy, Titus*. NAC 34. Nashville: Broadman, 1992.

Lightfoot, Joseph Barber. "The Colossian Heresy." n *Conflict at Colossae: A Problem in the Interpretation of Early Christianity, Illustrated by Selected Modern Studies*, edited by Fred O. Francis and Wayne A. Meeks, 13–59. Rev. ed. SBS 4. Missoula, MT: SBL/Scholars, 1975.

———. *Saint Paul's Epistles to the Colossians and to Philemon: A Revised Text with Introductions, Notes, and Dissertations*. Grand Rapids: Zondervan, 1959.

Lincoln, Andrew T. *Ephesians*. WBC 42. Dallas: Word, 1990.

———. *The Letter to the Colossians*. In *The New Interpreter's Bible*, vol. 6. Nashville: Abingdon, 2000.

Lincoln, Andrew T., and A. J. M. Wedderburn. *The Theology of the Later Pauline Letters*. NTT. Cambridge: Cambridge University Press, 1993.

Lindars, Barnabas. *New Testament Apologetic*. Philadelphia: Westminster, 1961.

Lindemann, Andreas. *Der Epheserbrief*. ZBK 8. Zürich: Theologischer, 1985.

———. *Der Kolosserbrief*. ZBK 10. Zürich: Theologischer, 1983.

Lock, Walter. *A Critical and Exegetical Commentary on the Pastoral Epistles: (I & II Timothy and Titus)*. ICC. Edinburgh: T. & T. Clark, 1989.

Lodge, John G. *Romans 9–11: A Reader-Response Analysis*. University of South Florida International Studies in Formative Christianity and Judaism 6. Atlanta: Scholars, 1996.

Loh, I-Jin. "A Study of an Early Christian Hymn in II Tim. 2:11–13." ThD diss., Princeton Theological Seminary, 1968.

Loh, I-Jin, and Eugene Albert Nida. *A Handbook on Paul's Letter to the Philippians*. UBSHS 19. New York: United Bible Societies, 1995.

Lohmeyer, Ernst, and Werner Schmauch. *Die Briefe an die Philipper, an die Kolosser und an Philemon*. KEK 9. Göttingen: Vandenhoeck & Ruprecht, 1964.

Lohse, Eduard. *Colossians and Philemon*. Hermeneia. Philadelphia: Fortress, 1971.

Long, Frederick J. *Ancient Rhetoric and Paul's Apology: The Compositional Unity of 2 Corinthians*. SNTSMS 131. Cambridge: Cambridge University Press, 2004.

———. "Ephesians: Paul's Political Theology in Greco-Roman Political Context." In *Christian Origins and Classical Culture: Social and Literary Contexts for the New Testament*, eEdited by S. E. Porter and A. W. Pitts. NTHC. Leiden: Brill, forthcoming.

Longenecker, Bruce W. *The Triumph of Abraham's God: The Transformation of Identity in Galatians*. Nashville: Abingdon; Edinburgh: T. & T. Clark, 1998.

Longenecker, Richard N. *Galatians*. WBC 41. Dallas: Word, 1990.

———. *Paul: Apostle of Liberty*. New York: Harper & Row, 1964.

Lopez, René. "Does the Vice List in 1 Corinthians 6:9–10 Describe Believers or Unbelievers?" *BSac* 164 (2007) 59–73.

Löverstam, Evald. *Spiritual Wakefulness in the New Testament*. Translated by W. F. Salisbury. Lunds Universitets Årsskrif 55. Lund: Gleerup, 1963.

Lüdemann, Gerd. *Opposition to Paul in Jewish Christianity*. Translated by M. Eugene Boring. Minneapolis: Fortress, 1989.

Lührmann, Dieter. *Galatians*. Translated by O. C. Dean. CC. Minneapolis: Fortress, 1992.

Lütgert, Wilhelm. *Die Vollkommenen im Philipperbrief und die Enthusiasten in Thessalonich*. BFCT 13. Gütersloh: Bertelsmann, 1909.

Luz, Ulrich. *Matthew 21–28*. Hermeneia. Minneapolis: Fortress, 2005.

———. "Paul as Mystic." In *The Holy Spirit and Christian Origins: Essays in Honor of James D. G. Dunn*, edited by Graham N. Stanton et al., 131–43. Grand Rapids: Eerdmans, 2004.

MacDonald, Margaret Y. *Colossians and Ephesians*. SP 17. Collegeville, MN: Liturgical, 2008.

———. *The Pauline Churches: A Socio-Historical Study of Institutionalization in the Pauline and Deutero-Pauline Writings*. SNTSMS 60. Cambridge: Cambridge University Press, 1988.

Maier, Gerhard. *Mensch und freier Wille: Nach der jüdischen Religionsparteien zwischen Ben Sira und Paulus*. WUNT 12. Tübingen: Mohr/Siebeck, 1971.

Malherbe, Abraham J. "'Gentle as a Nurse': The Cynic Background to 1 Thess. 2." *NovT* 12 (1970) 203–17.

———. *The Letters to the Thessalonians: A New Translation with Introduction and Commentary*. AB 32B. New York: Doubleday, 2000.

Malina, Bruce J. "Does *Porneia* mean Fornication?" *NovT* 14 (1972) 10–17.

Malina, Bruce J., and Jerome H. Neyrey. "First-Century Personality: Dyadic, Not Individual." In *The Social World of Luke-Acts: Models for Interpretation*, edited by Jerome H. Neyrey, 67–96. Peabody, MA: Hendrickson, 1991.

Malina, Bruce J., and John J. Pilch. *Social-Science Commentary on the Letters of Paul*. Minneapolis: Fortress, 2006.

Marshall, I. Howard. *A Critical and Exegetical Commentary on the Pastoral Epistles*. ICC. Edinburgh: T. & T. Clark, 1999.

———. "Election and Calling to Salvation in 1 and 2 Thessalonians." In *The Thessalonian Correspondence*, edited by Raymond F. Collins, 259–76. BETL 87. Leuven: Leuven University Press/Peeters, 1990.

———. *1 and 2 Thessalonians*. NCB. Grand Rapids: Eerdmans, 1983.

———. *Kept by the Power of God: A Study of Perseverance and Falling Away*. 3rd ed. Carlisle: Paternoster, 1995.

———. "Orthodoxy and Heresy in Earlier Christianity." *Themelios* 2 (1976) 5–14.

Marshall, Peter. *Enmity in Corinth: Social Conventions in Paul's Relations with the Corinthians*. WUNT 2/23. Tübingen: Mohr/Siebeck, 1987.

Martin, Dale B. *The Corinthian Body*. New Haven, CT: Yale University Press, 1995.

———. "Paul without Passion: On Paul's Rejection of Desire in Sex and Marriage." In *Constructing Early Christians Families: Family as Social Reality and Metaphor*, edited by Halvor Moxnes, 201–15. New York: Routledge, 1997.

————. *Slavery as Salvation: The Metaphor of Slavery in Pauline Christianity*. New Haven, CT: Yale University Press, 1990.

Martin, Ralph P. *Ephesians, Colossians, and Philemon*. Interpretation. Atlanta: John Knox, 1991.

————. *2 Corinthians*. WBC 40. Waco, TX: Word, 1986.

Martin, Troy W. "Apostasy to Paganism: The Rhetorical Stasis of the Galatian Controversy." *JBL* 114 (1995) 437–61.

————. *By Philosophy and Empty Deceit: Colossians as Response to a Cynic Critique*. JSNTSup 118. Sheffield: Sheffield Academic, 1996.

Martyn, J. Louis. "Epilogue: An Essay in Pauline Meta-Ethics." In *Divine and Human Agency in Paul and His Cultural Environment*, edited by John M. G. Barclay and Simon J. Gathercole, 173–83. LNTS 335. London: T. & T. Clark, 2006.

————. *Galatians: A New Translation with Introduction and Commentary*. AB 33A New York: Doubleday, 1997.

Matera, Frank J. *Galatians*. SP 9. Collegeville, MN: Liturgical, 1992.

————. *II Corinthians: A Commentary*. NTL. Louisville: Westminster John Knox, 2003.

Matthews, Victor H. "The Unwanted Gift: Implications of Obligatory Gift Giving in Ancient Israel." *Semeia* 87 (1999) 91–104.

McEleney, Neil J. "The Vice Lists of the Pastoral Epistles." *CBQ* 36 (1974) 203–19.

McKnight, Scot. *Galatians*. NIVAC. Grand Rapids: Zondervan, 1995.

Meade, David G. *Pseudonymity and Canon: An Investigation into the Relationship of Authorship and Authority in Jewish and Earliest Christian Tradition*. WUNT 39. Grand Rapids: Eerdmans, 1986.

Mearns, Christopher L. "The Identity of Paul's Opponents in Phillipi." *NTS* 33 (1987) 194–204.

Meeks, Wayne A. *The First Urban Christians: The Social World of the Apostle Paul*. New Haven, CT: Yale University Press, 1983.

————. "In One Body: The Unity of Humankind in Colossians and Ephesians." In *God's Christ and His People: Studies in Honour of Nils Alstrup Dahl*, edited by Jacob Jervell and Wayne A. Meeks, 209–211. Oslo: Universitetsforglaget, 1977.

Melick, Richard R. *Philippians, Colossians, Philemon*. NAC 32. Nashville: Broadman, 1991.

Menken, M. J. J. *2 Thessalonians*. NTR. New York: Routledge, 1994.

Merk, Otto. "1 Thessalonians 2:1–12: An Exegetical-Theological Study." In *The Thessalonians Debate: Methodological Discord or Methodological Synthesis?*, edited by Karl P. Donfried and Johannes Beutler, 89–113. Grand Rapids: Eerdmans, 2000.

Merkel, Helmut. *Die Pastoralbriefe: Übersetzt und erklärt*. NTD. 9 Göttingen: Vandenhoeck & Ruprecht, 1991.

Merklein, Helmut. "Die Bedeutung des Kreuzestodes Christi für die paulinische Gerechtigkeits und Gesetzesthematik." In *Studien zum Jesus und Paulus*, 1:1–106. WUNT 43. Tübingen: Mohr/Siebeck, 1987.

————. *Der erste Brief an die Korinther*. OTK NT 7. Gütersloh: Gütersloher Mohn, 1992.

Metzger, Bruce M. *A Textual Commentary on the Greek New Testament*. 2nd ed. Stuttgart: Deutsche Bibelgesellschaft/United Bible Societies, 1994.

Meurer, Siegfried. *Das Recht im Dienst der Versöhnung und des Friedens*. ATANT 63. Zürich: Theologischer, 1972.

Meyer, Ben F. "Election-Historical Thinking in Romans 9–11, and Ourselves." *Ex Auditu* 4 (1988) 1–7.

———. "The Expiation Motif in the Eucharistic Words: A Key to the History of Jesus?" In *One Loaf, One Cup: Ecumenical Studies of 1 Cor 11 and Other Eucharistic Texts*, edited by Otto Knoch and Ben F. Meyer, 11–33. NGS 6. Macon: Mercer University Press, 1993.

Meyer, L. V. "Remnant." In *ABD*, 5.699–71.

Michel, Otto. *Der Brief an die Römer*. Göttingen: Vandenhoeck & Ruprecht, 1978.

———. "κύων, κυνάριον." In *TDNT* 3.1101–04.

———. "φιλοσοφία,φιλόσοφος." In *TDNT* 9.172–88.

Miller, James C. *The Obedience of Faith: The Eschatological People of God, and the Purpose of Romans*. SBLDS 177. Atlanta: SBL, 2000.

Miller, James D. *The Pastoral Letters as Composite Documents*. SNTSMS 93. Cambridge: Cambridge University Press, 1997.

Minear, Paul S. *The Obedience of Faith: The Purposes of Paul in the Epistle* SBT 2/19. London: SCM, 1971.

Minn, Herbert R. *The Thorn that Remained: Materials for the Study of S. Paul's Thorn in the Flesh: 2 Corinthians XII.vv.1–10*. Auckland: Institute Press, 1972.

Mitchell, Margaret M. "1 and 2 Thessalonians." In *The Cambridge Companion to St. Paul*, edited by James D. G. Dunn, 51–63. CCR. Cambridge: Cambridge University Press, 2003.

———. *Paul and the Rhetoric of Reconciliation: An Exegetical Investigation of the Language and Composition of 1 Corinthians*. HUT 28. Tübingen: Mohr/Siebeck; Louisville: Westminster John Knox, 1991.

———. "Paul's Letters to Corinth: The Interpretative Intertwining of Literary and Historical Reconstruction." In *Urban Religion in Roman Corinth: Interdisciplinary Approaches*, edited by Daniel N. Schowalter and Steven J. Friesen, 307–38. HTS 53. Harvard: Harvard University Press, 2005.

———. Review of *The Letters to the Thessalonians*, by Abraham Malherbe. *RBL* 9 (2004) 1–12.

Moo, Douglas J. *The Epistle to the Romans*. NICNT. Grand Rapids: Eerdmans, 1996.

Moore, George Foot. *Judaism in the First Centuries of the Christian Era: The Age of the Tannaim*. 3 vols. Cambridge, MA: Harvard University Press, 1966.

Moritz, Thorsten. *A Profound Mystery: The Use of the Old Testament in Ephesians*. NovTSup 85. Leiden: Brill, 1996.

Morland, Kjell Arne. *The Rhetoric of Curse in Galatians: Paul Confronts Another Gospel*. Emory Studies in Early Christianity 5. Atlanta: Scholars, 1995.

Morris, Leon. *The First and Second Epistles to the Thessalonians*. NICNT. Grand Rapids: Eerdmans, 1991.

Moule, C. F. D. "The Judgment Theme in the Sacraments." In *The Background of the New Testament and Its Eschatology: In Honour of Charles Harold Dodd*, edited by W. D. Davies and David Daube, 464–81. Cambridge: Cambridge University Press, 1956.

———. "'The New Life' in Colossians 3:1–17." *RevExp* 70 (1973) 481–93.

Mounce, William D. *Pastoral Epistles*. WBC 46. Waco: Word, 2000.

Muddiman, John. *The Epistle to the Ephesians*. BNTC. New York: Continuum, 2001.

Müller, Jac. J. *The Epistles of Paul to the Philippians and to Philemon*. NICNT. Grand Rapids: Eerdmans, 1955.

Müller, Karlheinz. *Anstoss und Gericht. Eine Studie zum jüdischen Hintergrund des paulinischen Skandalon-Begriffs*. SANT 19. Munich: Kösel, 1969.

Murphy-O'Connor, Jerome. "Corinthian Slogans in 1 Cor. 6:12–20." *CBQ* 40 (1978) 391–96.

———. *Paul: A Critical Life.* Oxford: Clarendon, 1996.

———. *St. Paul's Ephesus: Texts and Archaeology.* Collegeville, MN: Liturgical, 2008.

———. *St. Paul's Corinth: Texts and Archaeology.* Good News Studies 6. Wilmington, DE. M. Glazier, 1983.

———. *The Theology of the Second Letter to the Corinthians.* NTT. Cambridge: Cambridge University Press, 1991.

Myllykoski, Matti. "James the Just in History and Tradition: Perspectives of Past and Present Scholarship (Part 1)." *CBR* 5 (2006) 73–122.

Nanos, Mark D. "'Intruding Spies' and 'Pseudo-Brethren': The Jewish Intra-Group Politics of Paul's Jerusalem Meeting (Gal 2:1–10)." In *Paul and His Opponents*, edited by Stanley E. Porter, 59–98. PS 2. Leiden: Brill, 2005.

———. "What Was at Stake in Peter's 'Eating with Gentiles' at Antioch?" In *The Galatians Debate: Contemporary Issues in Rhetorical and Historical Interpretation*, edited by Mark D. Nanos, 282–318. Peabody, MA: Hendrickson, 2002.

———. *The Irony of Galatians: Paul's Letter in First-Century Context.* Minneapolis: Fortress, 2002.

———. *The Mystery of Romans: The Jewish Context of Paul's Letter.* Minneapolis: Fortress, 1996.

———. "Paul's *Reversal* of Jews Calling Gentiles 'Dogs' (Philippians 3:2): 1600 Years of an Ideological Tale Wagging an Exegetical Dog?" *BibInt* 17 (2009) 448–82.

Neufeld, Thomas R. *Ephesians.* Believers Church Bible Commentary. Scottdale, PA: Herald, 2002.

Newton, Derek. *Deity and Diet: The Dilemma of Sacrificial Food in Corinth.* JSNTSup 169. Sheffield: Sheffield Academic, 1998.

Neyrey, Jerome H. *Paul, in Other Words: A Cultural Reading of His Letters.* Louisville: Westminster John Knox, 1990.

Nicholl, Colin R. *From Hope to Despair in Thessalonica: Situating 1 and 2 Thessalonians.* SNTSMS 126. Cambridge: Cambridge University Press, 2004.

Nielsen, Charles M. "Scripture in the Pastoral Epistles." *PRSt* 7 (1980) 4–23.

Nolland, John. *Luke.* 3 vols. WBC 35A, B, C. Dallas: Word, 1989, 1993.

Oakes, Peter. *Philippians: From People to Letter.* SNTSMS 110. Cambridge: Cambridge University Press, 2001.

O'Brien, Peter T. "Ephesians 1: An Unusual Introduction to a New Testament Letter." *NTS* 25 (1978–79) 504–16.

———. *The Letter to the Ephesians.* PNTC. Grand Rapids: Eerdmans, 1999.

———. "Was Paul a Covenantal Nomist?" In *Justification and Variegated Nomism*, edited by D. A. Carson, Peter T. O'Brien, and Mark A. Seifrid, 2.249–96. WUNT 181. Tübingen: Mohr/Siebeck; Grand Rapids: Baker Academic, 2004.

Oberlinner, Lorenz. *Die Pastoralbriefe, erste Folge: Kommentar zum Ersten Timotheusbrief.* HTKNT 11.2. Freiburg: Herder, 1994.

———. *Der Pastoralbriefe, zweite Folge: Kommentar zum Zweiten Timotheusbrief.* HTKNT 11.2. Freiburg: Herder, 1995.

———. *Colossians, Philemon.* WBC 44. Waco, TX: Word, 1982.

Oepke, Albrecht. "ἀπατάω, ἐξαπατάω, ἀπάτη." In *TDNT* 1.384–85.

———. "ἀπόλλυμι, ἀπώλεια, Ἀπολλύων." In *TDNT* 1.394–97.

Omanson, Roger L., and John Ellington. *A Handbook on Paul's Second Letter to the Corinthians.* UBSHS. New York: United Bible Societies, 1993.

Oostendorp, D. W. *Another Jesus: A Gospel of Jewish-Christian Superiority in II Corinthians.* Kampen: Kok, 1967.

Oropeza, B. J. "Echoes of Isaiah in the Rhetoric of Paul: New Exodus, Wisdom, and the Humility of the Cross in Utopian-Apocalyptic Expectations." In *The Intertexture of Apocalyptic Discourse in the New Testament*, edited by Duane F. Watson, 87–112. SBLSymS 14. Atlanta: Scholars, 2002.

———. "Laying to Rest the Midrash: Paul's Message on Meat Sacrificed to Idols in Light of the Deuteronomic Tradition." *Biblica* 79 (1998) 57–68.

———. *Paul and Apostasy: Eschatology, Perseverance, and Falling Away in the Corinthian Congregation.* WUNT 2/115. Tübingen: Mohr/Siebeck, 2000.

———. "Paul and Theodicy: Intertextual Thoughts on God's Justice and Faithfulness to Israel in Romans 9–11." *NTS* 53 (2007) 57–80.

———. "Running in Vain, but Not as an Athlete (Gal. 2:2) The Impact of Habakkuk 2:2–4 on Paul's Apostolic Commission." In *Jesus and Paul: Global Perspectives in Honor of James D. G. Dunn for his 70th Birthday*, edited by B. J. Oropeza, C. K. Robertson, and Douglas C. Mohrmann, 139–50. LNTS 414. London: T. & T. Clark, 2009.

———. "Situational Immorality: Paul's 'Vice Lists' at Corinth." *ExpTim* 110 (1998) 9–10.

———. "What Is Sex? Christians and Erotic Boundaries." In *Religion & Sexuality: Passionate Debates*, edited by C. K. Robertson, 27–63. New York: P. Lang, 2006.

Orr, William F., and James Arthur Walther. *1 Corinthians: A New Translation.* AB 32. Garden City, NY: Doubleday, 1976.

Oswalt, John N. *Book of Isaiah: Chapters 40–66.* NICOT. Grand Rapids: Eerdmans, 1998.

Paige, Terence. "Stoicism, ἐλευθερία and Community at Corinth." In *Worship, Theology and Ministry in the Early Church: Essays in Honor of Ralph P. Martin*, edited by M. J. Wilkins and T. Paige, 180–93. JSNTSup 87. Sheffield: Sheffield Academic, 1992.

Paschke, Boris A. "Ambiguity in Paul's References to Greco-Roman Sexual Ethics." *ETL* 83 (2007) 169–92.

Pascuzzi, Maria. *Ethics, Ecclesiology and Church Discipline: A Rhetorical Analysis of 1 Corinthians 5.* Tesi Gregoriana: Serie Teologia 32. Rome: Pontifical Gregorian University, 1997.

Patzia, Arthur G. *Ephesians, Colossians, Philemon.* NIBCNT 10. Peabody, MA: Hendrickson, 1990.

Pearson, Birger Albert. "Eusebius and Gnosticism." In *Eusebius, Christianity, and Judaism.* Edited by Harold W. Attridge and Gohei Hata, 291–310. Detroit: Wayne State University Press, 1992.

———. "1 Thessalonians 2,13–16: A Deutero-Pauline Interpolation." *HTR* 64 (1971) 79–94.

———. *The Pneumatikos—Psychikos Terminology in 1 Corinthians: A Study in the Theology of the Corinthian Opponents of Paul and Its Relation to Gnosticism.* SBLDS 12. Missoula, MT: SBL, 1973.

Penna, Romano. *Paul the Apostle: A Theological and Exegetical Study.* 2 vols. Translated by Thomas P. Wahl. Collegeville, MN: Liturgical, 1996.

Perkins, Pheme. *Ephesians.* ANTC. Nashville: Abingdon, 1997.

Perrot, Charles. "Les examples du désert (1 Co. 10.6–11)." *NTS* 29 (1983) 437–52.

Phua, Richard Liong-Seng. *Idolatry and Authority: A Study of 1 Corinthians 8.1—11.1 in Light of the Jewish Diapora.* LNTS 299. London: T. & T. Clark, 2005.

Pietersen, Lloyd K. "Women as Gossips and Busybodies? Another Look at 1 Timothy 5:13." *LTQ* 41 (2007) 18–35.

Pietersma, A. "Jannes and Jambres." In *ABD* 3.638–39.

Pietersma, A., and R. T., Lutz. "Jannes and Jambres." In *OTP* 2.427–42.

Pinker, Aron. "Was Habakkuk Presumptuous?" *JBQ* 32 (2004) 27–34.

Piper, John. *The Justification of God: An Exegetical and Theological Study of Romans 9:1–23*. Grand Rapids: Baker, 1983.

Plevnik, Joseph. "1 Thess 5,1–11: Its Authenticity, Intention and Message." *Biblica* 60 (1979) 71–90.

Plummer, Alfred. *A Critical and Exegetical Commentary on the Second Epistle of St. Paul to the Corinthians*. Edinburgh: T. & T. Clark, 1966.

Pogoloff, Stephen M. *Logos and Sophia: The Rhetorical Situation of 1 Corinthians*. SBLDS 134. Atlanta: Scholars, 1992.

Pokorný, Petr. *Colossians: A Commentary*. Translated by Siegfried S. Schatzmann. Peabody, MA: Hendrickson, 1991.

———. *Der Epheserbrief und die Gnosis*. Berlin: Evangelische Verlagsanstalt, 1965.

Popkes, Wiard. "Zum Aufbau und Charakter von Röm 1.18–32." *NTS* 28 (1982) 490–501.

Porter, Stanely E. "Did Paul Have Opponents in Rome and What Were They Opposing?" In *Paul and His Opponents*, edited by Stanley E. Porter, 149–168. PS 2. Leiden: Brill, 2005.

———. "Reconciliation and 2 Cor 5,18–21." In *The Corinthian Correspondence*, edited by Reimund Bieringer, 693–705. BETL 125. Leuven: Leuven University Press, 1996.

Powers, Janet Everts. "A 'Thorn in the Flesh': The Appropriation of Textual Meaning." *JPT* 18 (2001) 85–100.

Qualls, Paula Fontana, and John D. W. Watts. "Isaiah in Ephesians." *RevExp* 93 (1996) 249–59.

Quarles, Charles L. "From Faith to Faith: A Fresh Examination of the Prepositional Series in Romans 1.17." *NovT* 95 (2003) 1–21.

Quinn, Jerome D. "The Last Volume of Luke: The Relation of the Luke-Acts to the Pastoral Epistles." In *Perspectives on Luke-Acts*, edited by Charles H. Talbert, 62–75. PRS, Special Studies 5. Danville, VA: Association of Baptist Professors of Religion, 1978.

———. *The Letter to Titus: A New Translation with Notes and Commentary and an Introduction to Titus, I and II Timothy, the Pastoral Epistles*. AB 35. New York: Doubleday, 1990.

Quinn, Jerome D., and William C. Wacker. *The First and Second Letters to Timothy: A New Translation with Notes and Commentary*. ECC. Grand Rapids: Eerdmans, 2000.

Räisänen, Heiki. *Jesus, Paul, and the Torah: Collected Essays*. JSNTSup 43. Sheffield: Sheffield Academic, 1992.

Reasoner, Mark. *The Strong and the Weak: Romans 14.1—15.3 in Context*. SNTSMS 103. Cambridge: Cambridge University Press, 1999.

Redditt, Paul L. *Haggai, Zechariah, Malachi*. NCB. London: M. Pickering; Grand Rapids, Eerdmans, 1995.

Reed, Jeffrey T. *A Discourse Analysis of Philippians: Method and Rhetoric in the Debate over Literary Integrity*. JSNTSup 136. Sheffield: Sheffield Academic, 1997.

Reinmuth, Eckart. "'Nicht vergeblich' bei Paulus und Pseudo-Philo: Liber antiquitatum biblicarum." *NovT* 33.2 (1991) 97–123.

Rengstorff, Karl Heinrich. "πρόθυμος, προθυμία." In *TDNT* 6.694–700.

Reumann, John Henry Paul. *Philippians: A New Translation with Introduction and Commentary*. AYB 33B. New Haven, CT: Yale University Press, 2008.

Richard, Earl. *First and Second Thessalonians*. SP 11. Collegeville, MN: Liturgical, 1995.

Richlin, Amy, editor. *Pornography and Representation in Greece and Rome*. Oxford: Oxford University Press, 1992.

Ridderbos, Herman N. *Paul: An Outline of His Theology*. Translated by John Richard de Witt. Grand Rapids: Eerdmans, 1975.

Riesenfeld, Harald. "The Meaning of the Verb ἀρνεῖσθαι." *ConBNT* 11 (1947) 207–19.

Riesner, Rainer. *Die Frühzeit des Apostels Paulus: Studien zur Chronologie, Missionsstrategie und Theologie*. WUNT 71. Tübingen: Mohr/Siebeck, 1994.

Rigaux, Béda. *Saint Paul: Les Épitres aux Thessaloniciens*. 2 vols. EBib. Paris: J. Gabalda, 1956.

Roberts, J. H. "Jewish Mystical Experience in the Early Christian Era as Background to Understanding Colossians." *Neot* 32 (1998) 161–89.

Robertson, A. T. *Word Pictures in the New Testament*. Nashville: Broadman, 1930.

Robertson, A. T., and Alfred Plummer. *A Critical and Exegetical Commentary on the First Epistle of St. Paul to the Corinthians*. ICC. Edinburgh: T. & T. Clark, 1978.

Roetzel, Calvin J. "Election/Calling in Certain Pauline Letters: An Experimental Construction." In *SBL Seminar Papers 1990*, edited by David J. Lull, 552–69. Atlanta: Scholars, 1991.

———. *2 Corinthians*. ANTC. Nashville: Abingdon, 2007.

———. *Judgment in the Community: A Study of the Relationship between Eschatology and Ecclesiology in Paul*. Leiden: Brill, 1972.

———. *Paul: The Man and the Myth*. SPNT. Minneapolis: Fortress, 1999.

Roloff, Jürgen. *Der erste Brief an Timotheus*. EKKNT 15. Zürich: Benziger, 1988.

Rosner, Brian S. "Deuteronomy in 1 and 2 Corinthians." In *Deuteronomy in the New Testament*, edited by Maarten J. J. Menken and Steve Moyise, 118–35. LNTS 358. London: T. & T. Clark, 2007.

———. "'Drive Out the Wicked Person': A Biblical Theology of Exclusion." *EvQ* 71 (1999) 25–36.

———. *Greed as Idolatry: The Origin and Meaning of a Pauline Metaphor*. Grand Rapids: Eerdmans, 2007.

———. *Paul, Scripture and Ethics: A Study of 1 Corinthinas 5–7*. AGJU 22. Leiden: Brill, 1994.

Royalty, R. M. "Dwelling on Visions: On the Nature of the So-Called 'Colossian Heresy.'" *Biblica* 83 (2002) 329–57.

Sampley, J. Paul. *I and II Corinthians*. New York: Scribner's, 1989.

———. "Paul and Frank Speech." In *Paul and the Greco-Roman World: A Handbook*, edited by J. Paul Sampley, 293–318. Harrisburg, PA: Trinity, 2003.

Sanday, W., and Arthur C. Headlam. *A Critical and Exegetical Commentary on the Epistle to the Romans*. ICC. Edinburgh: T. & T. Clark, 1980.

Sanders, E. P. *Paul and Palestinian Judaism: A Comparison of Patterns of Religion*. London: SCM, 1977.

———. *Paul, the Law, and the Jewish People*. Philadelphia: Fortress, 1983.

Sanders, Jack T. "Paul Between Jews and Gentiles in Corinth." *JSNT* 65 (1997) 67–83.

Sappington, Thomas J. *Revelation and Redemption at Colossae*. JSNTMS 53. Sheffield: Sheffield Academic, 1991.

Schenk, Wolfgang. *Die Philipperbriefe des Paulus: Kommentar*. Stuttgart: W. Kohlhammer, 1984.

Schippers, Reinier. "ἄρτιος." In *NIDNTT* 3.49–51.

Schlarb, Egbert. *Die gesunde Lehre: Häresie und Wahrheit im Spiegel der Pastoralbriefe*. MTS 28. Margburg: Elwert, 1990.

Schlier, Heinrich. *Christus und die Kirche im Epheserbrief.* Nendeln (Liechtenstein) Kraus, 1966.

———. *Principalities and Powers in the New Testament.* London: Burns & Oates, 1961.

———. "αἱρέομαι, αἵρεσις, αἱρετικός, αἱρετίζω, διαιρέω, διαίρεσις." In *TDNT* 1.180–85.

———. "ἀρνέομαι." In *TDNT* 1.768–71.

Schlueter, Carol J. *Filling Up the Measure: Polemical Hyperbole in 1 Thessalonians 2:14–16.* JSNTSup 98. Sheffield: JSOT Press, 1993.

Schmidt, Karl Ludwig, and Martin Anton. "σκληρύνω." In *TDNT* 5.1030–31.

Schmidt, Ulrich. *"Nicht vergeblich empfangen"! Eine Untersuchung zum 2. Korintherbrief als Beitrag zur Frage nach der paulinischen Einschätzung des Handelns.* BWANT 2. Stuttgart: W. Kohlhammer, 2004.

Schmithals, Walter. *Gnosticism in Corinth: An Investigation of the Letters to the Corinthians.* Translated by John E. Steely. 3rd ed. Nashville: Abingdon, 1971.

———. *Paul & the Gnostics.* Abingdon: Nashville, 1972.

Schnackenburg, Rudolf. *Ephesians: A Commentary.* Edinburgh: T&T Clark, 1991.

———. "Ephesus: Entwicklung einer Gemeinde von Paulus zu Johannes." *BZ* 35 (1991) 41–64.

Schneider, Johannes. "σταυρός, σταυρόω, ἀνασταυρόω." In *TDNT* 7.572–84.

Schnelle, Udo. *Einleitung in das Neue Testament.* Göttingen: Vandenhoeck & Ruprecht, 1994. ET: *The History and Theology of the New Testament Writings.* Translated by M. Eugene Boring. Minneapolis: Fortress, 1998.

———. *Paulus: Leben und Denken.* Berlin: de Gruyter, 2003. ET: *Apostle Paul: His Life and Theology.* Translated by M. Eugene Boring. Grand Rapids: Baker, 2005.

Schoedel, William R. *Ignatius of Antioch: A Commentary on the Letters of Ignatius of Antioch.* Hermenia. Philadelphia: Fortress, 1985.

Schrage, Wolfgang. *Der erste Brief an die Korinther.* 4 vols. EKKNT 7. Dusseldorf: Benziger, 1991–2001.

Schreiner, Thomas R. "Corporate and Individual Election in Romans 9: A Response to Brian Abasciano." *JETS* 49 (2006) 373–86.

———. "Does Romans 9 Teach Individual Election unto Salvation?" In *The Grace of God, The Bondage of the Will,* edited by Thomas R. Schreiner and Bruce A. Ware, 1.89–106. Grand Rapids: Baker, 1995.

———. *Paul: Apostle of God's Glory in Christ: A Pauline Theology.* Leicester: Apollos; Downers Grove, IL: InterVarsity, 2001.

———. *Romans.* BECNT 6. Grand Rapids: Baker, 1998.

Schreiner, Thomas R., and Ardel B. Caneday. *The Race Set Before Us: A Biblical Theology of Perseverance and Assurance.* Downers Grove: InterVarsity Press, 2001.

Schweizer, Eduard. *The Letter to the Colossians: A Commentary.* Translated by Andrew Chester. Minneapolis: Augsburg, 1982.

Scott, James M. *Exile: Old Testament Jewish and Christian Conceptions.* JSJSup 56. Leiden: Brill, 1997.

Segal, Alan F. *Paul the Convert: The Apostolate and Apostasy of Saul the Pharisee.* New Haven, CT: Yale University Press, 1990.

Seifrid, Mark A. "Paul's Use of Righteousness Language against Its Hellneistic Background." In *Justification and Variegated Nomism,* edited by D. A. Carson, Peter T. O'Brien, and Mark A. Seifrid, 2.39–74. WUNT 181. Tübingen/Grand Rapids: Mohr/Siebeck/ Baker Academic, 2004.

Shanor, Jay. "Paul as Master Builder: Construction Terms in 1 Corinthians." *NTS* 34 (1988) 461–71.

Shum, Shiu-Lun. *Paul's Use of Isaiah in Romans: A Comparative Study of Paul's Letter to the Romans and the Sibylline and Qumran Sectarian Texts.* WUNT 2/156. Tübingen: Mohr/Siebeck, 2002.

Silva, Moisés. "Old Testament in Paul." In *DPL*, 630–42.

———. *Philippians.* 2nd ed. BECNT. Grand Rapids: Baker Academic, 2005.

Skarsaune, Oskar. "Heresy and the Pastoral Epistles." *Themelios* 20 (1994) 9–14.

Sloan, Robert B. "Paul and the Law: Why the Law Cannot Save." *NovT* 33 (1991) 35–60.

Smit, Joop F. M. "What Is Apollos? What Is Paul? In search for the Coherence of First Corinthians 1:10–4:21." *NovT* 44 (2002) 231–51.

Smith, Ian K. *Heavenly Perspective: A Study of the Apostle Paul's Response to a Jewish Mystical Movement at Colossae.* LNTS 326. London: T. & T. Clark, 2006.

Smith, J. Z. "The Garments of Shame." *HTR* 5 (1965) 217–38.

Smith, Jay E. "Another Look at 4Q416 2 ii.21, a Critical Parallel to First Thessalonians 4:4." *CBQ* 63 (2001) 499–504.

Snodgrass, Klyne. *Ephesians.* The NIV Application Commentary. Grand Rapids: Zondervan, 1996.

———. "Justification by Grace—to the Doers: An Analysis of the Place of Romans 2 in the Theology of Paul." *NTS* 32 (1986) 72–93.

———. "Spheres of Influence: A Possible Solution to the Problem of Paul and the Law." *JSNT* 32 (1988) 93–113.

Söding, Thomas. "Der Erst Thessalonicherbrief und die frühepaulinische Evangeliumsverkündigung: Zur Frage einer Entwicklung der paulinischen Theologie" *BZ* 35 (1991) 180–203.

Spicq, Ceslas. *Saint Paul: Les Épîtres pastorales.* EBib. Paris: J. Gabalda, 1947.

Stählin, Gustav. "μῦθος." In *TDNT* 4.762–95.

———. "προσκόπτω, πρόσκομμα, προσκοπή, ἀπρόσκοπος." In *TDNT* 6.744–58.

Standhartinger, A. *Studien zur Entstehungsgeschichte und Intention des Kolosserbriefs.* NovTSup 94. Leiden: Brill, 1999.

Stansell, Gary. "The Gift in Ancient Israel." *Semeia* 87 (1999) 65–90.

Steinmann, Andrew E., and Michael A. Eschelbach. "Walk This Way: A Theme from Proverbs Reflected and Extended in Paul's Letters." *CTQ* 70 (2006) 43–62.

Stendahl, Krister. "The Called and the Chosen: An Essay on Election." In *The Root of the Vine: Essays in Biblical Theology*, by Anton Fridrichsen et al., 63–80. Westminster: Dacre, 1953.

———. *Paul among Jews and Gentiles, and Other Essays.* Philadelphia: Fortress, 1976.

Stenger, Werner. "Biographisches und Idealbiographisches in Gal. 1,11—2,14." In *Kontinuität und Einheit: Für Franz Mussner*, edited by Paul-Gerhard Müller and Werner Stenger, 123–40. Freiburg: Herder, 1981.

Stettler, Christian. "The Opponents at Colossae." In *Paul and His Opponents*, edited by Stanley E. Porter, 169–200. PS 2. Leiden: Brill, 2005.

Still, E. Coye. "Paul's Aims Regarding εἰδωλόθυτος: A New Proposal for Interpreting 1 Corinthians 8:1—11:1." *NovT* 44 (2002) 333–43.

Still, Todd D. *Conflict at Thessalonica: A Pauline Church and Its Neighbours.* JSNTSup 183. Sheffield: Sheffield Academic, 1999.

———. "Interpretive Ambiguities and Scholarly Proclivities in Pauline Studies: A Treatment of Three Texts from 1 Thessalonians 4 as a Test Case." *CBR* 5 (2007) 207–19.

Stowers, Stanley K. *A Rereading of Romans: Justice, Jews, and Gentiles.* New Haven, CT: Yale University Press, 1994.

Strobel, August. "Schreiben des Lukas? Zum sprachlichen Problem der Pastoralbriefe." *NTS* 15 (1968–69) 191–210.

Strüder, Christof W. "Preferences Not Parties: The Background of 1 Cor 1,12." *ETL* 79 (2003) 431–455.

Stuart, Douglas. "Curse." In *ABD* 1.1218–19.

Stuckenbruck, Loren T. "Colossians and Philemon." In *The Cambridge Companion to St. Paul*, edited by James D. G. Dunn, 116–32. CCR. Cambridge: Cambridge University Press, 2003.

———. *Angel Veneration and Christology: A Study in Early Judaism and in the Christology of the Apocalypse of John.* WUNT 2/70. Tübingen: Mohr/Siebeck, 1995.

Stuhlmacher, Peter. *Paul's Letter to the Romans: A Commentary.* Translated by Scott J. Hafemann. Louisville: Westminster John Knox, 1994.

Sumney, Jerry L. "The Argument of Colossians." In *Rhetorical Argumentation in Biblical Texts: Essays from the Lund 2000 Conference*, edited by Anders Eriksson et al., 339–52. ESEC 8. Harrisburg, PA: Trinity, 2002.

———. "'I Fill Up What Is Lacking in the Afflictions of Christ': Paul's Vicarious Suffering in Colossians." *CBQ* 68.4 (2006) 664–680.

———. *Identifying Paul's Opponents: The Question of Method in 2 Corinthians.* JSNTSup 40. Sheffield: Sheffield Academic, 1990.

———. *'Servants of Satan', 'False Brothers' and Other Opponents of Paul.* JSNTSup 188. Sheffield: Sheffield Academic, 1999.

———. "Studying Paul's Opponents: Advances and Challenges." In *Paul and His Opponents*, edited by Stanley E. Porter, 7–58. PS 2. Leiden: Brill, 2005.

Talbert, Charles H. *Ephesians and Colossians.* Paideia. Grand Rapids: Baker Academic, 2007.

———. *Reading Acts: A Literary and Theological Commentary on the Acts of the Apostles.* RNTS. New York: Crossroad, 1997.

Tamez, Elsa. "God's Election, Exclusion and Mercy: A Bible Study of Romans 9–11." *IRM* 82 (1993) 29–37.

Taylor, John W. "From Faith to Faith: Romans 1.17 in the Light of Greek Idiom." *NTS* 50 (2004) 337–48.

Theissen, Gerd. "Social Integration and Sacramental Activity: An Analysis of 1 Cor 11:17–34." In *The Social Setting of Pauline Christianity: Essays on Corinth*, by Gerd Theissen, edited and translated by John H. Schültz, 145–74. Philadelphia: Fortress, 1982.

Thielman, Frank. *Paul & the Law: A Contextual Approach.* Downers Grove, IL: InterVarsity, 1994.

———. *Philippians.* NIVAC. Grand Rapids: Zondervan, 1995.

———. "Unexpected Mercy: Echoes of a Biblical Motif in Romans 9–11." *SJT* 47 (1994) 169–171.

Thiselton, Anthony C. *The First Epistle to the Corinthians: A Commentary on the Greek Text.* NIGTC. Grand Rapids: Eerdmans, 2000.

———. "Realized Eschatology at Corinth." *NTS* 24 (1977–78) 510–26.

Thomas, Rodney. "The Seal of the Spirit and the Religious Climate of Ephesus." *ResQ* 43 (2001) 155–66.

Thorsteinsson, Runar M. *Paul's Interlocutor in Romans 2: Function and Identity in Context of Ancient Epistolography.* ConBNT 40. Stockholm: Almqvist & Wiksell, 2003.

Thrall, Margaret E. *A Critical and Exegetical Commentary on the Second Epistle of the Corinthians*. 2 vols. ICC. London: T. & T. Clark, 1994, 2000.

Tobin, Thomas H. *Paul's Rhetoric in Its Contexts: The Argument of Romans*. Peabody, MA: Hendrickson, 2004.

Tomson, Peter J. *Paul and the Jewish Law: Halakha in the Letters of the Apostle to the Gentiles*. CRINT 3.1. Assen: Van Gorcum; Minneapolis: Fortress, 1990.

Toney, Carl N. *Paul's Inclusive Ethic: Resolving Community Conflicts and Promoting Mission in Romans 14–15*. WUNT 2/252. Tübingen: Mohr/Siebeck, 2008.

Towner, Philip H. "Gnosis and Realized Eschatology in Ephesus (of the Pastoral Epistles) and the Corinthian Enthusiasm." *JSNT* 31 (1987) 95–124.

———. *The Letters to Timothy and Titus*. NICNT. Grand Rapids: Eerdmans, 2006.

Townsend, John T. "1 Corinthians 3.15 and the School of Shammai." *HTR* 61 (1968) 500–04.

Trebilco, Paul R. *The Early Christians in Ephesus from Paul to Ignatius*. WUNT 166. Tübingen: Mohr/Siebeck, 2004.

———. *Jewish Communities in Asia Minor*. SNTSMS 69. Cambridge: Cambridge University Press, 1991.

Trilling, Wolfgang. *Untersuchung zum zweiten Thessalonicherbrief*. Leipzig: St. Bennon, 1972.

———. *Der zweite Brief an die Thessalonicher*. EKKNT 14. Zürich: Benziger, 1980.

Trummer, Peter. *Die Paulustradition der Pastoralbriefe*. BBET 8. Frankfurt: P. Lang, 1978.

Van Neste, Ray. *Cohesion and Structure in the Pastoral Epistles*. JSNTSup 280. London: T. & T. Clark, 2004.

VanLandingham, Chris. *Judgment & Justification in Early Judaism and the Apostle Paul*. Peabody, MA: Hendrickson, 2006.

Varona, Antonio. *Eroticism in Pompeii*. Los Angeles: Getty Museum, 2001.

Walker, William O. "Does the 'We' in Gal 2.15–17 Include Paul's Opponents?" *NTS* 49 (2003) 560–65.

Wallace, Daniel B. *Greek Grammar beyond the Basics: An Exegetical Syntax of the New Testament*. Grand Rapids: Zondervan, 1996.

Walter, Nikolaus. "Die Philipper und das Leiden: Aus den Anfängen einer heidenchristlichen Gemeinde." In *Die Kirche des Anfangs: Für Heinz Schümann*, edited by Rudolph Schnackenburg et al., 417–34. Freiburg: Herder, 1978.

———. "δόγμα, ατος, τό *dogma* opinion; decree, statute." In *EDNT* 1.339–40.

Wanamaker, Charles A. *The Epistles to the Thessalonians: A Commentary on the Greek Text*. NIGTC. Grand Rapids: Eerdmans, 1990.

Waters, Guy Prentiss. *The End of Deuteronomy in the Epistles of Paul*. WUNT 2/221. Tübingen: Mohr/Siebeck, 2006.

Waters, Kenneth L. "Saved Through Childbearing: Virtues as Children in 1 Timothy 2:11–15." *JBL* 123 (2004) 703–35.

Watson, Duane F. "A Rhetorical Analysis of Philippians and Its Implications for the Unity Question." *NovT* 30 (1988) 57–88.

Watson, Francis. *Paul and the Hermeneutics of Faith*. London: T. & T. Clark, 2004.

Watson, Nigel. *The First Epistle to the Corinthians*. EpC. London: Epworth, 2005.

Watts, John D. W. *Isaiah 34–66*. WBC 25. Waco, TX: Word, 1987.

Watts, Rikki E. "'For I Am Not Ashamed of the Gospel': Romans 1:16–17 and Habakkuk 2:4." In *Romans and the People of God: Essays in Honor of Gordon D. Fee on the Occasion of His 65th Birthday*, edited by Sven K. Soderlund and N. T. Wright, 3–25. Cambridge: Eerdmans, 1999.

Webb, William J. *Returning Home: New Covenant and Second Exodus as the Context for 2 Corinthians 6.14—7.1.* JSNTSup 85. Sheffield: JSOT Press, 1993.

Wedderburn, A. J. M. *The Reasons for Romans.* Edited by John Riches. SNTW. Edinburgh: T. & T. Clark, 1988.

Weima, Jeffrey A. D. "The Function of 1 Thessalonians 2:1–12 and the Use of Rhetorical Criticism: A Response to Otto Merk." In *The Thessalonians Debate: Methodological Discord or Methodological Synthesis?*, edited by Karl P. Donfried and Johannes Beutler, 114–31. Grand Rapids: Eerdmans, 2000.

———. "'How You Must Walk to Please God': Holiness and Discipleship in 1 Thessalonians." In *Patterns of Discipleship in the New Testament*, edited by Richard N. Longenecker, 98–119. McMNTS. Grand Rapids: Eerdmans, 1996.

Weiser, Alfons. *Der zweite Brief an Timotheus.* EKKNT 16/1. Düsseldorf: Benziger, 2003.

Westerholm, Stephen. "The New Perspective at Twenty-Five." In *Justification and Variegated Nomism*, edited by D. A. Carson, Peter T. O'Brien, and Mark A. Seifrid, 2.1–38. WUNT 181. Tübingen: Mohr/Siebeck; Grand Rapids: Baker Academic, 2004.

———. "Paul and the Law in Romans 9–11." In *Paul and the Mosaic Law*, edited by James D. G. Dunn, 215–37. WUNT 89. Tübingen: Mohr, 1996.

Wilckens, Ulrich. "ὑποκρίνομαι, συνυποκρίνομαι, ὑπόκρισις, ὑποκριτής, ἀνυπόκριτος." In *TDNT* 8.558–71.

———. *Der Brief an die Römer.* 3 vols. EKKNT 6. Zürich: Benziger, 1978, 1980, 2003.

Wilk, Florian. *Die Bedeutung des Jesajabuches für Paulus.* FRLANT 179. Göttingen: Vandenhoeck & Ruprecht, 1998.

———. "Isaiah in 1 and 2 Corinthians." In *Isaiah in the New Testament*, edited by Steve Moyise and Maarten J. J. Menken, 133–58. NTSI. London: T. & T. Clark, 2005.

Wilken, Robert Louis. *The Christians as the Romans Saw Them.* 2nd ed. New Haven, CT: Yale University Press, 2003.

Williams, Demetrius K. *Enemies of the Cross of Christ: The Terminology of the Cross and Conflict in Philippians.* JSNTSup 223. Sheffield: Sheffield Academic, 2002.

Willis, Wendell Lee. *Idol Meat in Corinth: The Pauline Argument in 1 Corinthians 8 and 10.* SBLDS 68. Chico, CA: Scholars, 1985.

———. "1 Corinthians 8–10: A Retrospective after Twenty-Five Years." *ResQ* 49 (2007) 103–12.

Wilson, R. McL. *A Critical and Exegetical Commentary on Colossians and Philemon.* ICC. London: T. & T. Clark, 2005.

Wilson, Stephen G. *Leaving the Fold: Apostates and Defectors in Antiquity.* Minneapolis: Fortress, 2004.

———. *Luke and the Pastoral Epistles.* London: SPCK, 1979.

Wilson, Todd. "Wilderness Apostasy and Paul's Portrayal of the Crisis in Galatians." *NTS* 50 (2004) 550–71.

Winter, Bruce W. *After Paul Left Corinth: The Influence of Secular Ethics and Social Change.* Grand Rapids: Eerdmans, 2001.

———. *Roman Wives, Roman Widows: The Appearance of New Women and the Pauline Communities.* Grand Rapids: Eerdmans, 2003.

———. *Seek the Welfare of the City: Christians as Benefactors and Citizens.* First-Century Christians in the Graeco-Roman World. Grand Rapids: Eerdmans; Carlisle: Paternoster, 1994.

Wire, Antoinette Clark. *The Corinthian Women Prophets: A Reconstruction through Paul's Rhetoric*. Minneapolis: Fortress, 1990.

Wisdom, Jeffrey R. *Blessing for the Nations and the Curse of the Law: Paul's Citation of Genesis and Deuteronomy in Galatians 3.8–10*. WUNT 2/133. Tübingen: Mohr/Siebeck, 2001.

Witherington, Ben. *Conflict and Community in Corinth: A Socio-Rhetorical Commentary on 1 and 2 Corinthians*. Grand Rapids: Eerdmans, 1995.

———. *1 and 2 Thessalonians: A Socio-Rhetorical Commentary*. Grand Rapids: Eerdmans, 2006.

———. *Grace in Galatia: A Commentary on St. Paul's Letter to the Galatians*. Grand Rapids: Eerdmans, 1998.

———. *Jesus, Paul and the End of the World: A Comparative Study in New Testament Eschatology*. Downers Grove, IL: InterVarsity, 1992.

———. "Not So Idle Thoughts about *Eidolothuton*." *TynBul* 44 (1993) 237–54.

———. *Paul's Narrative Thought World: The Tapestry of Tragedy and Triumph*. Louisville: Westminster John Knox, 1994.

———. *A Socio-Rhetorical Commentary on Titus, 1–2 Timothy and 1–3 John*. Vol. 1 of *Letters and Homilies for Hellenized Christians*. Downers Grove, IL: IVP Academic, 2006.

Witherington, Ben, and Darlene Hyatt. *Paul's Letter to the Romans: A Socio-Rhetorical Commentary*. Grand Rapids: Eerdmans, 2004.

Witherington, Ben, and G. Francois Wessels. "Do Everything in the Name of the Lord: Ethics and Ethos in Colossians." In *Identity, Ethics, and Ethos in the New Testament*, edited by Jan G. van der Watt and François S. Malan, 303–33. BZNW 141. Berlin: de Gruyter, 2006.

Witulski, Thomas. "*Gegenwart und Zukunft* in den eschatologischen Konzeptionen des Kolosser- *und* des Epheserbriefes." *ZNW* 96 (2005) 211–42.

Wolfson, Harry Austryn. *Philo: Foundations of Religious Philosophy in Judaism, Christianity, and Islam*. 2 vols. 4th ed. Cambridge: Harvard University Press, 1968.

Wolter, Michael. *Die Pastoralbriefe als Paulustradition*. FRLANT 146. Göttingen: Vandenhoeck & Ruprecht, 1988.

Woyke, Johannes. *Götter, Götzen, Götterbilder: Aspecte einer paulinischen "Theologie der Religionen."* BZNW 132. Berlin: de Gruyter, 2005.

Wright, N. T. *The Climax of the Covenant: Christ and the Law in Pauline Theology*. Edinburgh: T. & T. Clark, 1991.

———. *The Epistles of Paul to the Colossians and to Philemon: An Introduction and Commentary*. TNTC. Leicester: Inter-Varsity, 1988.

———. "New Exodus, New Inheritance: The Narrative Substructure of Romans 3–8." In *Romans and the People of God: Essays in Honor of Gordon D. Fee on the Occasion of his 65th Birthday*, edited by Sven K. Soderlund and N. T. Wright, 26–35. Grand Rapids: Eerdmans, 1999.

———. *The New Testament and the People of God*. Vol. 1 of *Christian Origins and the Question of God*. VMinneapolis: Fortress, 1992.

———. *Romans*. In *The New Interpreter's Bible*, vol. 10. Nashville: Abingdon, 2002.

Yamauchi, Edwin M. *Pre-Christian Gnosticism: A Survey of the Proposed Evidences*. Grand Rapids: Eerdmans; London: Tyndale, 1973.

Yarbrough, O. Larry. *Not Like the Gentiles: Marriage Rules in the Letters of Paul*. SBLDS 80. Atlanta: Scholars, 1985.

Yee, Tet-Lim N. *Jews, Gentiles and Ethnic Reconciliation: Paul's Jewish Identity and Ephesians.* SNTSMS 130. Cambridge: Cambridge University Press, 2005.

Yeo, K. K. "The Rhetoric of Election and Calling Language in 1 Thessalonians." In *Rhetorical Criticism and the Bible*, edited by Stanley E. Porter and Dennis L. Stamps, 526–47. JSNTSup 195. London: Sheffield Academic, 2002.

Yinger, Kent L. *Paul, Judaism, and Judgment According to Deeds.* SNTSMS 105. Cambridge: Cambridge University Press, 1999.

Yonge, C. D., translator. *The Works of Philo: Complete and Unabridged.* New updated ed.. Peabody, MA: Hendrickson, 1993.

Young, Frances M. *The Theology of the Pastoral Letters.* NTT. Cambridge: Cambridge University Press, 1994.

Young, Frances M., and David F. Ford. *Meaning and Truth in 2 Corinthians.* BFT. London: SPCK, 1987.

Zerwick, Max, and Mary Grosvenor. *A Grammatical Analysis of the Greek New Testament.* Unabridged 3rd ed. Rome: Pontifical Biblical Institute, 1988.

Ziesler, J. A. *The Meaning of Righteousness in Paul: A Linguistic and Theological Enquiry.* SNTSMS 20. Cambridge: Cambridge University Press, 1972.

Zoccali, Christopher. "'And So All Israel Will Be Saved': Competing Interpretations of Romans 11.26 in Pauline Scholarship." *JSNT* 30 (2008) 289–318.

Ancient Sources Index

343

11:1	97, 169
11:1–4	228
11:10–11	195
14:6–7	193

Joel
| 3:5 | 287 |
| 3:19 | 178 |

Amos
3:1–2	169
3:2	172
4:11	74
6:1	155
6:10	291
6:12	271
9:10	155

Micah
| 3:11 | 155 |
| 7:18–20 | 191 |

Habakkuk
| 2:1–10 | 56 |
| 2:4 | 10–11, 16, 18, 20, 24, 97, 146–48 |

Zephaniah
| 1:1–6 | 160 |

Haggai
| 2:10–14 | 297 |

Zechariah
2:15	229
3:2	74
9:9–10	229
11:16	271
14:11	175

Malachi
1:2–3	178
2:8	160
3:22	196
3:16	156
4:4	196

APOCRYPHA

Tobit
1:10–11	139
11:14–16	253
12:16–17	253
14:6	40

Judith
2:3	80
9:5–6	169
12:2	139
15:2	217
16:9	274

Additions to Esther
10:4	170
10:10	170
11:12	170
14:17	248

Wisdom
2:24	119
3:10	283
3:16–19	51, 54
4:12	152
8:8	169
10:15	24
11:15–16	152
12	187, 189
12–14	150, 152
12:3–18	187
12:10	155
12:10–11	187
12:12	184, 187
12:19	155
12:23–14:31	154
12:27	40
13:2	249
14:26	51
14:26–31	54
15:1	186
15:3	186
15:7	185–86

⮌

NEW TESTAMENT

Romans (*continued*)

14:12	120–21
14:13	28, 124, 131, 136–38, 143, 168
14:14	91, 93, 138–39, 142, 145
14:15	50, 95, 137–39, 141–43, 168, 173, 199
14:17	92, 139
14:17–18	138
14:19–20	140
14:20	50, 124, 137–39, 141
14:20–21	95, 137, 143, 168
14:20–22	92
14:21	124, 131, 139, 142
14:23	95, 137, 140–43, 145, 168, 172
15	191
15:1	142
15:1–13	139, 143
15:2	139
15:3	165
15:4	264
15:4–5	161
15:5	161
15:7	142, 165
15:7–13	191, 195
15:8–9	26
15:8–12	9
15:9–12	182
15:11–12	195
15:13	161
15:14	45
15:14–15	143–44, 166, 199
15:15	135, 143
15:15–16	136
15:18	144
15:18–19	164
15:20–21	9
15:24–28	135
15:25–26	134–35
15:25–32	36
15:27	146
15:28	126, 219
15:30	122
15:30–31	130
16	143
16:3–4	42, 136
16:5	142
16:5 [D]	62
16:7	136, 141
16:11	136, 141

16:13	172
16:16	50, 232
16:17	28, 131, 138, 160, 216, 236
16:17–18	136, 197
16:17–19	199
16:18	119, 136, 213
16:19	135, 143, 166
16:20	239
16:25	285
16:25–26	230
16:26	144–45

1 Corinthians

1:1	48
1:1–9	70, 72–73, 126
1:2	72, 99, 169
1:4	99
1:4–5	72
1:4–9	65
1:5–9	63
1:8	73–74, 229, 247
1:8–9	219
1:9	72, 99, 281
1:10	66, 186, 281
1:10–17	66–67, 102–3, 127
1:11	66, 216
1:12	14, 67–68, 71, 116–17, 298
1:13	70, 100
1:13–14	83
1:13–17	70
1:16	41
1:17	70
1:17–18	206
1:17–19	207
1:18	79, 81, 118, 214, 217, 232, 277
1:18–23	206
1:18–31	66, 69, 183
1:18–2:6	67
1:18–2:16	69, 108
1:19	69, 192
1:21	69, 79
1:26–31	69
1:23	28, 131
1:26	48, 80
1:26–28	99
1:26–29	179
1:29	80
1:29–31	70

Galatians (*continued*)

5:3–4	30
5:4	5, 30, 151, 192, 254
5:5	12, 30, 31
5:6	21, 26, 30, 50, 145
5:7	18
5:7–8	29
5:7–10	20
5:10	12, 19, 24, 216
5:11	15, 26, 28, 130, 131
5:12	6, 12, 19, 210
5:13	9
5:13–14	28
5:13–26	17
5:13–6:2	265
5:14	21, 23, 25, 51, 53, 157, 164, 256
5:14–16	151, 163
5:14–26	115
5:15	25, 211, 248
5:15–16	25
5:16	26, 31, 49, 157, 163, 208, 214, 235, 244
5:16–17	49
5:16–18	25
5:16–21	80, 235
5:16–25	27, 163, 164
5:16–6:10	223
5:18	9, 25, 26
5:19	25, 53, 92
5:19–21	24, 25, 33, 51, 87, 104, 121, 162, 214, 278
5:19–23	54
5:19–25	51
5:20	136, 216, 300
5:20–21	76
5:21	12, 24, 25, 29, 30, 31, 32, 33, 216
5:22	145, 236, 265, 278
5:22–23	26, 49
5:22–25	25, 163
5:23	25, 265
5:24	80
5:25	9, 26, 29, 235
5:26	25, 216
6	311
6:1	9, 26, 29, 32, 34, 45, 81, 104, 127, 186, 228
6:2	21, 31, 157
6:2–4	27

6:2–5	32
6:4	26
6:5	12
6:6–7	121
6:7–8	25, 29, 31, 33
6:7–9	12, 29
6:8	30
6:9	31
6:10	26
6:11	37
6:11–13	19
6:11–18	243
6:12	12, 15, 21, 130
6:12–13	9, 15, 23
6:13	23
6:15	28, 278
6:16	21, 178
6:18	9
6:12–13	10, 81
6:13	12
6:16	17

Ephesians

1	228, 230–31
1–3	226, 235
1:1	224, 227, 231
1:1–14	70, 227, 230, 240
1:3	227, 229
1:3–11	174
1:3–14	62, 227, 240
1:3–23	226
1:4	227–28, 230, 235, 238
1:4–5	229, 232
1:4–11	170, 285
1:5	17, 169, 233
1:6	227–28
1:7	227
1:9	227
1:9–10	230
1:10	227, 229, 230
1:11	169
1:11–12	229
1:12	227
1:13	126, 227, 231–33
1:13–14	229–30
1:15	231–32
1:17	233
1:19	231
1:20	227

Colossians (*continued*)

⮌

PSEUDEPIGRAPHA

෴

JOSEPHUS AND PHILO

Josephus

NEW TESTAMENT APOCRYPHA, GNOSTIC LITERATURE, AND EARLY CHURCH FATHERS

Author Index

Aageson, James W., 190
Abasciano, Brian J., 172, 177, 180
Achtemeier, Paul J., 157
Adams, Edward, 71, 106
Aejmelaeus, L., 113
Aletti, Jean-Noël, 158, 249
Alexander, Loveday, 12
Allen, Leslie C., 170
Allo, E. Bernard, 67, 104
Andrews, Scott B., 131
Arichea, D. C., and H. A. Hatton, 263, 266, 282
Arnold, Clinton E., 225, 227, 239, 243f, 250, 252
Ascough, Richard S., 142
Ashley, Timothy R., 291

Balla, Peter, 122
Bammel, Ernst, 39
Bandstra, Andrew J., 98
Barclay, John M. G., 6, 18, 26, 31, 41f, 44, 47, 63, 140, 144, 146, 154, 230, 245
Barnett, Paul W., 121, 129
Barré, M. L., 131
Barrett, C. K., 4, 31, 67f, 75, 113, 116, 119, 121, 123f, 129, 141, 148, 263, 265, 289, 294f
Barth, Markus, 224, 228, 231f, 244f, 248, 258
Bassler, Jouette M., 72, 275, 277, 281, 290, 294
Bateman, Herbert W., 205
Bauckham, Richard, 260
Bauer, Walter, 296, 300
Baumbach, Günther, 209
Baumert, Norbert, 272
Beale, G. K., 58, 257

Beasley-Murray, G. R., 56
Behm, Johannes, 84
Bell, Richard H., 156, 192, 194, 196
Bénétreau, Samuel, 298
Bertram, Georg, 262,
Best, Ernest, 36, 43, 46, 48, 50, 224, 227, 232f, 239
Betz, Hans Dieter, 15f, 18, 26, 28, 30f, 112
Bevere, Allan R., 243, 245, 249f, 253, 256
Bieringer, Reimand, 112f, 123f
Bjerkelund, Carl J., 18
Black, David Alan, 45f
Blanke, Helmut, 244f, 248, 258
Blenkinsopp, Joseph, 186
Bloomquist, L. Greg, 221
Bockmuehl, Markus N., 204, 210, 213, 218, 221f
Boer, Martinus C. de, 153
Borgen, Peter, 94
Bormann, L., 207
Bouttier, Michel, 7, 236
Boyarin, Daniel, 16
Brändl, Martin, 96
Bratcher, Robert G., 254
Braun, Herbert, 304
Bray, Gerald, 128
Brown, Raymond E., 135
Brox, Norbert, 185, 195
Bruce, F. F., 13, 28, 39, 61, 225
Brunt, John C., 92
Bryan, Steven M., 197
Bujard, W., 243
Bultmann, Rudolf, 118, 122
Burton, Ernest DeWitt, 11, 14
Byrne, Brendan, 169, 172, 189

Caird, George B., 187f
Calvert-Koyzis, Nancy, 16

Subject Index

Abraham, 6, 11, 21–24, 28, 33, 44, 59f,
  562, 137, 140, 158, 160, 172,
  176f, 179, 191, 193, 228
Accommodation, 6
Acculturation, 6
Adam, 85, 160, 169f, 257, 272–78, 294,
  297
Affliction (see Suffering), 18, 38f, 42, 44,
  64, 104, 129f, 132f, 310f
Anathema, 19, 73, 100, 107, 175
Anti-god powers (see also Demons,
  Satan), 60, 79, 81, 98, 109, 111,
  153, 182, 196, 247f, 256, 284,
  310f
Antinomian (ism) (see also Law), 136,
  157, 251
Antioch (Syrian), 11–15, 34f, 77, 110,
  199, 309, 311
Antiochus Epiphanes, 57
Apollos, 66, 68–71, 75, 112, 274
Apostasy (see also Unbelief, Persecution,
  Suffering, Vices, Restoration,
  Deny, Assimilation),
  Antagonistic, 5
  (in) communities (see Communities),
    1, 309–12
  consequences of (see Judgment), ix,
    2, 311
  definition, 1
  diversity of, 2, 312
  gradual 5, 82
  nature of, 2, 309f
  perceived, 1–2, 43, 118, 132, 263,
    298, 310
  precipitate 5, 81, 39
Apostles ("super-"), 68, 116, 127, 131
Ashamed, Shame, 39, 48, 65, 75, 108,
  146–48,161, 167, 191, 199, 211,
  213f, 285

Asia Minor, 13, 18, 130, 224f, 227, 233,
  236–41, 245f, 251, 258, 299,
  303f, 309f
Assimilation, 6, 33, 64, 102, 110f, 125,
  139, 164f, 227, 237, 240, 310
Assurance, 7, 35, 40, 55, 60f, 64f, 73,
  100f, 119, 132, 161, 167f, 173,
  180, 189, 227, 230, 249, 277, 281,
  291, 301f
ἄτακτοι, 45–48
Authority of Paul, 9, 19, 24, 32, 68, 71,
  78, 83–86, 89, 91, 93, 101f, 112–
  34, 138, 208, 298f, 309
Baptism, 70f, 83, 99f, 126, 162, 165, 175,
  225, 229, 236, 256f, 278–80,
  287f, 290
Behavior (see Moral Behavior), 6, 14f,
  23, 32, 39–41, 44–48, 50–51, 55,
  66, 73, 87, 95, 97f, 101–3, 106–8,
  118, 123, 125, 127, 138, 149, 163,
  165, 178, 200, 209, 212–16, 223,
  226, 231, 235–38, 240, 244, 249,
  258f, 265, 268, 270f, 310
Believe, Belief (see Faith; Unbelief), 1f,
  5–11, 14–18, 20–26, 28, 30–34,
  38–51, 53–55, 58, 60–65, 67–73,
  75–77, 79–97, 100–10, 113, 115f,
  118, 121–26, 130–32, 136–40,
  142, 144–51, 154–68, 170–75,
  177, 179, 181f, 185–86, 188–89,
  191, 193–94, 196–98, 200–02,
  205–09, 212–15, 217–20, 222,
  226–41, 244f, 249–51, 254–56,
  258f, 262, 267, 273, 275–91,
  294–96, 298–302, 306–12
Blameless, 20, 23, 44, 50, 72, 207, 210,
  215, 218, 221, 229f, 232, 238,
  240, 247, 258
Blasphemy, 3, 5, 266f, 269, 287